HAWAII RESTAURANT GUIDE 2004

Robert & Cindy Carpenter
www.hawaiirestaurantguide.com

HAWAII RESTAURANT GUIDE
2004

1st Edition

ISBN 1-931752-31-1
Library of Congress Control Number: 2004108834

Printed in the United States of America.

Holiday Publishing Inc.
Post Office Box 230
Havana, IL 62644-0230
holidaypublishing@yahoo.com

HAWAII RESTAURANT GUIDE
2004

TABLE OF CONTENTS

Hawaiian Islands

INTRODUCTION

Do you find yourself sitting down before a trip cross-referencing two or three destination guides just so you can get a more accurate picture of the place? Better yet have you ever finished reading a review and wondered if the person who wrote it had actually been there? Or how about the uneasy feeling you get when you suspect that you've just read a paid advertisement instead of an unbiased critique? It's all happened to us, and the lasting impressions we got from those experiences shaped our approach while writing HRG 2004.

Guidebooks by their very nature are compilations. Sometimes they draw their information from many people's research and the final copy is written from the collected data. That's all fine and well but who's the expert in charge of overseeing the accuracy of the end product? Not being quite comfortable with the management by committee approach, we chose to personally go through the entire process and perform every step along the way.

After deciding to write the Hawaii Restaurant Guide the next issue to be settled was determining our criteria. We settled on the following: Is the restaurant easy for a visitor to locate? Is there parking available? Is the facility pleasant, clean and appealing? Would we eat there? Would we recommend it to a friend? Is the food, setting, or service distinctive? Has the chef or restaurant won any awards? These questions became the baseline for the selection process in HRG 2004.

Attention then turned to the information people expect to find when reading a restaurant review. First they want accurate information concerning the physical location, phone number, website address, hours of operation, dress code, style of cuisine, credit cards, and price range. Then they like to see actual menu items and prices to go along with legend symbols and personal impressions. Regional listings of restaurants and glossaries are also helpful as are descriptions of new and interesting cuisines. These all became part of the HRG 2004 wish list.

The Hawaii Restaurant Guide includes complete information on over 400 dining establishments presented in a comprehensive directory style. Inside you will find special places to dine in all price ranges. There are no negative reviews. If we didn't think a place should be included it was quietly omitted. There was no solicitation or compensation offered or accepted to taint the data. It's hard to be objective when the owner rolls out the red carpet.

So plan to visit Hawaii! Explore the renowned pleasures of sights and sounds to be found in the islands. But while you're there be sure to discover some of the culturally diverse culinary experiences unique to America's Pacific Paradise!

AUTHORS' PERSONAL FAVORITES

If there's one question we hear more than any other, it's got to be "What is your favorite restaurant?" That's a tough one to answer. There are literally hundreds of great dining spots in Hawaii. However, just like beauty is in the eye of the beholder, individual tastes and preferences mean everything when making this call. Having said that, we would like to offer our list of personal favorites.

BIG ISLAND

HE SAID…	SHE SAID…	WE SAID…
Edelweiss	Pahu 'ia	Kilauea Lodge

KAUAI

HE SAID…	SHE SAID…	WE SAID…
Hamura Saimin	Tidepools	Café Portofino

LANAI

HE SAID…	SHE SAID…	WE SAID…
Ihilani	Formal Dining Room	Henry Clay's

MAUI

HE SAID…	SHE SAID…	WE SAID…
I'O	The Bay Club	Longhi's

MOLOKAI

HE SAID…	SHE SAID…	WE SAID…
Molokai Pizza Café	Maunaloa Room	Hotel Molokai

OAHU

HE SAID…	SHE SAID…	WE SAID…
Golden Dragon	La Mer	Alan Wong's

ALL OF HAWAII

HE SAID…	SHE SAID…	WE SAID…
3660 On The Rise Oahu	L'Uraku Oahu	David Paul's Maui

ISLAND
CUISINES

HAWAIIAN CUISINE

It has been said that everybody in Hawaii came from someplace else which also holds true for many of the food sources we think of as native to the island chain. The Hawaiian Islands are geologically very young. They are also among the most remote places on earth with nearly three thousand miles of open ocean separating the islands from any major land mass. Hawaii's youth and isolation led to the evolution of a unique but nutritionally sparse flora and fauna.

The first arrivals in Hawaii are thought to have been a small dark people whose origins hail back to Southeast Asia. Archaeologists believe that these people lived off what they found which didn't go much beyond fish, birds, and a few native plants. Many like to think of those earliest inhabitants as the legendary Menehune, but they, like their history, disappeared into the annals of time. It wasn't until the Polynesians voyaged to Hawaii with their domestic animals and "canoe" plants that the island food resources achieved any variety.

These ancestors of the modern Hawaiians were great mariners. A thousand years ago they began sailing their double-hulled voyaging canoes up from Tahiti bringing with them dogs, pigs, and fowl as well as coconuts, sweet potatoes, breadfruit, bananas, taro, yams, arrowroot, and sugarcane. They also brought the Polynesian style of cooking which includes broiling over hot coals, boiling with hot stones, and baking in an underground oven. It is this latter method, cooking in an imu, that holds center stage at Hawaiian luaus today.

Ancient Hawaiians lived in ahupua'a which were land divisions reaching from the top of the mountains down adjoining ridges to the ocean. These triangular watersheds theoretically contained all the elements required to sustain the community. Trees for building canoes grew up on the mountain. The uplands supported dry land crops like sweet potatoes and yams. Down along the stream beds taro was grown in paddies called loi. Then, beyond the coconut and breadfruit trees, lay the ocean with its wealth of fish, mollusks, and seaweeds.

The Hawaiian diet was simple but healthful. Fish provided the bulk of the common people's protein with domestic animals and fowl reserved primarily for the chiefs and special occasions. The staple starch was poi made from the steamed and pounded corms of the taro plant. When conditions wouldn't allow for taro cultivation sweet potatoes or breadfruit were used as substitutes. Taro greens and seaweed filled the need for leafy vegetables by supplying vitamins and minerals. Finally, bananas and coconuts were important for good health.

Today these traditions continue. Modern Hawaiians usually cook much like everyone else, but they make a point to hold luaus to celebrate milestones in life. Island favorites like kalua pig, lomi lomi salmon, chicken long rice, laulau, haupia, and of course poi are staples at these events. If you get the chance, try to attend a luau and experience the original Hawaiian cuisine.

CHINESE CUISINE

The Chinese have influenced the socio-economic and culinary scenes of the islands to the point that it would be hard to imagine Hawaii without them. Beginning in the mid 1800's they were the first immigrant group recruited to work in the sugar cane fields. From those humble beginnings the Chinese went on to become the merchant class and landlords of Honolulu.

The Chinese experience in Hawaii is more than a list of menu items and real estate investments. It's a meaningful part of Hawaiian history. The early Chinese immigrants came from southern China, so naturally they brought that style of cooking with them. After they arrived it didn't take long for them to figure out that there wasn't much of a future working on the plantations, so as soon as their contracts expired they moved on.

These free but unemployed farmers looked around and saw opportunity. Where the Hawaiians had once raised taro and fish the Chinese saw rice paddies and duck ponds. Intermarriage provided access to idle land that soon became truck gardens and small farms. Since trading is a way of life for the Chinese, the port of Honolulu quickly had its own Chinatown full of shops and small eateries.

Today you see the effects of this history throughout the islands. The dominant Chinese cuisine in Hawaii is Cantonese. This is what most North Americans picture when they think about eating Chinese, so the methods and menu items are quite well known. Preparations like dim sum and stir-fries are popular in that region and are standards on menus in Hawaii.

True Chinese cooking is a healthful cuisine. Chefs in China instinctively strive for balance and harmony in meal preparation. This can be accomplished by using a variety of cooking methods and ingredients. No Chinese cook would ever serve an entire deep-fried meal; rather he or she would always include vegetable dishes and serve steamed rice on the side.

To fully enjoy a Chinese meal make sure you choose a variety of dishes, levels of spiciness, and cooking methods. This is dining banquet style, but it can still be done at a fairly reasonable cost. Some restaurants have made things easier by selecting an assortment of dishes and offering them as a package, but those set menus can be a bit on the middle-of-the-road side. Make your meal an adventure and select the items yourself—just watch out for the chicken feet!

No trip to Honolulu is complete without a visit to Chinatown. Take a walk and look for the shops with the barbequed pork and smoked ducks hanging in the windows. Down off King Street you'll find markets packed with people selling vegetables you've never seen and fish so fresh they're still swimming. Finally, stop for lunch at a place where you're the only ones speaking English and there isn't a fork in sight. That's when you'll know why they call it Chinatown.

JAPANESE CUISINE

Like so many others the Japanese experience in Hawaii is tied to sugar. The first immigrants began arriving from Japan soon after the end of the American Civil War. At first it was a trickle, but after the Reciprocity Act Of 1876 removed tariffs on Hawaiian sugar, the trickle turned into a torrent. That was the age of industrialized sugar, and enormous amounts of manpower were required. Today Americans of Japanese ancestry play a major role in Hawaiian society. This is reflected through Hawaii's wide variety of Japanese dining venues.

It has been said that the Japanese eat with the eyes as well as the mouth. This becomes apparent after visiting one of their restaurants. Instead of having a single main entrée dominating the table, Japanese diners prefer a variety of smaller servings. The dishes are served separately on various plates and bowls artistically arranged around the table.

The ultimate fine dining experience is the kaiseki. This is also known as royal dining or dining in courses and involves considerable ceremony as well as an elegant dinner presentation. An elaborate array of special courses is served that might include items such as an exquisite appetizer, assorted sashimi and sushi, miso soup, a tempura course, a seafood dish, a small steak, pickled vegetables, steamed rice, cold noodles, and dessert.

A more common choice is the teishoku or complete meal. This Japanese equivalent of the prix fixe dinner consists of an appetizer, soup, pickled vegetables, one or two entrees, rice, and perhaps dessert. Anyone interested in exploring Japanese cuisine would do well to start with a teishoku as the variety allows the diner to do some sampling and not be overwhelmed by the menu.

Within the various meal presentations you will find a variety of preparation styles. Thanks to the spread of international dining, visitors to Hawaii often think of sushi and sashimi as typical Japanese food. While those are popular items in Japan, their cuisine goes far deeper than that. Beyond the temptations of the sushi bar you will find several major styles of cooking.

First comes yakimono, which are grilled or broiled dishes. Teriyaki and yakitori are classic examples of yakimono. That knife-wielding chef in a teppanyaki house is also doing a form of yakimono cooking. Then there's agemono where meats or vegetables are fried in oil. Tempura with its light puffy coating is probably the most recognizable form of agemono. Finally you have nabemono where thinly sliced pieces of meat and vegetables are gently simmered in a fragrant broth using a chaffing dish placed on the tabletop. Shabu shabu and sukiyaki are traditional nabemono dishes.

So walk into a Japanese restaurant with confidence, and after a half-bow to the hostess get ready for a truly unique and exceptional dining experience.

PORTUGUESE CUISINE

Portuguese culinary tradition is the odd man out among ethnic cuisines in Hawaii. Where all the rest are Asian in origin Portuguese is European. When the Asians serve a starch it is nearly always rice. For the Portuguese starch means bread or beans. Asians love stir-fries. The Portuguese prefer stews. In spite of all these differences, Portuguese cooking has become a valued part of the Hawaiian melting pot.

The Portuguese have always been a seafaring people. During the fourteenth and fifteenth centuries Portuguese ships embarked on a great wave of global exploration. Those adventurers brought back spices and foods that were unheard of in Europe. The resulting trade routes reached around the world exposing the Portuguese to exotic places and exotic places to the Portuguese.

The first Portuguese plantation laborers arrived in Hawaii during the 1870's and were actually from the Azores and Madeira. This was a rather natural development as sugarcane had been part of the Madeira agricultural scene for hundreds of years. These European immigrants differed from their Asian counterparts as they intended to stay in Hawaii permanently. Their families brought hearth and home along with the entire range of Portuguese cuisine.

Hearty soups, stews, and casseroles were a rather new concept in the islands but old favorites among the Portuguese. Usually these were enhanced with the wide variety of spices and flavors that had come into their possession through global exploration. Portuguese sausage or linguica with its garlicky zest has gone on to become a mainstay breakfast item across the islands. In Hawaii you'll find eggs and Portuguese sausage right next to Egg McMuffins and breakfast burritos on fast food restaurant menus.

Another island favorite is Portuguese Bean Soup. If Hawaii people had to name the recipes that make their top ten list, Portuguese Bean Soup would be there every time. Somehow it doesn't seem to matter what a restaurant normally serves or where its price range falls, this local comfort food combining beans and vegetables with ham hocks and Portuguese sausage manages to make its way into the rotation as soup of the day.

Finally, there is the Portuguese tradition of baking bread. Everywhere you go in Hawaii you'll find menus offering French toast made with Portuguese sweet bread. Also known as pao doce, this local favorite has taken on another identity as Molokai Sweet Bread. Visitors to that island will see local people boarding the plane carrying loaves for those at home. Another Portuguese specialty is the sugary doughnut without a hole known as the malasada. Traditionally served as a special treat the day before Ash Wednesday, malasadas were prepared using the family's remaining butter and eggs before starting the lean times of Lent.

KOREAN CUISINE

Immigrants from Korea began arriving in Hawaii during the early 1900's. Like their fellows, the early arrivals came to work on the plantations. Although that era is all but over, the migration continues today as Koreans seeking economic opportunity leave their homeland for Hawaii and other parts of North America.

Koreans strive for balance and harmony in all aspects of their lives. This is never more obvious than at the table, where they look to food as a cure for physical and mental ailments as well as for sustenance. Their cuisine is low in fat and very healthful with an emphasis on grilled or broiled meats, soups, and fresh vegetables. Some of the cooking methods favored by Koreans involve tableside preparation using a grill or by simmering meats and vegetables in broth, while others require pan or deep-frying.

One item that has almost come to mean Korean is kim chee. Interestingly enough both of this pickled relish's principal ingredients came from other places. The Dutch introduced cabbage to the Koreans and the chili peppers that give kim chee its fire were brought from Portugal. This zesty condiment is nearly always seen on Korean tables and adds zip to offset the mildness of rice.

Contrary to general impressions not all Korean food is highly seasoned. In fact many of their favorite menu items could pass as comfort food. If you like teriyaki then you'll enjoy the marinated grilled meats. Koreans are more of a beef-eating nation than other Asian countries. It is thought that invading Mongols introduced cattle to Korea hundreds of years ago. Other protein sources common to the Korean diet include poultry and fish as well as soybean products.

For those who really like to know the details, some of the ingredients used as flavoring in Korean cuisine include chrysanthemum leaves, daikon, ginger root, garlic, enokitake, shimeji and shiitake mushrooms, hot green and red peppers, green onions, mirin, miso, nori, sesame oil and seeds, pine nuts, soybean sprouts, soy sauce, tofu, and wakame.

Combination meals are usually offered giving the diner a chance to experience a variety of items. These dinners begin with several small dishes of salads and pickled vegetables. Turnips, potatoes, kim chee, seaweed, bean sprouts, and garlic bulb pickles among others will be offered. Soup made of oxtails, fish, chicken or vegetables, many times with the addition of a beaten egg or dumplings, are important courses in a Korean meal. Popular entrées commonly seen include bulgoki, kal bi ribs, and chun. As in other Asian cultures desserts are limited to fruits and special occasion items.

Most island Korean restaurants tend to be less formal establishments where one can enjoy a healthful dinner of wonderfully prepared foods at a reasonable cost.

FILIPINO CUISINE

Filipinos constituted the last major group of immigrants recruited to work on Hawaii's sugar cane and pineapple plantations. Their arrival during the early to mid-1900's was a reaction to legal restrictions placed by the US Congress on importing foreign workers. The Hawaiian planters needed cheap field labor, and as the Philippines were a US Territory, it became the logical alternative.

Although at first glance one might assume that Philippine culture would be Southeast Asian in nature that is not at all the case. Early visits from the east followed by three hundred years of Spanish occupation and fifty years as a US Territory heavily influenced Filipino daily life. The result is a cuisine that is truly global in nature.

Early traders from China and Malaysia are thought to have been the first outsiders to seriously impact the culinary traditions of the Filipino people. The use of egg roll wrappers in lumpia, rice, curry, coconut, coconut milk, patis, soy sauce, and noodles all had their origins in eastern cuisines.

Then came the Spanish who truly made an impression on the daily diet in the Philippines. Tomatoes, onion, garlic, beans, pimientos, and olive oil have become everyday components in Filipino dishes. During the late 1890's America was at war with Spain and the islands came under US military rule. Although Filipino people enjoy American dishes as well as their own, little of what we consider true Filipino food could be attributed to that period of history.

Today the Filipino influence on the culinary arts in Hawaii might not be as noticeable as that of some other Asian cuisines as there are not many restaurants serving an exclusively Filipino menu. However, that doesn't mean that visitors won't be exposed to Filipino food. Many island restaurants incorporate Filipino styles and dishes in their menus. You just have to know what to look for.

Filipino cooks like to mix all of a dish's ingredients together rather than preparing and serving them separately. A classic example of this is adobo, which is a stew made from pork and/or chicken that has been marinated in garlic and vinegar. Another is chicken relleno, which is a roasted and boned chicken that is stuffed with a pork, onion, raisin, pimiento, and hard-cooked egg stuffing.

Then come the veggies! Filipino culinary tradition calls for the use of an extremely wide variety of vegetables. Most Western visitors won't easily identify many of them, but a walk through a Filipino grocery or Chinatown will give you the idea. Of course, no meal would be complete without rice or pancit noodles to round things out.

Finally, the Filipinos are fond of sweets. Look for leche flan, fruit lumpia, or cascaron and you'll know you've found the dessert section of the menu.

THAI CUISINE

People from Thailand were among the first modern immigrants who did not come to Hawaii seeking work on the plantations. Their arrival over the last thirty years was part of a general movement out of Southeast Asia by those looking for more promising forms of economic opportunity. As many before them had already discovered, a quick way to create an income in a new land is to open a restaurant and introduce the neighborhood to your native cuisine. Hawaii with its large Asian ethnic population was a natural for these new entrepreneurs. Thai cuisine has quickly become a local favorite.

Thai cuisine reflects an interesting history of interaction between people throughout Indochina. Thanks to its central location Thailand became a crossroad for foreign travelers and exotic ideas. Immediately to the north lies China with its ancient traditions of stir-frying and the use of noodles. Among that group were Buddhists preparing vegetarian dishes. From the west came people from India making curries and Arabs cooking skewer-broiled meats. And of course don't forget the ever-present Portuguese and their tiny red hot peppers!

Chefs from Thailand have a whole arsenal of flavors at their disposal. Some of the ingredients commonly used include Thai chilies, Kaffir lime leaves, lemon grass, ginger, mint, basil, curry, peppers, and the ever-present fish sauce known as nam pla. Thai food may be ordered spiced mild, medium, or hot. However, since mild dishes can miss the point and hot is best reserved for the Thai's we suggest that people consider ordering medium. Then in order to moderate the spicy flavors, be sure to include at least one dish that is made with coconut milk and have it all served along side a steamer basket of sticky rice.

A meal in a Thai restaurant is generally served all at once and then shared between the diners, rather than in courses. Usually a number of dishes are presented giving everyone an opportunity to sample a variety of items. Great effort is made to balance out the contrasting tastes and textures in order to promote harmony in the meal. Unlike many Asian countries a fork and spoon are used in dining. The fork is used for cutting and pushing food onto the spoon, and the spoon gives the diner the ability to fully appreciate the flavorful sauces.

A good rule to follow in making dinner selections is to always ask, "What do the locals order?" Here there are favorites like anywhere else. Starting with the appetizer section consider the Thai Crispy Noodles or Satay Chicken. Then follow up with a Green Papaya Salad and a bowl of Tom Yum Soup. Next comes the main event where dishes like Evil Prince Shrimp, Pork Pad Pet, Chicken Panang Curry, and Beef with Thai Basil Sauce appear high on the list. Finally, make sure to include a dish of Pad Thai Noodles and dinner is served.

Try to visit a Thai restaurant while in you're in Hawaii. You'll discover an exciting new cuisine that truly broadens the horizons of culinary adventure.

VIETNAMESE CUISINE

The end of the Vietnam War signaled the beginning of a major migration of Vietnamese people to Hawaii and North America. What started out as a political exodus has turned into a classic movement of people seeking a better way of life. Hawaii has been an attractive location for resettlement because of its mild, temperate climate and the presence of other Asian cultures. Today their presence has become so visible that there are those who refer to the central part of the Honolulu Chinatown historic district as Little Saigon.

While you are walking around Chinatown notice the small Vietnamese eateries that seem to be popping up on every street corner. At one time, Chinese immigrants operated these shops. Now those people have moved on to other endeavors and the latest wave of arrivals have taken their place. Many of these places are pho shops. Pho is pronounced "fuh" and is an aromatic rice noodle soup made with a clear, rich beef stock. A plate of fresh herbs such as Thai basil and cilantro along with bean sprouts and jalapeños is served on a separate plate. You flavor this popular breakfast or lunch dish to your own specifications.

Vietnamese cuisine is the result of many years of cultural blending. Like the other countries in Southeast Asia, the ebb and flow of history brought in successive waves of new people and customs. The original inhabitants of Vietnam are thought to have moved down the coastline from southern China. Then others from the east and west arrived looking for trade. There were occupations, first by the Chinese and then by the French. Throughout that time the people of Vietnam were learning new culinary methods and techniques.

 As you peruse a Vietnamese menu you will witness those influences through the use of everything from lemongrass and curry paste to croissants and baguettes. Naturally, the Asian staple starch appears as a major item. Not only do you see rice served steamed as a side dish but it also appears in noodles and as rice paper for wrapping. Vietnamese foods have a delicate fresh taste and are never heavy in texture or flavor. Herbs are used as greens as well as for flavor. Dishes made with curry may be ordered spiced according to personal preference.

A Vietnamese meal is served family style where everyone samples each dish. Preparation is not a detailed or complicated endeavor but rather is a gathering of fresh healthful ingredients handled and cooked as little as possible. A favorite example is the banh hoi. This popular dish is made by taking grilled marinated meat slices and placing them onto a rice paper wrapper piled with pickled daikon and carrots, bean sprouts, romaine, rice vermicelli, and fresh mint leaves. This is then rolled up like a burrito and dipped into a light, flavorful sauce.

Vietnamese cuisine is the new kid on Hawaii's culinary block. Although some of the surroundings may be a little basic, go in and try this wonderful taste experience just once and you will find yourself wanting to go back for more!

LOCAL FOOD

Local food is the Hawaiian Everyman's version of homegrown comfort food. Its roots go back to the plantation days when people were recruited from around the world to work the sugar cane and pineapple fields. Although they lived in separate camps the workers gathered in small groups for lunch and that is where the blending of cultures began.

The field workers' diet was pretty simple. Just about everyone had a tin of rice and some kind of meat and vegetable. A Japanese worker might bring some teriyaki beef and his Portuguese comrade might have a can of sardines. The Koreans would certainly bring along some kim chee and the Filipinos their adobo and lumpia. Then in a kind of Hawaiian potluck the workers would share what they brought bringing variety to an otherwise ordinary lunch in the field.

That was the beginning of local food, but what does it look like today? When you think local food think of something simple a plantation family would keep in their pantry. First comes the staple starch, which is nearly always rice. Then you have canned meat of which Spam, Vienna Sausages, sardines, corned beef, and beef stew predominate. To add a little interest there would be a jar of mayonnaise and a bag of macaroni with which to make a simple mac salad. Then the upcountry farmers would bring down their cabbage and dinner would be served.

Most visitors to Hawaii experience local food at one of the diners that can be found just about everywhere in the islands. The standard offering is what is commonly called a plate lunch. For six or seven dollars you get a choice of meat such as teri chicken, katsu pork, or mahi mahi, "two scoop" rice, and a scoop of mac salad. The whole affair comes appropriately served in a Styrofoam carryout container complete with plastic table service. Bon Appetit!

Now if a big bowl of noodle soup is more your style, local food can accommodate you as well. The staple item here is known as saimin. The history of this dish is interesting. The Chinese say it has a Japanese origin and the Japanese say it came from China, so they both must be right! To make saimin, first you must have a stock. In the Japanese tradition this would be a dashi which is a broth made from nori flavored with bonito shavings. Since this is a little lean for many tastes the choices take off from there. Some places use a chicken stock and others a beef broth. Determining your preference and figuring out who is using what is part of the adventure of exploring the local food establishments.

Then come the noodles that by tradition are made from wheat flour, eggs, and water. This "long rice" is complemented with a little meat and perhaps an egg as well as some Chinese cabbage to top the whole thing off. Local diners will buy a teri beef stick or two to add flavor to their bowl or to eat along side with some hot mustard. Make sure you try adding a dash of hot sauce for added zest.

PACIFIC RIM CUISINE

In a geographical sense Pacific Rim refers to all of the nations that border the Pacific Ocean. This area not only includes Japan, Korea, China, and Southeast Asia but it also takes in Australia, New Zealand, and all of Polynesia as well as South, Central, and North America. However, no matter how large that seems physically, in a cultural sense the Pacific Rim involves even that much more.

People from diverse cultures have shared their culinary traditions since the beginning of time. This interaction has greatly accelerated as global commercial activity, improved communications, and personal travel experiences impacted the general public. During the 20th century our new awareness of different culinary tastes and practices began to change people's expectations regardless of where they stood on the economic ladder. Witness the evolving trends of American dietary culture as we went from Italian and Chinese to Mexican and Thai. Once we began to sample exciting new flavors we didn't want to stop.

This brings us to a better understanding of the dynamics behind the Pacific Rim movement. Watching the explosion of mass-produced ethnic convenience foods, what enterprising young chef wouldn't try to capitalize on a new trend? Taking advantage of opportunity, professional chefs began using their classic training to blend ingredients from one group of countries and cooking methods from another to produce results that are on a higher level than the sum of the parts.

For instance, grilled beef tenderloin with shiitake mushrooms in a Marsala demi glace served with mashed Hawaiian taro and Okinawan sweet potatoes is a far cry from a grilled steak and baked potato. The combination uses Chinese, French, Italian, Hawaiian, Okinawan, Continental European and American foods and methods to elevate the diner's experience. The chef's education and experience in blending flavors led to the resulting balanced and pleasing entree.

In the Hawaiian Islands visitors sometimes wonder if they are experiencing Pacific Rim or Hawaii Regional Cuisine. Hawaii Regional Cuisine showcases locally produced fish, meats, fruits, and vegetables combined with local ethnic styles and classic cooking techniques to produce an upscale contemporary version of Hawaiian "local food". Pacific Rim Cuisine draws upon a much broader geographic area when sourcing its ingredients and cooking methods and ends up as an innovative fusion of cuisines from all around the Pacific Rim.

A visit to a Pacific Rim restaurant is like a visit to a foodie theme park. As you read the menu, try and picture the ingredients and tastes the chef is combining before you make your selection. Not all the world's tastes and textures are to everyone's liking. By thinking about what you really enjoy and then following your own lead you will be much better prepared to select those dishes more likely to please and experience a truly enjoyable dining experience.

HAWAII REGIONAL CUISINE

There was a time when dining in Hawaii was less than a stellar experience. Much of what appeared on restaurant menus had to be shipped in over long distances. Things that could be arrived frozen and those that couldn't arrived tired. Then, in an attempt to please the visitors, the local chefs tried to prepare classic cuisine under less than ideal circumstances. As you can imagine, cooking Continental out of a can didn't work very well.

Along came the late '80's and a group of young chefs decided that something had to be done to change the situation. They began to talk with local farmers, fishermen, and ranchers about the types of products needed to raise the level of their culinary offerings. Then, in order to create new and exciting dishes, these chefs began merging local cultural influences with their newfound sources of supply and Hawaii Regional Cuisine was on its way to being born

In the original group there were twelve chefs who banded together and formally created the Hawaii Regional Cuisine movement. Those twelve are: Sam Choy, Roger Dikon, Mark Ellman, Bev Gannon, Jean Marie Josselin, George Mavrothalassitis (Mavro), Peter Merriman, Amy Ferguson Ota, Philippe Padovani, Gary Strehl, Alan Wong, and Roy Yamaguchi. Their goal was to combine fresh island products with local ethnic cooking styles and classic techniques in a contemporary upscale regional cuisine unique to Hawaii.

Hawaii Regional Cuisine is a fusion of elements from both eastern and western cultures. Much of the inspiration comes from the meager beginnings of the plantation camps and what islanders call "local food". Add that to an innovative group of classically trained chefs and the freshest of local products and you get truly unique preparations unlike anything you've ever experienced.

There are an amazing variety of offerings on a Hawaii Regional Cuisine menu. Naturally, fresh island fish like opakapaka and mahi-mahi appear regularly, but so do local aquaculture products like Kahuku prawns and Keahole lobster. Look for the Asian preparations and Polynesian sauces that take these specialties one-step beyond. Then to complement the seafood dishes, you might find innovative items like pineapple chicken or macadamia crusted lamb rounding things out.

While you are traveling in the islands keep an eye out for restaurants operated by any of the twelve original Hawaii Regional Cuisine chefs. They will surely provide you with a memorable evening of dining enjoyment. There is also a new group of young up and coming chefs who are doing wonderful work in Hawaii. These people call themselves the Hawaiian Island Chefs and include Steven Ariel, Chai Chaowasaree, Hiroshi Fukui, Teresa Gannon, George Gomes, Wayne Hirabayashi, D. K. Kodama, Lance Kosaka, Jacqueline Lau, Douglas Lum, James McDonald, Mark Okumura, Russell Siu, Goren Streng, and Corey Waite. Look for them. They are the new wave and they're here today.

Legend

Dress Code and Restaurant Price Symbols are based upon dinner. Lunch is usually a less expensive meal with more casual attire acceptable.

Restaurant Prices:

$	<$10
$$	$10-25
$$$	$25-$40
$$$$	$40+
Ent Card	Entertainment Card

The Entertainment Card travel discount card offers sizeable discounts and may be purchased for many geographic areas. You can view the benefits and order a directory and card at www.entertainment.com. At this writing the cost for the Hawaii package is $35.00. Fine, moderate, and casual dining choices are offered at many locations in Hawaii but are most common on Oahu. These books are released in limited quantities every November and do sell out. Either order early online or ask at your local bookstore. Make sure that you get the membership card with your copy. It should be attached inside the front cover.

Credit Cards Accepted:

AE	American Express
CB	Carte Blanche
DC	Diners Club
DIS	Discover
JCB	Japan Credit Bank
MC	Master Card
V	Visa

Days of Operation:

Su	Sunday
Mo	Monday
Tu	Tuesday
We	Wednesday
Th	Thursday
Fr	Friday
Sa	Saturday
X	Except

Example: XMo=Every Day Except Monday

Service Code:

Bru=Brunch   **Buf**-Buffet

Cuisine Code:

Amer	American
Asian	Asian
Braz	Brazilian
Car	Caribbean
Chi	Chinese
Cof	Coffee
Cont	Continental
Ec	Eclectic
Euro	European
Fili	Filipino
Fre	French
Ger	German
Grk	Greek
Haw-Reg	Hawaiian Regional
Haw	Hawaiian
Ind	Indian
Indo	Indonesian
Isl	Island
Ital	Italian
Japan	Japan
Kor	Korean
Local	Local
LatAm	Latin American
Med	Mediterranean
Mex	Mexican
Pac	Pacific
Pac-Rim	Pacific Rim
Port	Portuguese
Sea	Seafood
Spec	Specialty
Stk	Steak
Thai	Thailand
Trop	Tropical
Veg	Vegetarian
Viet	Vietnamese

Dress Code:

Casual	sandals, t shirts, shorts
Resort Casual	shirt with a collar, shorts with pockets, no flip-flops
Evening Aloha	long pants on gentlemen with closed-toed shoes
Formal	long sleeved dress shirt or jacket for gentlemen; inquire
Note:	Bathing suits and tank tops are suitable attire on the beach and by the pool. Cover-ups are an absolute must at even the most casual of dining spots.

Menu Items:

Nothing in the world of travel changes faster than restaurant menus. Everything from the seasonal availability of produce to which side of the bed the chef got up on impacts what you're offered when you sit down to dine. Nowhere is this more true than in Hawaii where the catch of the day really is caught that day. If the boats didn't bring opakapaka in, it just isn't available.

This guide attempts to help the reader come to his own conclusions. Menu items were chosen to give a well-rounded cross-section of the offerings and a sense of their depth and complexity. Signature dishes have been included whenever possible as they tend to be constants and best represent the expertise and direction of the chef. Finally, prices are always subject to change and should be viewed as guidelines of affordability.

Reservations:

It is always wise to call ahead. Even the most notable restaurants change their hours and days of operation. This is particularly true in travel destinations like Hawaii where business tends to be seasonal.

Spelling & Punctuation:

We have attempted to duplicate the spelling and punctuation as they appear on individual menus. If you think that some of them are unusual, you should have seen what they did to our spell check and grammar programs!

BIG ISLAND
DINING

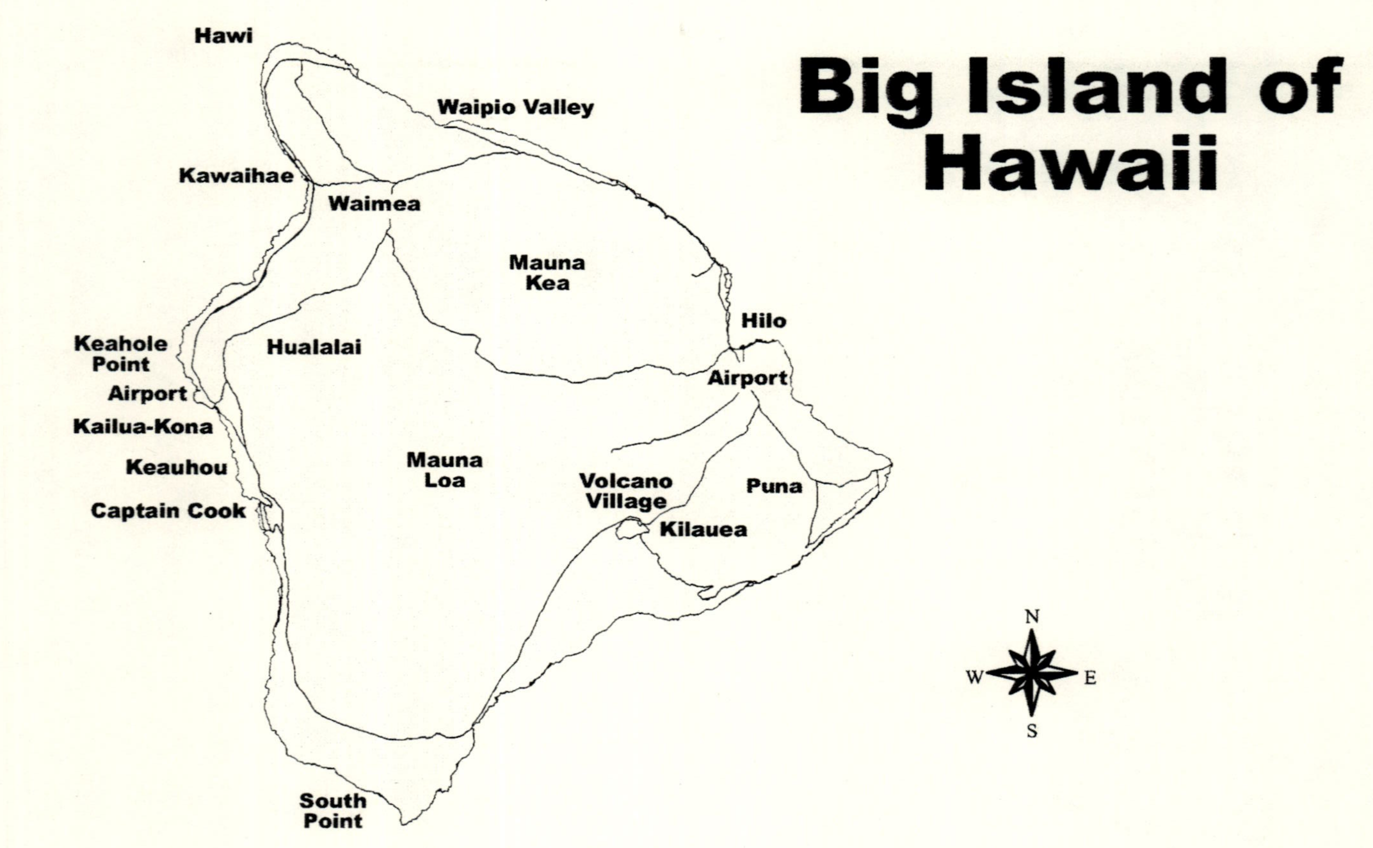

Big Island of Hawaii
Hawi
Waipio Valley
Kawaihae
Waimea
Mauna Kea
Hilo
Keahole Point
Hualalai
Airport
Airport
Kailua-Kona
Keauhou
Mauna Loa
Volcano Village
Puna
Captain Cook
Kilauea
South Point
N
E
S
W

Big Island Dining

Waimea

Aioli's
Opelo Plaza
65-1227A Opelo Rd
Waimea, HI 96743
808-885-6325
Web: None
Hours: L 11:00 AM-4:00 PM Tu-Sa
         D 5:00 PM-8:00 PM We-Th, 5:00 PM-9:00 PM Fr-Sa
Cards: MC V
Dress: Casual
Style: Cont $$

Menu Sampler:

Breakfast:
N/A
Lunch:
Self-serve gourmet sandwiches, soups, salads, and desserts run from $3-$9 and include house roasted turkey, ham, hamburgers, and fresh catch. Caesar Salad is featured on Wednesdays. All breads, cookies and desserts are homemade. Seating available in the adjoining dining room. Menu changes daily.
Dinner:
All dinners are served with a choice of salad or soup and a roll. Entrée selections change every three weeks. Creamy Garlic Soup is a specialty! Prime Rib of Beef (only on Friday or Saturday), herb crusted, baked potato, vegetable $22.95, Grilled Prime Flatiron Steak with béarnaise sauce, garlicky mashed potatoes, sautéed mushrooms $19.95, Frenched Rack of Young Lamb with garlicky mashed potatoes, mint yogurt sauce, local corn $20.95, Chili and Chipotle with vodka beurre blanc over a Hawaiian purple sweet potato cake $18.95, Rabbit, Mushroom and Andouille Gumbo over rice $18.95, Penne Pasta with Gorgonzola, side of garlic bread $13.95, Baked Stuffed Eggplant with rice, pine nuts, onion, and mint, lemon herb sauce, side of garlic bread $13.95

Impressions:

Aioli's offers innovative deli food during the day and gourmet table service at night. This small eatery serves an affordable, fine dining product in a casual atmosphere. Although they do not have a liquor license, tell Al at the Kamuela Liquor Store which entrées you're having, and he'll help you choose a wine from his amazingly serious wine selection. There's no corkage fee at Aioli's. Wander in for breakfast or lunch anytime, but dinner reservations are a must.

Big Island Dining

Kona

Aloha Angel Café
Highway 11
Kainaliu, HI 96750
808-322-3383
www.alohatheatre.com
Hours: BL 8:00 AM-2:30 PM
             D 5:00 PM-9:00 PM
Cards: AE JCB MC V
Dress: Resort Casual
Style: Ec/Isl $$

Menu Sampler:

Breakfast:
All egg dishes served with red garlic potatoes or rice, fruit and choice of multi-grain toast or homemade muffin. Surfer Special of two eggs your way, choice of bacon, ham, Portuguese or vegetable sausage links $7.95, 3 Egg Omelette or Scramble with spinach, mushrooms & cheese $7.95, French toast made with Hawaiian sweet bread $6.50, Fresh Fish of the day & Eggs $10.95

Lunch:
Chinese Salad of soba noodles, grilled tofu or chicken, cucumbers, bean sprouts & snow peas tossed in our creamy sesame dressing with crispy wontons on a bed of greens $10.95. Burger includes choice of chips, garlic red potatoes $7.50, Fish or Tofu Tacos with island greens and chipotle sauce $12.95

Dinner:
Appetizers: Hawaiian Sweet Potato Coconut Salad on Spinach $6.95, Chinese Soba Noodle Salad $10.95, New Zealand Green Lipped Mussels $7.95
Entrées: Filet Mignon-Two 4 oz. Medallions grilled with a cabernet & mushroom sauce $20.95, Seafood Curry with shrimp and scallops $21.95, Chef's Fresh Catch $Market Price, Lemon Grass Grilled Chicken Breast with tropical fruit salsa $15.95, Pork Picata Sauté with a lemon caper butter sauce $16.95, Lamb Chops grilled & served with port wine & mushroom sauce $20.95

Impressions:

The historic Aloha Theater building in Kainaliu is now home to the Aloha Angel Café. This trendy café/deli serves an eclectic breakfast and lunch menu on the picturesque south lanai and a more traditional dinner in their well-appointed dining room. For those on the run, the deli features wonderful home baked goodies and 100% Kona Coffee for a morning treat on the way to the volcano. Entertainment in the form of movies, plays and concerts is provided nightly.

Big Island Dining

Kohala Coast

Bamboo Restaurant & Gallery
Akoni Pule Hwy (Hwy 270)
Hawi, HI 96743
808-889-5555
www.thebamboorestaurant.com
Hours:　L 11:30 AM-2:30 PM Tu-Sa
　　　　D 6:00 PM-9:00 PM Tu-Sa
　　　　Su Bru 11:00 AM-2:00 PM
Cards:　DC MC V
Dress:　Casual
Style:　Pac-Rim $$

Menu Sampler:

Breakfast:
Sunday Brunch: Eggs Bamboo with lilikoi hollandaise sauce-one egg
$5.95/two eggs $7.95. Most items are under $9.95 except for a fish special.
Lunch:
Kohala Coconut Grilled Chicken with Thai coconut sauce served on fresh
vegetables & steamed rice $8.95, Kohala Quesadillas with kalua pork $8.95,
Teri Chicken Sandwich $7.95, BBQ Pork sandwich $7.95.
Dinner:
Pupus: Chicken Sate Pot Stickers of seasoned chicken, herbs, and peanuts
wrapped in won ton pi, steamed and served with sweet chili mint sauce $7.25
Entrées: Beef Tenderloin grilled to your taste and finished with a coffee brandy
cream sauce $17.95/$27.95, Macadamia Nut Crusted Chicken Cordon Bleu of
chicken breasts wrapped around ham & swiss cheese, quickly seared and then
topped with our spicy lilikoi sauce $18.95, Bamboo Bouillabaisse of a light
coconut, pineapple, and saffron broth with fresh shrimp & fish $Market Price

Impressions:

Housed in a historic hotel and general store in the plantation town of Hawi,
Bamboo is definitely Old Hawaii. This north end favorite offers an eclectic
menu blending island and Thai influences to create an interesting fusion cuisine.
The dining room shares the roomy lower floor with a gift shop offering silk
clothing and specialty items. Upstairs you'll find a couple more shops displaying
koa wood furniture and artwork. Try something different and take the sunset
drive up the coast highway for dinner. The experience is well worth the effort.

Big Island Dining

Kona

Bianelli's
Kuakini Hwy & Palani Road
Kailua-Kona, HI 96740
808-329-7062
www.bianellis.com
Hours: L/D 11:00 AM-10:00 PM Mo-Fr
        D 4:00 PM-10:00 PM Sa
Cards: AE DC DIS MC V
Dress: Casual
Style: Ital $$

Menu Sampler:

Breakfast:
N/A
Lunch/Dinner:
Gourmet Pizzas: New York Style or Deep Dish Chicago Style, 12" $12.45-$18.95, 14" $12.95-$20.95, 16" $13.95-$22.95, By the Slice 11AM-4PM $2, Combinations such as The Gorgonzola with garlic herb sauce, parmesan, gorgonzola, whole peeled tomatoes & fresh herbs, Bianelli's Combo with pepperoni, ham, sausage, mushrooms, green peppers, and black olives. Traditional and gourmet ingredients for toppings such as buffalo milk cheese, gorgonzola cheese, feta cheese, ricotta cheese, roasted red pepper, pesto, pine nuts, fresh spinach, Maui onion, shrimp, artichokes, green chilies, and eggplant. Garlic Cheese Bread $2.75, Greek Salad $4.50-$6.95, Calzones $9.95 & Amazones (for two) $16.90, "healthy" food menu, Sub sandwich (hot or cold) $6.95, Philly Steak $7.50, Sausage & Peppers $7.50, Grilled Pastrami $7.50
Pasta Dinners: With Dinner Salad add $2, Lasagna $11.95, Tiger Prawn Pasta $17.95, Spinach Manicotti $9.45, Eggplant Parmigiana $9.45
Desserts: Various cakes, cheesecakes, pies, etc. made in Kona from $3.25. Imported and domestic beers, draft beer, and house wines.

Impressions:

Excellent pizza, pastas, and salads are served promptly in the friendly confines of this Big Island favorite. In our opinion cheese makes or breaks a pizza, and Bianelli's comes through with top quality products. Likewise, the crust has just the right amount of crispness. This rambling bistro is popular with visitors and local residents alike so expect a crowd. Full bar service is offered complete with a fine list of imported beers and wines. Park on-site or walk up from the wharf.

Big Island Dining

Kona

Bistro Yokohama
Sunset Alii Plaza
75-5799 Alii Drive
Kailua-Kona, HI 96740
Phone: 808-329-9661/res 808-895-1373
Web: None
Hours: L 11:30 AM-1:30 PM Mo-Fr
         D 5:30 PM-9:00 PM Mo-Sa
Cards: AE JCB MC V
Dress: Casual
Style: Japan $$

Menu Sampler:

Breakfast:
N/A
Lunch:
Bentos including edamame, green salad, tsukemono, nimono (boiled vegetable
with soy sauce and sugar), tofu, shaomai, rice, and miso soup -- Teriyaki
Chicken Bento $12, Tonkatsu $12.00, Tempura $12.00, Sashimi $12.00,
Misoyaki Butterfish $13.50, Tempura Udon $12.00
Dinner:
Starter Pupu: Edamame $3.50, Fried Ahi $12.00, Tsukemono $5.25, Agedashi
Tofu $4.50, Salmon Shioyaki $8.75, Ahi Carpaccio $8.50, Shaomai $8.75
Salads: Maui Onion Salad $6.25, Seaweed Salad $6.25, Green Salad $4.75
Entrée: All include rice, miso soup, & tsukemono. Sashimi Platter $19.75,
Tempura Supreme $18.75, Tonkatsu $16.75, Misoyaki Butterfish $17.75,
Grilled Chicken Bistro $16.75, Grilled Salmon Bistro $17.55, Fried Salmon
$17.50, Steamed Opakapaka $19.75, Spicy Garlic Shrimp $18.75
"Pot & Pan": served with rice, miso soup and tsukemono, minimum of two
orders. Shabu Shabu $24.75 per order, Sukiyaki $24.75 per order
Wine, Sake, Domestic & Japanese Beer, Soft Drinks and Desserts

Impressions:

Bistro Yokohama is located in the back of the Sunset Alii Plaza. The pleasant
décor is Japanese minimalist with simple wooden chairs and tables arranged
symmetrically in an uncluttered atmosphere. The mood is one of peaceful
civility, which is a refreshing change in the midst of the hubbub along Alii
Drive. A wide range of traditional Japanese specialties is available at prices in
line with the level of presentation. Parking is free in the lot behind the plaza.

Big Island Dining

Kohala

Brown's Beach House
The Orchid At Mauna Lani
One N. Kaniku Drive
Kohala Coast, HI 96743
808-885-2000
www.orchid-maunalani.com
Hours: L 11:30 AM-3:00 PM
        D 6:00 PM-10:00 PM
Cards: AE DC DIS JCB MC V
Dress: Resort Casual
Style: Pac-Rim $$$

Menu Sampler:

Breakfast:
N/A
Lunch:
Brown's Beach House Clam Chowder $8, Oriental Chicken & Somen Noodle
Salad with sesame & soy vinaigrette $15, Fresh Island Taco-grilled & blackened
catch of the day, poblano cream $15, Open Faced Crab Melt with mozzarella
cheese & avocado, fruits $15, Grilled Hoisin Chicken Sandwich $14
Dinner:
Appetizers: Phyllo Crusted Tiger Prawn w/tropical fruit bbq sauce & balsamic
glaze $15, Misoyaki Butterfish (black cod) with Lomi Edamame $12
Salads: Island Baby Spinach & Radicchio Salad & crisp polenta, pancetta
vinaigrette $15, Caesar Salad with Lavosh Basket & Firecracker Shrimp $17
Soups: Lobster Bisque with fried won ton, anise liqueur, crème fraiche $8
Entrées: Macadamia Nut Crusted Rack of Lamb w/Kona Orange natural jus
$45, Seared Crisp Moi with basmati rice and citrus-shoyu sauce $36, Wok
Seared Kona Lobster with lobster won ton ravioli & wasabi butter sauce $45
Desserts: Tropical Fruit Soup w/macadamia nut biscotti and coconut sorbet $8,
Manago Cobbler with Tahitian vanilla bean ice cream $10

Impressions:

Stroll across the Orchid's beautiful grounds and you'll come to this outstanding
restaurant with its ocean front setting and breezy open-air atmosphere. Brown's
Beach House is a Kohala Coast favorite specializing in Pacific Rim cuisine. Not
only do they serve a wonderfully creative menu, but the servings are generous as
well. Try the Arnold Palmer Iced Tea for a lemony kick! Live entertainment
adds a special touch making this a great choice for romantic dining.

Hilo

Café Pesto
308 Kamehameha Ave.
Hilo, HI 96720
808-969-6640
www.cafepesto.com
Hours: L/D 11:00 AM-9:00 PM Su-Th
              L/D 11:00 AM-10:00 PM FrSa
Cards: AE DC DIS MC V
Dress: Casual
Style: Ec/Ital $$

Menu Sampler:

Breakfast:
N/A
Lunch/Dinner:
Appetizers: Asian Pacific Crab Cakes with honey-miso vinaigrette and pickled cucumber namasu $11.95, Focaccia with herbed goat cheese, Greek olive pesto, or rosemary gorgonzola $3.95, Sesame Big Island Goat Cheese $8.95
Salads: Thai Curry Shrimp over chilled fettuccine tossed with spinach, red onions, & a red curry vinaigrette $8.95, Greek Pasta Salad $7.95
Calzones: Toscana-prosciutto ham, mushrooms, and grainy Dijon mustard $9.95 at lunch or $14.95 at dinner with soup or salad
Gourmet Pizzas: 9" & 12" $7.95-$17.95, Variety of traditional & gourmet.
Entrées: Linguine al Pesto with grilled smoked chicken-apple sausage, vine-ripened tomatoes, roasted tomato-basil marinara $9.95/$14.95, Mango Glazed Chicken with caramelized mango chutney, garlic mashed potatoes, and Pahoa corn relish $17.95, Beef Tenderloin, Lobster Tempura & Garlic Prawns $28.95
Hot Sandwiches (Lunch Only): Milolii-garlic basted bay shrimp, Pacific crab, mushrooms, and blended cheeses on French bread $9.95, Hakalau-warm Kalua turkey, wilted spinach, caramelized onions, Poha-mango chutney, garlic basted French bread $8.95, Smoked Ham, Mushrooms, Dijon Mustard $7.95

Impressions:

Visit the downtown district behind Hilo Bay and you'll find Café Pesto with its classic bistro atmosphere. Here amidst the black and white tile flooring, high ceilings, and café style chairs, the proprietors offer an eclectic menu appropriate to the surroundings. When ordering, it's like, "Wow! Can I have one of these and one of those?" For patrons looking to spend time with casual company, Café Pesto has a full bar with an extensive wine and beer list.

Kohala

Café Pesto
Kawaihae Shopping Center
Kawaihae Harbor
North Kohala, HI 96743
808-882-1071
www.cafepesto.com
Hours: L/D 11:00 AM-9:00 PM Su-Th
          L/D 11:00 AM-10:00 PM FrSa
Cards: AE DC DIS MC V
Dress: Casual
Style: Ec/Ital $$

Menu Sampler:

Breakfast:
N/A
Lunch/Dinner:
Appetizers: Half Moon Nachos of Asian style chips, smoked mozzarella, jumbo shrimp, cilantro sour cream, mild chili dressing, corn relish $9.95, Crostini with a creamy herbed garlic butter $2.95, Smoked Salmon Pizzette $8.95
Salads: Seared Poke with Spinach Salad with green onion, ginger and grilled pineapple $Market Price, Thai Curry Shrimp w/red curry vinaigrette $8.95
Calzones: East West of sweet Japanese eggplant, marinated artichokes, sun dried tomatoes, and rosemary gorgonzola, or Onomea w/island fish, onions, peppers, & bean sprouts $9.95 at lunch or $14.95 at dinner with soup or salad
Gourmet Pizzas: 9" & 12" $7.95-$17.95 w/traditional & gourmet toppings
Entrées: Salmon Alfredo of smoked salmon, sun dried tomatoes, shiitake mushrooms and fettucine in a light cream sauce $10.95/$16.95, Mango Glazed Chicken w/caramelized mango chutney, garlic mashed potatoes, and Pahoa corn relish $17.95, Linguine al Pesto w/grilled smoked chicken-apple sausage $9.95
Hot Sandwiches (Lunch Only): Fresh Catch, parsley dressing, lettuce and vine ripened tomatoes on French bread or fajita $Market Price, Garlic Basted Bay Shrimp, Pacific Crab, mushrooms, and blended cheeses on French bread $9.95

Impressions:

When you drive up the Kohala Coast you'll come to a commercial harbor and the Kawaihae Shopping Center. Therein lies the original Café Pesto with its casual yet upscale dining menu. The specialties of the house switch back and forth between Italian and eclectic. Both are particularly good making this a popular spot with visitors and locals alike. Plan ahead. This place gets busy.

Kona

Cassandra's & My Place
75-5669 Alii Drive
Kailua-Kona, HI 96740
808-334-1066
Web: None
Hours: L 11:00 AM-4:00 PM Mo-Fr
        D 4:00 PM-10:00 PM
Cards: AE DC DIS JCB MC V
Dress: Casual
Style: Grk $$

Menu Sampler:

Breakfast:
N/A
Lunch:
Starters: Melitzanosalata of eggplant with fresh garlic, parsley, onions, olive oil and herbs $4.95, Spanokopita of spinach, feta cheese, and herbs in filo dough $5.95, Mushroom Caps stuffed w/scallops $8.95, Humus $4.50, Tiropita $5.95
Salads, etc: Greek Salad $7.95, with shrimp $10.95, Caesar Salad $6.95/$9.95 Omelets, 7" Pita Pizzas, Gyros sandwich $7.95, Fish and Chips $8.95
Burgers: Served w/French fries. Cheeseburger $7.95, Mushroom Burger $7.95
Dinner:
Starters: Garlic Prawns $8.95, Deep Fried Calamari $8.95, Dolmades-grape leaves stuffed with meat & rice in avgolemono sauce $7.95, Pita Bread $2.50
Salads: Sliced Tomatoes & Onions with oregano & vinaigrette dressing $6.95
Pasta's: Linguine-Greek with garlic butter and feta cheese $13.95
Entrées: Served with roasted potatoes, rice pilaf and vegetable of the day. Lamb Souvlaki $17.95, Chicken Souvlaki $16.95, Scallop Uvetsi-scallops baked in tomato, herb, garlic sauce and spinach topped with feta cheese and parsley $18.95, Filet of Salmon with olive oil, lemon, garlic, and fresh herbs $19.95, Moussaka with ground beef $14.95, Rack of Lamb $23.95, Dolmades $13.95

Impressions:

There's not a lot of Greek food served in these islands, so if you're craving a taste of the Aegean don't miss out on a visit to Cassandra's. This Kailua-Kona eatery is located upstairs across from the pier and serves a solid list of the old favorites. Even then, be sure to ask about daily specials before ordering. Price points are always of interest and most people will consider Cassandra's to be quite affordable. This is a pleasant place to while away an evening on the bay.

Big Island Dining

Kohala

Coast Grille
Hapuna Beach Prince Hotel
62-100 Kaunaoa Drive
Kohala Coast, HI 96743
808-880-1111
www.hapunabeachprincehotel.com
Hours: D 6:30-9:30 PM
Cards: AE JCB MC V
Dress: Resort Casual
Style: Pac-Rim/Sea $$$

Menu Sampler:

Breakfast/Lunch:
N/A
Dinner:
Raw Bar: Top Quality Assortment of oysters, clams, mussels $Market Price.
Appetizers: Manila Clam and Corn Chowder with roasted peppers $8, Shrimp Risotto, kabocha, sage pesto $18, Oven Roasted Scallops, pineapple jasmine rice, red curry glaze $12, Seared Hawaiian Ahi Summer Roll, green papaya salad, roasted peanut sauce $15, Bloody Mary Oyster Shooter w/spring onion $7
Entrées: Grilled Pork Tenderloin, smoked apple chutney, corn pudding, Waimea Haricot Verts $28, Crab Crusted Salmon, braised baby fennel, crispy potato pancake, coriander sauce $34, Grilled New York Steak, crispy Maui onion rings, grilled tomato salsa, soy garlic jus $33, Pancetta Wrapped Filet Mignon, forest mushroom compote, foie gras red wine sauce $34, Crispy Soft Shell Crab, pineapple jasmine rice, grilled Maui onions, mint shallot sauce $29
Desserts: Coconut Crème Brulee with mangoes, Waimea strawberries and toasted fresh coconut curls $11. Signature Dessert of White Chocolate Ginger Parfait with macadamia praline mousse, crème Anglaise & raspberry sauce $10, Warm Chocolate Cake w/ liquid center, nutmeg ice cream, mango compote $11

Impressions:

This spacious restaurant has an airy indoor seating area as well as a large outdoor terrace overlooking beautiful Hapuna Beach. The well stocked raw bar's wide variety of fresh oysters and homemade pokes challenge the diner to forgo dinner for an evening of pupus, but the upscale Pacific Rim entrées will tempt you to your table. Look for interesting dishes with complex flavors. The personable wait staff adds to the experience with informative, efficient service.

Big Island Dining

Waimea

Daniel Thiebaut

65-1259 Kawaihae Road (Hwy 19)
Waimea, HI 96743
808-887-2200
www.danielthiebaut.com
Hours: L 11:30 AM-2:00 PM Mo-Fr
            D 5:30 PM-9:00 PM
Cards: AE DC DIS JCB MC V
Dress: Resort Casual
Style: Fre/Asian $$$

Menu Sampler:

Breakfast:
N/A
Lunch:
Seafood Stir Fry w/chow fun noodles & lobster cream sauce $12.50, Slow cooked Lamb in Thai Curry Sauce w/coconut, mango chutney 7 jasmine rice $11.50, Mac Nut Tofu with stir-fry veggies and Tahini sauce $9.50
Dinner:
First Course: Lobster Bisque flavored with brandy and topped with cilantro coconut cream $6.50, Hilo Sweet Corn Crabcake w/lemongrass-coconut lobster sauce, annato crème fraiche & mango salsa $7.50, Spicy Chicken Wonton $6.50
Entrées: Grilled Shutome with green peppercorn, sweet and sour orange chili sauce, and jasmine rice $21.50, Hunan Style Rack of Lamb with lamb jus, eggplant compote, Puna goat cheese and roasted potatoes $24.50, Sautéed Macadamia Nut Chicken Breast with gingered mustard seed sauce, pickled pineapple and pave potatoes $20.50, Tomato-Fennel Risotto $18.00
Dessert: Fresh Papaya Millefeuille with vanilla sauce $6.50, Warm Strawberry Gratin with Tahitian vanilla ice cream $6.50, Chocolate & More $7.50
Prix Fixe: Three Course Prix Fixe $30.00 of first course, entrée, & dessert

Impressions:

Chef Daniel Thiebaut has transformed a quaint plantation general store into a wonderful setting for informal yet upscale dining. Note the counter and stools along one wall of the main room where the Parker Ranch paniolos used to sit and enjoy their beer. Some of their antique bottles are still on the shelves and even the old-fashioned fixtures remain in the bathrooms. The innovative menu uses fresh local ingredients and expert techniques with very pleasing results. This is a great addition to a small town widely known for culinary excellence.

Kohala

Donatoni's
Hilton Waikoloa Village
425 Waikoloa Beach Drive
Waikoloa, HI 96738
808-886-1234
www.hiltonwaikoloavillage.com
Hours: D 6:00 PM-9:30 PM
Cards: AE DIS DC JCB MC V
Dress: Evening Aloha
Style: Ital $$$

Menu Sampler:

Breakfast/Lunch:
N/A

Dinner:

Antipasta: Bruschetta al Pomodoro e Prosciutto of diced tomatoes, basil, and olives on toasted Italian bread with imported Parma ham $12, Carpaccio alla Boscaiola with thin slices of raw beef tenderloin, Reggiano cheese, celery and portabello mushrooms $13, Seared Fresh Tuna with citrus dressing $13

Insalate: Caprese con Mozzarella di Bufula of buffalo mozzarella, tomato, basil and roasted Maui onions $12, Insalata di Cesare $9, Spinach Salad $9

Zuppa: Minestrone alla Toscana with croutons and parmesan cheese $6

Pasta: Gnocchi di Patate al Gorgonzola-potato dumplings sautéed with arugula, walnuts, and gorgonzola cheese $21, Linguine ai Scampi of marinated shrimp with Italian fine herbs tossed with linguine pasta and a light white wine garlic butter sauce $26, Fettuccine Alfredo con Pollo and sun dried tomatoes $20

Secondi: Pesce del Giorno—sautéed fillet of fresh fish on marinated angel hair pasta with citrus butter sauce $27, Sella d'Agnello in Crosta di Pistacchio—pistachio crusted rack of lamb with pesto mashed potatoes and Cabernet sauce $32, Scalloppine al Marsala with mushrooms, shallots, and butter $25

Dolci: Tiramisu with Espresso Sauce $7, Hazelnut Crème Brulee $7

Impressions:

Donatoni's offers their patrons fine Northern Italian cuisine in a romantic canal side atmosphere. The formal setting provides a feeling of intimacy that can be hard to find in a resort the size of the Hilton Waikoloa. Diners can choose from inside tables or seating out on the terrace. Prime meat and seafood entrées are featured along with creative pasta selections. Flavors tend to be subtle without sacrificing depth. Reservations are definitely recommended.

Big Island Dining

Hilo

Don's Grill
485 Hinano Street
Hilo, HI 96720
808-935-9099
Web: None
Hours: B/L/D 10:30 AM-9:00 PM Tu-Fr
         B/L/D 10:00 AM-9:00 PM Sa-Su
Cards: AE MC V
Dress: Casual
Style: Amer/Isl $

Menu Sampler:

Breakfast:
Ham & Cheese Omelet with rice or hashed browns and toast $5.50, Loco Moco-an island original of a hamburger patty with a mound of rice, gravy and a fried egg $3.95, Double Loco Moco $6.95, Two Eggs with bacon, grilled fish, ham, or Portuguese sausage, Spam, link sausage, or corned beef hash $5.25, on weekends only-Sweetbread French Toast $3.25, Pancakes $2.75/$3.25

Lunch/Dinner:
Entrées: served with hot vegetables, fresh roll and choice of rice, mashed potatoes or French fries. Rotisseried Chicken $6.50/$7.95, Seafood Platter of breaded shrimp, breaded scallops and grilled filet of fish $8.95/$10.50, Lasagna with hot vegetables & garlic bread $6.50/$7.95, Grilled Teriyaki Beef $7.50/$8.95, Pork Chops $7.95/$9.50, Barbecue Ribs $8.95, Grilled Liver $7.50
Burgers and Sandwiches: with choice of French fries, cole slaw or macaroni salad $4.50-$6.75, Reuben Sandwich $5.50, Patti Melt $5.25, French Dip $6.50, Smoked Turkey Breast $4.95, Spam & Egg $5.25, Clubhouse $5.95
Soups: Saimin $4.50, Won Ton Mein $5.75, Chili & Rice with cheese $3.95
Salads: Cobb Salad $6.95, Taco Salad $5.95, Chicken Caesar $6.25
Sweet Treats: Homemade Pie $1.95, Ala Mode $2.95, Cheesecake $2.25, With Strawberries $2.75, Milkshakes $2.95, Apple-Lumpia Ala Mode $3.75

Impressions:

Not far from the airport there's a family dining spot serving a solid menu with substantial portions at reasonable prices. Don's Grill is a favorite with the local crowd and those visitors fortunate enough to find it. This isn't fine dining, but the offerings are tasty and well prepared. The menu includes favorites from the plantation days as well as choices from a variety of cuisines. Think of Don's as an international comfort food station. The modern facility with its airy solarium seating brings an outdoor feeling many find welcoming on a rainy Hilo day.

Big Island Dining

Kona

Drysdale's Two
Keauhou Shopping Center
78-6831 Alii Drive
Keauhou, HI 96739
808-322-0070
Web: None
Hours: 11:00 AM-11:30 PM Kitchen/10:00 AM-2:00 AM Bar
Cards: JCB MC V
Dress: Casual
Style: Amer $$

Menu Sampler:

Breakfast:
N/A
Lunch/Dinner:
Pupus: Chicken Fingers with hot sauce and French fries $7.70, Cheese Nachos & Jalapenos $7.60, Potato Skins $7.80, Shrimp Scampi with garlic toast $9.95
Burgers: $6.25-$8.95-Patty Melt on Grilled Rye, Baja Burger, Aloha Burger
Salads: Chef's Salad w/egg, ham, cheeses & turkey $10.25, Tuna Salad $8.85, Shrimp Salad w/1000 Island dressing $11.95, Cobb Salad w/crumbled blue cheese $10.85, Cajun Blackened Chicken Salad w/blue cheese dressing $9.50
Sandwiches: Fish Sandwich with fries $9.95, Italian Meatball Sandwich on a French roll with bell peppers & onions $7.95, Keauhou BLT with turkey $7.15
Plates: Tempura Fish & Chips $9.70, Pasta Primavera on spaghetti $10.85, Oriental Chicken Stir-Fry with rice $12.15, Greek Gyros Sandwich with yogurt dill sauce $7.80, BBQ Pork Baby Back Ribs & onion rings $14.90, Sesame Pasta Sauté with chicken breast chunks, zucchini, snow peas, onions, linguini $11.35, Shrimp Basket with Fries and cocktail sauce $8.75, Prime Rib of Beef with French fries and au jus $15.75, Liver & Onions with house potatoes $11.75

Impressions:

There are times when a sports bar with a solid menu and an ocean view are just the ticket. If that mood strikes you, visit Drysdale's Two in the Keauhou Shopping Center. Yes, Drysdale's, as in Mrs. Don (Ginger) Drysdale, as in Dodger Hall of Fame Pitcher. Casual dining is the rule in this friendly establishment, but the menu is quite broad and everyone should be able to find something to please. Check the daily board for fresh fish and ethnic specialty dishes. If you just want to hang out, have a seat at the bar and relax with your favorite beverage while watching the live sports telecasts. There always seems to be a lively discussion going on among the interesting crowd.

Big Island Dining

Waimea

Edelweiss

Kawaihae Road (Hwy 19)
Waimea, HI 96743
808-885-6800
Web: None
Hours: L 11:30 AM-1:30 PM XSuMo
        D 5:00 PM-8:30 PM XSuMo
Cards: MC V
Dress: Resort Casual
Style: Ger $$

Menu Sampler:

Breakfast:
N/A
Lunch:
Ranch Burger $8.75, Sautéed Chicken Breast with champignons $11.50
Venison Ragout $12.00, Beef Rouladen $12.00, listen to the many specials!!
Dinner:
Appetizers: Croute aux Champignons $4.95, Melon Prosciutto $4.95
Soups: Onion Soup $4.25, Soup of the Day $3.00
Salads: Caesar Salad $4.25, Waimea Tomatoes, Maui Onion and English Stilton
Cheese Salad $4.25, San Francisco Bay Shrimp Cocktail $5.95
Entrées: All dinners include soup of the day, salad, vegetable and coffee or tea.
Wednesday is Osso Buco Night in the winter—reservations are recommended,
as it is a local favorite. Wiener Schnitzel $21.50, Roast Duck Bigarade braised
with light orange sauce $22.50, Rack of Lamb (for two) basted in garlic,
mustard and fine herbs $55.00, Edelweiss Specialty of sauteed veal, lamb, beef,
& bacon with pfifferling $24.75, Filet Mignon with Green Pepper Sauce $26.50
Light Dinner: Specials announced every night $25.50, Bratwurst with
sauerkraut $10.50, Croute Edelweiss of Creamed Mushrooms on French Toast
with slice of ham, glaced with cheese $10.50

Impressions:

Edelweiss is the ultimate change of dining pace. While the Kohala Coast is all
about sunshine and seafood, this upcountry restaurant serves a robust German
menu in the cool misty environs of Waimea. Dinner here is like a visit to an Old
World inn. Chef Hans-Peter Hager owns and operates this long-time favorite.
His authentic preparations would sell just as well in Milwaukee or Munich.
Seating is limited, so make sure and call ahead for a reservation.

Big Island Dining

Kona

Edward's at Kanaloa
Kanaloa at Kona
78-261 Manukai
Keauhou, HI 96739
808-322-1434
www.edwardsatkanaloa.com
Hours: B 8:00 AM-11:30 AM
       L 11:30 AM-3:30 PM
       D 4:30 PM-9:00 PM
Cards: MC V
Dress: Resort Casual
Style: Cont/Med $$$

Menu Sampler:

Breakfast:
Bacon, chicken-apple sausage, O'Brien potatoes, eggs & toast $7.25, Cajun Omelet with Portuguese sausage $7.95, Salmon Gravlax on toasted bagel $7.95, Belgium Waffle with strawberries & whipped cream $7.25, Pancakes $6.25
Lunch:
Salad of field greens, blue cheese, walnuts, dried apricots, raspberry vinaigrette topped with a barbeque salmon filet $9.95, Fresh Fish Sandwich, grilled $9.50
Dinner:
Appetizers, Soups, Salads: Escargot in garlic butter & brie cheese $9, Two Sautéed Soft Shell Crabs in a creamy pommery mustard sauce $12, Lobster Bisque with vermouth $7, Ginger Chicken Orzo Soup $5, Caesar Salad topped with Parmesan & fried prosciutto ham $8, Greek Salad in an olive oil & red wine sauce $7, Big Island Salad of greens, mac nuts, blue cheese, cucumber & dried apricots in raspberry vinaigrette $7, Seared Ahi or Sashimi Style $Mkt
Entrées: Pork Tenderloin with herbs de Provence with potato tart & onion marmalade $24, Pepper Crusted 8 oz Filet Mignon in a brandy peppercorn sauce with potato tart & asparagus $28, Coq au vin and mashed potatoes $24, Chicken and Artichoke Strudel with roasted red pepper coulis $23, Seafood Orzo Pesto cooked in marsala butter $29, Twin Lobster Tails with cilantro beurre blanc, asparagus and baked potato $48, Mussels Provencal over pasta $26

Impressions:

If you're looking for ocean front dining, you've come to the right place. This intriguing menu uses fresh, full-flavored ingredients in its Mediterranean menu to create some truly exciting tastes. Beautiful setting and very romantic!

Kohala

Grand Palace
King's Shops
250 Waikoloa Beach Drive
Waikoloa, HI 96738
808-886-6668
Web: None
Hours: L 11:00 AM-2:00 PM
         D 2:00 PM-9:15 PM
Cards: AE DIS JCB MC V
Dress: Casual
Style: Chi $$

Menu Sampler:

Breakfast:
N/A
Lunch:
Luncheon specials include soup of the day, egg roll, choice of rice, and entrée.
Dinner:
Appetizers: Crab Rangoon $6.25, Pot Stickers $6.25, Spring Rolls $5.95
Soup: Chicken Creamy Corn Soup $9.95, Won Ton Soup $2.75/per person
Seafood: Sautéed Shrimp with Szechuan Sauce $17.95, Prawns in Pepper Salt $17.95, Crab Meat Fu Yong $15.95, Mussel with black bean sauce $12.95
Poultry: Cantonese Roast Duck $11.95, Rainbow Chicken $9.95, Crisp Duck $12.50, Chicken with Diced Vegetable and Cashew Nuts $9.50, Kung Po $9.95
Beef: Shredded Beef w/Orange Peel Sauce $10.95, Beef with Snow Peas $9.50
Pork: Mu Shu Pork $9.95, King Do Ribs $10.95, Pork with String Beans $9.95
Vegetables: Szechuan Eggplant $9.50, Lettuce with Oyster Sauce $9.50.
Hot pots, sizzling platters, rice and noodle specialties, desserts, and extensive family dinner combinations round out the menu.

Impressions:

We've got a little rule of thumb we use when sizing up an ethnic restaurant. If the menu is Chinese, but the patrons all look like they came from Cleveland, there might be a problem. That is definitely not the case at the Grand Palace. Although located in the mainland visitor haven of Waikoloa, this establishment attracts a large Asian following. Those people know good Oriental cooking when they find it and aren't afraid to drive a few miles to enjoy it. The Grand Palace is highly recommended to anyone who enjoys authentic Chinese cuisine.

Big Island Dining

Kona

Hard Rock Café
Coconut Grove Marketplace
75-5815 Alii Drive
Kona, HI 96740
808-329-8866
www.hardrockcafe.com
Hours: 11:00 AM-11:00 PM
Cards: AE DIS JCB MC V
Dress: Casual
Style: Amer/Ec $$

Menu Sampler:

Breakfast:
N/A
Lunch/Dinner:
Appetizers: Jumbo Combo of Handmade Onion Rings, Santa Fe Spring Rolls, Potato Skins, and Tupelo Chicken with a trio of sauces $8.99, Classic Chicken Wings served with celery and bleu cheese dressing $14.29, Potato Skins $7.39
Salads: Grilled Chinese Chicken Salad with homemade Oriental dressing $9.19, Haystack Chicken Salad with greens, vegetables, grilled or Tupelo fried chicken breast, spicy pecans and ranch dressing $8.99, Cobb Salad $9.19, Caesar Salad $7.79, Hard Rock House Salad with homemade croutons $6.99
Entrées and Sandwiches: "Pig Sandwich" Southern Style with fries, coleslaw and BBQ beans $9.19, Original BLT (BIG) with fries and coleslaw $8.99, HRC's Country Char-Broiled Burger with fries $8.39, Bruce's Famous BBQ Ribs (full rack) with fries, coleslaw, and BBQ beans $17.49, Hickory BBQ Chicken Dinner $10.29, Twisted Mac & Cheese with 3 cheese sauce, grilled chicken breast, and a side of garlic bread $9.99, HRC Shrimp Fajitas $14.99
Desserts: Chocolate Chip Cookie Pie $4.99, Down Home Apple Cobbler $4.99

Impressions:

If you're strolling around Alii Drive and find yourself in need of a cold beer and a good familiar sandwich, just walk up the stairs to the Hard Rock Café. Located along the harbor in the middle of town you'll find one of this chain's famous restaurant/nightclub locations. Every memory has a sound track, and the great tunes and memorabilia here are a rock 'n roll time trip. Menu offerings come in a wide variety and are surprisingly reasonable in price. This is a fun experience that appeals to a wide range of age groups. One note though, this is Kailua-Kona and the facility is smaller than those you may have visited in other locales.

Big Island Dining

Hilo

Harrington's
135 Kalanianole Ave
Hilo, HI 96720
808-961-4966
Web: None
Hours: L 11:00 AM-2:00 PM Mo-Fr
         D 5:30 PM-9:30 PM
Cards: AE MC V
Dress: Resort Casual
Style: Sea/Stk $$

Menu Sampler:

Breakfast:
N/A
Lunch:
Sandwiches: All sandwiches are served with seasoned waffle fries or coleslaw. Paniolo Prime Rib Sandwich with sauteed mushrooms and onions $8.95, Catch of the Day $8.95, Harrington's Burger $8.25, Vegetable Pita $7.25
Salads: Shrimp Caesar $8.95, Oriental Chicken Salad $8.25, Green $3.25/$4.75
Entrées: Prawns Chardonnay with mushrooms and Brie cheese $13.95, Fish & Chips $8.95, New York Steak broiled to order $14.75, Seafood Linguini $13.95
Dinner:
Appetizers: Escargot en Casserole with garlic butter, brandy, herbs on a bed of spinach and topped with cheeses $8.95, Seafood Chowder $2.95/ $3.95
Entrées: Opakapaka Meuniere topped with delicately browned lemon butter $18.95, Slavic Steak broiled and sliced thin and topped with a hearty garlic butter sauce $17.50, Chicken Marsala $18.95, Prime Rib au jus with horseradish sauce $22.95, New York Peppercorn Steak with an espanol sauce $22.75
Desserts: House Bread Pudding with a butter rum cream sauce $3.25, Lilikoi Sherbet $2.25, House Cheesecake with a mac nut/graham crust $3.25

Impressions:

This classic supper club is located on the waterfront near the Hilo airport. Guests are greeted by a warm, cozy atmosphere that perfectly complements cool, misty evenings. You can start with a visit to the lounge for cocktails and pupus before moving on to a relaxing dinner at a table overlooking the bay. The menu centers on traditional steak and seafood fare with daily specials. If you are looking for intimate and romantic in Hilo, this is where you'll find it. Harrington's is located right around the corner from the main Banyan Drive hotels.

Big Island Dining

Kohala

Hawaii Calls

Outrigger Waikoloa Hotel
69-275 Waikoloa Beach Drive
Waikoloa, HI 96738-5711
808-886-6789
www.outrigger.com
Hours: B 6:00 AM-11:00 AM
        D 5:30 PM-9:30 PM
Cards: AE DC DIS JCB MC V
Dress: Resort Casual
Style: Asian/Pac Rim $$$$

Menu Sampler:

Breakfast:
Buffet-$18.95/adult, $9.50/children, Continental Breakfast Buffet $11.95, Japanese Breakfast $17.75, A la Carte menu also available
Lunch:
N/A
Dinner:
Appetizers: Lobster Ahi Napoleon of a half sweet Keahole lobster tail, fresh ahi tartare with tobiko aioli $17, Pupu Platter for Two of coconut crusted shrimp, crispy calamari and mac nut ahi tempura $14/person, Lobster Nachos $16
Salads and Soups: Hawaii Calls Salad with mixed greens, vine ripened tomatoes and cucumbers on crispy rice paper $7, Outrigger Seafood Salad with scallops, shrimp, calamari and Waimea mixed greens served in a wonton basket with avocado and lemongrass vinaigrette $17, Salad Bar w/dinner $8, entrée $9
Entrées: Grilled Tournedos of Beef with boursin cheese scallion mashed potatoes topped with house made onion rings and wild mushroom demi-glace $34, Island Moi seared crispy with coconut jasmine rice, Asian vegetables with spicy cucumber salad and pickled ginger beurre blanc $33, Roasted Duck Breast char siu style w/steamed white rice, ratatouille and mandarin orange sauce $29
Desserts, Specialty Coffee Drinks, Fine Cognacs and Port Menu

Impressions:

Hawaii Calls is the Outrigger's beautiful signature restaurant. Diners have the choice of gracious indoor dining or seating out on the lanai where the great view and spacious grounds can best be appreciated. During breakfast hours the buffet provides an adequate selection of traditional items, but a nice ala carte menu is offered as well. Dinner becomes quite a bit more upscale and ambitious.

Big Island Dining

Kona

Huggo's
75-5828 Kahakai Road
Kailua-Kona, HI 96740
808-329-1493
www.huggos.com
Hours: B 6:30 AM-11:30AM
         L 11:30 AM-2:30 PM Mo-Fr
         D 5:30 PM-10:00 PM
Cards: AE DC DIS JCB MC V
Dress: Casual
Style: Amer/Ec $$

Menu Sampler:

Breakfast:
Java On The Rock-Two Egg Omelets with various fillings: American, Southwestern, Greek, Florentine with tortillas $6.75, with bagel or croissant $7.75, Lox & Bagels $6.00, Tropical Fruit $7.00

Lunch:
All sandwiches and burgers are served with choice of pineapple cole slaw, fries, rice, sliced tomatoes. Classic Huggo Burger with sautéed onions, mushrooms and choice of cheddar or swiss $8.95, Taro Burger $8.95, Mac Nut Chicken Katsu Plate Lunch with rice $9.95, Chinese Chicken Salad with sesame-hoisin vinaigrette $10.95, Fresh Catch broiled, grilled, sautéed, or blackened $Mkt

Dinner:
Appetizers: Fish Trap Shrimp in a net of fried, shredded phyllo dough with sweet chili dipping sauce $11.50, Garlic Bread Parmesan $4.50, Poke $11.50

Soups & Salads: Spinach Salad with goat cheese and orange segments $7.95, Seafood Chowder $3.95/$5.95, Classic Caesar $5.95/$8.95, Green Salad $7.95

Entrées: New York Steak with brandy green peppercorn sauce, wasabi mashed potatoes, asparagus, frizzled onions $29.95, Grilled Chicken Pasta with goat cheese cream sauce, sun dried tomatoes, mushrooms, diced pancetta, linguine $21.95, Crab Crusted Ono with mango vinaigrette glaze, rice, vegetables $29.50

Impressions:

This establishment comes in several incarnations. First there's Huggo's, which is their casual seaside dining spot. Then a few feet away there's Huggo's On The Rocks, which can best be described as a watering hole and place to see and be seen. Finally come dawn Java On The Rock appears serving coffee and breakfast items to bleary-eyed partygoers. Watch out for waves!!!

Big Island Dining

Kohala

Imari

Hilton Waikoloa Village
425 Waikoloa Beach Drive
Waikoloa, HI 96738
808-886-1234
www.hiltonwaikoloavillage.com
Hours: D 6:00 PM-9:30 PM
Cards: AE DIS JCB MC V
Dress: Evening Aloha
Style: Japan $$$$

Menu Sampler:

Breakfast/Lunch:
N/A
Dinner:
Appetizers, Soups, Salads: Edamame-boiled soy beans $6, Yasai Tempura-assorted tempura vegetables $9.50, Imari Salad w/Imari Dressing $6, Watarigani Kaarage-deep-fried soft-shell crab served with ginger ponzu sauce $16, Red Miso Soup $6, Fresh Clams in a light butter broth $13, Sunomono $9
Entrées: Catch of the Day-grilled, teriyaki, steamed $36, Wakadori Teriyaki of Grilled Breast of Chicken with teriyaki glaze $29, Live Maine Lobster grilled, teriyaki, steamed $55, Wafu Steak with grated daikon, and ponzu sauce $35
Specialty Dinners of Shabu Shabu, Sukiyaki, and Chef's Assorted Course with otoshi, tempura or sashimi, shabu shabu, sukiyaki, or three course assortment of grilled, steamed or deep fried, tsukemono, & dessert $47-$62 per person
Sashimi and Sushi: Maguro Sashimi of fresh ahi served with wasabi and soy sauce $16, California Roll of crab, avocado & cucumber $9, Spider Roll $17.50
Teppanyaki: with otoshi, rice, miso soup, & tsukemono. Filet Mignon $42, Shrimp and Jumbo Scallops $39, Steak and Shrimp $44, Catch of the Day $38, Lobster Tail $55, Breast of Chicken $32, Vegetarian Dinner $32

Impressions:

Upon entering Imari you will be immersed in all things Japanese. Kimono clad waitresses and attendants seat and serve you from a choice of traditional dining styles. Patrons can choose from teppanyaki tables, the sushi bar, tatami rooms, and conventional table seating. Chef Atsumi is classically trained and uses the freshest of ingredients to create his healthy selections. This restaurant has clean contemporary lines and makes generous use of wood to convey the decor of Japan. You won't find a better example in the neighbor islands.

Big Island Dining

Kona

Island Lava Java
75-5799 Alii Drive
Kona, HI 96740
808-327-2161
www.islandlavajava.com
Hours: 6:00 AM – 10:00 PM
Cards: DIS JCB MC V
Dress: Casual
Style: Cof $

Menu Items:

Breakfast:
Breakfast Sandwiches-6 AM-2 PM-Bagel and Cream Cheese $1.85, Bagelwich with cream cheese, tomato and sprouts $2.75, Denver Wrap $4.75, Egg/Veggie Wrap $4.75, Eggwich on English Muffin $2.25, Ham/Cheese Croissant $3.25
Breakfast Plates-6 AM-Noon-Waffles $3.95, Berry Pancakes $5.95

Lunch/Dinner:
Sandwiches all come with mayo, lettuce, tomato, sprouts, choice of cheese and bread, chips or small salad-Chicken Salad $6.95, Garden Burger $6.95, Lava Java of turkey and ham $7.95, Pita Pocket-choices $7.95, Polish Dog $3.75- w/chili and cheese or kraut $5.25, Taco Salad $6.75, Cup of Soup $3.50, Nachos $4.95, Greek Wrap with Chicken $8.95, Veggie Wrap $6.95, Caesar Salad $7.95

Beverages:
100% Kona Dark/Med Roast Coffee 12 oz $1.40, Refill $.60, 16 oz $2.00, Refill $1.00, Flavored, Kona Pohaberry, Decaf, Latte's, Café Au Lait, Chai, Espresso $2.50-$3.25, Hot Chocolate $1.50/$2.00, Milk Shakes $4.75, Coke Float $3.25
Now featuring a Kava and fresh fruit/veggie drinks bar.

Impressions:

Island Lava Java is a cross between a coffee house and the neighborhood delicatessen. Patrons order at the counter, and then find a seat on the lanai overlooking the bay. Things start early as the regulars straggle in before work and then continue on until the after-dinner crowd has headed off to bed. Some come for the specialty coffees, while others enjoy the reasonably priced wraps and sandwiches. Regardless of which you prefer you'll find it served throughout the day. As an added convenience, two internet terminals are available for those who feel the need to complicate their vacation by checking their e-mail. If the caffeine doesn't get you going, the news from your broker undoubtedly will!

Big Island Dining

Kona

Jameson's By The Sea
Magic Sands Beach
77-6452 Alii Drive
Kona, HI 96740
808-329-3195
Web: None
Hours: L 11:00 AM-3:00 PM Mo-Fr
         D 5:00 PM-9:30 PM
Cards: AE DC DIS JCB MC V
Dress: Casual
Style: Sea $$

Menu Sampler:

Breakfast:
N/A
Lunch:
Appetizers: Salmon Pâté $8.95, Fried Calamari $8.95, Sashimi $13.95
Burgers & Sandwiches: Cheeseburger $7.95, Grilled Crab & Shrimp $11.50, Reuben $9.95, BBQ Beef $9.25, Deep Fried Calamari Steak Sandwich $10.95
Entrées: Teriyaki Rib Eye Steak $13.95, Fried Tempura Shrimp $14.95, Seafood Quiche $10.95, Fresh Ono $14.95, New York Steak $18.95
Salads/Entrées: Curried Chicken Salad $11.95, Thai Chicken $10.95, Chicken or Shrimp Caesar Salad $11.95, Jameson's Crab Louie $14.95, Tempura Fried Shrimp $14.95, Seafood Quiche w/choice of salads $10.95, Ono $14.95
Dinner:
Appetizers: Sashimi $13.95, Crab Stuffed Mushrooms $9.95, Fried Calamari $9.95, Chilled Seafood Platter $14.95, Sautéed Mushrooms $4.95
Entrées: Opakapaka prepared five ways $Market Price usually $32-$34, Baked Stuffed Shrimp with crabmeat, cheese and hollandaise $23.95, Seafood Diablo $21.95, Shrimp Curry with mango chutney $22.95, New York Steak $29.95, Filet Mignon w/béarnaise $37.95, Shrimp Scampi over linguini $22.95

Impressions:

This is the kind of restaurant visitors picture when they think of dining in Hawaii. It's located on the lower floor of a 1960's vintage oceanfront condo building beside Magic Sands Beach. Diners have their choice of indoor/outdoor seating, both with lovely sunset views. Make no mistake, seafood is king here. Landlubbers might be happier elsewhere. After dinner try one of the homemade chiffon pies. The shortbread crust and island style fillings are delightful.

Big Island Dining

Kona

Kanaka Kava
Coconut Grove Marketplace
75-5803 Alii Drive-B6
Kailua-Kona, HI 96740
808-327-1660
www.puuala.com
Hours: LD 11:00 AM-10:00 PM Su-We
         LD 11:00 AM-11:00 PM Th-Sa
Cards: None
Dress: Casual
Style: Isl $$

Menu Sampler:

Breakfast:
N/A

Lunch/Dinner:
Ala Carte: Kalua Pork $4, Poke (Raw Fish) $4, Squid Luau $4, Opihi (Raw/Cooked) $4, Ulu (Breadfruit) steamed with coconut milk $3, Poi $2, Sweet Potato $2, Taro steamed with coconut milk $3, Garlic Bread $2, Haupia/Sweet Potato Pie $4

Plates: All plates come with two ala Carte items. Fresh Fish/Chicken/Tofu Plate $10, Lau Lau Plate $10, Seafood Plate-scallops, shrimp, fish $12, Pupu Platter-pork, sweet potato, poke, ulu, poi, squid luau $15

Salads: Seafood Salad-shrimp, scallops, fish, baked with sesame oil, garlic and oyster sauce over greens, carrots, tomato, cucumber, avocado, mushrooms & Zack's miso dressing $12, Chicken Breast/Fish Filet/Tofu Salad prepared as above $10, Poke Salad-fresh poke served as above $10, Kanaka Salad of greens, tomato, cucumber, carrots, mushrooms, avocado, & Zack's miso dressing $8

Kava Menu: Fresh Kava-with or without juice $3/$4, Kavalada-blended kava drink with coconut milk and pineapple juice $5, O2 Bar-15 minutes with aroma $10, Yerba Mate $3, Coffee $2, Fruit Juice $1, Bottled Water $1

Impressions:

Kanaka Kava is not your ordinary everyday eatery. This is a kava bar. If you're not familiar with kava bars, we should probably start at the beginning. Kava is an adult beverage made from the root of the intoxicating pepper. Although non-alcoholic, kava definitely has a kick to it hence the reason it is served at kava bars. The kava ritual begins with consuming several bowls of this interesting beverage followed by much eating and visiting. This is happy hour Polynesian style and is highly recommended for the adventurous traveler.

Hilo

Ken's House of Pancakes
1730 Kamehameha Ave.
Hilo, HI 96720
808-935-8711
Web: None
Hours: 24/7
Cards: AE DC DIS JCB MC V
Dress: Casual
Style: Amer/Isl $

Menu Sampler:

Breakfast/Lunch/Dinner:
The entire menu is available 24 hours a day seven days a week. Macadamia Nut
Waffles $6.50, Fresh Banana Pancakes $5.25, Eggs Benedict $6.95, Crab Cakes
Benedict $7.85, Loco Moco $4.95, Saimin $5.20, 23 Famous Omelettes,
Florentine Omelet with spinach and sour cream, hashed browns or white or
brown rice, and toast or pancakes $7.75, homemade muffin with honey butter
$1.00, Burgers $6.10-$7.65 with fries or salad, BBQ Kalua Pig Sandwich on a
grilled hoagie bun $7.35, Broiled Mahi Mahi Sandwich with cottage cheese or a
green salad $7.65, Hot Turkey Sandwich with mashed potatoes and gravy $8.35.
Dinner style entrees come with mac salad, choice of rice, fries, or mashed
potatoes: Broiled Teriyaki Chicken $8.25, Grilled Pork Chops $8.55, Honey
Stung Chicken $8.75, Liver Lovers with grilled onions, bacon and gravy $7.95,
Kalbi Ribs with Kim Chee $10.45, Vegetarian BLT $6.95, Oxtail Stew $9.95,
Every Wednesday after 3 PM is Paniolo Night with a Prime Rib special.
Desserts: Milk Shakes $2.95, Ice Cream Floats $2.85, Sundaes of strawberry,
blueberry, chocolate, lilikoi & coconut $1.95-$4.10, Sweet Potato Pie with
haupia topping $3.25, Macadamia Nut Pie $2.45, Fresh Papaya $1.85

Impressions:

This old Hilo standard serves a traditional mainland and island menu in a coffee
shop/diner setting. Ken's is especially convenient as it is located just to the north
of the airport entrance. Long distance travelers seem to suffer from maladjusted
body clocks, and this is where Ken's really shines. We're talking 24-hour dining
here which is a rarity on the neighbor islands. You can expect solid fare served
at reasonable prices in this clean, well-lit eatery. Parking can be scarce in the lot
along the highway, so if that one's full, try the area to the south and walk over.

Big Island Dining

Volcano Village

Kilauea Lodge & Restaurant
19-3948 Old Volcano Road
PO Box 116
Volcano, HI 96785
808-967-7366
www.kilauealodge.com
Hours: D 5:30 PM-9:00 PM
Cards: MC V
Dress: Resort Casual
Style: Cont/Haw-Reg $$

Menu Sampler:

Breakfast:
Offered for overnight guests only. Not open to the public.
Lunch:
N/A
Dinner:
Starters: Brie Cheese coated in an herb batter with coconut flakes and lightly fried with three grain mini-loaf and brandied apples $6.50, Stuffed Mushroom Caps $6.50, Hand Battered Big Island Zucchini Spears $5.50
Entrées: All are served with soup, salad, vegetables and our own three-grain bread. Fresh Catch of the Day served three ways; sautéed in piccata sauce, broiled and topped with a papaya ginger sauce or mango chutney glaze with crushed macadamia nuts, or blackened Cajun style with Hawaiian salsa $Mkt, Hasenpfeffer-Braised Rabbit in a hearty hunter's wine sauce $24, Lamb Provencal-rack of lamb baked with fresh herbs & seasoned bread crumbs, garnished with papaya apple mint sauce $28.50, Free Range Medallions of Venison flamed with brandy $28.50, Duck L'Orange with apricot mustard glaze $24.50, Osso Buco $34.50, Eggplant Supreme on pasta or rice pilaf $18.50

Impressions:

The Kilauea Lodge is located in a former YMCA camp that was refurbished as an inn back in 1987. On a cool, misty upcountry evening you just might get the feeling that you are in British Columbia instead of Hawaii. Here among the majestic pines and giant ferns the owner/chef serves an excellent Continental menu backed with touches of Hawaii Regional Cuisine. Diners can expect rich tastes and large portions from this Old World establishment. Be careful about over-ordering. Many patrons choose to split an entrée with their dining partner, which can be done for an additional $7.50. Reservations are a must.

Kona

Kona Brewing Co. Pub
75-5629 Kuakini Hwy
Kona, HI 96740
808-329-2739
www.KonaBrewingCo.com
Hours: L/D 11:00 AM-9:00 PM Su-Th, 11:00 AM-10:00 PM FrSa
Cards: DC DIS MC V
Dress: Casual
Style: Amer/Isl $$

Menu Sampler:

Breakfast:
N/A
Lunch/Dinner:
Pupus: Nachos layered with gourmet toppings $9.99, Mac Nut Pesto Cheese
Bread-focaccia topped with macadamia nut pesto, roasted garlic and mozzarella
and served with a side of marinara $6.99, Roasted Garlic served with toasted
spent grain focaccia and creamy gorgonzola cheese $5.99, Garlic Twists $3.25
Salads: Caesar Salad $5.49/$7.99, Mauna Loa Spinach Salad tossed in balsamic
vinaigrette with toasted macadamia nuts, chevre, organic tomatoes, and red
onions $6.99/9.49, Add Grilled Chicken or Rock Shrimp to salad $2.99/$3.99
Sandwiches: All are served on house made focaccia rolls with Kettle Chips.
Pololu-sliced chicken breast served hot with mozzarella cheese, roasted red
pepper coulis, pepperoni, and fresh basil leaves $8.49, Porterhouse Dip of Roast
Beef marinated and cooked in our Pahoehoe Porter, topped with grilled red
onions, melted cheddar and mozzarella cheeses with porter au jus for dipping
$9.99, Pacific Golden Ale Garlic Shrimp Melt with spinach and cheeses $10.99
Pizza: Small 10", Medium 12", and Large 14" from $8.99 to $22.99. Traditional
and gourmet ingredients such as Kalamata olives, macadamia nuts, pesto, wild
mushrooms, roasted red peppers, rock shrimp, lilikoi barbecued chicken.

Impressions:

If you like brewpubs, you need to check this one out. Although the Kona
Brewing Company produces quality-crafted award-winning beers that are sold
throughout the islands, they don't relegate the kitchen to the back seat.
Indoor/outdoor seating, innovative food, and a fun crowd are located just a block
mauka of the King Kamehameha Hotel in the heart of Kona. Occasional
appearances of live musicians such as Johnny Lang keep things hopping.

Big Island Dining

Kona

Kona Galley

75-5663 Palani Road
Kailua-Kona, HI 96740
808-329-5550
Web: None
Hours: L 11:00 AM-4:00 PM XSu
          D 4:00 PM-9:00 PM
          D 4:30 PM-9:00 PM Su
Cards: AE DC JCB MC V
Dress: Casual
Style: Cont/Isl $$

Menu Sampler:

Breakfast:
N/A
Lunch:
Soup and House Salad $6.95, Kona Galley Gourmet Burgers with lettuce, tomato, onion, pickles on a sesame bun and French fries $6.95-$9.95
Pizza: A variety of traditional and gourmet toppings $7.95-$8.95
Dinner:
Starters: Escargot in garlic herb butter topped with melted cheese $8.95, Galley House Green Salad $4.95, Poke $9.95, Shrimp Louie $10.95
Pasta: Angel Hair Pasta prepared with garlic, fresh tomato, Parmesan cheese $11.95, Baked Vegetable Lasagna $13.95, Shrimp Linguini with parmesan cream sauce $13.95
Entrées: Include fresh vegetables & choice of rice or potato. Chicken Puna w/a breast of chicken sautéed w/papaya wedges, bay shrimp, covered w/our special curry sauce $16.95, Steak Diablo of choice sirloin rubbed w/herbs, ground pepper, broiled and topped w/fresh green salsa & melted cheese (spicy!) $18.95

Impressions:

When you are looking for affordable upscale dining in Kailua- Kona, check out the Kona Galley. This open-air restaurant sits across the street from the King Kamehameha Hotel. There on the second floor overlooking Kona Bay diners are offered a selection of traditional items with interesting touches. If watching the sunset isn't relaxing enough for you, try one of Grandpa's Mai Tai's for a total mood adjuster. Look for the coupons being circulated by the hotels and activity desks. This is the quiet end of the bay front and there are deals to be had.

Kona

Kona Inn Restaurant
Kona Inn Village Shopping Center
75-5744 Alii Drive
Kona, HI 96740
808-329-4455
Web: None
Hours: L 11:30 AM-9:30 PM
         D 5:30 PM-9:00 PM
Cards: AE MC V
Dress: Resort Casual
Style: Sea/Stk $$

Menu Sampler:

Breakfast:
N/A
Lunch:
Café Grill 11:30 AM-9:30 PM-Pupus, Soups & Salads, Sandwiches
Soups & Salads: Clam Chowder $4.25 & $5.25, Grilled Chicken Caesar Salad $9.95,Caesar Seafood Salad $5.95, Seafood Cobb Salad $12.95, Poki $7.95
Entrees: Deluxe Burger with chips $6.95, Fresh Fish Sandwich with chips $Market Price, Sautéed Calamari Sandwich $8.95
Dinner:
Pupus: Sashimi $Market Price, Jumbo Shrimp Cocktail w/special sauce $10.95, Seared Rice Paper Ahi w/wasabi dipping sauce $Mkt, Thai Curry Lemongrass Soup $4.25, $5.25, Field Green Salad w/Hamakua Goat Cheese $7.95
Entrées: Seafood Pasta on Linguine in an olive oil, garlic, tomato, wine and herb butter $20.95. Each of the following includes potato, pilaf, or rice, a green vegetable and warm bread: Calamari sautéed golden brown $15.95, Hawaiian Chicken, broiled and topped with pineapple $16.95, Teriyaki Top Sirloin $19.95, Prime Rib $22.95 & $25.95, a large variety of locally caught fresh fish $Mkt Price, Fettucine with Mac Nut Pesto and Seared Shrimp $19.95

Impressions:

The Kona Inn was built to accommodate inter-island steamship passengers back in the 1920's. Although the original twenty-room inn has been replaced by a garish shopping venue, the dining room remains to this day surrounded by an expansive lawn out on an oceanfront point. The traditional steak and seafood menu has some innovative ethnic twists added recently which fit well with the setting. This romantic spot is a favorite with repeat visitors. Make sure to take time to view the displays in the outer lobby.

Big Island Dining

Volcano Village

Lava Rock Internet Café

Volcano Village
Old Volcano Road
Volcano, HI 96785
808-967-8526
Web: None
Hours: B 7:30 AM-10:30 AM
         L 10:30 AM-5:00 PM
         D 5:00 PM-9:00 PM XSu Mo
Cards: MC V
Dress: Casual
Style: Amer/Isl $$

Menu Sampler:

Breakfast:
Espresso $2.50, Latte $3.00, Mocha $3.50, Cappuccino $3.25, Sweet Bread
French Toast with homemade lilikoi butter, guava butter or ohelo berry syrup
and 2 eggs $6, Pancakes (3) with two eggs $5.50, Three Egg Omelets with rice
or potatoes, toast or biscuit $6.25, Loco Moco $4.95/$5.95, Fried Rice $4.25

Lunch:
Burgers/Entrées: served with choice of salad, French fries or chips $4.95-
$6.25, Chinese Chicken Salad $7.00, Philli Cheese Steak with choice of salad,
French fries or chips $6.75, Chicken, Steak, Veggie or Tempeh Fajitas $8.25

Dinner:
Dinner Plates: served with soup and garden salad, taro roll, mashed potatoes or
rice and potato-mac salad or cole slaw—Teriyaki Beef $9.00, Hamburger Steak
with gravy and onions $8.75, Chicken Katsu $8.75/$9.75, Kalbi Ribs $11.00

Meals: Served with soup and salad. Linguine and Meat Balls with garlic bread
$9.50, Southern Fried Chicken with French fries $9.75, New York Steak with
steamed vegetables, and choice of baked potato, rice or linguine $12.50, Grilled
Mahi Mahi $12.50, Nightly Specials Tu-Fr $9.95, Prime Rib $16.95/$20.95 Sat.

Desserts: Lilikoi, Manago or Ohelo Cheesecake $4.00, Haupia Crunch $3.00

Impressions:

You'll find this pleasant little coffee shop tucked behind a general store in
Volcano Village. The Lava Rock Internet Café serves generous portions of
mainland and island comfort food. Their extensive hours work well for visitors
who have to drive in from other parts of the island. This is a great place to go
online and check your e-mail while enjoying a meal or a great piece of pie.

Waimea

Maha's Café
Waimea Center
65-1148 Mamalohoa Highway
Kamuela, HI 96743
808-885-0693
Web: None
Hours: B 8:00 AM-10:30 AM XTuWe
         L 10:30 AM-4:30 PM XTuWe
Cards: DC DIS JCB MC V
Dress: Casual
Style: Amer/Isl $

Menu Sampler:

Breakfast:
Papaya with fresh lemon $2.75, Poi Pancakes with coconut syrup $3.75, Granola Parfait with fruit, nuts, and yogurt $4.25, Home Style Banana Bread, Papaya Coffee Cake, Croissants, or Pan Biscuits $2.75, Eggs 'n things $5.25
Lunch:
Entrées: Broiled Fresh Fish with sliced steamed taro and sweet potato on a bed of Kahua greens with a gingered vinaigrette $9.25, Kohala Harvest-a bountiful salad of veggies with Maha's house dressing and feta cheese and served with Waimea Sweet Corn Bread $7.75, The Hukilau-fresh fish daily $Market Price
Sandwiches: Freshly Roasted Turkey sliced on 12 Grain Bread with home style mushroom stuffing and cranberry relish $6.75, Smoked Ahi with lilikoi salsa baked in a flour tortilla with shredded cheese $10.75, Thinly Sliced Lamb on 12 Grain Bread with lettuce, tomato, light mayo and spicy mango chutney $8.00
Desserts: Hawaiian-Style Bread Pudding with guava-ginger sauce $3.00, Macadamia Shortbread with lilikoi curd $3.00, Spencer House Fruit Cobbler with vanilla hard sauce $3.00, One-is-not-enough Fudge Brownie $3.00
Dinner:
N/A

Impressions:

Maha's is located in Waimea's historic Spencer House surrounded by the hustle and bustle of the Waimea Center. The eclectic menu offers light breakfasts, lunches, and old-fashioned island desserts all prepared in a healthy fashion. Regulars swear by this place, but the selections change as the mood strikes, so be ready for the dining experience of the day when you visit Maha's Cafe.

Kona

Manago Hotel Restaurant
622-6155 Mamalahoa Hwy
Captain Cook, HI 96704
808-323-2642
www.managohotel.com
Hours: B 7:00 AM-9:00 AM XMo
        L 11:00 AM-2:00 PM XMo
        D 5:00 PM-7:30 PM XMo
Cards: DC DIS JCB MC V
Dress: Casual
Style: Amer/Isl $$

Menu Sampler:

Breakfast:
Choice of papaya or juice, coffee or tea, breakfast meat choice of link sausage, Portuguese Sausage, Vienna Sausage, Spam, Ham, or Bacon, toast/rice, & two eggs $4.50, Pancake $3.00, French toast $3.00, Japanese Green Tea $1.50/$2.50

Lunch/Dinner:
Entrées: All entrees include three side dishes and steamed rice: New York Steak $12.25, Shrimp Sauté $10.50, Butterfish $9.50, Opelo, Akule, Mahi Mahi or Pork Chops $8.50, Teriyaki Chicken $8.00, Liver or Beef Teriyaki $7.50, Hamburger Steak $7.00, Ahi (seasonal) $9.50

Sandwiches: Mahi Mahi $5.50, BLT $4.50, Cheeseburger $4.50, Hamburger $4.00, Tuna $4.00

Impressions:

The Manago Hotel is a "must see" even if it isn't mealtime. Built in 1917 for traveling salesmen and tourists on their way to see the volcano, the Manago looks much the same today as it did two generations ago. As part of your trip through time, you can step into the parlor and examine the old photos on the walls. To add to your experience, The Manago offers delicious island comfort food in a dining room reminiscent of roadside inns from the 40's and 50's. This entire area is a look at old Hawaii complete with wooden plantation style buildings clinging to the sides of cliffs and a narrow road cut into the hillside.

Big Island Dining

Waimea

Merriman's
Opelo Plaza
65-1227 Opelo Road
Kamuela, HI 96743-2349
808-885-6822
www.MerrimansHawaii.com
Hours: L 11:30 AM-2:30 PM Mo-Fr
           D 5:30 PM-9:00 PM
Cards: AE MC V
Dress: Resort Casual
Style: Haw-Reg/Pac-Rim $$$

Menu Sampler:

Breakfast:
N/A
Lunch:
Kalua Pig & Sweet Onion Quesadilla with Ahualoa jack cheese, kimchee & mango chili dipping sauce $7.95, Wainaku Corn & Shrimp Fritters with turtle bean relish &cilantro sour cream $7.95, Wok Char Ahi w/wasabi $Mkt
Dinner:
Appetizers: Mauna Kea Goat Cheese Baked in Phyllo with Hibara Farm organic greens and Waimea strawberry vinaigrette $8.95, Soup of the Day $5.95
Salads: Peter's Caesar with Szechuan Shrimp $10.95, Spinach Salad $7.95
Vegetable Dishes: Stir Fried Cake Noodle with sugar snap peas and vegetable stir fry with spicy black bean sauce $18.95, Lemon Pepper Pasta $19.95
Entrées: Merriman's Original Wok Charred Ahi $Market Price, Kung Pao Fresh Island Shrimp—hot & sour stir fried with macadamia nuts served with long rice salad $20.95/$24.95, Grilled Kahua Ranch Beef w/black bean $23.95
Sweet Endings: Caramel Mixed Nut Tart, sour cream cardamom topping, orange passion mango sauce, Coconut Crème Brulee, chocolate biscotti $6.95

Impressions:

Peter Merriman's charming restaurant is located in the town of Waimea just 20 minutes from the resorts on the Kohala Coast. This pioneer in Hawaii Regional Cuisine combines fresh island ingredients in a fusion of flavors and techniques representing every ethnic group in the islands. Check out the pictures of the local suppliers in the entryway. We especially like the one of the Puna Goat Cheese vendors posed at their establishment. The sign on the building says "Hippies Use Side Door". This takes on special meaning when you realize that they're all hippies! The party never stops in Puna.

Big Island Dining

Hilo

New China Restaurant
510 Kilauea Ave.
Hilo, HI 96720
808-961-5677
Web: None
Hours: 10:00 AM-9:00 PM Tu-Su
Cards: MC V
Dress: Casual
Style: Chi $

Menu Sampler:

Breakfast:
N/A
Lunch/Dinner:
Appetizers: Pupu Platter $12.00, Fried Pot Stickers (10) $5.50, Crispy Won Ton (10) $3.00, Spring Roll (5) $5.50, Breaded Shrimp (10 pcs.) $6.95
Combination Plates: Spare Ribs, Crispy Chicken, Mahi Fish & Vegetables $5.95, Shrimp and Cashew Nuts w/vegetables & Crispy Chicken $6.25
Soups: Abalone with Pork & Veg Soup $6.95, Tofu w/Vegetables Soup $5.50
Sizzling Platters: Shrimp with Ginger Onions $9.50, Bat Zhen (assorted meats & vegetables) $7.50, Shrimp & Chicken with Black Bean Sauce $7.75
Entrées: Char Siu Pork (Hong Kong Style) $6.25, Mongolian Beef $6.95, Crispy Chicken with Pineapple Sauce $5.50, Chicken with Black Bean Sauce $5.75, Egg Fu Yong $4.50, Fresh Scallops and Shrimp with Oyster Sauce $9.25
Noodles: Saimin (Large) $2.95, Wor Won Ton Mein $3.75, Singapore Style Rice Noodles $5.50, Beef Chow Fun (Hong Kong Style) $5.50, Shrimp Chow Mein with Vegetables $6.25, Chicken with Vegetables Cake Noodles $5.95
Rice: Young Chow Fried Rice (House Special) $5.95, Shrimp Fried Rice $5.50
Chop Suey and Vegetarian Food: Shrimp Chop Suey $5.95, Vegetables Chow Fun $4.95, Vegetables Cake Noodles $5.25, Garlic Broccoli $4.95

Impressions:

New China is the kind of place you look for when you no longer feel the need for elegant décor and fancy wine lists. This is the Cantonese-Hong Kong style of Chinese cooking with which most people are familiar. The menu is built around traditional favorites and is broad enough to satisfy without branching out so far as to mystify. Better yet, you don't come away feeling like everything came out of a box. Service is fast in this affordable dining spot regardless of whether you are eating in or taking out. There's plenty of parking in the lot by the building.

Hilo

Nihon Restaurant & Cultural Center
123 Lihiwai Street
Hilo, HI 96720
808-969-1133
Web:	None
Hours:	L 11:00 AM-1:30 PM XSu
	D 5:00 PM-8:00 PM XSu
Cards:	AE DC DIS JCB MC V
Dress:	Resort Casual
Style:	Japan $$

Menu Sampler:

Breakfast:
N/A
Lunch:
The Hatamoto is served with rice, kappa maki, potato salad, konomono, miso soup, and tossed salad. Add to this any two entrées from Butterfish Misoyaki, Shrimp Tempura, Sashimi, Broiled Chicken Teriyaki, Tonkatsu, Beef Sirloin Teriyaki, Chicken Katsu $11.95, Oriental Style Shrimp Salad with special miso dressing $9.95, Oyako Donburi of slices of chicken simmered with onions, egg, and donburi sauce $7.95, Tofu Nabe with chicken or beef in broth $12.95
Dinner:
Combination Dinner is served with sashimi, rice, konomono, miso soup, Japanese green tea, and vegetable salad. Add any two entrées from the above lunch list plus Seafood Batayaki $17.95, Sukiyaki of chicken or beef, vegetables and noodles simmered in an authentic sukiyaki sauce $14.95, Nabeyaki Udon of shrimp tempura, crablet, and egg served in a bowl of udon noodles and a light sauce and garnishes $10.95, Nihon Nabemono of vegetables, seafoods, and other garnishes in a light and flavorful broth $15.95, Sushi a la carte

Impressions:

This establishment sits on a point jutting out into Hilo Bay. From the beginning Nihon was conceived to be more than just a restaurant. It's also a cultural center with a small gallery featuring historic photographs and displays. Diners will find reasonably priced local style Japanese cuisine being served in traditional service. For those looking to experience Japanese food and culture as found in Hilo, this would be an interesting choice. One comment though, the restaurant is built up on stilts above the tsunami crest. So if you have problems climbing stairs, an elevator is located at the back of the building for your convenience.

Big Island Dining

Hilo

Nori's Saimin & Snacks
688 Kinoole Street
Hilo, HI 96720
808-935-9133
Web: None
Hours: LD 10:30 AM-3:00 PM Mo-Sa
         LD 4:00 PM-12:00 AM Tu-Th
         LD 4:00 PM-1:00 AM FrSa
         LD 10:30 AM-9:30 PM Su
Cards: MC V
Dress: Casual
Style: Local Japan $

Menu Sampler:

Lunch/Dinner:
Soups: Garnished with green onions, char siu, and eggs. Specials include cooked vegetables and a chicken stick on the side. Saimin S $3.50, L $4.20, Udon Won Ton S $4.55, L $5.75, Special $6.80, Seaweed Won Ton Min S $4.55, L $5.75, Mundoo Soup S $5.50, L $6.50, Hong Kong Style Noodle $5.75
Noodles: Fried Noodles, Fried Saimin, or Chow Fun served with a chicken stick $5.45. Fried Thai Curry Noodles with a BBQ stick $6.25, Cold Zaru Buckwheat Noodles $6.25, Bi Bim Kook Soo $6.50, Cold Zaru Wakana $6.25
Entrées: Include choice of macaroni salad or tossed salad. Teri Beef $6.25, Fresh Ono with Stir Fry Peppers $6.95, Miso Butterfish $7.45, Korean Shortribs $7.25, Teri Shrimp w/Calamari Combo $7.25, Ahi-choice of four preparations $6.95, Big Plate includes Ahi Tempura, Fried Noodles, Kalbi Ribs, Teri Beef, Chicken Sticks, Musubis and Macaroni Salad $15.95, Sizzling Salmon Tsukemono Steak w/one scoop of rice, mac salad & a tossed salad $7.25
Omiyage & Desserts: Nori's Chocolate Mochi- by the slice $1.15, mini-loaf $3.85, large loaf $8.75, Nori's Chocolate Mochi Cookies $5.00, Nori's Haupia Pies- slice $1.75, whole pie $12.00, Cherry Plum Seed $1.25, Shrimp Crackers $2.75, Nori's Mustard Cabbage Koko $3.75, Nori's Macadamia Nut Brittle $3.50, Dried Teri Tako $5.95, Dried Ahi Jerky $4.95, Nori's Hot Sauce $5.00

Impressions:

Nori's is definitely a cultural experience. This one's not easy to find, so you won't see a lot of tourists inside. What you will find is a very popular local establishment serving a home-style mélange of Japanese/Korean dishes. Hilo people really like this place. It's friendly and cozy, but what they enjoy most are the local favorites prepared the way they like them, like chocolate mochi cake!

Big Island Dining

Hilo

Ocean Sushi Deli
239 Keawe Street
Hilo, HI 96720
808-961-6625
www.oceansushideli.com
Hours: L 10:00 AM-2:00 PM XSu
          D 4:30 PM-9:00 PM XSu
Cards: AE DC JCB MC V
Dress: Casual
Style: Japan $

Menu Sampler:

Breakfast:
N/A
Lunch/Dinner:
Nigiri Sushi (2 pcs): Wakame (seaweed salad) $2.50, Chukakurage (seasoned jellyfish) $2.50, Ebi (shrimp) $2.50, Tsubugai (conch) $3.50, Special Scallops $3.50, Unagi (eel) $4.00, Awabi (abalone) $4.00, Negi Hama (yellowtail and green onions) $4.00, Lomi Salmon $4.50, Opihi $5.00, Uni (sea urchin) $7.00
Hosomaki & Temaki: Kappa (cucumber) $1.40, Salmon Skin $2.50, Ahi Poke $2.50, Tako Poke $2.50, California or Canadian $2.75, Unagi Avocado $3.50
Special Rolls: Big Island-ahi, avocado, macadamia nuts, spicy or special mayo $4.50, Mermaid Roll-special scallops (scallop with mayo and flying fish eggs), imitation crab, shredded daikon, shrimp, tobiko on the outside $4.50, Ebi-Ten roll-shrimp tempura with lettuce and spicy or special mayo $4.50, Tokyo Roll-ahi tempura, cucumber, & avocado wrapped in tofu skin w/a sweet sauce $5.50
Salads: Seaweed Salad $6.25, Cold Soba Salad $5.75, California Salad $7.50
Miscellaneous: Miso Soup $1.00, Steamed Rice $1.00, Ahi or Tako Poke $5.00
Sushi Boxes and Family Platters: Extensive selections from $4.30-$49.95

Impressions:

A waitress in a fancy Kohala resort turned us on to this place. She originally came from Hilo and raved about indulging in plates full of quality sushi at very reasonable prices. Intrigued by the thought, we did a little research and found that Ocean Sushi Deli is not only right across the street from one of our favorite spots, Tsunami Grill & Tempura, but it's owned by the same family. At first glance this little storefront looks a bit funky, but it's very clean and attracts a nice cross section of Hilo society. The menu is truly extensive. It's one of the only places you'll find that regularly offers opihi. No alcohol served but BYOB.

Big Island Dining

Kona

Ocean View Inn
75-5683 Alii Drive
Kailua-Kona, HI 96740
808-329-9998
Web: None
Hours: B 6:30 AM-11:00 AM XMo
         L 11:00 AM-2:45 PM XMo
         D 5:15 PM-9:00 PM XMo
Cards: None
Dress: Casual
Style: Amer/Chi/Haw $

Menu Sampler:

Breakfast:
Ham and Eggs $4.75, Spanish Omelet $4.95, Bagel and Cream Cheese $2.00,
Hot Cakes w/ ham, bacon or pork sausage $4.95, Papaya $1.50
Lunch:
Kalua Pork Sandwich w/ potato salad $6.95, Teriyaki w/ French fries $5.95, Hot
Beef Sandwich w/ mashed potatoes $6.50, Chinese Plate with rice $6.25
Dinner:
Dinners include soup or fruit cup, green salad w/ dressing, rice, French fries or
mashed potatoes, coffee or tea. Pork Chops with fried onions $8.95, Country
Fried Steak $10.50, Shoyu Chicken $8.25, Broiled Ono Steak $9.95
Hawaiian: Laulau & Poi $4.25, Lomi Salmon $1.50, Kalua Pig $4.75
Desserts: Pies with ice cream $3.50, Sliced Pineapple $1.50, Sherbet $1.50

Impressions:

The Ocean View Inn has been a part of the Alii Drive scene for a great many
years. Linoleum floors, Formica tables, a vintage jukebox, old photos, and
jalousie windows overlooking the bay set the stage for a scene from the past.
One can almost picture the sailors crowded around the adjacent bar and dancing
across the floor. The menu selections are traditional island favorites with some
Chinese items tossed in for variety. Portions are large, prices are reasonable, and
the food is respectable. This used to be the center of town, but progress keeps
moving along. The action is now located farther south down along Alii Drive.
Regardless, if it's mealtime and you are looking for value and a glimpse of Old
Hawaii, take a walk and go visit the Ocean View Inn.

Kona

Oodles of Noodles
Crossroads Shopping Center
75-1027 Henry Street
Kona, HI 96740
808-329-9222
www.oodleskona.com
Hours: L 10:00 AM-5:00 PM
        D 5:00 PM-9:00 PM
Cards: AE DC DIS JCB MC V
Dress: Resort Casual
Style: Haw-Reg $$

Menu Sampler:

Breakfast:
N/A
Lunch:
Appetizers: Veggie Summer Roll with hoisin peanut sauce $5.95, Upcountry Organic Greens, Edible Blossoms, Crisp Noodles, Guava Dressing $4.95
Soups: Pho-Vietnamese beef noodle, carpaccio, and table greens $8.95
Entrees: Grilled Vegetable Pasta Primavera with olive oil $10.95, Kona Style Wok Seared Ahi "Tuna Noodle" Casserole with orecchiette, shiitake cream, crisp onions, wok seared spiced ahi or cooked ahi $13.95, Pad Thai $10.95
Dinner:
Appetizers: Upcountry Organic Greens, plum dressing $4.95, Thai Style Crisp Calamari with lime fish sauce $7.95, Spicy Pacific Caesar with crunchy noodle croutons $4.95, Chinese Style Dumplings, Ginger Scallion Sauce $9.95
Soups: Oodles Saimin of duck broth, lup cheong, char siu, fish cake, bok choy, scallions $7.95, Tamarind Seafood Soup of glass noodle, fish, scallops, rock shrimp $19.95, Udon with Tsuyu Broth, Peking Duck and Kai Choy $13.95
Entrées: Southwestern Style Fettucine of grilled chicken, ancho-chipotle chili cream, sweet peppers, roasted corn, lime and cilantro $15.95, Curried Lemongrass Coconut Chicken with mung bean noodle $12.95

Impressions:

Owner-chef Amy Ferguson Ota has long been an island leader in Hawaii Regional Cuisine. Currently working out of a modest storefront that has been interestingly decorated with original art, she wows taste buds with her marvelous combinations of quality ingredients and imagination. If you're looking for something unusual yet reasonably priced, this one is a must!

Big Island Dining

Kohala

Pahu i'a
Four Seasons Hualalai Resort
100 Ka'upulehu Drive
Ka'upulehu-Kona, HI 96740
808-325-8000
www.fourseasons.com/hualalai
Hours: B 6-11 AM
             D 5:30-10 PM
Cards: AE DC DIS JCB MCV
Dress: Evening Aloha
Style: Pac Rim $$$$

Menu Sampler:

Breakfast:
Big Island Buffet of traditional and alternative breakfast items 25.00, A la Carte
Breakfast Specials: Huevos Rancheros with Chorizo, refried black beans, corn
tortilla, salsa rojo 16.00, Lemon Ricotta Pancakes 13.00, Japanese Breakfast
26.00, Crispy Belgian Waffle w/Kahlua Macadamia Nut Butter 13.00

Lunch:
N/A

Dinner:
Starters: Five Spice Duck Potstickers with wild mushroom poke 14, Dim Sum
Sampler 16, Carrot Ginger Soup with crème fraiche & chives 9, Pan Roasted
Foie Gras with caramelized gingered apple, Riesling sauce 18
Salads: Big Island Hearts of Palm Salad with candied macadamia nuts,
Gorgonzola cheese and Asian pear 13, Lobster Caesar Louie 17
Entrées: Wok Seared Shutome with pineapple fried rice, Singapore black
pepper sauce 33, Garlic Rib Eye Steak with roasted potatoes, red wine sauce 36,
Crispy Skin Opakapaka Meuniere with caramelized Maui onions, Fingerling
potatoes, roasted macadamia nut brown butter 38, Veal Oscar Hualalai with
black truffle potatoes, shrimp and crab ravioli, Asian béarnaise sauce 38, Spicy
Thai Barbeque Ali'i Prawns, pad Thai noodles, vegetable stir fry 38, Homemade
Vegetable Ravioli with Grilled Hearts of Palm, tomato ginger coulis 29

Impressions:

Pahu i'a is the casually luxurious signature restaurant at the Four Seasons
Hualalai Resort. Here along the oceanfront you'll find Pacific fusion cuisine
taken to a higher level. The chef creates particularly complex preparations to
give the diner full exposure to what's possible when diverse cultures collide.
Patrons can expect a combination of fine dining and setting second to none.

Waimea

Paniolo Country Inn
65-1214 Lindsey Road
Kamuela, HI 96743
808-885-4377
Web: None
Hours: B 7:00 AM-11 AM
        L/D 11:00 AM-8:00 PM
Cards: AE DIS MC V
Dress: Casual
Style: Amer/Mex $

Menu Sampler:

Breakfast:
Mac Nut Hotcakes 2/$3.35, 4/$6.50, Omelets served with rice, potatoes, or sliced tomatoes $4.50-$5.95, Breakfast Specials $3.25, Loko Moko with eggs $4.50, Eggs Benedict (1/2 order) $4.50 (full order) $6.50

Lunch/Dinner:
Sandwiches: All served on whole wheat or French roll with fries or cole slaw. Turkey Tom with sliced turkey breast topped with tomato, onion, melted cheese, mayonnaise and sprouts $6.95, Paniolo Club $6.95, Char Broiled Chicken $6.95
Hamburgers: Served with choice of bun w/lettuce, onion & pickles, fries or slaw. Paniolo Burger $5.95, Keiki Burger- children $3.00, Cheeseburger $6.35
Salads: Paniolo Taco Salad with beef, veggie or chicken $6.95, Tostada Grande Salad served on a crisp fried tortilla $6.95, Caesar Salad $$4.45/$6.75
Paniolo Platters: Served with a choice of soup or salad, rice or French fries, and a corn coblet. 12 oz T-Bone $16.95, Fried Chicken $9.95, 6 oz Top Sirloin $11.45, Barbecued Baby Back Pork Ribs $13.95, Seafood Platter $13.95
Paniolo Pizza: Pizza for one $2.95-$8.90, for two $5.50-$13.55, for four to six $11.95-$23.00 with a wide variety of toppings available
South of the Border Specials: Quesadilla with beef, chicken or ham $5.95, Burrito Supreme with veggies and beef, chicken or ham $7.35, Nachos $3.50

Impressions:

For such a small town, Waimea has much to offer in the way of culinary choices. The Paniolo Country Inn with its country café atmosphere and home-style menu might be a rural cousin to some of the gourmet finds in town, but the food is good and the portions satisfying. This is family dining American style and there should be something on the menu to please everyone in the group.

Big Island Dining

Kona

Peacock House
81-6587 Mamalahoa Hwy
Kealakekua, HI 96750
808-323-2366
Web: None
Hours: L 10:00 AM –2:00 PM Mo-Fr
         L 11:00 AM-2:00 PM Sa
         D 5:00 PM – 8:00 PM XSu
Cards: DC DIS JCB MC V
Dress: Casual
Style: Chi $

Menu Sampler:

Breakfast:
N/A

Lunch/Dinner:
Appetizers: Crispy Won Ton (12 pcs) $3.00, Fried Shrimp (10) $7.25, Chinese Chicken Salad $5.75, Char Siu-Sweet BBQ Pork $6.50, Pupu Platter $7.25
Soups: Scallop with Egg and Chicken Soup $7.50, Won Ton Soup $4.75, Egg Blossom with Minced Pork Soup $5.95, Pork Watercress Soup $5.95, Hot & Sour Soup with Chicken $5.95, Pork Mustard Cabbage Soup $5.95
Entrées: Kung Po Shrimp $7.25, Hong Kong Style Crispy Chicken $6.50, Roast Duck $6.75, Black Pepper Steak $7.25, Beef or Pork with ginger & green onion $7.25, Moo-Shu Pork $6.75, Scallops with black bean sauce and vegetables $8.75, House Special Chop Suey $6.95, Spicy Tofu $6.25, Char Siu Egg Fu Yung $5.75, House Special Fried Rice $5.75, Singapore Mai Fun $6.95, Steamed Pork Hash $6.25, Chop Suey $5.25, Combination Dinner Plates available $5.95-$6.50, Dinner for 2 $19.95, for 3 $27.95, for 4 $34.95

Impressions:

Peacock House is located on the makai side of the highway in the Pualani Terrace shopping plaza. This small but attractive establishment has a wonderful view overlooking the western shore of the Big Island 1000 feet below. Lunch can be ordered a la carte or selected from the buffet. The food is consistently good, and the staff will steer you in the right direction. We were once told, "Haole customer no like!" when considering a local favorite that turned out to be more fat than lean. MSG can be omitted upon request. Beer and wine are available. This makes a good stop between the Kona Coast and the volcano.

Hilo

Pescatore
235 Keawe Street
Hilo, HI 96720
808-969-9090
Web: None
Hours: B 7:30 AM-11:00 AM SaSu
         L 11:00 AM-2:00 PM
         D 5:30 PM-9:00 PM
Cards: AE DC DIS JCB MC V
Dress: Resort Casual
Style: Ital $$$

Menu Sampler:

Breakfast:
French Toast $4.25, with fresh strawberries & cream $4.95, Italian Omelet with Italian sausage, Fern Forest spinach, mushrooms, tomatoes and cheddar cheese topped with marinara sauce and served with home fries or rice $5.95
Lunch:
Panini Grill Sandwiches include fries or pasta salad: Grilled Chicken with prosciutto, provolone, fresh sage, and roasted pepper mayonnaise $7.95, Veggie Panini of grilled portobellos, spinach, garlic, roasted peppers and fresh mozzarella $6.50, Pasta Chicken Salad w/grilled chicken breast $7.95
Pizza: 8" & 12" $8.95-$18.95 Traditional & Gourmet Toppings.
Pasta: Pesto $4.25/$5.95, Alfredo $4.95/$6.95, Puttanesca $4.95/$7.95
Dinner:
Antipasti: Carpaccio de Pesce of ahi with garlic, capers, red onion, balsamic vinegar, olive oil & Parmesan $10, Garlic Bread with mozzarella and tomatoes $5, Scampi $9, Antipasto $7, Calamari Fritte $6, Sautéed Artichokes $6.00
Pasta: Puttanesca (includes soup or salad) olive oil, garlic, anchovies, capers, crushed red peppers, sun dried tomatoes and olives $16, Fra Diavolo $19.00
Entrée: Includes soup or salad & Fresh Baked Bread—Veal Scaloppini Marsala $22, Cioppino Classico $25, Lamb Chops marinated with mint pesto $24, Black Angus Ribeye Steak Grilled $25, Chicken Breast Parmesan Style $18

Impressions:

Pescatore is in the old part of downtown Hilo. With its high ceilings, bentwood chairs, and the evening mist falling outside one gets the feeling of being in a big city neighborhood instead of Hawaii. Expect a traditional Italian menu with all the regional classics. The black tie service is an appropriate match, and although the prices aren't in the budget category, you can spend a lot more for a lot less.

Big Island Dining

Hilo

Queen's Court
Hilo Hawaiian Hotel
71 Banyan Drive
Hilo, HI 96720
808-935-9361
www.castleresorts.com
Hours: B 6:30 AM-9:30 AM Mo-Sa
           B 6:30 AM-9:00 AM Su
           Bru Buf 10:30 AM-1:30 PM Su
           L 11:15 AM-1:15 PM XSu
           D 5:30 PM-9 PM
Cards: AE DC DIS JCB MC V
Dress: Resort Casual
Style: Amer/Ec/Isl $$$

Menu Sampler:

Breakfast:
Buffet Mo-Sa: Scrambled Eggs, French Toast, Meats, Rice, Potatoes, Toast, Fresh Fruits and Juices, Baked Goods, Japanese items such as Miso Soup, Tofu, Fishcake, Green Onions, Coffee and Tea $10.25/Adults, $6.75/Children
Sunday Champagne Brunch Buffet- Lavish spread of carved meats, traditional breakfast items; stir fry station, omelet station, curries, snow crab legs, pasta, unique salads, desserts and much champagne $24.25/Adults/$14.50/Children
Lunch:
Prime Rib Sandwich on grilled sourdough with fries or potato-mac salad $9.25, Saimin $3.75 & $4.75, Sesame Chicken Salad $6.75, Somen Salad $8.50
Dinner:
Prime Rib & Crab Dinner Buffet: Mo-Th with ethnic theme foods featured each night $24.25 (Mo-Paniolo night, Tu-Italy, We-Orient, Th-Country; Seafood Dinner Buffet: Fr- with carved meats and hot and cold fish, seafood $27.25, Seafood Hawaiian Dinner Buffet: SaSu-with carved meats and traditional Hawaiian foods $27.25; A la Carte Menu also offered.

Impressions:

Queen's Court has been voted the best buffet on the Big Island several years in a row. This cut above dining room overlooks Hilo Bay and is known for bountiful selections of fine traditional and island foods. They do what they do very well.

Kona

Quinn's Almost By The Sea
75-5655 Palani Road
Kona, HI 96740
808-329-3822
Web: None
Hours: L 11:00 AM-5:00 PM
        D 5:00 PM-11:00 PM
Cards: MC V
Dress: Casual
Style: Amer/Sea $$

Menu Sampler:

Breakfast:
N/A
Lunch:
Pupus: Sautéed Mushrooms w/garlic bread in brandy and garlic butter $6.50,
Quinn's Spicy Wings $7.25, Crab Stuffed Mushrooms $9.95, Kalbi Pupu
$10.25, Broiled Steak Strips-5 oz. Filet Mignon topped with grilled onions
$10.50, Deep Fry Pork Egg Rolls with sweet chili sauce $8.95
Burgers: served with fries, rice or salad. Char Broiled Burger $7.95
Sandwiches: served with fries, rice or salad. Snow Crab Mix on Sourdough
with jack cheese $10.25, Mahi Mahi on an onion bun $8.95, Monte Cristo $8.95
Soups & Salads: Clam Chowder $2.95/$3.95, Shrimp & Crab Salad $11.50
Dinner:
All of the items above plus the following: Served with soup or dinner salad,
vegetable, choice of rice, Quinn's Potatoes, fries—Catch of the Day $22.95,
Teriyaki Chicken smothered in mushrooms $18.95, Shrimp Scampi on a bed of
linguine $22.95, Steak & Broiled Shrimp $23.95, Filet Mignon $22.95

Impressions:

Across from the King Kamehameha Hotel you'll find an establishment that
looks deceivingly small from the street. Upon entering the premises a charming
courtyard patio and a respectable sized dining room reveal themselves. The
décor is "island funky" reminiscent of the Florida Keys. This hideaway serves
good, unpretentious food at very convenient hours in a friendly atmosphere.
After 9 PM it can be difficult to find restaurants that are still open in Kailua-
Kona, but Quinn's serves until 11 PM. So whether your body clock is upside
down or you simply stayed too long at happy hour, take a walk up Alii Drive
and try Quinn's for a casual late evening dinner.

Big Island Dining

Kona

Royal Jade Garden
Lanihau Center
75-5595 Palani Road
Kona, HI 96740
808-326-7288
Web: None
Hours: 10:30 AM-9:30 PM
Cards: JCB MC V
Dress: Casual
Style: Chi $

Menu Sampler:

Breakfast:
N/A

Lunch/Dinner:
Appetizers: Royal Jade Platter S- $9.50, L- $16.95, Egg Roll $3.25, Crisp Won Ton $4.25, Pot Stickers $6.25, Char Siu $4.25, Fried Shrimp Chips $1.95
Soups: Abalone Soup $9.25, Pork with Mustard Cabbage Soup $6.50, Hot & Sour Soup $7.25, Chicken Cream Corn Soup $6.50, Ox Tail Soup $7.95
Entrées: Fried Tofu Vegetable Black Bean Sauce $7.95, Cashew Nut Vegetable $7.50, Beef with Oyster Sauce $6.95, Steamed Pork Hash $7.95, Roast Duck $6.95, Kung Po Chicken $7.50, Chicken with Macadamia Nuts $7.75, Fish Filet with Vegetables $7.95, Spicy Shrimp $7.95, Abalone w/Black Mushrooms $13.95, Honey Glaze Walnut Shrimp $9.50, Char Siu Chop Suey $6.95, Royal Jade Chow Mein $8.50, Beef Chow Fun $7.95, Vegetarian Egg Fu Yong $6.95, Grandma's Tofu (spicy) $7.50, Shrimp a la Canton $8.25, Char Siu $7.25
House Special: Garlic Shrimp Hong Kong Style $9.50, Mandarin Sweet and Sour Chicken $7.95, Mongolian Lamb $8.95, Duck w/Mustard Cabbage $8.95
Noodles: Royal Jade Wor Mein Soup $6.25, Char Siu Sai Mein $3.95, Wor Won Ton Mein $5.95, Spicy Beef Mein $6.25, Gau Gee Soup $5.25
Rice: Char Siu, Beef, Chicken, or Vegetable Fried Rice $5.95, Shrimp Fried Rice $6.50, Royal Jade Fried Rice $6.50, Steam Rice $1.00

Impressions:

Don't be put off by the shopping plaza location--Royal Jade Garden is no Takee Outee. This family-owned establishment offers a wide range of Chinese classics with some unusual items presented for added interest. They offer a hot bar for the hurry-up crowd at lunch, but we always prefer to order from the menu. It just seems to play out better that way. Make sure to ask about the daily specials!

Hilo

Royal Siam Thai
70 Mamo Street
Hilo, HI 96720
808-961-6100
Web: None
Hours: L 11:00 AM-2:00 PM XSu
        D 5:00 PM-9:00 PM
Cards: AE DC DIS MC V
Dress: Casual
Style: Thai $$
        Ent Card

Menu Sampler:

Breakfast:
N/A
Lunch/Dinner:
Appetizers: Fried Fresh Tofu $4.95, Spring Rolls $5.95, Chicken Satay $5.95
Soups: Tom Yum Seafood Soup with a tangy broth of spices, straw mushrooms, tomatoes, lemongrass, lime leaves and vegetables in mild, medium, or hot $8.95, Coconut Chicken Soup $5.95, Thai Noodle Soup with Pork or Chicken $5.95
Salads: Mild, medium, or hot. Green Papaya Salad $5.50, Cucumber Salad $5.50, Royal Siam Tofu Salad $5.95, Hot & Sour Shrimp or Squid Salad $8.95
Entrées: Mild, medium, or hot. Budda Rama-chicken sautéed in peanut sauce on a bed of spinach $7.95, Red Curry with chicken or beef and bamboo or eggplant $7.95, Scallops with sweet basil $9.95, Thai Garlic Shrimp $9.95, Ginger Chicken, Beef or Pork $7.95, Yellow Curry with Chicken or Beef with potatoes and onions $7.95, Seafood Curry of shrimp, scallop, calamari & fish with yellow curry and vegetables and rice $10.95, Eggplant with Chicken $7.95, Cashew Chicken $7.95, Basil Chicken or Beef $7.95, Ong Choi Beef $7.95
Desserts: Tapioca Pudding $2.50, Thai Custard $1.95, Green Tea, Coconut, or Kona Coffee Ice Cream $1.95, Cheesecake $2.50, Thai Iced Tea or Coffee $1.95

Impressions:

Visitors and locals alike enjoy this small eatery in downtown Hilo. Service is fast, the prices are reasonable, and they have won awards for their consistently good food. Thai cuisine combines comforting tastes with zesty surprises. Ask about the Drunken Noodles. This delicious dish is prepared on request but is not on the menu. Ample street side parking is available.

Big Island Dining

Kohala

Roy's at Waikoloa
King's Shops
250 Waikoloa Beach Drive
Waikoloa, HI 96738
808-886-4321
www.roysrestaurant.com
Hours: L 11:30 AM-2 PM
            D 5:30-9:30 PM
Cards: AE DC JCB MC V
Dress: Resort Casual
Style: Haw-Reg $$$

Menu Sampler:

Breakfast:
N/A
Lunch:
Entrees: Big Island Teriyaki Beef Sandwich with sautéed onions and mozzarella cheese with furikake rice $10.95, other items $5.00-$14.00
Dinner:
Appetizers & Salads: Roy's Blackened Ahi with spicy soy mustard butter sauce $9.00, Caramelized Sweet Onion Tart with Puna goat cheese, wild berry vinegar and white truffle oil $6.95, Baby Romaine & Fresh Watercress with peppered walnuts and creamy blue cheese balsamic dressing $7.50
Kiawe Fired Pizzas: Herb Grilled Garden Vegetable Calzone with caper tapenade, peppered jack cheese, and walnut pesto $6.50, Pizzas $6.50/$7.50
Entrées: Candied Macadamia Nut Crusted Rack of Lamb with Kona coffee caramel sauce & apple pear chutney $27.95, Lemongrass Crusted Swordfish with ginger scented coconut cream with lingham, sweet mashed potatoes and lotus root $25.95, Cracked Seed Baked Half Chicken with garlic mushroom potato hash, fresh fennel and rosemary $16.95, Mac Nut Ono $25.95
Desserts: Wonderful tray of gourmet desserts changing daily!

Impressions:

We have never had a bad meal at Roy's--no matter which location! Roy Yamaguchi is one of the Hawaii Regional Cuisine pioneers, and his restaurants are now found worldwide. In Waikoloa, Hawaiian Island Chef member Jaqueline Lau uses fresh local ingredients with taste pleasing twists to make dining here a culinary experience. Don't miss it!! This is one Roy's in Hawaii that serves lunch. Reservations are strongly suggested during dinner hours.

Hilo

Seaside Restaurant
1790 Kalanianole Ave
Hilo, HI 96720
808-935-8825
Web: None
Hours: D 5:00 PM-8:30 PM XMo
Cards: AE DC JCB MC V
Dress: Resort Casual
Style: Isl $$

Menu Sampler:

Breakfast/Lunch:
N/A
Dinner:
Pupus: Sautéed Mushrooms $3.95, Spicy Chicken Wings $5.95, Calamari Strips $5.95, Shrimp Cocktail $6.95, New York Steak $8.95
Complete Dinners include fresh salad, hot vegetables, rice, and apple pie: Mullet $16.95, with Chicken $15.95, with New York Steak $20.95, Fried Aholehole $23.95, Grilled Ahi, Mahi, or Ono with butter garlic or pesto sauce $Market Price, Grilled Atlantic Salmon with butter garlic, teriyaki or miso $16.95, Furikake Salmon with teriyaki sauce and wasabi mayonnaise $18.95, Butterfish-fried, grilled, teriyaki or miso $17.95, Grilled Shrimp with Pasta with butter garlic, caper or marinara sauce $17.95, Vegetarian Pasta with butter garlic, pesto, or marinara sauce $8.95, Seaside Chicken w/brown gravy $10.50

Impressions:

Along the coast just south of the airport you'll find a Hilo institution. The Seaside Restaurant is unique among Hawaii's seafood eateries as it sits on the edge of an ancient fishpond that still operates as an aquaculture farm for their kitchen. Obviously, "When In Rome…" is the order of the day here, so plan on trying one of their fresh fish dishes. The menu is a classic example of cultural blending where surf and turf can mean steak with mullet, and the grilled salmon is offered prepared with butter garlic, teriyaki, or miso. For a more traditional touch, apple pie is served with every meal. This is very much a local place.

Big Island Dining

Kona

Sibu Café
Banyan Court Mall
75-5695 Alii Drive
Kona, HI 96740
808-329-1112
Web: None
Hours: L 11:30 AM-3:00 PM
        D 5:00 PM-9:00 PM
Cards: None
Dress: Casual
Style: Indo $

Menu Sampler:

Breakfast:
N/A

Lunch/Dinner:
Appetizers: Spring Rolls with a tangy dipping sauce $3.95, Shrimp Sate with peanut sauce $5.75, Garlic Shrimp in a sauce of garlic, basil, parsley, cilantro and ripe tomatoes with traces of black pepper and green chili over linguini-a Sibu original $5.95, Krupuk Udang-light, crispy shrimp wafers $1.95
Salad: Gado Gado-layered classic Indonesian salad of brown rice, carrots, green beans, egg and tofu with peanut sauce, lime and ground peanuts $11.50
Pasta: Tofu Laksa of tofu, baby corn, green beans, rice noodles & bean sprouts in a rich fragrant sauce, coconut milk, lemongrass and Indonesian spices $12.95
Entrées: Chicken Curry with rice and salad $12.50, Balinese Chicken—filets of chicken marinated in tarragon, garlic, onions, canola oil and a hint of vinegar, flame grilled and served with peanut sauce $13.75, Spicy Pork—trimmed pork in a hearty cumin, coriander, onion and garlic sauce with lots of hot green chilies $12.95, Vegetable Curry $11.95, Combination Plates $13.25-$14.95

Impressions:

The Sibu Café is located in the rear of the Banyan Court Mall on Alii Drive. The owner makes an extra effort to provide a quality dining experience by using filtered water, canola oil, and sweetening with dark brown sugar. No MSG or products containing MSG are used. You'll also find an interesting choice of vegetarian items. A tantalizing health-conscious menu, efficient service, and peaceful location make this a good casual dining choice. Please note that no credit cards are accepted. Free parking is available behind the building.

Big Island Dining

Kona

Teshima Restaurant
Highway 11
Honalo, HI 96750
808-322-9140
Web: None
Hours: B 6:30 AM-11:00 AM
         L 11:00 AM-1:45 PM
         D 5:00 PM-9:00PM
Cards: None
Dress: Casual
Style: Amer/Japan $

Menu Sampler:

Breakfast:
Two Eggs, Meat, choice of two-toast, hash browns or rice $4.75, Fried Rice with two eggs and ham $5.00, Japanese Breakfast of fried fish, one egg, miso soup, tsukemono, sunomono and Japanese Tea $5.50, Bento to go $5.75-$6.75
Lunch:
Daily Specials 11 AM-1:45 PM $8.25 includes rice, miso soup, tsukemono, sunomono and hot green tea-Sakura Tray, Chicken Katsu Teishoku, Teriyaki Chicken, Fish and Vegetable Tempura with Spare Ribs, Chazuke Tray, Pupu Tray. Hamburger Deluxe $4.50, BLT $4.75, Ono Breaded Pork Chops $9.95, Bento Box Lunch To Go with 2 rice balls $6.00, with 3 rice balls $7.00
Dinner:
Teishoku of miso soup, sashimi, sukiyaki, fried fish, sunomono, tsukemono, rice $9.75. Dinner Combos include rice, miso soup, tsukemono, sunomono and hot green tea-Steak and Shrimp Tempura $15.95, Beef Teriyaki and Shrimp Tempura $13.75, Deep Sea Trio with shrimp tempura, fried fish and sashimi $12.95. Sweet Sour Spare Ribs $8.50, Kona Beef Curry Stew $7.50, Homemade Corned Beef Hash Patties w/fresh island-laid egg $7.50, New York Steak $10.95

Impressions:

This family style café and dining room has been a Honalo Town gathering spot for many years. The reasonably priced menu is a blend of American, Hawaiian, and especially Japanese influences. One dish that successfully blends all three is the Fried Rice with two eggs and ham. This is breakfast and lunch all rolled into one. To accompany the traditional ham and eggs, the fried rice is rich with the flavors of green onions, bean sprouts, and sesame oil. If you are traveling to and from the volcano and need a convenient stop for anytime-of-day dining, just slide into a booth and experience their unique style of local comfort food.

Big Island Dining

Kona

Thai Rin
Alii Sunset Plaza
75-5799 Alii Drive
Kona, HI 96740
808-329-2929
Web: None
Hours: L 11:00 AM-2:30 PM
         D 5:00 PM-9:00 PM
Cards: AE DC DIS JCB MC V
Dress: Casual
Style: Thai $$

Menu Sampler:

Breakfast:
N/A
Lunch/Dinner:
Appetizer: Spring Rolls $4.95, Shrimp Toast $4.95, Chicken or Shrimp Satay $6.95/$7.95, Deep Fried Tofu $5.95, Spicy Chicken Wings $7.95
Salads: Green Papaya Salad $4.95, House Salad with peanut sauce $4.95, Roast Duck Salad with red wine dressing $9.95, Combination Seafood Salad with chili paste dressing $12.95, Chicken or Beef Salad with lime-chili dressing $7.95
Soups: Lemongrass Soup with Fish $9.95, Coconut Milk Soup with Chicken $8.95, Noodle Soup with Beef $7.95, Pork Soup with clear broth $7.95
Noodles and Rice: Pad Thai with Chicken $8.95, Spicy Noodles with Tofu $8.95, Pineapple Fried Rice with shrimp, cashews and raisins $9.95, Sautéed Rice Noodles with shrimp in soy sauce with eggs, broccoli, and cabbage $9.95
Entrées: Chicken with garlic, pepper, broccoli, carrots, cabbage and Thai garlic sauce $8.95, Tofu Stir Fried with bean thread, egg, onion and tomato $8.95, Chicken Panang Curry with peanut sauce, coconut milk, sweet basil and vegetables $8.95, Scallop Macadamia Nuts with onions & vegetables $11.95, Lobster Tail sauteed w/choice of sweet & sour sauce or Thai garlic sauce $21.95
Special Thai Rin Platter of Fried Spring Rolls, Chicken Satay, Beef Salad, Chicken Wings and Tom Yung Kung- Lemongrass Shrimp Soup $16.95
Dessert: Bananas in Coconut Milk $2.50, Fried Banana $1.95, Ice Cream $2.50

Impressions:

Thai Rin is located curbside on Alii Drive and comes complete with ocean and sunset views. Their award-winning menu is a favorite around Kailua-Kona. The prices are reasonable and the portions generous. If you're looking for a pleasant, convenient place to enjoy flavorful Thai cuisine, give Thai Rin a try.

Volcano Village

Thai Thai Restaurant
19-4084 Old Volcano Road
Volcano, HI 96785
808-967-7969
Web: None
Hours: D 5:00 PM-9:00 PM
Cards: AE DIS JCB MC V
Dress: Casual
Style: Thai $$

Menu Sampler:

Breakfast/Lunch:
N/A
Dinner:
Appetizers: Spring Rolls of long rice, carrots, cabbage and onion stuffed in a rice-paper wrapper and deep-fried to a golden brown, served with a special sweet and sour sauce $5.99/$8.99, Deep-fried Tofu with a peanut sauce $7.99
Salads: Long Rice Salad (Salafun Noodles) jelly noodles made from mung beans flavored with onions, chili peppers, lime juice, and fresh mint (hot, medium or mild) with ground pork $10.99, w/shrimp or mixed seafood $12.99
Soups: Shrimp Thai Ginger Soup made from coconut milk, Thai ginger &lime juice- hot, medium or mild $12.99, Chicken Long Rice Soup w/chicken broth, cabbage & roasted garlic-mild $8.99, Spicy Tofu Lemongrass Soup $12.99
Entrées: Beef Ong Choi-beef and Thai watercress stir fried with garlic-hot, medium or mild $9.99, Shrimp Red Curry with red chili peppers in a curry sauce, coconut milk, Thai eggplant, bamboo, and Thai basil $12.99, Chicken Panang Curry with red chili peppers, spices, coconut milk, long beans and seasonal vegetables $10.99, Beef Taypoh Curry is a special curry w/beef, leafy greens such as Thai watercress (ong choi) or spinach, Thai spices, & coconut milk w/peanut sauce $10.99, Shrimp Pad Thai w/Thai rice noodles $12.99

Impressions:

Nestled in the mists and rain forest on top of Mt. Kilauea visitors will find an unexpected surprise. This attractive Thai restaurant serves an extensive dinner menu and offers proof that a good Asian ethnic meal can be found anywhere in Hawaii. Pay attention to the waiter when he describes the degrees of spiciness, as Mainland medium and Thai medium are two completely different things. The cook won't understand if someone orders their dish seasoned hot and returns it.

Kohala

The Batik
Mauna Kea Beach Hotel
62-100 Mauna Kea Beach Drive
Kohala Coast, HI 96743
808-882-7222
www.maunakeabeachhotel.com
Hours: D 6:30 PM-9:00 PM SuThFr
Cards: AE DC DIS JCB MC V
Dress: Evening Aloha/Jac Opt
Style: Euro-Asian $$$$

Menu Sampler:

Breakfast/Lunch:
N/A
Dinner:
Starters: Whole Roasted Garlic and Escargots with wild mushrooms, basil and garlic bread 17.50, Lumpia of Roast Peking Duck w/sweet chili and hoisin dip 17.50, Kahua Ranch Butter Lettuce w/yellow pear tomatoes & walnut dressing 11.00, Langostinos sautéed in garlic, angel hair pasta w/lobster sauce 18.00
Entrées: Macadamia Nut Crusted Ono with baby bok choy and purple sweet potato lemongrass coconut emulsion 31.00, Grilled Tenderloin of Beef sliced on caper & onion whipped potato w/Sauce Poivrade 34.00, Roasted Colorado Rack of Lamb, Potatoes Soubise, Caramelized Garlic Balsamic Juice 38.00
Curries: Chicken 32.00, Shrimp 35.00, Lobster 48.00 served in a traditional mild Indonesian style with Biryani Rice or a spicy Thai style w/lemon grass, lime leaf & jasmine rice w/condiments of mango chutney, shredded roasted coconut, raisins, peanuts, pineapple & mint chutneys & vegetable achar
Desserts: Coconut Mousse on Grilled Pineapple w/bittersweet chocolate sauce 9.00, Passion Fruit & Valrhona Chocolate Mousse Terrine with raspberry & kiwi sauces 10.50, Hawaiian Sorbets w/fruits & Lilikoi Mint Sauce 10.50

Impressions:

The Mauna Kea is the quintessential Kohala Coast resort, and The Batik is their premier restaurant. The menu here mixes European with Asian and Pacific Rim cuisines served in the ambiance of a private club. As you would expect, the marvelous food is paired with excellent service. Live entertainment is featured when available. Reservations are a must for this special dining experience. Dining times are by seating, so call early if you have a preference.

Big Island Dining

Kohala

The Bay Terrace
Mauna Lani Bay Hotel
68-1400 Mauna Lani Drive
Kohala Coast, HI 96743
808-885-6622
www.maunalani.com
Hours:　B 6:30 AM-10:30 AM
　　　　 D 6:00 PM-9:00 PM
Cards:　AE DC DIS JCB MC V
Dress:　Resort Casual
Style:　Cont/Isl/Ital $$$

Menu Sampler:

Breakfast:
Continental Buffet $16.00, Full Buffet $24.00, Fresh Opakapaka Hash with Sweet Onions, Peppers, Yellow Finn Potatoes and Poached Eggs $14.00
Lunch:
N/A
Dinner:
Appetizers: Crab Cakes with arugula, Cipollini onions, lemon misto aioli $12.50, Seafood Antipasto of marinated calamari, shrimp, bay scallops with Tuscan beans, focaccia bread and truffle oil $16.00, Warm Calamari Salad $11
Salads: Waimea Beet Salad with roasted walnuts and gorgonzola dressing $10.00, Garden Arugula Salad with pine nuts and grated pecorino cheese $8.50
Entrées: Island Mahi Mahi on Israeli Couscous with red and gold tomatoes and roasted fennel $25.00, Seared Veal Loin with fricassee of artichokes, wild mushrooms and fingerling potatoes, and mustard-herb sauce $32.00
Desserts: Crepe Suzette with vanilla ice cream and hot strawberry compote $8.00, Tiramisu with white chocolate caramel vanilla sauce $8.00
Prime Rib and Seafood Buffet: Friday & Saturday Nights 6-9 PM $49.00 for adults, $20.00 for children 12 and under

Impressions:

This casually upscale restaurant is located in the beautiful Mauna Lani Bay Hotel. Resort guests can start their day here with the breakfast buffet but the real dining begins at night. In order to please a variety of tastes the ala carte dinner menu does a good job covering a lot of culinary territory. On Fridays and Saturdays an extensive dinner buffet is also offered. It would be a good idea to call ahead for evening reservations, particularly on the weekend.

Big Island Dining

Kohala

The Canoe House
Mauna Lani Bay Hotel
68-1400 Mauna Lani Bay Drive
Kohala Coast, HI 96743
808-885-6622
www.maunalani.com
Hours: D 6:00 PM-9:00 PM
Cards: AE DC DIS JCB MC V
Dress: Resort Casual
Style: Pac-Rim $$$$

Menu Sampler:

Breakfast/Lunch:
N/A
Dinner:
Appetizers: Keahole Lobster Summer Roll in a soybean wrap with sweet & sour mango dipping sauce $18, Grilled Baby Back Ribs with guava hoisin barbecue sauce $14.50, Cracked Kona Lobster & Crab Soup with coconut cream $9, Wasabi Lobster Tempura on Stick with Japanese cucumber, pickled plum salad in a two mustard butter sauce $19, Hamachi & Scallop Ceviche $17.00
Entrées: Miso-Sake Marinated Mahi Mahi with stir-fried Chuka noodles and a spicy sesame aioli $32, Canoe House Surf and Turf of Kona raised lobster and filet mignon with roasted shiitake mushrooms and furikake jasmine rice in a lilikoi butter sauce $50, Ginger Scallion Crusted Tofu with stir-fried mixed vegetables and pasta $27, Puna Honey-Glazed Lamb Chops with smashed garlic new potatoes, yellow tomatoes and a poha berry red wine sauce $38, Grilled Lemon-Pepper Scallops with wild mushroom mashed potatoes and a Chinese mustard-soy beurre blanc $34, Sautéed Island Ono with wasabi smashed potatoes, Asian vegetables, and roasted macadamia nut sauce $33 .
Wine recommendations are given for each entrée and are sold by the glass.

Impressions:

This classic Big Island restaurant is located oceanfront at the Mauna Lani Bay Resort. The island décor involves lots of teak and a huge outrigger canoe suspended from the ceiling. The Canoe House serves award-winning Pacific Rim Cuisine in a tropical garden setting. Expect high quality ingredients combined with Asian influences backed up with attentive service. Kohala sunsets are stunning from this dining spot. Reservations are a must.

Kohala

The Grill
The Orchid at Mauna Lani
One North Kaniku Drive
Kohala Coast, HI 96743
808-885-2000
www.orchid-maunalani.com
Hours: D 6:30 PM-9:00 PM XSuMo
Cards: AE DC DIS JCB MCV
Dress: Resort Casual
Style: Sea/Stk $$$$

Menu Sampler:

Breakfast/Lunch:
N/A
Dinner:
Appetizer: Seared Foie Gras and caramelized mango with shaved winter truffles and Madeira sauce 18, Exotic and Wild Mushrooms in Toasted Brioche w/butternut squash coulis & marsala mushroom essence 12, Sautéed Pancetta Wrapped Shrimp & Diver Scallop, warm radicchio, watercress puree 17
Soups: Traditional Gratinated Onion Soup 10

Salads: Mâche, Frisee and imported Stilton cheese with Ka'u oranges, fresh beets, candied walnuts & a walnut vinaigrette 12, Waimea Greens 11
Entrées: Black Angus Beef w/choice of sauces-wild mushroom, brandy peppercorn, béarnaise and choice of starch-creamy Yukon gold & basil smashed potato, classic baked potato, horseradish mashed potato or basmati rice-Center Cut Filet Mignon 5 oz 34, 10 oz 46, 16 oz dry aged Rib Eye 44, Pan Fried Onaga w/lobster scented lentils, roasted vine ripe tomatoes, greens, cabernet fennel jus 36, Roast Venison Rack w/Red Currant Habanero Glaze 40

Impressions:

The Grill has the atmosphere of a traditional city club. Everything from the koa wood paneling and chandeliers to the plush carpeting and upholstered armchairs speak of another time and another place. This beautiful dining room is renowned as the premier spot to enjoy steak on the Big Island. This is not a salt-and-sear steak house. Instead the high quality beef comes with an elaborate choice of sauces and mustards. For those with a lighter taste, the lamb and fish are also wonderfully prepared. The fantastic cuisine and attentive service makes for a very memorable evening. Reservations are a must at this popular restaurant.

Big Island Dining

Kohala

The Pavilion
Mauna Kea Beach Hotel
62-100 Mauna Kea Beach Drive
Kohala Coast, HI 96743
808-882-7222
www.maunakeabeachhotel.com
Hours: B Buf 6:30 AM-11:00 AM
             D 6:00 PM-9:30 PM
Cards: AE DC DIS JCB MC V
Dress: Evening Aloha
Style: Pac-Rim $$$

Menu Sampler:

Breakfast:
 Extensive A La Carte Menu or Breakfast Buffet $26/Adult, $13/Children
Lunch:
N/A
Dinner:
Starters: Pavilion Pupu Sampler Platter of "Mauka-Makai" Samplers $19, Ahi
Tuna Poke with shoyu citrus vinaigrette and crunchy seaweed $15
Soup and Salads: Waimea Tomato & Sweet Kula Onion w/aged balsamic
vinaigrette & Puna goat cheese $12, Manta Ray Point Salad of sweet onion,
Ka'u avocado, Waimea tomato, Enoki mushroom, red beets, Hilo hearts of palm
in a creamy macadamia nut pesto dressing $12, Seafood Won Ton Soup $7
Entrées: Smoked Breast of Chicken w/macadamia nut polenta & poha berry jus
$25, Grilled Lamb Chops w/balsamic cabernet sauce, lobster & taro hash $29,
Trio of Ahualoa Pork Medallions w/sweet onion & mango salsa, sweet potato &
ginger butter $26, Macadamia Nut Crusted Prawns w/grilled pineapple rice, chili
butter sauce $28, Garlic Salmon w/lemon pepper, spaetzle, scallion relish $30

Impressions:

You'll find The Pavilion at the Mauna Kea Beach Hotel overlooking world
famous Kaunaoa Bay. This resort has the atmosphere of a casually elegant
country club, and the same holds true for The Pavilion restaurant. Morning
begins here with breakfast on the patio. Patrons have their choice of selecting
from an upscale buffet or an ala carte menu. Dinner is served nightly with
Pacific Rim cuisine and Continental favorites taking center stage. Although
breakfast is quite casual, you'll want to step it up a notch in the evening.

Kona

The Royal Thai Café
Keauhou Shopping Center
78-6831 Alii Drive
Kona, HI 96740
808-322-8424
Web: None
Hours: L/D 11:00 AM-10:00 PM
Cards: AE DC DIS JCB MC V
Dress: Casual
Style: Thai $$

Menu Sampler:

Breakfast:
N/A
Lunch/Dinner:
Appetizers: Fresh Basil Rolls with shrimp, bean sprouts, basil, green leaf lettuce and plum dipping sauce (not deep fried) $5.95, Chicken Satay with peanut sauce and cucumber salad $5.95, Thai Fried Chicken Wings $8.95
Soup: Chicken Tom Kah Kai, a hot and sour soup with coconut milk, galanga, onion and mushrooms $2.50/$6.95, Thai Dumpling Soup $$2.50/$6.95
Thai Curries: Beef Green Curry with bamboo shoots, broccoli, cabbage, bell pepper, sweet basil and mushrooms in coconut milk $8.95, Seafood Curry with shrimp, squid, scallops, fillet of fish, red curry in coconut milk $13.95
Specials: Royal Thai Diamond Seafood with broiled lobster tail, giant shrimp, scallops, squid, and fillet of fish with mixed vegetables topped with oyster sauce $22.95, Fiery Jumbo Shrimp broiled in butter and topped with special royal spicy sauce $12.95, Royal Thai Foursome of shrimp, pork, beef and chicken sautéed with mixed vegetables served on a hot plate $11.95, Pork with Spicy Garlic Sauce & green romaine, garlic, and black & white pepper $9.95
Noodles and Fried Rice: Combination Fried Rice with chicken, pork, and beef pan-fried with rice, egg, onion, tomato and scallions $8.95, Pad Thai with shrimp, chicken, egg, garnished with peanut and bean sprout $8.95

Impressions:

This spacious Thai restaurant is located in the new Keauhou Shopping Center at the southern edge of Kona. Although shopping center locations conjure up images of little take-out places, that is not at all the case here. Patrons can expect to find a nicely decorated dining room with a helpful staff serving full-flavored Thai specialties at affordable prices. Try the lunch plates for a particular bargain.

Big Island Dining

Kohala

The Terrace
Mauna Kea Beach Hotel
62-100 Mauna Kea Beach Drive
Kohala Coast, HI 96743
808-882-7222
www.maunakeabeachhotel.com
Hours: B Bru Buf 11:00 AM-2:00 PM Su
Cards: AE DC DIS JCB MC V
Dress: Resort Casual
Style: Amer/Isl $$$

Menu Sampler:

Breakfast/Lunch:
Lavish buffet brunch on Sundays with fresh fruits, seasonal berries, omelets made to order, Traditional Eggs Benedict, Belgian "mini" waffles, imported and domestic cheeses, lobster bisque, shrimp cocktail, crab claws, sushi bar, sashimi, vegetable tempura, Caesar Salad made to order, grilled Waimea vegetable salad, chef's smoked salmon with Maui onions, capers, and cream cheese, carved meats, island catch, hot entrees, Build-your-own ice cream sundaes, pastries, and desserts Adult $38/Children $19

Dinner:
N/A

Impressions:

The reputation of The Terrace doesn't revolve around its view of the world's most beautiful beach or the fabulous décor of the hotel. Rather this dining spot's claim to fame is the one meal of the week served here. Sunday Brunch at The Terrace is considered by many to be the best on the Big Island if not in all of Hawaii. You'll find every upscale island treat imaginable presented. To start things off you can have your Caesar salad or mixed greens individually tossed. Then moving on you'll come to a sushi chef preparing made-to-order sushi and sashimi. On the other side of a bountiful grouping of baked goods, dim sum, entrees, and side dishes you'll discover the omelet and carved meat stations. Behind it all there's a wonderful collection of desserts where even the ice cream is hand scooped. For those who enjoy their adult beverages, full bar service is available at additional charge. Topping it all off, live entertainment is provided throughout the meal. Reservations are required for this special experience.

Big Island Dining

Kohala

Tres Hombres Beach Grill
Kawaihae Shopping Center
Highway 270
North Kohala, HI 96743
808-882-1031
Web: None
Hours: L/D 11:30 AM-9:00 PM Su-Th
         L/D 11:30 AM-10:00 PM FrSa
Cards: MC V
Dress: Casual
Style: Mex $$

Menu Sampler:

Breakfast:
N/A
Lunch/Dinner:
Antojitos: Tortilla Chips smothered in chile sauce and refried beans, topped with jack cheese, fresh tomatoes, green onions and jalapenos garnished with sour cream and guacamole $6.95/$9.95/$11.95, Plato Grande of taquitos, guacamole, quesadillas, calamari and nachos serving 4 or more $19.95
Soups and Salads: Island Salad of greens topped with sliced avocado, onion, tomato & fresh papaya $9.95, with chicken breast $11.95, steak $14.95, or Mahi Mahi $17.95, Soup of the Day $4.95, Mexican Salad with vegetables $10.95
The Beach Grill: Two Chicken Breasts with a honey mustard glaze $14.95, Large Pacific Shrimp basted in lime and cilantro butter $16.95, Full Rack of Baby Back Ribs with refried beans, small salad and a cheese quesadilla $20.95
Combinaciones: All are served with refried beans & Spanish rice. Enchilada $8.95, Taco $8.95, Tostada/Chile Relleno $10.95, Taquitos (4) $10.95
Comidas Especiales: All are served with refried beans & Spanish rice. Crab Enchilada with pepper cheese, topped with green sauce, guacamole & sour cream $18.95, Two Carne Asada Tacos with grilled seasoned steak in soft flour tortillas with cheese & pico de gallo and guacamole $14.95, Chile Poblano stuffed with crab, shrimp & jack cheese, battered and baked, topped with tomatillo cream sauce & sour cream $18.95, Two Shrimp Tacos $16.95
A la Carte: Beef or Chicken Taco $4.95, Fish Taco $6.95, Shrimp Taco $8.95

Impressions:

Welcome to Baja on the Big Island! This second floor ocean view lounge and dining spot is a welcome find on the sparsely settled Kohala coast. Andale!

Big Island Dining

Hilo

Tsunami Grill & Tempura
250 Keawe Street
Hilo, HI 96720
808-961-6789
Web: None
Hours: L 10:30 AM-2:00 PM XSu
             D 4:30 PM-9:00 PM XSu
             D Buf Only 4:30 PM-8:00 PM Su
Cards: AE DIS MC V
Dress: Casual
Style: Japan $

Menu Sampler:

Breakfast:
N/A
Lunch/Dinner:
Buffets: Lunch $10.95/adults-$6.95/children, Dinner $14.95/adults-$8.95/children
Appetizers & Side Orders: Ahi Sashimi (7 pcs) $6.95, Yakitori (2 sticks) $3.25, Gyoza (6 pcs) $3.75, Lau Lau $3.00, Kim Chee $3.00, Mushroom Tempura $3.50, Edamame $3.00, Tsukemono (local style) $2.50
Soups: Miso Soup $1.00, Oxtail Broth Soup $1.00, Saimin $5.95-$7.45
Salads: Soba-Tofu Salad $7.95, Seaweed Salad $6.95, Chicken Salad $5.95
Curry Rice: Served with salad. Chicken Curry $6.75, Beef Curry $6.95 Oxtail Curry $7.95, Ebi (shrimp) Curry $7.45, Seafood Curry $8.95, Pork Curry $6.95
Yakimono: (Broiled Meats) Served with rice, miso soup, tsukemono. New York Steak $12.95, Sliced Teri Beef $8.45, Teriyaki Pork $7.95, Misoyaki Pork $7.95
Tsunami Combination Plates: Served with rice, miso soup, and tsukemono. 32 choices of entrée selections-Bentos, Katsu, Tempura, Udon, Soba, Saimin, Broiled Fish, Stuffed Seafood, Butteryaki and Donburi: wide variety of choices available-all under $10.00. Two choices $7.95, three choices $9.95

Impressions:

This downtown Hilo café serves excellent, local style Japanese comfort food at unbeatable prices. The buffets are a particularly good value and include a nice variety for those who want to do some sampling. For the noodle soup crowd, there is a whole page of nothing but saimin choices that even offer a choice of dashi. From 9 PM to 1 AM on Friday and Saturday night take 15% off your bill.

Volcano Village

Volcano House
Ka Ohelo Dining Room
Hawaii Volcanoes National Park
Volcano Village, HI 96785
808-967-7321
www.volcanohousehotel.com
Hours:　B 7:00 AM-10:30 AM
　　　　L 11:00 AM-2:00 PM
　　　　D 5:30 PM-9:00 PM
Cards:　AE DC DIS JCB MC V
Dress:　Dinner-Resort Casual
Style:　Amer/Cont $$

Menu Sampler:

Breakfast:
Traditional Breakfast Items served buffet style-$9.50/Adult, $5.50/Children ages 2-12, Continental Breakfast is available for $5.50

Lunch:
Casual Buffet of hot American style entrees, salad bar, rolls, and desserts-$12.50/Adults, $7.50/Children 2-12, Snack Bar 9 AM-5 PM

Dinner:
Starters: Shrimp Cocktail $7.95, Sautéed Shrimp with herb garlic butter $8.95, Clam Chowder $4.25, Seasonal Fruit Platter $8.50, Soup du Jour $3.95

Entrées: All entrées include dinner salad, vegetable du jour, and choice of rice or potato du jour. Fisherman's Catch of the day sautéed, poached or grilled with chef's special sauce $Market Price, Fillet Mignon seared and glazed with a French red wine sauce $22.00, Roasted Prime Rib with a crust of Hawaiian salt and crushed peppercorns and glazed with a French red wine sauce-light cut $17.50-full cut $19.95, Pork Medallions with a rich brown sauce $14.50, Add mahimahi or shrimp, deep-fried or sautéed to any of the above entrees for $7.50

Pasta: Linguini Alfredo with cream and parmesan cheese, appetizer portion $7.50, a la carte $10.95, meal size with dinner salad $13.25, Seafood Linguini made with scallops, clams, shrimp, and fish with a white or red sauce, appetizer portion $9.50, a la carte $14.50, meal size with dinner salad $18.50

Impressions:

With a dining room overlooking a huge crater with jets of steam…well, how can you top that? Breakfast and lunch buffets are adequate and quick, and dinner has a casual fine-dining atmosphere, but the old lodge and its view steal the show!

Big Island Dining

Volcano Village

Volcano Golf & Country Club
991621 Piimauna Drive
Volcanoes National Park, HI 96718
808-967-8228
www.volcanogolfandrestaurant.com
Hours: BL 7:00 AM – 3:00 PM
Cards: AE DC DIS JCB MC V
Dress: Casual
Style: Amer/Isl $

Menu Sampler:

Breakfast:
Specials: Wiki Wiki Burrito filled with a scrambled egg, cheese, and choice of Portuguese sausage, ham, bacon or Spam, salsa and sour cream $2.50, Short Stack of two buttermilk pancakes with choice of syrup $3.00, Birdie on the First Hole-two eggs any style with choice of meat or mahimahi, with choice of toast and choice of rice or Country Club style potatoes $6.00, French Toast $6.00
Lunch:
Homemade Portuguese Bean Soup or Soup of the Day $2.25/$3.50
Salads & Sandwiches: Somen Salad w/kamaboko and char siu $6.75, Chef's Salad $7.25, Hamburger Deluxe w/fries $7.25, Mahi Mahi Burger sautéed, flame-broiled or deep fried $7.50, Teriyaki Beef Sandwich of flame-broiled beef marinated in Oriental sauce served on a sesame bun w/mac/potato salad $7.50
Hot Entrées & Local Favorites: Hot Entrées served w/rice, mashed potatoes or fries, Chicken Cutlet $7.75, Garlic Pepper Chicken $8.75, Teriyaki Beef $9.00, Mahi Mahi sautéed, broiled, deep-fried $9.25. Chili & Rice $5.75, Saimin w/teriyaki beef stick $6.50, Oriental Fried Rice $7.00, Loco Moco $7.25, Kalua Pork & Cabbage $7.50, Hawaiian Beef Stew $7.25
Side Orders: Fries $3.00, Beer Battered Onion Rings $3.75, Garlic Bread $1.25
Desserts: Macadamia Nut Pie or Cheese Cake $4.25, Ice Cream $3.00
Dinner:
N/A

Impressions:

Things aren't real formal in Volcano Village and the country club fits right in. Patrons will find an interesting menu made up of mainland and island favorites. Prices are quite reasonable, and nobody goes away hungry. Of course there's a 19th hole for those so inclined. This relaxing dining room is a good alternative for those who aren't up to the buffet breakfast and lunch served at the park.

Kona

Wasabi's Japanese Cuisine
Coconut Grove Marketplace
75-5803 Alii Drive
Kona, HI 96740
808-326-2352
Web: None
Hours: LD 10:00 AM - 9:00 PM
Cards: JCB MC V
Dress: Casual
Style: Japan $$

Menu Sampler:

Breakfast:
N/A
Lunch:
Teri Chicken and Rice Bowl $5.95, Katsu Chicken and Rice Bowl $8.50,
Yakisoba $8.50, Spicy Chow Funn Noodles-chef's special $8.50, Special
Combo-Teri Chicken, 4 pc California Roll, salad, rice $8.50, Bentos $8/$12,
Sushi Plates-9 pc $14.95 to 15 pc $18.95, Tempura Udon $9.50
Dinner:
Entrées: Tempura & Teri Chicken $12.95, Katsu Combo $12.95, Steak,
Tempura and Teri Salmon $18.95, Beef Shabu Shabu for Two $39.95, Steak and
Tempura $16.95, Unagi w/soup, salad & rice $16.95, Sukiyaki for Two $39.95
Sushi Plates: Oahu-5 pcs of nigiri & 10 pcs of rolled sushi $18.95, Alii Feast-4
pcs nigiri sushi, 8 pcs deluxe California roll & 2 hand rolled $21.95
Sushi: California Roll or Avocado Roll $6.50, Hamachi Roll $7.50, Fresh
Dungeness Crab Roll $10.50, Tempura Shrimp Roll $10.00, Crazy Roll of
tempura shrimp roll covered with spicy ahi sashimi-crispy $16.00, A Ling's
Special Roll-California Roll covered with Unagi & special sauce $15.00,
Tempura Veggie Roll $7.00, Salmon Skin Roll $7.50, Ume Roll $6.00,
Ensenada Roll of large spicy tuna roll with special sauce $10.00

Impressions:

Things have changed at Wasabi's Japanese Cuisine. The owners recently
expanded this little sushi shop into the world of full service dining. Patrons will
notice a considerably more ambitious dinner menu complete with nabemono
dishes such as sukiyaki and shabu shabu. Look for this establishment in the back
of the Coconut Grove Marketplace next to the kava bar. There's plenty of free
parking in the shopping center lot behind the main Ali'i Drive storefronts.

KAUAI
DINING

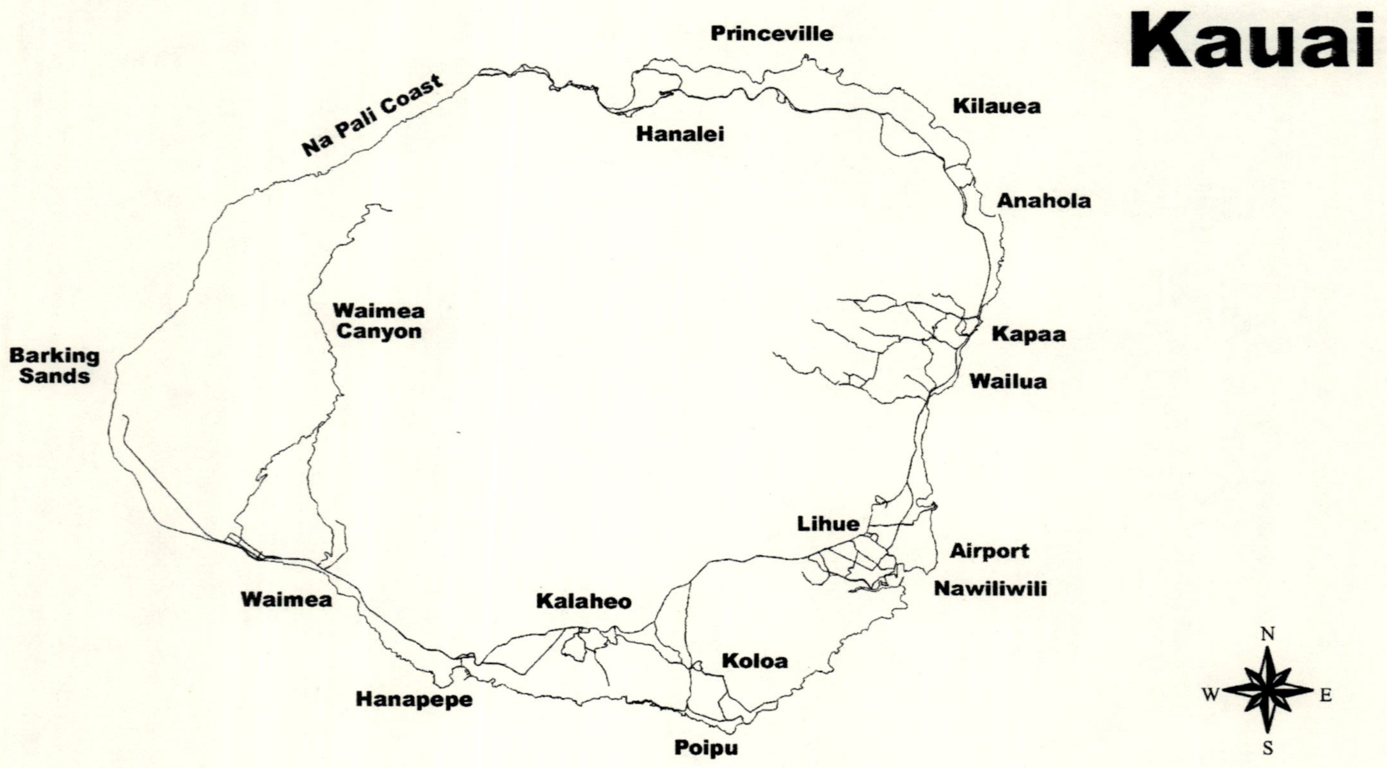
Kauai
Princeville
Na Pali Coast
Hanalei
Kilauea
Anahola
Waimea
Canyon
Barking
Sands
Kapaa
Wailua
Lihue
Airport
Nawiliwili
Waimea
Kalaheo
Koloa
Hanapepe
Poipu
N
W
E
S

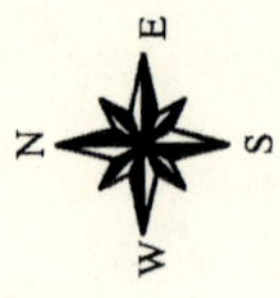

Kauai Dining

East Coast

A Pacific Café
Kauai Village Shopping Center
4-831 Kuhio Hwy (Hwy 56)
Kapa'a, HI 96746
808-822-0013
Web: None
Hours: D 5:30 PM-10:00 PM
Cards: AE DC DIS JCB MC V
Dress: Resort Casual
Style: Haw-Reg/Pac-Rim $$$

Menu Sampler:

Breakfast/ Lunch:
N/A
Dinner:
First Taste: Crispy Salmon "Firecracker", cucumber kim chee, sweet and sour sauce $8.75, Thai Style Tempura Calamari, sweet Thai chili sauce $9.25, "Tiger Eye" Ahi Sushi Tempura, soy wasabi beurre blanc $10.50
Dim Sum: Poached Scallop Ravioli, tobiko pearls, lime ginger beurre blanc, Sweet Shrimp and Imu Duck Lumpia, orange ginger glaze, avocado salsa $7.00
Soups & Salads: Thai Coconut Curry Soup with tiger prawn and ahi $6.50, Warm Duck Salad, goat cheese fritter, candied walnuts, pomegranate vinaigrette $7.50, Crispy Scallop Salad, mizuna, grapefruit, basil vanilla vinaigrette $7.50
Main Courses: The "Original" Wok Charred Mahi Mahi, garlic sesame crust, Asian stir fried vegetables, lime ginger beurre blanc $23.75, Mongolian Style Rack of Lamb, Chinese black bean Maui onion cabernet sauce $24.95, Fresh Herb Crusted Uku, crispy shrimp, saffron fennel sauce $23.25, "Surf & Turf", ahi, scallops, & foie gras, cherry port glaze $24.50, Coffee Smoked Double Pork Chop, garlic mashed potato, whole grain mustard sauce $21.95, Potato Crusted Onaga, white truffle mashed potato, cabernet thyme sauce $23.75
Desserts: Steamed White Chocolate layered with haupia and toasted macadamia nut mousse served over caramel sauce and Tahitian vanilla bean crème Anglaise Special Sampler Menus of various courses, dessert, and wines $59.00

Impressions:

Chef /Owner Jean Marie Josselin was one of the original chefs in the Hawaii Regional Cuisine movement. His intimate Kapa'a restaurant has won numerous awards and is guaranteed to take your taste buds for a great ride. Don't let the shopping center location fool you--this is world-class dining. An evening at A Pacific Café should be on every foodie's to-do list while visiting Kauai.

Kauai Dining

Lihue

Aromas
Harbor Mall
3501 Rice Street-Suite 207
Lihue, HI 96766
808-245-9192
Web: None
Hours: B 8:00 AM-11:30 AM XMoTuWe
         L 11:30 AM-4:30 PM XMoTuWe
         D 5:00 PM-9:30 PM XMo
Cards: AE DIS JCB MC V
Dress: Resort Casual
Style: Ecl/Med/PacRim $$

Menu Sampler:

Breakfast:
French Toast of Portuguese sweet bread dipped in vanilla, orange & cinnamon batter w/coconut or maple syrup $6.50, Kauai Crown Fried Rice & Eggs, guava toast points $7.25, Aromas Omelette w/potatoes/rice & toast $6.75-$8.25
Lunch:
Salads: Aegean Salad w/feta cheese, cucumbers, red onions, tomatoes, carrots, garbanzo beans, mixed greens, Kalamata olives, roasted red peppers $8.25
Entrees: Carolina Turkey Panini on sourdough with black olive tapenade, Maui chips/fries $7.95, Aromas Garlic Shrimp, penne pasta & griddled French bread $10.75, Bajitos (Fish Tacos Baja Style) $9.95, Kealia Vegetable Plate $7.95
Dinner:
Appetizers: Coconut, Ginger, Carrot Bisque topped with a green onion & shrimp ratia $7.25, Kalapaki Pot Stickers w/hoisin sesame dipping sauce $6.75
Entrees: Phuket Shrimp Boat-tiger prawns, vegetables, and a shrimp sweet & sour sauce in a pineapple boat over macadamia nut fried rice w/a banana & ginger lumpia $23.95, Grilled Kalbi Duck Breast w/baby bok choy, macadamia nut fried rice & light Kalbi sauce $18.50, Grilled New York Steak topped w/honey & red wine onions, cheeses, & buttermilk mashed potatoes $24.00

Impressions:

We particularly like chef-owned and operated dining venues, as they provide the perfect stage for culinary self-expression. This scenario plays well at Aroma's where the ambitious menu comes with bold accents and varied choices. Robert Moler has created this little gem on the second floor of the Harbor Mall complex overlooking Nawiliwili Bay just south of Lihue. Reservations are recommended.

Kauai Dining

East Coast

Aussie Tims Texas Barbeque
Waialua Shopping Plaza
4-361 Kuhio Highway
Kapa'a, HI 96746
808-822-0300
www.aussietims.com
Hours: L/D 1:00 PM-8:00 PM
Cards: AE MC V
Dress: Casual
Style: Amer $

Menu Sampler:

Breakfast:
N/A

Lunch/Dinner:
Barbeque Plates: Served with homemade beans and choice of one side, white bread and barbeque sauce. Smoked Texas Brisket $9.95, Pulled Pork Plate $8.95, Smoked Chicken Plate $7.95, Pecan Smoked Turkey Plate $9.95, Half Pound Cajun Smoked Shrimp with hot Cajun sauce $12.95
Sandwiches: Served on a bun with potato-mac salad or slaw. Pulled Pork $7.95, Texas Beef Brisket $7.95, Smoked Chicken $6.95, Smoked Turkey $8.95
Trash Can: Ribs, Barbeque Chicken, Brisket, and Cajun Shrimp, Slaw, Corn and Beans-family style-for two $30.00, each additional person $15.00
Sides: Homemade Potato Mac Salad $1.80, Cole Slaw $1.80, Barbeque Beans $2.50, Roasted Corn on the Cob $.95, Corn Bread Plain $1.50, Jalapeño and Cheese Corn Bread $1.75, Dill Pickles $.75, Steamed Rice $1.50
Specials: Jambalaya with shrimp, chicken, and Andouille sausage $6.95/$13.95, Cajun Fried Shrimp Basket with fries or slaw $9.95, Cajun Smoked Shrimp $12.95, Southern Fried Chicken Basket-3 pieces with slaw or fries $8.95, Chicken Fried Steak with country gravy, mashed potato, and one side $8.95
Desserts: Apple Strudel, Peach Cobbler, Raspberry Cheesecake $3.75 each

Impressions:

Texas BBQ on Kauai? Yep! Aussie Tims is a small storefront establishment in a strip mall behind Mema Thai. The friendly owners have concocted their own sauces in mild house, medium hot, or pyrotechnic habanero to use on their smoked meats. The brisket, pulled pork and chicken are favorites of ours and can be accompanied by a variety of side dishes. Everything is available packed as carryout for a beach picnic or the condo crowd.

North Shore

Bali Hai
Hanalei Bay Resort
5380 Honoiki Road
Princeville, HI 96722
808-826-6522
Web: None
Hours: B 7:00 AM-11:00 AM
        L 11:30 AM-2:00 PM
        D 5:30 PM-9:00 PM
Cards: AE DIS MC V
Dress: Resort Casual
Style: Haw-Reg/Pac-Rim $$

Menu Sampler:

Breakfast:
Traditional and island favorites such as Garden Island Omelet $10.50, Poi Pancakes $8.25, Seafood Omelet $13.50, Breakfast Burritos $8.25
Lunch: Kauai Onion Soup with melted provolone $4.95, BBQ Baby Back Pork Ribs with watermelon BBQ sauce, pineapple cole slaw, fresh vegetables and choice of fried rice, steamed rice or garlic linguini $14.95, Honey Dijon Chicken Sandwich with bacon and caramelized onions with fries or fruit $9.95
Dinner:
First Courses: Bali Hai Crabcakes served on roasted Kauai sweet corn with curry butter sauce & mango-papaya relish $12.75, Ahi Poke Tower $12.75
Entrées: Oven Roasted Lamb Chops with Dijon mustard, herb, and mac nut crust with mushroom risotto, garlic and rosemary demi glace $29.95, Fresh Catch prepared "Tropical Breeze" sautéed with a cool papaya and pineapple salsa, wasabi garlic mashed potatoes $27 or as "Rock Jumping Fisherman" broiled, topped with green coconut milk, sweet chili & peanut sate sauce $27, Curried Seafood & Saffron Risotto, Achote Chile & Cilantro Chive Oil $25.95

Impressions:

Perched on a cliff overlooking the famed Bali Hai setting from the movie "South Pacific" you'll find this beautiful restaurant with its high ceilings, stone work, bamboo, and rattan. An outrigger canoe hangs overhead in the Happy Talk Lounge adding to the exotic atmosphere. Every table enjoys a stunning panoramic view of the bay and the mountains beyond. The kitchen keeps pace with the surroundings serving innovative preparations combining ingredients and techniques from around the Pacific. This is a very romantic dining spot.

Kauai Dining

North Shore

Bamboo Bamboo
Hanalei Center
Kuhio Hwy
Hanalei, HI 96714
Phone: 808-826-1177
Web: None
Hours: L 11:30 AM-2:30 PM XMo
        D 5:30 PM-9:30 PM
Cards: AE JCB MC V
Dress: Resort Casual
Style: Cont/Pac-Rim $$$

Menu Sampler:

Breakfast:
N/A

Lunch:
Hanalei Taro Burger with lettuce, tomato, onion $8.95, Fish & Chips
w/seasoned fries $10.95, Chicken Pesto Sandwich on sourdough $8.95

Dinner:
Appetizers: Fresh Vegetable Summer Rolls w/sweet chili sauce $8.95, Kilauea
Goat Cheese Salad with mixed greens, cherry tomatoes, cucumbers, and pecans
$9.95, Crispy Ahi Spring Rolls with wasabi cream sauce $9.95, Calamari
Fritters with papaya cocktail sauce $8.95, Shrimp Cocktail $9.50

Pasta: Choose Penne, Linguini, Angel Hair Pasta- Top with Medley of Fresh
Vegetables in either marinara, butter garlic or cream sauce $14.95, Creamy
Pesto Sauce $15.95, Bamboo Special Meat Sauce 412.95, Tomato Herb $10.95

Entrées: Brick Oven Pizza (Fr, Sa, Su) Potato Crusted Mahi Mahi or Ono
served in a beurre rouge wine sauce with steamed rice $24.95, North Shore
Seafood Pasta in white wine, garlic, and herbs topped with a marinara $23.95,
Gina's Filet Mignon, 8 oz. grilled, served with a cabernet black peppercorn
sauce and garlic mashed potatoes $25.95, Catch of the Day $24.95

Desserts: Tiramisu $7.00, Apple Pie a la Mode $5.50

Impressions:

Near the end of the road in the quaint village of Hanalei travelers will find a
comfortable chef-owned restaurant known as Bamboo Bamboo. The spacious
indoor/outdoor dining area has a Pacific/Indonesian décor and features original
artwork on the walls. The innovative menu offers a little something for everyone
including pizza for the kids. The fine food is backed by a substantial wine list
and a full service bar. Espresso and Cappuccino fans come right this way!

111

Kauai Dining

South Shore

Beach House
5022 Lawai Road
Koloa, HI 96756
808-742-1424
www.the-beach-house.com
Hours: 5:30 PM-10:00 PM
Cards: AE DC MC V
Dress: Resort Casual
Style: Pac-Rim $$$

Menu Sampler:

Breakfast/Lunch:
N/A
Dinner:
Appetizers: Thai Curry Shrimp & Scallop Wonton, mango Thai basil, mint cucumber sauce $10.95, Wasabi Panko Crusted Mussels, black bean beurre blanc $8.50, Fish Nachos, refried black Thai rice, roasted corn/Hawaiian chili salsa, mango chipotle sauce $9.95, Fried Calamari w/wasabi lime sauce $8.95
Soup and Salad: Omoa Baby Lettuce, roasted sesame orange vinaigrette $5.50, Seafood Corn Chowder with fresh thyme and sherry $6.95, Blackened Ahi Caesar, romaine lettuce, feta & parmesan cheese, herb croutons $9.50
Entrées: Chinese Style Roasted Duck, lemon orange Grand Marnier demi, seared miso shiitake risotto cake, pickled vegetables, mac nut pesto $24.95, Cajun Spiced Ono with roasted garlic mashed potato and lobster chive sauce $24.95, Pulehu New York Strip, truffle butter, sweet onion confit, potato au gratin, red wine demi-glaze $24.95, Sun-dried Tomato pesto Linguine, shrimp, spinach, crimini & shiitake mushroom $23.95, BBQ Vegetable Kabobs $18.95
Desserts: Beach House Tiramisu $6.50, Bananas Foster $6.50, Molten Chocolate Desire (allow 20 minutes for preparation)

Impressions:

The Beach House has one of the most dramatic settings you'll find in Hawaii. Outside, there's the Pacific Ocean splashing up on the rocks. Inside, diners find fine Pacific Rim cuisine served in a casual yet upscale atmosphere. The menu has been broadened recently and offers a nice variety of enticing selections. This special dining spot is very busy so be sure to make reservations. Valet parking is almost a must as there is no lot on the premises and space is very limited in the surrounding area. Pupu and cocktail service begins at 5 PM so stop in early and secure your seat for the fabulous sunset viewing.

West Side

Brick Oven Pizza
2-2555 Kaumualii Hwy (Hwy 50)
Kalaheo, HI 96741
808-332-8561
Web: None
Hours: L/D 11:00 AM-10:00 PM XMo
Cards: MC V
Dress: Casual
Style: Ital $

Menu Sampler:

Breakfast:
N/A
Lunch/Dinner:
Pizza: Hearth Baked Pizzas made of whole wheat or white crust brushed with garlic butter $8.75-$26.35 in 10", 12", 15" sizes, Pizza Bread (one slice) $2.75 w/traditional ingredients such as Italian sausage (they make their own), salami, pepperoni, black olives, mushrooms, anchovies, or Seafood Style Pizza Bread w/bay shrimp, cheddar cheese, green onions, pizza sauce or garlic butter $3.30
Sandwiches: Hot Super Sandwich of smoked ham, salami, pepperoni, cheese, mustard, lettuce, tomatoes, onions $6.30, Italian Sausage Sandwich of homemade Italian sausage, pizza sauce, cheese, lettuce, tomatoes, white onions $6.50, Garlic Toast $.75/slice, with cheese $1.30/slice, Pizza Bread $2.75
Salads: Veggie Salad of greens, zucchini, mushrooms, bell pepper, black olives, onions, mozzarella and cheddar cheese in small $3.65 or large $5.95
Desserts: Aloha Pie $2.85, Chocolate/Strawberry Sundae Ice Cream Cups $.80

Impressions:

The village of Kalaheo is just a short distance from Poipu and Koloa. As you enter town from the north you'll see Brick Oven Pizza mauka of the highway. Here you'll find one of the best pizzas in Hawaii. The garlic butter-brushed crust is excellent and comes with a large variety of traditional toppings. Vegetarians will like the sauce as it's made without meat or poultry stock. Everybody will like the 100% real mozzarella cheese! Brick Oven Pizza has been family owned since 1970 and offers good food at reasonable prices backed up with quick, efficient service. In keeping with Italian tradition, wine and beer are available.

Kauai Dining

North Shore

Café Hanalei
Princeville Hotel
5520 Ka Haku Road
Princeville, HI 96722
808-826-2760
www.princeville.com
Hours: Su Bru 10:00 AM-2:00 PM
          B 6:30 AM-11:00 AM XSu
          L 11:00 AM-2:30 PM XSu
          D 5:30 PM-9:30 PM
Cards: AE JCB MC V
Dress: Resort Casual
Style: Pac-Rim $$$

Menu Sampler:

Breakfast:
Sunday Brunch: 10 AM-2 PM. $38.00 or $42.50 with Champagne. Buffet of a wide variety of exotic salads, seafood, pastas, carved meats, breakfast classics
Daily Breakfast: Breakfast buffet $23.95, Continental Breakfast $17.50, Japanese Breakfast $23.95/$19.50, Hanalei Taro Pancakes-apple bananas $10.95
Lunch:
Hawaiian style Chicken Salad w/sweet potato hash, organic greens & crispy tofu $15.95, Grilled Fresh Albacore sandwich w/sesame miso aioli & pickled vegetables $15.95, Passionfruit Mousse with Kula Strawberries $6.50
Dinner:
Appetizers: Hanalei Seafood Chowder with taro, luau leaf, coconut milk 8.00, Kalua Duck Lumpia with poha-ume dipping sauce, lomi tomato relish 16.00
Entrées: Mochiko Chicken stuffed with long rice and shiitake mushrooms, served with mochi rice risotto, citrus soy reduction, and mustard soy drizzle 29.00, Lemon Grass Crusted Ahi with shrimp dumplings 34.00
Dessert: Rum Roasted Pineapple served warm with coconut ice cream 7.00, Hawaiian Vanilla Bean Crème Brulee with macadamia nut biscotti 7.00
Friday Night Seafood Buffet: 5:30-9:30 PM $43.95/adults, $2.50/year - children. Salads, cold and hot seafood, carved items, wok station

Impressions:

This decidedly upscale restaurant is located in one of the most beautiful hotels in the islands. The fabulous setting high on a ridge overlooking Bali Hai is as good as it gets. The menu at Café Hanalei is quite ambitious and doesn't disappoint. Stop by the Princeville Resort and let the North Shore work it's magic!

Kauai Dining

Lihue

Café Portofino
Pacific Ocean Plaza
3501 Rice Street
Nawiliwili, HI 96766
808-245-2121
www.cafeportofino.com
Hours: D 5:00 PM-10:00 PM
Cards: AE DC DIS MC V
Dress: Resort Casual
Style: Ital $$$

Menu Sampler:

Breakfast/Lunch:
N/A
Dinner:
Antipasti: Escargot Maison 8.00, Calamari Fritti 8.75, Mozzarella Marinara 8.00, Pepperoni Arrostiti 8.00, Steamed Clams $Market Price
Zuppe: Minestrone alla Portofino-mixed fresh vegetables with garlic and oregano 4.00, Gaspacio-cold spiced fresh tomato soup 4.00, Soup of the Day
Pasta: Penne Broccoli Spinach 13.50, Fettuccine Alfredo 15.00, Linguine a la Carbonara 16.00, Fettuccine Shrimp & Mushroom in a creamy sauce 20.00
Insalate: Caesar Salad 8.00, Green Salad with house dressing 5.00
Specialite d'ella Casa: Osso Buco alla Portofino-veal shank in a traditional sauce on a bed of fettucine 26.00, Scampi a la Limone 19.00, Melanzanle a la Parmigiana 15.00, Scampi alla Provinciale w/butter, white wine, garlic 20.00
Secondi di Vitello: Scaloppine alla Parmigiana-medallions of veal in tomato sauce with mozzarella cheese 20.00, Scaloppine a la Piccata or Marsala 20.00, Scaloppine alla Portofino with lemon-sage butter sauce 20.00
D'Alla Griglia: Chicken Cacciatore 14.50, Pollo Porcini-chicken breast sautéed, and flambé in brandy with a light wild mushroom sauce 15.00
Daily specials are posted.

Impressions:

This romantic white linen and black tie restaurant is located on the second floor of the Pacific Ocean Plaza opposite Kalapaki Beach and the Marriott Resort. The specialty of the house is Northern Italian cuisine and you'll have to look hard to find better. Whether choosing to dine indoors or out you'll discover a gracious continental experience with tropical flair. This is one of our favorite dining experiences on the island of Kauai.

Kauai Dining

East Coast

Camp House Grill & Bar

Kauai Village Shopping Center
4-381 Kuhio Hwy (Hwy 56)
Kapa'a, HI 96746
808-822-2442
Web: None
Hours: B 6:30 AM-10:30 AM
         L/D till 9:00 PM
Cards: AE DIS MC V
Dress: Casual
Style: Amer $$

Menu Sampler:

Breakfast:
Camp House Breakfast Quesadilla topped with salsa and served with rice or hash browns $4.95, French Toast $3.95, Biscuit & Gravy Meal with two eggs, rice or hashed browns, and a biscuit covered in gravy $4.95, Eggs Benedict $8.95, Belgian waffle $4.95, Omelets $6.95-$8.95, Monte Cristo $5.95

Lunch:
Famous Camp House Burgers $3.95-$5.50, BBQ Pork Ribs $16.95, Huli Chicken-half bird seasoned with a secret blend of Hawaiian, Chinese, and Cajun spices $8.95, Chicken Sandwiches-four different preparations $4.95-$5.95

Dinner:
Dinners are served with a choice of soup/salad & choice of rice, potato salad, fries, or cucumber kim chee. New York Steak $14.95, King Crab Legs-1# $29.95, Prime Rib-16 oz.-$19.95, BBQ Pork Ribs with local style BBQ sauce $16.95, Shrimp Tempura $16.95, Pork Chops $11.95, Shrimp Scampi $15.95

Dessert:
PIES!! Homemade in flavors such as pineapple cream cheese macadamia nut, chocolate cream, sour cream apple, chocolate peanut butter cream cheese and Paradise (pineapple, macadamia nut and coconut) $3.50

Impressions:

Located in the busy Safeway Shopping Center behind Long Drugs in Kapa'a you'll find a homey diner/café style restaurant called the Camp House Grill & Bar. This reliable family dining spot is a good choice when you crave a taste of mainland fare or just need some comfort food. Prices are reasonable and the service is friendly. Ask them about their rich creamy pie--even at breakfast!

Kauai Dining

West Side

Camp House Grill
Kaumualii Hwy (Hwy 50)
Kalaheo, HI 96741
808-332-9755
Web: None
Hours: B 6:30 AM-10:30 AM
        L /D till 9:00 PM
Cards: AE DIS MC V
Dress: Casual
Style: Amer $$

Menu Sampler:

Breakfast:
French Toast $3.95, Biscuit & Gravy Meal with two eggs, rice or hashed
browns, and a biscuit covered in gravy $4.95, Eggs Benedict $8.95, Belgian
waffle $4.95, Monte Cristo $5.95, Omelets $6.95-$8.95 w/ many fillings
Lunch:
Famous Camp House Burgers $3.95-$5.50, Huli Chicken-half bird seasoned
with a secret blend of Hawaiian, Chinese, and Cajun spices $8.95, Chicken
Breast Sandwiches-four different preparations $4.95-$5.95, Quiche $2.95
Dinner:
Dinners are served with a choice of soup or salad and a choice of rice,
potato salad, fries, or cucumber kim chee. Pork Chops-broiled and covered with
mushrooms & brown Gravy $12.95, King Crab Legs-1# $29.95, Prime Rib (16
oz.) $19.95, BBQ Pork Ribs with local style BBQ Sauce $16.95, Camp House
Combo-ribs & BBQ chicken $16.95, Sirloin Steak Polynesian $11.95/$15.95
Dessert:
PIES!! Homemade in flavors such as pineapple cream cheese macadamia nut,
chocolate cream, sour cream apple, chocolate peanut butter cream cheese and
Paradise (pineapple, macadamia nut and coconut) $3.50

Impressions:

For a vivid time-warp depiction of 1950's Hawaii, stop at this plantation cottage
restaurant in Kalaheo. During our last visit there was a refrigerator with a beer
tap sticking out the side in the dining room, so you can forget worrying about
the dress code. Old photos and memorabilia from the plantation days line the
walls. This is a good stop if you get in the mood for comfort food while on your
way to Barking Sands Beach or the Waimea Canyon areas.

Kauai Dining

South Shore

Casablanca at Kiahuna
Kiahuna Tennis Club
2290 Poipu Road
Poipu, HI 96756
808-262-8196
Web: None
Hours: B 7:30 AM-11 AM Mo-Sa
         B 8:30 AM-Noon Su
         L 11:30 AM-3:00 PM Mo-Sa
         L Noon-3:00 PM Su
         D 6:00 PM-9:00 PM Tu-Sa
Cards: MC V
Dress: Resort Casual
Style: Med $$$

Menu Sampler:

Breakfast:
Waffles with fresh fruit or macadamia nuts 8, Omelette du Jour 8, Eggs
Benedict 9, Eggs Florentine 9, French Toast of Challah with fruit 9

Lunch:
Salads: Spanish Lobster Ensalada on sourdough toast, served with black beans,
mesclun, creamy vinaigrette & Romescu 13, Israeli salad of avocado, red onion,
cucumber, egg and caramelized walnuts, toasted cumin lemon vinaigrette, pita 7
Entrees: Panini of mozzarella & prosciutto with potato salad 8, Souvlaki of
skewered lamb with rice pilaf 13, Prawn & Scallop Skewer 13

Dinner:
Entrees: Fettuccine alla Toscana w/sautéed chicken & pancetta tossed in a light
rosemary cream sauce 14, Braciola di Maiale-pork tenderloin stuffed w/fig,
honey & balsamic vinegar, red wine & raisin sauce and ricotta mashed potatoes
19, Anatra con Succo-grilled duck breast w/an herbed jus & cognac pate, served
w/ricotta mashed potatoes 19, Filleto di Manzo-grilled beef tenderloin 26
Tapas: served Su Noon-3 PM, Mo 11:30 AM-6 PM, Tu-Sa 11:30 AM-10 PM
Crostini with two tapenades 6, Hummus with pita and cucumber 6, Grape
Leaves stuffed with basmati rice and spices, served with garlic yoghurt 9

Impressions:

Centered in the Kiahuna resort's pool and tennis court complex you'll find a
jewel of a restaurant serving exciting tastes from the Mediterranean. Throughout
the day Casablanca's patrons can enjoy a step away from the ordinary. This
alfresco fine dining restaurant is a good choice for wine and tapas.

Kauai Dining

South Shore

Casa di Amici
2301 Nalo Road
Poipu, HI 96756
808-742-1555
Web: None
Hours: D 6:00 PM-Closing
Cards: DC MC V
Dress: Resort Casual
Style: Ital/Sea/Cont $$$

Menu Sampler:

Breakfast/Lunch:
N/A

Dinner:
Pupus: Shrimp and Ahi Thai Sticks served with wasabi aioli, Thai sweet chili, sesame-ginger sauce and namasu $8, Gnocchi Quatro Formaggio with four cheese filling with a tomato-sage-pancetta sauce gratineed with Grana Padano Parmesan $8, Calamari Fritte breaded in Panko Flakes in a piccatta sauce $8
Salades: Insalata Di Pomodoro of sliced tomatoes, sweet red onions, fresh mozzarella, olive tapenade, and fresh basil with a raspberry vinaigrette $8, Caesar w/croutons $6, Fresh Romaine with creamy basil-tarragon vinaigrette $5
Risotto: Smoked Salmon Risotto of marinated salmon in pineapple and vanilla, smoked over hickory wood, prepared with fresh dill, tomato & horseradish $8
Pasta: Fettucine Alfredo $17, Scampi Di Amici with garlic & linguine $23
Entrée: Tournedos Rossini-sauteed medallions of filet finished in a Madeira-shallot sauce, served with an Asian spiced pate, fluted mushroom caps atop garlic croutons $24, Veal Piccatta of sautéed veal scaloppini finished in a chardonnay lemon-caper sauce-light $18/regular $23, Duck Confit $18.00/23.00
Desserts: Bananas Foster $8, Tiramisu $7, Frozen Mango Mousse $6.50

Impressions:

This intimate dining spot is located in a residential neighborhood behind Poipu Beach. Casa di Amici offers upscale Italian fare with touches of island influence on their ambitious, well-executed menu. Reservations are a must at this romantic little restaurant. Parking in the lot out front is limited and on the street nearly impossible, so we recommend dining early. On Friday and Saturday evenings live entertainment adds to the enjoyment of the patrons.

East Coast

Coconuts Island Style Grill & Bar

4-919 Kuhio Highway
Kapa'a, HI 96746
808-823-8777
Web: None
Hours: D 4:00 PM-10:00 PM XSu
Cards: AE DC JCB MC V
Dress: Resort Casual
Style: Pac Rim/Trop $$$

Menu Sampler:

Breakfast/Lunch:
N/A
Dinner:
Pupus: Lobster Ravioli with saffron sauce & two tobiko $7.00, Coconut Seafood Cigars served with sweet pineapple chili chutney $6.00, Dragon Fire Baby Back Ribs served with a cooling slaw & sesame-citrus dressing $8.95
Salads: Kapa'a Organic Greens with balsamic dressing, candied pecans & Gorgonzola cheese $5.50, Goat Cheese & Organic Garden Greens $7.75
Main Things: Big Crispy Veal Scaloppine with balsamic basil sauce, capellini & veggies $19.95, Thai Curry Pasta with linguine tossed with chicken, Roma tomato, eggplant & potato $10.00, Grilled & Teriyaki Dipped Salmon with passion fruit ponzu sauce, coconut scallion rice & veggies $13.95, Tempura Dipped Ono served with ginger wasabi aioli, stir fried rice & veggies $19.95, Seafood Paella with shrimp, scallops, mussels, calamari, saffron rice & veggies $17.95, A Very Tasty Burger with crispy house made potato chips $8.95
Desserts: Classic Crème Brulee topped w/caramelized bananas & raspberry sauce $5.75, Pineapple Upside Down Cake w/coconut sorbet & mango coulis $5.75, Chocolate Volcano Cake served warm with Kona Coffee Sauce $5.75

Impressions:

What a fun, lively place! The tropical décor and innovative cuisine really packs them in. Get there early to put your name in for a table as reservations are only taken for parties of six or more. After you've tried the Lobster Ravioli or Tempura Dipped Ono you'll know why the crowds are here. Don't be put off if the building looks like it used to be a fast food outlet--it was!

Kauai Dining

South Shore

Dali Deli
5492 Koloa Road
Koloa, HI 96756
808-742-8824
Web: None
Hours: B/L 8:00 AM-3:00 PM Mo-Sa
Cards: AE MC V
Dress: Casual
Style: Amer $

Menu Sampler:

Breakfast:
Two Eggs with ham, bacon, or sausage and home fries, toast or a bagel $6.95, French Toast made with challah bread and served with fresh island fruit $6.95, Breakfast Burrito with a spinach tortilla filled with scrambled eggs, refried beans, green chilies, sautéed onions and sour cream, topped with cheddar cheese and fresh salsa $7.95, Daily Dali Omelet with home fries, toast or a bagel $7.95, Pancakes (3) with fresh island fruit $6.95, Bacon & Cheese Bagelwich $7.95

Lunch:
Daily Soup $3.25/$5.75, Italian Sub on a French Roll with balsamic vinaigrette $7.25, Grilled Marinated Portobello Mushroom Sandwich with garlic mayo on a French roll with a choice of salad, fries $8.75, Cajun Shrimp Sandwich with red bell peppers, lettuce and Creole spices & garlic mayo on a French Roll $9.25, Meat Loaf Sandwich on a grilled French roll with salad or fries $7.95, Philly Cheese Steak with salad or fries $7.95, Hello Dali of fresh roast turkey, cranberry relish, and lettuce on a French roll $7.25, Caprisce Sandwich of fresh mozzarella, pesto, arugula, tomato and lemon olive oil on a French roll $6.95, Greek Salad $5.95 with hummus $6.75, Daily Mystery Salad $???, Dali Daily Soup $3.25/$5.75, with salad $4.75/$7.25

Dinner:
N/A

Impressions:

In Old Koloa Town there's a plantation style eatery that serves up comfort in class. Inside you'll find the Dali Deli serving breakfast and lunch items with interesting combinations of fresh ingredients. The baked goods displayed in the deli are a treat to the eyes as well as the palate, especially when accompanied by a latte, cappuccino, or espresso. This casual restaurant is colorful, comfortable, and friendly. Better yet it's a great value.

South Shore

Dondero's
Hyatt Regency Kauai Resort & Spa
1571 Poipu Road
Koloa, HI 96756
808-742-6260
www.kauai.hyatt.com
Hours: D 6:00 PM-10:00 PM
Cards: AE DC DIS JCB MC V
Dress: Resort Casual
Style: Ital $$$$

Menu Sampler:

Breakfast/Lunch:
N/A
Dinner:
Appetizers: Carpaccio Dimanzo Con Rugula E Parmigiano of sliced lean tenderloin of beef, arugula, roasted pepper, shaved Parmesan cheese, and artichoke $12.50, Insalata Di Gorgonzola E Pomodori-tomato & Gorgonzola salad w/cracked black pepper, extra virgin olive oil, sweet basil $9.50
Pasta: Black Ink Fettucine with scallops, shrimps, mussels, salmon, clams, lobster, cognac bisque sauce, and black truffle $33.00, Lobster Picata with pistachio fettucine, sun dried tomato, truffle cream sauce $35.00
Entrée: Veal Loin Sautéed in Olive Oil with Parmesan cheese, fresh baby spinach, semolina cakes, porcini mushroom sauce $28.00, Roast Lamb Rack with herb crust, homemade gnocchi, asparagus, baby carrots, and lamb jus reduction $36.00, Grilled Beef Tenderloin on Mashed Eggplant, black truffle sauce and artichoke fritters $32.50, Chicken Parmigiana $27.00, Grilled Opakapaka w/roasted vegetables, tomatoes, olives, garlic, balsamic glaze $28.00
Desserts: Tiramisu $8.00, Amaretto Cheesecake & fresh berry sauce $8.50, Vanilla Crème Brulee with fresh berries $9.50, Fresh Fruit Sorbet $9.50

Impressions:

Dondero's offers a dining experience that's completely in step with its location in Poipu's benchmark resort. Just like The Hyatt Kauai Resort & Spa focuses on indulging oneself, their signature Italian restaurant can be counted on for an evening of superb fine dining. The perfect ending to a busy day begins when you are escorted into the elegantly appointed room or out onto the terrace. Then things move on to choices from an extensive wine list before choosing from the gourmet level Northern Italian menu. After dinner, remain at your table for a cognac, or retire to the Library for an after dinner drink and a bit of live music.

Lihue

Duke's Canoe Club
Kauai Marriott Resort
3610 Rice Street
Lihue, HI 96766
808-246-9599
www.dukeskauai.com
Hours: L 11:00 AM-11:30 PM
              D 5:00 PM-10:00 PM
Cards: AE DC DIS MC V
Dress: Resort Casual
Style: Amer/Sea $$

Menu Sampler:

Breakfast:
N/A

Lunch:
Barefoot Bar—Mac Nut and Dungeness Crab Wonton $6.95, Duke's Nachos $7.95, Beachside Burger $6.45, Stir-Fry Chicken Cashew $8.95, Pizzas $7.95, Fresh Fish Tacos $8.95, Large Caesar Salad with grilled chicken or mahi $9.95

Dinner:
Each selection includes our salad bar serving Duke's tossed Caesar Salad, freshly baked muffins, and sourdough bread. Fresh island fish prepared several ways such as baked in a garlic, lemon and sweet basil glaze, or marinated in shoyu and ginger, grilled and served with papaya lime relish, or roasted firecracker which is with tomato, chili, cumin aioli and served with black beans, Maui onion, and avocado relish, grilled with pineapple salsa, or Parmesan and Herb Crusted sautéed and topped with lemon and capers—all at $Market Price. Prime Rib $17.95/$24.95, Seafood Coconut Curry-Thai Style-with fish, shrimp, and scallops served on white rice $17.95, Shrimp and Steak $19.95

Impressions:

Duke's Canoe Club is located down the beach from the Kauai Marriott Resort. This large open-air restaurant centers around a tropical garden that would fit well on a Hollywood sound stage. Even the tabletops are made from native woods and have been labeled with their island names. The terraced dining room and spacious Barefoot Bar offer patrons a front seat on Nawiliwili Bay. Dinner is the real hit here with the affordable steak and seafood menu served in generous portions. A light menu is available throughout the day for those looking for a late lunch or just coming in off the beach.

Kauai Dining

West Side

Grinds Café & Espresso
4469 Waialo Road
Eleele, HI 96705
808-335-6027
www.grindscafe.net
Hours: BLD 5:30 AM – 9:00 PM
Cards: JCB MC V
Dress: Casual
Style: Amer/Ec/Isl $

Menu Sampler:

Breakfast:
Served All Day. Skillets are served with rice or potatoes. Portuguese Skillet with grilled Portuguese sausage, onions and green peppers with white cheeses $6.75, Farmers Skillet with homemade sausage grilled with green peppers and onions smothered with homemade country gravy $6.75, Omelets are served with rice or potatoes. Chili & Cheddar Cheese Omelet $6.00, Smoked Turkey, Mushrooms, and Monterey Jack Cheese Omelet $5.95, Mahi Mahi Breakfast of grilled mahi, choice of rice or potatoes, and two eggs any style $7.00, Loco Moco $5.75

Lunch:
Sandwiches: All come with condiments and choice of bread. Italian Sandwich $5.95, Super Veggie Sandwich $5.65, Cajun Ono Sandwich $6.50, Crispy Chicken Sandwich with grilled mushrooms, jack cheese and Dijon mustard $6.50, Grinds Burger (1/2 #) $5.75, Swiss Mushroom Burger $6.50
Salads: Chicken Walnut Salad topped with hot sliced chicken slices $8.25, Italian Salad with red onion ranch dressing $7.75, Organic Caesar $7.00
Pizza: 15" and 18", Wheat or white crust with a wide variety of toppings. The Sicilian $17.50/$23, The Veggie $17.00/$22.00, Cajun Chicken $17.50/$22.50

Dinner:
Mahi Mahi lightly breaded, grilled and served with homemade tartar sauce, rice and choice of mac salad or cole slaw $7.50, Sweet Shoyu Chicken with a pineapple honey shoyu sauce, rice and choice of salad $6.95, Cajon Ono $6.75
Pastas: Cajun Chicken Linguine with green peppers, onions, celery and carrots and Cajun Sauce $12.75, Veggie and Pesto Linguine $10.50, add Ono $2.50

Impressions:

Grinds is an affordable little place along the highway on the way to the Waimea Canyon. This local eatery does it all--all day long. Their breads and pastries are baked in house adding a nice touch to the big portions and extensive menu.

Kauai Dining

Lihue

Hamura Saimin Stand
2956 Kress Street
Lihue, HI 96766
808-245-3271
Web: None
Hours: L/D 10:00 AM-11:00 PM Mo-Th
        L/D 10:00 AM-1:00 AM Fr-Sa
        L/D 10:00 AM-9:30 PM Su
Cards: None
Dress: Casual
Style: Island $

Menu Sampler:

Breakfast/Lunch/Dinner:
Saimin-noodle soup with a garnish of green onions, fish cake and chopped ham in small $3.25, medium $3.50, large $3.75, and ex-large $4.00, or Won Ton Mein-saimin with pork and shrimp filled dumplings $4.75, Shrimp Saimin with two pieces deep fried tempura shrimp $5.00, BBQ Sticks-grilled chicken or beef skewers dipped in a teriyaki sauce $1.00 each, Crispy Won Tons (6) $3.00, Manapua $.90,Lilikoi Chiffon Pie $1.50 per piece or a whole pie $10.00

Impressions:

Time travel to Old Hawaii is today's reality at Hamura's Saimin Stand. Take your place at the diminutive counter lined with tiny stools zigzagging across the front of this plantation-style building and let the ladies dish you up some of the best Asian style noodle soup you've ever tasted. Don't be shy about sitting next to another patron and talking story. Everyone is friendly and will offer advice about the hot mustard and other condiments. Order a BBQ Stick with your saimin and you're on your way to living local. One word of caution though, only Hawaiians and teenage boys have the stamina to finish an extra large bowl of Hamura's saimin, so think about ordering something smaller.

Over by the side door you'll see the shave ice and halo halo stand with tropical flavored syrups and extras like li hing mui and azuki beans. But then the lilikoi chiffon pie is very light, refreshing, and at $1.00 a slice why not sample some? This cultural icon is very crowded around lunchtime so plan accordingly.

Kauai Dining

North Shore

Hanalei Dolphin Restaurant & Fish Market
5-5016 Kuhio Hwy (Hwy 56)
Hanalei, HI 96714
808-826-6113
Web: None
Hours: L 11:00 AM-3:30 PM, Light Menu 3:30 PM-5:30 PM
          D 5:30 PM-10:30 PM
Cards: MC V
Dress: Casual
Style: Sea/Stk $$$

Menu Sampler:

Breakfast:
N/A
Lunch:
Fin Burger charbroiled or Cajun with lettuce, tomato and onion $6, Calamari Sandwich-deep-fried, lettuce, tomato, and onion $8, Fish & Chips in beer batter with fries $11, Main Dish Salads $5-$9, Seafood Chowder-cup/$3, bowl/$6
Dinner:
Appetizers: Artichoke Crowns stuffed with garlic, butter, bread crumbs and cheese $8, Ceviche of raw fish marinated in lemon juice with tomatoes, celery, chili, Chinese parsley and green olives $6, Sashimi Plate $Mkt
Entrées: All entrees are served with a family style salad with our own dressing, penne pasta, steak fries, rice, or marinated veggie kabob, and hot homemade bread. Baked potato a la carte $2.50 with condiments. Fresh Scallops baked in wine, smothered in mozzarella $27, Dolphin Shrimp baked in butter and wine with our special seasonings topped with sour cream $27, Hawaiian Chicken-breast marinated in soy sauce and ginger $20/child's plate $16, 8 oz. Filet Mignon $24, Fish 'n Chips $20, Australian Lobster 20-24 oz. $Mkt
Desserts: Dolphin Ice Cream Pie $7, New York Cheesecake $5, Sundae $5

Impressions:

For us the atmosphere at this open-air restaurant catches the magic of the Hanalei Valley. It sits alongside the Hanalei River, and at night the tiny lights in the palms and plants reflect upon the water. This traditional steak and seafood house has been around for a long time. The menu avoids trendy contrivances and comes at you straight on. There is a fish market in the back, so you can be sure that today's catch is fresh. Plan ahead as reservations are not accepted.

Kauai Dining

Lihue

Hanama'ulu Restaurant
3-4291 Kuhio Hwy (Hwy 56)
Lihue, HI 96715
808-245-2511
Web: None
Hours: L 9:00 AM-1:00 PM Tu-Fr
         D 4:30 PM-Close Tu-Su
         D Buf 5:30 PM-8:30 PM Su
Cards: MC V
Dress: Casual
Style: Chi/Japan $$

Menu Sampler:

Breakfast:
N/A
Lunch:
Deluxe Chinese Plate Lunch-soup, fried chicken, fried shrimp, chop suey, crisp
won ton, sweet and sour spare ribs, char siu or kau yuk, served with rice and tea
$8.00, Japanese Special Plate Lunch includes miso soup, rice and tea and
includes choice of one-calamari steak, sukiyaki with tofu, tonkatsu, teriyaki fish,
teriyaki beef, teriyaki chicken, fish tempura, donburi $7.50, Won Ton Soup $7
Dinner:
Pupus: Crispy Won Ton $5.00, Spring Rolls $7.50, Potstickers $7.50
Entrées: Pork and Vegetables with tomato $8.00, Beef and Broccoli with
mushrooms $8.00, Crisp Fried Ginger Chicken $6.75, Shrimp Canton $9.50,
Shrimp Tempura with traditional dipping sauce $10.95, Tofu Tempura $5.00
Complete Dinners: Family Style 9 Course Chef's Deluxe Chinese or Chef's
Special Japanese Dinners $17.00 per person, Hanama'ulu Special Platter $15.00
Oriental Buffet: Sunday Nights 5:30-8:30 PM $15.95
Dessert: Azuki Tempura $3.50, Green Tea Ice Cream $2.00

Impressions:

The proper name of this establishment is the Hanama'ulu Restaurant, Tea
House, and Sushi Bar. Try putting that in a phone book! This rambling 80-year
old Chinese/Japanese restaurant is located on the Lihue highway bypass across
from the 7-11 store. If you are coming for dinner, add to your evening and make
a reservation in one of the traditional Japanese tatami rooms where you can
enjoy dining by the gardens and koi ponds. Park in the Hanama'ulu Plaza lot
just north of the building and enter through the gates.

Kauai Dining

East Coast

Hong Kong Café
Wailua Shopping Center
4-361 Kuhio Highway
Kapa'a, HI 96746
808-822-3288
Web: None
Hours: L/D 11:00 AM – 9:30 PM
         L/D 2:00 PM – 9:30 PM Su
Cards: MC V
Dress: Casual
Style: Chi $

Menu Sampler:

Breakfast:
N/A
Lunch/Dinner:
Plate Lunches: Include two-scoop rice, one scoop mac salad, and chilled sweet
& sour cabbage. Deep Fried Stuffed Eggplant $5.75, Char Siu $5.95, Duck with
Ginger Chicken $5.95, Lup Cheong with Sweet and Sour Rib $5.75
Super Bentos: Crispy Chicken, Sweet & Sour Ribs, Kau Gee, Fried Shrimp,
Vegetable Gon Lo Mein, Rice $6.65, Beef Broccoli, Lemon Shoyu Chicken,
Kau Gee, Fried Shrimp, Vegetable Gon Lo Mein, Rice $6.95
Appetizers: Deep Fried Crab & Cheese Won Ton (6 pcs) $4.50, Deep Fried
Won Ton (12 pcs) $3.65, Deep Fried Kau Gee (6 pcs) 4.25, S & S Sauce $.50
Soups: Won Ton Soup $5.75, Hot & Sour Soup (vegetarian) $6.75, Large
Saimin $3.95, Crispy Chicken Look Funn $5.75, Egg Drop Soup $5.95
Entrees: Sizzling Happy Family $9.95, Shrimp with Cashew Nuts $7.95, Kung
Pao Chicken $6.50, Pork with Bitter Melon & Black Bean $6.75, Szechuan
Broccoli $6.50, Chicken Choy Sum (Ham Ha) $6.50, Kung Pao Tofu $6.50
Rice: Shrimp Fried Rice $6.25, Mixed Vegetable Fried Rice $5.95, Steam $.50
Mein: House Chow Mein/ Kau Gee Mein $6.50, Spicy Chicken Lo Mein $5.75

Impressions:

This busy little place features Chinese food cooked by chefs from China. Will
wonders ever cease! The owner is a local realtor who divides his time between
selling property and helping recent immigrants achieve their dreams of owning
their own restaurants. The menu is varied and authentic, but the big hit is the
specials board. Local specialties like fresh fish and Kauai shrimp make their
way to the kitchen daily. This is condo country and carryout is a top seller.

North Shore

Java Kai Hanalei
Hanalei Center
Hanalei, HI 96714
808-826-6717
www.tastethefun.com
Hours: 6:30 AM-6:00 PM
Cards: MC V
Dress: Casual
Style: Cof/Spec $

Menu Sampler:

Breakfast:
Collection of pastries, traditional offerings, and great Belgian waffles! Try the Kauai Waffle with strawberry papaya, apple banana, macadamia nuts and whipped cream on a fresh hot Belgian waffle for $7.50. Other treats are the Surfer's Sandwich with egg, bacon slices and cheese on an English Muffin $5.95, Bali Hai Burrito with eggs, potatoes, onions, tomatoes, cilantro, chili and cheese wrapped in a tortilla with papaya salsa and sour cream $8.50, Granola with milk or soy $4.95, Lattes, Smoothies, Chai, Juices, and Lemonade Baked Items: Aloha Bars of toasted coconut, macadamia nuts and chocolate chips on a shortbread cookie crust; bagels, smoothies, specialty flavored coffee drinks, lemon bars, homemade muffins, apple pie, chocolate chip macadamia nut & oatmeal raisin cookies, shortbread with lemon topping.
Lunch/Dinner:
N/A

Impressions:

Your first impression upon entering Java Kai might be the smell of freshly brewed coffee, but they make a fine showing with their menu items as well. Patrons order breakfast sandwiches and baked goodies at the counter for delivery to their table. Besides the over-the-counter items Java Kai offers more than twenty types of coffee for sale with shipping available. Inquire within. This is an enjoyable place to while away some time on a misty Hanalei morning.

Lihue

JJ's Broiler
Anchor Cove Shopping Plaza
3416 Rice Street
Lihue, HI 96766
808-246-4422
Web: None
Hours: L 11:00 AM-5:00 PM
          D 5:00 PM-10:00 PM
Cards: DC DIS JCB MC V
Dress: Casual
Style: Amer/Pac Rim $$$

Menu Sampler:

Breakfast:
N/A
Lunch:
Hawaiian Ocean Chowder $6.75, French Onion Soup $6.75, Fish & Chips with seasoned fries and malt vinegar $11.95, Asian Grilled Chicken Salad with crisp vegetables and rice noodles served with hoisin dressing and a grilled chicken breast $10.95, Philly Steak Sandwich with rice or fries and pickle $9.95, Sautéed Mushroom Cheeseburger w/rice or fries and pickle $9.75, Fish 'n Chips $11.95
Dinner:
Appetizers, Salads & Soups: Onion Soup with glazed cheese and onion $6.25, Clam Bucket, 2 lbs. in white wine, garlic and herbs $19.95, Peking Chicken Taco of tender strips of chicken, shiitake mushrooms & vegetables wrapped in Peking pancakes with garlic oyster sauce $9.95, JJ's House Escargot $9.95
Entrées: All entrees include table salad bar & choice of steamed or house rice: Roasted Macadamia Lamb Rack with juniper garlic sauce $23.95, Prime Rib of Beef with au jus and horseradish $27.95, Coconut Shrimp with curried coconut crumbs, mango sauce and chutney $19.95, Beef Medallions with Lobster Sauce in a shiitake cream sauce $29.95, Hoisin Salmon Skewers on a warm soba salad with vegetables $23.95, Herbed Seafood Linguini with fresh basil, garlic $23.95

Impressions:

You'll find JJ's Broiler near the Marriott overlooking the beach on Nawiliwili Bay. Casual meals are served downstairs either inside or out on the lanai with the second floor open for dinner. Portions are quite generous, so sharing is apropos. After work a lively crowd gathers in the lounge to relive the day's events and enjoy their favorite adult beverages.

Kauai Dining

South Shore

Joe's On The Green

2545 Kiahuna Plantation Drive
Poipu, HI 96756
808-742-9696
Web: None
Hours: B 7:00 AM-11:30 AM
           L 11:30 AM-2:30 PM
           D 5:30 PM-8:30 PM WeTh
Cards: MC V
Dress: Casual
Style: Amer $

Menu Sampler:

Breakfast:

Breakfast Specials include choice of hash browns or rice. Michael's Eggs
Benedict $9.50, Create your own 3-egg omelet $8.50, J.B.'s Breakfast Burrito-a
flour tortilla, beans, scrambled eggs, salsa, cheese, olives, and sour cream $8.25,
French Toast $6.95, Banana Macadamia Nut Pancakes $7.75, Miso Soup $2.75,
Anahola Granola $4.00, Half Papaya with yogurt or cottage cheese $3.75

Lunch:

"Personalized" House Salad served with a focaccia breadstick $7.25, New
England Style Seafood Chowder-cup $3.25, with a half turkey or tuna sandwich
$7.25, with a small house salad $6.95, or a bowl of chowder $5.50. Sandwiches
are served with French fries, island coleslaw, potato-mac salad, or steamed rice.
Joe's Mama Burger $7.95, Chicken Avocado with jack cheese-grilled $8.75.
Lunch Specials are Fish and Chips w/cole slaw & fries $8.95, Linguini with
Chicken-Artichoke Sausage & vegetables $8.50, Chicken Cutlet served with
sautéed veggie's, rice and gravy $7.75, Loco Moco-1/3# hamburger $6.50
Desserts: Lilikoi Dream Ice Cream Pie $4.95, Kauai Ice Cream Pie $4.95

Dinner:

Wednesday & Thursday from 5:30-8:30 PM with live Hawaiian music

Impressions:

This popular chef-owned dining spot is located on the golf course of the
beautiful Kiahuna Plantation. Going by the informal name of Joe's On The
Green this establishment offers an affordable upscale menu with a choice of
inside or outside seating. If you've watched birds trying to mooch a meal at a
restaurant in Hawaii, wait until you see the native island chickens try to outsmart
the waitresses at Joe's. Hey, they live on Kauai too!

West Side

Kalaheo Coffee Co & Café

22-2436 Kaumualii Hwy (Hwy 50)
Kalaheo, HI 96741
808-332-5858
www.kalaheo.com
Hours: B/L 6:00 AM-3:00 PM Mo-Fr
         B/L 6:30 AM-3:00 PM Sa
         B/L 6:30 AM-2:00 PM Su
Cards: MC V
Dress: Casual
Style: Cof/Spec $
         Ent Card

Menu Sampler:

Breakfast/Lunch:

Gourmet coffees, wonderful pastries and baked goods such as pie, caramel rolls, fruit scones, croissants, muffins and cinnamon buns are produced daily on the premises. Belgian Waffles, Pancakes, Eggs with Portuguese sausage, ham or bacon, rice or potatoes, Bonzo Burrito with sauteed ham, peppers, mushrooms, onions and olives scrambled with two eggs, wrapped in a burrito with cheddar and Monterey jack. Sandwiches such as Hot Pastrami Kalaheo Style on fresh baked bread, Grilled Herb Chicken Sandwich with our tomato-onion relish, Soup and Salad Combo. The most expensive item on the menu costs $8.25.
Dinner: N/A

Impressions:

Kalaheo Coffee Co & Café is a serve-yourself-at-the-counter kind of place. You'll find this to be a convenient stop on that trip to Barking Sands Beach or the Waimea Canyon. Although you couldn't really call this a restaurant there are a few tables available for limited seating. The reasonably priced breakfast and lunch offerings are surprisingly interesting and varied for this style of meal service. The staff is friendly and the surroundings are pleasant, but it's the baked goods that make this a definite recommendation.

Kauai Dining

West Side

Kalaheo Steak House
4444 Papalina Road
Kalaheo, HI 96741
808-332-9780
Web: None
Hours: 6:00 PM-10:00 PM
Cards: AE DIS MC V
Dress: Resort Casual
Style: Stk $$$

Menu Sampler:

Breakfast/Lunch:
N/A
Dinner:
Appetizers: Steamer Clams by the pound $5.95, Mussels- ½ # steamed in Tabasco, butter, garlic, green onions and lemon juice $5.95, Teriyaki Steak Stix of sirloin and strip loin skewered and marinated in teriyaki and barbecued $4.75, Mushrooms sautéed w/butter, garlic, red wine topped with Parmesan cheese & parsley $6.25, Artichokes steamed in an herb marinade $6.75 (seasonal)
Entrées: All dinners include House or Caesar salad and rolls with baked potato or white rice sliced bread and butter. Top Sirloin-12 oz.-$18.75, with a teriyaki marinade $18.95, Filet Mignon with sautéed mushrooms $24.95, Prime Rib slow roasted for 8 hours with au jus gravy and blended horseradish sauce- 12 oz cut $20.95, Teriyaki Chicken Breast $16.95, Cornish Game Hen, marinated, oven roasted, flame broiled, topped with parmesan and chopped parsley $16.95, Baby Back Pork Ribs roasted then flame broiled with sauce $18.95, Kalaheo Shrimp sautéed in butter, lemon and fresh garlic, topped with parmesan and parsley and served on white rice $19.95, Alaskan King Crab Legs-1# $28.95, Broiled Fresh Island Fish $Market Price, Combos are offered $20.95/$24.95
Side Orders: Portuguese Bean Soup $4.95, Scalloped Potatoes $2.95
Desserts: Rum Cake & Ice Cream $3.95, Melinda's Cheesecake $4.95

Impressions:

Kalaheo Steak House has the friendly atmosphere you expect to find in a small town dining spot. However, as soon as you open the menu you're back on Main Street. This restaurant offers a metropolitan steak and seafood menu without the usual big-city prices. To find this little gem, drive a few miles south from Poipu Beach to Kalaheo and take a left at the stoplight on Papalina Road. Then go one block, look on your left, and you've found it. A small parking lot is off to the side of the building and there is plenty of street-side parking.

Kauai Dining

South Shore

Keoki's Paradise
Poipu Shopping Village
2360 Kiahuna Plantation Drive
Poipu, HI 96756
808-742-7535
www.keokisparadise.com
Hours: L 11:00 AM-11:30 PM
         D 5:00 PM-10:00 PM
Cards: AE DC DIS JCB MC V
Dress: Resort Casual
Style: Stk/Sea/Island $$

Menu Sampler:

Breakfast:
 N/A
Lunch:
Plate Lunch has "two scoop" rice. Choices are Koloa Pork Ribs $9.95, Grilled
Island Fresh Fish $9.95, Hawaiian Fish and Chips $9.95, Stir-Fry Chicken
Cashew $9.95, Veggie and Cashew Stir Fry $8.95, Bamboo Special $Mkt
Sandwiches: Keoki's Fish Sandwich $9.95, Keoki's Paradise Burger $5.95,
Cheeseburger $6.95, Tuna & Cheddar $6.95, Grilled Roast Beef & Cheddar
$6.95. Cobb Salad $9.95, Grilled Chicken Caesar Salad $9.95. Nachos $5.95
Dinner:
Pupus: Thai Shrimp Sticks-grilled and served with a tangy guava cocktail sauce
$8.95, Panko Crusted Scallops with Wasabi Butter Sauce $9.95.
Fish: Prepared five different ways-baked or sautéed with sauces $19.95-$23.95
Entrées: All entrées are served with Keoki's Caesar Salad & a basket of freshly
baked bread. Coconut Crusted Chicken with coconut & mango sauce $15.95,
Prime Rib $24.95, Koloa Pork Ribs $16.95, and Coconut Crust Chicken with
mango sauce $15.95, Pesto Shrimp Macadamia over rice pilaf $16.95

Impressions:

Keoki's Paradise has great tropical atmosphere with lots of bamboo, torches,
umbrella drinks, indoor/outdoor dining, and live Hawaiian music. The menu
revolves around old-time favorites prepared with island twists. Portions are very
generous and come at reasonable prices. This combination attracts a lively
crowd and makes for a fun time. Keoki's is a large place with lots of parking.
The long hours and café menu make this a great late night stop.

North Shore

Kilauea Bakery & Pau Hana Pizza
Kong Lung Center
Kilauea. HI 96754
808-828-2020
Web: None
Hours: Pizza 11:00 AM-9:00 PM
            Bakery 6:30 AM-9:00 PM
Cards: MC V
Dress: Casual
Style: Spec $

Menu Sampler:

Breakfast:
Coffee made by the cup in the bakery with scones, and sweet cinnamon buns.
Breakfast pastries and Danishes use fresh mango, cheese, lilikoi, coconut, and
Key Lime flavors. Full service gourmet coffee and espresso bar available.

Lunch/Dinner:
Tuscan Style Pizza as traditional or as gourmet as you like it. Sizes are small 8",
medium 12", and large 16" ranging in price from $7.25-$27.85. Fresh
vegetables, seafood, meats, specially prepared vegetables, and assorted cheeses
make any combination possible. Specialty Pizzas are small $10.95, medium
$16.95, and large $23.75 and are wonderful gourmet combinations such as
Pomodoro-fresh tomatoes, Kilauea goat cheese, house marinated artichokes,
black olives and mozzarella cheese, or the Billie Holliday of smoked ono, Swiss
chard, roasted onions, gorgonzola rosemary sauce, and mozzarella cheese.

Impressions:

Take the turnoff from the main highway to the Kilauea National Marine and
Wildlife Reserve and you will find yourself in the small north shore village of
Kilauea. Then follow the road toward the Kilauea Lighthouse until you reach the
Kong Lung Center. There in the garden courtyard resides the Kilauea Bakery &
Pau Hana Pizza. This is a very popular place with the locals—they line up in the
morning with their coffee cups in hand. You'll know why when your eyes start
to shine after the first cup! The pastries are an excellent accompaniment to their
specialty coffees and teas. Lunch and dinner patrons find the pizza to be hearty,
authentic, and delicious. There are a few indoor and outdoor tables for dining
convenience. This is a great stop while you're out exploring the north shore.

East Coast

Kountry Style Kitchen
1485 Kuhio Highway
Kapa'a, HI 96746
808-822-3511
Web: None
Hours: BL 6:00 AM-2:00 PM
Cards: MC V
Dress: Casual
Style: Amer $

Menu Sampler:

Breakfast:
Ham & Cheese Omelette with hash browns or rice, toast & jelly or cornbread $7.25, 8 oz. Steak & Eggs with hashed browns or rice, toast & jelly or cornbread $11.75, Omelette Bar $5.00 plus $1.45 for meats, $1.25 for cheese, $1.00 for veggies, 3 Banana or Strawberry Pancakes $5.25, French Toast $5.00, Fresh Chilled Papaya $1.75, Loco Moco $5.50, Eggs Benedict with hash browns or rice $8.75, Garden Benedict with mushrooms, spinach, tomatoes, and olives served with hash browns or rice $8.25, Keiki Specials $3.25-$3.50

Lunch:
All burgers are served with Krispy Fries. Burger Bar $4.75 plus mushrooms & bacon $1.50 each, plus cheese & veggies $1.00 each, BLT or Patty Melt served with French fries or potato salad $7.25, Grilled Mahi Mahi with vegetables, rice or fries, tartar sauce and hot corn bread $9.25, Kountry Fried Chicken (3 pcs) with rice or fries, vegetables, and hot corn bread $7.25, Chef Salad $7.25

Dinner:
N/A

Impressions:

The Kountry Style Kitchen Restaurant is a classic small town coffee shop. It's located in a roadside storefront and has the standard booths and tables for seating. Coffee pots held high by waitresses weaving through the tables and specials hand written on the board complete the scene. The atmosphere here is comfortable and welcoming helped along by the homey menu offerings. Quality ingredients are used and the solid fare delivers as intended. As Kapa'a is the mid-point of Kauai's crescent-shaped highway this would be a convenient breakfast stop while touring. Parking is available in the rear of the restaurant.

East Coast

La Playita Azul
4-831 Kuhio Hwy
Kapa'a, HI 96746
808-821-2323
Web: None
Hours: L 11:00 AM-3:00 PM XSu
         D 5:30 PM-9:00 PM
Cards: AE MC V
Dress: Casual
Style: Mex $$

Menu Sampler:

Breakfast:
N/A

Lunch/Dinner:
Entrees: Tacos Dorados-two crispy tacos with shredded beef or chicken, salsa fresca, guacamole, rice and beans $9.95, Chicken Mole Enchilada-two chicken enchiladas served with homemade mole sauce, rice and beans $9.95, Quesadilla filled with cheese and chicken or beef, served with rice, beans, guacamole and sour cream $10.95, Chimichanga with an herb flour tortilla stuffed with chicken or beef, deep fried and served with rice and beans $10.95, Burrito Con Pollo with shredded chicken, rice and beans, and fresh tomatillo or tomato sauce $10.95, Taco de Pescado-two soft shell tacos made with sautéed fresh fish, served with salsa fresca, rice and beans $12.95, Chile Rellenos-traditional chile poblano stuffed with Monterey jack cheese, served with a fresh ranchero sauce, rice, beans, and tortillas $13.95, Fajitas of grilled chopped steak or chicken and fresh mixed vegetables, served with rice, beans, tortillas $15.95, Camarones Al Mojo De Ajo (garlic shrimp) served with rice, beans, tortillas $16.95, Camarones Ala Diabla-large shrimp sautéed in a chipotle sauce with rice, beans and tortillas $17.95, Seafood Burrito-an herb flour tortilla stuffed with jumbo scallop, shrimp, fresh fish, sautéed mixed vegetables, rice and beans and a fresh sour cream-jalapeño sauce $18.95, Seafood Fajita $21.95

Impressions:

La Playita Azul is another of the storefront eateries so common in Hawaii. It isn't very large, but the kitchen does a great job serving an extensive menu of authentic Mexican specialties. This isn't just a taco house. Besides the quick lunch items we all enjoy, they offer upscale entrees made with steak, chicken, and fresh seafood. Dining is very casual with seating both inside and out.

East Coast

Lemon Grass Grill, Seafood and Sushi Bar

4-885 Kuhio Highway
Kapa'a, HI 96746
808-821-2888
Web: None
Hours: D 5:00 PM-9:30 PM
Cards: AE DC DIS JCB MC V
Dress: Resort Casual
Style: Japan/Pac Rim $$$

Menu Sampler:

Breakfast/Lunch:
N/A

Dinner:
Starters: Tempura Fried Ahi of nori wrap with seasoned rice, ahi, deep fried, masago and wasabi aioli $8.75, Kalua Won Ton with ginger sweet potato, lomi tomato, poi vinaigrette, pineapple relish and our Kalua won ton $7.25
Salads: Moloa'a Shrimp and Papaya Salad with local greens, papaya, sprouts, pine nuts served with the spicy mango vinaigrette dressing $7.25
Specialties: Jumbo Scallop Sauté with jade sauce, fried long rice, shiitake relish, garlic mashed potatoes and balsamic syrup $19.00, Broiled Herb Lamb Loin with ratatouille, garlic mashed potatoes, pineapple relish and lamb au jus $20.95, Hoisin BBQ Chicken Breast with slaw and won ton pi, black bean relish, pineapple relish, and papaya relish $15.25, Huli Huli Chicken $15.25
Sushi Bar: Nigiri Sushi $3.50-$7.50, Cut Rolls- 9-1-1 of spicy tuna roll topped with avocado, katsuo bushi $9.50, Rainbow $9.50, Hand Rolls-California $4.00, Spicy Tuna $5.00, Eel $5.00, Sushi Combos-Waipoli Combo with miso soup, maguro, sake, Hamachi, ebi, Tamago, and California Roll $14.50, Viva Las Vegas Roll of tempura shrimp, crab, ahi, cucumber, deep fried and served with a sweet, spicy sauce $12.50, Spider Roll of soft shell crab and cucumber $11.50

Impressions:

Our first impression upon entering Lemon Grass was, "Wow! What a beautiful wood building!" Inside, you go up a staircase to the main dining room or stay downstairs for lanai dining. The sushi bar is unique with floating boats that were originally intended to convey fresh creations to diners. Unfortunately the corners proved too tight so the boat parade ended, but the sushi just keeps coming. After sampling the sushi experience, don't miss out on the Pacific Rim inspired menu. You won't find some of these innovative preparations elsewhere.

Kauai Dining

Lihue

Lihue Barbecue Inn
2982 Kress Street
Lihue, HI 96766
808-245-2921
Web: None
Hours: B 7:00 AM-10:30 AM XSu
         L 10:30 AM-1:30 PM XSu
         D 5:00 PM-8:30 PM XSu
Cards: MC V
Dress: Casual
Style: Amer/Filip/Japan/Haw $$

Menu Sampler:

Breakfast:
Shortstack Special of two pancakes, one egg and choice of either bacon or Portuguese sausage $5.95, Three Egg Omelet with chicken, onions, tomatoes, green peppers, spinach and cheese $8.95, Oriental Breakfast of miso, fish teriyaki, egg with green onions, tsukemono, and steamed rice $7.95

Lunch:
All entrees and sandwiches include soup or fresh fruit, dessert and choice of coffee or tea. Grilled or Sautéed Fish of the Day with fruit salsa $12.95, Mahi Fish & Chips w/fries, cole slaw & tartar sauce $10.95, Teriyaki Chicken Sandwich w/fries & slaw $8.95, Hamburger $4.50, Katsu Donburi $8.95

Dinner:
Appetizers: Tri-Sampler of fire-grilled chili rubbed prawns served with a BBQ Hollandaise sauce, furikake deep fried squid with honey-curry dipping sauce, and seared teriyaki top sirloin $16.95, Winter Crab Cakes w/curry sauce $14.95

Entrées: Baby Back Ribs $19.95, Baked Stuffed Mahi Mahi w/snow crab, veggies & cheese, Dijon & ginger aioli $18.95, Mac Nut Crusted Chicken Breast w/papaya/pineapple marmalade $18.95, Rack of Lamb w/chutney $23.95

Desserts: The greatest homemade cream pies in flavors such as peanut butter, chocolate, lemon, banana, cherry, etc. $1.00 per slice!!

Impressions:

Years ago soldiers used to line up in the street to enjoy the Lihue Barbecue Inn's home-style food and atmosphere. Not that much has changed as a solid group of loyal customers keeps the friendly staff busy serving a wide variety of island favorites. The diner/café decor includes booths and tables and there is a separate lounge area. You won't find a more reasonably priced menu in Hawaii.

East Coast

Mema Thai Chinese Cuisine

Wailua Shopping Plaza
4-369 Kuhio Hwy (Hwy 56)
Kapa'a, HI 96746
808-823-0899
www.hanaleihaven.com
Hours: L 11:00 AM-2:00 PM XSaSu
         D 5:00 PM-9:30 PM
Cards: AE DC DIS MC V
Dress: Casual
Style: Chi/Thai $$

Menu Sampler:

Breakfast:
N/A

Lunch/Dinner:
Appetizers: Shrimp Rolls of rice paper stuffed with long rice, onion, black mushrooms, water chestnuts and shrimp served with lettuce, mint leaves and cucumber $7.95, Sa-the—coconut milk, peanut butter, kaffir lime leaves, seasoning, cucumber sauce on the side, choices are tofu or vegetable $7.95, Chicken on the Stick $8.95, Fish battered and deep fried $10.95, Shrimp $10.95
Soups: Thai Ginger Coconut Soup with kaffir lime leaves $7.95-$14.95, Long Rice Soup $7.95-$10.95, Spicy Lemongrass Soup with Shrimp $10.95
Salad: Fresh Island Papaya Salad $6.95, Calamari Salad w/lemongrass $10.95
Noodles and Rice: Pad Thai of stir fried Thai rice noodles with eggs, chives, and bean sprouts topped with peanuts and lemon on the side-chicken or pork $9.95, shrimp $11.95, seafood $17.95, Broccoli Noodles with Pork $9.95
Entrées: Fried Garlic Pork with garlic & black pepper served on a bed of chopped cabbage with sweet & sour sauce $9.95, Pad Ped $8.95-17.95, Lemon Chicken $8.95, House Curry with kaffir lime leaves, fresh ground lemon grass, peas and coconut milk- chicken, pork, or beef $9.95, Mema's Beef Curry $9.95

Impressions:

Mema Thai is located across the highway from Restaurant Kintaro at the southern edge of Kapa'a. As you walk up to the door, the first things you'll notice are the rosewood furnishings and ornate Asian art objects that give this restaurant its distinctive and exotic atmosphere. From there the enticing aromas take off and give a hint to the fabulous flavors to be experienced herein. Thai food will never be referred to as boring. This is affordable dining with panache.

Kauai Dining

North Shore

Neide's Salsa & Samba
Hanalei Center
5-5161 Kuhio Highway
Hanalei, HI 96714
808-826-1851
Web: None
Hours: L 11:30 AM-2:30 PM
          D 5:00 PM-Closing
Cards: MC V
Dress: Casual
Style: Braz/Mex $

Menu Sampler:

Breakfast:
N/A
Lunch/Dinner:
Mexican Dishes:
Macho Burrito with refried beans, cheese and onions, choice of shredded beef, chicken, pork or veggies, topped with ranchera sauce, melted cheese, sour cream and black olives $7.95, Huevos Ranchera of two eggs sunny side up on a crisp, flat corn tortilla with refried beans, ranchera sauce, sour cream and black olives, served with Spanish rice and flour tortilla $8.95, Nachos w/black olives $4.50
Brazilian Dishes: Panqueca of a crepe with pumpkin stuffing and fresh vegetables, smothered in Neide's own special sauce with melted cheese and fresh vegetables & cheese served with Brazilian rice $8.95, Ensopado of chicken and fresh vegetables baked with a special Brazilian sauce, served with Brazilian rice and black beans $8.95, Bife Acebolado-a tender, juicy beef steak smothered in fresh Maui onions, served with Brazilian rice and black beans $13.95
Child's Plate: Choice of a taco, enchilada, or quesadilla served with Spanish rice and beans $5.50

Impressions:

Neide's Salsa & Samba is located in the back of the Hanalei Center and shares a courtyard dining area with Bamboo Bamboo. Indoor dining is offered in an attractively decorated room set with wooden tables and chairs. Since opening in 1998 Neide's has developed a loyal following of locals and visitors with their large servings of Mexican and Brazilian dishes. For those new to Brazilian cuisine, it is long on meat courses and comes in sizeable portions. All of the entrées here are mildly seasoned, as in the Brazilian tradition.

East Coast

Norberto's El Café
4-1373 Kuhio Hwy (Hwy 56)
Kapa'a, HI 96746
808-822-3362
Web: None
Hours: D 5:00 PM-9:00 PM XSu
Cards: AE DIS MC V
Dress: Casual
Style: Mex $$

Menu Sampler:

Breakfast:/Lunch:
N/A
Dinner:
All dinners are served with soup, Spanish rice, refried beans, corn chips, and plenty of hot Mexican salsa. Burrito Ranchero of shredded or ground beef $14.45, Beef Tostada-Enchilada Combination made with a crispy corn tortilla with seasoned beef, refried beans, cheddar cheese, lettuce, Spanish enchilada sauce, and tomatoes served with one jack and cheddar cheese enchilada $14.45, Rellenos Tampico-a select green chile stuffed with natural Monterey Jack cheese, dipped in whipped egg and sautéed to a golden brown, with Spanish sauce and cheese and a tasty cheese enchilada $16.95, Mex-Mix Plate with a chicken chimichanga, a chicken taquito, and a cheese enchilada with guacamole $16.95. A la carte items range from a $4.25 Taco, $8.45 for a Nachos Supreme, $8.45 for a Burrito Outrageous, to $13.95 for a Rellenos Plate for adults.
Dessert: Hula Pie $3.50, Rum Cake 3.00, Ice Cream $2.00

Impressions:

Norberto's is located in the heart of Kapa'a Town in an old-fashioned high ceiling building. This eatery has long been a favorite on Kauai. The menu is traditional zesty Mexican with some notable twists. First, in order to meet heart-healthy standards, no lard or animal fat is used in preparation. Then, as an added spin, many of the dishes may be requested vegetarian. In fact, one of their house favorite enchilada offerings is stuffed with eggplant rather than meat. For a total local touch the restaurant also features homegrown taro leaf enchiladas. Fish specials are offered when available. The cantina in the back serves Margarita's by the glass or pitcher as well as domestic and imported beer.

Kauai Dining

East Coast

Ono Family Restaurant
1292 Kuhio Hwy (Hwy 56)
Kapa'a, HI 96746
808-822-1710
Web: None
Hours: B 7:00 AM-1:00 PM
         L 11:00 AM-2:00 PM
Cards: AE DC JCB MC V
Dress: Casual
Style: Amer/Island $

Menu Sampler:

Breakfast:
Eggs Hash--corned beef hash with two poached eggs, toast, side of hollandaise and a slice of papaya $6.75, Eggs Canterbury-poached eggs, ham, turkey, jack cheese, tomato, hollandaise sauce and mushrooms on an English muffin with a slice of papaya $7.95. Three-Egg Omelets include a wide choice of fillings, & a choice of hash browns, rice, fried rice or toast $5.75-$7.50, Tropical Stack with bananas, macadamia nuts, coconut, and whipped cream $6.25

Lunch:
Farmer's Sandwich of turkey, ham, jack cheese, lettuce, tomato and mayonnaise on Branola bread with French fries and soup $7.50, Chicken Breast Plate served with rice or fries and choice of teriyaki or BBQ sauce and soup or salad $8.20, Saimin-Chinese noodle soup topped with wonbok, carrots, green onions, & a half hard-boiled egg-small $3.50, large $5.50, Burgers served with fries or salad $5.70-$8.20, Oriental Chicken Salad with a stir-fried chicken breast $7.75

Dessert: Coconut or Macadamia Nut Custard Homemade Pie $3.50/slice.

Dinner:
N/A

Impressions:

This plantation-style restaurant is an excellent choice for breakfast or lunch. Their lengthy menu features two pages of egg dishes alone! Other ingredients such as homemade chorizo, lup cheong, and kim chee reflect the multi-cultural population of the island. Although steamed rice or potatoes accompany most offerings, the fried rice is a real hit. This local and visitor favorite is full of aloha style hospitality and is a "must try" for the adventurous traveler.

West Side

Pacific Pizza & Deli
9852 Kaumualii Highway
Waimea. HI 96796
808-338-1020
Web: None
Hours: L/D 11:00 AM-9:00 PM
Cards: DIS MC V
Dress: Casual
Style: Amer/Spec $

Menu Sampler:

Breakfast:
N/A
Lunch/Dinner:
Pizzas & Calzones:
Pacific Pepperoni Pizza-S $7.25, M $11.95, L $16.25/Pepperoni Calzone $4.75
Surfa Deluxe with pesto sauce, Canadian bacon, shrimp, faux crab, pineapple-S $8.95, M $14.95, L $19.95/Surfa Deluxe Calzone $5.50
Lomi Lomi with cheeses, fresh tomatoes, diced salmon, diced onions & green onions-S $8.95, M $14.95, L $19.95/Lomi Lomi Calzone $5.50
Hapa Haole with pesto sauce, cheeses, sun-dried tomatoes, mushrooms, zucchini, olives, Canadian bacon, and pineapple-S 8.95, M $14.95, L $19.95/Hapa Haole Calzone $5.50
Portuguese with our own Portuguese sausage, onions, and olives & more - S $8.50, M $13.95, L $18.95/Portuguese Calzone $5.00
Cold Wraps with turkey, chicken, roast beef, pastrami, ham or veggies $5.25-seafood $6.25 in a tomato-basil tortilla with our own special dressing
Deli Sandwiches with choice of meat and bread with fresh toppings $5.25

Impressions:

Located in a large plantation style building alongside Wrangler's Steakhouse you'll find the Pacific Pizza & Deli. High ceilings, wood floors, and antiques are a proper setting for the quality pizza and calzones coming out of the kitchen. The yeasty crust is puffy on the edges while thin and crispy in the center, even with all the toppings. Sometimes it is difficult to obtain good Italian sausage in the islands, but theirs' has that tantalizing taste of fennel. A small pizza will feed two people generously making this a very affordable stop for lunch or dinner.

Kauai Dining

East Coast

Panda Garden
4-831 Kuhio Hwy
Kapa'a, HI 96746
808-822-0092
Web: None
Hours: L 10:30 AM-2:00 PM X We
        D 4:00 PM-9:30 PM
Cards: AE DIS JCB MC V
Dress: Casual
Style: Chi $$

Menu Sampler:

Breakfast:
N/A
Lunch/Dinner:
Appetizer: Spring Roll $4.95, Shrimp and Bacon Roll $5.95, Squid with Pepper Salt $10.95, Steam Dumpling $5.95, Roasted Pork $5.50, Fried Kau Gee $4.50
Soup: Bird's Nest Soup $10.95, Minced Chicken Cream Corn Soup $6.50
Seafood: Kung Pao Shrimp $9.50, Sweet and Sour Shrimp with Pineapple $8.95, Squid with Garlic-Ginger Sauce $8.95, Lobster Tail w/Black Bean Sauce $19.95, Fish Fillet in Szechuan Sauce $12.95, Scallop w/Chinese Peas $9.95
Chicken: Curry Chicken $7.50, Dry Fry Chicken $8.50, Hong Kong Crispy Chicken $6.95, Sesame Sauce Chicken $8.50, Lemon Chicken $6.95
Beef: Mongolian Beef $7.50, Beef with Black Mushroom $8.50, Beef with Oyster Sauce $7.50, Green Onion Beef $8.50, Beef with Green Pepper $8.50
Pork: Shredded Pork with Garlic-Ginger Sauce $7.95, Steam Pork Hash $7.50
Other Entrees: Duck with Oyster Sauce $8.50, Mu Shu Pork $8.95, Seafood Pineapple Fried Rice $9.95, Seafood Hong Kong Noodle $11.95
House Specialties: Walnut Shrimp $14.95, Szechuan Triple Crown w/Gulf shrimp, tender beef & pork -hot & spicy $13.95, Orange Flavored Beef $11.95
Lunch Specials: Mo-Fr 10.30 AM-2:00 PM-served w/soup, fried won ton, & rice-Cashew Nut Chicken $5.95, Mongolian Beef $6.95, Beef w/Broccoli $5.95
Family Dinners: $12.95/$15.95 per person (two person minimum-one entrée choice per person) includes Spring Roll, Soup, Entrees and Rice

Impressions:

Panda Garden might be located in a storefront, but it is definitely a restaurant. Besides their solid Hong Kong and Szechuan menu, they offer full bar service and an attractive facility. Find them in the Kauai Village Shopping Center.

Kauai Dining

South Shore

Pizzetta
5408 Koloa Road
Koloa, HI 96756
808-742-8881
Web: None
Hours: L 11:00 AM-3:00 PM
         Happy Hour 3:00 PM-6:00 PM
         D 4:00 PM-9:00 PM
Cards: MC V
Dress: Casual
Style: Amer/Ital $$

Menu Sampler:

Breakfast:
N/A
Lunch:
Sandwiches & Pasta: Veneto of blackened chicken, Cajun dressing, mozzarella cheese, lettuce & tomato w/pasta salad $6.95, Homemade Meatball-oven baked w/marinara, roasted garlic cream sauce & mozzarella, open-faced w/pasta salad $6.95, Pasta Lunch Special-penne w/choice of sauce, house salad & bread $7.95
Pizza: Thin Crust or Regular. Medium $13.95-$17.95, Large $17.95-$22.95, additional toppings-Medium $1.75, Large $2.25 each, Slices only $2.95-$3.70
Happy Hour: 3:00 PM-6:00 PM
Dinner:
Antipasti, Salads & Sides: Hot Crab & Artichoke Dip with Crostini $9.95, Garlic Bread Sticks with marinara sauce $5.95, Caesar Salad $4.95/$7.95
Entrees: Fettuccini Quattro Formaggio $9.95, Chicken Marsala w/side of penne Marsala or garlic mashed potatoes $16.95, Eggplant Parmesan w/pasta or garlic mashed potatoes $13.95, Pesto & Mushrooms Calzone $8.95, Lasagne $13.95, Fettucini Scampi w/white wine, roasted garlic & parmesan cheese $15.95
Pizza: Handmade herb crust thin or regular, medium or large $13.95-$22.95, Pizza By The Slice $2.95-$3.70 served 11:00 AM-6:00 PM

Impressions:

After several days of fine dining experiences you might crave a casual, affordable meal. That's where Pizzetta comes in. Here you'll find pizza and pasta parlor favorites served in a convivial family atmosphere. This happening spot is not just for visitors though, as local patrons throng here for happy hour and revelry late into the evening. Delivery is free anywhere on the south shore.

Kauai Dining

South Shore

Plantation Gardens
Kiahuna Plantation Resort
2253 Poipu Road
Poipu, HI 96756
808-742-2216
Web: None
Hours: 5:30 PM-10:00PM
Cards: AE DC MC V
Dress: Resort Casual
Style: Pac-Rim/Med $$$

Menu Sampler:

Breakfast/Lunch:
N/A
Dinner:
Pupus: Crab and Rock Shrimp Stuffed Shiitake Mushrooms imu baked with macadamia nut aioli $10.95, Island Shrimp & Fresh Fish Wontons with mango guava chili sauce $9.95, Mixed Sashimi Platter with wasabi shoyu sauce $12.95
Salads: Poipu Seafood Salad w/wasabi lemon aioli $11.95, Caesar Salad with macadamia nut garden pesto croutons and pecorino cheese $6.95
Pizza: Koloa Pizza with grilled lemongrass chicken, mozzarella & pepper jack cheese, Kamuela tomato, Kauai avocado, Hawaiian chili pepper aioli $8.95, Plantation Pizza with Brenda's Portuguese sausage, Maui onions, roasted red bell peppers, smoked mozzarella cheese and tomato sauce $8.95
Entrées: Parker Ranch Black Angus New York Steak grilled with Hawaiian salt, kiawe roasted wild mushrooms, Maui onions, sweet corn, tomatoes $23.95, House Smoked Pork Tenderloin, sugar cane skewered, grilled tamarind hoisin plum sauce, caramelized Maui pineapple $17.95, Jumbo Scallops Stir Fry-smoked bacon wrapped scallops, kiawe grilled, Koloa asparagus, Asian vegetable stir fry and soba noodles $16.95, Grilled Chicken Breast with sesame papaya teriyaki sauce, rice noodles, hearts of palm, watercress, snow peas, asparagus, and soy vinaigrette $14.95, Fish and Shrimp Stir Fry $16.95

Impressions:

This historic plantation home with its cherry floors, koa trim, hand painted murals, and high ceilings was once the home of the Kiahuna Plantation manager. Today it's a luxurious open-air dining venue serving award-winning Pacific Rim cuisine with an occasional Mediterranean spin. Whether enjoying pupus in the lounge or dining on the veranda, a gracious island experience awaits.

South Shore

Poipu Beach Broiler
1941 Poipu Road
Koloa, HI 96756
808-742-6433
Web: None
Hours: Su Bru 10:00 AM-2:00 PM
         L 11:00 AM-5:00 PM
         D 5:00 PM-10:00 PM
Cards: AE DIS MC V
Dress: Resort Casual
Style: Isl/Pac-Rim $$

Menu Sampler:

Breakfast:
Sunday Brunch: Eggs to order with choice of meat, starch and toast $8, Traditional Eggs Benedict with rice or potatoes $10, French Toast with cinnamon and macadamia nuts $7, Omelettes with starch & toast $9
Lunch:
Appetizers: Sea Scallops dusted with togarashi, pan seared & served with strawberry sweet and sour sauce $10, Baby Back Ribs w/bourbon-pineapple $10
Salads: Salad Bar $7, Caesar Salad with lemon anchovy vinaigrette $6
Main Courses: Fish & Chips w/fries & lemon remoulade sauce $9, Teriyaki Chicken Sandwich with caramelized pineapple $8, Fresh Tuna Sandwich $7
Dinner:
Appetizers: Chicken Sticks-coconut breaded & served w/chili orange sauce $7
Entrées: Macadamia Mahi Mahi pan fried & served with jasmine rice and Kahana Royale beurre blanc $17, Seafood Fettucine with smoked bacon & button mushrooms, and Chablis garlic cream $21, Grilled New York Steak with garlic whipped potatoes, crispy straw onions $20, Baby Back Pork Ribs with Hawaiian salt baked potato, house made bourbon & pineapple bbq sauce $20
Desserts: Chocolate Temptation Cake, molten lava center, Kauai vanilla bean ice cream $6, Three Types of Chocolate Mousse with crème Anglaise $6

Impressions:

This used to be The House Of Seafood. Recently new owners came in and took the place down to the bare walls. Not only did the atmosphere improve but so did the menu. Chef Brant Hunt prepares exciting dishes with layers upon layers of flavor. His gift is taking something common and adding spins to come up with results that far exceed the sum of the parts. Fun and affordable!

Kauai Dining

West Side

Pomodoro Restaurant

Rainbow Plaza
2-2514 Kaumualii Hwy (Hwy 50)
Kalaheo, HI 96741
808-332-5945
Web: None
Hours: D 5:30 PM-9:30 PM
Cards: MC V
Dress: Resort Casual
Style: Ital $$

Menu Sampler:

Breakfast/Lunch:
N/A
Dinner:
All dinners include our home baked foccacia.
Antipasti: Calamari Fritti $10.50, Mozzarella Marinara $7.50, Prosciutto &
Melon (or seasonal fruit) $8.50
Insalate: Caesar $6.95, Mixed Greens with light balsamic vinaigrette $5.95
Zuppe: Minestrone alla Pomodoro $4.25
Pasta: Spaghetti with Bolognese or Marinara Sauce $11.95, with meatballs
$12.95, Tortellini alla Panna $14.95, Manicotti filled with a blend of cheeses
$14.50, Lasagne (House Special) with Italian sausage and choice beef $14.95,
Linguini with white or red clam sauce $14.50, Fettuccine Alfredo $12.95
Specialties: All dishes are served with farfelle pasta with seasonal vegetables.
Veal Pizzaiola with roasted peppers and onions in our special wine sauce
$19.95, Chicken Saltimbocca $18.95, Eggplant Parmigiana $17.95, Scampi
$19.95, Veal Scaloppini Al Marsala $19.95, Scampi in a fresh garlic, caper and
wine sauce $19.95, Veal Piccata $19.95, Calamari Steak Parmigiana $17.95
Desserts: Assorted Italian desserts daily $5.50

Impressions:

This intimate bistro-style restaurant is located on the second floor of the
Rainbow Plaza at the eastern edge of Kalaheo. After cocktails, dinner begins
with prompt and professional servers delivering the authentic Italian cuisine for
which this family-run establishment is known. Afterwards there is a wonderful
dessert tray to tempt you. For this kind of quality combined with reasonable
prices, a visit to Pomodoro is definitely worth the short drive from Poipu.

Kauai Dining

North Shore

Postcards Café
5-5075A Kuhio Hwy (Hwy 56)
Hanalei, HI 96714
808-826-1191
www.postcardscafe.com
Hours: D 6:00 PM-9:00 PM
Cards: AE MC V
Dress: Casual
Style: Sea/Veg $$

Menu Sampler:

Breakfast/Lunch:
N/A
Dinner:
Pupus: Island Taro Fritters-polenta crusted with pineapple chutney salsa $9.00,
Thai Summer Rolls, fresh or seared with spicy peanut sauce $9.00, Salmon
Rockets wrapped in lumpia with a sweet spicy chili sauce $10.00, Porcini
Crusted Scallops sautéed with mushrooms & greens, cashew-date dressing
$10.00, Butterfly Prawns broiled, served with pineapple-coconut-macadamia
topping $10.00, Cajun Crusted Ahi with chipotle chili sauce $11.00
Salads: Poki Salad with cucumbers, celery, red onions, scallions, diced tofu and
sesame tamari marinade $6.00, Caesar Salad with homemade croutons $8.00
Entrées: Seafood Sorrento-a pasta with medallions of fresh fish and shrimp
sautéed with onions, mushrooms, tomatoes, bell peppers, Kalamata olives and
capers in a garlic-sherry sauce $22.00, Taj Triangles are warm phyllo crescents
filled with seasonal vegetables and spices with a delectable sauce and fresh
tropical chutney $16.00, Thai Coconut Curry with fresh vegetables & tempeh
sautéed with Thai spices over organic rice with pungent peanut sauce $16.00,
Island Fish grilled or blackened, with rice, vegetables and a choice of sauces-
honey ginger Dijon, macadamia nut butter, or peppered pineapple sage $Mkt

Impressions:

Look for the quaint plantation cottage home of Postcards mauka of the highway
as you enter Hanalei. Indoor/outdoor dining is offered in this picturesque village
setting. The vegetarian oriented menu features natural and organic ingredients,
although fish and shellfish are offered. This little spot seems to attract its fair
share of celebrities and loyal patrons, so call ahead as dinner reservations are
necessary. Hours are subject to change seasonally.

Kauai Dining

East Coast

Restaurant Kintaro
4370 Kuhio Hwy (Hwy 56)
Kapa'a, HI 96746
808-822-3341
Web: None
Hours: D 5:30 PM-9:30 PM XSu
Cards: AE DC DIS JCB MC V
Dress: Resort Casual
Style: Japan $$

Menu Sampler:

Breakfast/Lunch:
N/A
Dinner:
Sushi: Maki Sushi (cut rolls) and Temaki Sushi (hand rolls) Kilauea Roll-slightly smoked salmon, tuna (ahi), avocado, & Maui onions $9.00/half roll $5.50, Shrimp Tempura Roll with cucumber, radish sprouts & tobiko rolled in seasoned rice & seaweed $10.00-with unagi $12.95, Nigiri Plate $13.95
Appetizers: Lemon Buttered Mussels in shell (4 pcs) $3.95, Gyoza -fried dumpling (5 pcs) $5.50, Crispy Won Ton from owner's factory (8 pcs) $3.50
Dinners: Served with chilled buckwheat noodles and sauce, miso soup, rice, Japanese pickles and tea. Tempura Combination of local fish, shrimp, and a variety of fresh vegetables $13.95, Yakitori-chicken with onion, bell pepper, teriyaki sauce and salad $13.50, Various Nabemono $10.95-$14.95
Teppan Yaki: Chef is entertaining as he prepares the meal on a tableside grill. Dinners are served with miso soup or salad, shellfish, seafood, mushroom, and fresh island vegetables prepared teppan style. Oysters sautéed with olive oil $14.95, Filet Mignon $20.95, Hibachi Shrimp $17.95, Island Chicken Teriyaki $14.95, Steak Teriyaki $19.95, Fresh Island Fish with Scallops $Market Price
Nabe Mono: One pot chafing dish with seafood and vegetables $10.95, $14.95

Impressions:

Even though Restaurant Kintaro is much larger than it looks from the outside, you need to decide which style of Japanese dining you're interested in before making reservations. This rambling establishment offers a sushi bar, teppanyaki tables, teishoku, and tatami seating. If we had to choose one place on Kauai to experience Japanese cuisine this would be it. As one patron said, "Best sukiyaki I ever had, and I eat it a lot". Reservations are a must in this popular place.

South Shore

Roy's Poipu Bar & Grill
Poipu Shopping Village
2360 Kiahuna Plantation Drive
Poipu, HI 96756
808-742-5000
www.roysrestaurant.com
Hours: D 5:30 PM-9:30 PM
Cards: AE DC JCB MC V
Dress: Resort Casual
Style: Haw-Reg $$$

Menu Sampler:

Breakfast/Lunch:
N/A
Dinner:
Appetizers: Minted Chicken & Basil Spring Rolls w/sweet chili peanut vinaigrette $7.50, Shrimp & Asparagus Crepes w/chevre, pesto & rosemary demi-glace $9.50, Seared Shrimp-on-a-stick w/spicy wasabi sauce $10.50
Salads: Granny Smith Apple & Gorgonzola Salad w/candied walnuts & a sesame miso vinaigrette $7.50, Herb Calamari Caesar Style Salad w/croutons & shaved pecorino romano cheese $9.50, Greens w/sesame soy rice wine vinaigrette $6.50, Mongolian Grilled Chicken Breast Salad $8.50
Entrées: Jade Pesto Steamed Hawaiian Whitefish w/a Chinese sizzling cilantro ginger peanut oil $29.50, Asian Seared Peking Duck Breast w/ a star anise mango basil sauce $28.50, Imu Roasted Pork Pot Roast w/ a pineapple ginger apple sauce $19.50, Yama Mama's Meatloaf with onion rings & mushroom pan sauce $8.50/ $17.50 (entrée), Hibachi Style Salmon with a citrus ponzu sauce $12.50/$24.50 (entrée), Garlic & Honey Mustard Short Ribs w/fresh poi & lomi tomatoes $24.50, Kiawe Grilled Tiger Shrimp $24.50, 20-25 Nightly Specials

Impressions:

Chef Roy Yamaguchi was one of the founders of the Hawaii Regional Cuisine movement begun in the late '80's to promote the use of fresh local produce, fish, and meats in island cooking. His style of culinary fusion launched Roy's into the global marketplace of fine dining. Every dish offered at this casual but upscale eatery uses herbs and spices from diverse cuisines for a real taste explosion! Look for the nightly specials, and don't miss the dessert tray. Roy's in Poipu is smaller than some of his other locations, so reservations are an absolute must.

Kauai Dining

South Shore

Sheraton Kauai Resort Restaurants
Sheraton Kauai Resort
2440 Hoonani Road
Poipu, HI 96756
808-742-4012
www.sheraton-kauai.com
Hours: See Below
Cards: AE DC JCB MC V
Dress: Resort Casual
Style: Ital/Stk/Sea/Japan $$$

Menu Sampler:

Galleria Dining Rooms
Shells: B-Traditional Breakfast Buffet $17.95, Extensive a la carte menu available.
D: Filet Mignon seared & roasted served w/cognac peppercorn sauce $30, Sautéed Opakapaka with a lemon caper sauce $28, Broiled Lobster Tail $36
Amore Ristorante: D-Lobster stuffed in half moon ravioli w/ricotta cheese in a light lobster lemon cream reduction $21, Sautéed Jumbo Shrimp in a garlic, white wine and butter with a touch of lemon on a bed of fettuccini $26
Naniwa: D-Wafu'u Steak of Black Angus Strip Loin Steak w/Sudachi ponzu radish sauce & sautéed vegetables $29/$35, Wakadori Chicken $25/$31
The Point: 11 AM-Midnight. Portuguese Bean Soup $8.95, Coconut Shrimp w/Thai sweet and sour $16.95, Saimin $8.95, Vegetarian Spring Rolls $10.95, Cheese & Pepperoni Pizza $14.95, Triple Chip Nachos $10.95.
Entrees- 6-10 PM- Roasted Chicken w/garlic & rosemary glaze, mashed potatoes & veggies $19.95, NY Steak w/mashed potatoes $25.95
Oasis Bar & Grill: Grilled Angus Beef w/trimmings & fries $11.95, Fried Mahimahi Sandwich with fries $14.95, Turkey Club w/fries $11.95

Impressions:

 The Sheraton Kauai Resort sits on one of the most beautiful stretches of beach on the entire island. Capitalizing on the hypnotic views, they have assembled a notable collection of dining rooms covering the waterfront from casual dining to international cuisine. Shells is the anchor serving the daily upmarket breakfast buffet before changing over to a steak and seafood format. When the time comes for drinks and pupus, don't miss sunset at The Point. Lunch service is available at the casual Oasis Bar & Grill while adventurous dinner patrons will find gourmet Italian in Amore Ristorante and outstanding Japanese in Naniwa.

Kauai Dining

East Coast

The Bull Shed
4-796 Kuhio Hwy (Hwy 56)
Kapa'a, HI 96746
808-822-3791
Web: None
Hours: D 5:30 PM-10 PM
Cards: AE DC DIS MC V
Dress: Casual
Style: Amer/Sea $$

Menu Sampler:

Breakfast/Lunch:
 N/A

Dinner: All dinners include steamed rice, bread & butter and a trip to the salad bar. Broiled Shrimp or Teriyaki Broiled Shrimp $15.95, Scallops Bull Shed-sea scallops sprinkled with parmesan cheese and baked in white wine sauce with sliced mushrooms $17.95, Prime Rib (house specialty) $20.95, Pork Baby Back Ribs $17.95, Garlic Tenderloin or Tenderloin Filet $17.95, Grilled Teriyaki Chicken $13.95, Garlic Chicken $13.95, Australian Lamb Rack-a full rack marinated in an herbal red wine recipe and broiled $23.95, Teriyaki Beef Kebobs broiled with crisp vegetables $10.95, Teriyaki Top Sirloin marinated in a sauce of brown sugar, pineapple juice and shoyu $14.95, Black Pepper Tenderloin, broiled, smothered in pepper sauce with onion, mushroom and beef au jus mix $17.95, Alaskan King Crab/Grilled Catch of the Day $Market Price Children's menu is available.
Desserts: homemade ice cream pies and cheesecakes $3.50

Impressions:

This oceanfront restaurant is Kauai's answer to supper club dining. With a salad bar, cocktail lounge, and prime rib in a starring role, this moderately priced steak-and-seafooder strikes a note of comfort and familiarity. Although the interior décor is not a strong suit, the seaside atmosphere, good food, and friendly service continue to please. On warm evenings try to get a table by the oceanfront windows for a cooling breeze. Finding the entrance to The Bull Shed can be an interesting experience. Look across the highway from the McDonald's at the Waipouli Town Center stoplight and follow the lane to the ocean.

South Shore

Tidepools

Hyatt Regency Kauai Resort and Spa
1571 Poipu Road
Koloa, HI 96756
808-742-1234
www.kauai-hyatt.com
Hours: D 6:00 PM-10:00 PM
Cards: AE DC DIS JCB MC V
Dress: Resort Casual
Style: Contemporary Haw $$$

Menu Sampler:

Breakfast/Lunch:

N/A

Dinner:

Appetizer: Charred Hawaiian Ahi Sashimi with wasabi and sweet ginger dip 12.75, Kimo's Crab Cake with avocado salsa and passion fruit sauce 11.00, Steamed Mussels and Clams in a lemon grass, ginger, and garlic broth 10.75
Soup and Salads: Coconut Lobster Soup with Tahitian vanilla bean crème 7.50, East Kauai Onion Soup baked with four cheeses 7.00, Grilled Kauai Sweet Onions and Vine Ripened Tomatoes with Omao mizuna and arugula, Hanalei feta cheese and black pepper lychee vinaigrette 8.75, Grilled Japanese Eggplant Salad with Kauai Kunana feta cheese, rosemary and thyme vinaigrette 8.75
Entrées: Macadamia Nut Crusted Mahi with kahlua, lime, ginger butter sauce and served with jasmine rice 28.50, Seafood Mixed Grill-a selection of lobster, scallops, shrimp and island fish with stir-fry vegetables 34.00, Prime Rib with creamy horseradish 28.50, Roasted Sonoma Lamb Rack with eggplant and goat cheese risotto and oregano scented demi $36.00, Kauai Spiced Opah stuffed with lump crab meat, shiitake mushrooms and asparagus 29.00

Impressions:

Tidepools is the signature restaurant of the Hyatt Regency Kauai Resort and Spa in Koloa. Dining here means sitting under a thatched roof surrounded by bamboo décor, torches, and koi fishponds while the ocean surf pounds in the distance. This is truly an Old Hawaii setting. The wait staff proudly presents the freshest island ingredients fused in creative preparations. A must try is the Coconut Lobster Soup with Tahitian Vanilla Bean Crème. Don't pass up the dessert offerings! This is a personal favorite and would be a good choice for the splurge night of a special visit. Reservations are strongly recommended.

Kauai Dining

Lihue

Tip Top Motel & Café
3173 Akahi Street
Lihue, HI 96766
808-245-2333
Web: None
Hours: B 6:30 AM-11:30 AM XMo
        L 11:00 AM-2:00 PM XMo
        D 5:30 PM-9:30 PM XMo
Cards: MC V
Dress: Casual
Style: Amer/Haw/Japan $

Menu Sampler:

Breakfast:
Ham & Cheese Omelet with rice or hash browns $6.25, Macadamia Nut
Pancakes $3.75/$4.25, Our Famous Oxtail Soup $7.00, Loco Moco $6.00, Sweet
Bread French Toast $3.75, French Toast $3.50, Fried Rice $3.00, Soft Fried
Noodles $5.25, Beef Stew $5.75, Bento of chicken, corned beef hash, teri meat,
egg roll, goteburg sausage, potato salad, pickled vegetables, rice $6.00
Lunch:
All entrées and daily specials are served with vegetable, choice of rice, French
fries or mashed potatoes. Country Style Boneless Chicken $5.95, Pork Chops
$6.00, Baked Meat Loaf with gravy $5.75, Roast Pork $6.50, Hamburger $3.20
Dinner:
Sushi Combination of 7 different kinds of Nigiri Sushi and Maki Mono $19.95,
Chirashi Sushi-a fresh seafood combination artistically over vinegared rice
$16.95, Fresh Salmon Roll $5.00, Unagi Roll $5.50, Spicy Ahi Roll $5.50, Soft
Shell Crab Roll $6.95, Big California Roll $9.00, Assorted Sashimi $16.95
Entrees: Include soup & rice. Shrimp Tempura $12.95, Teriyaki Beef $10.95,
Chicken Katsu $9.50, Oyaku Donburi $8.95, Saimin Special $6.95

Impressions:

Are there motels in Hawaii? A few. Does this establishment cater mostly to
locals? Sure does. Is the food good? It is. The Tip Top Café offers local style
dining in spotless surroundings. A visit to the Tip Top is a cultural experience.
Local businessmen and groups of ladies as well as retirees and keiki gather in
the roomy booths to enjoy the local cuisine and discuss all that's happening in
Lihue. Oxtail Soup is a top choice in the café section of the restaurant during
breakfast and lunch. For a change of pace, the sushi bar serves lunch and dinner.

Kauai Dining

Lihue

Tokyo Lobby

Pacific Ocean Plaza
3501 Rice Street
Lihue, HI 96766
808-245-8989
Web: None
Hours: L 11:00 AM-2:00 PM XSaSu
              D 4:30 PM-9:30 PM
Cards: AE JCB MC V
Dress: Resort Casual
Style: Japan $$

Menu Sampler:

Breakfast:
N/A

Lunch:
Sashimi and Sushi: Served w/soup. Nigiri asst $14.95, Inari Sushi $10.95
Donburi: Served with soup. Oyako Donburi of sliced chicken, onions, and eggs over rice with special sauce $6.50, Katsu Donburi of fried pork cutlet, onions, and eggs over rice with special sauce $7.50, Curry Chicken Donburi $6.95
Entrécs: Served with soup, pickled vegetable, and rice. Shrimp and Vegetable Tempura $7.95, Yaki Sakana (Grilled Mackerel) $7.95, Katsu $7.95

Dinner:
Appetizer: Gyoza-seasoned ground pork wrapped in ravioli and pan-fried $4.50, Shu-Mai—shrimp dumplings $3.95, Edamame $2.95, Sashimi $9.50
Side Order: Miso Soup $1.50, Ochitashi—steamed spinach with light soy sauce $4.50, Oshinko (pickled vegetables) 4.50, Green Salad w/house dressing $4.50
Sashimi and Sushi: Served with soup. Sashimi with rice $13.95, Makimono Combination—nori rolled sushi $14.95, Sashimi Deluxe with rice $21.95
Entrées: Served with soup, pickled vegetable, salad and rice. Hibachi Lemon Herb Chicken $12.95, Beef Teriyaki $14.95, BBQ Salmon or Fish in season $13.95, Tokyo Love Boat-complete dinner for $22.50/person, min. of two

Impressions:

The menu at Tokyo Lobby can best be described as provincial Japanese. No, this isn't kaiseki dining, but it isn't local style either. The menu offers a wide variety of traditional Japanese dishes at very reasonable prices. Look for this restaurant on the first floor of the Pacific Ocean Plaza across from the entrance to the Kauai Marriott. There's ample parking in the shopping center lot.

North Shore

Tropical Taco
Halelea Building
5088 Kuhio Hwy (Hwy 56)
Hanalei, HI 96714
808-827-8226
Web: None
Hours: 11:00 AM-5:00 PM XSu
Cards: None
Dress: Casual
Style: Mex $

Menu Sampler:

Breakfast:
N/A
Lunch/Dinner:
Tropical Taco-deep fried or just warm $6.50, Tropical Fish Taco-fish dipped in beer batter and fried golden brown or grilled $7.50, Regular Taco $4.50, Fat Jack—ten inches of flour tortilla with cheese, meat, beans, deep fried, topped with lettuce, salsa, cheese, and sour cream $7.50, Fresh Fish Burrito of catch of the day fried and topped with the works of beans, lettuce, salsa, cheese, and sour cream $6.50, Veggie Burrito-everything but the meat $5.50. Recently Roger added "taro tacos" made with taro grown behind his house.

Impressions:

Roger and Barbara Kennedy would like to welcome you to their new taco eatery in Hanalei. For a look at its predecessor ask to see the old green panel van where it all began. In days gone by that truck was Roger's taco shop. Local lore has it that during a hurricane back in the early '90's, Roger chained his taco truck to a palm tree in a desperate attempt to protect his investment and after donning a bicycle helmet rode out the storm inside! There is another version of the story that says he did it because his truck was safer than his house. We leave it up to you to decide which version you prefer.

Eventually Roger bowed to progress and relocated in the new Halelea Building. In order to remain true to the spirit of his original business, his artistically inclined friends designed a silhouette of the truck's side panel and mounted it on the kitchen wall of his new establishment. Through this "van window" orders are placed and delivered as they always have been. Fun people, nice restaurant, simple but tasty menu, very large portions, and a good time!

Kauai Dining

West Side

Waimea Brewing Co.
Waimea Plantation Cottages
9400 Kaumualii Hwy (Hwy 50)
Waimea, HI 96796
808-338-9733
www.wbcbrew.com
Hours: 11:00 AM-9:00 PM Su-Th
         11:00 AM-11:00 PM Fr-Sa
Cards: AE DC DIS MC V
Dress: Casual
Style: Amer/Island $$

Menu Sampler:

Breakfast:
N/A

Lunch/ Dinner:
Pupus: Ale Steamed Shrimp, ½ # served with sweet Thai chili sauce $12.95, Nui Nachos $9.95, Taro Leaf Goat Cheese Dip with grilled pita bread $9.50
Salads: Asian Chicken Salad w/citrus vinaigrette $9.95, Thai Beef Salad $10.95
Sandwiches: All are served with brewpub fries & Java slaw. Kalua Pork Sandwich—pork roasted Hawaiian style topped with smoked provolone cheese on a Maui onion bun with lettuce, tomato and kosher pickle $9.95, Island Catch Sandwich with grilled fish on an onion roll with wasabi aioli, lettuce, tomato and sprouts $8.95, Seared Poke Wrap with wasabi aioli and fresh veggies $10.95
Pastas: Penne w/Grilled Chicken & Portuguese Sausage $16.95, Shrimp Fettucine $18.95, Poke Pasta w/ahi poke, bok choy & marinara sauce $16.95
Entrées: Honey-Mango Barbeque Ribs with choice of sticky rice or wasabi mashed potatoes $24.95, Jawaiian Chicken is a breast of chicken grilled with jerk seasonings, served with our Caribbean Rice 'N Beans $15.95
Brews: Wai'ale'ale Ale, Pakala Porter, Captain Cook's Original India Pale Ale, and Na Pali Pale Ale, West Side Wheat, Leilani Light, Cane Fire Red

Impressions:

Want an unlikely combination? How about a brewpub in an old plantation village at the end of the road in Waimea! Waimea Brewing Co. serves distinctive pupus and large servings of fun, tasty salads, sandwiches, and entrees in the pub or out on the veranda. After sightseeing on the sunny west side the surprisingly good on-site brewed beers offer a great way to relax and cool off.

West Side

Wrangler's Steakhouse
9852 Kaumualii Highway
Waimea, HI 96796
808-338-1218
Web: None
Hours: L 11:00 AM-4:00 PM Mo-Fr
        D 4:00 PM-9:00 PM Mo-Fr
        D 5:00 PM-9:00 PM Sa
Cards: AE MC V
Dress: Casual
Style: Sea/Stk $$$

Menu Sampler:

Breakfast:
N/A
Lunch:
Chicken Caesar Salad with grilled chicken slices, greens and garlic toast $8.95, Shrimp Louie with bay shrimp, egg, and fresh veggies $8.95, Wrangler Burger-grilled steak patty with mushrooms, cheese, onions and sprouts and steak fries $8.95, Kau Kau Tin with beef teriyaki, tempura shrimp and veggies $8.95, Pulehu Steak of grilled New York Steak with special garlic sauce $11.95
Dinner:
Grilled Filet Mignon served on a sizzling platter $24, Rib Eye with mashed potatoes or steamed rice and vegetables $20, Grilled Sirloin Steak & Scampi $28, 25 oz Porterhouse with capers $32, Japanese Kobe New York-Wagyu Beef $60, Pork Chops with crispy sweet & sour onions $18, Fresh Island Fish $Market Price, Prefixe menu for two $55
Desserts: Warm Peach Cobbler $5.50, other fine choices $5.50

Impressions:

Wrangler's Steakhouse is located in the last town you pass through when driving to the Waimea Canyon. This restaurant is a wonderful addition to the west shore dining scene. It combines the area's picturesque past with an upscale menu. Better yet they do it at lunch as well as dinner. The focus might be steak and seafood, but it's done with flair and offers some local culinary treats as well. Look for high quality food and a cheerful wait staff. There's even a unique gift shop inside. This is a solid choice for visitors to this side of the island.

Kauai Dining

North Shore

Zelo's Beach House
Ching Young Village
5-8420 Kuhio Hwy (Hwy 56)
Hanalei, HI 96714
808-826-9700
www.zelosbeachhouse.com
Hours: L 11:00 AM-3:30 PM, Light Menu 3:30 PM-5:30 PM
         D 5:30 PM-9:30 PM
Cards: MC V
Dress: Casual
Style: Amer/Sea/Mex $$

Menu Sampler:

Breakfast:
N/A

Lunch:
Gourmet Onions Rings 5.95, Calamari Steak Wedges with cocktail sauce 9.95, Beer Battered Fish & Chips 13.95, French Dip 9.50, Chinese Chicken Salad 12.95, Puebla Style Fresh Fish Tacos with Spanish rice & black beans 13.95, Burgers—1/3# served with fries or rice 8.25-9.95

Dinner:
Pupus: Beer Battered Artichoke Hearts with bleu cheese dip 9.95, Spicy Shrimp Sushi Tiki-layers of spicy shrimp, sushi rice & tobiko on a bed of wild greens 11.95, Macho Nachos with all the works 10.95
Salads: Wild Organic Greens Salad $5.00, Caesar 9.95
Entrées: Prime Rib with Shiitake Mushroom Au Jus 26.00, Slow Cooked Baby Back Ribs---1½ #-with roasted red potatoes 19.00, Crab Stuffed Ono Wrapped in Shredded Phyllo, baked and served with a light lemon sauce 26.00, Mac Nut Crusted Ono with lemon ginger sauce 25.00, Beer Battered Fresh Fish and Chips with fries 15.00, Pine Nut Mahimahi with basil pesto relish 23.00, Seafood Burrito, beans & rice, salsa verde & sour cream 16.95, Chef Vene's Tequila Seafood Tostada in a tequila salsa verde with black beans & Mexican rice 19.95

Impressions:

Zelo's might not be on a beach, but it's the kind of place people from the upper Midwest dream about when the Alberta Clipper starts blowing snow down their shorts. With its great tunes, large bar, casual atmosphere, and wide variety of tasty food, Zelo's fulfills many needs. This open-air establishment is a fun place to grab a quick lunch or spend an entire evening while visiting the north shore.

LANAI
DINING

Lanai

Kaena Point
Shipwreck Beach
Halepalaoa Landing
Lanai City
Airport
Kaumalapau Harbor
Manele Bay
N
E
S
W

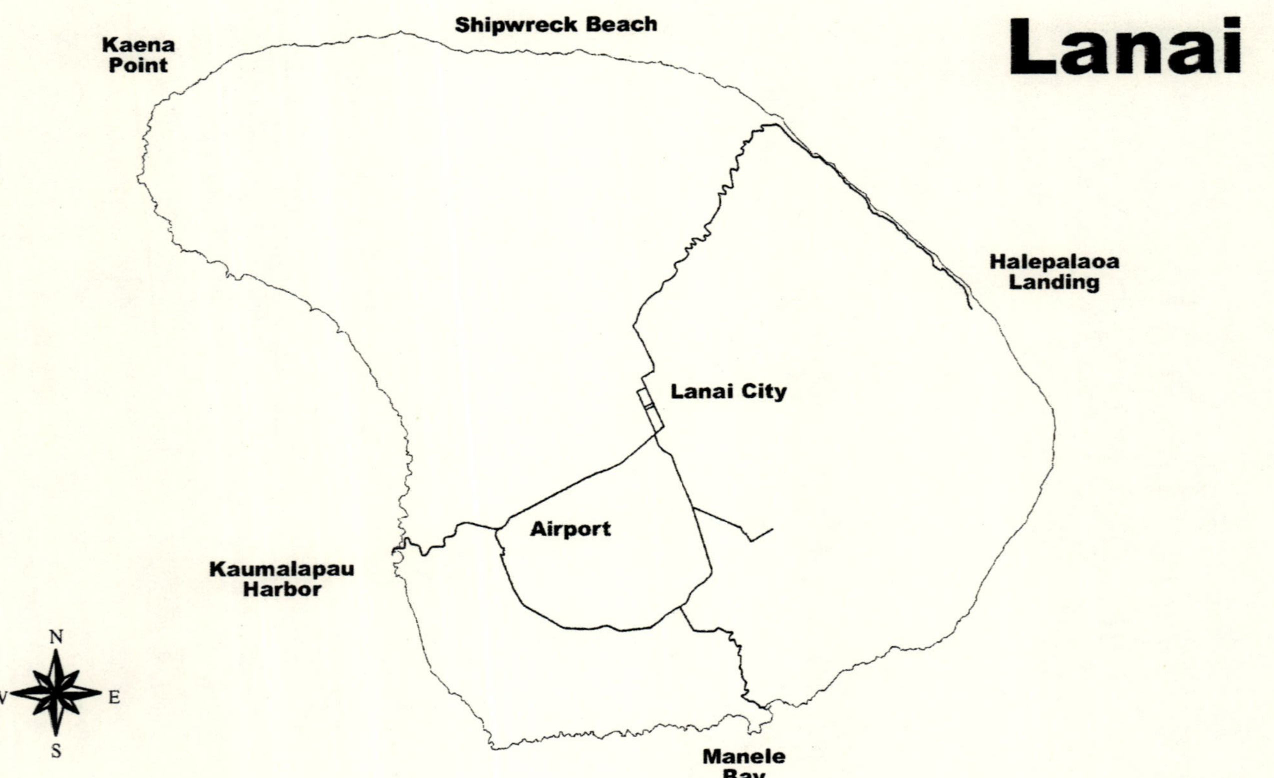

Lanai Dining

Lanai City

Blue Ginger Café
409 Seventh Street
Lanai City, HI 96763
808-565-6363
Web: None
Hours: BLD 6:00 AM-8:00 PM
         BLD 6:00 AM-9:00 PM weekends
Cards: None
Dress: Casual
Style: Amer/Isl $/$$

Menu Sampler:

Breakfast:
Check the breakfast board on the wall for specials-seasonal fruits, omelets, and pancakes. Three Egg Omelets with rice and toast $5.00, Western Omelet with rice and toast $6.50, French Toast-one slice $1.75, two slices $3.00, Pancakes-one $2.00, two $3.25, three $4.50, Pastries are wonderful for $1.25

Lunch/Dinner:
Plates with rice, macaroni salad, or tossed salad: Hamburger Steak $6.50, Roast Pork $7.00, Mahi Mahi $8.50, Chicken Katsu $7.50, Pizzas $11.75-$18.75.
Sandwiches: Hamburger $3.50, Teriyaki Burger $4.00
Ice Cream specialties such as shakes, malts, etc., Dole bottled juice.

Impressions:

This busy little restaurant is a glimpse of Old Hawaii complete with plantation styling, small-town friendliness, and a variety of comfort food. Blue Ginger is located on the north side of Dole Square in the center of town. Orders are taken at the counter and then brought to your table. The tableau of patrons talking story over coffee seems quite ordinary until you realize that you are on a small island in the middle of the Pacific Ocean. Is it really that different out here? The food is well prepared, the portions large, and the prices reasonable. Sitting down for breakfast at the Blue Ginger is a great way to start the day.

Lanai Dining

Manele Bay

Challenge at Manele Clubhouse
Manele Bay Hotel
One Manele Road
Lanai City, HI 96763
808-565-2222
www.lanai-resorts.com
Hours: L 11:00 AM-3:30 PM
         D 6:00 PM-9:00 PM XTuWe
Cards: AE DC DIS JCB MC V
Dress: Resort Casual
Style: Eclec/Pac-Rim $$

Menu Sampler:

Breakfast:
N/A
Lunch:
Appetizers: Made-to-Order Hot Salt-and-Pepper Potato Chips with caramelized onion dip $6, Lanai Seafood Chowder w/Portuguese Sweet Bread Croutons $8
Luncheon Salads: Asian Tuna-Grilled Ahi Tuna, island greens, sesame Lychee dressing $18, Caesar $10, with Fresh Island Fish $18, Prawns $16
Sandwiches and Entrées: Served w/choice of fries, Maui chips, cole slaw or fruit. Prawn BLT in pita bread w/grilled onion, Creole remoulade $15, Fish and Chips-crispy fried fresh fish, pineapple tartar sauce, fries $14
Afternoon Temptations: Crispy Calamari $11, Dim Sum & dipping sauces $12
Dinner:
Appetizers: Volcano-Spiced Soft Shell Crab, ponzu mango coulis $14, Hulopo'e Firecracker Shrimp, green papaya relish, kim chee $17
Entrées: Island Mahimahi, turmeric, carrot, Absolute essence $26, Flank Steak with port blue cheese, spinach, Indonesian blue crab $27, Pad-Thai Noodles with rice noodles, bean sprouts, green onions $19, Thai-hitian Seafood Stew with fresh seafood, saffron curry sauce $29, Manele Chicken with grilled chicken breast, ginger, black beans, green onions $23

Impressions:

The clubhouse at this coastline golf course houses a posh little restaurant with one of the most beautiful views in the world. Here guests find an upscale yet relaxed dining experience that comes as a welcome change to the norm at most destination resorts. This is a great call when you're looking to really get away.

Lanai Dining

Lanai City

Experience at Koele Clubhouse
Lodge at Koele
One Keomoku Highway
Lanai City, HI 96763
808-565-4580
www.lanai-resorts.com
Hours: L 10:30 AM-5:00 PM
Cards: AE DIS MC V
Dress: Casual
Style: Amer/Ec $$

Menu Sampler:

Breakfast:
N/A
Lunch:
Soup "n" Pupus: Today's Soup $7, Kalua Pork Springrolls, shredded cabbage, lomi lomi tomatoes $12.50, Sweet Chili Crab Cakes & Lemon Aioli $13.50
Entrees: All sandwiches include seasoned fries. Moroccan Spiced Catch on Israeli Cous Cous with cucumber mango yogurt dressing $13.50, Char-Broiled Cheddar Burger with roasted onions $10.50, and bacon $13.00, Smoked Turkey Club with avocado and black pepper mayonnaise $10.50, Shredded BBQ Chicken Sandwich with caramelized onion and cracked pepper jam on fresh corn bread $11.50, "The Judges Special" Shaved Roast Beef Sandwich with roasted peppers, onions and jack cheese $13.00, Fresh Catch Sandwich on Sourdough Bread with butter lettuce, Roma tomatoes and caper lemon dressing $13.50, Herb Roasted Vegetables on Fresh Foccassio Bread with butter lettuce, Roma tomatoes, provolone cheese and pesto dressing $9.50, Romaine Lettuce Salad with garlic croutons & Caesar Dressing $7.00, with Grilled Chicken $12.50, with Grilled Catch of the Day $14.50
Desserts: Fresh Baked Cookie $2.00, Fruit Sorbet $5.00
Dinner:
N/A

Impressions:

This is the smaller of the two Lanai Resort clubhouse restaurants. It's located in the cool uplands above Lanai City. Diners are seated on a veranda overlooking the golf course and a small lake. Lunch and pupus offer a good variety with depth in the preparation. Be sure to ask about the catch of the day. It can be rainy here, so pick a sunny day to fully appreciate the experience.

Lanai Dining

Lanai City

Formal Dining Room
Lodge at Koele
One Keomoku Highway
Lanai City, HI 96763
808-565-4580
www.lanai-resorts.com
Hours: D 6:00 PM-9:30 PM
Cards: AE DIS MC V
Dress: Jackets Req-Tie Opt/Formal
Style: Amer/Pac-Rim $$$$

Menu Sampler:

Breakfast/Lunch:
N/A
Dinner:
Starters: Seared Foie Gras on mango-croissant bread w/spicy walnuts & ten year old balsamico $18, Orange Scented Venison Carpaccio with baby arugula, shaved parmesan, drizzled with Port Syrup and white truffle oil $16
Soups: Spring Squash Bisque with leeks, pancetta and whiskey crema $13
Salads: Manchego Cheese Tart with frisee salad, dried pear relish and lemon vinaigrette $14.00, Grilled Lobster Salad with leeks, morels, Dijon aioli, Roma tomato and basis essence $16, Red and Gold Beet Salad $13
Entrées: Chef's Special Seafood Selection $Mkt Price, Seared Tenderloin of Beef on truffle-potato 2x4's, grilled white asparagus, fava beans, tomato jam and truffle-cabernet reduction $43, Grilled "Mignon" of Ahi on parsnip-potato cake, leek, fennel and pancetta salad and red wine reduction $42, Crispy Seared Breast of Muscovy Duck on apple-sweet potato puree, arugula leaves with shaven Maui onion and cider glace $43

Impressions:

The Lodge at Koele conjures up images of a Victorian era hunting lodge. At one end of the Great Hall you'll find the Formal Dining Room with its linen and crystal appointments. Here Executive Chef Bradley J. Czaika serves award-winning cuisine apropos for the elegant setting. The menu combines Continental and Pacific Rim influences with a fresh country spin. Dining in this upscale restaurant is a very special treat. The romantic atmosphere makes this a natural for honeymooners. Make sure to dress for dinner. Reservations are required. There's a free shuttle for those staying elsewhere on the island.

Lanai City

Henry Clay's Rotisserie
Hotel Lanai
828 Lanai Ave
Lanai City, HI 96763
808-565-7211
www.hotellanai.com
Hours: D 5:30 PM-9:00PM
Cards: MC V
Dress: Resort Casual
Style: Cajun/Ec/Isl $$$

Menu Sampler:

Breakfast/Lunch:
N/A
Dinner:
Appetizers: Rajun Cajun Clay's Shrimp of bayou-seasoned gulf shrimp in a garlic, spices and seafood butter sauce $10.95, Cockie Leekie and Maui Onion Soup Au Gratin with leeks and sweet Maui onions topped with browned cheeses $8.50, Ragout of Wild Mushrooms Rustic Pie $12.50, Washington Manila Clams or Penn Cove Mussels in white wine and herb-buttered broth $10.75
Chilled Starters: Henry Clay's Pâté $8.95, Pacific Northwest Oyster Shooters $1.75 each, Caesar Salad $8.50, Grilled Vegetable Antipasto $12.95
Entrées: Kiawe Grilled Rib Eye Steak with whole grained mustard sauce $27.95, Louisiana Style Ribs lightly smoked $19.95, Toasted Butternut Squash Ravioli with tomato fondue $18.95, Free Range Lanai Axis Deer prepared in various ways $Mkt, Seafood Crab Gumbo $28.95, Eggplant Creole on Angel Hair Pasta $18.95, Gourmet Pizza $12.95+

Impressions:

Chef/Owner Henry Clay Richardson combines his New Orleans heritage with island experience at this casually upscale restaurant. The menu could best be described as eclectic. One minute you're looking at Cajun specialties and the next it's Continental cuisine. One thing though, it's all done very well. The wait staff has an impeccable politeness that is a mixture of southern hospitality and island aloha. Henry Clay's is not a big place. Akamai diners go early in order to have a full selection. If you are staying at the Koele Lodge or Manele Bay Hotel, charges may be made to your room. Shuttles running between the two major resorts will convey you to and from this dining establishment.

Lanai Dining

Manele Bay

Hulopo'e Court
Manele Bay Hotel
One Manele Road
Lanai City, HI 96763
<u>www.lanai-resorts.com</u>
808-565-2290
Hours:　B Buf 7:00 AM-11:00 AM
　　　　D 6:00 PM-9:30 PM
Cards:　AE DC DIS JCB MC V
Dress:　Resort Casual
Style:　Pac Rim/Trop $$$$

Menu Sampler:

Breakfast:
Buffet: 24/adults, 12/children - with a wide selection of hot and cold foods.
Continental Buffet: Pastries, Sliced Fruit w/yogurt and cereal, juice 15
From the Menu: Kauai Shrimp Benedict on taro and sweet potato cakes, spinach with poached eggs and blue crab hollandaise sauce 15, Lanai Pineapple Upside Down Pancake 11, Hawaiian Waffle with coconut tapioca and caramelized Lanai bananas 11.50, Hash of pan-seared Onaga 15
Lunch:
N/A
Dinner:
Appetizers: Lobster Quesadilla with avocado, jack cheese, and mango sauce 14, Crispy Fried Calamari with a spiced cabbage slaw, tamarind dressing 11, Grilled Scallops on the Half Shell, Hawaiian chili-soy, ocean salad 15
Salads: Hearts of Palm, Orange & Avocado 13, Big Island Papaya & Pine Nuts, avocado, Mauna Kea chevre, pine nuts, balsamic vinaigrette 13
Entrées: Lanai Style Mahimahi with lobster fried rice, miso-butter sauce 30, New York Steak, grilled, potato puree, sake sauce 35, Spicy Asian Noodles wok-fried with island tofu & vegetables, soy-ginger-garlic sauce 23, Kiawe Smoked New Zealand Rack of Lamb, warm potato salad, poha berry au jus 34.

Impressions:

Hulopo'e Court is the more casual of the Manele Bay Hotel's main dining rooms. At this luxury resort that still means innovative fare and quality service. In addition to the fine tropical cuisine served here, Hulopo'e also offers a reasonably priced children's menu. Celebrity watching can be a plus.

Lanai Dining

Manele Bay

Ihilani Restaurant
Manele Bay Hotel
One Manele Road
Lanai City, HI 96763
808-565-2296
www.lanai-resorts.com
Hours: D 6:00 PM-9:00 PM
Cards: AE DC DIS JCB MC V
Dress: Resort Casual
Style: Med/Haw-Reg $$$$

Menu Sampler:

Breakfast/Lunch:
N/A
Dinner:
Appetizers: Seared Sea Scallops, spinach salad, Kula onions, parsley aioli 14, Gratinee of Pacific Blue Prawns with mushroom risotto$15, Seared Ahi & Caramelized Maui Onion Flatbread with lavender-infused olive oil 14
Antipasto: Vegetarian of roasted bell pepper trio, grilled tomato & orange salad, spiced eggplant, shaved mushrooms with lemon & thyme, grilled curry zucchini, baby artichokes, asparagus & truffle oil 16
Salads: Warm Sainte Maure Goat Cheese Frisee Salad with Maui onion, apple compote, pancetta 15, Ihilani Salad of watercress, arugula, baby fennel, Asian pear, jerez vinaigrette 13, Hirabara Farms Specialty Salad 12
Entrées: Lanai Venison Foursome of chop, loin, saddle and stew, cranberry, pear & lilikoi pairings 41, Grilled Beef Tenderloin with crispy potato & spinach cake, red wine sauce 40, Baked Onaga in a sea salt crust, caramelized onion tart, dungeness crab fondue, rose wine shallots sauce 38, Grilled Mediterranean Style Yellowfin Tuna, roasted garlic mashed potatoes, basil sauce 38, Oven Roasted Lobster, homemade chestnut fettuccini, banyuls red wine sauce 44

Impressions:

The Ihilani Restaurant is the award-winning signature dining room of the Manele Bay Hotel. The decidedly upscale menu features Hawaii Regional Cuisine with definite Mediterranean influences. The flavors experienced here are not shy. Tastes are complex and tend toward edgy holding the diner's interest. Attention to detail makes this one of Hawaii's finest dining experiences. Please note the dress code. Though stated as resort casual, this is one of the few places in Hawaii where leaning toward the more formal is appropriate. As you would expect, reservations are required.

Lanai Dining

Lanai City

Pele's Other Garden
Dole Square
Lanai City, HI 96763
808-565-9628
Web: None
Hours: L 10:00 AM-2:30 PM XSu
             D 5:00 PM-8:00 PM XSu
Cards: AE DIS JCB MC V
Dress: Casual
Style: Deli $$

Menu Sampler:

Breakfast:
N/A
Lunch:
Sandwiches and Hot Stuff: Italian Hoagie on French $6.99, Hot Meatball Sub $6.59, Pastrami and Swiss on French with honey-mustard $6.99, Veggie Wrap with shiitake sauce $6.89, Bean and Rice Burrito with salsa and cheese $3.99, Cheese Quesadilla $3.99, Cheese and Smoked Ham Quesadilla $5.79, Meatball Sub $6.99, Mixed Organic Greens Salad $3.99, Cheese on French $6.89
Pizza: 8" $6.50-$7.99, 16" $12.99-$19.75, Five Varieties-Thirteen Ingredients
Dinner:
Appetizers: Smoked Salmon with capers and red onion, sour cream $7.99, Bruscetta with diced fresh tomato, basil and olive oil on toasted baguette $6.25
Salads: Caesar Salad with garlic croutons $7.99, Mixed Organic Greens $7.99
Entrées: Bowtie Pasta in a creamy pesto sauce with prosciutto and butterflied garlic shrimp $18.99, Fettucini & Smoked Salmon tossed with olive oil and garlic, capers & lime zest $19.99, Spaghetti and Meat Balls $16.99, Rainbow Tortellini filled with three cheeses in Alfredo Sauce $16.99, Potato Gnocchi with marinara sauce $16.99, Heart Shaped Ravioli stuffed with fontina cheese and zucchini, covered with marinara sauce $17.99
Pizza: $7.99-$21.99, Individual and Family Size available. Homemade crusts.
Desserts: Tiramisu with Kahlua, Apple Granny with caramel glaze $6.75

Impressions:

Top quality gourmet ingredients and reasonable prices make this an inviting stop for lunch or dinner. Picnic baskets are a specialty at Pele's Other Garden. Lanai is a great place for off-road exploring, and having lunch in the boondocks makes the adventure that much more memorable. There's indoor/outdoor seating for those who choose not to travel. Look for Pele's on Dole Square in Lanai City.

Lanai Dining

Lanai City

Tanigawa's
419 Seventh Street
Lanai, HI 96763
808-565-6537
Web: None
Hours: B/L 6:30 AM-1:00 PM X We
Cards: None
Dress: Casual
Style: Amer/ Is $

Menu Sampler:

Breakfast:
Islanders Choice-Choice of Portuguese Sausage, bacon, Spam, Vienna sausage or pork link sausage with 2 eggs and served with rice, hash brown or toast $5.50, Garden Omelet- served with rice, hash brown or toast $6.50, Fried Rice with 1 egg $5.00, Homemade Corn Beef Hash with 2 eggs, rice, hash brown or toast $6.00, Grilled Ham Steak served with rice or hash brown, salad $7.00, Short Stack Special includes 2 pancake with breakfast sausage and 2 scrambled eggs $5.50, Short Stack (3 cakes) $3.75, Ham & 2 Eggs with starch $7.00

Lunch:
Spam Musubi $1.50, Bento $5.50, Saimin $3.50/$5.00, Won Ton Saimin $6.00, Loco Moco $6.00, Breaded Shrimp, rice and salad $7.50, Philly Cheese Steak Sandwich $4.75, Shrimp Tempura, rice and salad $8.50, Beef Stew with rice and mac salad $7.00, BBQ Short Ribs, rice and salad $8.00, Maui Hot Dog $2.00

Sandwiches: Teriyaki Beef Sandwich $3.00, Grilled Tuna Sandwich $3.75, Grilled Cheese $3.00, Grilled Ham & Cheese $4.50, BLT $4.00, Fish Sandwich with tartar sauce, lettuce, sliced tomatoes and French fries $7.00, Hot Dog $2.00

Burgers: Hamburger $2.00, Hamburger Deluxe with lettuce, tomato and onions $3.00, Cheeseburger $2.50, Bacon Burger $3.00, Bacon Cheese Burger $4.00, Old Fashion Teriyaki Burger Char-Broiled $3.75, Borge's Special includes a hamburger patty with cheese, bacon and egg $4.75

Dinner:
N/A

Impressions:

Father Time hasn't touched Tanigawa's. Everything about this place is Old Hawaii. The menu is simple and straightforward, but the food is solid fare, and the place is spotless. Don't let yourself be put off by appearances. Leave your preconceptions at the door, and get ready for a unique cultural experience.

Lanai Dining

Lodge at Koele

Terrace Restaurant
Lodge at Koele
1 Keomuku Hwy
Lanai City, HI 96763
808-565-4580
www.lanai-resorts.com
Hours: B 6:30 AM-11:00 AM
         L 11:00 AM-6:00 PM
         D 6:00 PM-9:30 PM
Cards: AE DC DIS MC V
Dress: Evening Aloha
Style: Cont/Isl $$$$

Menu Sampler:

Breakfast:
Poached Eggs on Blue Crab Cakes with blood orange hollandaise $16.00, Meyer Lemon Pancake with fresh berries and Vermont maple syrup $10.50
Lunch:
Entrées: Fresh Catch Sandwich with choice of fries, fruit salad or chips $13.50, Lanai Venison Pastrami Melt Sandwich with caramelized red onions, whole grain mustard, gruyere cheese & Hawaiian potato chips $14.50, Grilled Salmon on Arugula Salad w/walnut vinaigrette $14.50, Lobster Salad Sandwich $18.00
Dinner:
Starters: Crispy Calamari Salad w/caramelized red onions, sweet peppers & sherry vinaigrette $13.50, Macadamia Honey Glazed Prawns w/green papaya slaw $14.50, Caesar Salad w/garlic croutons & shaved Reggiano $13.00
Entrées: Hawaiian Seafood Selection $Mkt Price, Mustard Crusted Salmon on baby beet salad, sweet onions, leeks w/chive potato dumplings & lemon-dill butter sauce $27.50, Seared NY Striploin w/sweet corn blue cheese potatoes, braised chard, applewood smoked bacon w/grain mustard sauce $32.00, Roast Chicken on spicy Pecan wild rice, asparagus with thyme-chicken jus $28.00

Impressions:

The Terrace Restaurant serves a wonderful variety of fusion cuisine unlike any other you are likely to experience. It's almost as if the layers of flavor will never stop. Even breakfast has been taken to a higher level. At The Terrace simple items like poached eggs and pancakes become exotic dishes. Lunch is affordable considering the quality of the offerings. Dinner is elegant and romantic. Whatever meal you choose here will be a memorable experience.

MAUI
DINING

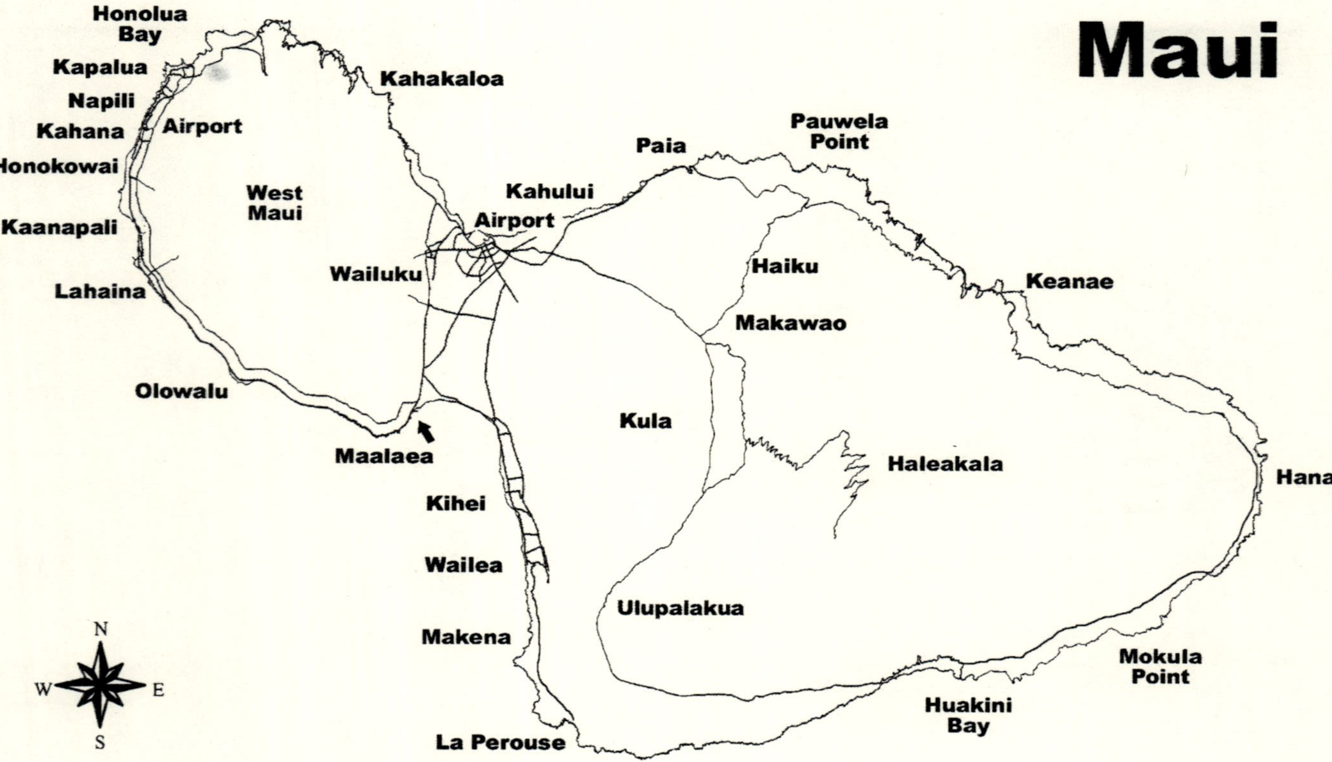

Maui
Honolua Bay
Kapalua
Napili
Kahana
Honokowai
Kaanapali
Lahaina
Airport
West Maui
Wailuku
Olowalu
Kahakaloa
Kahului
Airport
Maalaea
Kihei
Wailea
Makena
La Perouse
Paia
Pauwela Point
Haiku
Makawao
Kula
Keanae
Haleakala
Ulupalakua
Hana
Huakini Bay
Mokula Point
N
E
W
S

Maui Dining

Central Valley

A Saigon Café
1792 Main
Wailuku, HI 96793
808-243-9560
www.asaigoncafe.com
Hours: L/D 10:00 AM-9:30 PM Mo-Sa
         L/D 10:00 AM-8:30 PM Su
Cards: MC V
Dress: Casual
Style: Viet $$

Menu Sampler:

Breakfast:
N/A
Lunch/Dinner:
Appetizers: Fresh Summer Rolls with a special peanut sauce $4.25, Shrimp Pops-ground shrimp marinated and pasted on a sugar cane stick served with peanut sauce or sweet and sour garlic sauce (2) $8.25, Crisp Calamari served with lemon sauce $6.75, Fried Chicken Wings w/garlic & curry (4) $4.25
Salads: Rare Lemon Shrimps cooked in lemon, ginger & onion served on romaine $11.95, Green Papaya Salad with shrimp & basil in a spicy sauce $6.25
Soups: Meat Ball Pho $6.95, Rare Steak Pho $6.95, Noodle Soup Special with chicken & seafood $7.25, Hot and Sour Fish Soup $9.95, Won Ton Egg $7.25
Entrées: Banh Hoi-a Vietnamese burrito you create and roll with fresh basil, mint leaves, cucumber, romaine lettuce, bean sprouts, vermicelli cake noodles, pickled carrots and daikon wrapped in rice paper with sweet and sour dipping sauce-Chicken Breast with Garlic $9.25 or Grilled Tofu and Vegetable Platter with sweet garlic sauce $9.50, Sautéed Lemon Grass & Curry Chicken $7.25, Shredded Pork, Grilled Beef & Egg Cake $7.95, Sautéed Shrimp $10.25, Crisp Egg Noodles with Seafood $9.25, Sautéed Chicken with Ginger served on a bed of fresh lettuce and bean sprouts $7.25, Rice In A Clay Pot with Chicken $7.95

Impressions:

The owner of this Wailuku restaurant took Maui by storm a few years ago by introducing Vietnamese cuisine to the local dining scene. This is light and healthy fare with a Southeast Asian twist. Island residents, visitors, and celebrities throng here to enjoy the authentic Vietnamese preparations with their unique flavors and exotic ingredients. Look for this restaurant on the right side of the viaduct as you are entering Wailuku from Kahului.

Maui Dining

Central Valley

Ale House
355 E. Kamehameha Ave.
Kahului, HI 96732
808-877-9001
www.alehouse.net
Hours: LD 11:00AM – Midnight
Cards: DIS MC V
Dress: Casual
Style: Amer $$ Ent Card

Menu Sampler:

Breakfast:
N/A
Lunch/Dinner:
Pregame Warmups: Peel-N-Eat Pacific Shrimp $9.95, Shrimp and Veggie Springrolls $8.95, Coconut Breaded Chicken Tenders $7.95, Onion Blossom with chili mayo dipping sauce $7.95, Fresh Island Sashimi w/wasabi $9.95
Burgers & Sandwiches: ½ # with lettuce, tomato, onion and choice of fries or slaw-Golden Glove Burger $6.95, add any topping $1.00, Mushroom Burger $8.95, Smoked BBQ Pork $7.95, Seared Ahi Poke Roll-up $8.95, Reuben $8.95
Homemade Pizzas & Calzones: Metcalfe's Special Pizza $12.95, Garlic Herbed Chicken Calzone $11.95, Stromboli Pizza Roll-up $8.95, toppings $1.00
Soups: Bouya-spicy Louisiana dish with ham, shrimp, chicken, clams and sausage in a bread bowl $6.95, Portuguese Bean Soup $2.95/$4.95
Salads: Taco Salad $8.95, Chinese Chicken Salad w/Chinese vinaigrette $9.95
Nightly Specials: home style dinner selections under $9.00
Desserts: Hot Fudge Sundae $7.95, Strawberry Shortcake $5.95

Impressions:

There's a quirk about departing Maui that doesn't occur to people until the day they leave. Checkout time at the resorts is usually around noon, but the flights to the mainland don't take off until evening. The question then becomes what do you do with your spare time? One possible answer is to drive up near the airport and visit the Ale House. Many active people enjoy sports bars and the Ale House is Maui's best. Everywhere you look there's a television, and the video game selection should keep the most energetic young travelers happy. The menu is a perfect match. The selections cover everything from pizzas and calzones to home style entrees. Not only do they offer a quality product—it's priced right. And like all Maui restaurants the Ale House is smoke free! One caveat though, regardless of how you spend that last afternoon secure your baggage first.

Maui Dining

Lahaina

Aloha Mixed Plate
1285 Front Street
Lahaina, HI 96761
808-661-3322
www.alohamixedplate.com
Hours: LD 10:30 AM-10:00 PM
Cards: MC V
Dress: Casual
Style: Isl $

Menu Sampler:

Breakfast:
N/A
Lunch/Dinner:
Pupus: Coconut Prawns (4) with island chutney $7.95, Pupu Platter of drummettes, onion rings, and breaded teriyaki beef $7.95, Cajun Fries $3.25
Plate Lunches: Mini is a half portion with 1 scoop rice; Regular is a regular portion with 2 scoops rice and 1 scoop macaroni salad; Jumbo Plate-One and a half portions, 2 scoops rice, 1 scoop of macaroni salad. Shoyu Chicken $2.95/$4.95/$6.95, Grilled Teriyaki Beef $3.75/$6.50/$8.50, Sautéed or Deep Fried Mahi Mahi $4.25/$6.95/$8.50, Coconut Prawns $--/$9.95/$13.95
Burgers & Sandwiches: Kalua Pig Sandwich with fries and cole slaw $6.95, Taro Burger with fries and cole slaw $6.95, Hamburger with fries $4.50
Noodles: Saimin with char siu, green onion and fish cake $3.25, Look Funn of fresh noodle stir fried with thinly sliced marinated beef, Chinese peas, and black bean garlic sauce $6.95, Chow Mein with thin soft noodle & oyster sauce $3.95
Drink Specials: Hawaiian Angel of coconut rum, cranberry and pineapple juices $4.00, Mai Tai $4.00, Daily Special $3.50, beer and wine

Impressions:

If you are looking for an introduction to local food, you couldn't find a better place to start than Aloha Mixed Plate. Located beachfront next to the Old Lahaina Luau grounds this outdoor eatery serves up all the island favorites. When you first enter and are told to sit anywhere, be akamai and sit out next to the ocean. It is much cooler there under the trees than on the upper deck near the bar. Everyone seems to enjoy the food, reasonable prices, and peaceful setting. If you are a shellfish fan try the Coconut Prawns either as an appetizer or a plate lunch. They're excellent! After a busy day, stop by for happy hour between 3 PM and 6 PM. Parking is plentiful in the lot out front.

Kihei

Antonio's
Long's Center
1215 S Kihei Road
Kihei, HI 96753
808-875-8800
Web: None
Hours: D 5:00 PM-9:00 PM XMo
Cards: MC V
Dress: Resort Casual
Style: Ital $$

Menu Sampler:

Breakfast/Lunch:
N/A
Dinner:
Antipasti: Calamari quickly fried and served with homemade sauce $7.95, Sautéed Eggplant Slices layered with buffalo mozzarella and tomatoes $7.95, Bruschetta of tomatoes, onions, herbs, extra virgin olive oil on toasted Italian bread $5.95, Garlic Bread with roasted garlic and herbs $4.95
Pasta: Puttanesca with fresh tomato, celery, olives, capers, onion and garlic $9.95, Smoked Salmon Pasta with sautéed onion, garlic, sundried tomatoes and peas with creamy vodka tomato sauce $16.95, Wild Mushroom Pasta $15.95
Entrées: Meat Lasagna with homemade pasta, tomato sauce and special seasonings $16.95, Osso Buco-veal shank baked with zesty sauce over risotto $23.95, Ravioli with Sautéed Spinach with onion and garlic with Gorgonzola and ricotta cheese, tomato or cream sauce $15.95, Seafood Risotto with shrimp, scallops, calamari and clams $17.95, Homemade Italian Sausage with red & green peppers, onion, garlic and chunky tomato sauce over pasta $14.95
Dessert & Beverages: Tiramisu $6.95, Espresso $2.50, Cappuccino $4.25, Mango Ice Tea $1.75, Moretti Italian Beer $4.75

Impressions:

This intimate, cozy storefront restaurant is located in the Long's Center in North Kihei. The wonderful Italian/Sicilian cuisine comes as no surprise as the chef uses fresh pastas and cheeses and relies upon his mother's recipes for absolute authenticity. Good food and attentive service in a casual atmosphere provide a pleasant dining experience. Be sure to save room for the excellent tiramisu.

Maui Dining

Kihei

Aroma D'Italia
1881 S Kihei Road
Kihei Town Center
Kihei, HI 96753
808-879-0133
Web: None
Hours: D 5:00 PM-9:00 PM XSu
Cards: AE MC V
Dress: Resort Casual
Style: Ital $$

Menu Sampler:

Breakfast/Lunch:
N/A
Dinner:
Antipastos & Salads: Special Antipasto Salad $8.95, Fresh Tomato & Onion Salad with tomatoes, onions, provolone cheese, olive oil, balsamic vinegar and fresh basil $5.95, Caesar Salad $5.95, with marinated grilled shrimp $8.95
Entrées: Chicken Parmigiana with meatless sauce and pasta $16.95, Veal Marsala with fresh mixed vegetables & pasta $18.95, Fettucine Alfredo $12.95, Shrimp Scampi on a bed of linguine $17.95, Grilled Eggplant with marinara sauce and romano cheese, served with orzo pastini with garlic, olive oil and fresh diced tomatoes $12.95, Italian Sausage in a red sauce with red and green bell peppers & onions over linguine $13.95, Chicken Piccata served with fresh mixed vegetables and pasta $16.95, Spinach & Sausage Lasagna $13.95, Spaghetti with meat sauce $8.95, ¼ # Meatball $2.95, Large Garlic Bread $3.00
Desserts: Spumoni Wedge with maraschino cherries & pistachio nuts $4.95, Tira Misu $4.95, Fresh Made Cannoli $4.95, Gelato Truffle Turtle $4.95
Bambino Menu is available.

Impressions:

Aroma D' Italia is located a couple doors down from Foodland in Kihei Town Center. This popular family dining spot offers indoor/outdoor seating and a traditional décor. The food is mainstream Italian focused on old family favorites. Owner Marie Palazzolo-Akina makes fantastic quarter-pound meatballs ($2.95) that can be added to any pasta dish. Expect to find warm, welcoming service. A children's menu is available as adult portions are quite large and invite sharing.

Lahaina

BJ's Chicago Pizzeria
730 Front St
Lahaina, HI 96761
808-661-0700
Web: None
Hours: L/D 11:00 AM-Late PM
Cards: AE MC V
Dress: Casual
Style: Pizza $$

Menu Sampler:

Breakfast:
N/A

Lunch/Dinner:
Appetizers: Spinach & Artichoke Pizza-Dilla (like quesadilla) $6.95, Bruschetta with pear tomatoes, basil, garlic, onions, olive oil, vinegar, and parmesan cheese $5.95, Buffalo Wings $6.95/$9.95, Toasted Ravioli $6.95
Specialty Salads: Sesame Chicken Salad with toasted almonds and toasted wontons $7.95, Chopped Italian Salad $6.95/$9.70, Caesar Salad $4.95/$7.95
Soups & Salads: Minestrone $2.75/$3.50, New England Style Clam Chowder (Fr & Sa only) $3.00/$3.75, Angel Hair Pasta Salad with herb-garlic olive oil, tomatoes and pine nuts $4.50, Dinner Salad with croutons $2.95
Pizza: Classic Deep-Dish Style-Small-4 slices $8.95-$15.35, Medium-6 slices $12.95-$20.95, Large-8 slices $14.95-$23.55, Calzones $5.95-$9.95
Pastas: Grilled Chicken Pasta on rotelle noodles with a rich cream sauce and fresh broccoli $10.95, Lasagne $9.45, Shrimp Pasta with creamy thermidor sauce, spinach, mushrooms and shrimp over rotelle noodles $13.95
Sandwiches: Meatball Sandwich topped with marinara sauce and melted provolone cheese with capellini salad $6.95, BBQ Chicken Sandwich with tomatoes, lettuce, red onions and mayonnaise served with capellini salad $7.25
Desserts: Pizookie 'N Cream (hot cookie) $4.95, Sorbet $3.50

Impressions:

Perched in second floor quarters above Front Street you'll find a really fun dining opportunity. BJ's serves award-winning deep-dish pizza along with other Italian specialties from their affordable menu. A full bar with domestic and imported beers, wines, and mixed drinks complete the offerings. If you like people watching, try to get a table overlooking the street and the ocean beyond.

Central Valley

Blue Marlin Grill & Bar

Maalaea Harbor Village
Maalaea, HI 96793
808-244-8844
Web: None
Hours: L/D 11:00 AM-Closing
Cards: AE DC MC V
Dress: Casual
Style: Amer/Isl $$$

Menu Sampler:

Breakfast:
N/A

Lunch/Dinner:
Appetizers: Crab & Shrimp Stuffed Mushrooms $8.25, Ahi Poke-1/2# $6.95, Oysters on the half shell (6) $10.95, Oyster Shooters $1.75 each, Summer Rolls $7.50, California Roll $8.95, Nachos $7.95, Onion Rings $5.95, Peel and Eat Shrimp $11.95, Spicy Chicken Wings $6.95, Quesadillas $8.95, Pizza $6.95
Burgers and Sandwiches: Served with green salad or fries. Hamburger $8.50, Fresh Fish Sandwich $9.95, Vegetable Foccacia $6.95, Shrimp Burger with Louie dressing $8.95, Grilled Chicken Sandwich with Dijonaise $7.95
Soups and Salads: Clam Chowder 12 oz. $5.95, Island Style Saimin $6.95, Blue Marlin Saimin with shrimp, egg, veggies & charsiu $8.95, Soup Of The Day-12 oz. mug $5.50, Classic Caesar $7.95-add fresh catch, grilled chicken, or shrimp $9.95, Old Fashioned Garden Salad Bowl for Two $7.95
Entrées: Served with veggies, rice or fries & warm crusty sourdough bread. Free Range Roast Chicken $14.95, Baby Back Pork Ribs $20.95, Maalaea "Famous" Tiger Prawns $28.95, Meat Platter (serves two), roast chicken, Maalaea prawns, and fresh fish $29.95, Sizzling New York Steak $22.95, Hawaiian Style Teriyaki Steak $17.95, Seafood Platter for Two of King Crab, Maalaea Prawns and fresh fish $48.95, Fresh Fish & Chips $12.95

Impressions:

If your idea of vacation dining leans toward the nautical, you will enjoy this open-air spot overlooking Maalaea Harbor. Fishermen and boaters, locals and visitors alike, enjoy the drinks, plentiful food, and friendly atmosphere at this dockside hang out. You'll find a nice selection of pupus during happy hour and a menu built around traditional American and island favorites. This is a great place for winter-weary travelers to connect with the land of perpetual summer.

Central Valley

Buzz's Wharf

Maalaea Harbor
Maalaea, HI 96753
808-244-5426
www.buzzswharf.com
Hours: L/D 11:00 AM-9:00 PM
Cards: AE DC DIS JCB MC V
Dress: Casual
Style: Sea/Stk $$$

Menu Sampler:

Breakfast:
N/A
Lunch:
Appetizers: Coconut Panko Shrimp served with a lime dill aioli $11.95,
Colossal Onion Rings in special beer batter $7.95, Crab Cakes $7.95
Soups and Salads: Maui Onion Soup baked with a trio of cheeses $5.95
Sandwiches: Fresh Catch with toppings and fries $9.95, Cajun Chicken and
fries $8.95, Coconut Shrimp Sandwich with lime dill aioli $12.95
Favorites: Teriyaki Chicken with vegetables, rice or fries $14.95, Fish & Chips
$12.95, Shrimp & Chips $13.95, Broiled Hawaiian Teriyaki Steak $15.95
Dinner:
Appetizers: Escargot with garlic butter and herbs $8.95, Buzz's Famous
Steamers in our special broth $12.95, Volcano Seared Ahi $Market Price
Soups & Salads: Buzz's Maui Onion Soup baked with a trio of Cheeses $5.95,
New England Clam Chowder $3.25/$4.95, Tuscan Salad with local mixed
greens, roasted red bell peppers, prosciutto, feta cheese, toasted pine nuts and
Calamata olives in balsamic vinaigrette $11.95, House Salad $7.95
Entrées: 12 oz. New York Steak $22.95, Clam Linguini $20.95, Paradise
Prawns Tahitian with dry vermouth, dill & parmesan cheese $26.95, BBQ Ribs
$18.95, Chicken Marsala with garlic, herb butter, mushrooms, tomatoes $17.95

Impressions:

There was a time when about the only place on Maalaea Harbor was Buzz's
Wharf. Not anymore. But Buzz's continues on serving fun tropical drinks and
their Hawaiianized steak and seafood menu. This centrally located establishment
serves both lunch and dinner, which works well for visitors touring the island.
Anyone looking to dine by the water will find that Buzz's certainly fits the bill.

Maui Dining

Lahaina

Café O'Lei Lahaina
839 Front Street
Lahaina, HI 96761
808-661-9491
Web: None
Hours: L 10:00 AM-4:30 PM
        D 5:00 PM-9:00 PM
Cards: MC V
Dress: Casual
Style: Haw-Reg $$

Menu Sampler:

Breakfast:
N/A
Lunch:
Salads: Curry Chicken Salad with boneless breast of chicken, mango curry dressing, fresh papaya and Kula greens $8.95, Quinoa Salad of quinoa, baby greens, grilled eggplant, roast peppers and tomatoes, crumbled goat cheese, basil vinaigrette $8.50, Asian Chicken Salad with fresh mint & Chinese noodles $7.95
Sandwiches: Served with today's specialty salad. Crab Club of a snowcrab salad with crisp bacon, Kula greens, tomatoes and avocado on foccacia $9.50, Seared Ahi Sandwich with wasabi mayonnaise on focaccia $10.95
Dinner:
Appetizers and Salads: Maui Onion Soup En Croute with gruyere cheese, brandy and a light pastry crust $6.95, Taro Salad with blue cheese, crisp Okinawan sweet potatoes, fresh vegetables, balsamic vinaigrette $8.95
Dinner Entrées: Roast Prime Ribs of Beef w/Hawaiian Alaea salt, jus, popover, creamed horseradish, mashed russet potatoes $19.95, Creamy Chicken Fettucine w/garlic, basil pesto, tomatoes, olive oil, Parma Reggiano, cream $15.95, Sautéed Mahi Mahi w/ginger butter, papaya salsa, pea shoots & rice $15.95
Desserts: Homemade and wonderful!

Impressions:

The owners of Café O'Lei have a way of controlling costs while providing quality dining that few in the islands have matched. At their Lahaina location they have trumped their formula by locating directly over the water on Front Street and maintaining a menu that is priced within the reach of just about anyone. The tasty fresh foods coming from the kitchen are prepared using a wide variety of techniques making ordering easy. There's a lot here to like.

Maui Dining

Lahaina

Café Sauvage
844 Front Street
Lahaina, HI 96761
808-661-7600
www.cafesauvage.com
Hours: D 5:00 PM-9:30 PM
Cards: AE DC DIS JCB MC V
Dress: Resort Casual
Style: Isl/Sea/Stk $$$

Menu Items:

Breakfast/Lunch:
N/A
Dinner:
Starters: Soup du Jour 3.50, Mixed Green Salad with candied nuts, fresh pears, and a sesame vinaigrette 4.95, Appetizer Pizzas with fresh tomatoes, roasted garlic, fresh pesto, and mozzarella & parmesan cheeses 7.95, Smoked Kalua Pig shredded and served with chipotle aioli & chips 5.95, Crispy Calamari dredged in spicy cornmeal, served with tartar sauce 6.95, Spinach Salad 5.95
Entrées: Shrimp-Scallop Scampi sautéed with garlic, spinach, tomatoes and cream on pasta 18.95, Black Sesame Tempura Prawns-crispy prawns with roasted red pepper aioli 19.95, Peppered Ahi $Market Price, Filet and prawn Combo, bacon wrapped filet with Cajun prawns 22.95, Plum-Glazed Lamb "Lollichops" 24.95, Mixed Grill Platter $Mkt, Chicken Penne with mushrooms, olives, and tomato-cream sauce 15.95, Pasta Primavera with fresh sautéed vegetables with pesto pasta 14.95, Crispy Chicken Roulade 16.95
Three Course Gourmet Meal: Soup or Salad, Entrée-choice of Filet & prawns Combo, 12 oz. NY Steak, Fresh Fish of the Day, or Tempura Prawns, Dessert, Coffee or Iced Tea $25.95/person
Prix Fixe Menu: Early Dinner offered from 5-6:30 PM-Soup du Jour or House Salad, Choice of 8 oz. NY Steak, Garlic Shrimp Scampi, Crispy Stuffed Chicken Breast, or Fresh Peppered Ahi Tuna, Ice Cream or Crème Brulee $19.95

Impressions:

Chef Dean Louie came to Maui from his home in San Francisco via Honolulu and Guam. His unusual background comes through in the delicious twists applied to his steak and seafood menu. Although Café Sauvage is located right in the middle of the Front Street high-rent district, the menu prices belie that fact. This is affordable fine dining in a picturesque courtyard setting.

Maui Dining

Wailea

Caffé Ciao
Kea Lani Fairmont
4100 Wailea Alanui Drive
Wailea, HI 96753
808-875-4100
www.fairmont.com
Hours: BLD 6:30 AM-10:00 PM Deli
        L 12:00 PM-3:00 PM
        D 5:30 PM-10:00 PM
Cards: AE DC DIS JCB MC V
Dress: Resort Casual
Style: Ital $$$

Menu Items:

Breakfast:
Deli/Bakery goodies and coffees, Lunch & Dinner Entrees & Salads, breads available. Counter service with tables outside.

Lunch:
Appetizers: Seared Sashimi with mango-butter sauce $10.95
Soup: Soup of the Day Specialty Soup Selection with Parmesan Bread $5.00
Salads: Wailea Seafood Salad with poached shrimp, calamari, scallops, mussels, fish, vegetables and herb-lemon dressing $14.00, Cobb Salad $14.00
Sandwiches: Ciabatta Steak Sandwich with Maui onions, bell peppers, mushrooms and provolone cheese on Ciabatta bread $15.95, Crab Melt $17.95

Dinner:
Antipasti: Manila clams sautéed in garlic, white wine and butter $12.00
Pizzas: Ciao-homemade Italian sausage, mushrooms and marinara sauce $18.95
Pastas: Capellini Genovese with pesto, lobster, scallops, baby spinach and oven roasted tomatoes $23.95, Seafood Linguini Piccanti w/Kalamata olives $23.95
Entrées: Grilled Island Snapper with sautéed Maui onions, sun dried tomatoes, artichokes and scallions in a demi glace infused red sauce $28.95, Sautéed Veal Scaloppini with caramelized Maui onions in a Marsala demi glace $28.95

Impressions:

Caffé Ciao offers a lot of versatility to Kea Lani visitors. On one hand, there's the deli/bakery with its upscale specialties, and on the other, there's a courtyard trattoria. During the day this is an excellent source for picnic goodies. At night the outdoor dining area with its rotisserie and kiawe wood-fired brick oven creates cozy warmth. The interesting assortment of party foods and beverages makes for good browsing even when you're not out looking for a meal.

Maui Dining

Lahaina

Canoes
1450 Front Street
Lahaina, HI 96761
808-661-0937
Web: None
Hours: D 5:00 PM-9:30 PM
Cards: AE DC DIS JCB MC V
Dress: Resort Casual
Style: Haw-Reg $$$

Menu Items:

Breakfast/Lunch:
N/A
Dinner:
Appetizers: Crispy Coconut Shrimp with lilikoi mustard sauce and mango salsa $9.95, Garlic Clams with Maui onions and kaffir lime $9.95, Herbed Steamed Artichoke with lemon basil aioli sauce $7.95, Seared Ahi with ginger tomato relish and Chinese mustard sauce $Market, Ahi Sashimi $12.95
Soups, Salads, & Sides: Best Salad Bar on Maui-over 60 items $14.95 without an entrée, New England Clam Chowder $4.95, Sautéed Mushrooms $5.95
Entrées: Macadamia Nut Crusted Mahi with Lilikoi Sauce $Mkt, Miso Glazed Broiled Pacific Salmon with pickled cucumber mango salad and citrus soy vinaigrette $22.95, Lahaina Baby Back Ribs with orange mango BBQ sauce $17.95/$24.95, Fresh Catch-prepared Grilled with Kula tomatoes, fresh herbs, garlic and herb butter sauce, Sautéed with rock shrimp, capers and butter sauce $Market Price, Crispy Piña Colada Shrimp with mango salsa and pineapple Hana Bay rum sauce $23.95, Slow Roasted Herb Crusted Prime Rib with natural juices $24.95, Linguini Pasta with Roasted Vegetables, sundried tomatoes, garlic chips, extra virgin olive oil, fresh garden herbs $18.95
Desserts: Dessert tray choice $6.95 including our award winning Maui Pineapple Crème Brulee in a fresh pineapple ring presentation

Impressions:

Along the main highway between Lahaina and Kaanapali you'll see a longhouse style building reminiscent of Old Hawaii. Inside the island atmosphere continues with a koa wood bar in the lounge and outrigger canoes hanging from the ceiling. Ambitious preparations and wide variety are highlights on the Hawaii Regional Cuisine menu. There's plenty of parking on the premises.

Maui Dining

Kihei

Canton Chef
Kamaole Shopping Center
2463 S Kihei Rd
Kihei, Hi 96753
808-879-1988
Web: None
Hours: L 11:00 AM-1:30 PM
        D 5:00 PM-9:00 PM
Cards: AE DC JCB MC V
Dress: Casual
Style: Chi $$

Menu Items:

Breakfast:
N/A
Lunch/Dinner:
Appetizers: Crispy Won Ton Chicken $5.50, Potstickers $8.00, Combo Plate of egg roll, char siu, and BBQ chicken $8.00, Shrimp baked with pepper and spicy salt $16.95, Steamed Shrimp ½ # $16.95, Jelly Fish $10.00, Chicken Stick $6.75
Soup: Seafood Hot & Sour Soup $9.00, Abalone Soup $9.00, Chicken Egg Drop Soup $5.50, Tofu Vegetable Seaweed and Seafood Soup $10.50
Vegetables: Black Mushrooms with snow peas $8.00, Egg Fu Young $6.85, Garlic String Beans $7.00, Chinese Cabbage with White Cream Sauce $8.50
Entrées: Pork with hot garlic sauce $7.00, Kung Pau Shrimp $12.00, Braised Tofu with black mushrooms $13.00, House Pot of chicken, char siu, vegetables and Chinese mushrooms in an earthen pot $8.00, Stir Fried Scallops $14.00, Beef Tenderloin Sizzling Platter $10.00, Canton Fried Rice $6.00, Lemon Chicken or Sweet Sour $8.00, Canton Roast Duck $7.00, Boneless Duck $13.00, Steam Beef w/ginger & onions $8.00, Curry Chicken (hot!) $7.00

Impressions:

A decent, reasonably priced Chinese restaurant is always a welcome find while traveling. The familiar smells and tastes can be a safe haven for jangled taste buds in need of comfort food. On the second floor of the Kamaole Shopping Center in South Kihei you'll find Canton Chef serving a variety of flavorful Cantonese and Szechuan dishes. The dining area is large and airy and has an interesting Oriental décor. Carry out is offered for the condo crowd. They also have a full service bar and plenty of free parking is available in the lot out front.

Wailea

Capische

Diamond Resort Wailea
555 Kaukahi Street
Wailea, HI 96753
808-879-2224
Web: None
Hours: 5:00 PM-9:00 PM
Cards: AE DC DIS JCB MC V
Dress: Resort Casual
Style: Ital $$$$

Menu Items:

Breakfast/Lunch:
N/A
Dinner:
Appetizers: Lobster Ravioli-quenelle of sun dried tomatoes and sherry shellfish cappuccino $14, Sautéed Calamari with fresh herbs, tomatoes, white wine and olive pesto $10, Portabello Mushroom with herb goat cheese and red wine reduction $13, Antipasti of Chef's Daily Selection $Market Quote
Soup & Salad: Peppercress of crispy pancetta, Asian pears, toasted almonds, tarragon vinaigrette and shower of gorgonzola $11, Caprese of buffalo mozzarella, big isle tomatoes, baby basil, and coriander vinaigrette $12, Caesar $9, Roasted Tomato Soup with goat cheese croutons and parsley pesto $8
Pasta & Risotto: Shrimp Carbonara with pancetta wrapped prawns, caramelized Maui onion, parmesan cream and spinach tagliatelle $30, Cioppino with lobster, prawns, scallops, calamari, fresh fish, saffron fennel broth and capellini $32, Vegetable Risotto with sautéed portabellos, asparagus, wilted arugula, white truffle and parmesan chards $26, Saffron Vongole w/clams $28
Meat & Fish: Veal Three Ways-Picatta, Marsala, Parmesan $29, Roasted Rack of Lamb with herbed risotto and candied fig jus $36, Beef Tenderloin with green peppercorns, pomme puree, and cognac sauce $31, Quail Saltimboca with apple smoked bacon wrapped quail, potato nest, fennel and apple stuffing, shallot sage brown butter $35, Savory Braised Diver Scallops with fried shallots $30

Impressions:

With its stone walls, koi ponds and waterfalls, the Diamond Resort is a beautiful setting for Capische. The view alone is worth a visit, but the food is right up there with the best. Classic Italian dishes with a definite contemporary twist will satisfy any diner's culinary cravings. As seating on the terrace and in the lounge is limited at this popular establishment, reservations are a must.

Maui Dining

Kaanapali

Cascades Grille & Sushi Bar

Hyatt Regency Maui
200 Nohea Kai Drive
Kaanapali, HI 96761
808-667-4727
www.maui.hyatt.com
Hours: D 5:45 PM-10:00 PM
Cards: AE DC DIS JCB MC V
Dress: Evening Aloha
Style: Pac-Rim/Sea $$$

Menu Items:

Breakfast/Lunch:
N/A
Dinner:
Starters: Maui Pupu Platter of shrimp, crab, spring roll, onion rings and tenderloin skewers $21.95, Chilled Vietnamese Summer Rolls $8.75,Shrimp Nokekula of beer-battered coconut shrimp with orange horseradish sauce $11.75, Hawaiian Ahi Poke w/Maui onion, seaweed, sesame and ponzu $8.95, Sweet Maui Onion Rings w/Hawaiian bbq sauce $6.95, California Roll Sushi $7.75, Hawaiian Roll Sushi $7.50, Spicy Salmon Roll $8.00
Soups & Salads: Hawaiian Seafood Chowder $5.50, cascade's Salad with Upcountry lettuce, vegetables, pineapple and caramelized pineapple dressing $6.75, Miso Soup $3.50, Kula Caesar with fresh parmesan croutons $7.50
Entrées: Island Fish Baked with a macadamia nut crust, chardonnay and fresh herbs or Bamboo Steamed with shiitake mushrooms, shoyu-cilantro butter sauce $Mkt, Spicy Shrimp & Scallop Stirfry, crisp vegetables in a chili garlic sauce $31.00, Moyer Farms Filet Mignon, cabernet gorgonzola demi glace $29.00, Mac-Nut Crusted Tofu, grilled vegetables, wild rice, island fruit salsa $22.75

Impressions:

Whoever designed Cascades certainly got the job done. This casually upscale restaurant is located above the Hyatt Regency water park but does not participate in the activity going on below. Only the island breezes and views of the ocean are apparent to dining patrons. The menu covers a lot of territory. You'll find everything from traditional favorites to exciting new tastes. Dining here by torchlight can be an unforgettable experience. The sushi bar is a particular favorite. Be sure to try some of their contemporary specialties.

Maui Dining

Kaanapali

Castaway Café
Maui Kaanapali Villas
45 Kai Ala Drive
Kaanapali, HI 96761
808-661-9091
Web: None
Hours: B 7:30 AM-2:00 PM
           L 11:00 AM-5:00 PM
           D 5:00 PM-9:00 PM
Cards: AE DC MC V
Dress: Resort Casual
Style: Amer/Isl $$

Menu Items:

Breakfast:
Loco Moko $7.95, Big Island Omelet $7.75, Eggs Benedict $7.95
Griddle: (before 11AM) Pineapple, Banana or Macadamia Nut Pancakes $5.95, Kula Cinnamon Raisin French Toast $5.95, Belgian Waffle w/fresh fruit $6.95
Lunch:
Fish & Chips $9.95, French Dip $8.95, Paradise Chicken Salad $8.95, Fresh Catch Sandwich $8.95, Caesar Salad $7.25, Hamburger $6.50, BLT $6.95
Dinner:
Pupus: Coconut Shrimp $8.95, Asian Sampler $7.95, Buffalo Wings $6.95
Entrées: Fresh Catch Dinner $19.95, Gorgonzola Shrimp $19.95, Hawaiian Cordon Bleu $17.95, Pineapple Shoyu Chicken $15.95, Seafood Alfredo $18.95
Tuesday Night is Pasta Night: Two-for-one pasta selections; Bolognese Sauce $14.50, White Clam Sauce $15.50, Alfredo Sauce $14.50, Carbonara Sauce $15.50, Lasagna Bolognese $15.50, Pietro Sauce (spicy tomato) $13.50
Desserts: Castaway Chocolate Treasure Chest $4.95, Macadamia Nut Ice Cream $2.95, Sosume Macadamia Nut Pie $4.50, After Dinner Drinks

Impressions:

This relaxing dining spot is located next to one of the most beautiful stretches of beach in the world. The scene is truly Hawaiian/South Pacific with open-air seating and thatched roof décor framing sunset views spied between Lanai and Molokai. An award-winning wine cellar complements the varied menu. Prices are quite reasonable considering the setting and quality. Who says Kaanapali Beach has to be expensive? Reservations are recommended at dinner.

Maui Dining

Lahaina

Cheeseburger In Paradise
811 Front Street
Lahaina, HI 96761
808-661-4855
www.cheeseburgermaui.com
Hours: B 8:00 AM-11:00 AM
             L/D 11:00 AM-10:00 PM
Cards: AE DIS JCB MC V
Dress: Casual
Style: Amer $$

Menu Items:

Breakfast:
Eggs with potatoes or rice, wheat toast, and choice of meat $6.95, Omelets $6.95, Eggs Benedict $7.95, French Toast from Portuguese Sweet Bread $5.95
Lunch/Dinner:
Burgers are made from Meyer Natural Angus Beef Patties and are served with 1000 Island dressing, tomatoes, lettuce and sauteed onions on sesame seed or whole-wheat buns. Cheeseburger In Paradise with a special blend of jack and cheddar or Jarlsberg Swiss $7.25, Best Burger In Paradise $6.75, Cajun Chicken Sandwich $8.25, Jumbo Cheese Dog with cheese and sautéed onions (chili $1.00 extra) $6.50, Classic BLT on a sesame seed bun $6.75, Grilled Chicken $8.25
Sides: Fries (large basket) $3.75, Chili Cheese Fries $6.00, Cheese Fries $5.50, Calamari-Scallop Combo with cocktail sauce $6.95, Onion Rings $4.75
Salads: Upcountry Salad of greens, tomatoes, mushrooms, cucumbers and crunchy croutons $7.50, Caesar Salad $7.95, add Chicken Breast to either $3.25
Entrées: Polynesian Shrimp & Fries-coconut shrimp and seasoned fries $10.95, Fish Sandwich-lightly battered, fried, on a French roll w/lettuce & tomato $8.75

Impressions:

What do you do when you're hanging out in Lahaina, don't want to go back to the mainland, and can't find a decent cheeseburger? You set up shop on Front Street and start Cheeseburger In Paradise! Cheeseburger is two floors of hustle and bustle built out over the water filled with food, music, and fun. This is a great stop when casual American food is on the agenda. Visitors throng to this Maui icon to sample the large burgers and the crisp-crunchy seasoned fries.

Wailea

Cheeseburgers, Mai Tais & Rock-n-Roll
Shops at Wailea
3750 Wailea Alanui Drive
Wailea, HI 96753
808-874-8990
www.cheeseburgerland.com
Hours: B 8:00 AM-11:00 AM
         L/D 11:00 AM-10:00 PM
Cards: AE DC DIS JCB MC V
Dress: Casual
Style: Amer $$

Menu Items:

Breakfast:
Just Eggs with rice or potatoes, meat and toast $6.95, Eggs Benedict $7.95, Loco Moco $6.95, French Toast $5.95, Cheeseburger $7.75, Macadamia Nut Cakes $5.95/with two eggs $6.95, Pineapple Boat $4.95, Ham & Cheese Omelet $6.95

Lunch/Dinner:
Sides: Famous Seasoned Fries $3.75, Ono Onion Rings $4.75, Cheese Fries $5.50, Chili Cheese Fries with onions $6.00, Pineapple Mac Nut Coleslaw $3.50

Burgers: Large and all are served with 1000 Island dressing, tomatoes, lettuce, sauteed onions and fresh buns. Cheeseburger in Paradise with a blend of colby and jack or a slice of Swiss $7.75, Da Kine $6.95

Sandwiches: Polynesian Chicken Salad Sandwich $8.25, BLT $6.75, Jumbo Cheese Dog $6.50, Calamari Steak Sandwich grilled and served with pineapple mac nut coleslaw $8.25

Salads: Mandarin Shrimp Salad with greens, cashews, jumbo shrimp, Mandarin orange slices and tangy ginger dressing $10.95, Caesar Salad $7.95

Entrées: Mahi Mahi Sandwich on a Sesame bun with lettuce and tomato $10.25, Aloha Fish and Fries $10.25, Polynesian Shrimp and Fries-coconut breaded fried shrimp with seasoned fries and pineapple mac nut cole slaw $14.95

Impressions:

On the makai side of the first floor at the Shops of Wailea there's a fun, casual dining spot that is a sister restaurant to Cheeseburger In Paradise. Between the thatched roof décor, fabulous views, and great music, you'll find the carefree feeling of hanging out on holiday alive and well. The bar actually offers Cheap Red Wine and Cheap White Wine! When you feel the need for something familiar, stop by for quality food and drink in this friendly atmosphere.

Maui Dining

Lahaina

Chez Paul
One Olowalu Village
Lahaina, HI 96761
808-661-3843
Web: None
Hours: D 6:30 PM & 8:30 PM
Cards: AE DC DIS JCB MC V
Dress: Resort Casual
Style: Cont/Fre $$$$

Menu Items:

Breakfast/Lunch:
N/A

Dinner:
Chilled Appetizers: Chilled Leek & Potato Soup w/chives $9, Imported Duck Liver Terrine w/ brioche $24, Homemade Duck Pate w/Mustard Seed $10

Hot Appetizers: Cappucino of Lobster Soup with Cognac $10, Traditional Bourgogne Escargot in their shells $12, Wild Mushroom and Goat Cheese baked in a flaky puff pastry, old Port wine sauce $12

Salads: Warm Goat Cheese Brushetta on Greens with extra virgin olive oil vinaigrette and roasted pine nuts $8, Shrimp and Artichoke Salad with mangos and fine herb vinaigrette $16, Volcano Greens, shaved Manchego cheese, poached Asian pears, raspberry mustard vinaigrette $9

Entrées: Fresh Island Fish poached in champagne, leeks, and capers with beurre blanc $36, Black Angus Filet with green, pink, and black peppercorns sauce $38, Rack of Lamb grilled, Paniolo marinade, exotic mango fruit chutney $39, Boneless Crispy Duck with exotic fruits and pineapple sauce bigarade $36

Desserts: French Style Fruit Cobbler with coconut ice cream $9, Pineapple and Vanilla Crème Brulee in a pineapple shell $9, Hot & Runny Chocolate Cake with vanilla bean ice cream $9, Assorted Cheeses $9

Impressions:

Newcomers usually crane their necks at the quaint scene surrounding Chez Paul. On one side is a local general store selling Spam Musubi at the counter, while on the other there's a wonderful French restaurant offering classic selections. Listen carefully as the French waiter recites specials and wine suggestions. If you just nod your head agreeably you might be surprised! Reservations are necessary for the two nightly seatings. Be extra careful pulling on and off the highway.

Northwest

China Boat
4474 Lower Honoapiilani Rd
Kahana, HI 96761
808-669-5089
www.chinaboatmaui.com
Hours: L 11:30 AM-2:00 PM Mo-Sa
           D 5:00 PM-10:00 PM
Cards: AE DIS JCB MC V
Dress: Resort Casual
Style: Chi $$

Menu Sampler:

Breakfast:
N/A

Lunch/Dinner:
Appetizers: Potstickers (6) 6.75, Fried Shrimp Won Ton (6) 4.75, Crab Claw 5.75, Cream Cheese and Crab Meat Fried Wonton (6) 6.75, Vegetable Egg Roll (2) 3.75, Salted Duck 9.75, Jelly Fish 7.75, Spicy Won Ton 6.75

Soup: For (1) or (2)--Hot and Sour Soup 3.75/6.75, Sizzling Rice Soup 4.25/8.25, Assorted Wonton Soup 4.25/8.25, Sweet Corn & Crab Meat Soup 5.50/9.50, Shark Fin and Crab Meat Soup 21.50/38.95

Fried Rice & Noodle: Seafood Noodle Soup 12.95, Soft Chow Mein with choice of chicken, pork, beef, or vegetable 7.95, House Fried Rice 8.95, Seafood Pan Fried Noodles 14.95, Pineapple Seafood Fried Rice 14.95

Entrées: Shrimp with Lobster Sauce 12.95, Jade Scallop 17.95, Happy Family 21.95, Beef with Broccoli 10.75, Orange Flavored Beef 14.95, Moo-Shu Pork 9.95, Shredded Pork with Peking Sauce 9.75, Hot Szechuan Beef 10.95, Spiced Chicken in garlic sauce 10.95, Crispy Duck 18.95, Lemon Chicken 9.75, Hot Spiced Eggplant with shredded pork 8.75, Sautéed Fresh Dungeness Crab 38.95, Sliced Fish with Black Bean Sauce 14.95, Hot Szechuan Bean Curd 8.75, Sautéed Chinese Greens 8.25, Peking Duck 42.95, Kung Pao Chicken 9.75

Impressions:

China Boat excels in the flavorful and zesty styles of Mandarin and Szechuan cooking. The owners emigrated from China bringing their traditional recipes with them. Although seafood preparations are their forte, other choices shine as well. China Boat is located across from the beach in Kahana with convenient parking on site. We view this as the best Chinese dining in West Maui.

Maui Dining

Lahaina

Coconut Grove
1312 Front Street
Lahaina, HI 96761
808-661-5648
Web: None
Hours: D 5:30 PM-9:00 PM We-Sa
         D 5:00 PM-9:00 PM Su Buf
Cards: AE DC JCB MC V
Dress: Resort Casual
Style: Isl/Pac $$

Menu Sampler:

Breakfast/Lunch:
N/A
Dinner:
Appetizers: Coconut Shrimp deep-fried, served with sweet chili sauce and shoyu mustard sauce $7.95, Asian Potstickers filled with shrimp, herbs and vegetables served with peanut sauce and sweet chili sauce $5.95, Mahimahi Tempura served with tartar sauce and sweet chili sauce $4.95
Grilled Specialties: Rib Eye Steak basted with garlic butter and topped with Madeira wine sauce $17.50, Hibachi Beef & Shrimp-a grilled New York Steak and plump shrimp marinated in a miso-sake Oriental sauce with sweet peppers, onions and mushrooms $22.95, Kiawe Smoked Barbecued Ribs, spicy or mild, a full rack smoked in our kiawe smoker with our Maui Plantation Paniolo BBQ sauce $19.50/half rack $15.50
Seafood Specialties: Lobster Tahitian-classic lobster epicurean dish w/our famous family Tahitian Sauce $29.50, w/prawns $16.50, Crusted Mahimahi w/macadamia nuts, cilantro, deglazed w/sake, lemon, & sweet shoyu $16.50
Fresh Hawaiian Fish Preparations: Catch of the Day charbroiled, sautéed, or baked with the following sauces-lemon caper butter sauce, pineapple beurre blanc, beurre blanc w/mushrooms and tomato concasse, teriyaki $16.50-$21.95
Desserts: Sweet Temptations: Hot Lava Chocolate Cake with raspberry and whipping cream $5.50, Cheesecake with Strawberry Coulis $5.50

Impressions:

Coconut Grove has a familiar ring on the Maui dining scene. Before moving on to take a chef's position in Kaanapali, the owner ran a restaurant by the same name in this location. Now that he's retired what does he do? He returns to his origins and hangs the shingle back up! The experience can best be described as traditional island dining. We have yet to find anything here that didn't please.

Maui Dining

Lahaina

David Paul's Lahaina Grill

127 Lahainaluna Road
Lahaina, HI 96761
808-667-5117
<u>www.lahainagrill.com</u>
Hours: D 6:00 PM-10:00 PM
Cards: AE DC DIS MC V
Dress: Evening Aloha
Style: Haw-Reg/Pac-Rim $$$$

Menu Sampler:

Breakfast/Lunch:
N/A
Dinner:
Appetizers: Kona Lobster Crab Cake with a cool avocado relish and mustard cream 15, Kalua Duck Quesadilla w/roasted Maui onions & poblano peppers 12, Eggplant Napoleon of smoked mozzarella, mushrooms, olives, roasted peppers and tomato-balsamic vinaigrette 13, Seared Ahi & Foie Gras with a sweet & sour fresh fig compote and Maui onion flavored duck demi glace 18
Soups and Salads: Warm Pecan Crusted Goat Cheese and Baby Arugula Salad tossed in poha honey-mustard dressing 14, Sweet Kula Corn and Lobster Soup with cilantro crème fraiche 11, Maui Onion Soup with gruyere & provolone 9
Entrées: Tequila Shrimp and Firecracker Rice w/Southwestern herbs and spices and a tequila butter 29, Maui Onion Crusted Seared Ahi with vanilla bean jasmine rice & an apple cider-soy butter vinaigrette 38, Oven Roasted Chicken Breast filled w/Upcountry mushrooms, braised apples, Kula spinach, Gruyere cheese, wrapped in pancetta, served on tomato risotto w/Madeira wine jus 29, Grilled Polenta Stacks w/goat cheese, tomatoes, grilled eggplant, marinated Portobello mushrooms & roasted red bell peppers, Maui onion sauce 23
Desserts: YES! A very enticing selection.
Chef's Tasting Menu: 74 per person, two-person minimum

Impressions:

David Paul's has been voted best Maui restaurant several years running. This restaurant is sophisticated yet casual in its décor, and the upscale cuisine is the ultimate in fantastic fusion. Besides traditional table seating, they have a counter top area for fun informal meals and tapas. Although housed on the first floor of the historic Lahaina Inn (from the 1890's), the restaurant is air conditioned for comfort. It can get hot in Lahaina! Reservations are a definite must here.

Central Valley

Dragon Dragon
Maui Mall
70 E. Kaahumanu Ave.
Kahului, HI 96732
808-893-1628
Web: None
Hours: L 10:30 AM-2:00 PM
         D 5:00 PM-9:00 PM
Cards: AE MC V
Dress: Resort Casual
Style: Chi $

Menu Sampler:

Breakfast:
N/A
Lunch/Dinner:
Appetizers: Honey Walnut Prawns $13.95, Crispy Egg Rolls (4 pcs) $5.95
Soup: Seafood Tofu Soup $11.95, Spicy Hot & Sour Soup $8.95
Entrées: Stir Fried Prawns with Broccoli $13.95, Clams with Black Bean Sauce $11.95, Five Flavor Roast Duck (Half) $11.50, Kung Pao Chicken $8.95, Spareribs with Garlic Supreme Sauce $9.95, Braised Tenderloin Chinese Style $11.95, Assorted Seafood on Sizzling Platter $13.95, Mongolian Beef $9.50
Funn/Noodles/Rice: Yin and Yang Fried Rice $13.95, Pan Fried Noodles with Shredded Pork $7.50, Fried Rice with Chicken and Pineapple $8.95
Vegetable: Mixed Vegetables with Long Rice Casserole $8.50
Dim Sum: Served Only At Lunch. Steamed Shrimp Dumplings (3 pcs) $2.85, Steamed Pork Hash (3 pcs) $2.85, Deep Fried Shrimp Dumplings (3 pcs) $2.85, Steamed Mochi Rice with Mixed Meat wrapped in Lotus Leaf (1 pc) $2.00

Impressions:

Dragon Dragon is a lovely example of Chinese design and decoration. The room was planned in accordance with the principles of Feng Shui and decorated with original artwork from China. This is as close as you can get to Chinese fine dining on Maui. The menu selections are upscale and although they might appear a little pricey at first glance, the portions are ample limiting how much you need to order. For lunch there is a selection of dim sum at very reasonable prices, so once again the budget alternative is to make the mid-day meal your splurge and go light for dinner. There's lots of parking in the lot out front.

Maui Dining

Upcountry

Duncan's & Rockin' Sushi
3647 Baldwin Ave
Makawao, HI 96768
808-573-9075
Web: None
Hours: RS L 11:30 AM-3:00 PM Mo-Sa
             RS D 5:00 PM-9:00 PM Mo-Th
             RS D 5:00 PM-10:00 PM FrSa
             RS 3:30 PM-9:00 PM Su
             Dun BLD 6:30 AM-5:00 PM
Cards: AE DC MC V
Dress: Casual
Style: RS-Sushi $$, Dun-Bakery $

Menu Sampler:

Breakfast/ Lunch:
Duncan's-Breakfast Wrap of scrambled eggs, mozzarella cheese, tomato & basil $5.95, w/lox add $1.00, Breakfast Bagel w/scrambled eggs, ham & cheddar $3.95, Cinnamon Raisin Toast $2.75, Tuna Bagel with cheddar & tomato $3.95, Greek or Caesar Salad $5.95, Makawao Blend Coffee $1.25/$1.50/$1.75, Teas $1.50, Espresso, $1.75, Cappucino $2.75, Mocha $3.25, Hot Chocolate $2.65, Apple Pie $2.75, Roselani Ice Cream, Cinnamon Buns $2.50
Lunch/Dinner:
Sushi- (1 pc) Toro $3.50, Amaebi $3.50, Mirugai $3.50, Uni $3.50, Hamachi $3, Unagi $3, Maguro $2.50, Saba $2.50, Tamago $2, Tako $2, Ika $2
Sashimi-(9 pc) $12-$17, **Combo Platters** $15-$33.95, **Sushi Rolls** (6 pc) $5-$7, **Temaki** (hand roll) $6-$7, **Specialty Rolls**-Rainbow Roll $12, Spider Roll $12, Dynamite Roll $15, Baked California Roll $15, Shrimp Tempura Roll $12
Soft Beverages $2, BYOB is OK

Impressions:

Upcountry Maui people are a resourceful lot when it comes to business. Every storefront, courtyard, and alleyway in the paniolo village of Makawao is utilized in some commercial pursuit. Duncan's & Rockin' Sushi is a excellent example of entrepreneurial symbiosis. In this pleasant plantation style building you'll find a counter serving luscious baked goods and sandwiches, while in the back there is a sushi bar serving the freshest of seafood. During a recent visit the sushi chef unwrapped a loin of ahi with the fatty belly attached. He asked which part we preferred and we enthusiastically replied "Toro!" He smiled and served us an exceptional combination sushi and sashimi plate. Ah… the joys of Upcountry!

Lahaina

Erik's Seafood & Sushi
Old Lahaina Shopping Center
843 Wainee Street
Lahaina, HI 96761
808-662-8780
Web: None
Hours: L 11:00 AM-2:00 PM
              Lite Menu 2:00 PM-5:00 PM
              D 5:00 PM-10:00 PM
Cards: MC V
Dress: Resort Casual
Style: Sea $$$

Menu Sampler:

Breakfast:
N/A
Lunch:
Fish & Chips: Choice of panko crusted, beer battered, or grilled and comes with fries or rice-Mahimahi, Ono, Ahi, Snapper, Shrimp, Scallops $7.95, Oysters $10.95, Chicken Strips $6.95, Captain's Platter $12.95.
Sandwiches: Fried Lobster Sandwich with fries $16.95, Erik's ½ # Burger with fries $5.95, Seafood Club with grilled mahi, snow crab, bay shrimp, bacon & fries $9.95, Crab Melt with fries $7.95, Fish Sandwich with home fries $6.95
Specialties: Boullabaise with garlic cheese bread $12.95, Cioppino $12.95
Dinner:
Sushi: Nigiri (2 pc) $2-$8, Maki Sushi $5-$14, Combination Platters $16-$30
Appetizers: BBQ Shrimp wrapped in bacon $6.95, Oysters Far East broiled w/ chili garlic, soy, lemon, scallions, sesame seeds, sprouts & watercress $6.95
Entrées: Baked Stuffed Jumbo Prawns $30.95, Roasted Rack of Lamb with minted lamb demi-glace $28.95, Seafood Curry $21.95, Cioppino $30.95
Fresh Fish Preps: Teriyaki, Mac Nut, Gratinee, Florentine & others $Mkt

Impressions:

Erik's spent twenty years up the coast in Kahana but recently moved to the Old Lahaina Shopping Center. The new facility is more spacious and offers better parking, but there's even better news-- Erik's new space came with a sushi bar! Not only can you get the wide range of fresh fish dishes that this restaurant built its reputation on, but now they offer some of the highest quality sushi on the island. Lunch is a great value as are the early bird specials between 5 and 6.

Wailea

Ferraro's At Seaside
Four Seasons Resort
3900 Wailea Alanui
Wailea, HI 96753
808-874-8000
www.fourseasons.com/maui
Hours: L 11:30 AM-3:00 PM
         D 6:00 PM-9:00 PM
Cards: AE DC DIS JCB MC V
Dress: Evening Aloha
Style: Ital/Med $$$$

Menu Sampler:

Breakfast:
N/A
Lunch:
Rejuvenate: Hawaiian Tuna Sashimi & California Roll $19.00
Venture: Maine Lobster Sandwich on toasted sourdough bread $19.00
Comfort: Cobb Salad with grilled chicken breast, avocado, bacon $17.00
Rustic: Prawns & Scallop Pizza with grilled asparagus $20.00
Dinner:
Antipasti: Gamberoni Gratinati-herb breaded jumbo shrimp gratinati, lemon mosto oil $17.00, Carpaccio Di Manzo-beef Carpaccio, roasted porcini $15.00
Zuppa E Insalate: Pasta E Fagioli-Toscana Borlotti Bean and Stracci Pasta Soup $13.00, Insalata Ferraro's-arugula, endive, mac nuts $13.00
Primi Piatti: Risotto All' Aragosta-Maine Lobster and Mascarpone Risotto $39.00, Capellini Alla Checca-angel hair pasta, pan fried garlic, tomato $23.00
Secondi Piatti: Cotoletta Milanese-veal milanese, arugula, vine ripened tomato and mozzarella salad $35.00, Tonno in Crosta con Panzanella-olive and caper crusted seared ahi tuna, panzanella salad $33.00, Costolette Allo Scottadito-grilled lamb chop, mascarpone polenta, rapini, mint fig sauce $37.00

Impressions:

At lunch Ferraro's offers a casually upscale poolside menu, but at dinner the umbrellas disappear and candlelight, tablecloths, and musicians transform the venue into a completely different experience. This is oceanside dining under the stars. The fine Italian cuisine and innovative preparations complete the scene.

Northwest

Fish & Game Brewing Co
Kahana Gateway Shopping Center
4405 Honoapiilani Hwy
Kahana, HI 96761
808-669-3474
www.fishandgamerestaurant.com
Hours: L 11:00 AM-3:00 PM, Happy Hour 3 PM-5 PM
           D 5:00-10:00 PM/10:30 PM-2:00 AM
Cards: AE DC DIS JCB MC V
Dress: Casual
Style: Ec/Sea/Stk $$$

Menu Sampler:

Breakfast:
N/A
Lunch:
Appetizers: Steamed Clams ½# $5.95/ 1# $10.95, Spicy Chicken Wings $5.95
Soups and Salads: Clam or Oyster Chowder $6.95, Cioppino $9.95
Sandwiches: All are served with fries. Philly Cheese Steak with caramelized onions & peppers and swiss cheese $10.95, Shrimp and Crab Melt $9.95
Specialties: Shrimp in Beer Batter $9.95 Farmer's Salad $6.95
Dinner:
Appetizers: Crispy Fried Calamari with chipotle remoulade $7.95, Oysters Rockefeller $9.95, Six Oysters on the Half Shell $9.95, Cajun Shrimp $10.95
Soups and Salads: Clam or Oyster Chowder $6.95, Caesar Salad $5.95
Entrées: Live Dungeness Crab $Mkt Price, Fresh Island Fish prepared four different ways $Market Price, Kiawe Grilled One Pound Ribeye Steak with roasted garlic & fresh herb demi-glaze $25.95, Char-Broiled Rack of Lamb with Rosemary demi-glaze $28.95, Hoisin Glazed Duck w/wild rice pilaf $20.95
Pastas: Shrimp Pasta w/gorgonzola & roasted garlic cream sauce $21.95

Impressions:

Under the clock tower at the Kahana Shopping Center you'll find a special brewpub restaurant. The fine woodwork, leather seating, and open fireplace convey elegant comfort but don't come across as stuffy. The menu is a fun collection of meats, fishes and seafood with classic yet innovative tastes. Fresh house-brewed beers add to the experience. This is one of the few places of its kind where you will find an in-house brewed Pilsner. A late night menu is also available. This casually upscale dining spot comes highly recommended.

Kihei

Five Palms Beach Grill

Mana Kai Resort
2960 S Kihei Road
Kihei, HI 96753
808-879-2607
Web: None
Hours: Su Bru 8:00 AM-2:45 PM
         B 8:00 AM-11:30 AM XSu
         L 11:00 AM-2:30 PM
         D 5:00 PM-9:30 PM
Cards: AE DC DIS MC V
Dress: Resort Casual
Style: Haw-Reg $$$

Menu Sampler:

Breakfast:
Molokai Sweet Bread French Toast with grilled banana and crystallized ginger $7.95, Eggs Benedict $10.95, Hickory Smoked Salmon Benedict with wilted watercress and caper hollandaise $13.95, Crab & Avocado Omelette $14.95
Lunch:
Paniolo Salad with BBQ chicken, avocado, jicama, sweet corn, tomatoes and ranch style dressing $11.95, Grilled Ahi Sandwich with pickled ginger, furikake and tartar sauce $12.95, Kung Pao Chicken $11.95, BBQ Hoisin Chicken $12.95
Dinner:
First Tastes: Seared Ahi and Pohole Fern Shoots with three citrus ponzu and chile pepper oil $14.00, Grilled Asparagus Bruschetta w/roasted garlic $10
Soups & Salads: Mauiterranean Salad $6.00, Hot and Sour Duck Soup with pepeau, tofu, scallion and Hawaiian chile pepper $7.00, Lobster Chowder $8
Entrées: Flambéed Tiger Prawns with garlic butter, fresh garden herbs on angel hair pasta $25.00, Hawaiian Seafood Bouillabaisse with ginger and lemon grass broth $29.00, Pulehu Rack of Lamb with potato palao and Asian vegetable ratatouille $30.00, NY Steak with Maytag Blue Cheese Crumble $27

Impressions:

Five Palms has one of the most beautiful settings in the islands with a view all the way down the coast to Big Beach. Breakfast and lunch are offered all day, which works well for those devoting their day to sun and surf. The creative menu and excellent food quality speak well of this restaurant. Look for the awards in their trophy case. Reservations for dinner are a must.

Northwest

Gardenia Court
Kapalua Bay Hotel
1 Bay Drive
Kapalua, HI 96761
808-669-5656
www.kapaluabayhotel.com
Hours: B Buf 6:30 AM-11:00 AM XSu
           B Buf 9:30 AM-1:30 PM Su
           D 6:30 PM-8:30 PM Tu, Th, Sa
Cards: AE DC DIS JCB MC V
Dress: Resort Casual
Style: Ital/Pac $$$

Menu Sampler:

Breakfast:
Japanese Breakfast $24.50, American Breakfast $19.50, Breakfast Buffet $21.95, Continental Buffet $14.95, Sunday Champagne Brunch Buffet $32.00, Eggs Benedict $15.50, French Toast $11.50, Waffles $11.50, Omelets $16.50
Lunch:
N/A
Dinner:
Lau'ai & Pupu: Ahi Sashimi $16, Crispy Thai Calamari with volcano remoulade $13, Seafood Chowder $7, Steamed Manila Clams with fresh ginger, lemongrass and white wine $12, Baja Grilled Chicken Breast, mango slaw, Puna goat cheese crostini $9, Baby Spinach Salad w/warm raspberry vinaigrette $10
Makai & Mauka: Petite Filet of Beef, wild mushroom ragout and pinot noir sauce $32, Grilled Yellow Fin Ahi Nicoise-olive oil, garlic caper, lemon, tomato and anchovy butter w/seasonal vegetables and potato du jour $22, Macadamia Nut Crusted Local Mahimahi w/seasonal vegetables and jasmine rice w/light citrus beurre blanc $27, Seafood Pasta w/tiger prawns, bay scallops, Atlantic salmon, angel hair pasta, and island vegetables $28, Chef's Daily Special $32
Seafood Buffet: Friday nights 5:30 PM-9:00 PM $41

Impressions:

The Kapalua Bay Hotel is one of the few places in modern Hawaii that seems to have escaped the fast pace of mass tourism. In this upscale establishment you'll find a genteel open-air restaurant known as Gardenia Court. Nearly all Hawaiian resorts provide their patrons with a breakfast buffet, but this one is particularly well done. The fine ala carte menu at dinner is a fitting complement.

Maui Dining

Lahaina

Gerard's
The Plantation Inn
174 Lahainaluna Road
Lahaina, HI 96761
808-661-8939
www.gerardsmaui.com
Hours: D 6:00 PM-8:00 PM Seatings
Cards: AE DC DIS JCB MC V
Dress: Evening Aloha
Style: Fre/Isl $$$$

Menu Sampler:

Breakfast/Lunch:
N/A
Dinner:
Appetizers: Shiitake and Oyster Mushrooms in puff pastry $10.50, Shrimp sauteed in hazelnut oil, fresh pasta with truffle butter and wild mushrooms $18.50, Sautéed Calamari with lime and ginger $10.50, Ahi and Hawaiian Snapper Carpaccio with wild fennel and extra virgin olive oil $12.50
Soups: Chilled Cucumber Soup with dill $8.50, Fisherman's Ahi Stew $12.50
Salads: Spinach Salad w/grilled scallops, Reggiano Parmesan cheese shavings, balsamic vinaigrette $14.50, Warm Shrimp Salad w/asparagus & garden peas $12.50, Kona Lobster & Avocado Salad w/fine herb vinaigrette $19.50
Entrées: Ragout of Kona Lobster with pasta and morel mushrooms $42.50, Grilled Rack of Lamb with mint crust, jus with poached garlic, puree of carrot and potato $34.50, Veal Fricasee with cider and roquefort cheese, caramelized apples and Calvados brandy, jasmine rice $32.50, Roasted Hawaiian Snapper with star anise, fennel fondue, emulsion of orange and ginger $32.50
Desserts: Soufflé Glace au Grand Marnier served with caramel sauce $8.50, Gerard's Crème Brulee caramelized with a thick crust of Hawaiian raw sugar $8.50, Macadamia Nut Chocolate Cake $8.50, Fruit Tarte Tatin $8.50

Impressions:

Chef Gerard Reversade blends classic French techniques with fresh island produce to create preparations that come in just one notch below sinful. His restaurant is definitely the benchmark for French dining on Maui. The gracious plantation setting puts the finishing touch on a great evening. If you love fine dining but have blown your budget, cruise the appetizers. You won't regret it. Reservations are a must at this old Lahaina favorite.

Maui Dining

Kihei

Greek Bistro
2511 S Kihei Road
Kihei, HI 96753
808-879-9330
Web: None
Hours: L 11:00 AM – 4:00 PM
           D 4:00 PM –10:00 PM
Cards: MC V
Dress: Resort Casual
Style: Grk $$

Menu Sampler:

Breakfast:
N/A
Lunch:
Luncheon Specials: Sliced Leg of Lamb Gyros $10.00, 1 piece of Spanokopita
$7.00, Fresh Fish on pita $12.00, Salads: Special Greek Salad $7.00
Dinner:
Appetizers: Stuffed Grape Leaves with rice, herbs, spices with marinated
onions & tzatziki dressing $8, Mediterranean Style Calamari sautéed in white
wine lemon sauce $9, Sautéed Mushrooms w/garlic rosemary merlot sauce $8
Salads: Bistro's Original Greek with mixed greens, cucumbers, tomatoes,
onions feta cheese and Kalamata olives, topped with our tzatziki dressing $6/$10
Specialties From Greece: Homemade Spanokopita-phyllo dough, chopped
spinach, onions, feta & parmesan cheese $18, Lamb Souvlakia served w/ choice
of sautéed new potatoes, rice pilaf or pasta $19, Sliced Leg of Lamb served with
pita bread, onions & tzatziki sauce w/choice of sautéed new potatoes, rice pilaf
or pasta $19, Moussaka Saloniki of eggplant, potatoes, lamb & beef $19
From The Mediterranean Region: Jumbo Shrimp Santorini sautéed with
garlic, onions, red bell pepper, tomatoes, mushrooms, fresh herbs and spices in a
light white wine fish sauce $25, Lamb & Chicken Shish Kabob with bell
peppers, onions & mushrooms finished with rosemary Merlot wine sauce $21

Impressions:

The Greek Bistro has been owned by the Arabatzis family for years and is
definitely your destination if you are looking for good Greek food on Maui. So
much of what is found in the islands revolves around Pacific Rim cuisine that
it's nice to find an alternative. Lamb and seafood are the soul of Greek cooking,
and they hold center court on this menu. This is lanai dining at its best. A small
private party room is available for those special occasions.

Wailea

Hakone
Maui Prince Hotel
5400 Makena Alanui
Wailea, HI 96753
808-875-5888
www.princehotels.co.jp/maui-e/
Hours: D 6:00 PM-9:00 PM XSu
Cards: AE DC DIS JCB MC V
Dress: Evening Aloha
Style: Japan $$$$
         Ent Card

Menu Sampler:

Breakfast/Lunch:
N/A
Dinner:
Monday: Japanese Dinner Buffet 6-9 PM, $44/Adult, $25/ Child. Salads, sushi, rolls, hot entrees, seafood, noodles, dumplings, edamame, desserts
Tuesday through Saturday: A la Carte Service, Dinners and Sushi Bar:
Starters: Deep Fried Tofu with garnish and sauce 6, Snow Crab, Cucumber & seaweed in vinaigrette sauce 8, Marinated Raw Squid 4
A La Carte: Appetizer Sushi 15, Assorted Sashimi 28, Grilled Butterfish marinated in sweet miso 12, Lobster Tail baked with creamy white miso sauce 28, Stir-fried clam, vegetable, mushrooms & udon noodles 16
Rakuen Kaiseki: Tropical Course Menu includes rice and pickled vegetables 58, has Chef's special appetizer, catch of the day sashimi, delicate clear soup with seasonal ingredients, an assortment of tempura, choice of nigiri sushi, choice of baked lobster or miso butterfish, choice from sweet selections. Nabemono: served & cooked tableside (two person minimum) 38/person- Sakizuke-chef's special appetizer & edamame, Sukiyaki, Shabu Shabu
Sweets: Momotaro of delicate white peach compote in peach juice gelatin 6, Macadamia Nut Creamy Mousse with Hawaiian vintage chocolate sauce 6

Impressions:

Chef Katsuhiko Sato prepares Japanese cuisine with an occasional Hawaiian twist. This is traditional dining in a relaxed and friendly atmosphere. For those who prefer the truly casual approach there's a sushi bar in the rear of the room. Newcomers to Japanese cuisine will appreciate the Monday night buffet with its variety of dishes and techniques. Reservations are required.

Maui Dining

Upcountry

Hali'imaile General Store
900 Haliimaile Road
Haliimaile, HI 96768
808-572-4946
www.bevgannonrestaurants.com
Hours: L 11:00 AM-2:30 PM Mo-Fr
         D 5:30 PM-9:30 PM
Cards: AE CB DC MC V
Dress: Resort Casual
Style: Haw-Reg $$$

Menu Sampler:

Breakfast:
N/A
Lunch:
Bev's Crab Pizza 8, Brie and Grape Quesadilla with sweet pea guacamole 9,
Sashimi Napoleon with crispy wontons, smoked salmon, ahi tartar, sashimi and
wasabi vinaigrette 17, House Salad with onions, oranges, walnuts 6
Entrées: Oven Roasted Chicken Club with caramelized onions, brie & bacon 9,
Baby Back Ribs with Asian Slaw & Crispy Onion Strings 12
Dinner:
Appetizers: Asian Pear & Duck Tostada with Asian spiced duck confit with
sundried cranberries, carrot, jicama, won bok slaw, toasted macadamia nuts &
ginger chili cream dressing 11, Ahi Taro Cakes w/wasabi miso vinaigrette 12
Salads: Wasabi Pea Crusted Goat Cheese Salad with jicama, carrots, sunflower
sprouts, snow peas, citrus vinaigrette 10, Caesar with garlic croutons 7
Entrées: Rack of Lamb Hunan Style marinated in hoisin, sesame, black bean
sauce with mashed potatoes 28, Baby Back Pork Ribs in homemade BBQ sauce,
mashed potatoes & onion strings 22, Brick Pressed Breast of Chicken with
garlic wilted spinach, mashed potatoes, honey Dijon sauce 22, Coconut Seafood
Curry w/mixed fresh catch in coconut milk, green curry paste, jasmine rice 24

Impressions:

Chef Bev Gannon is one of the charter members of the Hawaii Regional Cuisine
movement. When you taste her imaginative yet comforting creations you will
understand her popularity. Fresh local ingredients highlight this culinary style,
and Chef Bev is definitely not cooking out of a box. Her restaurant is located in
an old Upcountry plantation store complete with high ceilings and loaded
shelves. Be sure to make reservations during dinner hours.

Wailea

Hana Gion
Renaissance Wailea Beach Resort
3550 Wailea Alanui
Wailea, HI 96753
808-879-4900
www.renaissancehotels.com
Hours: D 5:30 PM-9:00 PM XTuTh
Cards: AE DC DIS JCB MC V
Dress: Evening Aloha
Style: Japan $$$$

Menu Sampler:

Breakfast/Lunch:
N/A
Dinner:
Sushi and Sashimi: Chef's Selection of nine pieces of fresh sashimi $18, Sashimi Moriawase-selection of twenty-two pieces 38.00, Sushi combination of chef's selection of eight pieces nigiri and six pieces of roll sushi 28.00
Side Dishes: Miso soup 2.00, Steamed Rice 2.00, Edamame 3.50
Teppanyaki: Seating at 5:30, 7:00, and 8:30 PM. Teppanyaki dinners include shrimp appetizer, Japanese pickled vegetables, miso soup, rice and sautéed vegetables-Scallops with butter and lemon 31.00, Teriyaki Chicken-chicken breast sautéed with traditional teriyaki sauce 28.00, Tiger Prawns sautéed in butter 34.00, Fresh Island Fish-chef's preparation 34.00, New York Steak grilled to your taste 31.00, Steak and Lobster 45.00, Combinations of any two items 33.00
Sake, Domestic and Imported Beers, Tropical Drinks

Impressions:

Hana Gion is a labyrinth of Japanese dining styles. As you enter this intimate restaurant you are greeted by a ten-seat sushi bar flanked by a tatami room. Then proceeding further inside you come upon a teppanyaki table adjoining the traditional dining room. The menu makes full use of the various styles available. At the sushi bar the casual crowd can enjoy specialties that are done just a little bit better than usual. Then for a more complete experience go to the main dining room for tableside or tabletop preparations. Finally, if you are looking for dinner and a show try the teppanyaki room. Reservations are recommended.

Maui Dining

Upcountry

Hana Hou Café
810 Haiku Road
Haiku, HI 96708
808-575-2661
Web: None
Hours: 10:00 AM-10:00 PM
Cards: AE DC MC V
Dress: Casual
Style: Isl/Haw-Reg $$

Menu Sampler:

Breakfast:
N/A
Lunch:
Starters: French Fries $2.95, Onion Rings $4.25, Fish & Chips $9.95
Plate Lunches: served with two scoops rice and macaroni salad-Hamburger
Steak with onions & mushrooms, smothered in brown gravy $6.95
Hawaiian Plates: All served with rice or poi, macaroni salad and haupia. Lau
Lau-pork & butterfish wrapped in taro leaves and steamed $7.95, Combo of
Laulau or Kalua pork, w/choice of chicken long rice, squid luau or lomi $9.95
Burgers: all come with lettuce, tomato, onion, pickles and macaroni salad-Hana
Hou Burger $5.95, Teriyaki Hamburger $6.95, Grilled Mahi Burger $7.95
Dinner:
Starters: Shrimp Tempura $9.95, Calamari $8.95, Sashimi $8.95, Seared Ahi
$12.95, Crab Cakes $8.95, Tempura Ahi Roll $9.95, Ahi Poke $9.95
Salads: Chinese Chicken Salad $8.50, Caesar Salad with homemade croutons
$6.95, Haiku Green Salad with Mandarin oranges, walnuts, blue cheese $7.95
Pastas: Wild Mushroom Pasta $12.95, with chicken $14.95, with shrimp $16.95
Steak & Seafood: Fresh Catch served with tropical salsa, garlic lemon butter, or
teriyaki sauce $Mkt, Rib Eye Steak 10 oz $16.95, New York Steak 10 oz
$16.95, Shrimp Curry $16.95, Fish & Chips $9.95, wonderful specials nightly

Impressions:

Those who are interested in exploring upcountry Maui might find themselves in
the small community of Haiku. There on the site of the former Haiku pineapple
cannery sits the Haiku Town Center and the Hana Hou Café. When entering, go
past the take-out window and step inside where you'll find a pleasant dining
room serving a complete menu including full bar service. This is a great place to
try Hawaiian food, as they also do catering and specialize in luaus.

Lahaina

Hard Rock Café
Lahaina Center
900 Front Street
Lahaina, HI 96761
808-667-7400
www.hardrock.com
Hours: L/D 11:00 AM-10:00 PM
Cards: AE DIS JCB MC V
Dress: Casual
Style: Amer/Ec $$

Menu Sampler:

Breakfast:
N/A
Lunch/Dinner:
Starters: Santa Fe Spring Rolls with fresh salsa and guacamole dressing $6.99, Classic Chicken Wings, medium, hot, or tangy bbq, celery, bleu cheese $7.79
Salads: Grilled Chinese Chicken Salad with greens, snow peas, cabbage, carrots, bell peppers, water chestnuts, scallions, broccoli florets topped with marinated grilled chicken and Oriental dressing $9.19, Haystack Fried Chicken Salad $8.99, Hard Rock House Salad with veggies, bacon, croutons $6.99
Burger Platters: Each half-pound burger comes with lettuce, tomato, red onion and pickle and a full plate of French fries. Char-Broiled Burger $8.39, Cheeseburger $8.99, Hickory Barbecue Bacon Cheeseburger $9.29
Sandwiches: Cajun Chicken Sandwich $9.19, Stacked Roast Beef Sandwich $9.19, Hickory Smoked Pig Sandwich w/fries, cole slaw, bbq beans $9.19
Specialties: Twisted Mac & Cheese-lightly spiced 3 cheese sauce, grilled chicken breast, garlic bread $9.99, Grilled Sirloin Steak with horseradish demi sauce and "frizzled" onions, mac & cheese and fresh vegetables $14.99, Famous Grilled Fajitas with chicken, beef or veggies with toppings, rice, and pinto beans $12.29, Roasted Vegetable Pasta with Pesto with garlic toast $9.99

Impressions:

This establishment is part of a worldwide chain that displays rock 'n roll memorabilia, sells T-shirts, and serves spirits, shooters, and suds alongside good casual food. The Lahaina rendition has a great location right on Front Street complete with an unobstructed view of the ocean for great turtle and people watching. The tunes crank up here, and there is always a friendly group at the bar. This place crosses generational lines and is popular with kids of all ages.

Maui Dining

Kihei

Harlow's
2511 S Kihei Road
Kihei, HI 96753
808-879-1954
www.harlowsmaui.com
Hours: D 5:00 PM-?
Cards: AE DC DIS JCB MC V
Dress: Evening Aloha
Style: Sea/Stk $$$

Menu Sampler:

Breakfast/Lunch:
N/A
Dinner:
Starters: Oysters-half dozen with papaya-wasabi mignonette Mkt Price, Toasted Macadamia Nut Encrusted Brie with roasted elephant garlic 12
Salads: Grilled Asparagus & Goat Cheese Salad with walnut oil dressing and sun dried tomato crouton 9, Mixed Seasonal Greens with walnut oil dressing, bacon & walnuts 5, Harlow's Caesar Salad with cheese sails 6
Entrées: Opakapaka Mac Nut in a browned butter, lemon and parsley sauce 30, Teriyaki Grilled Pork Loin w/teriyaki glaze, baked, grilled pineapple 19, Prime Rib 22/26/34, Filet Mignon 23/35, Giant Thai Scallops sautéed w/shiitake mushrooms, red bell pepper, Maui onions & scallions in a spicy lemongrass, ginger, coconut milk & shoyu glaze 28, Fresh Catch of the Day-pan seared, charbroiled or volcano served w/daily salsa & lemon aioli Mkt Price, Hawaiian Seafood Casserole of lobster tail, white fish, scallops, Shiitake mushrooms & Maui onions baked with a wasabi aioli, panko flakes, papaya puree 29

Impressions:

Long time Maui visitors will find Harlow's in the former location of the Kihei Prime Rib & Seafood House. In fact this is the Kihei Prime Rib & Seafood House! The owners wanted to update their menu and the name got changed in the process. Today you'll find the same high quality meats and fish prepared with a definite Pacific Rim flair. For those who want to try something special but aren't looking for a big dinner, give the Starters section of the menu a try. They're just the ticket for the cocktail and sunset watcher set. Parking is at a premium in the lot and on the street, but an evening attendant will assist you.

Hana

Hotel Hana Maui Dining Room
Hotel Hana Maui at Hana Ranch
5031 Hana Hwy
Hana, HI 96713
808-248-8211
www.hotelhanamaui.com
Hours: B 7:30 AM-10:30 AM
            L 11:30 AM-2:30 PM
            D 6:15 PM-9:00 PM
Cards: AE DC DIS JCB MC V
Dress: Resort Casual
Style: Isl/Pac-Rim $$$

Menu Sampler:

Breakfast:
Rain Forest Omelet-3 eggs w/pohole fern shoots, mushrooms, tomato, jack cheese, hash browns, toast $13, Orange French Toast w/coconut syrup $13
Lunch:
Starters: Grilled Char Siu Baby Back Ribs with a hoisin BBQ Sauce $12.50, Tomato and Lemongrass Gazpacho with rockshrimp and avocado $12.00/$7.00
Salads: Baby Greens w/balsamic vinaigrette & goat cheese crouton $8.00
Sandwiches: Fresh Catch Club w/lemongrass aioli & furikake fries $16.00
Dinner:
Appetizers: Miso Risotto w/shiitake mushroom, English peas & baby onions $13.00, Crispy Tofu Roll with shichimi-sesame-soy sauce $14.00
Soups & Salads: Upcountry Baby Lettuces with Asian pear and candied macadamia nuts w/honey-mustard-sesame dressing $8.50, Kula Baby Romaine Caesar Salad w/Parmigiano-Reggiano, egg, anchovy and croutons $9.50
Entrées: Herb Crusted Beef Tenderloin w/tutu potatoes, garden vegetable fricassee, red wine sauce $30.00, Seared Ahi Peppersteak w/crispy potato stix and pea sprout salad tossed in a wasabi vinaigrette, pinot noir sauce $29.00

Impressions:

The Hotel Hana Maui may be at the end of the proverbial road, but don't expect to find pantry food on the menu. The fare is strictly upscale in this paradise found resort. One of the first things you'll notice is the layers of flavor that come through in the preparations. Simple pleasures are great, but complex ones are so much more interesting. This resort and restaurant offer both while giving the rare experience of living life at the old Hawaiian pace. Revel in it!

Maui Dining

Kaanapali

Hula Grill
Whalers Village
2435 Kaanapali Parkway
Kaanapali, HI 96761
808-667-6636
www.hulapie.com
Hours: L 11:00 AM-11:00 PM
         D 5:00 PM-9:30 PM
Cards: AE DC DIS JCB MC V
Dress: Resort Casual
Style: Haw-Reg $$$

Menu Sampler:

Breakfast:
N/A
Lunch (Barefoot Bar):
Pupus: Macadamia Nut and Crab Won Tons with mustard and shoyu dipping sauce 7.00, Chicken, Corn and Cilantro Eggroll, Southwestern Style 8.00
Sandwiches: Hula Cheeseburger, ½# beef w/bacon, white cheddar on an onion roll with fries and smoked guava ketchup 9.00, Grilled Fish Sandwich 11.00
Entrées: Gado-Gado Salad of fresh chilled vegetables & brown rice w/Thai peanut dressing 9.00, w/chicken 11.00, w/fish 13, Island Fish & Chips 11.00
Dinner:
Starters: Scallop and Lobster Potsticker with guava plum sauce 9.50, Shrimp & Goat Cheese Quesadilla with mac nuts & black bean Maui onion relish 9.50
Entrées: Shrimp Scampi sautéed in garlic butter and tossed with udon noodles, tomatoes and capers 19.50, Screamin Sesame Opah roasted Szechuan style 23.00, Banana Barbecued Ribs w/mango barbecue sauce 21.00, Asian Style Crab Cake w/lump crab & sugar snaps, pickled plum vinaigrette 21.00
Dessert: Coconut Crème Brulee (for two) 9.50

Impressions:

Chef/owner Peter Merriman was the driving force behind the Hawaii Regional Cuisine movement. His specialties are always a pleasing spin for the taste buds. Hula Grill has a casual setting reminiscent of a 1930's Hawaiian beach house. The open-air bar and feet-in-the-sand seating are perfect for lunch at the beach. Then come sunset, patrons can expect an exciting dining experience. Lunch is come as you are, but dress it up a notch for dinner. The Kaanapali crowd walks.

Wailea

Hula Moons

Wailea Marriott & Outrigger Resort
3700 Wailea Alanui
Wailea, HI 96753
808-874-7831
www.outrigger.com
Hours:　Bru 10:00 AM-2:00 PM Su
　　　　B 6:00 AM-11:00 AM
　　　　D 5:30 PM-9:30 PM
Cards:　AE DC DIS JCB MC V
Dress:　Resort Casual
Style:　Haw-Reg/Isl/Pac-Rim $$$

Menu Sampler:

Breakfast:
Champagne Sunday Brunch: blintzes, omelet station, eggs benedict, pasta station, island satés station, cold seafood, hot entrees, desserts $37/adults, $15/children.
Traditional Breakfast Buffet: weekdays $17.95/adults, $8.75/children 6-12.
Lunch:
N/A
Dinner:
Appetizers: Lobster & Shrimp Martini served warm with a cream lobster sauce $13.95, Signature Crab Cakes with shiitake mushrooms & roasted corn $9.95
Salads: Warm Spinach and Feta Salad w/ orange segments & bacon $7.95
Entrées: Filet and Jumbo Tiger Shrimp, wild mushroom bordelaise, garlic mashed potatoes, crispy Kula onions $34.95, Fresh Island Catch grilled with ginger lemon grass beurre blanc, vegetables, jasmine rice $26.95, Lilikoi Glazed Lamb Chops with Maalaea Asparagus, Asian pear chutney, garlic mashed potatoes $19.95, Grilled Ahi Filet & Tiger Shrimp, fried rice $27.95
Desserts: Tropical Flambé Dessert Buffet $6.95/person

Impressions:

Hula Moons is the main dining room at the Wailea Marriott & Outrigger Resort. The upscale retro décor brings back images of Old Hawaii through the extensive use of bamboo and vintage fabrics. In the morning they serve the standard resort breakfast buffet, but in the evening the menu tilts over to fine dining. Local fruits and vegetables are featured along with fresh fish and prime cuts of meat in a mélange of island style fusion dishes. Entertainment is featured nightly.

Wailea

Humuhumunukunukuapua'a
Grand Wailea Resort Hotel & Spa
3850 Wailea Alanui Drive
Wailea, HI 96753
808-875-1234
www.grandwailea.com
Hours: D 5:30 PM-9:00 PM
Cards: AE DC DIS JCB MC V
Dress: Evening Aloha
Style: Sea/Stk $$$$

Menu Sampler:

Breakfast/Lunch:
N/A
Dinner:
Appetizers: Crispy Crab & Lobster Cake, island seven spice crust, Maui sweet corn relish and roasted red pepper aioli $14, Coconut Prawns with a cranberry ginger sauce & Asian coleslaw $14, Humu Ribs w/tamarind-habanero sauce $11
Soup and Salad: Lobster Bisque topped with crème fraiche $10, Vine Ripened Tomatoes with baby greens, shaved Maui onions, balsamic reduction & Thai basil vinaigrette $9, Shrimp Cocktail w/avocado, salsa, chips $12
Entrées: Pacific Spiny Lobster-up to 2 # $52/#, Kona raised Maine Lobster-2# minimum $34/#, Macadamia Nut Crusted Mahi Mahi with coconut rice, baby bok choy and a ginger black bean sauce $29, Steamed Island Sea Bass marinated in Darjeeling tea, with blood orange demi-glace, soba noodles and seasonal vegetables $29, Garlic & Herb Grilled Prawns w/lemon grass ginger rice, sautéed spinach, pineapple teriyaki sauce $32, Nightly Specials
Desserts: Humu Sampler with banana crème brulee in macadamia nut short bread cup, rhubarb cobbler with Ulupalakua strawberry coulis, and Hawaiian vintage chocolate mousse banana crème brulee $13, Kona Coffee Mud Pie $10

Impressions:

Everything about the Grand Wailea Resort is done on a Las Vegas scale, and their signature restaurant follows suit. Humuhumu is a fantasy depiction of a South Sea village set on pilings over a shallow lagoon. Diners are seated in thatch-roofed pavilions where tropically clad waiters attend to their needs. The cuisine is imaginative Polynesian with culinary influences from all around the Pacific Rim. For an unusual touch, the lagoon is stocked with both Hawaiian spiny and Maine clawed lobsters. Patrons can then select their own dinner from the trap. This is a popular spot for that splurge evening while staying in Wailea.

Maui Dining

Lahaina

I'O
505 Front Street
Lahaina, HI 96761
808-661-8422
www.iomaui.com
Hours: D 5:30 PM-9:30 PM
Cards: AE DC DIS MC V
Dress: Evening Aloha
Style: Euro/Asian $$$$

Menu Sampler:

Breakfast/Lunch:
N/A
Dinner:
Appetizers: Silken Purse-steamed won tons stuffed with roasted peppers, mushrooms, spinach, mac nuts & silken tofu over a fragrant tomato coulis with a creamy basil yogurt puree $8.50, Grilled Baby Back Ribs with a hoisin barbecue glaze and a green apple confit $9.00, Lobster Egg Rolls, passion fruit dip $12.00
Soups and Salads: Thai Curry Asparagus Soup of green Thai curry, asparagus topped with lobster and tarragon $12.00, Duck Salad with watercress and Kula greens, bleu cheese, seasonal berries and a truffle mango dressing $11.00
Main Course: Lobster Thai-hitian: wok stir fry of lobster, sweet peppers, Maui pineapple flamed with dark cane rum, served with mango Thai curry sauce 8oz-$32, 16oz-$59, Lamb 'Pa'-rack of lamb dusted with Madras curry and Porcini mushroom powder, sautéed greens, caramelized pineapple demi-glace and a lavender yogurt accent $28, Grilled Duck Breast, grilled asparagus, and seared foie gras served with Molokai sweet potato and a prickly pear Merlot Sauce $34
Desserts: Chocolate Pate of creamy Hawaiian chocolate fudge with passion fruit Anglaise and fresh Kula strawberries $6.50, Apple Tart of Granny Smith apples, mac nuts, and Calvados in a puff pastry w/crème Anglaise & caramel sauce $7

Impressions:

Owner James McDonald has catapulted himself from his beginnings as a culinary student on Maui to the top tier of Hawaii's fusion cuisine chefs. In the I'O kitchen he combines a Pacific Rim style with strong European influences to create dishes with extraordinarily complex tastes. Relaxing on the open-air veranda or beachside patio with an excellent vintage makes for an evening to remember. The professional staff and artistic décor add much to the experience.

Kihei

Isana Restaurant
515 S. Kihei Road
Kihei, HI 96753
808-874-5700
Web: None
Hours: D 5:00 PM-10:00 PM
Cards: MC V
Dress: Resort Casual
Style: Japan/Kor $$

Menu Sampler:

Breakfast/Lunch:
N/A

Dinner:
Sushi Bar: Sushi Combo $24.50, "69" Roll $13.00, Rainbow Roll $13.00, Baked Mussels $5.50, Shrimp Tempura Roll $9.75, Spicy Salmon Roll $6.50, Hamachi Roll $6.75, Mirugai Dynamite $12.50, Spicy Hamachi Roll $7.00, Salmon/Avocado Roll $7.50, Dynamite $8.50, Ahi Poke $7.50, Spicy Tuna Roll $6.50, Soft Shell Crab Roll $12.00, Eel/Avocado Roll $7.50, Salmon Skin Roll $6.50, **Nigiri:** (2 pc) Tuna $5.50, Hamachi $5.75, Tako $5.50, Saba $5.25, Toro $6.50, Amaebi $7.00, Unagi $5.95, Uni (urchin) $7.50, **Hand Rolls:** Tuna Hand Roll, Salmon Hand Roll, Hamachi Hand Roll, Spicy Tuna Hand Roll, Spicy Salmon Hand Roll, Spicy Hamachi Hand Roll-all $4.90
Appetizers: Shrimp Jhun-shrimp & vegetable pancake $9.95, Onion Jhun $8.95, Fried Man Doo-Korean dumplings $7.50, Shrimp Salad $7.95
Korean Barbecue: Cook over a hot grill at your table-includes rice & assorted vegetables-Traditional Kalbi $18.50, Bul Go Gi $16.50, Shrimp & Vegetable $17.50, Spicy Pork Loin $16.50, Marinated Chicken $13.95, Brisket $15.50
Korean Dinner Specials: Seaweed Soup $7.95, Oxtail Soup $12.95, Man Doo Kook-Korean dumpling soup $9.95, Bibhim Bhap in a stone pot $10.95

Impressions:

Isana is a yakiniku bar, which probably doesn't tell you much unless you are from Japan. The Japanese love their seafood and grilled meats, so they took things one-step further and combined quality sushi and sashimi with Korean marinated barbeque. The result is really quite tempting. First, diners start out around the sushi bar with their favorite aquatic combinations. Then afterwards, those still able retire to the yakiniku tables where they grill their dinner on steel plates recessed into the table. This dining adventure is sure to be a highlight.

Upcountry

Jacques Bistro
120 Hana Hwy
Paia, HI 96779
808-579-8844
Web: None
Hours: L 11:00 AM-3:00 PM
         D 5:00 PM-10:00 PM
Cards: AE DIS JCB MC V
Dress: Resort Casual
Style: Euro/Asian $$

Menu Sampler:

Breakfast: N/A
Lunch:
Grilled Sandwiches $6.50, Beer Specials
Dinner:
Appetizers: Soup Pauvert-a special pumpkin coconut soup with diced scallops $4.25, Mini Pesto Caper Pancakes served with crème fraiche and smoked salmon $7.25, Smoked Chicken Quesadilla with avocado salsa & cucumber salad $9.95, Malibu Coconut Shrimp with ginger & served with Malibu rum, lime cilantro butter & side salad $9.95, Steamed Clams from New Zealand with miso butter sauce $11.95, Sashimi Plate with white rice & mixed greens $11.95
Salads: Spinach & Shrimp Salad w/walnuts, coconut and oranges in a citrus vinaigrette $8.95, Fresh Lobster Meat Salad, onion sesame vinaigrette $19.95
Entrées: Vegetable Tofu Curry-coconut curry with bananas and oranges $11.95, Smoked Chicken Pasta served in a gorgonzola, white wine & cream sauce over farfalle, onion, garlic $12.95, Roasted Duckling served with a sauce of lilikoi, pumpkin, sugar, cumin, cinnamon, caramelized $18.95, Seared Ahi crusted with spices $18.95, Sautéed Beef with a sauce of sake, shoyu, ginger & mirin $11.95
Dessert: Mousse au Chocolat $6.00, Tiramisu $6.00, Crème Brulee $6.00

Impressions:

For a taste of the Mediterranean with a big dollop of Maui, try Jacques Bistro in Paia. The alternative scene found in this former plantation town is one to be savored, and Jacques lends his own offbeat yet cosmopolitan air. Fresh island ingredients and classic techniques combine in the tasty bites found on his menu. Awning topped tables with waitresses wrapped in pareos spread the fun in this Bohemian destination along the Hana Highway. Party on!!

Northwest

Jameson's Grill & Bar

Kapalua Bay Golf Course
200 Kapalua Drive
Kapalua, HI 96761
808-669-5653
www.jamesonsgrillandbar.com
Hours: B 7:00 AM-11:00 AM
         L 11:00 AM-3:00 PM
         D 5:00 PM-10:00 PM
Cards: AE DC DIS JCB MC V
Dress: Evening Aloha
Style: Sea/Stk $$$
         Ent Card

Menu Sampler:

Breakfast:
Eggs Kapalua made with pan fried crab cakes with wild mushroom sauce $12.95, Omelets $8.95, Cinnamon-Raisin French Toast $6.95

Lunch:
Starters: Furikake Seared Ahi $13.95, Baked Artichoke $9.95
Soup: Island Seafood Chowder/Portuguese Bean Soup $4.95
Main Courses: Maui Chicken Salad $9.95, Calamari Spinach Salad $9.95, Roast Beef Sandwich with Maui Chips $5.95, BBQ Chicken Pizza on a Boboli crust with caramelized onion pineapple and cheese blend $9.95

Dinner:
Appetizers: Kapalua Crab & Shrimp Cakes with mango chili coulis $10.95, Porcini Crusted Sea Scallops with goat cheese polenta, roasted corn coulis $12.95, Tiger Prawn Martini with Kula greens and spicy sauce $11.95
Entrées: Fish of the Day grilled w/salsa verde, pan-sautéed w/an herb crust & caper butter sauce, baked w/shiitake mushrooms, artichoke hearts, sundried tomatoes & roasted garlic, or chef's special $Mkt Price, NY Strip w/brandy green peppercorn demi-glace $26.95, Miso Sake Prawns $23.95

Impressions:

Jameson's at Kapalua is one of those versatile establishments that serve as both a beautiful golf course/tennis court clubhouse and a fine dining establishment. The menu offers traditional steak and seafood fare with enticing European and Asian influences added for interest. With its pleasant staff, convenient hours, and first-rate food, Jameson's has long been a West Maui favorite.

Maui Dining

Wailea

Joe's Bar & Grill
 Wailea Tennis Center
131 Wailea Ike Place
Wailea, HI 96753
808-875-7767
www.bevgannonrestaurants.com
Hours: D 5:30 PM-10:00 PM
Cards: AE DC DIS JCB MC V
Dress: Resort Casual
Style: Amer $$$

Menu Sampler:

Breakfast/Lunch:
N/A
Dinner:
Appetizers and Salads: Bev's "World Famous" Crab Dip baked in a crock with crisp flour tortillas 8, Asian Fried Calamari with nuoc cham dipping sauce and wasabi cocktail sauce 12, Seared Blackened Ahi Sashimi with a ginger sauce with shiitake mushrooms 14, Ahi Carpaccio with truffle oil, capers, asiago cheese, and lemon dill aioli 14, Boursin Cheese Crab Cake seared, w/pickled ginger, wasabi puree over cucumber noodles 14, Roasted Portobello Salad w/warm applewood bacon vinaigrette, greens, cherry tomatoes, blue cheese 12
House Specialties: Joe's Favorite Meatloaf with Bev's Texas BBQ Sauce and garlic whipped potatoes 23, Pan Seared New York Steak with sautéed baby spinach, whole roasted garlic and garlic whipped potatoes 34, Black Market Ribs with grilled corn and steak fries 25, Traditional Roasted Prime Rib of Beef with garlic whipped potatoes, island vegetables and au jus 30, Pan Seared Scallops with roasted sweet pepper vinaigrette, mixed island vegetables, fingerling potatoes 28, Smoked Chicken Penne Pasta with pine nuts 25
Desserts: Wonderful selection created by Joe's daughter, Cheech Gannon

Impressions:

Joe's Bar & Grill is located in a perch above the courts at the Wailea Tennis Center. Evidence of Joe's years as a production and set manager for various rock groups and celebrities adorn the walls. Maybe his years on the road gave him an appreciation for home-style comfort food because Joe's Bar & Grill serves just that, although with interesting twists. Portions are large so consider sharing, although a $10 split plate charge dampens our enthusiasm for that approach. If you're in need of some upscale down-home cooking try eating at Joe's!

Kihei

Joy's Place
Island Surf Building
1993 S Kihei Rd
Kihei, HI 96753
808-879-9258
Web: None
Hours: L/D 10:00 AM-5:00 PM Mo-Sa
Cards: AE MC V
Dress: Casual
Style: Deli $

Menu Sampler:

Breakfast:
N/A
Lunch/Dinner:
Organic Salads: Salad Plate of fresh tuna or organic turkey salad with vegan potato or pasta salad and greens with homemade dressing $5.75
Organic Soups: 12 oz $3.95, 16 oz $4.50, different choices daily Organic Chili: Vegetable Chili and Rice $3.95/$4.25-with grated cheese & chopped onion $.30
Organic Sandwiches: All sandwiches include lettuce, tomato, onion, grated carrot and clover sprouts, mayo or Vegenaise, bread, sprouted wheat tortilla, (wheat free bread or rice wrapper $.50 extra), Turkey, avocado, provolone $7.50, Fresh Tuna Salad $7.50-with avocado and cheese $7.95
Organic Tortilla Wraps: Curried Hummus $6.50, Black Bean $5.95
Beverages: Fresh Lemonade $2.70, Ginger Lemonade $2.95, Spiced Herbal Tea $.170, Fruit Smoothies $3.95, Joy's Tropical Delight w/apple juice $3.95
Homemade Goodies: Raisin Oatmeal Cookies, Chocolate Brownie with Oat Crust, Coconut Macaroon

Impressions:

This small storefront deli is up a side street across from Cove Park. Although there are a few tables available for inside dining, much of what is sold here gets carried out. Joy's has a totally fresh organic menu with items that are low fat, low salt, wheat-free, and fabulous! Until you have tasted a fresh tuna salad sandwich made without using canned fish you really haven't eaten tuna. The condo crowd would do well to ask about Joy's Take Out Meal Packages for healthy evening meals at a reasonable cost.

Maui Dining

Lahaina

Kimo's
845 Front Street
Lahaina, HI 96761
808-661-4811
www.hulapie.com
Hours: L 11:30 AM-3:00 PM
         D 5:00 PM-10:30 PM
Cards: AE DC DIS MC V
Dress: Resort Casual
Style: Isl/ Stk $$$

Menu Sampler:

Breakfast:
N/A
Lunch:
Pupus: Koloa Pork Ribs with our plum BBQ sauce $6.95, Smoked Marlin $6.95
Entrées: Coconut Crusted Island Fish w/peanut sauce, tropical salsa & jasmine rice $11.95, Lahainaluna Tuna Melt w/capers on grilled sourdough $6.95
Salads: Wo Hing Salad w/teri chicken, won tons, sesame dressing $10.95
Dinner:
Appetizers: Mu Shu Kalua Pork $6.95, Fisherman's Chowder $3.95, Sashimi $Market Price, Caesar Salad $3.95, Shrimp Cocktail $7.95
Entrées: Each selection includes Kimo's Caesar salad, a basket of carrot muffins and sourdough rolls, and steamed herb rice. Fresh Fish with five different preps including orange ginger baked with macadamia nuts, parmesan crusted with caper and herb beurre blanc $19.95-$25.95, Prime Rib with garlic mashed potatoes $24.95, Teriyaki Sirloin Steak with garlic mashed potatoes $18.95, Seafood Newburg in a sweet sherry cream sauce $16.95, Polynesian Teriyaki Chicken $15.95, Koloa Pork Ribs glazed with plum sauce $17.95
Desserts: The Original Hula Pie $5.95, Macadamia Nut Ice Cream $3.95

Impressions:

While traveling in the islands you might notice the difference between Hawaii size meat portions and those on the mainland. For whatever reason, Hawaii chefs tend to follow the nutritionalist guideline that lists four ounces as the proper size portion for protein. Not at Kimo's! The purveyor at this place is definitely a carnivore. When we want to eat a meal centered around a large portion of high quality island fish or mainland beef, this is where we go. Don't be afraid to share an entrée. This is great waterfront dining Maui style.

Upcountry

Kimura's Saimin Shop
Haiku Town Center
810 Haiku Road
Haiku, HI 96708
808-575-5228
Web: None
Hours: BLD 6:00 AM-2:00 PM Mo
            BLD 6:00 AM-9:00 PM Tu-Sa
Cards: None
Dress: Casual
Style: Isl $

Menu Sampler:

Breakfast/Lunch/Dinner:
Saimin-with char siu, green onion, egg-Large $6.50 w/choice of extra char siu, roast pork, 3 BBQ sticks, Medium $5.50 w/choice of extra char siu, roast pork, 2 BBQ sticks, Small $4.50 w/choice of extra char siu, roast pork, 1 BBQ stick, Dry Noodles-with char siu, bean sprouts, green onion $4.50, Wet Noodle adds saimin broth to dry noodles $4.50, Hamburger w/mayo, ketchup, mustard, lettuce $1.75, Deluxe $2.00, add cheese $.25, Teriyaki Sandwich w/mayo & lettuce $1.99, BBQ Sticks 2/$1.99, Roast Pork $1.99

Impressions:

You won't find an extensive menu at Kimura's. This is a saimin shop of the old order, and the offerings don't go much beyond what you see on this page. In fact, there are those who might question why we even included it. For us the answer is quite simple; Kimura's typifies the utter simplicity of the plantation diet in the days before jumbo jets and destination resorts. In keeping with its time warp mentality, the shop is located in a remnant of the old Haiku pineapple cannery. This becomes apparent when you pull in and realize that the parking lot is actually the floor of the original building.

Inside the simple shop you'll find several tables and the local ladies waiting to prepare your order. The ample servings of saimin come with a choice of extra trimmings. For those who'd like to try something even more provincial than the local noodle soup, Kimura's version of dry noodle and its cousin wet noodle is some of the tastiest we've had in the islands. Incidentally, all noodle jokes aside, dry noodle can be described as an egg noodle chow mein made even better with the addition of a ladle full of saimin dashi in its wet noodle version.

Maui Dining

Wailea

Kincha
Grand Wailea Resort Hotel & Spa
3850 Wailea Alanui Drive
Wailea, HI 96753
808-875-1234
www.grandwailea.com
Hours: D 6:00 PM-9:00 PM XTuWe
Cards: AE DC DIS JCB MC V
Dress: Evening Aloha
Style: Cont/Japan $$$$

Menu Sampler:

Breakfast/Lunch:
N/A
Dinner:
Appetizers: Edamame (boiled salted soy beans) $4, Crispy Foie Gras of sauteed goose liver in a shiso crust topped with an ume plum paste $18, Broiled Sea Scallops with a mirin barbeque glaze, miso marinated asparagus $10
Tempura Courses: Eggplant, pumpkin, sweet potato, and Japanese mushrooms $11, Pacific Shrimp with Maui onions and shiso $13, Shiitake and Shrimp $12
Soups and Salads: Miso Soup $3, Red Soy Bean Soup $5, Maui onion, carrots, sprouts, scallions, shiso bonito flakes, sesame seeds, lettuce tossed w/Calamansi Ponzu sauce $9.50
Entrées: Broiled Alaskan king crab legs with lemon, ponzu and steamed asparagus $39,Grilled Sake Marinated Duck Breast with Maui onions, citrus and lychee $28, Boneless Breast of Chicken w/a light teriyaki sauce & tropical fruit relish $26, Seared Opakapaka w/seven Japanese lemon-miso butter sauce $29
Traditional Main Courses: Each includes steamed rice, miso soup and pickled vegetables. Grilled Filet Mignon with crispy potato, Kincha's steak sauce $32, Broiled Salmon basted with a light teriyaki sauce or salted with lemon $28, Chef's Assortment of five fish $39, Grilled Filet Mignon with crispy potato $34
Omakase: Experience the traditional dining experience of Japan as the chef walks you through the artwork of Japanese cuisine- Fixed Price $65

Impressions:

This traditional Japanese restaurant comes with gardens, koi ponds, stone bridges, and rock waterfalls. The diverse dining styles and menu items offered reflect the multi-faceted nature of Japanese cuisine when tweaked by continental influences. This contemporary fusion successfully adds interest and excitement.

Maui Dining

Kihei

KKO
2511 S Kihei Rd
Kihei, HI 96753
808-879-1954
www.kaikuono.com
Hours: B 8:00 AM-11:30 AM
          L 11:30 AM-2:00 PM
          D 5:00 PM-10:00 PM
Cards: AE DIS JCB MC V
Dress: Resort Casual
Style: Isl $$$

Menu Sampler:

Breakfast:
Half Egg Benedict $5.25, Half Salmon Benedict $6.25, Egg Burrito with cheese, potato and bacon $5.25, Mini Pancakes $5.95, Fresh Fruit Smoothie $5.25

Lunch:
Soups & Salads: Upcountry Greens, walnuts, apples, raisins & blue cheese w/raspberry vinaigrette $6.95, Greek Salad $7.95, Soup du Jour $5.95
Sandwiches: Maui Taro Burger $7.95, BBQ Kalua Pig Sandwich $7.95, Cajun or Pan Seared Fresh Catch $9.95, French Dip w/creamy horseradish $8.95

Dinner:
Pupus: Thai Grilled Calamari with a chipotle aioli dipping sauce $8.95, Fresh Fish Quesadilla w/caramelized Maui onions $10.95, Steamers-1/4# Italian style w/white wine, garlic, vermouth, oregano, tomatoes, red pepper $12.95
Entrées: Toasted Macadamia Nut Boneless Chicken Breast topped with mango aioli $14.95, Fish & Chips in beer batter with French fries & tartar sauce $14.95, Mango Barbecued Baby Back Ribs w/mango bbq sauce $16.95, Peppered New York Steak with a trio of peppercorns & topped with garlic butter $17.95
Sushi Bar: Ono Kai Sushi 5 PM-10 PM

Impressions:

This is the kind of place most visitors are naturally attracted to. It's open air, has good ocean views, and won't break the budget. The menu offers solid middle-of-the-road fare with some island twists. Things can be a little quiet down at this end of Kihei, but the party goes on later than usual at KKO. You'll find a late night menu served after 10 PM and a happening seafood bar. Parking is dicey, so you've got to be flexible. Arrive early or late and avoid the problem.

Lahaina

Kobe Japanese Steak House
136 Dickenson
Lahaina, HI 96761
808-667-5555
www.kobemaui.com
Hours: D 5:30 PM-10:00 PM
Cards: AE DC DIS JCB MC V
Dress: Resort Casual
Style: Japan $$$
         Ent Card

Menu Sampler:

Breakfast/Lunch:
N/A

Dinner:
Sushi Appetizers: Kobe Assorted of 6 pieces nigiri and 1 tuna roll sushi $18.95, Emperor Assorted of 8 pieces nigiri and 1 tuna roll sushi $21.95, Sashimi Hawaiian Maguro (caught fresh daily) $11.00, Samurai Assorted $12.90

Teppanyaki Style Dinners: Each dinner includes teppan shrimp appetizer, shabu-shabu soup, grilled vegetables consisting of mushrooms, onions, zucchini and bean sprouts, rice & hot tea. Teriyaki Chicken $14.95, Sukiyaki Steak $18.95, Kobe Emperor Steak $28.95, Teriyaki Chicken & Steak Combo $19.95, Vegetarian Dinner $12.95, Tofu Steak Dinner $9.95, Filet Mignon $27.95

Teppanyaki Fish and Seafood Combinations: Scallops and Steak $25.95, Shrimp and Scallops $23.95, Lobster Tail $Market Price, Teppan Scallops $24.95, Opakapaka $18.95, Lobster Tail $39.95, Calamari Steak $22.95

Super Sunset Specials: 5:30-6:30 PM Teriyaki Steak & Chicken $15.95, Teriyaki Chicken $11.95, Opakapaka $14.95, Sukiyaki Steak $14.95

A keiki menu is available for children under age 10 $7.95-$12.95.

Impressions:

The teppanyaki experience is as much a form of entertainment as it is a type of dining. Participants sit around a large table-front grill while the chef slices, dices, and grills. This is time for table talk. The patrons get to know each other quickly, and the chef keeps things hopping with his patented banter. In the Japanese tradition presentation, variety, and taste are paramount. Expect quality to hold sway over quantity. Their "Dynamite" at the sushi bar is one of the best on the island! Look for coupons. Be sure to ask about complimentary parking in the Baldwin House lot.

Maui Dining

Upcountry

Kula Lodge and Restaurant
Haleakala Hwy
Kula, HI 96790
808-878-1535
www.kulalodge.com
Hours: B 6:30 AM-11:00 AM
         L 11:30 AM-4:30 PM
         D 5:00 PM-8:30 PM
Cards: MC V
Dress: Resort Casual
Style: Isl/Pac-Rim $$$

Menu Sampler:

Breakfast:
Classic Eggs Benedict $11, Two Eggs, bacon, ham or Portuguese sausage with cottage fries & toast $8.50, Bananas Foster Pancakes w/macadamia nuts $11.75
Lunch:
Soups, Salads and Appetizers: Maui Onion Soup with a focaccia crostini and smoked mozzarella cheese $6.00, Papaya Shrimp Salad $14.00, Miso Oysters Rockefeller $12.00, Warm Spinach Salad w/gorgonzola cheese, Granny Smith apples, spicy pecans & drizzled w/warm smoked bacon-balsamic vinaigrette $8.00, Kula Corn Chowder with Pancetta & roasted red peppers $6.00
Main Courses: Black Angus Burger –1/2 # on a toasted onion bun with oven roasted garlic potato spears $11.00, Macadamia Nut Pesto Pasta $16.00
Dinner:
Appetizers: Thai Summer Rolls with peanut and chili sauces $12.00
Entrées: Sautéed Lilikoi Prawns, shallots, and Hawaiian passion fruit with lemon grass risotto and baby bok choy $24.00, Sugarcane Baby Back Ribs with mango BBQ sauce and roasted garlic mashed potatoes $18.00, Fresh Fish served dragon seared or macadamia nut crusted $24.00

Impressions:

A trip Upcountry is like entering a special world that is sometimes ethereal and always interesting. The Kula Lodge fits right in with its "Tolkienesque" gardens nested around brick and stone patios overlooking panoramic bi-coastal views. Check out the outdoor stone and brick oven where bread, pizza, and calzones are baked. This is a lovely stop when touring Upcountry Maui.

Lahaina

Lahaina Coolers
180 Dickenson
Lahaina, HI 96761
808-661-7082
www.lahainacoolers.com
Hours: B 8:00 AM-11:15 AM
              L 11:15 AM-5:00 PM
              D 5:00 PM-Midnight
Cards: AE DC MC V
Dress: Casual
Style: Ec $$

Menu Sampler:

Breakfast:
Huevos Rancheros $8.95, Fried Rice Plate of jasmine rice with eggs, ham &
Portuguese sausage and veggies $7.25, Local Benedict of Hawaiian sweet bread
and Portuguese sausage $8.95, Macadamia Nut Pancakes $7.50, Mediterranean
Omelet w/bacon, tomato, fresh basil, & feta cheese $8.75, Fruit Bowl $5.50
Lunch:
Sandwiches: Grilled Chicken Breast on garlic herb bread with Canadian bacon,
grilled red bell peppers, jack cheese, Dijon mayo, lettuce, tomato, onion and
sprouts $8.95, BBQ Pork Sandwich $8.50, BLT with cheese $8.50
Entrées: Hibachi Chicken with jasmine rice and mac salad $9.95, Kalua Pig
with sides $8.95, Fish Tacos with salsa aioli, jasmine rice & black beans $10.95
Dinner:
Pupus: Tempura Calamari with Gorgonzola herb dip $6.95, Grilled Artichoke
over couscous with lemon & parsley aioli $8.95, Crab Wontons $8.50
Salads: Soba Noodle Salad w/greens & grilled tofu $5.50/$8.50
Entrées: Evil Jungle Pasta of chicken breast, onions, red & green peppers and
spicy Thai peanut sauce over linguine $15.95, Pepperoni Pizza $12.95, Bistro
Burger $9.95, Vegetarian Shepherd's Pie $14.95

Impressions:

When you walk up Dickenson St. and see a place that looks like it belongs in
Key West, you'll know you've found Lahaina Coolers. This local favorite is
known for its interesting menu and just-right portions. The Cooler stays open
late, so if you've been running with the night owls and forgot about dinner, give
it a try. Look behind the complex for some of the cheapest parking in Lahaina.

Maui Dining

Lahaina

Lahaina Fish Company
831 Front Street
Lahaina, HI 96761
808-661-3472
Web: None
Hours: L 11:00 AM-Midnight
        D 5:00 PM-10:00 PM
Cards: AE JCB MC V
Dress: Resort Casual
Style: Sea/Stk $$$

Menu Sampler:

Breakfast:
N/A
Lunch:
 Salads & Soups: Maui Onion & Tomato Salad with Gorgonzola, macadamia nut oil & balsamic vinegar $4.99, Seafood Chowder $3.99
Pupus: Crispy Pork Potstickers with sweet chili sauce $6.99
Sandwich: All served in a basket with fries. Mahi Mahi Sandwich $8.99, Chicken Caesar Sandwich $10.99, Crabcake Melt w/jalapeño jack $9.99
Baskets: Wela Chicken Wings & Chips $8.99, Fan Tail Fried Shrimp $11.99
Dinner:
Pupus: Oysters Rockefeller $9.99, Grilled Zucchini & Eggplant Balsamico topped with gorgonzola cheese $8.99, Fried Calamari $9.99, Ahi Katsu $12.99
Entrées: All are served with sourdough rolls, and choice of steamed rice, garlic pesto pasta or French fries. Seven Fresh Fish Choices with three different preps-grilled with garlic lemon butter, broiled with garlic butter, blackened Cajun style $19.99-$23.99, Sautéed Sea Scallops in garlic, wine & lemon butter $16.99, Seafood Puttanesca $19.99, Top Sirloin Steak $10.99/$12.99, Luau Style Pork Ribs $15.99/$19.95, Island Fish & Chips $9.99, Hawaiian Teriyaki Chicken topped with pineapple salsa $12.99, Lobster & Scallops Primavera $21.99

Impressions:

Visitors to the islands all seem to have one thing in common; they want to dine by the ocean. At Lahaina Fish Company you don't just dine by the ocean, you dine over it! If immersing yourself in the seafood experience is high on your list, this place will scratch that itch. Leave your preconceived notions at home, and go with the waiter's recommendations. He knows the varieties and preparations of choice. For a budget minded lunch, try a bowl of the seafood chowder.

Maui Dining

Wailea

Le Gunji
Diamond Resort
555 Kaukahi St
Wailea, HI 96753
808-874-0500
www.diamondresort.com/maui
Hours: D 6:00 PM & 8:00 PM seating
Cards: AE DC DIS JCB MC V
Dress: Evening Aloha
Style: Fre/Japan $$$$

Menu Sampler:

Breakfast/Lunch:
N/A
Dinner:
Complete Teppanyaki Dinners:
Diamond Course with fresh catch, lobster tail and grilled steak served with appetizer, soup, sorbet, steamed or garlic fried rice, grilled vegetables $70.00
Mini-Diamond Course with fresh fish of the day and steak served with appetizer, soup, sorbet, steamed or garlic fried rice, grilled vegetables $45.00
Mini-Diamond Course with steak and lobster tail served with appetizer, soup, sorbet, steamed rice or garlic fried rice, grilled vegetables $55.00
Seafood Course with lobster tail and fresh catch of the day served with appetizer, soup, sorbet, steamed or garlic fried rice, grilled vegetables $55.00
Beef Steak Course with appetizer, soup, sirloin or tenderloin steak, sorbet, steamed or garlic fried rice, grilled vegetables $50.00
Dessert and coffee or tea is included in the above dinners.

Impressions:

The dramatic wood and stone architecture of the Diamond Resort includes a waterfall and stream that actually flows under the building. Both the Le Gunji and Taiko restaurants are well positioned to take advantage of this spectacular setting. Of the two Le Gunji is the more intimate. Here there are only two teppanyaki tables seating eight diners each. For comfort's sake the grill and the chef are positioned at a distance while still affording patrons a view of the cooking process. Look for definite French influences in some of the dishes. Another unusual touch is the rolling preparation where the steak courses are cooked in two separate servings. This assures that the meat is always served hot. Reservations are required for the two nightly seatings.

Maui Dining

Kaanapali

Leilani's on the Beach
Whaler's Village
Kaanapali, HI 96761
808-661-4495
www.leilanis.com
Hours: L 11:00 AM-11:00 PM
            D 5:00 PM-10:00 PM
Cards: AE DC DIS MC V
Dress: Casual
Style: Sea/Stk $$

Menu Sampler:

Breakfast:
N/A
Lunch:
Appetizers: House Made Fresh Fish Chowder 4.00, Crispy Calamari Strips 7.00, Beach Fries 2.00, Maui Onion Strings 7.00, and Artichoke Fritters 7.00
Hawaiian Local Plates: Includes two-scoop rice and one scoop mac salad. Paniolo Teriyaki Sirloin Steak 12.00, Stir Fry Chicken Cashew 10.00
Sandwiches: All w/Maui chips. Grilled Tuna Salad and Cheddar 7.50, Beachside Burger 8.00, Teriyaki Grilled Chicken Breast Sandwich 8.95
Dinner:
Pupus: Sashimi w/wasabi & pickled ginger Market Price, Yin and Yang Calamari panko crusted w/fiery tomato coulis 7.00, Ginger Shrimp Cocktail 9
Entrées: All dinners include house salad. Kiawe Smoked Baby Back Ribs w/buttermilk & garlic topped baked potato 17, Pepper Crusted Filet Mignon w/chimichurra sauce, Maui onion stack & Hawaiian sweet potatoes 24.50, Citrus Grilled Ono w/chardonnay & lemon beurre blanc 21, Teriyaki Style Char Broiled Ahi Steak marinated in sesame oil, Dijon & shoyu, with cucumber namasu 19.50, Fried Coconut Prawns with ginger cocktail sauce 16
Desserts: Hula Pie 6.00, Messy Apple Crisp w/mac nut ice cream 6.00

Impressions:

This happening dining spot is located on beautiful Kaanapali Beach. If you came to Hawaii expecting an $8 hamburger, this is one place where you'd expect to find it. But what a hamburger! Finish the one half-pound Beachside Burger basket, and you'll be looking for a tree to go to sleep under. People watching is a primary activity here and goes well with the good food, tropical drinks, and friendly service. This Whaler's Village favorite attracts locals as well as visitors.

Maui Dining

Lahaina

Longhi's
888 Front Street
Lahaina, HI 96761
808-667-2288
www.longhi-maui.com
Hours: B 7:30 AM-11:30 AM
           L 11:30 AM-5:00 PM
           D 5:00 PM-10:00 PM
Cards: AE DIS JCB MC V
Dress: Resort Casual
Style: Ec/Sea $$$$

Menu Sampler:

Breakfast:
Two Poached Eggs Benedict or Florentine with hollandaise on toasted French bread $13.50, Today's Quiche $9.25, French Toast with Grand Marnier, powdered sugar butter and maple syrup $9.25, Fresh Cinnamon Roll $4.25

Lunch:
Appetizers: Penn Cove Mussels $13.50, Ahi Carpaccio $15.50, Clams $14.50
Sandwiches: Peking Duck $11.00, Steak Sandwich with mushrooms and onions $16.00, Cheese Steak $12.50, Chicken Picatta Sauté w/butter & lemon $12.00
Entrées: Maine Lobster Salad on fresh greens $20.50, Sicilian Pasta with calamari $14.50, Prawns Venice with garlic butter, lemon and parsley $16.00

Dinner:
Appetizers: Pacific Manila Clams $14.50, Zucchini Fritta $12.50
Salads and Sides: Greek Salad $7.25/$10.25, Sugar Snap Peas $7.75
Entrées: Filet Longhi sliced thin and served with sautéed bell peppers and topped with sautéed basil $31.00, Chicken or Veal Saute as Piccata, Marsala, Parmesan or Mediterranean $24.00/$30.00, Prawns Amaretto sautéed in brandy, amaretto with fresh orange juice & cream $29.00

Impressions:

Longhi's is reminiscent of the French Riviera with its black and white marble floors, round café style tables, and open-air ambiance. The Front Street location is the perfect spot for sunset viewing and people watching. Pay close attention as the wait staff recites the menu, or you'll miss some of the innovative selections. Whether you're looking for breakfast, lunch, or dinner, this top choice provides fabulous food and great atmosphere. Don't miss it!

Maui Dining

Wailea

Longhi's
The Shops at Wailea
3750 Wailea Alanui
Wailea, HI 96753
808-891-8883
www.longhi-maui.com
Hours: B 7:30 AM-11:30 AM SaSu
          B 8 :00 AM-11:30 AM Mo-Fr
          L 11:30 AM-5:00 PM
          D 5:00 PM-10:00 PM
Cards: AE DIS JCB MC V
Dress: Resort Casual
Style: Ec/Sea $$$$

Menu Sampler:

Breakfast:
Baked Italian Frittata with Meat & Vegetables or Vegetables with hollandaise on toasted French bread $10.00, Today's Quiche $9.00, French Toast with Grand Marnier, powdered sugar, butter and maple syrup $9.25

Lunch:
Appetizers: Fruitta De Mare $16.50, Potato Crusted Crab Cakes $15.00
Sandwiches: New York Steak with mushrooms and onions $16.00, Chicken Piccata $13.00, Classic New York Reuben $10.50, Italian Hoagie $9.00
Entrées: Ahi Torino-sautéed with macadamia nuts $15.00, Manicotti with four cheeses topped with béchamel and Pomodoro sauces $9.50, Fresh Catch $15

Dinner:
Appetizers: Potato Crusted Crab Cakes with a bell pepper coulis $15.00
Salads and Sides: Caprese Salad $14.50, Artichoke Longhi $11.25
Entrées: Lamb Chops with Raspberry-Mint Sauce $31.00, Chicken or Veal Saute as Piccata, Marsala, Parmesan or Mediterranean $24.00/$30.00, Prawns Amaretto sautéed in brandy, amaretto with fresh orange juice & cream $29.00

Impressions:

Bob Longhi recently brought his version of casual dining elegance to The Shops at Wailea. This sister restaurant to Longhi's original Lahaina location provides the same café style ambiance and fantastic cuisine that repeat visitors have come to expect. The menu also stays true to form so those hoping to revisit a particular preparation won't be disappointed. This is one big-name restaurant where the prices are appropriate for what's offered. Look for entertainment in the evening.

Central Valley

Maalaea Grill
300 Maalaea Road
Maalaea, HI 96793
808-243-2206
Web: None
Hours: L 10:30 AM-3:00 PM
        D 5:30 PM-9:00 PM XMo
Cards: MC V
Dress: Resort Casual
Style: Isl/Pac-Rim $$

Menu Sampler:

Breakfast:
N/A
Lunch:
Salads: Curry Chicken Salad w/fresh papaya & Kula greens $7.95, Taro Salad with blue cheese, crisp Okinawan sweet potatoes, balsamic vinaigrette $8.95
Entrées: Served with today's specialty salad. Blackened Mahi Mahi with fresh papaya salsa, steamed rice $8.95, Creamy Chicken Fettucine with garlic, tomato and fresh basil in a light parmesan cream sauce $7.95, Today's Plate $6.50
Sandwiches: Served with today's specialty salad. Crab Club-snow crab salad with crisp bacon, Kula greens, tomatoes and avocado on foccacia $8.50, Prime Rib Dip on garlic grilled baguette, jus $8.95, Seared Ahi w/wasabi mayo $7.95
Dinner:
Appetizers and Salads: Manoa Lettuce Wraps with chicken, water chestnuts and shiitake mushrooms $6.95, Maui Onion Soup en Croute with gruyere cheese, brandy, light pastry crust $5.95, Feta Potato Cakes $5.95
Entrées: Served with today's specialty salad. Seafood Zarzuella of clams, shrimp, mussels, fresh fish, lobster, tomato saffron broth and linguine $18.95, Roast Prime Ribs of Beef with au jus, popover, horseradish, and the "Grill" potatoes $14.95/$18.95, Macadamia Nut Roast Duckling with honey $15.95

Impressions:

This island themed restaurant is located in the Maalaea Harbor Village. With a view overlooking the marina and lots of bamboo in the décor, the chef-owners have created a perfect backdrop for this island eatery. They also have a knack for keeping costs in line and passing the savings along through their reasonably priced menu while offering creative fusion cuisine. This is an excellent choice for the culinary adventurer traveling on a budget.

Maui Dining

Upcountry

Mama's Fish House
Hana Hwy
Kuau, HI 96779
808-579-8488
www.mamasfishhouse.com
Hours: L 11:00 AM-2:30 PM
         D 4:45 PM-9:00 PM
Cards: AE JCB MC V
Dress: Resort Casual
Style: Sea $$$$

Menu Sampler:

Breakfast:
N/A
Lunch:
Grilled Ahi Sandwich with smoked bacon, Kula greens and tomatoes on cheddar cheese focaccia bread with Maui onion dressing 23, Sugarcane Grilled Chicken Salad with macadamia nut-mustard dressing 20, Kalua Pig with Molokai sweet potato , baked banana, tropical fruit and fresh coconut 36, Panang Curry Fish 29
Dinner:
First Course: Seared Ahi Sashimi with pineapple-tamarind sauce and hot mustard 18, Macadamia Nut Crab Cake with fire and ice relish 16, Polynesian Lobster Soup with coconut, fresh spinach and Hana breadfruit crisps 15
Entrées: Crispy Kalua Duck with mango-mui glaze, baby bok choy, rice pilaf 29, Mahi Mahi cooked in ti leaf package with coconut milk and mango, opened at your table, with slow roasted Kalua pig and Hanalei poi, lomi-lomi salmon 38, Onaga sautéed with tomatoes, wine and capers, with Vermont cheddar scalloped potatoes 40, New York Steak with shiitake mushroom bordelaise sauce 39, Bouillabaisse of fresh fish, shellfish, and lobster simmered in a fragrant saffron broth and capellini pasta and garlic rouille 46

Impressions:

When you head east out of Paia on the Hana Highway you'll come to what has to be the perfect location for a Hawaiian seafood restaurant. There in a private cove surrounded with palm trees sits Mama's Fish House. For many Mama's means seafood on Maui. In order for the chef to get what he wants when he wants it, Mama's actually has its own fishing fleet. Talk about fresh! Daily menu changes are generated depending upon the catch. Be sure to check out the specials list. Reservations are strongly recommended. Valet parking is available.

Maui Dining

Central Valley

Mañana Garage
33 Lono Ave
Kahului, HI 96733
808-873-0220
www.mananagarage.com
Hours: L 11:30 AM-2:30 PM Mo-Sa
            Midday Menu 2:30 PM-5:00 PM
            D 5:00 PM-9:00 PM Late Night Menu 9:00-10:30 PM We-Sa
Cards: AE DIS JCB MC V
Dress: Resort Casual
Style: LatAm/PacRim $$

Menu Sampler:

Breakfast:
N/A
Lunch:
Chicken Tortilla Epozote Soup with jalapeño corn bread 10.50, Cubano Classico-a pressed and grilled Cuban Sandwich with chile spiced fries and Kool Slaw 9.25, Guava Chicken w/fried plantains, black beans & rice 10.50
Dinner:
Appetizers: Fried Green Tomatoes with smoked mozzarella, red onion, arugula, balsamic syrup & chili olive oil 8.25, Adobo BBQ Duck and Sweet potato Quesadilla w/chipotle chili salsa 9.95, Manana Caesar with jalapeño corn bread croutons 6.50, Ceviche Bar aka Nuevo-Latino Poke 13.00
Dinner: Pumpkin Seed Crusted Shrimp with vegetable enchilada, mole dulce, cucumber pico de gallo and mac nut kool slaw 24.00, Citrus-Jalapeño Glazed Salmon with black bean salsa & red rice 19.50, Chile Adobo Pulled Pork with fried plantains, black beans, and tomatillo salsa and flour tortillas 17.50
Sides: Fried Plantains 3.50, Black Beans and Red Rice 3.00
Desserts: Dulce de Leche Strawberry Trifle $6, Chocolate Dulce de Leche $6

Impressions:

This highly regarded Kahului eatery has a Latin American auto shop décor straight out of Little Havana. Their innovative menu was derived from a fusion of Caribbean and Pacific cuisines and has been designed to please an eclectic, upscale clientele. Live entertainment and special event theme parties are always a possibility, so check with them to see what's happening. On Wednesday through Saturday nights there's a late night menu from 9-10:30 PM. For a Miami-meets-Maui experience try the Mañana Garage!

Maui Dining

Central Valley

Marcos Grill & Deli
444 Hana Hwy
Kahului, HI 96733
808-877-4446
Web: None
Hours: B 7:30 AM-Noon, Su till 1 PM
         L /D 10:00 AM-10:00 PM
Cards: AE DC DIS JCB MC V
Dress: Resort Casual
Style: Amer/Ital $$

Menu Sampler:

Breakfast:
Classic Eggs Benedict $12.95, Breakfast Sandwiches $8.95, Chocolate Cinnamon French Toast $6.95, Banana Nut or Strawberry Pancakes $6.95
Omelets: Served with oven-roasted potatoes, choice of toast and jelly. Veggies w/ Swiss $7.95, Mexican $8.95, Mushroom $8.95, Portuguese Sausage $7.95
Lunch/Dinner:
Deli Sandwiches with toppings and a choice of pasta salad or garden salad: Smoked Turkey Breast $10.95. Homemade Italian Sausage $11.95, The Club Sandwich $13.95, Grilled Ono $12.95, Chicken Parmigiana $12.95, The Italian Sub $11.95, Triple BLT $9.95, Rib Eye Sandwich $13.95, Reuben $12.95
Appetizers: Gnocchi in a basil and herb tomato sauce $7.95; Sweet Red Pepper stuffed with eggplant, mushrooms, garlic, prosciutto and provolone cheese $8.95
Salads: Classic Caesar $7.95, Greek Salad $6.95/$10.95, Italian Salad $10.95
Pizzas: $10.95-$19.95, Clams and Garlic $14.45, Pepperoni $13.45
Entrées: Pasta Primavera with choice of fresh garlic and olive oil, Alfredo Sauce, or marinara sauce $15.95, Clams & Linguini $19.95, Grilled Salmon w/ bowtie pasta & sugar snap peas $19.95, Mushroom chicken in a light cream sauce over fettucine $20.95, Seafood Pasta $24.95, Ravioli w/pink sauce $16.95
Desserts: Tiramisu, White Chocolate Amore Gelato $5.50 and up

Impressions:

If you're on the way to the airport and want to start your trip back to the mainland with something better than an airline micro-meal, stop by Marco's Grill & Deli. This is upscale Italian dining with fine sauces and subtle flavors leading the way. Their pastas, salads, pizzas, and entrees come in bountiful portions so sharing might be a good idea. Just about everything they serve is made in house, so freshness and quality are assured.

Kihei

Marcos South Side Grill
1445 S Kihei Road
Kihei, HI 96753
808-874-4041
Web: None
Hours: B 7:30 AM-10:45 AM Su till 1 PM
        L /D 10:00 AM-10:00 PM
Cards: AE DC DIS JCB MC V
Dress: Resort Casual
Style: Amer/Ital $$

Menu Sampler:

Breakfast:
Classic Eggs Benedict $12.95, Roasted Peppers, Eggs, & Cheese Breakfast
Sandwich $7.95, Chocolate Cinnamon French Toast $6.95, Apple Cinnamon
Pancakes $6.95, Granola with strawberries & bananas $6.95
Omelets: Served with oven-roasted potatoes, choice of toast & jelly. Veggie
w/Swiss $7.95, Mexican $8.95, Mushroom $8.95, Portuguese Sausage $7.95
Lunch/Dinner:
Deli Sandwiches with toppings and a choice of Pasta Salad or Garden Salad:
Smoked Tavern Ham $9.95, Pastrami $10.95. The Italian Sub $11.95, Meatball
Parmigiano $12.95, Reuben $12.95, Rib Eye Steak Sandwich $14.95
Appetizers: Bruschetta with tomatoes, basil, garlic, olive oil and romano cheese
$5.95, Gnocchi w/basil herb $7.95, Buffalo Wings w/ Blue Cheese $8.95
Salads: Classic Caesar $7.95, Italian Salad $10.95, Blue Cheese Salad $9.95
Pizzas: $10.95-$19.95, Clams and Garlic $14.45, Pepperoni $13.45
Entrées: Vodka Rigatoni with prosciutto, romano and mozzarella $16.95,
Fettucine Alfredo $14.95, Clams & Linguini $19.95, Grilled Salmon with
bowtie pasta and sugar snap peas $20.95, Veal Parmigiano over fettucine
$22.95, Ravioli with Prosciutto in a pink sauce $16.95, Pasta Primavera $14.95
Desserts: Tiramisu, White Grand Marnier Seashell Gelato $5.50 and up

Impressions:

Marcos built their new Kihei location in a grand style reminiscent of a fine
Italian home. The quality menu items come in portions large enough to share.
That approach makes particular sense if you and your dining partner like to
sample courses. Don't worry about being difficult. The wait staff has heard that
request before. Marcos is a fine addition to the South Maui dining scene.

Maui Dining

Central Valley

Maui Bake Shop & Deli
2092 Vineyard Street
Wailuku, HI 96793
808-242-0064
Web: None
Hours: 6:00 AM-4:00 PM Mo-Fr
         7:00 AM-2:00 PM Sa
Cards: AE DC DIS JCB MC V
Dress: Casual
Style: Spec $

Menu Sampler:

Breakfast:
Apple, Cherry, Blueberry, or Peach Turnovers $2.50, Muffins-Oat Bran
w/raisins & nuts, Blueberry, Chocolate w/ chocolate chips, banana $1.20,
Cinnamon Rolls of brioche dough with custard, cinnamon, and raisins $1.99,
Hawaiian Strudel-apples with a touch of pineapple, raisins, and almonds $2.50
Coffees: Maui Blend Coffee, Small $.85, Large $.95, Hot Chocolate $1.75,
Espresso $1.75, Capuccino $1.95, Café au Lait $1.95, Latte $2.25, Mocha $2.50
Lunch:
Sandwiches $3.95 with the following choices: Turkey, Ham, Pastrami, Roast
Beef, Tuna, garnished with lettuce, tomatoes, onions, Dijon & Mayo, Cheese
$.25, and served on homemade breads such as baguette, whole wheat, white,
sourdough, rye. 12 Oz. Soup & ½ Sandwich $5.25, Soup & Sandwich $7.75, 12
Oz. Soup with bread $3.95, Whole Mini Quiche Lorraine or Spinach Quiche
$6.50, Caesar Salad with grilled chicken $6.95, Greek Salad $6.95, Lox &
Bagels $6.50, Pizza $2.75/slice, 9" Pies-peach, cherry, apple, mac-nut, custard
$8.95, pumpkin or pumpkin custard $11.95, mac nut or cream pie $12.95
Dinner:
N/A

Impressions:

Maui Bake Shop & Deli is a longtime favorite among the local business and
professional crowd. You can tell when coffee break time is approaching by the
large orders being boxed up for carryout. Although this is self-service style
dining, several tables are available along the front of the shop. When you enter
check the board for the daily specials. Besides what sounded good to the chef
that morning, they recently offered 10 different sandwiches and six types of
salads. This is a great little stop while touring the Wailuku historic sites.

Maui Dining

Central Valley

Maui Culinary Academy
Maui Community College
310 Kaahumanu Ave
Kahului, HI 96732
808-984-3280
Web: None
Hours: BL Cafeteria 7 AM-5 PM Mo-Th,
        BL Cafeteria 7 AM-2:30 PM Fr
        L The Class Act WeFr
Cards: MC V
Dress: Casual
Style: Cont/Intl L $$, D-$$$$

Menu Sampler:

Breakfast/Lunch:
Cafeteria style service arranged in stations.
Farm To Table- features quality sandwiches and salads. Caesar Salad $5.00, Chinese Chicken Salad $6.00, Turkey Club with side salad or fruit $5.50
World Plate $6.50, may be ordered a la carte- entrée $3.00, starch $1.50, vegetable $1.50, soup $1.50-$3.00, **Pizza:** $5.50, Veggie Wrap $5.75
Raw Fish Camp: Selection of hand rolled sushi $4.00 with edamame and condiments, **Campus Café:** Burgers & Sandwiches-Cheese Steak Sandwich w/rice or salad $4.75, **Patisserie:** Selection of Cookies & Muffins $1.00-$1.50
Lunch:
The Class Act: Complete **Lunch** for $20 + gratuity. Reservations will be taken 7 days in advance, Monday-Friday 8:00 AM-4:30 PM. Example: French Lunch-Seafood Sausage with Tomato Beurre Blanc, Endive Salad with Pate Maison and Mustard Vinaigrette, choice of Tournedos au Poivre with Brie and Cabernet Demi-Glace or Fish Baked En Papillotte, Frozen Grand Marnier Soufflé.
Dinners are offered two times a semester with a multi-course prix-fixe gourmet dinner with entertainment for $65.00. These are popular, so plan ahead!

Impressions:

When young Maui residents choose a career in the restaurant industry their first stop is often the culinary arts department at the local community college. There overlooking the harbor in Kahului the University of Hawaii has developed a first rate program for these aspiring young chefs. The centerpieces of this effort are the Pa'ina Food Court and The Class Act restaurant in the new Pa'ina building. On the main floor options include display stations with interesting self-service selections, while the more discriminating will find a gourmet lunch upstairs.

Maui Dining

Upcountry

Moana Bakery & Café
71 Baldwin Ave
Paia, HI 96779
808-579-9999
www.moanacafe.com
Hours: B 8:00 AM-11:00 AM
          L 11:00 AM-3:00 PM
          D 3:00 PM-9:00 PM
Cards: MC V
Dress: Resort Casual
Style: Cont/Isl $$$

Menu Sampler:

Breakfast:
Ham & Cheese Omelet served with tomato salsa, potatoes, and toast $8.95,
North Shore Saimin with fresh udon noodles & fish cake $6.95, Crab Cake or
Mahi Mahi Benedict with roasted potatoes and fresh hollandaise sauce $12.95
Lunch:
Thai Chicken Salad served in a crispy noodle basket $9.95, Roast Lamb and
Hummus wrapped in a sun dried tomato tortilla with mixed greens and potato
salad $9.95, Grilled Mahi Mahi Sandwich with Asian slaw and onion rings on
French flat bread with potato salad and mixed greens $9.95, Soup $5.95
Dinner:
Crispy Veggie Spring Roll with bean thread noodles, shiitake mushrooms,
carrots, and fresh herbs served with sweet chili dipping sauce and macadamia
nuts $8.95, Chili Seared Ahi served rare with Molokai sweet potatoes, taro
leaves and mango salsa $21.95, Rack of Lamb Roasted with garlic and
rosemary, deglazed with port wine and finished with a demi-glace $28.95,
Medallions of Filet Mignon w/tarragon beurre $24.95, Island Fish Specials
$23.95, Crab Cakes w/pineapple remoulade, guava puree, Kula greens $12.95

Impressions:

Paia is home to an interesting collection of offbeat shops and people. There in a
quaint Baldwin Avenue storefront you'll find a gem of a restaurant. This chef-
owned European style bistro serves consistently great food. Every morning the
kitchen comes up with interesting specials so be sure to ask. In keeping with
their name, there's a display case in front featuring a sinful variety of house
baked gourmet tarts, rolls, and desserts. The sticky buns are the best on the
island. Get some to go for breakfast on the run when taking the drive to Hana.

Lahaina

Moose McGillycuddy's
844 Front Street
Lahaina, HI 96761
808-667-7758
Web: None
Hours: B 7:30 AM – 11:00 AM
          L 11:00 AM – 4:00 PM
          D 4:00 PM – 10:00 PM
Cards: AE MC V
Style: Amer $$

Menu Sampler:

Breakfast:
7:30-8:30 AM—Early Bird Special $1.99, Eggs Benedict $6.95, Famous
Omelettes-4 eggs, country potatoes & toast $6.95, Beggar's Banquet-3 eggs,
potatoes & toast $4.25, Moose Cakes-buttermilk, macadamia or banana $3.95-
$5.45, Super Bloody Mary's-22 oz. with 2 ½ oz vodka $3.75
Lunch:
Sandwiches: All served w/crispy fries. Fresh Fish Sandwich of char-broiled ahi
on a whole wheat bun $7.25, French Dip w/au jus $6.95, Bird of Paradise-char-
broiled teriyaki chicken breast topped w/tavern ham & melted Swiss $7.25
Gourmet Burgers: ½ # certified Angus beef w/toppings & fries. Basic Burger
$5.95, w/cheese $6.25, w/bacon & cheddar $6.95, w/teriyaki & pineapple $6.45
Specialties: Fish & Chips $8.95, BBQ Chicken (1/2) $13.95, Fish Tacos $8.95
Dinner:
Pupus: Chicken Quesadilla $5.95, Combo Pupu Platter (2-4 people) $11.95
Salads: Fajita Salad $9.95, Chicken Caesar $7.95, Garden Salad $4.50
Entrées: All served with fresh steamed veggies. Mahi Mahi Macadamia $9.95,
Roast Beef & Mashed Potatoes $8.95, Fresh Teriyaki Ahi char-broiled $10.95,
Koko Shrimp-coconut beer battered shrimp $12.95, Lasagna $9.95

Impressions:

Moose's is the kind of place you'd picture on a college campus. It's loud, it's
funky, and it's happening. This place isn't known for haute cuisine, but the fare
is solid and, more importantly, affordable. Here you'll find a lengthy menu that
offers something for the entire family. The daily happy hour runs from 3 to 6
when locals and visitors alike gather around the bar to enjoy some of the lowest
priced adult beverages in Lahaina. Then afterwards, the late night revelry crowd
fills the place as the scene changes over to live music and misbehavior!!

Wailea

Mulligan's On The Blue
100 Kaukahi Street
Wailea, HI 96753
808-874-1131
www.mulligansontheblue.com
Hours: BLD 8:00 AM-9:00 PM
           D Specials 5:00 PM-9:00 PM
Cards: AE DC JCB MC V
Dress: Casual
Style: Irish $$

Menu Sampler:

Breakfast:
All hot breakfasts include your choice of home fries or steamed rice and toast, croissant or Irish muffin. Blue Course Breakfast-three eggs any style, your choice of bacon, Irish or Portuguese sausage $8, Steak & Eggs-8 oz. Sirloin steak with two eggs any style $11, Smoked Salmon Bagel with cream cheese and capers $7, Irish Benedict w/corned beef $9, Irish Breakfast-2 eggs, Irish sausage, bacon, grilled tomato, baked beans $10, Loco Moco $9

Lunch/Dinner:
All sandwiches come with Irish chips (French fries) and cole slaw. Fresh Fish Sandwich with tartar sauce, lettuce & tomato on a toasted Kaiser roll $11, Sirloin Steak Sandwich-8 oz. Sirloin on garlic toast with sautéed mushrooms $10, Mulligan Burger with choice of cheese, lettuce, tomato & sliced onion $9, Fish & Chips with Harp battered mahi mahi with Irish chips and homemade tartar sauce $11, Traditional Shepherd's Pie of fresh ground beef & vegetables simmered in a savory sauce, topped with creamy mashed potatoes and baked $12, Chicken Curry of tender chicken and vegetables in a coconut curry sauce served with rice $11, Gaelic Steak with Irish Whiskey Cream Sauce $14

Dinner Specials:
Chef's creation of daily dinner specials and catch of the day

Impressions:

Mulligan's is another of Maui's special clubhouse restaurants. This time the menu isn't built around fusion cuisine. Instead the offerings come straight from the Emerald Isle. You can start the day off with an Irish breakfast or finish it with shepherd's pie. Even some of the waitresses have been imported from Ireland! Live entertainment is a regular event. This is a great place to have a cold one, even if you're not a golfer. Do happy hour for two-for-one pupus.

Northwest

Nachos Grande
3350 Lower Honoapiilani Rd
Honokowai, HI 96761
808-662-0890
Web: None
Hours: B 7:00 AM–11:00 AM
         L/D 11:00 AM-11:00 PM
Cards: None
Dress: Casual
Style: Mex $

Menu Sampler:

Breakfast:
Two Eggs Huevos Rancheros w/beans, potatoes, salsa $5.99, Ham & Cheese Omelet w/beans, potatoes, toast, beverage $5.99, 3 pancakes $2.49

Lunch/Dinner:
Nachos with Beef, Pork or Chicken and cheese, beans, sour cream, guacamole, tomato and olives $6.95, Taco Plate includes two tacos of hard or soft shell tortilla, with beef, pork or chicken, lettuce, tomato and cheese with Spanish rice and beans $6.25, Large Soft Shell Fish Taco filled with beans, fresh island fish, sour cream, lettuce, cucumber, tomato and cheese served with chips $6.99, Chicken Burritos filled with Spanish rice, beans, lettuce, tomato and sour cream $6.99, Chimichanga with Beef $6.99, Tostada Salad in a crisp tortilla shell with beans, rice, lettuce, guacamole, sour cream, tomato, olives, black beans and cheese $5.99, Island Fish & Chips with French fries $7.99
Children's menu: Bean & Cheese Burrito $3.25, Bean Taco w/rice $2.75
Side Orders: Chips and Salsa $2.59, Guacamole and Chips $2.99, Guacamole $.75, Sour Cream $.75, Spanish Rice $1.00, Beans $1.00, Fries $1.50

Impressions:

There's an interesting collection of eateries at the Honokowai Marketplace. Out in the parking lot you'll see a building where Nacho's Grande shares space with a small sushi restaurant and a bar featuring a large selection of premium agave tequilas. All manage to co-exist here and stay open until the wee hours, much to the delight of the West Maui party crowd. It's casual, cozy, and crazy, but it works! This Mexican self-serve eatery offers delicious food in very adequate portions. Everything is made to order, so find a seat at the bar and enjoy a Margarita while waiting for your meal. Service in this conveniently located establishment is available from 11 AM until 12 Midnight.

Maui Dining

Wailea

Nick's Fishmarket Maui

The Fairmont Kea Lani Resort
4100 Wailea Nui
Wailea, HI 96753
808-879-7224
www.tri-star-restaurants.com
Hours:　D 5:30 PM-10:00 PM
Cards:　AE DC DIS JCB MC V
Dress:　Evening Aloha
Style:　Sea $$$$

Menu Sampler:

Breakfast/Lunch:
N/A
Dinner:
Appetizers: Alaskan Crab Cakes served with spicy avocado remoulade sauce, pea sprout & lemon $13.95, "Firecracker" Salmon Roll with green papaya salad & sweet & sour chili vinaigrette $13.95, "Original" Tiger Eye Sushi tempura style with pear tomato salad & sake mustard sauce $14.95
Soup: Chef's Creation of the Evening $7.95
Salads: Greek Maui Wowie w/chopped onions, tomatoes, avocado, shredded romaine, feta & bay shrimp $11.95, "Just Sliced" Heirloom Tomatoes w/fig balsamic, extra virgin olive oil & Hawaiian sea salt $10.95, Ahi Nicoise, blackened ahi over greens, olives, haricot vert & red wine vinaigrette $13.95
Entrées: Potato "Scaled" Mahi Mahi with truffle potatoes, cabernet-pepper sauce & white truffle oil $29.95, Opakapaka-Hawaiian pink snapper sautéed with rock shrimp, lemon, butter & capers $34.95, Live Kona lobster steamed & prepared tableside $29.95/#, Grilled Beef Filet with potato terrine, shallot confit & Port Sauce $30.95, Mongolian Style Rack of Lamb w/sweet potatoes $41.95 A keiki menu is available.

Impressions:

Have you ever gotten the feeling that service levels on Maui are a little too laid back? Forget that at Nick's Fishmarket. From the second you walk in it's obvious that your every need will be anticipated. In fact, sometimes you might wonder how many people really are waiting on you. Then the fabulous food arrives. Naturally Nick's only uses the finest ingredients, but look past the obvious to the depth of preparation. The layers of flavor just keep coming at you. Even the steak dishes are taken an extra step. Reservations are a must.

Maui Dining

Lahaina

pacific 'O
505 Front Street
Lahaina, HI 96761
808-667-4341
www.pacificomaui.com
Hours: L 11:00 AM-4:00 PM
            D 5:30 PM-10:00 PM
Cards: AE DC DIS MC V
Dress: Resort Casual
Style: Pac-Rim $$$

Menu Sampler:

Breakfast:
N/A
Lunch:
Appetizers: Chicken Gyoza-crispy dumplings w/peanut sauce & kim chee $9
Salads/Entrees: O'o Caesar Salad w/Asian Caesar dressing $6.50, Macaroni & Cheese—sautéed lemongrass crusted prawns, shiitake mushrooms & asparagus w/Gemelli pasta in a creamy white cheddar sauce & tomato mirin accent $14.50
Dinner:
Appetizers: Prawn and Basil Won Tons served with a spicy sweet and sour sauce and Hawaiian salsa $12, Blackened Ahi Tower w/wasabi aioli $12
Salads: Roasted Maui Onion and Big Island Puna Goat Cheese Salad with a smoked tomato dressing $9.5, Shogun Caesar w/tempura anchovies, Enoki mushrooms, parmesan sesame tuiles, miso samurai dressing $9
Entrées: Painted Fish—fresh fish painted with Indonesian soy, grilled and served w/grilled pineapple & red pepper salsa w/ginger sweet and sour sauce $26, Thai Dye Duck—braised duck colored in spices served with Thai rice noodles & Thai curry coconut sauce $25, Pink Peppered Beef-grilled filet mignon topped w/gorgonzola cheese & sautéed spinach, greens & glaze $29
Desserts: Banana Pineapple Lumpia $8.50, Macadamia Nut Ice Cream $7

Impressions:

pacific 'O can be found ocean side at 505 Front Street in Lahaina. This upscale beachfront bistro is operated by highly regarded chef/owner James McDonald. Here you'll find award-winning Pac-Rim cuisine with a heavy Asian spin. Get ready to enjoy some truly intriguing taste combinations. For those with lighter appetites, lunch presents an affordable opportunity to experience this wonderful cooking style. The fine wine list is available by the bottle or the glass.

Maui Dining

Wailea

Palm Court
Renaissance Wailea Beach Resort
3550 Wailea Alanui
Wailea, HI 96753
808-879-4900
www.renaissancehotels.com
Hours: B 6:00 AM-11:00 AM
           D 5:30 PM-9:30 PM
Cards: AE DC DIS JCB MC V
Dress: Resort Casual
Style: Med $$$$

Menu Sampler:

Breakfast:
Full Buffet: $19.00/adults, $9.50/children, Continental Buffet $15.00, Palm Court Benedict with crab cakes $13.00, Three Egg Omelette $11.50

Lunch:
N/A

Dinner:
Buffets: Wednesday & Saturday-Oriental $32, Tuesday & Friday-Seafood $32, Sunday-Mediterranean $32, Monday & Thursday -Pacific Rim $32
Starters: Maui Onion Soup Gratinee $6, Crispy Calamari with caper aioli $10, Ohana Pupu Sampler with ginger duck potstickers, crisp calamari and rock shrimp with chipotle aioli, and crab Rangoon on a sugar cane stick $18.00
Salads and Sandwiches: Baby Greens with gorgonzola, apples, raisins and walnuts with raspberry vinaigrette $8, Island Mahi Mahi Sandwich with lemon-dill aioli and French fries $12, Classic Caesar Salad $6.00/$10.00
Pizza: Create Your Own Pizza from a variety of toppings, Small $13, Large $17 with choice of 3 toppings, Wild Mushroom & Grilled Vegetable Pizza $16.00
Entrées: Lobster Ravioli with tarragon cream $26.00, Linguine with prawns and fresh basil cream $28.00, Roasted Rack of Lamb with port wine sauce $30.00, Ginger-Orange Chicken with cilantro $21.00, Island Style Bouillabaisse $30.00

Impressions:

Palm Court is the Renaissance's casual yet upscale main dining room. There in an airy courtyard you'll find better than usual buffets offered along with an appealing a la carte menu. In addition to their more elaborate meal service, diners can choose from affordable family-oriented items like sandwiches and pizza. The crossover is done quite nicely without the appearance of afterthought.

Maui Dining

Lahaina

Penne Pasta Café
180 Dickenson
Lahaina, HI 96761
808-661-6633
www.mauitacos.com
Hours: L/D 11:00 AM-9:30 PM Mo-Th
   L/D 11:00 AM-10:00 PM Fr
   D 5:00 PM-10:00 PM Sa, 5:00 PM-9:00 PM Su
Cards: AE DIS MC V
Dress: Casual
Style: Ital $

Menu Sampler:

Breakfast:
N/A
Lunch/Dinner:
Pastas: Linguine Pesto $6.95, Penne Puttanesca-Pomodoro sauce with olives, capers, hot peppers, anchovies & garlic $7.95, Bolognese Fettuccine with slow braised beef with red wine, garlic, and tomato and fettucine $7.95, Linguine Clam Sauce $9.95, Chicken Picatta with Linguini $8.95
Flatbreads: With olives, capers, basil, oregano & roasted peppers $5.95
Salads & Primi's: Mixed Greens, tomatoes & feta $5.95, Broccoli with olive oil & garlic $4.95, Nicoise of island tuna confit, olives, peppers, potatoes, tomatoes, capers & greens with a red onion Dijon vinaigrette $9.95
Sandwiches: All are served with house made potato salad. Mozzarella, tomato, basil & greens $5.95, Roast Chicken Salad Sandwich with tomatoes, greens & Dijon $6.95, Salami and Provolone with Dijon $6.95, Island Tuna $8.95
Dessert: Panna Cotta or Chocolate Pot de crème $3.95, Tiramisu $5.95

Impressions:

While enjoying Front Street is great fun, mealtime can be a challenge for those on a budget. Sure, there are always the fast food outlets, but let's get real, you didn't come to Maui to eat McBurgers! Mark Ellman of Maui Taco fame saw this dilemma and met it by bringing innovative yet affordable dining to Lahaina. Mark starts with fresh ingredients and zesty flavors in the sauces that are the key to his pastas. He then goes on to feature elaborate salads and sandwiches as well as nightly specials like Osso Buco. You order at the counter and are served at your table in this casual establishment. Beer and wine are also available. As an added plus, there's inexpensive parking in the lot behind the building.

Maui Dining

Kihei

Pita Paradise
Kihei Kalama Village
1913 S Kihei Rd
Kihei, HI 96753
808-875-7679
Web: None
Hours: L/D 11:00 AM-9:30 PM XSu
         D 5:00 PM-9:30 PM XSu
Cards: MC V
Dress: Casual
Style: Grk $$

Menu Sampler:

Breakfast:
N/A
Lunch:
Appetizers: Ziziki Bread $3.95, Potato Skins $5.95, Grilled Pita $2.95
Salads: Greek Salad $6.25, Caesar Salad $5.95, Fresh Island Catch $11.95
Entrées: Lamb Gyro Pita served with sauteed new potatoes $8.95, Caesar Salad
Pita $6.95, Lamb, Chicken, or Steak Kabob Pita served with mixed grilled
veggies and sautéed new potatoes $12.95, Grilled Veggie Delight Pita $6.95
Dinner:
Pupus: Hummus and Grilled Pita $5.95, Calamari pan seared with lemon, garlic
and white wine $7.95, Ziziki Bread grilled with cheeses and herbs $3.95
Pitas: All served with choice of roasted potatoes or rice pilaf. Mediterranean
Chicken $8.95, Steak n' Kula Onion $10.95, Fresh Catch Pita $12.95
Pastas: Fresh Fish of the Day, Calamari, and Jumbo Prawns pan seared with
fresh veggies and a light seafood broth $18.95, Grilled Chicken Pasta $13.95
Kabobs: Served with grilled veggies, potatoes or rice pilaf and grilled pita.
Chicken Kabobs $13.95, Fresh Fish Kabobs $15.95, Lamb Kabobs $13.95
Dessert: Baklava Ice Cream Cake $5.95

Impressions:

Pita Paradise is a casual dining spot offering savory tastes of the Aegean. The
outside deck seating provides a pleasant anytime atmosphere with plants all
around and tiny lights in the landscaping. The change of pace menu highlights
Mediterranean food with a heavy Greek orientation. Lunch is self-serve, while a
wait staff is provided at dinner. Beer and wine are available. Free parking is
abundant in the surrounding Kalama Village lot.

Upcountry

Polli's
1202 Makawao Ave
Makawao, HI 96768
808-572-7808
Web: None
Hours: B 8:00 AM-11:00 AM
         L 11:00 AM-5:00 PM
         D 5:00 PM-10:00 PM
Cards: AE DIS MC V
Dress: Casual
Style: Mex $

Menu Sampler:

Breakfast:
Huevos Rancheros, French Toast, Banana Pancakes, Paniolo Breakfast, Loco Moco, Omelettes, and Eggs Benedict and Mahi Benedict-all under $6.95
Lunch:
Appetizers: Nachos-corn and flour tortilla chips topped with cheddar and jack cheese $3.95/$5.95, Buffalo or BBQ Wings $5.25/$8.25, Mexican Pizza $6.75
Entrées: Taco Salad $7.25, Taco Plate $7.95, Chimichanga $7.75, Shrimp Fajitas for Two $15.95, Beef Burrito $7.95, Seafood Enchilada Plate $8.75
Dinner:
Appetizers: Makawowie Nachos with cheddar/jack cheese, guacamole, sour cream, salsa and olives $6.75/$8.25 with chicken, pork, beef or veggie taco mix
Entrées: Fiesta Tostada $10.50, Fish Taco Plate with rice, beans and guacamole $8.95, Seafood Burrito stuffed with sautéed shrimp and fish, beans, cheddar/jack cheese, rice, onions and jalapenos, smothered in creamy jack cheese sauce with side toppings $10.95, Carnitas Plate with tender roasted pork, chili verde sauce, served with rice, beans, guacamole and tortillas $9.25, Chile Queso $7.95, Baby Back Ribs Dinner $9.95, $13.50, $17.50, Barbecued Chicken Dinner $9.25
Desserts: Bunuelos topped with Ice Cream $4.50

Impressions:

At the junction of Baldwin and Makawao Avenues you'll find a funky little eatery with a banner above the door announcing, "If you don't eat here we'll both starve". That just might be true, so if you're cruising Upcountry Maui stop by Polli's for large servings of flavorful Mexican food served by a personable wait staff. While there check out the awesome surfing pictures on the walls. In the morning Haleakala downhill bike tours pile in here, so plan breakfast late.

Maui Dining

Wailea

Prince Court
Maui Prince Hotel
Makena, HI 96753
808-875-5888
www.mauiprincehotel.com
Hours: SuBru 9:00 AM-1:00 PM
         D 6:00 PM-9:00 PM
Cards: AE DC DIS JCB MC V
Dress: Evening Aloha
Style: Isl/Japan $$$$
       Ent Card

Menu Sampler:

Breakfast:
Sunday Champagne Brunch: $39/adults, $25/children (6-12, under 6 free).
Lunch:
N/A
Dinner:
Appetizers: Lobster and Salmon Mousse Ravioli, roasted Maui onion butter sauce, fresh herbs, spring mushrooms 9.00, Tiger Shrimp Martini 9.00
Soups and Salads: Spring Vegetable Minestrone Soup with rock shrimp, white beans, Italian herbs, asiago cheese crisp 7.50, Kamuela Tomato Salad with mozzarella cheese, shaved Maui onion, white truffle oil, balsamic vinegar 9.00
Entrées: Char Broiled Rack of Lamb with minted Maui onion jelly, julienne vegetables, Yukon Gold potato mash 30.00, Pacific Rim Seafood Mixed Grill-tiger shrimp, fresh catch, lobster, scallops, Asian herb butter, grilled vegetables, jasmine rice 29.00, Chicken Breast with Wild Mushroom Risotto with tomato vinaigrette 22.00, Tenderloin of Beef and Half Stuffed Lobster-char-broiled steak, port wine sauce, baked lobster stuffed with crabmeat, seasonal vegetables, Yukon Gold potato mash 32.00, Farfalle Pasta with Roasted Mushrooms 21.00
Friday Night Seafood & Prime Rib Buffet: $40/adults, $25/children

Impressions:

If you are looking for a great Sunday Brunch, drive down to Makena and visit the award-winning Prince Court. This weekly event isn't cheap, but it attracts lots of locals so you know it's got to be something special. But the good times don't stop there. This fine dining room makes things happen seven nights a week. The menu offers specialties like moi and venison that are generally hard to find. We particularly like the sophisticated preparations. Make reservations!

Northwest

Roy's Kahana Bar & Grill

Kahana Gateway Shopping Center
4405 Honoapiilani Hwy
Kahana, HI 96761
808-669-6999
www.roysrestaurant.com
Hours: D 5:30 PM-10:00 PM
Cards: AE DC JCB MC V
Dress: Resort Casual
Style: Haw-Reg/Pac-Rim $$$

Menu Sampler:

Breakfast/Lunch:
N/A
Dinner:
Appetizers: Hawaii Kai Style Crispy Crab Cakes with a spicy sesame butter sauce $11.5, Seared Tiger Shrimp on a Stick with spicy wasabi cocktail sauce & kim chee $8.5, Vegetable Parmesan Risotto, mushrooms & edamame $8.5
Salads: Mongolian Grilled Chicken Breast Salad with candied pecans & sesame soy vinaigrette $8.5, Hau'ula Tomato and Warm Onion Salad with blue cheese, spinach & balsamic pancetta vinaigrette $8.5, Vine Ripened Tomato Carpaccio with fried capers, red onions, goat cheese herb olive oil $7.5
Entrées: Kiawe Grilled Rack of Lamb with scallion infused potatoes, minted berry cabernet sauce $29.5, Teriyaki Seared Breast of Duck with sugar snap peas, citrus chile natural, crispy gyoza & ponzu salad $22.5, Sweet Soy Grilled Hawaiian King Moi with steamed rice, stir-fry veggies, sweet soy ginger sauce $30.5, Lemongrass Mahi Mahi with fried rice, grilled Wailua asparagus spears, garlic wasabi soy butter $28.5, Basil Flashed Black Tiger Shrimp with feta mashed potatoes, island pesto, balsamic drizzle $24.5, "Return of the Killer" Japanese Misoyaki Butterfish with sizzled soy vinaigrette $13.5/$27
Desserts: Fabulous Dessert Tray!

Impressions:

We like all the Roy's locations, but this is our favorite on the island of Maui. It's hard to say why, but the mood and feel just seem closer to that of his Hawaii Kai flagship restaurant. As expected, the menu features fresh fish, game, and local produce fused with island herbs and exotic spices in taste-tingling creations. The atmosphere is casual yet upscale with an open display kitchen and the hustle and bustle of the bright young servers who just want to see you have a good time.

Kihei

Roy's Kihei Bar & Grill
Piilani Village Shopping Center
300 Piikea Ave
Kihei, HI 96753
808-891-1120
www.roysrestaurant.com
Hours: D 5:30 PM-10:00 PM
Cards: AE DC JCB MC V
Dress: Resort Casual
Style: Haw-Reg/Pac-Rim $$$

Menu Sampler:

Breakfast/Lunch:
N/A
Dinner:
Ohana Appetizers: Plum Glazed Duck Breast with Chinese Black Bean Dragon Syrup $10.50/$22.50, Crispy Crab Cakes with spicy sesame sauce $11.50
Fresh Salads: Mongolian Grilled Chicken Breast Salad with candied pecans & sesame soy vinaigrette $8.50, Poached D'Anjou Pear Salad with walnuts, bleu cheese, red wine lemongrass vinaigrette $8.50, "Nalo Farms" Mixed Green Salad with Dean Okimoto's creamy herb garlic dressing $5.95
Entrées: Hibachi Teriyaki Salmon, spun vegetable salad, citrus ponzu sauce $10.50/$25.50, Roy's Original Blackened Island Ahi with spicy soy mustard butter $27.50, Kiawe Grilled Filet mignon, fingerling potatoes, Enoki mushrooms, Roy's Desolation Reduction $29.50, Roy's Classic Roasted Macadamia Nut Crusted Lehi with Kona Maine lobster sauce $28.50, Jade Pesto Steamed Hawaiian White Fish with sizzling peanut oil, ginger, cilantro, soy $28.50, Misoyaki Pork Pot Roast with New Fashioned pineapple-apple sauce $17.50, Misoyaki Butterfish with sizzling soy vinaigrette $13.50/$27.50
Desserts: Fantastic Tray!

Impressions:

This is one of the newer additions to Roy Yamaguchi's Hawaiian restaurant empire. Here in South Maui, Roy continues to create award-winning dishes by combining classic techniques and fresh island ingredients with Asian flavors. The resulting fusion cuisine provides excitement "In da mout". To accompany these exotic tastes, Roy now produces his own sake. Look for the Y Sake Tasting Menu of five courses paired with four glasses of Roy's Y Sakes at a cost of $55.00. Reservations are highly recommended at all of Roy's fine restaurants.

Northwest

Roy's Nicolina
Kahana Gateway Shopping Center
4405 Honoapiilani Hwy
Kahana, HI 96761
808-669-5000
www.roysrestaurant.com
Hours: D 5:30 PM-10:00 PM
Cards: AE DC JCB MC V
Dress: Resort Casual
Style: Haw-Reg/Pac-Rim $$$

Menu Sampler:

Breakfast/Lunch:
N/A
Dinner:
Appetizers: Furikake Crusted Calamari-stacked in a butter leaf cup with garlic chili aioli $9.5, Asian Udon Noodle Primavera, lemon kabayaki glaze $7.5/14.5, Roy's Original Blackened Ahi-spicy soy mustard butter $13.5/27
Salads: Roy's "New Wave" Caesar Salad w/Nalo tomatoes, Parmesan wafer & croutons $8.5, Roy's Butter Lettuce Salad, buttermilk blue cheese dressing $8.5
Entrées: Garlic Honey Mustard Beef Short Ribs-scalloped potatoes, poi & lomi tomatoes $24.5, The Original Yama's Mama's Meatloaf-crispy onion rings & mushroom pan gravy $8.5/17, Macadamia Nut Crusted White Fish with Kona lobster butter sauce $29.5, Balsamic Herb Grilled Chicken Breast-sautéed vegetables & sweet onion tomato napoletana $18.5, Sweet Soy Grilled Hawaiian King Moi-steamed rice, stir-fry veggies, sweet soy ginger sauce $30.5, Herb Grilled Filet Mignon-scalloped potatoes, baby carrots, peppercorn kukui nut sauce $30.5, Lemongrass Mahi Mahi, fried rice, grilled asparagus $28.5
Desserts: Tray of Fabulous, Wicked Things

Impressions:

When you pull into the Kahana Gateway Shopping Center you'll notice that there are not one but two Roy's locations to choose from. What is the difference between them? Not a whole lot. In fact, people who don't work there might think that they are virtually identical. All of Roy's fine restaurants are award winners and have loyal local and visitor followings. The food is always an exciting blend of fresh island ingredients and Pacific Rim influences. Check out the Nightly Specials Sheet for truly innovative expressions by the house chef. Make it a point to have at least one dinner at Roy's during your visit to Hawaii.

Maui Dining

Central Valley

Ruby's Diner
Queen Kaahumanu Center
Kahului, HI 96732
808-248-7829
www.rubys.com
Hours: B 7:00 AM-11:30 AM
        L/D 11:30 AM-9:00 PM Su-Th
        L/D 11:00 AM-10:00 PM FrSa
Cards: AE DC DIS JCB MC V
Dress: Casual
Style: Amer $

Menu Sampler:

Breakfast:
Eggs Benedict with a rich Hollandaise Sauce and RubySpuds $9.29, Huevos Rancheros $8.89, Cinnamon Roll French Toast $7.39, Cinnamon Apple Pancakes $6.29, Denver Omelet with RubySpuds and toast $8.79

Lunch/Dinner:
Starters: Chicken Fingers with a trio of dipping sauces $7.99, Frings, a combination of fries and RubyRings (onion rings) $5.39, Quesadilla $7.59
RubyBurgers: with a choice of 100% USDA Choice Beef, Turkey, or Veggie patty or a grilled chicken breast on a traditional or whole wheat RubyBun with tomato, lettuce and RubySauce. For $1.99 add a half order of fries (five kinds), or a half order onion rings $2.99, RubyBurger $7.09, Cheeseburger $7.69
Favorites: Chicken Tacos filled with grilled chicken breast, vegetarian black beans, lettuce, salsa, cheese, green onion, taco sauce, guacamole, sour cream $8.99, Alaskan Halibut Fish & Chips with French fries, cole slaw and tartar sauce $10.69, BBQ Ranch Chicken Salad with Zesty Cilantro Dressing $8.69, Ruby's Chili $3.99/$4.99, Ruby's Clam Chowder $3.99/$4.99, Shrimp & Chips w/fries & slaw, $9.39, Fresh Baked Turkey Pot Pie served w/seasonal fruit $7.49
Fountain Favorites: Deluxe Shakes & Malts $4.29, Original Shakes & Malts $3.99, Jumbo Flavored Cokes $2.39, Barq's Root Beer or Coke Float $3.29

Impressions:

We can all remember that favorite hamburger stand or malt shop back in our hometown, and Ruby's caters to the best of those collective memories. The retro décor was designed to make time travel possible if for only a short time. While the prices aren't cheap for this style of dining, the food is high in quality and comes in ample portions. This a great stop to make while touring the island.

Kaanapali

Rusty Harpoon
Whaler's Village
Kaanapali, HI 96761
808-661-3123
www.rustyharpoon.com
Hours: B 8:00 AM-11:00 AM
         L 11:00 AM-5:00 PM
         D 5:00 PM-10:00 PM
         Bistro 10:00 PM-2:00 AM
Cards: MC V
Dress: Resort Casual
Style: Ec/Sea/Stk $$$
         Ent Card

Menu Sampler:

Breakfast:
Hawaiian Breakfast Casserole with fresh fruit $9.95, Smoked Salmon Benedict $11.95, Ultimate Omelet with potatoes and toast $10.95, Harpoon Mary $6.95, Cappuccino $3.95, Lattes $4.25, Espresso $2.75, Glass of Champagne $5.25
Lunch:
Lunch Specials: Bouya-ham, chicken, shrimp, clams and spicy sausage simmered in a Louisiana style red sauce, rice $14.95, Taco Salad $12.95, Mushrooms Galore Burger $9.95, Chicken Caesar Roll-up $11.95, Reuben on Grilled Rye, salad $10.95, Spicy Peanut Chicken Salad $13.95
Dinner:
Appetizers: Jumbo Coconut Shrimp with ginger mango cream sauce & tropical salsa $10.95, Crispy Maui style onion rings with hoisin BBQ sauce $8.95
Soups: Clam Chowder with bacon bits $3.95, served in a bread bowl $6.95
Specialties: Deep Fried Shrimp with Panko flakes $25.95, Seafood Curry over rice pilaf $21.95, Fresh Catch Harpoon Style-baked, broiled or sauteed, served on a bed of caramelized Maui onion with an Asian cream sauce $26.95, Grilled Beef Tenderloin w/barbecued Maui onions, potato or tropical rice pilaf $27.95, Maui Onion Stuffed Salmon Roulade, sweet chili beurre blanc $29.95
Desserts: Crème Brulee with seasonal berries $9.95, Root Beer Float $6.95

Impressions:

This isn't one of those sports bars that serves food just to keep a liquor license. Yes, you can join the lively crowd around the bar watching a football game, but afterwards sit down at a table and experience some of the wonderful offerings from the kitchen. The Entertainment Card makes this an enticing selection.

Maui Dining

Lahaina

Ruth's Chris
900 Front Street
Lahaina, HI 96761
808-661-8815
www.ruthschris.com
Hours: D 5:00 PM-10:00PM
Cards: AE DC JCB MC V
Dress: Resort Casual
Style: Stk $$$$

Menu Sampler:

Breakfast/Lunch:
N/A
Dinner:
Appetizers: Mushrooms Stuffed With Crabmeat $9.50, Barbecued Shrimp with white wine, butter, garlic and spices $9.95, Onion Soup Au Gratin $5.25, French Fried Maui Onion Rings $4.75, Seared Ahi Tuna $Market Price
Salads: Caesar $6.25, Combination $4.95, Asparagus & Hearts of Palm $6.95
Entrées: All steaks are USDA Prime, custom-aged and cut extra thick. Filet $27.50, Petite Filet $22.95, Rib Eye $26.95, T-Bone $33.25, Pork Chops $21.50, Veal Chop $29.25, Lamb Chops $30.50, Broiled Marinated Chicken $19.25
Side Orders: Seven kinds of potatoes are featured as is rice and a variety of vegetables. Au Gratin Potatoes $5.25, Shoestring Potatoes $4.75, Sautéed Mushrooms $5.25, Creamed Fresh Spinach $5.00, Broccoli Au Gratin $5.25
Desserts: Chocolate Praline Encore-pecan pie with the addition of bittersweet chocolate cream, topped with whipped cream and chocolate shavings $6.00, Bread Pudding with Whiskey Sauce $5.00, Crème Brulee with fresh berries and mint $6.25, Cheesecake $5.50, Espresso $3.00, Cappuccino $3.50

Impressions:

Starched white tablecloths, black tie service, polished woodwork, and a club-like atmosphere…what more could a steak lover ask for? How about an ocean view across Front Street in Lahaina! Ruth's Chris is a traditional steak house serving USDA Prime steaks broiled at 1800 degrees and presented sizzling on a heated platter. To accompany these primo aged meats, the a la carte menu offers a choice of seven potato preparations, crisp salads with fresh dressings, and various vegetable selections. Side dishes are portioned for two so don't over-order! High quality food and service standards are maintained at every Ruth's Chris. Although it isn't always necessary, we recommend reservations.

Wailea

Ruth's Chris
Shops at Wailea
Alanui Drive
Wailea, HI 96753
808-874-8880
www.ruthschris.com
Hours: D 5:00 PM-9:30 PM
Cards: AE DC JCB MC V
Dress: Evening Aloha
Style: Stk $$$$

Menu Sampler:

Breakfast/Lunch:
N/A
Dinner:
Appetizers: Shrimp Cocktail $9.95, Shrimp Remoulade $9.95, Barbecued Shrimp with white wine, butter, garlic and spices $9.95, Onion Soup Au Gratin $5.25, French Fried Maui Onion Rings $4.75, Crab Stuffed Mushrooms $9.50
Salads: Sliced Tomato and Maui Onion with crumbled bleu cheese and vinaigrette dressing $6.50, Caesar $6.25, Combination of mixed greens $4.95, Fresh Asparagus and Hearts of Palm $6.95, Italian Salad $5.95
Entrées: Filet $27.50, Petite Filet $22.95, Rib Eye $26.95, Veal Chop $29.25, Three Broiled Lamb Chops with mint jelly $30.50, Broiled Marinated Double Breast Chicken $19.25, Two Center Cut Pork Chops w/ sweet and spicy apple slices $21.50, Steak & Lobster $Market Price, Lobster Tails $Market Price
Side Orders: Au Gratin Potatoes $5.25, Shoestring Potatoes $4.75, Sautéed Mushrooms $5.25, Creamed Fresh Spinach $5.00, Broccoli Au Gratin $5.25
Desserts: Chocolate Praline Encore-pecan pie with the addition of bittersweet chocolate cream, topped with whipped cream and chocolate shavings $6.00, Bread Pudding with Whiskey Sauce $5.00, Crème Brulee with berries $6.25

Impressions:

Up on the second level of the new Shops at Wailea you'll find one of Ruth's Chris newest locations. As always, diners will find starched white tablecloths and a hushed, yet convivial, club-like atmosphere accompanying the fine USDA Prime steaks. Although the entrees are superb, cruising the appetizer, soup, salad, and dessert items provides wonderful possibilities for all sorts of lighter meals. High quality food and service standards are maintained at every one of Ruth's Chris restaurants. Reservations are definitely recommended.

Central Valley

Saeng's Thai
2119 Vineyard St
Wailuku, HI 96793
808-244-1567
Web: None
Hours: L 11:00 AM-2:30 PM Mo-Fr
          D 5:00 PM-9:30 PM
Cards: MC V
Dress: Casual
Style: Thai $$
          Ent Card

Menu Sampler:

Breakfast:
N/A
Lunch/Dinner:
Appetizers: Chicken or Beef Satay-chicken or beef strips skewered and marinated, grilled and served with peanut sauce and cucumber salad $6.95, Stuffed Chicken Wings-boned wings stuffed with mixed vegetables, long rice and spices $7.50, Crispy Calamari with sweet and sour sauce $7.50
Salads: Silver Noodle Salad-crystal bean thread noodle mixed with chicken and spicy lemon sauce $6.95, Green Papaya Salad $6.50, Tofu Salad $6.50
Soups: Shrimp Coconut Soup $9.50, Chicken Tom Yum Soup $8.50
Noodles: Pad Thai $8.50, Pad Si-iu (Chow Fun) $9.25, Rad Na $9.50
Entrées: Green, Red or Yellow Curry with Chicken, Beef or Pork $8.95, Shrimp Matsaman Curry $9.95, Chicken Panang Curry $8.95, Evil Prince with Beef-beef sautéed with spices, coconut milk, bamboo shoots, basil & chopped cabbage $8.50, Beef Larb $8.50, Honey Lemon Shrimp with steamed vegetables $9.50, Kung Pao Chicken $8.50 All may be ordered mild, medium or hot.
Desserts: Thai Tapioca Pudding $2.50, Fried Banana w/ Ice Cream $3.50

Impressions:

Wailuku Town is a cultural experience all of its own. Saeng's Thai fits right in with the adventure. Viewed from the street the narrow sidewalk and wooden façade give no clue to the gem hidden inside. The interior décor features a lush garden complete with koi pond and an intriguing bent wood ceiling. Menu items have fiery yet soothing flavors created by blending coconut milk, curry pastes, herbs, and spices. The Thai food served here is some of the best we've found.

Maui Dining

Kihei

Sala Thai
Kihei Kalama Village
1913 S Kihei Rd
Kihei, HI 96753
808-874-8667
Web: None
Hours: L 11:30 AM-2:30 PM XSu
        D 5:00 PM-9:30 PM
Cards: AE DC DIS JCB MC V
Dress: Casual
Style: Thai $$
        Ent Card

Menu Sampler:

Breakfast:
N/A

Lunch/Dinner:
Appetizers: Marinated Prawn & Sausages wrapped in bo-pia, deep fried and served with sweet chili sauce $9.95, Sateh Tofu steamed and served on a bed of cabbage and served with special peanut sauce $7.95, Spring Roll $8.95
Salads: Green Papaya Salad $7.50, Sliced Chicken, mint leaves, cucumber, long rice, onion, chili, Thai pickle sauce $7.95, Calamari Salad, cashews $9.95
Soups: Spicy Shrimp Soup, lemongrass, kaffir lime leaves $11.95
Entrées: Pad Thai-rice noodles stir fried with bean sprouts and tofu $8.95, Beef Evil Prince $10.95, Chicken Cashew Basil $10.95, Chicken Panang Curry $10.95, Deep Fried Whole Fish topped with spicy sweet and sour ginger sauce and topped with crushed cashew nuts $14.95, Eggplant Tofu $8.95, Mike's Award Winning Cornish Game Hen with garlic and black pepper $12.95, Spicy Mussel Delight served on the half shell $11.95, Labb Beef w/mint leaves $9.95
Desserts: Gluey Churm-Banana in Brown Sugar with Coconut Milk and Grand Marnier with Ice Cream Scoop $7.95, Sticky Rice with mangoes $5.95

Impressions:

In the back of Kalama Village there's a delightful little restaurant serving zesty Thai cuisine. The owner has taught many others to cook Thai, and now he has returned from Bangkok to once again serve his own special dishes on Maui. The Panang Curry is almost bisque-like and Mike's Cornish Game Hen is fabulous! Seating is offered indoors or out on the porches. If you have never experienced Thai food, this restaurant would be a great place to start. Take it easy on the degree of spiciness, as the dishes served here are full-flavored.

Maui Dining

Central Valley

Sam Sato's
1750 Wili Pa Loop
Wailuku, HI 96793
808-244-7124
Web: None
Hours: BL 7:00 AM-2:00 PM Mo-Sa
         Manju Pick Up 7:00 AM-4:00 PM Mo-Sa
Cards: None
Dress: Casual
Style: Local $

Menu Sampler:

Breakfast:
Two Eggs, choice of rice, toast, hash browns and choice of one: bacon, ham, Portuguese sausage, Vienna sausage, hamburger patty, Spam, link sausage $4.50, Omelettes-three eggs, choice of rice, toast, or hash browns-Hama & Cheese 5.00, Denver 5.25, Vegetarian 5.25, Hot Cakes (1 pc.) $2.00, Banana Hotcakes (1 pc.) $2.75, Fried Rice topped with green onion, sprouts, egg $4.00

Lunch:
Sandwiches: Hamburger $2.35, Hamburger Deluxe 2.50, Cheeseburger 2.60, Cheeseburger Deluxe 2.75, Teriyaki 2.60, Teriyaki Deluxe 2.75, BLT 2.75

Noodles: Dry Noodles small $3.75, Dry Noodles large 4.50, Dry Noodles double 6.05, Super Dry with vegetables 5.20, Saimin small 3.50, Saimin large 4.25, Saimin extra large 4.95, Won Ton Mein 4.50, Chow Fun large 4.75

Plate Lunches: Hamburger Steak 5.75, Combination (chop suey vegetable, spare ribs, egg foo young, char siu 6.25, Yakitori Plate 6.00, Teriyaki 6.00 Manju (Lime/Azuki) $.50 each, Turn Overs (peach, apple, coconut, pineapple, pineapple peach) $.80 each, Kim Chee side order $1.50, BBQ stick $.95

Impressions:

Sam Sato's began as a plantation camp store back in the heydays of Big Sugar. The camp and original store are gone, but Sam's diner lives on as a gathering place for the descendants of his early clientele. Today's version of this popular dining spot is located in a commercial area of Wailuku known as The Millyard.

If you're looking to experience local style dining with everyday islanders, this is a great place to visit. The simple menu matches the setting with headliners like dry noodles and saimin complementing breakfast choices and plate lunches. The house specialties come in a variety of sizes to suit all appetites. Please be aware that this local favorite can get very busy, so you may have to wait for a table.

Northwest

Sansei Seafood Restaurant & Sushi Bar
Kapalua Shops
115 Bay Drive
Kapalua, HI 96761
808-669-6286
www.sanseihawaii.com
Hours: D 5:30 PM-10:00 PM
Cards: AE DIS MC V
Dress: Resort Casual
Style: Pac-Rim/Sea $$$

Menu Sampler:

Breakfast/Lunch:
N/A
Dinner:
Sushi Rolls: Asian Rock Shrimp Cake crusted with crispy Chinese noodles in ginger-lime chili butter and cilantro pesto $6.95, Mango Crab Salad Handroll of ripe mango, snow crab & Kula greens with a spicy Thai vinaigrette $7.95, Yaki Maki Sushi-California roll wrapped w/smoked salmon and baked with dynamite sauce $14.95, Spider Roll w/sweet Thai chili sauce & unagi glaze $10.95
Appetizers & Salads: Tea Duck Egg Roll with slow roasted duck and fresh spring vegetables served w/plum sauce & cane mustard $4.95, Sliced Tenderloin of Beef served over rich glazed Japanese udon noodles $12.95/$21.95, Sansei's Rock Shrimp Dynamite-crispy tempura rock shrimp tossed w/creamy garlic masago aioli $8.95, Nori Ravioli of Lobster & Crab w/shiitake sauce $9.95
Entrées: Sansei's Seafood Pasta of black tiger prawns & sweet ocean scallops with Japanese papardelle noodles and fresh veggies tossed in spicy black bean chili butter $19.95, Roasted Peking Duck Breast over wild mushroom & potato risotto with a rich foie gras demi-glace $21.95, Pepper Crusted Pork Tenderloins served over roasted garlic mashed potatoes in an Asian sweet & sour glazed fig chutney $18.95, Shrimp & Vegetable Tempura w/dipping sauces $14.95/$19.95

Impressions:

Chef/Owner D.K. Kodama has won numerous awards for his unique approach to Pacific Rim cuisine. Here at Sansei's original Kapalua Shops restaurant, diners can experience these intriguing creations with their contemporary Japanese touches. The innovative yet reasonably priced sushi and entrees have made this a popular place for locals and visitors alike. Dining at Sansei is grazing at its best. In addition to the usual bar service they have a fine selection of sake.

Maui Dining

Kihei

Sansei Seafood Restaurant & Sushi Bar
Kihei Town Center
1881 South Kihei Road
Kihei, HI 96753
808-879-0004
www.sanseihawaii.com
Hours: D 5:30 PM-10:00 PM
Cards: AE DIS MC V
Dress: Resort Casual
Style: Pac-Rim/Sea $$$

Menu Sampler:

Breakfast/Lunch:
N/A
Dinner:
Sushi Rolls: Kapalua "Butterfry" of fresh snapper, smoked salmon, crab and veggies in a crispy panko batter roll with a tangy ponzu sauce $11.95, California Roll with crab, avocado & cucumber $6.25, Sansei Special Roll of spicy crab, fresh cilantro and veggies inside out with sweet Thai chili sauce $8.95
Appetizers & Salads: Japanese Calamari Salad with a won ton basket stuffed with fresh Kula greens & topped with crispy calamari in a spicy kochujang vinaigrette $9.95, Ahi Tataki of seared Hawaiian tuna, Maui onions and kaiware sprouts with a mild ponzu sauce $9.95, Broiled Miso Garlic Prawns $8.95
Entrées: Grilled Fresh Hawaiian Ahi and Award Winning Asian Rock Shrimp Cake served over a grilled furikake rice cake in ginger-lime chili butter with cilantro pesto $22.95, Spicy Crab Stuffed Whole Lobster Tail served on garlic mashed potatoes w/ginger-lime-chili butter & shiitake cabernet sauces $37.95
Noodles: Japanese Udon Noodles with fresh julienne veggies and roast pork in a homemade dashi broth topped with a traditional tempura shrimp $10.95

Impressions:

D.K. Kodama just opened his newest sushi restaurant to the delight of every foodie in South Maui. Not only are his creations unique, but the prices are affordable for nearly every budget. Sansei's contemporary island cuisine goes way beyond traditional Pac-Rim fusion. Chef Dave draws upon global influences to create dishes with great complexity. All this is presented in a fun, welcoming atmosphere. For the night owls and really budget-minded, stop by Thursday, Friday, and Saturday nights from 10 PM to 2 AM when all sushi and food are 50% off. Drink specials and karaoke add to the late night party scene.

Wailea

Sarento's On The Beach
2980 S. Kihei Rd
Kihei, HI 96753
808-875-7555
www.tri-star-restaurants.com
Hours: D 5:30 PM-10:00 PM
Cards: AE DC DIS JCB MC V
Dress: Resort Casual
Style: Cont/Ital $$$$

Menu Sampler:

Breakfast/Lunch:
N/A
Dinner:
Appetizers: Calamari Fritti with tomato-caper sauce & lemon aioli $9.95, Grilled Portobello Napoleon of prosciutto, eggplant, mozzarella & tomato w/arugula pesto $10.95, Mussels in broth with grilled Tuscan bread $11.95
Salads: Salad "Caprese" $8.95, Greek Salad with feta cheese, tomatoes, Kula Onions & cucumbers $7.95, Salad Gabriela of grilled marinated baby artichokes, plum tomatoes, Puna goat cheese and caper vinaigrette $10.95
Entrées: Fusilli Veneziana of sauteed beef tenderloin, cremini mushrooms, sun dried tomatoes in a Barolo wine sauce $26.95, Rack of Lamb Herb Butter Crusted w/fig balsamic jus and salted fingerling potato $39.95, 20 oz Porterhouse Plack w/Hawaiian red rock salt, herbed olive oil, butter $39.95, Lobster Cannelloni w/braised greens, grilled mushroom ragu, and lobster cream sauce $29.95, Osso Buco with saffron risotto $27.95, Cotolette Capricciosa of herb coated veal Milanese style w/white truffle oil vinaigrette $27.95, Swordfish Saltimbocca w/prosciutto, Bel Paese cheese & grilled radicchio with porcini mushroom $28.95, Seafood Fra Diavolo $37.95, Penne Calabrese $25.95
Desserts: Ever changing, always fabulous!

Impressions:

Sarento's is located on one of the most beautiful beaches in Hawaii. Celebrities and notables alike frequent this establishment, not only for the views, but also for the five-star Italian cuisine. Chef George Gomes of the Hawaiian Island Chefs group is in charge of the kitchen. His traditional menu items often come with wicked Mediterranean spins. The large wine cellar houses more than 1500 bottles of domestic and imported vintages. Reservations and valet parking are highly recommended. An evening at Sarento's is splurge dining well spent.

Maui Dining

Northwest

Sea House Restaurant
Napili Kai Beach Resort
5900 Honoapiilani Road
Napili, HI 96761
808-669-1500
www.napilikai.com
Hours: B 8:00 AM-10:30 AM
         L 11:30 AM-2:00 PM
         D 6:00 PM-9:00 PM
Cards: AE MC V
Dress: Resort Casual
Style: Ec/Pac-Rim $$$

Menu Sampler:

Breakfast:
American Breakfast-two eggs, meat, starch, & beverage $8.95, Omelets-vegetarian, seafood, Spanish $9.95, Poached Eggs Napili Kai-benedicts with hollandaise sauce & choice of crab & spinach, Canadian bacon & fresh turkey breast $8.95, Banana Macadamia Nut Hot Cakes $4.95/$5.95
Lunch:
Shrimp Greek Salad $9.00, Kona Maine Lobster Caesar Salad $12.00, Shrimp BLT with choice of fries, onion rings or salad $9.00, Cioppino $12.00
Dinner:
Pupus: Coconut-Macadamia Nut-Crusted Shrimp with Thai chili sauce $11.00, Crisp Pacific Sushi of white rice, crab, and avocado rolled in nori with a macadamia nut crust and a red Thai curry sauce $10.00, Steamed Clams $12.00
Entrées: Steak Gallagher-Black Angus Tenderloin porcini-pepper crusted, pan seared in a Maui onion-Irish whiskey demi-glace $27.00, Hawaiian Snapper w/Lilikoi hollandaise sautéed and topped with Alaskan Snow Crab legs $30.00, Asian Lamb Chops with pickled mango and cucumber salad $22.00/$27.00, Veal Piccata a la Milanese in an herb-egg crust sautéed with caramelized shallots, baby spinach, capers, and served with a lemon beurre blanc $24.00

Impressions:

Sea House Restaurant offers relaxing beachfront dining on beautiful Napili Bay. The eclectic island-inspired menu is well conceived with interesting specialties offered at every meal. Many of the selections can be ordered in either light or full portions to suit the diners' appetite. The mood of the patrons and wait staff is definitely "island kine" in this laid-back vacation favorite.

Wailea

SeaWatch
Wailca Golf Club
100 Wailea Golf Club Drive
Wailea, HI 96753
808-875-8080
www.seawatchrestaurant.com
Hours: B/L 8:00 AM-3:00 PM
           D 6:00 PM-10:00 PM
Cards: AE DC DIS JCB MC V
Dress: Resort Casual
Style: Pac-Rim $$$

Menu Sampler:

Breakfast:
French Toast made with Molokai Sweet Bread 7, Classic Eggs Benedict 9.50, Crab Cake Benedict with roasted pepper hollandaise 9.75, Smoked Salmon Benedict with caper hollandaise 10.00. Half orders are available.
Lunch:
Chinese Chicken Salad 9.50, Teriyaki Ahi on Upcountry greens 14, ½# Kiawe Broiled Hamburger 8, Grilled Fresh Catch Sandwich with Kula lime aioli 12.5, Mango Chutney Cashew Chicken Wrap 9, Kiawe Broiled Chicken Caesar Salad 8.50, Soup 3.50/4.50, Wok Stir-fried Upcountry Vegetables in black bean 9
Dinner:
Appetizers: Macadamia Nut Brie, pineapple chutney and crostini 11, Pepper Crusted Seared Ahi, Asian slaw in a spicy lilikoi ponzu sauce 15
Salads: Baby Spinach, Lehua honey dressing, wonton chips, tiger prawn sate 10, Caesar Salad with sourdough croutons and Reggiano parmesan cheese 7
Entrées: New York Steak grilled, on roasted garlic mashed potatoes, Burgundy demi glace 28, Miso Glazed Tiger Prawns and coriander ginger sauce 26, Roasted Rack of Lamb with mango chutney 29, Mac Nut-Fresh Catch, Mango Chutney Macadamia Crusted, mashed Molokai potato, lemongrass butter sauce $Market Price, Muscovy Duck with a Bing cherry demi glace 26

Impressions:

SeaWatch is definitely more than just another golf course restaurant. The impressive facility sits high on the South Maui coastline and has stunning views of Wailea and Molokini. Their menu offers comfortable Pacific Rim cuisine. This is an excellent choice for breakfast that first morning on the island, or light pupus from 3-10 in the lounge area. Dinner reservations are recommended at this gracious dining spot.

Maui Dining

Northwest

Soup Nutz & Java Jazz
Honokowai Marketplace
3350 L Honoapiilani Road
Lahaina, HI 96761
808-667-0787
www.javajazz.net
Hours: BLD 6:00 AM-9:00 PM Mo-Sa
         BL 6:00 AM-5:00 PM Su
Cards: MC V
Dress: Casual
Style: Amer/Ec $$

Menu Sampler:

Breakfast:
Three Egg Omelettes served with curry home fries & toast 7.95-9.95, French Toast w/brioche, cream cheese, raspberry coulis 7.95, Two Eggs, Meat, home fries, toast $7.95, Short Stack $4.95, Sunday-Eggs Benedict 9.95

Lunch:
Sandwiches also served at dinner. Tuscany Chicken Sandwich on focaccia 8.95, Falafel on pita w/ancho chili sauce 7.95, Blackened Fish, red pepper aioli 8.95
Salads: Chicken Caesar 9.95, Spinach Salad with shaved red onion, candied walnuts, blue cheese, tomatoes, apples and a warm balsamic & bacon vinaigrette 8.95, Chinese Chicken Salad with won ton chips 8.95, Soup of the Day 4.75

Dinner:
Appetizers: Sun Dried Tomato Goat Cheese with fresh tomato basil dip and wedges of warm pita, for two 8.95, Grilled Quesadilla du jour 8.95
Entrées: Served with vegetables and choice of rice or potatoes. Beef Filet Mignon grilled and topped with a red wine herb butter sauce 24.95, Oven Roasted Lobster Tail with a lemon butter sauce 24.95, Angel Hair Pomodoro with fresh tomatoes, basil, garlic, white wine, capers & butter 9.95, w/chicken 13.95, w/shrimp 17.95, w/vegetables 9.95, Chicken Picatta 17.95
Desserts: Chocolate Truffle Mousse Cake with Kahlua $5.95

Impressions:

Once again we're at a strip mall, but you won't believe what people can do with a little bit of space. On one side, you can get coffees and pastries to go, and on the other, a full menu is served three meals a day. Then, just to make sure that every square foot is productive, an area is set aside between the two restroom doors for the jazz musicians. Think tasty, big food in a Bohemian setting!

Maui Dining

Wailea

Spago
Four Seasons Resort Maui
3900 Wailea Alanui Drive
Wailea, HI 96753
808-879-2999
www.wolfgangpuck.com
Hours: D 5:30 PM-9:00 PM
Cards: AE DC DIS JCB MC V
Dress: Evening Aloha
Style: Euro/Haw/Pac-Rim $$$$

Menu Sampler:

Breakfast/Lunch:
N/A
Dinner:
Appetizers: Spicy Ahi Tuna Poke in Sesame-Miso Cones 14, Thai Coconut Soup with Keahole Lobster, Keffir, Chili and Galangal 18, Risotto with Sweet Shrimp "Ama Ebi", Uni and Fried Ginger 18, Sautéed Oysters with Hot-Sweet Chinese Mustard or Iced Raw with Maui Onion-Soy Mignonette 18
Entrées: Roasted Salmon with Ginger-Macadamia Nut Crust, Molokai yams and black pepper 28, Chinois Lamb Chops grilled with Hunan eggplant and chili-mint vinaigrette 38, Kona Lobster with "sweet and sour" banana curry, coconut rice and dry-fried green beans 42, Ahi Tuna Grilled Rare with Plum-Miso Sauce, wasabi potatoes, and crispy Maui onions 32, Caramelized Pork Chop with lomi lomi tomatoes, fried garlic and creamy sage polenta 29
Desserts: Warm Guanaja Chocolate Tart with Tahitian vanilla bean ice cream 10, Baked Maui Pineapple Upside Down Cake with sour cream sorbet 10

Impressions:

The Four Seasons Resort Maui recently became home to one of the newer of Wolfgang Puck's acclaimed Spago restaurants. Diners are seated in a spacious terrace with a raised bar and lounge at its center. The wonderfully upscale but comfortable menu combines California and Hawaiian cuisines with a Euro base. To accompany an evening of memorable dining, Spago offers an extensive wine list with selections from around the world. For the younger set, there's a menu designed specifically for children. With its beachfront setting, gracious facility, and world-class cuisine, this new member of Wolfgang Puck's Fine Dining Group has all the ingredients to provide an outstanding culinary experience.

Maui Dining

Kaanapali

Spats Trattoria
Hyatt Regency Maui
200 Nohea Kai Drive
Kaanapali, HI 96761
808-667-4727
www.maui.hyatt.com
Hours: D 6:00 PM-9:00 PM SuMoWeFr
Cards: AE DC DIS JCB MC V
Dress: Evening Aloha
Style: Ital $$$

Menu Sampler:

Breakfast/Lunch:
N/A
Dinner:
Antipasti: Manila Clams, fresh herbs, garlic, white wine and extra virgin olive oil $12.00, Spats Antipasti Platter For Two-A selection of Italian specialty meats & cheeses, marinated salads, fresh seafood, grilled and roasted vegetables 22.50, Bruschetta de la casa $8.00, Carpaccio-thinly sliced beef tenderloin $10.00
Zuppe e Insalate: Minestrone with pesto crouton $6.50, Insalata Spats of baby lettuce, imported olives, tomatoes, Maui onions, and balsamic vinaigrette $7.50, Insalata Caesar w/fresh Parmesan, focaccia croutons and white anchovy $9.00
Entrées: Veal as piccata, marsala, saltimbocca, milanese or francaise $26.00, Pescatore Alla Griglia of grilled marinated baby lobster tail, island fish & shrimp in lobster broth $32.00, Pollo ala Caterina-francaised battered chicken breast w/jumbo crabmeat, roasted peppers, asparagus & fontina cheese $24.00
Pasta: Fettucine Carbonara with fresh cream, pancetta bacon, peas and parmesan cheese $19.00, Penne con Funghi w/roasted chicken & fresh sage in a creamy marsala sauce $20.00, Tortelloni Melanzane of cheese tortelloni with roasted eggplant, Pomodoro, fresh ricotta & basil $20.00, Gemelli Puttanesca w/rock shrimp, olives, capers, garlic & artichokes in spicy tomato sauce $21.50

Impressions:

Spats Trattoria conveys a big-city atmosphere with its old world décor of stained glass, brocade upholstery, private booths, and dark colors. This intimate scene is very grand and forms the perfect backdrop for the upscale Italian cuisine served here. The menu is built around traditional favorites at prices that aren't scary, that is if you remember that you're in the Hyatt Regency Maui.

Kihei

Stella Blues Café
1279 S. Kihei Road
Kihei, HI 96753
808-874-3779
Web: None
Hours: B 7:30 AM-11:00 AM Mo-Sa
         B 7:30 AM-2:00 PM Su
         L 11:00 AM-5:00 PM
         D 5:00 PM-10:00 PM
Cards: DIS MC V
Dress: Casual
Style: Isl/Pac-Rim $$

Menu Sampler:

Breakfast:
Eggs Benedict $9.95, with Lox add $2.00, Tofu Scramble with tofu, vegetables, cheeses, & tahini sauce with toast $7.95, Banana Mac-Nut Pancakes $4.95/$7.95
Lunch:
Salads & Soups: All served w/homemade focaccia bread. Cobb Salad $10.95, Shrimp Caesar $12.95, Fruit Salad w/vanilla black pepper vinaigrette $10.95, Stella's Homemade Chicken Chili with ancho chili roasted chicken $2.95/$3.95
Entrees: Stella's Special of spiced grilled eggplant, roasted garlic, sweet red peppers, feta, cucumbers, on homemade herb bread, chips & a pickle $8.95, Mom's Egg Salad on a Croissant, chips & a pickle $6.95, Grilled Roast Beef & Cheddar, grilled onions, spicy mustard, sourdough bread $8.95, Plate Lunches w/rice & potato salad- Chicken Teriyaki $8.50, Kalua Pork & Cabbage $9.50
Dinner:
Small Plates: Baked mussels smothered with garlic aioli and baked $6.95, Smoked Fish Dip w/cream cheese, spices and baked, with pita bread $6.95
Pasta: Carbonara-bacon, shallots, garlic, cream, eggs & parmesan $14.95
Big Plates: Fresh Local Fish Roasted with a mac-nut crust and tropical sauce, mashed purple sweet potatoes $Mkt, Baby Back Ribs, skillet cornbread, cole slaw $18.95, Miso Shrimp (8) with forbidden black rice, baby bok choy $18.95

Impressions:

What a difference a move makes! Stella Blues Café always served a solid menu of interesting fare, but the surroundings were a little bit lacking. They recently moved a short distance away into the former digs of a high-end restaurant and viva la difference! Now this family oriented establishment can seat their patrons in comfort while they enjoy healthy cuisine from morning till night.

Maui Dining

Kaanapali

Swan Court

Hyatt Regency Maui
200 Nohea Kai Drive
Kaanapali, HI 96761
808-667-4727
www.maui.hyatt.com

Hours: B Buf 6:30 AM-11:30 AM Mo-Sa
           Brunch 6:30 AM-12:00 PM Su
           D 6:00 PM-9:00 PM TuThSa
Cards: AE DC DIS JCB MC V
Dress: Evening Aloha
Style: Cont/Pac-Rim $$$$

Menu Sampler:

Breakfast:

Buffet daily-Traditional breakfast items. $21.95/adults, $10.95/children 5-12, children under 4 are free. A la Carte menu offering traditional items.

Lunch:

N/A

Dinner:

Appetizers: Plantation Shrimp with cocktail sauce & fresh Napili pineapple 13, Guava Painted Baby Back Ribs with Haiku papaya relish 13, Kauai Corn and Ginger Bisque with a crispy seafood fritter 8, Lobster, Crab and Shrimp Spring Roll with fresh mango, spicy Thai remoulade 15, Seared Forest Mushroom Potsticker w/ micro greens and sweet chili drizzle 13, Kula Greens 8

Entrées: Filet Mignon with roasted baby potatoes, Maui onions with marsala demi 35, Seared Opakapaka w/Thai rice, snow pea shoots, crystallized ginger vinaigrette 35, Vegetarian Sampler of exotic mushrooms, truffled asparagus, almond crusted tofu 30, Maui Sugar Cane Skewered Ahi tempura sushi roll with Asian greens 36, Tempura lobster with Seared Scallops 38

Dessert: Banana Crème Brulee $9, Guava Lilikoi Cheesecake with macadamia nut crust $7, Apple Macadamia Strudel with Tahitian Vanilla Sauce $7

Impressions:

Swan Court plays a dual role at the Hyatt Regency. In the morning, a bountiful breakfast buffet is offered along with creative a la carte items. Come evening the tables are set with candlelight to provide a more formal experience. The dinner menu focuses on sophisticated Pacific Rim cuisine with noticeable Continental influences. The breakfast bedlam goes GQ at night, so dress accordingly.

Maui Dining

Wailea

Taiko
Diamond Resort
555 Kaukahi Street
Wailea, HI 96753
808-874-0500
www.diamondresort.com/maui
Hours: B 7:00 AM-10:00 AM XTu
         L 11:00 AM-1:45 PM XTu
         D 6:00 PM-9:00 PM XTu
Cards: AE DC DIS JCB MC V
Dress: Evening Aloha
Style: Fre/Japan $$$$

Menu Sampler:

Breakfast:
Japanese Breakfast: $13, Traditional Breakfast $13, French Toast $6
Lunch:
Original Udon Salad $11, Diamond Burger $8, Teriyaki Chicken Sandwich
$9.50, Beef Curry & Rice $12, Tempura Udon in hot broth $12
Dinner:
Appetizers: Sushi Bar. Foie Gras and Scallop sauté in white wine, butter and
shoyu $13, Spicy maguro Poke of fresh island ahi served with a spicy sauce $8,
Black Pepper Duckling-chilled breast of duck served with black pepper sauce
and pommery mustard $9, Fried Tofu served with tempura sauce $6
Soup & Salad: Miso Soup with tofu and wakame $2, Kaiso Salad of seaweed
and sesame dressing $6, Kinoko Caesar with sautéed mushrooms $9
Entrées: Tenderloin Steak with secret ginger sauce $25, Sukiyaki with beef,
tofu, vegetables, udon and raw egg $28, Herb Butter Salmon on a bed of garden
fresh vegetables $23, Boursin Garlic & Fine Herb Stuffed Duck Cotolette-an
award winning crisp, panko-crusted breast of duck with shiitake mushrooms,
Maui onions and imported boursin garlic and fine herb gournay cheese $33

Impressions:

When you take a Japanese chef and train him in classic French culinary
technique, an interesting transition takes place. Chef Ishikawa calls on his
background as well as his education to create a unique fusion dining experience.
The impressive results are served in a three-story beamed ceiling room with
stone and glass walls and polished wood floors. Add a major waterfall and a
stream flowing under the building and you're not in Kansas anymore.

Lahaina

Thai Chef
Old Lahaina Shopping Center
Lahaina, HI 96761
808-667-2814
www.thaichefmaui.com
Hours: L 11:00 AM-2:00 PM Mo-Fr
             D 5:00 PM-9:30 PM
Cards: DC DIS JCB MC V
Dress: Casual
Style: Thai $$

Menu Sampler:

Breakfast:
N/A
Lunch/Dinner:
Appetizers: Thai Crisp Noodles $6.95, Thai Spring Rolls with chicken, long rice, carrots, eggs, onions, cabbage and spices in a pastry wrapper $7.50, Combo Plate-Thai spring rolls, fish patties, Thai toast with tangy cucumber $10.50
Salads: Green Papaya Salad $7.95, Beef Salad with grilled beef, onions, lemongrass, mint, Kaffir lime leaves, carrots and spicy lemongrass-ginger $9.50
Soup: Chicken Ginger Coconut Soup $9.95, Hot & Sour Soup $9.95, Tom Yum Soup w/Chicken $9.95, w/Shrimp $10.95 Spicy Seafood Combo Soup $14.50
Noodles: Pad Thai w/shrimp or chicken $10.95, Thai Chef Special Noodles with shrimp or chicken and vegetables in special gravy sauce $11.95
Entrées: Beef Chiang Mai (Larb) of minced beef, mint, onions, bean sprouts $9.95, Thai Garlic Chicken $9.95, Crab with Spicy Sauce $15.95, Shrimp with Garlic Vegetables $12.95, Chicken Thai Basil Sauce $9.95, Shrimp Panang Curry with red curry paste, red bell peppers, green peas, basil, and ground peanut simmered in coconut milk $11.50, Eggplant with Tofu $9.25
Dinners: For Two-6 items $36.95, For Three $48.95, For Four-10 items $72.95
Desserts: Thai Tapioca Pudding $2.95, Thai Coconut Ice Cream $3.25

Impressions:

Behind the bustle of Front Street you'll find the Old Lahaina Shopping Center and the Thai Chef restaurant. This small storefront eatery serves an excellent Thai meal at reasonable prices. The seasoning tends toward spicy, so when your server asks whether you want your dinner prepared mild, medium, or hot, be a little conservative. If you get carried away you'll appreciate the air-conditioning, which is a nice touch anyway, as the name Lahaina means "merciless sun".

Kihei

Thailand Cuisine
1819 S. Kihei Rd
Kihei, HI 96753
808-875-0839
www.thailandcuisinemaui.com
Hours: L 11:00 AM-2:30 PM Mo-Sa
        D 5:00 PM-10:00 PM
Cards: AE DC DIS JCB MC V
Dress: Resort Casual
Style: Thai $$

Menu Sampler:

Breakfast:
N/A

Lunch/Dinner:
Appetizers: Thai Spring Rolls (4) $7.95, Green Mussel Delight $7.95, Crispy Calamari $8.95, Fresh Summer Rolls (4) $8.50, Thai Crispy Noodles $5.95
Salads: Green Papaya Salad-shredded green papaya with garlic, tomatoes, dried shrimp and chili in a spicy sauce $7.95, Shrimp Salad $9.95, Beef Salad $8.95
Soup: Tom Yum Chicken with chicken, lemongrass, kaffir lime leaves, mushrooms, onions, simmered in a special broth with green onions and cilantro $8.95, Long Rice $8.95, Won Ton Soup $8.95, Hot and Sour Soup $8.95
Entrées: Beef Pad Thai-thin rice noodles stir fried with beef, eggs, bean sprouts, green onions, ground peanuts and special sauce $9.50, Crispy Egg Noodles with chicken $9.95, Chicken Panang Curry $9.95, Thai Red Curry Shrimp with pineapple, prawns, bean thread noodle, bell pepper, basil simmered in red curry paste and coconut milk $11.50, Beef Thai Basil Sauce $9.75, Thai Garlic Chicken $9.75,Shrimp with honey lemon sauce $10.95, Seafood Pad Pet-seafood sautéed with carrot, bell pepper, onion, fresh basil, and spiced sauce $15.95, Pad Pet Clams with basil spiced sauce $14.95, Siam Duck (crispy duck) of roast duck marinated in Thai sauce and served with lettuce, cucumbers, tomatoes, sweet and sour sauce $15.95, Garlic Calamari $11.95

Impressions:

Thai cuisine has been a new kid on the culinary block for some time now. As its popularity increases so does the investment level of the restaurateurs. This will become obvious as you enter Thailand Cuisine. But don't let the up market decor throw you off the point. The food here is as good as the setting. Check their schedule and plan dinner for an evening when the Thai dancers perform.

Maui Dining

Northwest

The Banyan Tree
Ritz-Carlton Kapalua
One Ritz-Carlton Drive
Kapalua, HI 96761
808-669-6200
www.ritzcarlton.com
Hours: L 11:30 AM-3:30 PM
         D 5:30 PM-9:30 PM
Cards: AE DC DIS JCB MC V
Dress: Resort Casual
Style: Cont/Haw-Reg/Pac-Rim $$$

Menu Sampler:

Breakfast:
N/A
Lunch:
Perfect Beginnings $8.50-Beverages such as Guava Chiffon, Frozen Raspberry-Mint Lemonade, Hibiscus Martini, Blended Mango Margarita, Lava Flow
Appetizers: Crisp Maui Onion Peels, ginger-red pepper dipping sauce $8
Salads: Big Island Lobster Salad-whole spiny lobster tail, upcountry greens, fresh mango, avocado and passion fruit dressing $24
Sandwiches: All served with choice of fresh fruit, French fries or Maui potato chips-Kona Crab Melt-thinly sliced prosciutto, artichokes, Maui onions $15
Dinner:
Appetizers: Chef's Signature Soup of coconut, sweet corn and lemongrass garnished with sweet crab meat $9, Spicy Pesto Grilled Shrimp $13
Entrées: Ahi Tuna & Seared Foie Gras-arugula, grilled Maui onions, sour cherry sauce $34, Colorado Rack of Lamb-"En Persillade", roasted garlic potato puree, truffled lamb reduction $32, Grilled Filet Mignon-gnocchi gallette, sweet corn, port wine demi glace $30
Sides: Cheese Raviolinis, Whipped Potatoes, butter poached asparagus, sautéed green beans $7

Impressions:

The Ritz Carlton Kapalua occupies an immense area along the West Maui coast. In the center of all that and beside the pool complex you'll find The Banyan Tree restaurant. This dual-identity dining venue does a casually upscale lunch during the day before switching over to their more ambitious dinner service at night. Regardless, expect quality fusion cuisine and an attentive wait staff.

Maui Dining

Northwest

The Bay Club
1 Bay Drive
Kapalua, HI 96761
808-669-5656
www.kapaluabayhotel.com
Hours: Lounge opens at 6:00 PM
         D 6:30 PM-9:30 PM
Cards: AE DC DIS JCB MC V
Dress: Evening Aloha
Style: Sea/Pac-Rim $$$$

Menu Sampler:

Breakfast/Lunch:
N/A
Dinner:
Appetizers: Maui Onion, Kamuela Tomato Salad- fresh buffalo Mozzarella, Thai basil, and Balsamic Glaze $12, Seared Tiger Prawns, watercress bruschetta, pine nut brown butter $14, Puna Goat Cheese and Caramelized Maui Onion Tart with micro green salad and truffle oil $10, Pan Seared Hudson Valley Foie Gras with toasted Hawaiian ginger sweet bread, parsnip puree, and truffled micro greens $18, Heirloom Tomato Gazpacho, Ama Ebi $9, Bay Club Sampler $20
Entrées: Three Course Lobster Sampler-Kona Lobster a la Plancha, Kona Maine Lobster Salad, Grilled Spiny Lobster Tail, Sherry Cream Sauce $70, Whole Crispy Moi with soba noodle and upcountry stir-fry finished with crystallized ginger and soy reduction $35, Roast Rack of Colorado Lamb with Kona coffee and fresh coca bean crust, finished with a cinnamon leaf and D'Anjou pear relish $36, Maui Onion Tenderloin of Beef, buttermilk mashed potatoes, island vegetables, Maui onion pinot noir sauce $38, Grilled Tofu Steak with sautéed veggies, coconut jasmine rice, roasted tomato fondue $26, Seared Ahi Saltimbocca, Serrano ham, sage, herb mash potato, reduced Marsala $34

Impressions:

You'll find The Bay Club sitting on top of a lava rock peninsula jutting out into Kapalua Bay. This used to be a private retreat for a few select residents. Today it's a fine dining establishment focusing on seafood and Pacific Rim cuisine. If a single choice from their wonderful menu isn't enough, ask for one of the tasting collections. Even the most jaded food enthusiast is sure to be impressed. We view the extensive wine collection as one of the best on the island. This is a genteel experience and patrons should plan to dress accordingly.

Maui Dining

Kihei

The Palm at Elleair
1345 Piilani Highway
Kihei, HI 96753
808-879-5100
Web: None
Hours: D 5:00 PM-10:00 PM XMo
Cards: MC V
Dress: Resort Casual
Style: Cont/Pac-Rim $$$

Menu Sampler:

Breakfast:
N/A
Lunch:
Kalua Pork Sandwich with crispy Maui onions & French fries $8, Hamburger
with French fries $7, Cheeseburger with French fries $8, NY Steak Sandwich
with French fries $10, Fish & Chips $8, Daily Specials $Mkt
Dinner:
King Crab & Prime Rib Buffet-Sa & Su- 5:00 PM-8:00 PM, $36/Adult,
$18/children under 12, Under 5 free. Mahi Mahi, Roasted Pork Loin, Spicy Thai
Shrimp, Smoked Salmon, Desserts made on premises.
Appetizers: Bamboo Forest-bamboo skewers of shrimp with a pineapple glaze
or chicken with spicy peanut curry sauce $8, Surf's Up-seared scallops with
white truffle scented mashed potatoes $10, Thai Sticks-shrimp wrapped in soba
noodles, deep fried & drenched w/spicy chili orange sauce $10, Mt. Fuji-Fuji
apples & roquefort cheese on Maui greens w/reduced port vinaigrette $9
Entrées: Fresh Island Ono seared, glazed with orange hoisin then roasted,
served with shiitake polenta & fried leeks $24, Shrimp & Scallop Kabobs with
grilled pineapple & red curry steamed rice $25, Grilled Free Range Rack of
lamb $2/oz-cut to order, Grilled Pork Tenderloin, pineapple chutney $24
Desserts: A tray of wonderful homemade pastries and delectable items

Impressions:

People driving down the Piilani Highway naturally spend much of their time
looking out at the ocean. Next time you're in that area, look the other way and
you'll notice a golf course at the Lipoa Street stoplight. There in the Elleair
clubhouse you'll find a lovely indoor-outdoor restaurant. The Palm is a chef-
owned venue, which means that diners have a real treat in store. The menu
features fine Pacific-Rim cuisine with a continental influence. Grazers will
certainly enjoy the extensive pupu list. Don't forget to sample the desserts!

Northwest

The Plantation House
Plantation Golf Course
2000 Plantation Club Drive
Kapalua, HI 96761
808-669-6299
www.theplantationhouse.com
Hours: BL 8:00 AM-3:00 PM
        D 5:30 PM-Closing
Cards: AE DC MC V
Dress: Resort Casual
Style: Ec/Isl/Med $$$

Menu Sampler:

Breakfast:
Classic Eggs Benedict $8.50, French Toast island style with fruit $7, Plantation House Potato Pancakes with salmon lox and applesauce $12, Smoked Ham & Cheese Omelet $8, Crabcakes Benedict with roasted pepper hollandaise $9
Lunch:
Starters: Crab Cakes with roasted pepper aioli $8, Soup du Jour $3/$4
Salads: Oriental Chicken Salad $8.50, Plantation Caesar Salad with fresh blackened fish $10.50, Upcountry Baby Spinach Salad w/ blackened ahi $16
Sandwiches & Specials: ½ # Burgers $7.50, Penne Pasta tossed with herb roasted Kula vegetables $10, with grilled chicken $13, Fresh Hawaiian Catch in a chef's preparation $15, Rosemary-Garlic Chicken Breast Sandwich $9
Dinner:
Starters: Warm Macadamia Nut Goat Cheese with mixed Maui greens and passion fruit vinaigrette $7.50, Sweet Chili Glazed Rimfire Shrimp Cocktail $9
Entrées: Pan Roasted Filet Mignon with bearnaise and Maui onion strings $24, Fresh Island Fish Sesame Crusted on a soba noodle and Maui vegetable stir-fry with a ginger-sesame broth $Market Price, Linguini tossed with Maui tomato, basil, garlic, olive oil $16, with chicken $19, scallops or shrimp $21

Impressions:

What a wonderful place to dine! The stunning ocean and golf course views are a fitting backdrop to this beautiful restaurant and its island style menu. Chef Alex Stanislaw has justly earned awards for his innovative, flavorful cuisine. Of course an extensive wine list accompanies the creative offerings. Lunch and dinner are popular here, but our personal favorite is the quiet time during a late breakfast when the crowds are gone and lingering takes on new meaning.

Maui Dining

Wailea

Tommy Bahama Café
The Shops at Wailea
3750 Wailea Alanui Drive
Wailea, HI 96753
808-875-9983
www.tommybahama.com
Hours:　L 11:00 AM-5:00 PM
　　　　 D 5:00 PM-10:00 PM
Cards:　AE MC V
Dress:　Resort Casual
Style:　Ec/Isl $$$

Menu Sampler:

Breakfast:
N/A
Lunch:
Appetizers: Warm Goat Cheese rolled in macadamia nuts with balsamic rum syrup, mango salsa and toasted baguette $8, Sweet Chilly Shrimp $13
Soups and Salads: Black Bean and Chorizo Soup with island spices $4/$5
Sandwiches and Entrées: Tahitian Tacos with won ton shells, black rice, grilled mahi mahi and mango salsa, avocado relish and sour cream $11
Dinner:
Appetizers: Jumbo Deep Fried Coconut Shrimp with papaya-mango chutney $14, Dr. Mambo's Plantain Combo of crispy plantain chips dusted with cinnamon sugar, served with black bean salsa and sour cream $7
Soups and Salads: Cooper Island Crab Bisque with toasted chili crostini, sherry and scallions $5/$7, House Vegetable Salad with a tangy citrus vinaigrette $7
Entrées: Char-Grilled Baby Back Ribs with Tommy's own blackberry brandy BBQ sauce, island slaw, mashed potatoes and cornbread $24, Chicken Breast stuffed with alouette cheese, sauteed in a roasted red pepper cream sauce and served with honey roasted onion mashed potatoes and fresh vegetable $21

Impressions:

Every item on Tommy Bahama's menu is a tasty memory of Florida and the Caribbean. Interestingly enough, the interpretations translate quite well to the middle of the Pacific. We have yet to try anything that we wouldn't order again. Entrée portions are large enough to invite sharing. Split the appetizers or they could easily be the limit of your culinary wanderings. This is probably good, as the prices aren't cheap, and we've yet to find a coupon or deal at Tommy's.

Kihei

Vietnamese Cuisine
Azeka Place I
1280 S. Kihei Rd
Kihei, HI 96753
808-875-2088
www.mauivietnameserestaurant.com
Hours: L/D 11:00 AM-10:00 PM
Cards: AE DC DIS JCB MC V
Dress: Resort Casual
Style: Viet $$

Menu Sampler:

Breakfast:
N/A
Lunch/Dinner:
Appetizers: Fresh Summer Rolls with shrimp (2) $3.95, Shrimp Pops $7.95,
Green Papaya Salad $6.95, BBQ Lemon Grass Beef or Chicken $7.25
Soup (Pho): (traditional noodle soup)-Chicken Pho $6.95, Rare Steak Pho $6.95
Noodle Soup: Rice Noodle with Seafood $7.25, Won Ton Chicken $7.25
Noodle Specialties: Crispy Egg Noodle with Beef and mixed vegetables $9.50
Soups: Hot & Sour Fish Soup w/green vegetables & herbs in a fire pot $9.95
Entrées: Sautéed Lemon Grass Chicken with somen noodles, fresh mint leaves,
bean sprouts, lettuce, cucumber, pickled carrots & daikon, toasted peanuts,
sauteed green onion with sweet & sour garlic sauce $7.25, Combination Fried
Rice $8.50, Create-Your-Own-Vietnamese Burritos (Banh Hoi) with chicken
breast and garlic, fresh mint leaves, pickled daikon, cucumber and carrot, somen
noodles, romaine $10.95, Crispy Orange Chicken wok fried with mixed
vegetables and served with jasmine rice $8.25, Curried Beef with Lemon Grass
and jasmine rice $8.50, Scallops with Snow Peas garnished with shredded
ginger, onion, garlic and green onion with steamed broccoli, carrots and
mushrooms $10.95, Pork in Clay Pot braised with black pepper sauce $9.95

Impressions:

If you like fresh delicate flavors and could stand to eat a more health-conscious
diet, you've got to try Vietnamese Cuisine. The food served in this restaurant
owes as much to the extensive use of locally grown vegetables and fresh herbs
as to the unique seasonings. These elements combine to create flavors that can
best be described as subtly addictive. In this beautifully decorated dining room
the owner has created a tradition of fine food and efficient professional service.

Maui Dining

Northwest

Vino

Kapalua Village Clubhouse
2000 Village Road
Kapalua, HI 96761
808-661-8466
Web: None
Hours: L 11:00 AM-2:00 PM
          D 5:30 PM-10:00 PM
Cards: AE DC DIS JCB MC V
Dress: Resort Casual
Style: Ital $$$

Menu Sampler:

Breakfast:
N/A

Lunch:
Salads: Herb-Roasted Chicken Salad with Upcountry greens, marinated vegetables, Gorgonzola dulce, and crisp peppercorn dusted pasta chips and Proseco pear vinaigrette 9.95, Caesar with lemon pepper croutons 7.95
Sandwiches: All served with Maui Potato Chips. Smoked Ham & Brie on a toasted roll with lettuce, tomato and sweet Maui onion honey Dijon 6.95

Dinner:
Antipasti: Grilled Local Asparagus on Bruschetta with farm fresh egg and white truffle oil, sprinkled with toasted garlic breadcrumbs 5.95
Salads: Giovanni's House Salad of upcountry greens, grape tomatoes, shaved fennel, and Kula onion with balsamic herb vinaigrette and olivada crostini 6.95
Large Plates: Pappardelle Pasta-ribbons of fresh tender pasta tossed with duck confit, slow-roasted chestnuts, rainbow chard, orange zest, and rosemary infused Marsala jus 12.95, Silk Handkerchiefs-house-made squares of egg pasta tossed in local basil pesto with oven-roasted Roma tomatoes, toasted salted almonds, and Pecorino Romano 11.95, Tuscan Style Rib Eye-salt cured and marinated in garlic and extra virgin olive oil, lightly grilled and served with fresh arugula, topped with lemon-rosemary gremolata 23.95, Rich Braised Lamb Shank 23.95

Impressions:

Will wonders from this guy ever cease? D.K. Kodama earned his reputation as an innovative sushi chef. When he opened a fine Italian dining establishment, eyebrows went up. Well, the verdict is in. Vino has been acclaimed for its world class cuisine and extensive wine list. D.K.'s talent for tweaking traditional tastes comes through across the menu. This one is worth driving a few extra miles.

Central Valley

Waterfront
Milowai Condominium
50 Hauoli Street
Ma'alaea, HI 96793
808-244-9028
www.waterfrontrestaurant.net
Hours: D 5:00 PM-Closing
Cards: AE DC DIS JCB MC V
Dress: Evening Aloha
Style: Ec/Sea $$$

Menu Sampler:

Breakfast/Lunch:
N/A
Dinner:
Appetizers: Sesame Pan Seared Sashimi Salad $12.00, Caesar Salad prepared tableside for two or more $12.00 per person, Steamed Pacific Cold Water Clams $14.00, Shrimp Tempura Nobashi w/macadamia nut honey mustard dip $11.00
Entrées: Fresh Fish prepared nine different ways-A La Meuniere, En Papillote, Hawaiian Salsa, Cajun Spice, Sicilian Style Provencale, Island Style with Prawns, En Bastille, Baked with crab meat stuffing, Southwestern Flair $Market Price, Jumbo Scallops sauteed and served with a Thai peanut sauce, macadamia nut and coconut risotto drizzled with hoisin vinaigrette and garnished with tobiko caviar $27.95, Exotic Game du Jour $Market Price, Cioppino over fettucine $38.00, Roasted Lamb Rack with a Szechuan peppercorn demi-glace $27.00/$30.00, Tournedos Au Poivre with pan seared medallions, crushed black and green peppercorns in a light cognac cream demi-glace $28.00, Veal Scaloppine a la Piccata over a bed of fettucine $29.00

Impressions:

The Waterfront Restaurant consistently wins awards for their wonderful food and black tie service. Diners have a choice of indoor or outdoor seating, and although most tables view the harbor, the lanai tables go fast, so plan to arrive early if you want to sit out front for the sunset. Evenings are romantic with lights reflecting on the water and surf sounds for background. When it comes time to order, your waiter will describe one of the most extensive selections of fresh fish available in the islands. Then the real fun begins! Patrons get to choose from some of the finest traditional and innovative fish preparations found anywhere. A lengthy list of great meat and game preparations round out the menu.

MOLOKAI
DINING

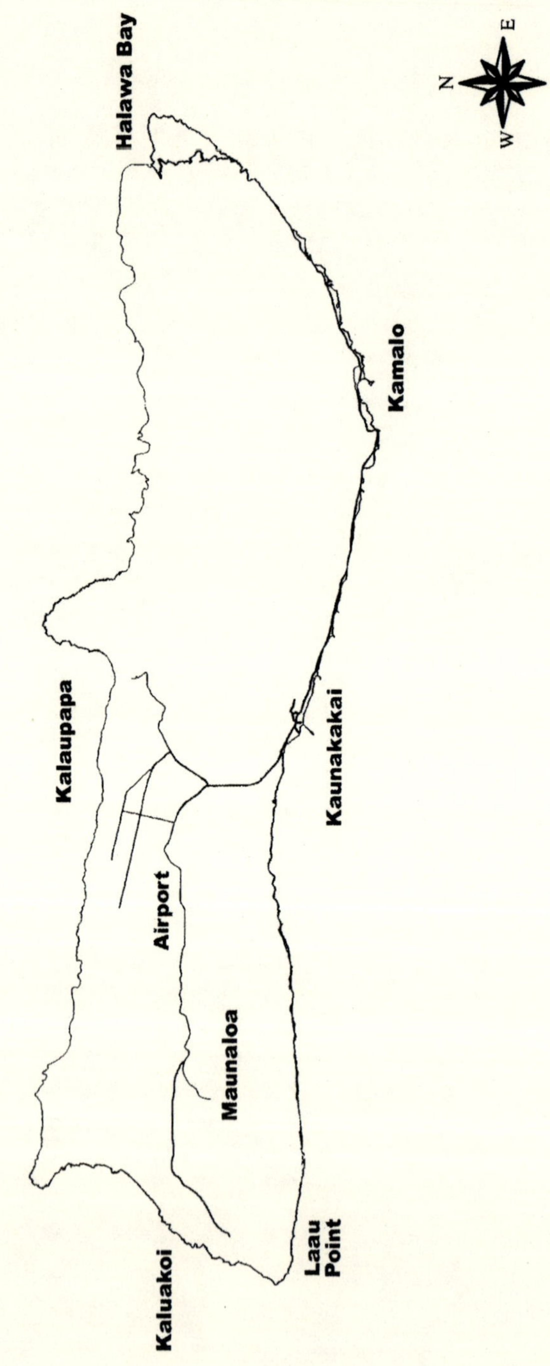

Molokai
Halawa Bay
Kamalo
Kalaupapa
Kaunakakai
Airport
Maunaloa
Kaluakoi
Laau Point
N
E
S
W

Molokai Dining

Kaunakakai

Hotel Molokai Restaurant
Hotel Molokai
Kamehameha V Hwy, PO Box 1020
Kaunakakai, HI 96748
808-553-5347
www.hotelmolokai.com
Hours: B 7:00 AM-10:00 AM
         L 11:30 AM-1:30 PM
         D 6:00 PM-9:00 PM
Cards: AE CB DC DIS JCB MC V
Dress: Casual
Style: Amer/Isl $$

Menu Sampler:

Breakfast:
Molokai French Toast $5.50, Create Your Own Three Egg Omelet with rice or hash browns $7.50, Eggs Benedict with rice or hash browns $7.25
Lunch:
Soups and Salads: Saimin $6.00, Won Ton Min $7.50, Chinese Chicken Salad with Oriental dressing $7.50, Caesar Salad w/chicken $7.50; w/shrimp $8.50
Sandwiches: Molokai Slider of open-faced, hot roast beef with gravy, sautéed onions and mushrooms on a French sourdough roll $8.25, Big Island Burger $7.00, Kauai Club Sandwich $7.50, Maui Reuben on Dark Rye Bread $7.50
Entrées: Charbroiled Kalbi Ribs with rice and pickled vegetables $8.00, Char Broiled Garlic Chicken Breast with a honey mustard cream sauce $7.50
Dinner:
Appetizers: Cream Cheese Poppers w/ranch dressing $5.50, Mushrooms $5.50
Soup, Salad, Pasta: Saimin with an Oriental shrimp broth $6.50, Caesar Salad with chicken or shrimp $9.50, Seafood Fettucine-choice of sauce $18.50
Entrées: All include soup or salad, steamed white rice or potato and fresh vegetables. Molokai Coconut Shrimp with special rum sauce $17.50, Fresh Catch $Market Price, BBQ Pork Ribs, Prime Rib-Fridays & Saturdays $19.50

Impressions:

The Hotel Molokai and its restaurant depict Hawaii before development turned villages into towns and cities. Here you'll find an oceanfront dining room with a menu in step with the slower pace of Molokai. This isn't fine resort dining, but budget-minded visitors will appreciate the reasonable prices and hearty fare. Local musicians present live entertainment in the evenings.

Molokai Dining

Kaunakakai

Kanemitsu Bakery & Restaurant
79 Ala Malama St
Kaunakakai, HI 96748
808-553-5855
Web: None
Hours: B 5:30 AM-11:00 AM XTu
        L/D 11:00 AM-6:30 PM XTu
Cards: None
Dress: Casual
Style: Isl/Spec $

Menu Sampler:

Breakfast:
Two Eggs, choice of meat, choice of starch, coffee or tea $5.46, Loco Moco
$6.52, Omelets with rice or toast $5.72-$6.50, Buttermilk, Blueberry, or Banana
Hotcakes $4.15-$4.42, French Toast $4.68, Breakfast Sandwich $4.15
Lunch/Dinner:
Sandwiches: Hamburger $1.82, Cheeseburger Deluxe $2.18, Teriburger $3.33,
Mahi Burger $4.16, BLT $3.54, Grilled Ham & Cheese $4.04, Tuna $2.50
Sides: Onion Rings $2.34, French Fries $2.07, Macaroni Salad $1.30
Plate Lunch: Includes tossed salad and rice. Hamburger Steak $5.72, Liver &
Onions with Bacon $6.66, Beef Teriyaki $4.95, Breaded Tenderloin Cutlet
$5.98, Mahi $6.66, Pork Chops $5.98, Fried Chicken $6.34, Chop Steak $5.15

Impressions:

Visiting Kanemitsu's is a trip back to the 1950's. This old storefront is actually a
bakery that doubles as a local style café. Besides the counter up front there are
tables along one side and a menu on the wall. The big draw here is the fantastic
bread. It comes in some pretty wild flavors-Banana Wheat, Cheese, Raisin Nut,
Onion-Cheese, Sweet Strawberry, Coconut-Pineapple, Pull Apart Cinnamon and
others, all priced under $4.00 a loaf. You might see visitors from neighboring
islands carrying bags of Molokai bread with them on their plane rides home.
Although the restaurant closes at 6:30 PM the bakery stays open to make bread
for the next morning's business. Residents of small towns have traditionally
come up with interesting ways to entertain themselves, and Kaunakakai is no
exception. People gather in the alley behind Kanemitsu's at 10:30 PM every
night except Monday to eat hot bread straight from the oven.

Molokai Dining

West Molokai

Maunaloa Room
Sheraton Molokai Lodge
PO Box 259
Maunaloa, HI 96770
808-660-2704
www.molokairanch.com
Hours: B 7-10 AM
         L 10 AM-4 PM
         D 6-9 PM
Cards: AE MC V
Dress: Evening Aloha
Style: Euro-Isl $$$

Menu Sampler:

Breakfast:
Eggs Maunaloa: Toasted English Muffin with Island Fish, two poached eggs, avocado and diced tomatoes 11, Create Your Own Omelet with choice of taro hash, hash browns or steamed white rice and choice of bacon, ham, link or Portuguese sausage and a selection of toasts 12, Belgian Waffle 9.

Lunch:
Served in the Paniolo Bar. All sandwiches are served with choice of ranch fries, cole slaw or fresh fruit. Paniolo Burger with sauteed mushrooms and onions and jack or cheddar cheese 9.5, Grilled Chicken Breast Sandwich with smoked mozzarella, guava and honey glaze 8.75, Vegetable Tortilla Wrap 7.50

Dinner:
Starters: Salt Fired Molokai Shrimp, herbed goat cheese bruschetta 12, Kaupoa Corn & Crab Chowder, Molokai sweet bread croutons 8, Kalua Pork Lumpia 9

Entrées: Herb-Crusted Tenderloin of Beef, mushroom ragout, roasted garlic 28, Mai Tai Mahimahi, balsamic rum syrup, li hing mui pineapple chutney, sesame rice 24, Pineapple-Guava BBQ Pork Ribs, grilled corn, smashed potatoes 24, Hawaiian Salt Roasted Half Chicken, garlic mashed potatoes 21

Impressions:

The Sheraton Molokai Lodge's Maunaloa Room is an upscale resort restaurant designed in keeping with the Lodge's rustic atmosphere. Patrons have a choice of indoor or veranda seating. The upscale island cuisine comes across quite well considering the remoteness of the location. Diners have a panoramic view of the ranch set against an ocean backdrop with windward Oahu in the distance. Weekend entertainment is an added plus at this unusual oasis.

Molokai Dining

Kaunakakai

Molokai Pizza Café
Kaunakakai Plaza
15 Kaunakakai Place
Kaunakakai, HI 96748
808-553-3288
Web: None
Hours: L/D 10:00 AM-10:00 PM
Cards: None
Dress: Casual
Style: Amer/Ec $
        Ent Card

Menu Sampler:

Breakfast:
N/A
Lunch/Dinner:
Salads: Caesar Salad $4.29, Super Chef Salad $6.99, Fresh Garden $3.59
Sides: Fresh Baked Bread Stix $1.99, Dipping Sauces-Tangy Red or Ranch
$.99. Pepperoni Bread Braids $2.29, All fresh baked on premises.
Specialties: Meatball Sub $7.99, Gyro Pocket with Spinach Pie $8.99, Chili
with Rice-homemade chili with beans $4.25, Italian Sausage Sub $8.99
Sandwiches: Classic Burger on a fresh baked bun $6.99, Fresh Baked
Submarine $7.99 or Pockets $7.59, Bacon Cheeseburger $8.99
Pasta: Linguini-with marinara $7.59, with meat balls/chili $8.99, Four Cheese
Lasagna $8.99, linguini Alfredo $8.99, all served with fresh baked Bread Stix.
Dinners: BBQ Baby Back Ribs $11.99, Huli Huli Chicken $9.99, Today's
Catch $Market Price, BBQ Chicken $9.99, Prime Rib on Sunday only $13.99
Pizza: Small 10" $9.44-$17.04, Medium 12" $11.94-$20.34, Large $14.44-
$23.64. Pizza by the slice $2.50, traditional and gourmet ingredients.
Desserts: Homemade Pies and Soft Serve Ice Cream & Sundaes
Kid's Menu Available

Impressions:

On an island the size of Molokai you're bound to find some eclectic dining
choices, and the Molokai Pizza Café definitely fills the bill. This all-things-to-
all-people establishment even serves prime rib on Sundays! The food is really
quite respectable with the pizza that gives the place its name leading the way.
You'll find this "island kine" eatery in a small business plaza off the harbor road
in Kaunakakai. Parking—why worry? There isn't even a stoplight on Molokai!

Molokai Dining

Kaunakakai

Sundown Deli
145 Puali Place
Kaunakakai, HI 96748
808-553-3713
Web: None
Hours: B 7:00 AM-10:30 AM Mo-Sa
         L 10:30 AM-4:00 PM Mo-Fr
         L 10:30 AM-2:00 PM Sa
Cards: None
Dress: Casual
Style: Amer $

Menu Sampler:

Breakfast:
Papaya w/lemon wedge $1.50, Fresh Cinnamon Rolls $1.50, Molokai Style Corn Bread $1.50, Hot Ham & Cheese Croissant $3.50, Hot Roast Beef & Swiss on French Roll $3.50, Canadian Bacon, Egg & Cheese Sandwich $4.00, Grilled Cheese Sandwich $2.25, Bacon, Egg, Cheese Sandwich $4.00, Bagel & Cream Cheese $1.50, Lox & Bagel $9.95

Lunch:
Daily Specials: All of the following dishes include garden salad, fruit and your choice of dressing. Vegetarian Quiche $6.50, Spinach Pie $6.50, Crab Cakes $6.50, Club Sandwich $6.95, Reuben Sandwich $5.95, Tuna Melt $5.95, French Dip $5.95, Chicken Fajita $5.95, Crab and Avocado on Croissant $7.50, Gourmet Saimin or Corn Chowder $3.95, Variety of Salads $3.25-$5.50

Beverages: Soft Drinks $.75, Juices $.75, Hansen's Kiwi Strawberry, Mandarin Lime, Cherry Vanilla $.85, Juice Squeeze-Wild Berry, Kiwi Lime, Passion Fruit and Mango, Mountain Raspberry $1.89

Fresh baked goods individually wrapped are available at the counter.

Dinner:
N/A

Impressions:

Molokai is a great place to escape the hustle and bustle of the main islands. We like to compare the west end of this island to Wyoming surrounded by an ocean. Amidst all this open space 8,000 people live and work. Naturally, their needs are on the same scale as their numbers. The town of Kaunakakai is small, the main street is small, and the delicatessen is small. In the midst of all this glorious emptiness you can still get some of your favorite deli items. Sundown Deli only has three tables; so carryout is the order of the day. Picnickers come hither!

OAHU
DINING

Oahu 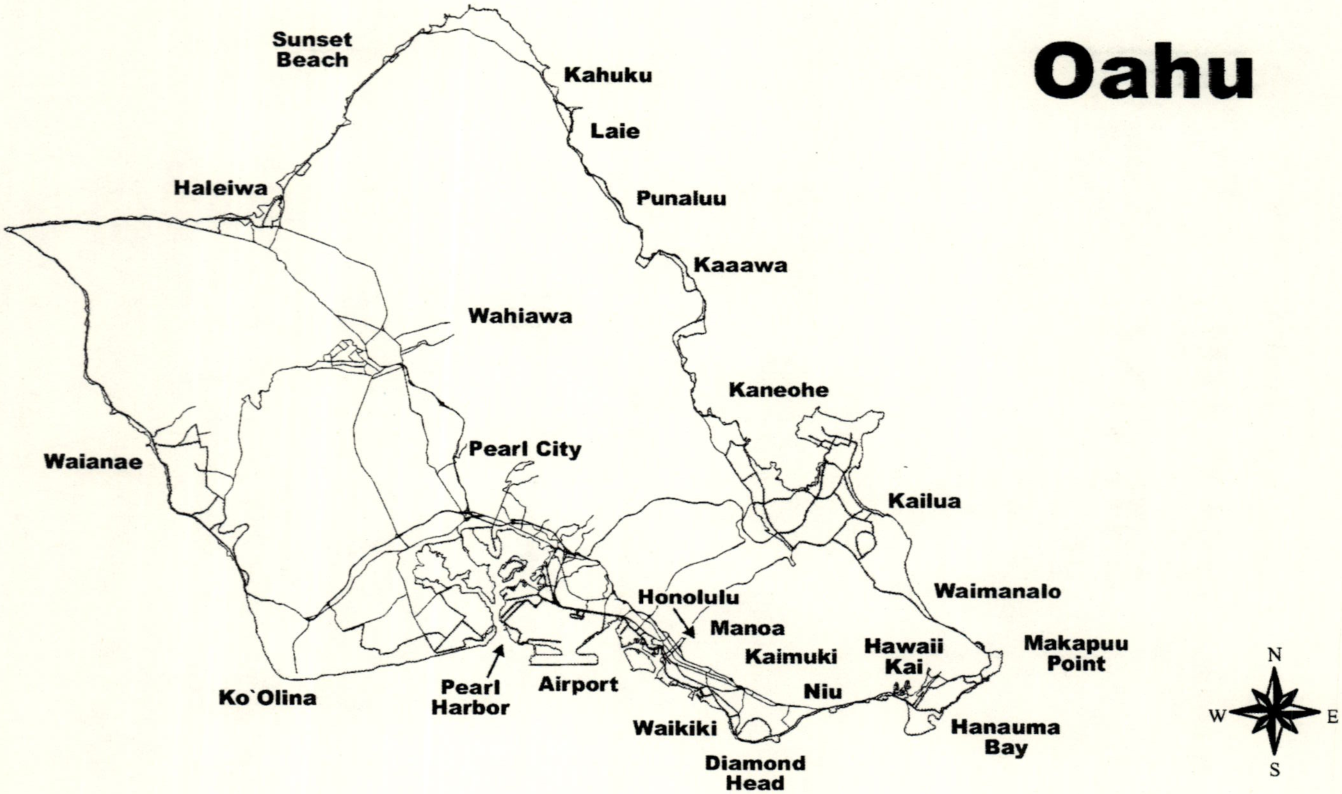
N
E
S
W
Sunset Beach
Kahuku
Laie
Punaluu
Kaaawa
Haleiwa
Wahiawa
Kaneohe
Pearl City
Kailua
Waianae
Waimanalo
Honolulu
Manoa
Kaimuki
Hawaii Kai
Makapuu Point
Ko'Olina
Pearl Harbor
Airport
Niu
Hanauma Bay
Waikiki
Diamond Head

Kaimuki

3660 On The Rise
3660 Waialae Ave
Honolulu, HI 96816
808-737-1177
www.3660.com
Hours: D 5:30 PM-9:00 PM XMo
Cards: AE DC DIS JCB MC V
Dress: Evening Aloha
Style: Euro/Isl $$$

Menu Sampler:

Breakfast/Lunch:
N/A
Dinner:
First Flavors: Signature Dish of Ahi Katsu of ahi wrapped in nori and deep fried medium rare, wasabi-ginger sauce $10.25, 3660 Sampler Platter for Two-Oxtail and Foie Gras Tortellini, Sautéed Mushroom & Natural Jus; Ahi & Salmon Hash, Lomi Tomato with Ogo; Crispy Shrimp Won Tons, Spicy Soy Sauce; Shichimi Seared Ahi, Asian Slaw $15.75
Second Flavors: Clam & Corn Chowder with roasted red pepper crème fraiche $5.95, Furikake Popcorn Shrimp Salad with garlic miso dressing $9.25
Entrées: Roast Rack of Macadamia Nut Crusted Lamb with cabernet mint sauce $27.25, New York Steak Alae pan seared with garlic, Hawaiian salt and butter, crisp onions $26.00, Chinese Steamed Fillet of Snapper in a Chinese black bean broth $24.50, Tempura Farm Raised Catfish with ponzu sauce $21.95
Taste of 3660: Four Courses-Pan Seared Scallop Salad, Crispy Calamari Spinach Salad, Medallions of Beef Tenderloin, Prawn, Dessert $36.60, wine $10
Sweet Endings: Harlequin Crème Brulee of vanilla bean custard and chocolate mousse glazed with a caramelized crust $6.95, White Chocolate Lemon napoleon with fluffy white chocolate, lemon mousse and fresh raspberries between layers of phyllo, lemon and raspberry sauces $6.95

Impressions:

3660 On The Rise has been a major part of the Honolulu dining buzz since it opened ten years ago. There behind Diamond Head, Russell Siu creates award-winning fusion cuisine complemented by an excellent selection of wines from around the globe. Waialae Avenue might be a bit distant from the normal visitor haunts, but 3660 is quite easy to find. Park in the deck under the building, and take the elevator up to the lobby. Make sure to get your ticket validated.

Chinatown

A Little Bit of Saigon
1160 Maunakea Street
Honolulu, HI 96817
808-528-3663
Web: None
Hours: BLD 7:00 AM-10:00 PM
Cards: AE DC DIS MC V
Dress: Casual
Style: Viet $

Menu Sampler:

Breakfast:
Traditional Fare-2 Eggs & 3 Pancakes $1.95
Lunch/Dinner:
Appetizer: Summer Rolls with peanut or lemon garlic sauce $3.50, Steamed Squids stuffed with pork hash, crab meat & minced shrimp $6.95
Salad: Beef Salad with sauteed beef mixed with shredded onion, basil leaves with peanut and lemon juice $6.95, Green Papaya Salad with shredded green papaya, shrimp, tropical herbs, peanuts and special fish sauce $7.95/$10.95
Soup: Chicken Noodle Soup with shredded chicken, green onion, cilantro and rice noodle $4.50/$4.95, Seafood Noodle Soup $5.50/$6.60, Spicy Noodle Soup with chili & spicy leaves, bean sprouts, lime jalapeno & rice noodle $4.95/$5.95
Fondue: Includes a tray of fresh tropical herbs, fresh vegetables, rice paper wrappers w/ sauce for dipping-Beef $14.95, Squid, Prawn, Beef Fondue $19.95
Entrées: Ginger Chicken $6.95, Pan Fried Fish topped with ginger sauce & green mango $7.95, Shelled Prawn with garlic pepper $8.95, Coconut Chicken-twice roasted chicken, marinated in garlic, shallots, fish sauce, then slowly roasted with fresh coconut water $6.95, Sautéed Mussels $8.95
Desserts: Banana Tapioca with apple banana, tapioca, coconut milk and topped with roasted peanuts and sesame seeds $2.50, Pineapple Milk Shake $1.95
Beverage: French Coffee w/Condensed Milk$2.00/$3.00, Carrot Juice $3.00, Soy Milk $2.00, Jelly Grass Drink $2.00, Lemonade $2.00, Beer $2.50/$3.00

Impressions:

The restaurants in Chinatown have largely been given over to immigrants from Vietnam. This is one of the better ones, so if you have never tried Vietnamese cuisine, here is your chance. Besides everything else this particular restaurant does a tremendous job with beef dishes. The extensive menu includes red meat in interesting ways. The owners will help you order, so be adventurous!

Honolulu

Aaron's

Ala Moana Hotel
410 Atkinson Drive
Honolulu, HI 94814
808-955-4466
www.tri-star-restaurants.com
Hours: D 5:30 PM-10:30 PM Su-Tu
       D 5:30 PM-11:30 PM We-Sa
Cards: AE DC DIS JCB MC V
Dress: Resort Casual
Style: Amer/Cont/Sea $$$$

Menu Sampler:

Breakfast/Lunch:

N/A

Dinner:

Appetizers: Black & Blue Ahi seared in Cajun spice $13.95, Escargot with sweet garlic & Parmesan Reggiano Gratinee $10.95, Foie Gras pan seared with a balsamic raspberry port wine reduction $18.00, Tiger Eye Sushi Tempura done tempura style with pear tomato salad and Chinese mustard sauce $13.95
Soups & Salads: Classic French Onion Soup $6.50, Daily Selection $6.00, Grilled Asparagus with goat cheese & walnut oil vinaigrette $7.50, Greek Maui Wowee Special with chopped tomatoes, avocado, Maui onions, feta cheese & bay shrimp $8.95, Caesar Sarento's Style with roasted garlic cloves $7.50
Entrées: Beef Filet ala 'Lexi" with Boursin cheese, olive oil mashed potatoes, & portobello mushroom $29.95, Steamed Island Onaga with baby Shanghai cabbage, soy-nori vinaigrette & sizzling hot peanut oil $29.95, Diver Sea Scallops with herb gnocchi, asparagus and shiitake mushrooms $27.95, Roasted Salmon with a smoked shrimp crust, mushroom orzo, red wine and honey thyme sauce $25.95, Grilled Rack of Lamb-herb crusted, sundried tomato jam, natural fennel jus $33.95, Clams Spaghettini w/slow roasted Pomodoro sauce, arugula, & olive oil $25.95, Veal Scallopine-porcini mushrooms & Madeira sauce $27.95

Impressions:

Those searching for a romantic dining experience would do well to consider an evening at Aaron's. Raised banquettes overlook the small window-side tables allowing everyone to enjoy the beautiful 36th floor view. The menu is upscale, the atmosphere clubby, and the service impeccable. Sophisticated patrons will appreciate the late night entertainment and extensive wine cellar. Valet parking is available at the hotel entrance street level on Atkinson Drive.

Honolulu

Akasaka
1646 B Kona Street
Honolulu, HI 96814
808-942-4466
Web: None
Hours: L 11:00 AM-2:30 PM Mo-Sa
         D 5:00 PM-2:00 AM, 5:00 PM-12:00 AM Su
Cards: AE DC DIS JCB MC V
Dress: Resort Casual
Style: Japan $$

Menu Sampler:

Breakfast:
N/A
Lunch:
Sushi Combinations served with Kobachi, Miso Soup and Salad $12.95/$14.95
Teishoku-served with Miso Soup, Salad, Pickled Vegetables and Rice, Sashimi
$12.95, Chicken Teriyaki $8.50, Butterfish Misoyaki $10.95, Combination
Lunches include miso soup, salad, pickled vegetables and rice-choice of two
entrees $12.95, choice of three entrees $16.95-choices include sashimi, tempura,
beef or chicken teriyaki, chicken katsu, tonkatsu, udon or soba
Dinner:
Nabe Mono: For two or more people only. Akasaka Nabe of fresh seafood and
seasonal vegetables $30.00
A la Carte: Shrimp Tempura $9.95, Teishoku Dinner Combinations served with
Vegetable Salad, Miso Soup, Pickled Vegetables & Rice, Scallop Butteryaki
$12.95, Beef Teriyaki Teishoku 412.95, or choice of two entrees $18.95, choice
of three entrees $24.95. NY Steak Dinner $15.50, King Crab Legs & NY Steak
$23.95, Shrimp & Vegetable Tempura $8.95, Yakitori $6.75

Impressions:

If you are a sushi lover and are looking for the ultimate hideaway, you can't do
any better than Akasaka. This diminutive eatery is located behind the Ala
Moana Shopping Center on a lane paralleling a parking lot off Kapiolani
Boulevard. Inside you'll find a few tables, one tatami room, and a ten-seat sushi
bar. The kitchen serves a surprisingly wide variety of Japanese specialties at
prices that are quite reasonable by Honolulu standards. Akasaka serves until the
wee hours making this a good choice for night owls.

Honolulu

Alan Wong's Restaurant
1857 S. King
Honolulu, HI 96826
808-949-2526
www.alanwongs.com
Hours: D 5:00 PM-10:00 PM
Cards: AE DC JCB MC V
Dress: Resort Casual
Style: Haw-Reg/Pac-Rim $$$$

Menu Sampler:

Breakfast/Lunch:
N/A
Dinner:
Appetizers: "Poki Pines" of crispy won ton ahi poke balls on avocado with wasabi sauce $12.50, Hot "California" Rolls…but with no rice-baked Kona lobster mousse wrapped in nori with crab avocado stuffing $14.00, Chinatown Roast Duck Nacho with homemade tapioca chips, avocado salsa $11.00
Salads: Ahi Cake-seared ahi and tomato terrine layered with grilled eggplant, Maui onions, basil, Big Island goat cheese lemongrass dressing $8.00, Whole Vine Ripened Tomato Salad with a li hing mui dressing $7.50, House Salad of greens with our Alan Wong's Special Oil Blend Vinaigrette $6.50
Entrées: Selections change nightly. Kiawe Wood Grilled Mahi Mahi with stir fried vegetables, wasabi sauce $27.00, Ginger Crusted Onaga, miso sesame vinaigrette, shiitake Enoki mushroom corn $33.00, Macadamia Nut-Coconut Crusted Lamb Chops with Asian ratatouille, roasted garlic smashed potatoes, red wine reduction $37.00, Pan Stew of Shrimp and Clams, Penne Pasta, chili garlic lemongrass black bean sauce $25.00, Braised Chinese Roast Duck Leg $28.00
Menu Tasting: Five Course without wines $65, with wines $90
Chef's Tasting: Seven Courses for $85/person (entire table must order)

Impressions:

Chef Alan Wong was a pioneer in the Hawaii Regional Cuisine movement. Back when many island chefs were still cooking out of boxes Chef Alan was out developing local sources of supply. Today only the freshest ingredients are used in his fusion creations. These unique combinations are guaranteed to excite even the most jaded diner. Despite the world-class reputation, you'll find an informal, friendly atmosphere at this establishment. If you can find any way possible, try and include Alan Wong's in your visit to Honolulu. Reservations are a must!

Oahu Dining

Honolulu

Anna Miller's 24 Hour Restaurant

Pearlridge West
Kamehameha Highway
Aiea, HI 96701
808-487-2421
Web: None
Hours: BLD 24/7
Cards: AE MC V
Dress: Casual
Style: Amer/Isl $$

Menu Sampler:

Breakfast:
Two Eggs, Choice of Toast, Rice, Hash Browns or Cornbread-with Ham, Spam or Link Sausage $5.95, Bacon or Portuguese Sausage $6.25, Corned Beef Hash $6.95, Chicken Fried Steak $7.25. Banana Pancakes (3) $4.45

Lunch/Dinner:
1/3# Hamburger w/choice of cole slaw, macaroni salad, fries, or rice $6.45, Pastrami Reuben w/choice of cole slaw, macaroni salad, fries, or rice $7.25, French Dip w/au jus & choice of whipped potatoes, fries, rice, cole slaw, or mac salad $7.95, Mahi Mahi Sandwich w/cole slaw, mac salad, fries or rice $7.25

Entrees: Served with choice of rice, fries, or whipped potatoes and hot roll or cornbread- Chicken Katsu $8.75, Homestyle Meatloaf $8.95, Liver & Onions $8.65, Turkey & Stuffing $9.95, Fish & Chips $9.45, Deep Fried Scallops $9.75. Chicken Pot Pie with green salad and hot roll or cornbread $8.75, New York Steak $11.95 or T-Bone Steak $16.95 served with soup or salad, rice, fries, baked or whipped potato, hot roll or cornbread. Caesar Salad $6.95, with grilled chicken $7.95, with bay shrimp $7.75, Soup & Salad with roll $6.45

Desserts & Pies: Brownie Fudge Sundae $5.45, Malts & Shakes $3.95, Root Beer Float $2.95, Fresh Strawberry, Pecan, Cheesecake, or Macadamia Nut Pie $3.25, Fruit, Cream, Custard or Meringue Pie $2.95, Ala Mode $1.55

Impressions:

Honolulu people will drive from miles around to dine at Anna Miller's 24 Hour Restaurant. This crowd pleasing family dining spot serves their extensive menu all-day-every-day. If somebody wants dinner at six in the morning, they get it. How about a sunset breakfast? No problem! But the flexible service isn't all that brings in the patrons. The food is genuinely good and fairly priced. This would be a good choice for a traditional mainland meal in an eclectic social setting.

Hawaii Kai

Assaggio
Koko Head Marina Shopping Center
7192 Kalanianole Hwy.
Honolulu, HI 96825
808-396-0756
Web: None
Hours: L 11:30 AM-2:30 PM
         D 5 PM-9:30 PM Su-Th
         D 5 PM-10 PM FrSa
Cards: AE DC DIS JCB MC V
Dress: Casual
Style: Ital $$

Menu Sampler:

Breakfast:
N/A

Lunch:
Appetizers, Soups, Salads: Fresh Clams Scampi Style $8.90, Minestrone or Tortellini in Brodo (broth) $2.90/$3.90, Tossed Green Salad $2.90
Entrées: Chicken Sorrentino with eggplant, cheese, and mushrooms in wine sauce $11.90, Fettuccini Alfredo with Broccoli $9.90, Lasagna $11.90, Meatball Sandwich $7.90, Eggplant Parmigiana Sandwich $7.90, Shrimp Scampi $13.90

Dinner:
Appetizers, Soups, Salads: Artichoke Pepperonata $7.90, Carpaccio with filet mignon $7.90, Vichyssoise or Pasta Fagioli $2.90/$3.90, Calamari Vinaigrette Salad $5.90, Caesar Salad (2 orders min.) $5.90 Sweet Broccoli Sauté $5.90
Entrées: Fettucine Alfredo w/broccoli $11.90/$14.90, Calamari Vegetable with squid strips and vegetables in garlic sauce with pasta $14.90/$16.90, Chicken Putanesca with garlic, anchovy, chili peppers and tomato sauce $14.90/$16.90
Desserts: Italian Spumoni $4.00, Homemade Cheesecake $4.50, Homemade Tiramisu $5.00, Zabaglione w/imported Marsala wine $4.50, Irish Coffee $5.00

Impressions:

As you head up the coast past Diamond Head you'll come to an area that would fit as well in Fort Lauderdale as it does in Hawaii. This is Hawaii Kai, home to Assaggio and the Koko Head Marina. Here at Assaggio's waterfront restaurant they take an upscale approach to décor and menu selections while maintaining reasonable prices. Tasty Italian food in generous portions makes Assaggio a great lunch choice while traveling around the island.

Honolulu

Auntie Pasto's
1099 S. Beretania
Honolulu, HI 96826
808-523-8855
Web: None
Hours: L/D 11 AM-10:30 PM
        D Su 4 PM-10:30 PM
Cards: MC V
Dress: Casual
Style: Ital $$

Menu Sampler:

Breakfast:
N/A

Lunch/ Dinner:
Antipasti: Garlic Bread $3.50, Red Pepper Calamari $6.50, Garlicky Clams & Mussels $8.95, Garlic Bread $3.00, Mozzarella Marinara $5.95, Fire Roasted Artichokes $7.50, Soup-cup $2.95, bowl $3.95

Salads: Garden Salad $4.50/$7.95, Original Caesar $4.95/$7.95 with shrimp add $4.00, Caprese- Tomato Mozzarella Salad $5.95, Kitchen Sink Salad $8.95, It's Greek To Me $5.95, Romaine & Gorgonzola $4.95, Pimento & Anchovy $5.50

Pasta: Sausage & Peppers $8.25, Meatball or Meat Sauce $7.95, Spinach & Cream $8.95, Creamy Pesto $8.95, Carbonara $8.95, Seafood $8.95, Tuna with Tomato & Onion $7.95, Fried Eggplant $8.50, Fresh Mushrooms $8.50, Tomato or Butter & Garlic $7.25, Clams $9.25, Fresh Vegetables $7.95

Entrées: Veal Marsala $14.50, Chicken Piccata $11.95, Grilled Calamari $11.95, Eggplant Parmesan $8.95, Lasagna Roll $8.95, Manicotti $7.25, Calamari Steak $11.25, Cacciuco (seafood stew) $15.95, Homemade Gnocchi $8.25, Cheese Pizza $8.95, Sausage, Oregano, Ricotta, Peppers, Onions $10.50

Desserts: Tiramisu $4.95, Cheesecake $4.50, Crème Brulee $3.95, Sorbet $4.50

Impressions:

Auntie Pasto's is a warm, welcoming establishment with waiters in white aprons and tables laid with red checked linens. Besides the comfortable atmosphere this restaurant provides a tasty menu. The salads are crisp with zesty dressings, and the pasta dishes are well seasoned with full-flavored meats and sauces. Espresso, Cappuccino, and a complete bar are available as are wonderful desserts. The prices are reasonable, but you'll have to look for parking on the street. Visitors will find this to be a convenient stop after touring the museums and galleries.

Leeward

Azul
Ihilani Resort & Spa
92-1001 Olani
Kapolei, HI 96707
808-679-0079
www.ihilani.com
Hours: D 6:00 PM-9:00 PM Tu-Sa
Cards: AE DC DIS JCB MC V
Dress: Evening Aloha
Style: Med $$$$

Menu Sampler:

Breakfast/Lunch:
N/A
Dinner:
Appetizers: French Vineyard Escargots in garlic herb butter $13.00, Open Faced Seafood Ravioli with wild mushroom basil and garlic cream sauce $14.50, Azul Antipasto $14.50, Mango Crab Cake crusted with angel hair pasta and roasted garlic cream sauce $15.00, Salad of Sautéed Foie Gras on potato pancake and oven dried pineapple with raspberry balsamic dressing $16.50
Soups & Salads: Roasted Red Bell Pepper Soup and seafood ravioli $8.00, Tomato Caprese with buffalo mozzarella and balsamic vinaigrette $8.00, Consommé of Shrimp with spring asparagus risotto cake and crispy house cured ham $8.00, Big Island Mesclun Salad, Jerez Vinaigrette $8.00
Entrées: Grilled Herbs and Garlic Marinated Tiger Prawns on mushroom risotto, tarragon beurre blanc $34.00, Rosemary Walnut Crusted Veal Rib Eye, celery root puree and port wine demi glace $36.00, Roasted Lobster with Molokai sweet potatoes and tarragon butter sauce $41.00, Ahi Tournedos of pepper crusted ahi topped with seared foie gras, parsnip mashed potatoes, syrah glace $35.00, Roast Muscovy Duck w/mango chutney, sauce de cassis $32.00
Chef's Fixed Price Menus $55 and $75

Impressions:

The Ihilani Resort & Spa is located in the wide-open spaces of southwestern Oahu, far from the hustle and bustle of Waikiki. This oasis of peace and serenity is the hub of the burgeoning Ko'Olina resort. Here you'll find Azul, the Ihilani's signature restaurant. The continentally influenced Mediterranean cuisine comes elegantly served and is complemented by an extensive wine list. Patrons will find that the setting and service are impeccable. Reservations are required.

Waikiki

Bali By The Sea
Hilton Hawaiian Village Hotel
2005 Kalia Road
Honolulu, HI 96815
808-941-2254
www.hawaiianvillage.hilton.com
Hours: D 6-9:30 PM XSu
Cards: AE DIS JCB MC V
Dress: Evening Aloha
Style: Euro-Asian $$$$

Menu Sampler:

Breakfast/Lunch:
N/A
Dinner:
First Tastes: Seared Diver Scallops and Wild Mushrooms with sautéed celery root, truffle vinaigrette and watercress coulis $13.00, Escargot and Wild Mushroom En Croute with Raclette cheese $7.50, Bali By The Sea Sampler of crispy prawns, seared scallops, beet salad, and ahi avocado cake $18.00
Soups: Island Bouillabaisse-a savory seafood stew of shrimp and scallops and fresh island catch $9.75, Gingered Maui Onion Soup w/coconut milk $7.00
Entrées: Sautéed Island Opakapaka crusted with Macadamia nuts, chopped cilantro and sweet potato mousseline, asparagus, baby carrots and kaffir lime sauce $34.00, Roasted Duck Breast and Confit Leg with wild rice risotto croquette, French beans, squash and sauce cassis $30.00, Roast Rack of Sonoma Lamb with orange hoisin glaze, Molokai sweet potato mousseline, touille of fresh vegetables and spicy peanut demi glaze $39.50, Scallion Crusted Ahi Tempura with fern shoots and hearts of palm salad, sweet potato lemon grass trap and ponzu butter sauce $36.00, Poached Kona Lobster $44.00

Impressions:

For an outstanding evening's entertainment of romantic dining, take a stroll through the Hilton Hawaiian Village to Bali By The Sea. This award-winning restaurant combines a comfortable upscale atmosphere with a fine dining menu in one of the nicest oceanfront locations on Waikiki Beach. The chef combines French, Asian, and island influences to produce wonderful taste and texture combinations. Bali's pupus display the chef's talents and can become a complete meal with little prompting. When the sunset starts to fade and the lights come on along the shore, you'll know why you made the reservation.

Honolulu

Bali Indonesia
1901 Kapiolani Blvd.
Honolulu, HI 96826
808-949-2254
Web: None
Hours: L 11:30 AM-2:00 PM, Buffet or Menu
            D 6:00 PM-9:00 PM, Buffet Mo-Th
Cards: AE MC V
Dress: Casual
Style: Indo $ Ent Card

Menu Sampler:

Breakfast:
N/A
Lunch:
Daily Buffet-$5.95/adult, $4.95/child-assortment of regular menu dishes
Dinner:
Dinner Buffet: Mo-Th $7.95/adult, $6.95/child-assortment from regular menu
Crackers: Shrimp Crackers w/Indonesian sauce $1.95, Belinjo crackers $1.95
Appetizers: BBQ Fish Cake wrapped in banana leaf with peanut sauce $6.95,
Indonesian style egg roll stuffed with chicken, shrimp, carrots, bamboo shoots,
and green onion, served with spicy peanut sauce $5.95, Deep Fried Tofu $5.95
Salads and Soups: Gado Gado-Mixed vegetables, tofu, eggs and shrimp
crackers with peanut dressing $7.95, Beef Ball & vegetables in soup $8.95
Satays: Asst. Satay-marinated chicken, lamb & shrimp w/peanut sauce $12.95
Entrées: Javanese Style BBQ Chicken $8.95, Indonesian Style Curry Chicken,
Egg, & Potatoes $8.95, Fried Spicy Beef w/chili sauce $9.95, Lamb cooked
w/coconut milk sauce $9.95, Margarine Sautéed Prawns w/black sweet & sour
sauce $9.95, Asst. Stir Fried Vegetables w/chicken, beef ball, and mushroom
$8.95, Indonesian Style Fried Egg Noodle w/ meats & vegetables $8.95

Impressions:

Bali Indonesia's location is typical Hawaii. Instead of occupying a freestanding
building, this dining spot can be found at the end of a strip mall. Inside, patrons
will find a comfortably busy yet gentle atmosphere. The menu features fresh
fruits and vegetables combined with ingredients like coconut milk, peanuts, and
fresh herbs. Vegetarians would love this place, but those of us who like a little
meat in our diet aren't left behind. Go online and check for coupons. A recent
offering provided an eight-course banquet for $13.95 per person.

Oahu Dining

Honolulu

Big City Diner
Ward Entertainment Center
1060 Auahi Street
Honolulu, HI 96814
808-591-8891
Web: None
Hours: B 7:00 AM-10:30 AM Mo-Fr
         B 7:00 AM-11:00 AM SaSu
         L 11:00 AM-4:00 PM Mo-Fr
         L 11:30 AM-3:30 PM SaSu
         D 4:30 PM-Closing FrSaSu
Cards: AE DIS JCB MC V
Dress: Casual
Style: Amer/Isl $

Menu Sampler:

Breakfast:
Broiled NY Steak & Eggs with choice of starch $8.95, Loco Moco $5.95, Fried Rice & Eggs $5.75, Kimchee Fried Rice $5.75, Murphy's Famous Apple Pancakes with warm cinnamon sauce $6.50, Grilled Oatmeal Cakes $5.95

Lunch/Dinner:
Pupus: Wings Over Kaimuki with a guava bbq sauce $6.50, Calamari Tempura Strips $6.50, Roasted Garlic Fries $3.95, Chips & Homemade Salsa $3.95

Salads: Paniolo Chicken Salad with lime marinated chicken, roasted corn, tomato, cheeses, chips & cilantro over greens $7.95, Citrus Grilled Salmon Salad with ponzu vinaigrette $9.50, Oriental Chicken Salad $7.95

Big Burgers & Specialty Sandwiches: All served with fries. Burgers are ½ lb. patties cooked medium or otherwise. Magic Mushroom Burger-mushrooms sautéed in garlic, Marsala wine & butter $7.95, Grandma's Famous Kimchee Burger $7.95, The Big City Club adding avocado, jack and cheddar cheeses $8.50, Ultimate Grilled Eggplant Sandwich with roasted red peppers, caramelized onion, melted jack cheese and roasted garlic mayo on sourdough roll $7.95, Pacific Fresh Fish Sandwich on a potato bun $8.95

Entrees: Served w/choice of white or brown rice, soup or salad. Chinatown Chow Mein noodles stir-fried w/fresh veggies $7.95, Herb Roasted Tequila Chicken $9.95, Fresh Catch Pan Seared &Glazed $9.95, Baby Back Ribs $16.95

Impressions:

This bustling anytime diner has a menu to tempt any taste or appetite. There is plenty of parking in the Ward Center lots making it easy to visit this fun place.

Oahu Dining

Honolulu

Bravo Restaurant-Bar
Pearlridge West
Kamehameha Highway
Aiea, HI 96701
808-487-5544
Web: None
Hours: LD 11:00 AM-10:00 PM Su-Th
          LD 11:00 AM-11:00 PM FrSa
Cards: AE DC DIS JCB MC V
Dress: Casual
Style: Ital $$

Menu Sampler:

Lunch/Dinner:
Pizza: 8" & 12", Classic Cheese $7.25/$11.25, Veggie Gourmet $8.75/$14.75, Artichoke & Prosciutto $8.95/$14.95, Garlic Roma $8.75/$14.75
Sandwiches: choice of fries, pasta salad, rice or today's pasta, Homemade Meatball Sandwich $6.50, Chicken Parmigiana Sandwich $7.25
Salads & Soup: Spinach Salad $4.95/$8.95, Chopped Salad $6.95/$8.95, Chinese Chicken Salad with sesame dressing $8.95, Minestrone $2.95
Steak & Veal: choice of pasta, rice, or fries-Veal Parmigiana $13.95, T-Bone $16.95, Steak Sinatra with sautéed mushrooms, onions & peppers $18.95
Pasta: Seafood Harvest Linguine in a light tomato cream sauce $16.95, Sautéed Scallops with fresh mushrooms in a cream sauce on linguine $13.95, Baked Chicken Canneloni $10.95, Eggplant Parmigiana $9.75, Lasagna $12.95, Penne Pasta with Artichokes & Chicken $13.95, Homemade Ravioli $9.95, Baked Rigatoni $10.95, Fettucine Pasta w/Sliced Chicken & Mushrooms in a garlic cream sauce $13.95, Eggplant Siciliana $11.95, Combo Platters-2 items $12.95
Desserts: Fresh Fruit Italian Ices $3.25, Cappucino Ice Cream Sundae $3.95, Tiramisu $4.95, Death By Chocolate $4.75, Haupia Chocolate Pie $3.25

Impressions:

Visitors to the USS Arizona Memorial are close at hand to one of Honolulu's favorite Italian restaurants. Just up the hill from Pearl Harbor you'll find the Pearlridge shopping complex and Bravo Restaurant-Bar. This establishment serves an extensive menu of affordable Italian specialties. Don't be intimidated by the crowds or large size of the room. Service is efficient and accommodating. During peak meal times the parking lot around the restaurant fills up. However, if you're not afraid to walk a bit, you'll find plenty of room behind the stores.

Windward

Brent's Restaurant & Delicatessen
Kailua Business Plaza
629-A Kailua Road
Kailua Business Plaza
Kailua, HI 96734
808-262-8588
Web: None
Hours: 7:00 AM-2:00 PM
Cards: MC V
Dress: Casual
Style: Amer/Ec $$

Menu Sampler:

Breakfast: (served till 2 PM)
All items served with choice of rice, hash browns, country fries or tomato; toast, bagel or English muffin; butter or cream cheese. Bruschetta Poached Eggs $8.75, Spicy Chicken Frittata $8.95, Four Pancakes $4.25, Strawberry Waffle $5.75 (SaSu only), Cheese Blintzes $8.75, Potato Latkes $7.95, Denver Omelet $8.95, Steak & Eggs $10.95, Fresh Mixed Fruit with Yogurt $3.25/$4.95
Lunch:
All served with choice of potato salad, cole slaw, macaroni salad or three-bean salad. Hot Corned Beef, Pastrami, & Swiss cheese with tomato & Russian dressing $9.75, Hot Brisket, Jack cheese, Ortega chili, grilled onion on grilled sourdough with fries $10.95, Meatloaf Sandwich on sourdough toast with grilled onions, gravy & fries $8.25, Hot Corned Beef Thick Deli Sandwich $8.50, Grilled Fresh Ahi or Salmon Club Sandwich w/fries $10.50, Kosher Salami $7.95, Latte $3.00, Cappuccino $2.75, Espresso $2.25, Cheesecake $4.50
Soups: Chicken Matzo Ball Soup (Jewish Saimin) $4.50, Clam Chowder $3.95
Dinner:
N/A

Impressions:

We normally try to highlight places that are easy to locate. That's not Brent's! Naturally this means that most of their patrons are locals. For the rest of us, take Kailua Road into Kailua, and as the road curves right, make a right turn into the driveway between the Ford dealership and First Hawaiian Bank. There in a back courtyard you'll find Brent's. The food served here makes this bit of extra effort worth it. Large servings of delicious mainland style meals are available most of the day. This place bustles. Bring your paper and have a seat indoors or out.

Honolulu

Brew Moon Restaurant & Microbrewery
Ward Center-2nd Level
1200 Ala Moana Blvd.
Honolulu, HI 96814
808-539-0088
Web: None
Hours: L/D 11:00 AM-10:00 PM
Cards: AE DC JCB MC V
Dress: Resort Casual
Style: Haw-Reg/Pac Rim $$ Ent Card

Menu Sampler:

Breakfast:
N/A
Lunch/Dinner:
Small Stuff: Ahi Sampler-a trio of blackened, sashimi, and spiked poke $13,
Steamed Manila Clams in a white wine garlic broth $10, Teri Wings $7.5
Soups: Chicken and Andouille Sausage Gumbo-mug $3, bowl $4.5
Salads: Spinach Salad w/shiitake mushroom, pecans, bacon, crispy sweet
potato, Bermuda onion, with moonberry vinaigrette $8, Ahi Poke Salad $12
Grilled Pizzas: Three Cheese Pizza $11, Barbeque Chicken Pizza $13
Sandwiches: All served with fries or rice. Beer Battered Mahi Burger $9,
Crabcake Sandwich w/Cajun mayo $9, Kalua Pork Sandwich $8
Lunch/Dinner Plates: Jambalaya w/spiced meats & seafood, smoked pork,
chicken, shrimp, Andouille, ham $13/$18, Chicken Curry w/pineapple, banana,
mango, long beans, Jasmine rice $10/$16, Manila Clam Pasta $11/$16.50, Sake
Steamed Mahi Mahi, coconut fried banana, rice & vegetables $12/$17.5
Dinner Plates: NY Strip Steak w/grilled tomato, green peppercorn sauce, whole
grain mustard mashed potatoes $24, Fire Roasted Ribs w/Mardi Gras slaw, mash
potato, mustard soy sauce $18, Pacific Bouillabaise in tomato saffron broth $19
Sweet Stuff: Bananas On The Moon with fried bananas, haupia sauce, vanilla
ice cream, chocolate sauce, macadamia nuts $5, Ice Cream or Sorbet $4
Beers: Handcrafted beers, Happy Hour 3 PM-7 PM Daily.

Impressions:

Up on the second floor of Ward Center you'll find Brew Moon with its Pacific
Rim centered menu. This contemporary restaurant offers dishes that you just
won't find elsewhere in Honolulu. Besides the Cajun/Creole and island
specialties, they offer a wide range of Pacific Rim selections. Look for late night
entertainment offering jazz, Hawaiian, contemporary, comedy, etc.

Windward

Buzz's Original Steakhouse
413 Kawailea Road (Hwy 61)
Lanikai, HI 96734
808-261-4661
Web: None
Hours: L 11:00 AM-2:00 PM
         D 5:00 PM-9:00 PM
Cards: None
Dress: Casual
Style: Sea/Stk $$

Menu Sampler:

Breakfast:
N/A
Lunch:
Burgers: Kiawe Charcoal Broiled Burgers are all served with lettuce and tomato on a sesame seed bun with your choice of a cup of soup or our tempura fries. Buzz Burger Deluxe-a 6 oz. Patty with house dressing and optional Swiss cheese and onions $7.95, Teriyaki/Thai Chicken Burger Thai peanut sauce & sprouts, $7.95 w/marinated beef & mayo dressing $8.95, Fresh Fish Burger char-broiled with Tartar Sauce $8.95, Mushroom Garden Burger $7.95
Salads: All served with French bread & olive oil. Thai Chicken Salad with peanut sauce $8.95, Scampi Salad with tomato, onion bleu cheese, capers, and charbroiled scampi $12.95, BLT Salad $6.00/$7.95, Caesar Salad $6.00/$7.95
Dinner:
Firsts: Tempura French Fries $2.50, Artichoke Surprise $6.95, Escargot $5.95
Soup and Salad Bar: $11.95, Salad Bar $8.95, Soup of the Day $2.50/$4.00
Entrées: Include salad bar, bread & butter. Top Sirloin 10 oz. $17.95, Baby Top $13.95, Ground Sirloin Special w/mushrooms & onions $12.95, Rack of Lamb $25.95, Prime Rib 13 oz. $21.95/Lanikai Cut 17 oz. $26.95, Lobster Tail $31.95, Scampi $22.95, Fresh Fish $Market Price, Chicken Teriyaki $13.95
Desserts: Buzz's Own Ice Cream Pies, Grasshopper Pie or Cheesecake $5.00

Impressions:

Buzz's doubles as both a beachside burger joint and steakhouse. During lunch this weathered wood restaurant serves a casual menu, while in the evening it makes the conversion to supper club fare. Although Buzz's is quite informal, bathing suits are not permitted, so wear a cover-up. Reservations are wise on weekend evenings. There's plenty of parking. Credit cards are not accepted.

Kaimuki

C & C Pasta Company
3605 Waialae Avenue
Honolulu, HI 96816
808-732-5999
Web: None
Hours: L 11:00 AM-3:00 PM Tu-Sa
        D 5:00 PM-10:00 PM Tu-Su
Cards: MC V
Dress: Casual
Style: Ital $$

Menu Sampler:

Breakfast:
N/A
Lunch:
Appetizers: Char-Grilled Vegetable Appetizer $9.00, Arugula Salad with pear, pecorino, watercress, and candied walnut salad with red wine dressing $8.00
Sandwiches: Fresh Mozzarella with tomato, sweet basil, drizzled with extra virgin olive oil and topped with cracked pepper $8.50, Roasted Pork Tenderloin & Provolone Cheese with aioli, baby greens, roasted onion and tomato $9.50
Pastas: Fettucine with Roasted Eggplant, tomatoes, smoked mozzarella & basil $10.50, Tagliatelle with Sweet Sausage, peas, and mixed mushrooms in a tomato cream sauce $10.50, Linguine with Clams, white wine, garlic $10.50
Dinner:
Appetizers: Escargot in Pastry with garlic, white wine, parsley & butter sauce $8.50, Warm Shrimp Salad, ricotta salata, green beans, tomatoes $9.00
Pasta: Fettuccine with Chicken, asparagus, porcini mushrooms, prosciutto and cream $17.50, Chef's Signature-Tagliatelle with Roasted Duck, Gorgonzola, pears and arugula $19.00, Fettuccine with Langoustino, beurre blanc $21.50
Entrees: Veal Involtini of pan fried escalope of veal stuffed with fontina and mortadella, fresh asparagus and house potatoes $22.50, House Roasted Pork Rib Florentine w/rosemary, thyme, garlic served with potatoes, grilled pear $25.00

Impressions:

C & C Pasta Company is a fine example of the restaurant evolution happening in Kaimuki. "Build it and they will come" really works here. The rustic style room has a deli counter in the rear displaying salame, cheeses, olives and pastry for sale, but take a seat in the dining room to enjoy pleasant service and excellent food. From appetizers to desserts, the tastes here are rich and flavorful.

North Shore

Café Haleiwa
66-460 Kamehameha Hwy
Haleiwa, HI 96712
808-637-5516
Web: None
Hours: B 7:00 AM-12:30 PM Mo-Fr
          B 7:00 AM-2:00 PM SaSu
          L 11:00 AM-2:00 PM Mo-Sa
Cards: AE MC V
Dress: Casual
Style: Amer/Mex $

Menu Sampler:

Breakfast:
Café Egg Sandwich of a one egg omelet style, cheese, Canadian bacon, toasted English muffin, tomato and sprouts with home fries $5.60, w/avocado $6.70, Huevos Rancheros w/beans & rice, $6.55, Quesadilla with home fries/beans/rice $6.65, Dawn Patrol of two large buttermilk pancakes and two eggs any style-offered between 7 and 8 AM for $3.10, after 8 AM $3.75, ½ papaya $1.10, Homemade Banana Nut Bread $2.50, fruit w/yogurt topped w/granola $4.00

Lunch:
Sandwiches: All served with home fries or potato salad and come with lettuce and tomato, with grilled onion on request. Mahi Mahi-6 oz broiled filet on a poorboy roll $6.95, Kama'aina Burger-1/3# w/cheddar cheese, mushrooms & bacon w/ homefries $8.50, Blue's Chicken Sandwich w/grilled chicken breast, jack cheese, grilled onions & mushrooms w/homefries $7.95, Veggie Sandwich on grilled sourdough bread with melted cheese $4.25 with avocado $5.25
Mexican Lunches-All plates are served with rice & beans or home fries. Fish Tacos with grilled mahi mahi, diced onion, tomatoes, cilantro and a lime on a steamed corn tortilla $6.35, Combination Plates $8.75-$10.50

Dinner:
N/A

Impressions:

Café Haleiwa is the abode of one Duncan Campbell, champion surfer and board designer emeritus. Everything else about the place follows suit. This casual café provides a glimpse of the laid-back North Shore lifestyle with its alternative crowd. The food is good, healthy, and plentiful with daily menu specials and fresh fruits listed on the board inside the front door. Locals and visitors alike love this place. There is plenty of free parking behind the restaurant.

Kaimuki

Café Laufer
3565 Waialae Avenue
Honolulu, HI 96816
808-735-7717
www.cafelaufer.com
Hours: BLD 10:00 AM-10:00 PM SuMoWeTh
             BLD 10:00 AM-11:00 PM FrSa
Cards: AE JCB MC V
Dress: Casual
Style: Amer/Pac-Rim $

Menu Sampler:

Breakfast:
Pastries-All our pastries are made with 100% butter $.65-$1.50

Cakes and Tortes-over a dozen daily to choose from $4.00-$5.75
Fresh Strawberries with Sour Cream & Brown Sugar $6.75
Beverages: Espresso $2.00, Latte $2.75, Cappuccino $2.75, Mocha $3.00, Thai Coffee $3.00, Thai Mocha $3.25, Hot Chocolate $3.00, Hot Tea $1.75

Lunch/Dinner:
Salads: Chinese Chicken Salad of lettuce, sliced chicken topped with sliced almonds, won ton pi, green onion, Chinese parsley, toasted sesame seeds $5.50/$7.50, Spinach Salad with our own honey mustard dressing, Gorgonzola cheese, craisins and sugar coated almonds $7.50, Orange Seared Shrimp Salad with a warm Orange Balsamic Vinaigrette dressing over Mesclun greens $9.50

Entrees & Sandwiches: Daily Entrée Specials $8.95-$18.95, Bratwurst made from coarse ground pork & spices, grilled, served with sauerkraut and country French bread $8.75, Vegetable Burger with choice of cheese and pasta salad $6.75, Salmon & Pumpernickel of smoked Atlantic salmon, pumpernickel bread, cream cheese, Maui onions, and capers $8.95, Vegetable Burger with pasta salad $6.75, Sandwiches with choice of bread, fillings, cheeses, and choice of pasta or green salad with lettuce, tomato and pickle $6.00

Impressions:

A quick glance into Café Laufer's front window reveals what appears to be a small bakery, but then they open for the day's business. The dining area is soon packed with patrons noshing on simple but tasty deli fare. Management insists that only the finest ingredients are used. The light-dining menu is brief yet creative. You can enter the building street side or from the parking lot in the rear. This restaurant is definitely an asset in Kaimuki's restaurant row.

Honolulu

Café Sistina
1314 S. King Street
Honolulu, HI 96814
808-596-0061
www.cafesistina.com
Hours: L 11:00 AM-2:00 PM Mo-Fr
        D 5:30 PM-9:30 PM
Cards: AE DC DIS JCB MC V
Dress: Resort Casual
Style: Ital $$

Menu Sampler:

Breakfast:
N/A
Lunch/Dinner:
Appetizers: Bruschetta Alle Vongole of grilled bread rubbed with garlic and covered with chopped clam in a wine garlic sauce $5.75, Oven Roasted Red Bell Pepper covered with bagna cauda and served with scamorza cheese $7.50
Salads: Insalata Contadina of mixed greens, grilled vegetables, frittata, feta cheese and balsamic vinaigrette $8.75, Verde Della Casa $4.75, Caesar $7.50
The Classics: Linguine Puttanesca with Kalamata olives, garlic, onions, capers, anchovies in a zesty tomato sauce $12.50, Veal Piccata with scaloppine sautéed in butter, capers and lemon wine sauce $16.75, Veal Piccata $16.75
The Contemporary: Pollo Porcini with a chicken breast sautéed with garlic, onions in an Italian wild mushroom sauce $15.50, Scampi San Remo of shrimp Riviera style with artichoke heart, red bell pepper, olives, and pancetta in a pink sauce with linguine $15.50, Mussels alla Toscana with linguine $13.85
The Cutting Edge: Lobster Ravioli with bay scallops, fresh tomatoes, basil in a dry Vermouth butter sauce $16.50, Spicy Tutto Mare with opakapaka, scallops, shrimp, calamari, shellfish in an exotic saffron prosciutto sauce over risotto $18.00, Gnocchi al Gorgonzola with asparagus and fresh tomatoes $14.50

Impressions:

Not only does he cook, he paints as well! Chef Sergio Mitrotti has decorated the walls and ceiling of this bistro-style restaurant with amazingly accurate frescoes from the Sistine Chapel. The chef also prepares fine Northern Italian cuisine. From classics to cutting edge the food is rich, delicious, and varied. This place bustles with a solid following of neighborhood regulars who like the large portions and reasonable prices. Live entertainment is often featured.

Oahu Dining

Honolulu

California Beach Rock 'N Sushi
404 Ward Avenue
Honolulu, HI 96814
808-597-8000
Web: None
Cards: AE DIS MC V
Hours: L 11:00 AM-2:00 PM Mo-Fr
         D 5:00 PM-10:00 PM Su-Th
         D 5:00 PM-11:00 PM FrSa
Dress: Casual
Style: Japan $$ Ent Card

Menu Sampler:

Breakfast:
N/A
Lunch:
Specials: Chicken Teriyaki $5.25, Beef Teriyaki $7.25, Shrimp & Assorted
Vegetable Tempura $6.95, Mahi Mahi Katsu $6.95, Fish Combo of broiled
salmon or mahi mahi, California roll, croquette, shumai, and a chicken wing
$7.95, Lunch Sushi Platter-six pieces of nigiri and a California roll $7.95
Dinner:
Special Rolls: Crunchy Roll-shrimp tempura, cucumber, yamagobo, kaiware &
spicy mayo coated with crunchy flakes and smelt roe $8.95, Rattlesnake Roll-
baked eel layered over a shrimp tempura roll, kaiware, yamagobo, & cucumber,
topped with eel sauce $9.25, Crunchy King Crab Roll with smelt roe $9.50
Appetizers: Edamame $2.25, Agedashi Tofu-deep fried tofu in tempura sauce,
topped with daikon and green onions $3.75, Beef or Chicken Gyoza-pan fried
dumplings $4.75, Seafood Dynamite baked with a masago mayo sauce $10.95
Entrees & Combos: all include rice, miso soup & salad. Chicken-charbroiled &
served w/teriyaki, mustard or ponzu $9.95, Supreme Salmon-pan fried fillets
topped w/garlic butter soy sauce $11.95, King Crab Legs w/garlic butter on the
side $26.95, Katsu or Miso Katsu-Chicken $9.95, Beef, Salmon, or Mahi $11.95
Salads: Salmon Skin Salad with ponzu dressing $6.95, Ahi Tataki Caesar $9.95

Impressions:

This is what you would call a "happening" Japanese restaurant and sushi bar.
While it certainly serves up a good lunch, the fun here really begins at night.
That's when you'll find a lively young crowd shouting local kine greetings,
wearing colorful fashions, and listening to great tunes. Rock 'N Sushi! Park
behind the restaurant or across the street at Sports Authority.

Honolulu

Chai's Island Bistro
Aloha Tower Marketplace
Honolulu, HI 96814
808-585-0011
www.chaisislandbistro.com
Hours: L 11:00 AM-4:00 PM XSaSu
              D 4:00 PM-10:00 PM
Cards: AE DC JCB MC V
Dress: Resort Casual
Style: Haw-Reg/Pac-Rim $$$$

Menu Sampler:

Breakfast:
N/A
Lunch:
Appetizers, Soups & Salads: Crispy Duck Lumpia with spicy hoisin sauce & fresh mango tomato salsa $7.95, Big Island Baby Greens with balsamic tamarind dressing $4.95, Combo Platter for Two of king crab cake, ahi katsu, crispy duck lumpia, and kaffir mac-nut encrusted jumbo prawns $26.95
Entrées: Grilled Breast of Chicken Sate with Thai peanut sauce with greens and toasted Asian flat bread $11.95, Crunchy Potato Seared Ahi Sandwich with caramelized pearl onion ponzu demi glace, greens and smashed potato $14.95, Seafood Risotto with heart of palm with prawns, scallops and crab meat $15.95
Dinner:
Appetizers: Honey & Hoisin Marinated BBQ Baby Back Ribs $9.95, Soft Shell Crab Tempura w/chili miso beurre blanc $11.95, Lobster Potstickers $10.95
Entrées: Long Island Duck Bistro Style with spicy port demi glace $33.95, Pan Fried Crispy Whole Moi with sun dried tomato citrus beurre blanc and Asian stir fried vegetables $36.95, Grilled Mongolian Style Lamb Chops with brandy demi glace $37.95, Grilled Garlic & Pepper Crusted Veal Chop with caramelized pearl onion demiglace, mashed taro & Asian stir fried vegetables $38.95

Impressions:

Chai's Island Bistro gives patrons a unique look at the local dining scene. Here at his Aloha Tower location Chef/owner Chai Chaowasaree draws upon his Thai background to create Pac-Rim cuisine that is both exciting and comforting at the same time. The resulting preparations are a feast for the senses. This is one of the few places of its type where lunch is an option. If you'd like to try fine Pac-Rim dining but are watching your budget, schedule a mid-day meal at Chai's.

Oahu Dining

Honolulu

Champion Malasadas
1926 S. Beretania
Honolulu, HI 96826
808-947-8778
Web: None
Hours: 6:00 AM-9:00 PM Tu-Sa
         6:30 AM-7:00 PM Su
Cards: None
Dress: Casual
Style: Spec $

Menu Sampler:

Breakfast/Lunch/Dinner:
Malasadas $.50 each. Coffee, tea, soda and bottled water are offered. Other pastries are also available.

Impressions:

This local establishment specializes in making a Portuguese treat called a malasada. For those of us new to Portuguese cuisine, malasadas are loosely defined as fried sugary donuts without a hole. The similarity to your standard donut shop offering ends there. Joc Miw, the Chinese owner, certainly improved upon the original recipe. His heavenly concoction is more an egg-rich popover than a donut. Champion Malasadas' sweets are so moist and rich that all it takes is a cup of tea or coffee and you've got breakfast. But have we mentioned that they are addictive? No tables are available, but who cares? The malasada sack is empty before the car starts anyway. Parking is available in front of the store.

Waikiki

Chart House Honolulu Lounge
1765 Ala Moana
Honolulu, HI 96815
808-941-6669
www.charthousehonolulu.com
Hours: D 5:30 PM-9:30 PM
               Lounge 4 PM-2 AM
Cards: AE DC DIS JCB MC V
Dress: Resort Casual
Style: Amer/Isl $$$

Menu Sampler:

Breakfast/Lunch:
N/A
Dinner:
Appetizers: Oysters Rockefeller $11.50, Sizzling Szechuan Shrimp $12.95, Escargot Bourguignonne with garlic, basil and bleu cheese butter and French rolls $8.75, Garlic Chicken $7.50, Fried Calamari $6.95, Steamed Clams $11.25
Soups and Salads: New England Clam Chowder $3.95, Seafood Salad on Nalo greens with jumbo shrimp, fried scallops, fried calamari, Maui onion and ripe tomato $14.50, Chart House Salad with Bay Shrimp $5.75/$8.25, Caesar $5.75
Shellfish: Abalone Dore dipped in egg and sautéed in olive oil $Market Price, Seafood Linguini with jumbo shrimp, fresh fish, sweet clams, ocean scallops, asparagus, onions, carrots, & shiitake mushrooms in a tomato garlic cream sauce served over linguini $26.95, Spiny Lobster Tail 1¼ # $34.95, 2-6# $29.95/#
House Specialties: Dinners are served w/squaw bread & New England Clam Chowder or green salad, & choice of steamed white rice, garlic mashed potatoes or ranch fries. Bouillabaisse w/fresh fish, clams, bay scallops, Gulf shrimp, and King crab legs in a tomato-wine court bouillon $29.95, Chinese Steamed Opakapaka w/ginger, cilantro, green onions, sesame oil & soy sauce $29.75, Slavonic Steak marinated, charbroiled, then sautéed in garlic & butter $30.75, Prime Grade Beef-Prime Rib $27.50/Lite $21.50, New York Cut $28.95/$35.75

Impressions:

If hanging out at the yacht club is a feel-good memory, you will enjoy the atmosphere at the Chart House. Although the address is listed as Ala Moana Blvd., this restaurant actually faces the marina opposite that address. This airy dining spot has been serving good food and drinks for about 35 years. For a late night meal the Chart House offers a satisfying menu and live entertainment nightly until 12:30 AM.

Waikiki

Cheeseburger In Paradise
2500 Kalakaua Ave
Honolulu, HI 96815
808-923-3731
www.cheeseburgerwaikiki.com
Hours: B 7:00 AM-11:00 AM
             L/D 11:00 AM-11:00 PM
Cards: AE DC DIS JCB MC V
Dress: Casual
Style: Amer $$

Menu Sampler:

Breakfast:
Three Egg Omelets served with wheat toast and home fries or rice $7.95, Eggs
Benedict $8.95, Spam & Eggs $7.25, French Toast $5.95, Macadamia Nut
Pancakes $5.95,Three Pancakes 4.95, Pineapple Boat $4.95, Half Papaya $3.95

Lunch/Dinner:
Sandwiches: All burgers use Meyer Natural Angus beef and are served with
1000 Island dressing, fresh tomatoes, lettuce and sautéed onions on sesame seed
or whole-wheat buns. Cheeseburger in Paradise with a blend of jack and cheddar
cheeses or swiss $7.25, Best Burger $6.75, Kalakaua Cajun Chicken Sandwich
$8.25, Polynesian Chicken Salad Sandwich of grilled chicken blended with
celery, cashews, pineapple bits, ginger sauce and topped with toasted coconut on
a whole wheat bun $8.25, Fresh Fish Sandwich w/a red Provencal sauce $8.95,
Calamari Steak Sandwich w/pineapple mac-nut slaw $8.25, Tofu Burger $7.50
Sides: Ono Onion Rings $4.75,Our Famous Seasoned Fries $3.75, Cheese Fries
$5.50, Chili Cheese Fries $6.00, Pineapple Mac Nut Cole Slaw $3.50
Salads: Caesar Salad $7.95, Chinese Chicken Salad with Oriental dressing
$10.95, Mandarin Shrimp Salad with a tangy ginger dressing $10.95
Entrées: Coconut Shrimp and Fries with pineapple mac-nut cole slaw $10.95

Impressions:

Legend has it that two girls arrived on Maui back in the 80's and didn't want to
leave. After looking around and realizing that they needed to earn some money
and finding that they couldn't get a good cheeseburger on the island, they started
a small restaurant. The rest is history. Cheeseburger's serves a casual menu with
something to please every member of the family. Be aware that the portions are
quite large! This is a fun place to listen to DJ tunes or enjoy live entertainment
in the evening while having a cold beer and a good meal.

Honolulu

Chef Mavro
1969 S. King St
Honolulu, HI 96826
808-944-4714
www.chefmavro.com
Hours: D 6:00 PM-9:30 PM Tu-Sa
Cards: AE DC JCB MC V
Dress: Evening Aloha
Style: Fre/Haw-Reg/Pac-Rim $$$$

Menu Sampler:

Breakfast/Lunch:
N/A

Dinner:

Appetizers: Ahi Seared, Provencale Salad with hearts of palm, anchovy sauce 19.00, Fillets, Opihi in a salad of arugula. opihi coral crouton 16.00, Moulard Duck Foie Gras sautéed with ginger, poached pear, julienne of savoy cabbage 20.00, Osetra Caviar from Iran, served with blinis and crème fraiche 89.00

Entrées: Day Boat Hawaiian Catch aioli crusted, saffron broth, tomato-fennel marinade 37.00, Long-Tail Snapper (Onaga) Medallions, sea urchin foam, leek etuveé 39.00, Keahole Lobster Pot-au-Feu flavored with sweet basil, braised Upcountry root vegetables 42.00, Island "Suckling Pig" Loin roasted served with crispy rind, red bell pepper basquaise, essence of cepe creamy polenta, Diamond Head kiawe honey glaze 32.00, Filet Mignon of Beef Tenderloin, pancetta wrapped, North Shore sweet corn, tender spinach, ogo-tarragon tomato sauce 37.00, Lamb Chateau, tapenade, puree of flageolets, confit tomato 39.00

Cheese: Brie de Meaux, baked Brie dome, red grape-star anise coulis 12.00

Desserts: Lilikoi Malasadas, guava coulis, pineapple-coconut ice cream 10

Three course 56/76, **four course** 65/95, and **six course** menus 93/132 are available, with/without wines.

Impressions:

At the corner of King & McCully you'll discover an inviting fine dining experience that ranks among the finest in Honolulu. The chef/owner is from Provence in France and has won numerous awards for his French-influenced Hawaii Regional Cuisine. World-class menu selections have been expertly paired with wines by the glass from the restaurant's extensive collection. Take the entire evening to savor all that is so graciously offered. Chef Mavro's is an easy drive from Waikiki. Just go to the corner of the Ala Wai Canal and straight out McCully. Valet parking is available on site.

North Shore

Cholo's Homestyle Mexican
North Shore Marketplace
Haleiwa, HI 96712
808-637-3059
Web: None
Hours: B 8-11 AM
        L/D 11 AM-9 PM
Cards: None
Dress: Casual
Style: Mex $$

Menu Sampler:

Breakfast:
Chillaquillas (Tortilla Casserole) topped with two eggs with rice, beans and tortillas $5.95, Two Soft Corn Tortillas filled with scrambled eggs, cheese, tomato, chile, onion and cilantro with chips $4.95, Pancakes (3) $3.75, Huevos Rancheros $5.95, Mexican Breakfast Sandwich of grilled sourdough bread, cheese, green chili, sliced tomato & omelet style egg, served w/potatoes $4.95

Lunch/Dinner:
Everything comes ala carte, plate, or dinner. Plate includes beans and rice; dinner includes salad, beans, rice, chips and salsa. Taco a la carte $3.00, plate $5.25, dinner $7.50, Enchilada $4.00/$6.75/$9.25, Chimi Changa $6.50/$9.25/$11.50, Gordita $4.95/$7.75/$10.25, Tostada $4.00/$6.75/$9.25, Nachos-homemade chips, fresh salsa, cheddar, jack and jalapenos $4.00, Side Orders of Guacamole $2.00, Sour Cream $1.00, Beans $2.00, Black Beans $2.25 Special Quesadillas-Spinach Quesadilla, black beans, spinach, tomatoes, cheese $5.25/$7.75/$10.25, Cholo's Fish Tacos Plates of local ahi or mahi grilled and spiced $6.75/$9.25/$10.00/$12.50, Shrimp Taco Plates $6.75/$9.25/$10.00/ $12.50, Chicken, Shrimp or Steak Fajitas plates and dinners $9.95-$17.50

Impressions:

When you're up on the North Shore watching killer waves and suddenly feel the need for a Mexican food fix, give Cholo's a try. This open-air storefront eatery is located in the back tier of the North Shore Marketplace in Haleiwa. Cholo's specializes in serving large portions of homemade traditional Mexican fare for breakfast, lunch, and dinner. This popular spot always manages to have room for another diner. The bustling North Shore Marketplace serves as the commercial hub for the entire area and makes an interesting stop while touring.

Oahu Dining

Waikiki

Ciao Mein
Hyatt Regency
2424 Kalakaua Ave
Honolulu, HI 96815
808-923-2426
www.ciaomein.com
Hours: D 6:00 PM-10:00PM
Cards: AE MC V
Dress: Evening Aloha
Style: Chi/Ital $$$

Menu Sampler:

Breakfast/Lunch:
N/A

Dinner:
Appetizers: Spring Rolls with shrimp, bamboo shoots $9.75, Carpaccio-slices of beef tenderloin with capers, olive oil, lemon and pepper $10.75, Szechuan Eggplant-wok fried in a spicy Szechuan sauce $9.25, Focaccia $9.00

Soups & Salads: Hearty Minestrone Soup with braised sausage $5.50, Soup Ciao Mein-a clear chicken broth w/lobster won tons $6.75, Chinese Salad $7.50

Entrées: Risotto $6.75, Fried Rice with egg, char siu pork, peas and choice of shrimp or Chinese sausage $7.25, Honey Walnut Shrimp-shrimp with snap peas and honey glazed walnuts $22.75, Seafood Funn Lasagna of assorted seafood, Boursin cheese, smoked mozzarella, spinach, eggplant, look funn noodles and marinara sauce $19.75, Mongolian Sizzle (Beef) $18.25, Bistecca Di Manzo Alle Erbe-marinated sirloin of beef in olive oil, basil, garlic herbs and pine nuts $20.75, Roast Duck Breast w/steamed buns, green onions & hoisin sauce $25.00

Desserts: Tiramisu Sculptures with espresso and sambuca $5.75, Marco Polo Frozen Delight of Napolitan spumone and espresso ice cream rolled in chocolate shavings, lychee sorbet, and white chocolate and ginger ice cream $5.75

Impressions:

H-m-m…Chinese and Italian prepared in the same kitchen and then combined in the same dish? Yes, and it works! In fact, it works extremely well. On the third floor of the Hyatt Regency there's a sleek yet fun restaurant that has been winning awards and pleasing diners with Marco Polo style culinary adventures for a number of years now. When the wait staff suggests interesting pairings of the delicious foods and beverages, follow their lead. Exotic set dinners are available for $30.00, $36.00 and $42.00 per person if your decisions waver.

Windward

Cinnamon's Restaurant
315 Uluniu Street
Kailua, HI 96734
808-261-8724
Web: None
Hours: B 7:00 AM-2:00 PM
         L 11:00 AM-2:00 PM
         D 6:30 PM-8:30 PM Th-Sa
Cards: DC DIS JCB MC V
Dress: Casual
Style: Ecl/Pac Rim $$

Menu Sampler:

Breakfast:
Omelettes with 3 eggs, choice of country home fries, rice, biscuit, pancakes, or hash browns $7.95-$9.95, Mahi Mahi Benedict $6.75/$8.75 or Traditional Benedict $6.95/$8.95 with home fries or hash browns, Frittata with basil pesto, artichoke hearts, spinach, onions & olives & melted parmesan cheese $9.25, Carrot Pancakes with Cream Cheese Sauce $3.95/$5.95, Portuguese Sweet Bread French Toast $3.95, Broiled Prime Rib & Eggs $9.75

Lunch:
Salads: Mandarin-char siu pork, Chinese roast chicken, won ton chips, peanuts, greens, mandarin oranges, Oriental dressing $8.75, Spinach & Bacon $8.50
Sandwiches: Curried Chicken Salad on grilled Portuguese sweet bread with cashew nuts $8.70, Mahi Mahi broiled or dipped in egg and sautéed $8.25
Entrees: Roast Beef with choice of starch, gravy, fresh vegetables $8.25, Stir Fry with mahi, chicken or beef, fresh vegetables, teriyaki sauce, rice $7.95

Dinner:
Specialties of the House: choice of starch and cole slaw garnish-Shrimp Curry with mango chutney $18.95, Mahi Mahi Scampi-sautéed in dairy butter, fresh garlic, vermouth, parmesan cheese $14.50, Chicken or Mahi Mahi prepared picatta style, marsala, chateau in a rich wine sauce, and fantasy-using fresh spinach, broccoli, Swiss Cheese and the house hollandaise sauce $14.95

Impressions:

Those looking for something special and not afraid of reading a map will really enjoy this island favorite. Just off the main highway near McDonalds you'll find Kailua Square and Cinnamon's. This quaint but upscale dining spot serves an ambitious menu of well-executed selections regardless of time of day. This is a great stop for those taking the circle island tour. Park in the courtyard lot.

Windward

Crouching Lion Inn

51-666 Kamehameha Hwy
Ka'a'awa, HI 96730
808-237-8511
Web: None
Hours: L 11:00 AM-3:00 PM
        D 5:00 PM-9:00 PM
Cards: AE DIS MC V
Dress: Resort Casual
Style: Amer/Isl $$/Ent Card

Menu Sampler:

Breakfast:
N/A
Lunch:
Appetizers: Honey Garlic Shrimp with a light tempura batter and sauce $9.25, Gourmet Sautéed Mushrooms in a butter, garlic and sherry sauce $7.50
Salads: Oriental Chicken Salad $9.25, Shrimp Parmesan Salad $10.25
Sandwiches: All served with fries. Kalua Pork $8.95, Mahi Mahi Melt $8.50
Gourmet Burgers: All served with fries. Cheeseburger Deluxe $8.00
Entrées: Various entrees served with fries, rice or mashed potatoes, vegetables and homemade buns. Kalua Pork Plate with sweet steamed cabbage $10.25, Sautéed Mahimahi $10.95, Chicken Macadamia $10.95, Teriyaki Steak $10.95
Dinner:
Appetizers: Steamed Clams $9.50, Escargot Bourgignonne $9.25
Specialties: Slavonic Steak (Signature Dish)-marinated tenderloin, charbroiled, and served from a sizzling platter of garlic butter $Market Price, Kalua Pork with steamed cabbage and poi bread pudding $14.95, Mahi Mahi sautéed in garlic butter $14.95, Teriyaki New York Steak (8 oz) $19.50, Chicken Macadamia-dipped in an egg and brandy batter, deep fried and served with sweet and sour sauce and macadamia nuts $15.75, Peppersteak $21.50

Impressions:

Whether you are traveling around Oahu or staying on the north shore, stop along the Windward Coast and enjoy the timelessness of the surroundings. Here you'll find a quaint stone building housing the Crouching Lion Inn. This famous Oahu landmark serves comfort food with island influences. Patrons will find The Livingston Galleries downstairs for after-meal browsing. The Crouching Lion Inn is located near a curve. Watch the address numbers so you don't miss it.

Waikiki

Diamond Head Grill
W Hotel
2885 Kalakaua Ave
Honolulu, HI 96815
808-922-3734
www.diamondheadgrill.com
Hours: D 6:00 PM-10:00 PM
Cards: AE DIS DC JCB MC V
Dress: Evening Aloha
Style: Haw-Reg/Pac-Rim $$$$

Menu Sampler:

Dinner:
Pupus: Sweet Potato Gnocchi, mascarpone cream, Hamakua mushrooms 12, DHG Crabcakes 13, Sugar Cane Skewer Petite Lobster Tempura, spicy Nalo greens, daikon, ponzu 15, Seared Foie Gras, baby beets, crouton 18
Greens & Soup: Waimanalo Arugula, Stilton blue cheese, macadamia nuts, Fuji apples, white wine vinaigrette 9, Housemade Buffalo Mozzarella, Hau'ula vine ripened tomatoes, Waimanalo greens 9, Hau'ula Tomato Gazpacho, fresh island ceviche 8, Caesar of Waimanalo Romaine, white anchovies $9
Entrées: Grilled Mahi Mahi, ogo relish, stir fry baby bok choy, furikake rice 28, Seared Island Ahi, duck hash, caramelized apple demi glace 29, Macadamia Nut Crusted Lamb Chops, potato gratin, roasted garlic sauce 38, Beef Tenderloin, Yukon gold puree, Hamakua Big Island mushrooms 33, Cioppino, fresh island seafood assortment, prawns, lobster and clams, tomato basil broth 27, Grilled Pork Chop, savory Kahuku corn pancetta pudding, maple jus 26
Desserts: Warm Kula Strawberry and Candied Ginger Cobbler with white chocolate gelato 8, Warm Lava Cake with Honey Gelato, coffee and vanilla crème Anglaise, assorted fruits 9, Piña Colada Cake, rum, shredded coconut, piña colada crème Anglaise 7.50, Dessert of the Day 8

Impressions:

This upscale restaurant is located on the second floor of the sophisticated W Hotel at the quiet Diamond Head end of Waikiki. The dinner selections are an intriguing fusion of island flavors and classic techniques. However, this is more than just a dining spot—it's a night scene. If you like your cocktails made with top shelf liquor that you can actually taste and smell, you've come to the right place. Live entertainment and a great pupu menu round out the picture. Call ahead for the weekly line-up. Use the valet parking or park out along the street.

Diamond Head

Diamond Head Market & Grill
3158 Monsarrat Ave.
Honolulu, HI 96815
808-732-0077
Web: None
Hours: 7:30 AM-9:30 PM
Cards: AE DIS JCB MC V
Dress: Casual
Style: Isl/Pac-Rim $

Menu Sampler:

Breakfast/Lunch/Dinner:
Bakery: Selections very daily. Whole Pies and Tarts- Chocolate Raspberry 9" $24.00, Hawaiian Carrot Cake 9" $21.00, Fresh Fruit Tart 9" $25.00, Lilikoi Cream Cake 7" $17.00, Individual servings of brownies, lilikoi bars, apple-blueberry crisp, Hawaiian spice cake, white chocolate mac-nut lemon cake, butter mochi, blueberry and cream cheese scones, energy bars, cookies
Market: Deli carryout meals-selections vary daily-Prime Rib, Kalbi Ribs, Osso Bucco, Garlic Braised Pork Roast, Kalua Pork, Potato and Rice Dishes, Hot Vegetables, Salads, Sushi, Appetizers, Entrees-Thai Red Curry Beef, Jambalaya, Shrimp Linguine, Black Bean Shrimp Stir Fry, Eggplant Parmesan, Beef Stew
Grill: Sandwiches offered alone, as a mini-plate, or as a plate lunch-Char Siu Pork $4.50/$5.75/$6.75, Teriyaki Chicken $4.00/$5.50/$6.50, Grilled Ahi Steak $6.50/$6.75/$8.75, Portobello Mushroom $4.00/$5.50/$7.50
Specials: bbq pork rib plate $8.75, ny steak plate $9.50, chicken eggplant sandwich $6.75, kal bi beef rib plate $8.50, western bacon burger $6.75

Impressions:

Carryout dining is very popular in Hawaii. Most island family members work, including Mom, so dinner often gets picked up on the way home. Local style restaurants many times get the nod, but the Diamond Head Market & Grill takes things up a notch. At the outside service window, you can order a good selection of sandwiches and upscale plate lunches cooked to order. However, the culinary fun really begins inside the store. The bakery counter offers tasty pies, cakes and confections in single servings or entire displays. In the gourmet case, you'll find a particularly nice assortment of prepared entrees and side dishes. Then there's a pantry section with many choice coffees, sauces, chutneys, relishes, and party foods to accompany it all. This bountiful array of foods is perfect for that picnic in Kapiolani Park or a special stay-at-home meal in your condo.

Honolulu

Dixie Grill BBQ & Crab Shack
404 Ward Avenue
Honolulu, HI 96814
808-596-8359
www.dixiegrill.com
Hours: B 8:00 AM-11:00 AM SaSu
           L/D 11:00 AM-10:00 PM
Cards: AE DC DIS MC V
Dress: Casual
Style: Amer $$

Menu Sampler:

Breakfast:
Cajun Biscuits & Gravy $3.50, Smokehouse Scramble $8.50, Blueberry Cream
Cheese Stuffed Toast $7, Crab Shack Omelette w/hashbrown casserole $12.00
Lunch/Dinner:
Appetizers: Pile 'O' Rings with BBQ aioli $5, Jumbo Coconut Shrimp $9,
Bucket of Cowboy Wings $7.99, Southern Fried Okra $6, Nacho Fries $8
Soup/Salad: Big Daddy's Crab & Shrimp $9.50, BBQ Chop Chicken Salad
with cheese & avocado $9, Gulf Coast Gumbo $7/$4, She-Crab Soup $7/$4
Sides: Mashed. Fries, Hush Puppies, Rice, Baked Beans, Co' Slaw, Corn on the
Cobb, Garden Green Salad, Garlic Bread, Mac Salad $3, all tasty!
BBQ: Served w/beans and a choice of one side. Baby Back Ribs $19/$13,
Hawaiian BBQ Glazed Smoked BBQ Chicken $11, Dixie Mixed Grill of baby
back ribs, fresh sausage, pulled pork & chicken $18, T-Bone Steak (20 oz) $24
Meals: Beer Battered Fish Basket with slaw & Dixie fries $9.50, Buttermilk
Fried Chicken (1/2) with mashers & slaw $9.50, Southern Fried Catfish with
rice & corn $13, Fried Shrimp Platter (7) with fries, corn & hushpuppies $14
Sandwiches: Pulled BBQ Chicken, Beef Brisket, or Pork Sandwich with fries or
mac salad $6.95, Fresh Fish Sandwich grilled or beer battered $9
Desserts: Pecan Pie topped with ice cream $5.00, Jack Daniels Mousse Pie with
Oreo cookie crust $5.00, Key Lime Pie with a granola & graham crust $4.85

Impressions:

Dixie Grill has an atmosphere that would fit right in on the Tamiami Trail. All
that's missing is the guy wrestling the rubber alligator. But then, hey! They
make great southern barbeque, and that's a rarity in Hawaii. If you are looking
for a change of pace or just like good barbeque, be sure to visit the Dixie Grill.

Manoa Valley

Donato's
Manoa Marketplace
2756 Woodlawn Drive, Suite 6-203
Honolulu, HI 96822
808-988-2000
http://donatosrestaurant.com
Hours: D 5:30 PM-Closing Tu-Su
        Sunset Menu 5:30 PM-6:30 PM Tu-Su
Cards: AE DIS JCB MC V
Dress: Resort Casual
Style: Ital $$$

Menu Sampler:

Breakfast/Lunch:
N/A
Dinner:
Antipasti: Bruschetta Rustica-toasted Asiago rustic bread topped w/roasted eggplant, tomatoes, basil & ricotta salata $4.95; Mozzarella Farcita-fresh homemade mozzarella stuffed w/roasted peppers, arugula, and Soppressata salami $9.95, Sautéed Black Mussels & a white wine tomato broth $10.95
Insalate: Fresh local grown arugula salad with toasted walnuts, crispy pancetta, & imported Gorgonzola tossed with lemon & olive oil $6.95
Pizzette: Pizzetta with tomato sauce, mozzarella, sautéed mushrooms, Italian sausage $9.25, Margherita- sauce, cheese and fresh basil $6.00
Pasta & Risotto: Risotto con Funghi w/white truffle oil $15.95, Ribbon pasta w/roasted duck breast, prosciutto, capers, & tomato white wine sauce $16.00
Specialita' Della Casa: Saltimbocca di Vitello- sautéed veal scaloppini topped with sage, prosciutto, and fresh mozzarella, served with sautéed spinach $23.95, Filetto di Pesce Moi in Padella-pan sautéed fresh Moi fillet served with Hauula tomato Puttanesca relish, rock shrimp, and asparagus risotto $18.95
Sunset Dinner Menu: 5:30-6:30-Starter, Entrée, Dessert $19.95 + tax/person
Sunday Evening Family Style: 3 course-$19.95/person, 4 course-$24.95
Tasting Menus: 3-5 courses $25.00/person-$60.00/person

Impressions:

Donato's is in a charming area of the city called the Manoa Valley. Chef Owner Donato Perfido moved his fine dining restaurant here not long ago and loyal patrons followed. Sample his full-flavored pupus, pastas and entrees and you too will become a fan. For a taste of his talents, specials on tapas or pizza and drinks are offered Tuesday through Thursday 5:30-7:30. Out of the way but worth it!

Chinatown

Duc's Bistro
1188 Maunakea
Honolulu, HI 96817
808-531-6325
Web: None
Hours: L 11:30 AM-2:00 PM XSaSu
         D 5:00 PM-10:00 PM
Cards: AE DC DIS JCB MC V
Dress: Evening Aloha
Style: Asian/Fre $$$

Menu Sampler:

Breakfast:
N/A
Lunch:
Appetizer: Crab Cake w/herb thermidor sauce $7.95, Shrimp Spring Roll $7.95
Salad: Duck Beaulieu-seared breast of duck with a raspberry vinaigrette $13.95
Entrée: Lamb Chops with Bordeaux Chivry Sauce $19.95, Spicy Lemongrass Chicken $12.95, Fresh Catch sautéed with a fresh tomato dill sauce $14.95
Dinner:
Appetizer: Chesapeake Bay Crab Cakes w/herb flavored thermidor sauce $7.95, Cha Goi Tom-fried spring rolls filled w/shrimp, taro and mushrooms $6.95
Soup: Bisque of Tomato and Lobster $5.95, Asparagus Princess $5.95
Salad: En Bataille of organic baby greens, mushrooms, goat cheese, walnuts, apples, balsamic vinaigrette $5.95, Avocado & Papaya w/greens $5.95
Entrée: Soup or salad included w/main course. Seafood Feuillete Joinville of prawns, scallops, morels, shiitakes folded in crayfish sauce and served in a puff pastry shell $21.95, Steak Aux Poivres-NY Steak flambé with VSOP Cognac, served with pink, green, and black peppercorn sauce $22.95, Spicy Lemongrass Chicken $12.95, Spinach Fettuccini- sautéed with strips of chicken breast, prosciutto and julienne of fresh vegetables in an herb supreme sauce $14.95

Impressions:

Duc's Bistro is a cool oasis of sophistication, which is an interesting contrast to the street scene outside in Chinatown. The menu blends French recipes with Vietnamese influences and throws in a little Cajun attitude just for spice. This is all complemented by a very adequate wine list. Duc's is a wonderfully relaxing dining spot. We were pleased to find live entertainment, even at lunch. Ask the waiter to take care of your parking tab in the lot across the street.

Waikiki

Duke's Canoe Club
Outrigger Waikiki Hotel
2335 Kalakaua Ave
Honolulu, HI 96815
808-922-2268
www.dukeswaikiki.com
Hours: B Buf 7:00 AM-10:30 AM
           L 11:00 AM-5:00 PM
           D 5:00 PM-10 PM
Cards: AE DC DIS MC V
Dress: Casual
Style: Sea/Stk $$

Menu Sampler:

Breakfast:
Buffet of traditional and island favorites, omelet station & juice $10.50
Lunch:
Fresh Fish Tacos $8.95, Roast Turkey and Avocado Sandwich $7.95, Thai Chicken Pizza $7.95Fisherman's Chowder $3.95, Beachside Burger $6.95,
Dinner:
Pupus: Mac Nut and Dungeness Crab Won Ton with mustard plum sauce $7.95, Poke Rolls w/raw ahi, Maui onions, sautéed in rice paper $9.95, Calamari $6.95
Entrées: Include salad bar and muffins and sourdough bread. Huli Huli Chicken-breast of chicken marinated in garlic, ginger, shoyu sauce and brown sugar $14.95, Fresh Island Fish of the Day prepared five ways $19.95-$24.95, Shrimp Scampi-shrimp sautéed in garlic butter on linguine with mushrooms, fresh tomatoes and capers $17.95, Prime Rib $17.95/$24.95, Big Island Pork Ribs glazed with a mango barbecue sauce & grilled $16.95

Impressions:

This Waikiki favorite was named after famed Olympic athlete and surfer Duke Kahanamoku. You'll find it on the beach at the Outrigger Waikiki Hotel. The breakfast buffet is a tremendous value and a great way to start the day. On the other end of the spectrum, the Barefoot Bar serves a light menu from 5 PM-12 AM and often has live local musicians performing. In between times people wander through for lunch and dinner or to enjoy their favorite adult beverages. While you're there checkout the surfing memorabilia on the walls. And yes, the "Beachboys of Waikiki" really do hang out here. They're just a little older now.

Waikiki

Eggs'n Things
1911-B Kalakaua Ave.
Honolulu, HI 96815
808-949-0820
www.eggsnthings.com
Hours: B 11:00 PM-2:00 PM XMoTuWe
           B 6:00 AM-2:00 PM MoTuWe
Cards: None
Dress: Casual
Style: Amer/Isl $$

Menu Sampler:

Breakfast:
Eggs: All orders served with 3 buttermilk pancakes or rice or potatoes and 2 eggs any style. Vienna Sausage & Eggs, Spam & Eggs, Corned Beef Hash & Eggs, Link Sausage & Eggs, Portuguese Sausage & Eggs, Ham & Eggs $7.00
Omelettes: 3 eggs, w/3 pancakes, rice or potatoes-toast extra. Cheese, Fresh Mushroom, Green Onion, Canadian bacon, Vegetarian, Corned Beef Hash $8.00
Crepes Suzettes: Sprinkled w/powdered sugar; choice of Sour Cream, Fresh Lemon, Banana, Strawberry, Blueberry $7.25, Choice of Sour Cream Lemon, Sour Cream Banana, Sour Cream Blueberry, Sour Cream Strawberry $8.00
Pancakes: Buttermilk $5.00, Choice of Banana, Blueberry, Coconut, Chocolate Chip, Bran, Buckwheat $6.00, Choice of Macadamia Nut, Pecan $7.00
Waffles: Plain $5.50, Choice of Blueberry, Coconut, Bran, Banana $6.25, Choice of Macadamia Nut, Pecan $7.00, Strawberry or Banana Whip Cream $8
Early Riser Special: 5 AM-9 AM-3 pancakes and 2 eggs $3.75
Late Riser Special: 1 PM-2 PM/1 AM-2 AM-same as Early Riser Special
Juices: Orange/Guava/Pineapple/Apple/Grapefruit/Passion/Carrot/Papaya $3/$6

Impressions:

The first thing that hits you about Eggs'n Things is the odd hours. This place doesn't open until late and then serves all night straight through to the following afternoon. As you can imagine, the crowd changes with the clock! Around midnight, expect to find the late night party crowd finishing off their revelry with a stack of pancakes. Then, in the wee hours, the local characters take the stage. Finally, come morning, a steady stream of visitors parades through the door. But regardless of who they are, they all come for the excellent breakfast menu. This is the kind of place where you're not only asked how you want your eggs cooked, you're asked how you want your waffle—soft, medium, or crisp. Don't be put off if there's a wait. Take a seat outside and watch the world go by.

Honolulu

Elena's Filipino Foods
94-300 Farrington Highway
Waipahu, HI 96797
808-671-3279
Web: None
Hours: B 5:00 AM-10:00 AM
         LD 10:00 AM-8:45 PM Su-Th
         LD 10:00 AM-9:00 PM FrSa
Cards: AE DIS MC V
Dress: Casual
Style: Fil $

Menu Sampler:

Breakfast:
Omelette Specials: Fried Rice Omelette (Bacon, Spam, Portuguese Sausage, Ham) ® 6.00, Pork Adobo Fried Rice Omelette ® 6.00, Chicken Fried Rice Omelette ® 6.00, Stuff Fried Rice Omelette ® 6.00, French Toast made with sweet bread 3.00, 3 Hotcakes 3.50, Waffle 3.00, Longaniza (pork & garlic sausage) with 2 eggs, rice, toast, or hotcake 5.00

Lunch/Dinner:
Adobo-pork marinated with vinegar & soy sauce 7.50, Dinugan-pork with blood 7.50, Gisantis-pork with green peas & tomato paste 7.50, Pinakbet-pork with mixed vegetables, eggplant, bitter melon, beans 7.50, Monggo Beans with Pork $7.50, Pansit-noodles & fresh vegetables (noodles imported from the Philippines) 7.50, Mixed Plate-any 4 listed above 7.75, Oxtail Soup 7.95, Sari-Sari of mixed vegetables, eggplant, squash, onchoi, crispy pork 7.50, Shrimp Sarciado- sautéed with tomato, onion, egg 8.95, Fried Bangus (milkfish) 9.50, Bangus Sinigang (soup) 9.75, Kare-Kare- oxtail sautéed with peanut butter 7.95, Beef Asada-filet beef steak 7.95, Lechon-crispy pork 8.50

Desserts: Banana Lumpia, 3 for 3.50, ArrozCaldo 7.00, Halo-Halo 3.50

Impressions:

When you feel the need to immerse yourself in local culture, drive on out to Waipahu and experience Elena's. This is a largely Filipino neighborhood, so guess what? Elena's is a Filipino restaurant with a largely Filipino clientele! Although some of the dishes may be unfamiliar, the friendly staff is always willing to help with explanations and suggestions. A luncheon buffet is also offered for those with big appetites or curiosities. After 30 years in business, this island favorite has become a local institution.

Kapahulu

Genki Sushi
900 Kapahulu Ave
Honolulu, HI 96816
808-735-8889
Web: None
Hours: L/D 11:00 AM-9:00 PM Su-Th
        L/D 11:00 AM-10:00 PM FrSa
Cards: AE DC DIS JCB MC V
Dress: Casual
Style: Japan $

Menu Sampler:

Breakfast:
N/A
Lunch/Dinner:
Nigiri Sushi-2 pc $1.20-$4.00, 5 pc $3.10-$5.60, choices include ocean salad, ika (squid), tako (octopus), tamago (egg), shiokara (salted squid), tobikko (caplin roe), seafood salad, tako poke, abalone salad, maguro (ahi), hotate (scallop), ebi (shrimp), salmon, unagi (freshwater eel), iwashi (sardine)
Makimono: California roll (2 pcs.), Canadian roll (2 pcs.), Nishiki roll (2 pcs.)$1.20, Tekka Maki $1.70, 8 pcs. California Roll or Canadian Roll $4.80
Temaki-Handrolls: Tuna Salad Maki or Negitoro Maki $1.20, Seafood Temaki, Spicy Tuna Temaki, California Temaki $1.70, Salad/ Miso Soup $1.20
Party Platters to go $7.40-$38.65, Beer, Wine & Sake available now.

Impressions:

If you would like to try sushi in a friendly fast-food atmosphere, try the Kaiten sushi service at Genki Sushi. In the Kaiten system, the sushi is rolled past your counter seat on a conveyor belt. You select what you want to eat and are billed by the number and color of plates chosen. Reasonable prices, a fun experience, and a chance to experiment with Japanese specialties draw many to their doors. This style of sushi service has become global in its popularity. There's even a drive-up window for take-out platters and combinations.

Waikiki

Golden Dragon
Hilton Hawaiian Village Hotel
2005 Kalia Road
Honolulu, HI 96815
808-946-5336
www.hawaiianvillage.hilton.com
Hours: D 6-9:30 PM XMo
Cards: AE DIS JCB MC V
Dress: Evening Aloha
Style: Chi $$$$
         Ent Card

Menu Sampler:

Breakfast/Lunch:
N/A
Dinner:
Appetizers: Golden Phoenix Shrimp $8.95, Crispy Crab Meat Won Ton $7.50, Spicy Roast Duck Salad $8.95, Chicken & Black Mushroom Potstickers $9.95
Soups: Hot and Sour Soup with diced tofu $5.50, Fresh Scallop Soup with pork loin & shiitake mushrooms $5.95, Shark Fin Soup $12.50, Won Ton Soup $5.50
Entrées: Mongolian Loin of Lamb with ginger and scallions $25.50, Cashew Nut Chicken w/water chestnuts & Chinese vegetables $16.50, Cantonese Roast Duck $15.75, Kung Pao Shrimp sautéed w/red chili-Szechuan style $19.50
Signature Selection: $36.00 per person, two-person minimum. Ten items.
The Lotus Dinner: $43.00 per person-Island Pork Char Siu, Chicken Egg Rolls, Crispy Won Tons, Fresh Scallop Soup, Kung Pao Chicken, Szechuan Tenderloin of Beef w/hoisin sauce & fresh tomatoes, Lobster in Curry Sauce w/Haupia, Stir Fried Shrimp w/snow peas & cashew nuts, Duck Fried Rice, Chilled Almond Float, Selection of Chinese Teas and Fortune Cookies

Impressions:

Golden Dragon is one of those places that is almost too good to be true. They have a beautiful setting, the food is outstanding, and the service impeccable. Now that we've got your attention, let's take things in detail. First, reservations are a must. This restaurant tailors it's evening around serving a certain number of diners, and you don't want to be disappointed. Next, if there ever was a time to order a complete fixed price dinner, this is it. The dishes Chef Steve Chiang prepares are truly superb, and these menus have been selected to give the diner a complete experience. Finally, this is a dinner to linger over. Don't eat and run!

Oahu Dining

Honolulu

Gordon Biersch Brewery Restaurant

Aloha Tower Marketplace
Ala Moana Blvd
Honolulu, HI 96814
808-599-4877
Web: None
Hours: L 10:30 AM-5:00 PM
        D 5:00 PM-10:00 PM Su-Th, 5:00 PM-11:00 PM FrSa
Cards: AE DC DIS JCB MC V
Dress: Resort Casual
Style: Amer/Pac-Rim $$

Menu Sampler:

Breakfast:
N/A
Lunch:
Pupus: Sweet Chili and Ginger Glazed Chicken Wings $7.95, Cornmeal Dusted Crab Cakes w/Asian Slaw $9.95, Spicy Ahi Spring Rolls w/sriracha aioli $9.95
Salads: Chopped Salad of chicken, pepper jack cheese, artichoke hearts, pepperoni in an Olive Lemon Vinaigrette $10.95, Asian Chicken Salad $7.25
Sandwiches: Marzen Barbecue Burger w/bacon, cheddar cheese, garlic fries $8.95, Blackened Mahi w/Cajun remoulade and garlic fries $8.95
Entrées: Goat Cheese Ravioli w/mushrooms, pine nuts, rosemary $13.50
Dinner:
Pastas: Sweet & Spicy Asian Vegetable Stir Fry with Jasmine rice $10.95
Pizzas: $8.95-$11.50-Italian Sausage w/basil $10.95, Classic Pepperoni $10.95
Pupus: Crispy Artichoke Hearts w/Parmesan & lemon aioli $7.95, Gordon Biersch Garlic Fries $4.95, Quick Fried Calamari w/spicy marinara $8.95
Salads: Hummus Salad with peppers, goat cheese and flat bread $9.95
Entrées: Hanger Steak with mustard demi & garlic mashed potatoes $16.50, BBQ Salmon w/grilled red onion, arugula, sweet ginger rice $18.50, Fresh Catch $Market, Hawaiian Rib Eye (16 oz) in a ginger teriyaki pineapple marinade, herb bliss potatoes $23.95, Lemon Ginger Crusted Salmon with sweet ginger rice and julienne vegetables $16.95

Impressions:

Find a seat overlooking the harbor and watch the ships go by. With a glass of house brewed beer, exotic pupus, and interesting menu items to accompany the dockside atmosphere, you can't help but relax and enjoy yourself.

Waikiki

Hakone
Hawaii Prince Waikiki Hotel
100 Holomoana St
Honolulu, HI 96815
808-944-4494
www.westinhawaiiprincehotel.com
Hours: D 6:00 PM-9:30 PM Ala Carte SuWeTh
            D 6:00 PM-9:30 PM Buffet & Limited Ala Carte FrSa
Cards: AE DC DIS JCB MC V
Dress: Resort Casual
Style: Japan $$$$ Ent Card

Menu Sampler:

Breakfast/ Lunch:
N/A

Dinner:
Appetizers: Ika Shiokara-salted marinated squid $4.00, Chawan Mushi-Egg Custard with shrimp & shiitake mushrooms $4.50, Tonkatsu $14.00
Nabemono-Chafing dish style "cook your own meal"-includes miso soup, oshinko, rice & veg.- Minimum two-person order. Sukiyaki with prime strip loin and vegetables with sweet sukiyaki sauce $31, Shabu Shabu with prime strip loin and vegetables w/ponzu & sesame sauce $31
Teishoku Combination Dinners: Daily-$36 includes rice, miso soup, kobachi, oshinko, and dessert plus two of the featured entree items-tempura, wafu filet mignon, Panko Fried Shrimp, Chicken, and Vegetables, Lobster Nogarayaki and broiled fish of the day
Hakone Buffet: Sushi Buffet with salads, shabu shabu, shrimp & vegetable tempura, noodles, sashimi, nigiri sushi, temaki, rice, oshinko, specials and dessert station- Adults $42, Child $21

Impressions:

Dining at Hakone is an authentic cultural experience where one can discover classic Japanese cuisine. You can choose a nabemono chafing dish, select from the a la carte menu, or enjoy the Hakone Buffet. The buffet features a wide variety of hot and cold dishes such as crispy shrimp, rib eye steak with teri-glaze, steamed Manila clams, salmon, butterfish, and Alaskan crab legs. The Prince is a lovely hotel with dining rooms overlooking the marina. Parking is readily available either by valet, in the adjoining deck, or along the marina.

North Shore

Haleiwa Joe's Seafood Grill
66-001 Kamehameha Hwy
Haleiwa, HI 96712
808-637-8005
Web: None
Hours: L 11:30 AM-4:15 PM Mo-Sa
        L 11:30 AM-3:45 PM Su
        D 5:30 PM-10:30 PM FrSa
        D 5:30 PM-9:30 PM Mo-Th
        D 5:00 PM-9:30 PM Su
Cards:
Dress: Casual
Style: Isl/Sea $$$

Menu Sampler:

Breakfast:
N/A
Lunch:
Small Plates: Ahi Spring Rolls $9.95, Thai Fried Calamari $6.50, Sweet Kalbi
Ribs with a scoop of white rice $7.50, Peel & Eat Fire Shrimp $8.75
Soups & Salads: Tropical Grilled Shrimp Salad on greens with our lilikoi
vinaigrette $12.25, Roasted Garlic Bread $4.25, Fish Monger Soup $4.25
Lunch Plates & Sandwiches: Haleiwa Joe's Hamburger on a poppy seed bun
with toppings & fries $6.25, Crunchy Coconut Shrimp with steamed rice $14.95
Dinner:
Small Plates: Island Ceviche with cilantro, tomato and jalapeno $6.95, Joe's
Tempura Crab Roll $9.25, Luau lumpia with Kahlua pig and taro leaf $8.25
Soup, Salads & Other Stuff: Ginger Peanut Chicken Salad on greens with a
spicy ginger dressing $9.75, House Salad with a sesame-miso dressing $3.95
Big Plates: Seared Fresh Ahi with spicy seasonings, on a bed of sautéed noodles
and ginger glazed baby carrots $19.75, Chinese Style Steamed Fish in Ti leaves
with sesame oil, fresh ginger, cilantro, and green onion $19.95, Prime Rib
roasted bone-in with creamy horseradish sauce & garlic mashed potatoes $22.95
Desserts: Key Lime Pie $5.50, Mango Sorbet $4.25, Love Cake $6.25

Impressions:

Offering an eclectic island menu, a marina in front, the quaint village of Haleiwa
behind, and the Pacific Ocean surrounding all, this casual full-service restaurant
has what every visitor imagines in a Hawaii dining experience. Visitors and
locals alike appreciate Haleiwa Joe's and patronize this establishment heavily.

Kaimuki

Hale Vietnam
1140 12th Avenue
Honolulu, HI 96816
808-735-7581
Web: None
Hours: LD 11:00 AM-10:00 PM
Cards: AE DIS MC V
Dress: Casual
Style: Viet $$

Menu Sampler:

Breakfast:
N/A
Lunch/Dinner:
Appetizers: Summer Rolls-boiled shrimp, seasoned pork, fresh mint, bean sprouts and rice noodles rolled in rice paper with special peanut sauce $4.75
Salads: Green Papaya of shredded papaya, roast pork, boiled shrimp, mint leaves $8.25, Lemon Beef-char-broiled beef slices, romaine, cucumber, tomatoes, toasted peanuts, onion flakes, Chinese parsley $8.25
House Specials: Pho-Famous Beef Noodle Soup of Vietnam-Medium Bowl $6.00, Large Bowl $6.50-your choice of rare steak, brisket, flank, tendon, tripe, chicken balls, beef balls, lean cooked chicken. Side plate of bean sprouts, fresh basil, chili pepper, and a lemon wedge. Oxtail Soup with noodle or rice $7.50
Vietnamese Sour Soup: Popular soup in Vietnam with fresh lemon grass, bean sprouts, bamboo shoots, celery, tomatoes, and fresh herbs-Catfish $11.75, Shrimp $11.75, Chicken $10.50, Vegetarian $9.50
Seafood Soup $6.95, Long Rice Soup $6.75, Vegetarian Long Rice Soup $6.75, Spicy Beef and Pork Noodle Soup $7.95, Fried Egg Noodle $8.95
Vietnamese Plate: Includes consommé, steamed rice, lettuce, cucumber and tomato slices $8.50-choices of BBQ Pork Chop, Shredded Pork, Chicken, BBQ Shrimp, Sautéed Lemongrass Shrimp or Beef, BBQ Beef
Entrees: Vietnamese Fondue $15.95-$17.95, Sautéed Beef, Chicken, Shrimp, or Tofu with Vegetables, or Lemongrass, Peanut Sauce, Black Beans $9.50-$11.75

Impressions:

Looking at the patrons sitting around the dining room of Hale Vietnam you'll find a wonderful cross-section of the cultures found in Honolulu. People from all backgrounds gather here to enjoy the healthy, fresh Vietnamese cuisine served in this attractive restaurant. Located in Kaimuki's restaurant row, this busy dining spot has metered parking in a large city lot behind the complex.

Oahu Dining

Manoa Valley

Hanaki Japanese Buffet
Manoa Marketplace
2756 Woodlawn Drive
Honolulu, HI 96822
808-988-1551
Web: None
Hours: L 11:00 AM-2:00 PM Mo-Fr, XTu
        L 10:30 AM-2:00 PM SaSu
        D 5:00 PM-9:00 PM
Cards: AE DC DIS MC V
Dress: Casual
Style: Japan $$

Menu Sampler:

Lunch:
Buffet: Seating at 11:00 AM and 12.30 PM, Monday-Friday, Miso Soup &
Soba Noodles, Shrimp & Vegetable Tempura Station, Contemporary Sushi Bar,
Sashimi and Assorted Cold Salads, Yaki Soba, Chicken Teriyaki, Traditional
and Creative Chef's Specials, Shaved Ice and Dessert Bar $12.95, Seniors 55+
$10.95, Kids under 4 ½ feet tall $4.95
Buffet: Monday through Friday Dinner Buffet and Saturday and Sunday Lunch
Buffet features the above items with more sushi, poke and dungeness crab legs
$17.95, $8.95 Kids under 4 ½ feet tall, Seniors 55+ $15.95 Monday-Friday
Dinner, no special seniors price Saturday and Sunday Lunch Buffet
Buffet: Saturday and Sunday Evenings features a seafood extravaganza,
including Dungeness Crab Legs, Miso Butterfish, and the Chef's Seafood
Creations and tender Prime Rib carved to order plus the above items $24.95 for
adults and $11.95 for Kids under 4 ½ feet tall. No senior specials.

Impressions:

Back in the Manoa Valley behind the University of Hawaii, culinary adventurers
will discover a special dining experience. There around the corner from Safeway
in the Manoa Marketplace you'll find Hanaki Japanese Buffet. The first things
that strike you when you walk through the door are the clean lines and civilized
atmosphere of this traditional establishment. Then, after being escorted to one of
the simple tables, you'll have the opportunity to experience a variety of Japanese
centered cuisine. The hallmark here is quality. Everything from the selections
offered to the levels of preparation and presentation exceed one's expectations.
The staff is very helpful to all, but as local people and Japanese visitors favor
this place, expect your visit to be a cultural encounter.

Honolulu

Hard Rock Café
1837 Kapiolani Blvd.
Honolulu, HI 96814
808-955-9383
www.hardrock.com
Hours: L/D 11:30 AM-12:30 AM
Cards: AE DIS JCB MC V
Dress: Resort Casual
Style: Amer/Ec $$

Menu Sampler:

Breakfast:
N/A

Lunch/Dinner:
Starters: Santa Fe Spring Rolls with fresh salsa and guacamole dressing $6.99, Hickory Smoked Chicken & Spinach Dip served with chips, melted cheddar and jack cheese and fresh salsa $5.99, French Onion Soup topped with melted provolone cheese $3.79, Jumbo Combo (all kine goodies!) $14.29

Salads: Grilled Chinese Chicken Salad $9.19, Haystack Fried Chicken Salad $8.99, Hard Rock Caesar Salad $7.79, Cobb Salad $9.19, House Salad $6.99

Burger Platters: Each half-pound burger comes with toppings and a full plate of French fries. Char-Broiled Burger $8.39, Cheeseburger $8.99, Bacon Cheeseburger $9.19, Natural Veggie Burger with Cajun mayonnaise, served with cole slaw and baked potato $8.39, Turkey Burger w/mustard-mayo $8.59

Specialties: Grilled Sirloin Steak (9 oz) grilled, topped with a horseradish demi sauce and frizzled onions with a side of "twisted mac n cheese" and fresh seasonal vegetables $14.99, Famous Grilled Fajitas of chicken, beef or fresh veggies, numerous condiments, pinto beans and seasoned rice $12.29

Desserts: Cheesecake $4.79, Dessert Nachos $7.99, Down Home Apple Cobbler $4.99, Seasonal Shortcake $5.99, Thick Shakes & Malts $3.99

Impressions:

You'll find the Hard Rock Café on the downtown side of Waikiki. Not only is this rock-n-roll icon a fun place for great tunes and fabulous memorabilia, but they also serve a solid casual dining menu. The burgers are made with high quality ground beef and the entrées add interesting twists to everyday comfort food. Make sure you ask to see the dessert menu! Check the website for a listing of entertainment and upcoming special events. There is a parking lot on site, but it can get crowded. Plan ahead if you drive. Better yet, walk or take a cab.

Oahu Dining

Waikiki

Hau Tree Lanai
The New Otani Kaimana Beach Hotel
2863 Kalakaua Avenue
Honolulu, HI 96815
808-921-7066
www.kaimana.com
Hours: B 7:00 AM-11:00 AM
         L 11:30 AM-2:00 PM Mo-Sa
         L 12:00 PM-2:00 PM Su
         D 5:30 PM-9:00 PM
Cards: AE DIS JCB MC V
Dress: Resort Casual
Style: Haw-Reg/Pac Rim $$$ Ent Card

Menu Sampler:

Breakfast:
Poi or Buttermilk Pancakes 8.25, Salmon Benedict Florentine-seared salmon, spinach, bacon, and poached eggs on a pepper-cheddar scone topped with a dill hollandaise, served with breakfast potatoes 14.25, Asian Breakfast of longanisa sausage, garlic fried rice, two eggs any style, pickled green papaya salad, and sliced Japanese cucumbers 11.25, Lox and Poi Bagel 11.25

Lunch:
Ahi Cobb Salad with seared island ahi, red potato salad, asparagus, Nicoise olives, anchovy fillets, balsamic vinaigrette 16.75, Crab Cake Burger on a whole wheat bun with seasoned curly Q fries 14.25, Jumbo Shrimp and Scallop Penne Pasta, choice of sauce 16.50, Seafood Omelet with rice or fries 13.50

Dinner:
Appetizers: Escargot in Puff Pastry w/mushrooms and demi glace 10.95, Pan Smoked Hoisin Duck Breast on a poi-green onion-wild rice pancake 8.50
Soups/Salads: Portuguese Bean Soup 6.25, Margherita Salad 9.95
Entrees: Balsamic-Soy Grilled Lamb Chops w/a watercress, mint, walnut salad and garlic-mashed potatoes 32.50, Surimi-Shrimp-Avocado Crusted Fresh Mahimahi glazed with garlic aioli with citrus beurre blanc sauce 28.50

Impressions:

Remember the beautiful beach scenes from the Magnum P.I. television series? Many of them were shot in front of this restaurant. Hau Tree Lanai is located on a terrace overlooking San Souci Beach at the quiet end of Waikiki. The setting is lovely at any time, but becomes almost stunning at sunset. A high level of preparation and presentation is maintained three meals a day.

Kapahulu

Hee Hing Restaurant
449 Kapahulu Ave
Honolulu, HI 96815
808-735-5544
Web: None
Hours: L/D 10:30 AM-9:30 PM
Cards: AE DC DIS JCB MC V
Dress: Resort Casual
Style: Chi $$

Menu Sampler:

Breakfast:
N/A

Lunch/Dinner:
Appetizers: Shrimp Pouches with salad sauce $5.95, Crisp Kau Chee $4.95, Spring Rolls $6.95, Crisp Won Ton $4.95, Golden Fried Spring Rolls $6.95
Soups: Hot and Sour Soup $7.25, Chicken Sweet Corn Soup $7.25, Kup Dai Fish Cake Rice Soup $6.25, Mustard Cabbage Soup $7.25, Egg Flower $7.25
Rice: Yang Chow Style Fried Rice $7.25, Chicken and Salt Fish Fried Rice $9.50, Char Siu and Roast Duck on rice $7.95, Minced Beef Fried Rice $7.25
Noodles: Chicken Lobster Noodles $15.95, Chow Fun w/beef, bell peppers and black bean sauce $7.50, Singapore Rice Noodles $7.50, Beef Chow Fun $7.50
Entrées: Roast Pork and Tofu Casserole in earthen pot $9.25, Scallops with Chinese peas in taro nest $13.50, Curry Lobster $24.95, Sauteed Sea Bass with ginger and onion $11.95, Crabmeat on poached hearts of lettuce $16.95, Shrimp with pineapple $7.95, Abalone with black mushrooms and oyster sauce $27.95, Almond Chicken $7.25, Mongolian Beef Tenderloin $8.95, Sweet and Sour Spare Ribs with pineapple $6.95, Spicy Szechuan Beef $7.95, Steamed Pork Hash $6.75, Sweet and Sour Roast Duck $7.50, Mochi Rice Duck $7.95
Dessert: Almond Float $1.95, Lychee Ice Cream $2.75, Almond cookie (3) $.35

Impressions:

Hee Hing shares a building with Sam Choy's Diamond Head Restaurant on the park side of Kapahulu Avenue. There's parking under the building for the use of both. The Lee family operates this restaurant and serves up an extensive menu of Szechuan, Cantonese, and Northern Chinese delicacies. Besides the ala carte items, Hong Kong style dim sum is served at lunch. They also offer a complete section for vegetarians. No MSG is used in their preparations. This is a good choice for Chinese food lovers who don't want to venture away from Waikiki.

Oahu Dining

Honolulu

Helena's Hawaiian Foods
1240 North School Street
Honolulu, HI 96819
808-845-8044
Web: None
Hours: LD 10:00 AM-7:30 PM Tu-Fr
Cards: None
Dress: Casual
Style: Isl $

Menu Sampler:

Breakfast:
N/A
Lunch/Dinner:
Ala Carte: Poi 1.75/2.00, Rice .60/.90, Kalua Pig 2.50/3.50/6.50, Kalua Pig &
Cabbage 2.75, Laulau 2.75, Tripe Stew 2.75, Beef Stew 2.75, Salt Beef with
Watercress 2.75, Luau Squid 2.75, Luau Chicken 2.75, Long Rice Chicken 2.75,
Short Ribs Pipikaula Style 3.50/6.95, Lomi Salmon 2.60, Lomi Salmon with
Raw Fish & Limu 2.75, Lomi or Poke (Aku or Ahi) 2.75, Opihi 2.75, Poke Fish
with Opihi 2.75, Fried Butterfish Collar 3.25, Boiled Butterfish Collar (with
stew gravy or plain) 3.25, Fried Aku or Ahi 2.75, Fried Aku or Ahi Bone (when
available) 3.25, Haupia 1.25/2.50/9.00, Soda 1.00
Combos: Menu A includes Kalua Pig and Lomi Salmon with two scoops rice
6.00, small poi 6.85, large poi 7.10; **Menu B** includes Kalua Pig and Pipikaula
Short Ribs with two scoops rice 6.90, small poi 7.75, large poi 8.00; **Menu C**
includes Kalua Pig, Lomi Salmon, and Pipikaula Short Ribs with two scoops
rice 9.50, with small poi 10.35, with large poi 10.60; **Menu D** includes Kalua
Pig, Lomi Salmon, Pipikaula Short Ribs, Luau Squid with two scoops rice
12.25, with small poi 13.10, with large poi 13.35

Impressions:

Helen Chock is an institution on the Honolulu restaurant scene. She has been
cooking and serving great regional food so long that most people have forgotten
when it all began. Her North School Street restaurant isn't easy to find, but all
the locals know where it's at, so that's "No problem!" The draw here is the
traditional Hawaiian food served in a variety of combinations. Luau favorites
like kalua pig and lomi salmon are available for workday lunches and dinners
instead of only on special occasions. When visiting Helena's be sure to check
out the awards on the walls. Even the James Beard crowd is sold on this one!
There is parking in front of this modest eatery, but go early to find a spot.

Diamond Head

Hoku's
Mandarin Oriental Hotel
5000 Kahala Ave
Honolulu, HI 96815
808-739-8780
www.mandarin-oriental.com
Hours:　SuBru 10:30 AM-2:30 PM
　　　　L 11:00 AM-1:00 PM Mo-Fr
　　　　D 5:30 PM-10 PM
Cards:　AE DC DIS JCB MC V
Dress:　Evening Aloha
Style:　Asian/Ec/Haw $$$$

Menu Sampler:

Breakfast:
Brunch Buffet: $44/adults, $22/child. Fresh Oysters, Crab Claws, Smoked Salmon, Ahi, Caesar Salad, Tandoori Chicken Salad, soups and desserts including a choice of a **regular menu entrée:** King Crab Omelet $22.00, Hoku's Eggs Benedict $19.00, Portuguese Sweet Bread French Toast $15.00
Lunch:
Three-Course Business Lunch $29.75, Ala Carte entrees and salads.
Dinner:
Starters: Lobster and Sweet Kahuku Corn Chowder $9.75, Oxtail Soup with chive pancakes $8.00, Hoisin Duck Taco w/pineapple mango salsa $12.00
Salads: Warm Lobster and Baby Spinach Salad w/truffle vinaigrette $21
Main Courses: Herb Crusted Fresh Island Onaga (Signature Dish) w/creamed spinach, red wine shallots and garlic mashed potatoes $37, Wood Fired Australian Rack of Lamb, Nicoise olive crushed Yukon Gold potatoes, yellow beans and natural jus $35, Mahi-Mahi Baked in Pandan Leaf, Okinawan sweet potatoes, kabocha pumpkin and long beans, w/vanilla orange sauce $29
Desserts: Chocolate Lovers Variation of Melting Chocolate Cake, Frangelico Soufflé, Chocolate Crème Brulee $7.75, Asian Pear & Pistachio Crisp $7.75

Impressions:

This contemporary dining room overlooks the ocean at the Kahala Mandarin Hotel. Chef Wayne Hirabayashi of the Hawaiian Island Chef's group oversees the operation of the display kitchen and its menu of innovative fusion cuisine. The pupus are like mini-entrees and can easily become dinner by themselves. This is truly fine dining in a matching locale. Reservations are recommended.

Honolulu

Hong Kong Harbour View Seafood Restaurant
1 Aloha Tower Drive
Honolulu, HI 96813
808-566-9989
Web: None
Hours: 9:30 AM-10:00 PM
Cards: AE DC DIS JCB MC V
Dress: Resort Casual
Style: Chi $$

Menu Sampler:

Breakfast/Lunch:
Dim Sum: 9:30 AM-2:30 PM-40-50 choices, Lunch 11:30 AM-2:30 PM
Lunch/Dinner:
Appetizers: Fried Bacon with Prawns Scallop Roll (5) $14.95, Minced Seafood in Lettuce $12.95, Cha Sho Pork $9.95, Fried Egg Roll/Crispy Won Ton $6.50
Sizzling Platters: Sizzling Oyster with Black Bean Sauce $16.95, Sizzling Beef w/Satay Sauce $12.95, Sizzling Tenderloin Steak w/Black Pepper Sauce $16.95
Soup: Dried Scallop Soup $14.95, Hot and Sour Soup/Won Ton Soup $10.95
Live Seafood: Live Maine Lobster sautéed with garlic & butter sauce/live Dungeness Crab sautéed with ginger & green onion/ live Hawaiian Prawns scalded with special sauce/ Oysters with black bean sauce in shell (4) $Mkt
Entrées: Braised Abalone with Black Mushrooms $26.95, Kung Pao Prawns $15.95, Hot Pot of Chicken & Tofu with Salted Fish $15.95, Crispy Roast Chicken $10.95, Lemon Sauce Chicken/Mu Shu Chicken $10.95, Pork Chop Peking Style/Sweet and Sour Pork $10.95, Egg Fu Yong $8.95, Fried Ground Tofu and Shrimp with Brown Sauce (5) $12.95, House Special Fried Rice with Assorted Seafood $14.95, Shrimp Pan-Fried Noodle $12.95, BBQ Pork Noodle in Soup $10.95, Duck with Vegetable Noodle in Soup $10.95
Dessert: Almond Pudding $2.50, Sweet Mochi Dumpling in Soup $3.50

Impressions:

The Aloha Tower Marketplace is home to several notable restaurants. Here on the second floor overlooking the water you'll find the Hong Kong Harbour View Seafood Restaurant. Naturally this elegantly furnished establishment specializes in Hong Kong style seafood, but is also known for its dim sum service at lunch. You'll see five dim sum wagons circulating around the room. Each one takes a different culinary approach with the group offering between 40 to 50 items in total. Midday shoppers will find this to be an affordable way of sampling many "delicate bites". Make sure to get your parking ticket validated.

Oahu Dining

Waikiki

House Without A Key
Halekulani Hotel
2199 Kalia Road
Honolulu, HI 96815
808-923-2311
www.halekulani.com
Hours: B Buf 7:00 AM-10:30 AM Mo-Sa
        B Buf 7:00 AM-11:30 AM Su
        L 11:00 AM-5:00 PM Mo-Sa, Noon-5 PM Su
        D 5:00 PM-9 PM
Cards: AE DC DIS JCB MC V
Dress: Resort Casual
Style: PacRim $$$

Menu Sampler:

Breakfast:
Buffet of traditional and Japanese entrees and salads $21.95
Lunch:
Appetizers: Premium Grade Ahi Sashimi w/shredded daikon & ginger $16.00
Salads: Caesar Salad with Poached Shrimp & garlic bread $15.50
Sandwiches: Grilled Lemongrass Chicken Sandwich on a croissant $14.00
Entrees: Sautéed Hawaiian Mahimahi w/lemon pepper basil crab sauce $16.50
Desserts: Almond Float with Seasonal Fruit & Lychee Sorbet $6.50
Dinner:
Cocktail Appetizers: Hot Pupu Assortment of Coconut Shrimp, Teriyaki Beef Brochettes and Vegetable Spring Rolls $14.00, Calamari Fritte $9.00
Salads and Soups: Spicy Chicken Salad with lilikoi mustard emulsion $7.50, Maui Onion Soup Gratinee with Swiss & Gruyere Cheese $8.50
Entrees: Ka'u Orange and Poha Berry Glazed Island Chicken Breast with seasonal vegetables and Lemon Verbano Saffron Rice $17.50, Seared New York Steak with Roasted Mushroom Shallot Sauce and vegetable $22.00
Desserts: Chocolate Macadamia Nut Haupia Tart w/raspberry coulis $6.50

Impressions:

House Without A Key has the relaxed pace and feel of neighbor island resort dining. Yes, it's located in a fine hotel, but no, patrons don't feel the need to dress for dinner. This casual but upscale restaurant overlooks the ocean from the courtyard of the Halekulani. We view it as an oasis in the midst of the hustle and bustle of Waikiki. House Without A Key offers exemplary meals and civilized service throughout the day. Entertainment is offered nightly.

Oahu Dining

Waikiki

Hy's Steak House
2440 Kuhio Ave
Honolulu, HI 96815
808-922-5555
www.hyshawaii.com
Hours: D 6:00 PM-10:00 PM Su-Th, D 5:30 PM-10:00 PM SaSu
Cards: AE DC DIS JCB MC V
Dress: Evening Aloha
Style: Sea/Stk $$$$

Menu Sampler:

Breakfast/Lunch:
N/A
Dinner:
Appetizers: Filet Mignon Tartare $10.95, Crab Cake with roasted garlic, pine nuts & basil $11.50, Escargot a la Hy's $11.50, Ahi and Scallops Katsu $14.95
Soups: Onion Soup Gratinee $5.95, New England Clam Chowder $5.25
Salads: Hawaiian Salad a la Hy's $9.95, Caesar Salad $10.95, Hy's Seafood and Avocado Salad $11.95, Warm Spinach Salad (tableside prep) $9.95
Entrées: NY Peppercorn Steak glazed with Madagascar peppercorn sauce $30.95, Roast Rack of Lamb $39.95, Filet Mignon $30.95/$35.95, Prime Rib $21.95/$28.95/$33.95, Steak Teriyaki $27.95, Chateaubriand for Two with a bouquet of fresh vegetables and sauce bearnaise $35.95 per person, Filet of Beef Wellington topped with pate maison and mushroom duxelles baked in a light pastry and served with a cabernet truffle sauce $33.95, Broiled Veal Chop Forestiere with shiitake and oyster mushrooms and Marsala wine sauce $32.95, Scallops charred and served with a Thai style sauce accented with basil, lemon grass and ginger $28.95, Chicken Marsala or Piccata $17.95/Veal choice $22.95
Accompaniments: Sauteed Onions $5.50, Creamed Spinach $4.95, Mushroom and Onion Sauté $6.50, Hollandaise or Bearnaise $1.95, Fresh Asparagus $8.50

Impressions:

Hy's main floor typifies the classic steak house with low lighting, starched tablecloths, and dark woods surrounding an open-hearth grill. However, up a few stairs patrons enter a plush tropical-toned dining room where a quieter experience awaits. Regardless, tuxedoed waiters serve a diverse menu of kiawe grilled meats, seafood, and Continental specialties. Tableside preparation might be a dying art, but not at Hy's. Diners can enjoy wines by the bottle or by the glass from the house's extensive wine list. Valet parking is available at the door.

Oahu Dining

Honolulu

India House Restaurant
University Square Shopping Center
2633 South King Street
Honolulu, HI 96826
808-955-7552
Web: None
Hours: L 11:00 AM-2:00 PM Mo-Sa
           D 5:00 PM-9:30 PM Mo-Sa
           D 5:00 PM-9:00 PM Su
Cards: MC V
Dress: Casual
Style: Indian $$

Menu Sampler:

Breakfast:
N/A

Lunch/Dinner:

Appetizers: Samosas-crisp pastry cones stuffed with potatoes, vegetables, and peas (4 pieces) $6.50, Pakoras-spicy vegetable fritters (tempura) $6.50, Paneer Pakoras $8.75, Papdums-delicious spicy crisp wafers $3.00

Soups: Mulligatawny-delicately spiced chicken soup cooked in tandoori oven $2.50, Vegetarian Soup $3.50

House Specialties: All served with naan bread, rice pullao, vegetable curry. Tandoori Chicken-chicken marinated in spices, herbs and yogurt and baked in a tandoori oven $15.95, Boti Kabob-choice cubes of marinated lamb, skewered w/onion, bell pepper and tomato $16.95, Fish Tikka-marinated, skewered $16.95

Ala Carte: Tandoori Specials using fish, chicken, lamb $9.95, Chicken Curry $9.95, Chicken or Lamb Vindaloo-highly spiced chicken or lamb cooked with potatoes in a tangy sauce $10.95, Lamb Spinach-lamb cooked with spinach and fresh Indian spices $10.95, Chana Masala-garbanzo beans cooked with fresh ginger and tomato $8.95, Palak Paneer-cottage cheese and spinach $8.95

Desserts: Halwas-cream of wheat pudding w/raisins, nuts and coconut $4.50

Impressions:

There is an area of South King Street near the University of Hawaii housing some great ethnic and alternative restaurants. This is where you'll find India House with its marvelous Northern Indian cuisine. Tablecloths and gracious service separate this establishment from your run of the mill storefront eatery. Park in the Central Pacific Bank lot on the corner, and get your ticket validated.

Chinatown

Indigo Eurasian Cuisine
1121 Nuuanu Ave
Honolulu, HI 96817
808-521-2900
www.indigo-hawaii.com
Hours: L 11:30 AM-2:00 PM Tu-Fr
         D 6:00 PM-9:30 PM Tu-Sa
Cards: DC DIS MC V
Dress: Resort Casual
Style: Euro-Asian $$$

Menu Sampler:

Breakfast:
N/A
Lunch:
Cool Island Buffet: Trio of Dim Sum $13.95, Lobster Potstickers $8.00, Lumpia Wrapped Shrimp w/chipotle aioli $9.00, Buddhist Bao Buns $7.00
Starters: Garden Spring Roll of vegetables & couscous pilaf w/tangerine sauce $6.75, Roasted Tomato Garlic Crab Soup w/blue crab & cilantro pesto $6.50
Entrées: Grilled Island Breast of Chicken with Indigo peanut sauce $13.50
Dinner:
Starters: Chinese Gin Doi w/roasted duck and dried apricots $7.50
Soups & Salads: Toasted Pecan Crusted Chevre and grilled portabella mushrooms w/plum vinaigrette $9.75, Nalo Farms Mesclen Greens with hibiscus mango vinaigrette $6.25, Asian Caesar Salad $7.95
Entrées: Grilled Shrimp with Thai macadamia nut pesto and green papaya slaw $21.25, Grilled Rib Eye Beef w/Black Bean Beurre Blanc Sauce & mashed potatoes $22.95, Mongolian Lamb Chops w/minted tangerine sauce $25.75, Cates Ocean Raised Moi Roasted in Banana Leaf & cocoa bean curry $21.50
Desserts: Apple Lemongrass Crisp served with Vanilla Gelato $6.25, Ginger Crème Brulee $5.25, Rich Goat Cheesecake with ginger lime sauce $5.50

Impressions:

Indigo invokes a New Orleans atmosphere with its brick walls, iron balconies, and hanging plants. Located in one of the oldest buildings in Chinatown, this upscale restaurant delivers exotic flavors borrowed with abandon from all around the world. The proprietor refers to his offerings as Eurasian, but from our viewpoint it looks more like Eclectic Global. This is a lively place in the evening with unique pupu offerings, live music, and interesting crowd.

North Shore

Jameson's By The Sea

62-540 Kamehameha Hwy
Haleiwa, HI 96712
808-637-4336
Web: None
Hours: B 9:00 AM-12:00 PM SaSu
          L 11:00 AM-5:00 PM
          D 5:00 PM-9:00 PM
Cards: AE DC DIS JCB MC V
Dress: Casual
Style: Amer/Sea $$$

Menu Sampler:

Breakfast:
Saturday and Sunday only from 9AM-12 PM. All menu items under $12.00.
Lunch:
Appetizers: Cajun Chicken Wings $7.95, Thai Shrimp Summer Rolls with avocado, mint, carrots and greens in rice paper with a spicy dipping sauce $9.95
Entrées: Grilled Crab and Shrimp with cheddar cheese on sourdough bread with choice of fries or cole slaw $11.50, Curried Chicken Salad served in a papaya $10.95, Teriyaki Chicken with sides $14.95, New York Steak with sides $19.95.
Dinner:
Appetizers: Salmon Pate $8.95, Fried Calamari with marinara sauce $8.95, Stuffed Mushrooms-minced escargot and herbs in mushroom caps $9.95
Entrées: All served with steamed white rice, garlic linguini, Oriental fried rice or potatoes and steamed vegetables in season. New York Steak, broiled to order $22.95, Sweet Australian Lobster Tail, broiled, served with Beurre Blanc Sauce and Drawn Butter $Market Price, Baked Stuffed Shrimp (Great!) stuffed with breadcrumbs, crabmeat and cheese topped with hollandaise $20.95, Thai, Teriyaki, or Cajun Chicken, boneless breast marinated and sautéed to a golden brown $14.95. Note the daily fresh fish specials and their creative preparations.

Impressions:

Jameson's is one of those places that pulls people in off the highway. Travelers circling the island will be particularly interested in the weekend breakfast and daily lunch offerings. As things quiet down in the evening, this North Shore beach house goes to a traditional steak and seafood menu. The laid back setting is a perfect fit for most island visitors; it's called sunshine, seafood, and suds!

Honolulu

Jimbo's Restaurant
1936 South King Street
Honolulu, HI 96826
808-947-2211
Web: None
Hours: L 11:00 AM-2:50 PM
         D 5:00 PM-9:50 PM
Cards: MC V-Cash Only for Carryout
Dress: Casual
Style: Japan $

Menu Sampler:

Breakfast:
N/A
Lunch/Dinner:
Udon- homemade noodles hot, cold or yaki (stir-fried) with: Fish Cake and Green Onions $5.40, Beef & Vegetable $6.75, Bukkake-Tempura Chip & Vegetable with dark broth $7.40, Udon with dipping sauce $5.40, Stir Fried Udon with tofu & vegetables $6.75, Hot Chicken Udon $6.75 Salad Udon of cold skinny udon w/fresh vegetables & shrimp or chicken $8.25, Katsu or Tako & Vegetable $7.75. All above may be made w/skinny udon or soba $1.50 extra
Donburi: Various toppings of meats, seafood, vegetable or tempura with egg on hot rice- Chicken & Egg $6.95, Pork Katsu & Egg $7.95, Shrimp & Vegetable Tempura with egg $9.45, Tofu & Egg $6.95, Shrimp Tempura $7.95
Curry Rice: Corn Curry w/chicken or beef on rice $7.60,with pork katsu $8.65, Pork Katsu Curry on rice $7.65, Beef or Chicken Curry $6.60, Plain $5.60
Side Orders: Miso Soup $1.50, Green Salad $4.05, Rice $1.10, Hiyayakko-cold tofu $3.50, Ten Mori-mix tempura platter $8.10, Octopus Tempura $3.95, Vegetable Tempura Platter $6.95, Kayaku Musubi $1.85, Potato Salad $1.50,
Dessert: Green Tea Ice Cream with Azuki Beans $2.50, Lychee Sorbet $2.50

Impressions:

Jimbo's is the kind of place local Japanese families and businessmen go to eat. The menu offers dishes that ordinary people enjoy as they get on with their daily lives. Call it Japanese comfort food if you will, but udon and katsu have a lot more in common with hamburgers and fried chicken than they do with sukiyaki or shabu shabu. We were impressed with the relaxed atmosphere, as the small restaurant filled up quickly after they opened, but never seemed overly busy. Parking is limited out front, so plan on arriving early or look along the street.

Honolulu

John Dominis Restaurant
Kewalo Basin
43 Ahui St
Honolulu, HI 96813
808-523-0955
www.johndominis.com
Hours: Su Bru 9:00 AM-1:00 PM
        D 6:00 PM-9:00 PM
Cards: AE CB DC JCB MC V
Dress: Evening Aloha
Style: Sea $$$$

Menu Sampler:

Breakfast:
Sunday Brunch $31.95 Extensive selection of seafood and traditional foods
Lunch:
N/A
Dinner:
Appetizers: Smoked Salmon w/condiments $9.95, Escargot Dijonaise Style in Puff Pastry $9.95, Pacific Crab Salad w/Papaya $10.50, Steamed Clams $10.95
Salads: Spinach Salad of pan-seared scallops flavored with curry spice, orange vinaigrette and orange segments $7.50, Caesar Salad in a bread basket $6.95
Entrées: Fresh Island Moi steamed with thin slices of ginger, scallions, lemon shoyu, cilantro & hot peanut oil; Szechuan style with a spicy sweet-sour sauce $29.95, Seafood Bouillabaisse $35.00, Grilled Miso Salmon in sake broth with baby bok choy $28.95, Angus Tenderloin of Beef with potato, vegetables, green peppercorn and brandy $29.95, Macadamia Nut Breaded Veal Piccata with lemon butter, capers and Japanese eggplant $22.95, Wok Fried Caramelized Tiger Prawns with fried rice and Oriental vegetables $34.95

Impressions:

In the midst of all the commercial activity between Waikiki and downtown Honolulu, you'll find a jewel of a restaurant. There, out on the end of a wharf, sits John Dominis. Although the surrounding neighborhood speaks of early industrial revolution, the panoramic view enjoyed by diners is unparalleled. Inside, the koi pond winds its way through the restaurant further enhancing the upscale atmosphere. The menu reflects the fresh fish brought into the docks, so be sure to inquire about the daily specials. Sunday Brunch is a bountiful feast, and dinner has never disappointed us. Reservations are always recommended.

Oahu Dining

North Shore

Kahuku Shrimp Trucks
Kamehameha Hwy
Kahuku, HI 96731
Phone: -------
Web: None
Hours: Approximately 10:00 AM-6:00 PM
Cards: None
Dress: Casual
Style: Sea $$

Menu Sampler:

Breakfast:
N/A
Lunch/Dinner:
Plate Lunch Style Shrimp includes two-scoop rice and one scoop macaroni
salad: Garlic Butter, Tempura, Western BBQ, Cocktail, Hot and Spicy, or
Coconut Lemon Sauce $10. You can also add their 8 oz NY Steak to your plate
for $7.00. A combo of 3 shrimp and steak/mahi/beef is $12.00. Other choices
include Whole Head-On Shrimp boiled or fried $10, Mahi Mahi $7.00, Teri
Beef $7.00, or Stir-Fry Shrimp with fresh vegetables $7.00

Impressions:

Up on the north tip of Oahu in and around the town of Kahuku you'll find the
center of a thriving cottage industry. Here industrious entrepreneurs have set up
businesses centered around one of the areas locally produced products. Fresh
shrimp are the specialty of the house and come from the aquaculture farms just
up the road. You'll find picnic tables positioned under canvas roofs beside the
vans and shrimp shacks, so don't let a little rain scare you away. Besides the
obligatory two scoop rice and mac salad that comes with the lunch plates, soda,
bottled water, and plenty of napkins are available. Theses are great places to
stop and talk story while you're on your way around the island.

Oahu Dining

Honolulu

Kaka'ako Kitchen
Ward Center
1200 Ala Moana Blvd-Bay1
Honolulu, HI 96813
808-596-7488
Web: None
Hours: B 7:00 AM-10:00 AM Mo-Fr
         B 7:00 AM-11:00 AM SaSu
         L/D 10:30 AM-9:00 PM Mo-Fr
         L/D 11:30 AM-9:00 PM Sa
         L/D 11:30 AM-5:00 PM Su
Cards: AE DC JCB MC V
Dress: Casual
Style: Haw-Reg $

Menu Sampler:

Breakfast:
Fried Rice 4.95, with one egg add .95, Banana Poi Bread 1.75, Huevos Rancheros-two eggs, brown rice, corn tortilla topped with chipotle vegetable chili & cheddar cheese 7.25. All the following served with white rice and a homemade biscuit with lilikoi butter, Pan-Seared Mahimahi and Two Eggs 6.95, Loco Moco 6.50, Kaka'ako Kitchen Omelet with three eggs, bacon, Spam, char siu chicken, Portuguese sausage, kamaboko and green onion 6.75

Lunch/Dinner:
Local Plates: Shichimi Seared Ahi Sandwich with tobiko aioli, soy-sake drizzle on taro bun $7.95, Sweet and Sour Spare Ribs w/rice, greens or mac salad $5.95
Sandwiches: Tempura Mahimahi on taro roll $6.50, Grilled Pastrami with Swiss cheese, house-made Russian dressing, on whole wheat hoagie bun $6.75, BLT and Crab Sandwich with basil mayonnaise on toasted herb bread $7.95
Gourmet Plates: Crispy Fried Sweet Chili Chicken with rice, greens or mac salad $8.25, Chicken Piccata over Linguine w/lemon caper sauce, taro roll $8.25, Char Broiled Ahi Steak medium rare, Asian salsa, soy-sake drizzle $Mkt

Impressions:

Kaka'ako Kitchen is an affordable fast food outlet for Chef Russell Siu's Hawaii Regional Cuisine. The approach here is plate lunch gourmet style. This means patrons can expect concrete floors, plastic chairs, and food served in styrofoam containers. It also means exciting cuisine can be purchased for lunch wagon prices. Try to avoid peak meal times, as this place is very popular with the local business crowd. Parking is free in the Ward Center deck adjacent to the shop.

Oahu Dining

Diamond Head

Kapiolani Community College
Ka'ikena Dining Room
Ohelo Building, 2nd Floor
4303 Diamond Head Road
Honolulu, HI 96816
808-734-9499
http://food.kcc.hawaii.edu/kaikena
Hours: L Seating at 11:00 AM, 11:30 AM, Noon
          D Seating at 5:15 PM & 5:45 PM
Cards: MC V
Dress: Resort Casual
Style: Fine $$

Menu Sampler:

Lunch:
Menus rotate frequently. Complete lunch includes choice of soup or salad, entrée, dessert, and beverage. Choice of Starters: Mixed Greens with Asparagus Vinaigrette or Tuscan White Bean Soup. Choice of Entrée: Grilled Snapper with Sauce Vierge, saffron spinach, garlic whipped potatoes, vegetables $14.95, Ravioli with Sundried Tomatoes and Ricotta Stuffing, creamy mushroom sauce $12.95, Scampi Style Shrimp with Pasta in Garlic Butter Sauce, vegetables $13.95, Braised Lamb Shanks, polenta, tomato confit, vegetables $14.95, Roast Cornish Game Hen, polenta, grilled vegetables $13.95
Dessert: Your choice of items such as Fresh Baked Apple Pie, Strawberry Shortcake, Chocolate Cream Pie, Orange Passion Chiffon Pie, Assorted French Pastries on a luscious pastry cart.
Beverages: Kona Coffee, Decaf Coffee, Hot or Iced Tea

Impressions:

If you would like to see where some of Hawaii's finest chefs got their start, drive up the side of Diamond Head to Kapiolani Community College and check out their Culinary Arts Program. As part of their education students operate the Ka 'Ikena Laua'e Restaurant. Inside this fine dining room students prepare and present a series of gourmet menus. Reservations are a must for these events so be sure to call ahead. Its also a good idea to check their website as the schedule varies with the school year. BYOB is permitted so don't forget the wine!

Waikiki

Keo's in Waikiki
2028 Kuhio Ave
Honolulu, HI 96815
808-951-9355
www.keosthaicuisine.com
Hours: B 7:30 AM-11:00 AM
           L 11:00 AM-2:00 PM
           D 5:00 PM-10:30 PM
Cards: AE DC DIS JCB MC V
Dress: Resort Casual
Style: Thai $$

Menu Sampler:

Breakfast:
Two Eggs with choice of meat and rice or hash brown $4.95, Asian Breakfast of broiled salmon, seasoned seaweed, pickled vegetables, steamed rice, miso soup and one egg $8.95, Buttermilk Pancakes with bananas or strawberries $3.95

Lunch/Dinner:
Appetizers: Golden Triangles (4)-tiger prawns wrapped in pastry triangle shells with shiitake mushrooms, water chestnuts, chives and fresh spices, deep-fried and served with tangerine hot sauce $7.95, Crispy Shrimp or Calamari lightly coated with rice flour, deep-fried, served with a vinaigrette hot sauce $10.95

Soups: Thai Ginger Soup with fresh Thai ginger from our farms, vegetables, coconut milk, green onion, spices, Thai parsley and seafood $4.25

Salads: Glass Noodle Salad with shrimp, onion, mint, lime juice, spices $13.95, Beef Larb-famous spicy salad with fresh lettuce and cabbage $13.95

Entrées: Thai Style Pork Chops marinated in spices $14.95, Hot Basil with chicken or beef $11.95, Honey Glazed Grilled Thai Style Spare Ribs $14.95, Chicken Panang Curry $12.95, Thai Crispy Fish with chili sauce $17.95

Desserts: Thai Tapioca $3.95, Mango Sorbet $5.95, Flan $3.95, Mud Pie $6.95

Impressions:

Twenty-five years ago Keo broke new ground by being the first to serve Thai cuisine in Honolulu. This was a natural success in a market attuned to Asian dining styles. Here you had ingredients people were accustomed to being served with zest like no one had experienced. Today this spacious Waikiki restaurant features tropical café style dining complete with rattan chairs and umbrella-covered tables. Normally Thai restaurants are lunch and dinner venues but Keo opens up for breakfast as well. All three are expertly prepared and fairly priced.

Kaimuki

Kim Chee II
3569 Waialae Ave.
Honolulu, HI 96816
808-737-7733
Web: None
Hours: LD 10:30 AM-9:00 PM
Cards: AE MC V
Dress: Casual
Style: Kor $

Menu Sampler:

Breakfast:
N/A

Lunch/Dinner:
Lunch Special includes Bar-B-Q Chicken, Meat Jun, & Man Doo with vegetables & rice $6.90, **Dinner Special** includes Bar-B-Q Short Rib, Shrimp Tempura, Fried Man Doo & Meat Jun $10.90
Combo Plates: Combo Plate of Bar-B-Q Beef, Chicken & Fried Man Doo with vegetables & rice $6.90, Kal Bee of Bar-B-Q Short Ribs with vegetables & rice $14.90, Chicken Katsu with vegetables & rice $7.50, Bibim Bap-Rice with vegetables, egg, and beef or chicken $7.50, Bibim Kooksoo of noodles with vegetables and beef or chicken $6.30, Fried Man Doo with vegetables & rice $6.30, Spicy Shoyu Chicken with vegetables & rice $7.50, Chicken Tofu with vegetables $7.50, Kim Chee Restaurant Special of Bar-B-Q Short Rib, Beef, Chicken, Meat Jun & Fried Man Doo with vegetables & rice $14.90
Fish: Fried Corvina Fish with rice $8.50, Shrimp Tempura with rice $8.50
Soup: Miso Soup with rice $7.50, Man Doo Kook-dumpling soup $7.50, Oxtail Soup with rice $9.00, Duk Man Doo-rice cake and man doo in soup $7.50
Side Orders: Butterfish $9.90, Mackeral $7.50, Fried Tofu $3.90, Kim Chee $2.00, Squid $7.50, Mahimahi Katsu $7.50, Dried Radish $4.00, Fish Jun $7.50

Impressions:

Kim Chee II is another one of those local favorites that has become an island institution. Kaimuki residents gather in this over-sized diner for the good food, fair prices, and convivial atmosphere. In keeping with tradition, the Korean menu stresses lean meats, fresh vegetables, and healthy preparations. Some items are offered in small portions for children and light appetites. If you've never tried Korean food, this would be a good place to start. You'll find Kim Chee II in Kaimuki's restaurant row. There's a large parking lot in the rear.

Honolulu

Kincaid's Fish, Chop, and Steak House
Ward Warehouse
1050 Ala Moana Blvd
Honolulu, HI 96813
808-591-2005
Web: None
Hours: L 11 AM-5 PM
        D 5-10 PM
Cards: AE DC DIS JCB MC V
Dress: Resort Casual
Style: Ec/Stk $$$

Menu Sampler:

Breakfast:
N/A
Lunch:
Starters: Broadway Pea Salad with peas, water chestnuts, sugar snap peas and bacon with white pepper dressing $5.50, Onion Soup baked with cheeses $6.95
Entrées: Sesame Chicken Salad $10.95, Prime Rib French Dip on a garlic butter toasted roll with au jus $11.95, Dungeness Crab and Artichoke Sandwich $11.95, Oven Roasted Chicken Dijon with panko flakes and parmesan $12.95
Dinner:
Appetizers: Warm Brie with Macadamia Nut Crust, seared and drizzled with balsamic-honey glaze $9.50, Coconut Tiger Prawns w/Cajun Marmalade $10.95
Entrées: Almond Crusted Sea Scallops with champagne beurre blanc $21.95, Roasted Chicken Breast Dijon with panko flakes and parmesan $16.95, Filet Mignon grilled, served with steakhouse butter and crispy onion strings $32.50, Baby Back Ribs with Hawaiian Barbecue Sauce, fries, slaw $18.95, Grilled New Zealand Rack of Lamb, in a Hunan Style Barbecue Sauce $25.95
Desserts: Kincaid's Original Burnt Cream $4.50, Roasted Pear Bread Pudding with Bourbon-Custard Sauce $6.50, Island Style Cheesecake $5.50

Impressions:

Beveled glass, multi-level floors, lots of brass, and a glossy wood décor are all part of the pleasant atmosphere you'll find at Kincaid's. Of course the view out over the park to the ocean doesn't hurt either. The menu does a first rate job of combining variety with innovative preparations. Kincaid's is known for their consistent quality, friendly staff, and reasonable prices. This is a favorite with the local business set. There's plenty of free parking in the shopping center lot.

Windward

Kin Wah Chop Suey
45-588 Kamehameha Hwy
Kaneohe, HI 96744
808-247-4812
Web: None
Hours: LD 10:00 AM-9:00 PM
Cards: MC V
Dress: Casual
Style: Chi $

Menu Sampler:

Breakfast:
N/A
Lunch/Dinner:
Soup: Bird Nest Soup 10.00, Scallop Soup 7.75, Watercress with Fishcake Soup 5.00, Hot Sour Soup 5.50, Shark Fin Soup 18.50, Long Rice with Pork Soup 5.00
Chop Suey: Kin Wah Chop Suey 5.00, Shrimp Chop Suey 5.50
Entrees: Pork or Beef with Ginger & Green Onion 5.75, with Green Pepper & Black Bean Sauce 5.25, with Tomato 5.25, with Eggplant 5.75; Char Siu 4.50, Sweet Sour Pork 5.25, Shrimp Pineapple 7.00, Kun Pao Shrimp 7.75, lobster with Curry Sauce 14.50, Oyster Roll with Pork 5.75, Pot Roast Chicken with Oyster Sauce 5.75, Chicken with Chinese Peas 5.75, Lemon Chicken 5.75, Crispy Chicken 5.75, Roast Duck with Gravy 6.00, Stuffed Duck 7.50
Chow Mein: Kin Wah Chow Mein 5.25, Chicken & Lobster Chow Mein 8.75
Gau Gee: Plain Crispy Gau Gee (10 pcs.) 4.50, Soft Gau Gee with Chicken & Vegetables (Gravy) 5.75, Wor Gau Gee Mein Soup 5.25, Gau Gee Soup 4.75
Sizzling Platters: Mongolian Beef 6.25, Stuffed Tofu with Pork 5.50
Plates: "A" -Beef with Broccoli, Gon Lo Mein, Lemon Chicken, Crispy Wun Ton & Rice $5.00, "B"-Pot Roast Pork, Spareribs, Beef Broccoli, Crispy Gau Gee, Fried Shrimp, Rice $5.75

Impressions:

Kin Wah Chop Suey is local party heaven. Visitors will have no problem getting a table for lunch, but watch out for dinnertime! That's when you'll find groups of 30, 45, or 60 residents sitting together celebrating one of life's milestones. This is a chop suey house with the comfort food and reasonable prices we have come to expect from such establishments. Now here's an inside tip you won't see anywhere else; this place has got to have the most reasonably priced top-shelf call drinks in Hawaii. Maybe that's why their functions are so popular! Look for Kin Wah in the shopping building behind the Island Mini-Mart.

Honolulu

Kirin

2518 S. Beretania
Honolulu, HI 96826
808-942-1888
Web: None
Hours: L 11:00 AM-2:00 PM
          D 5:00 PM-Midnight
Cards: AE DC DIS JCB MC V
Dress: Resort Casual
Style: Chi $$$

Menu Sampler:

Breakfast:
N/A
Lunch:
Appetizer: Deep Fried Bacon Roll with scallop & shrimp $14.95, Drunken Chicken-northern style $7.95, Spring Rolls $6.95, Deep Fried Won Ton $6.95
Entrées: Fried Shrimp with honey glazed walnut $15.95, Fried Fillet of Squid with peppery salt-spicy $9.95, Fried Saucy Spare Ribs "Wu Shi" Style $10.95
Dinner:
Appetizer: Sliced Five Spiced Beef Shank-spicy $9.95, Spring Rolls $7.95
Soup: Each serves 4 people. Hot & Sour Soup-spicy northern style $8.95, Crab Meat with dried fish maw soup $15.95, Shredded Dried Scallop with yellow chive soup $15.95, Eight Treasures & Tofu Soup $9.95, Chicken & Corn $8.95
Entrées: Fried Fillet of Uhu with peppery salt-spicy $14.95, Braised Sea Cucumber with shrimp roe-northern style $16.95, Saute Oyster with Szechuan garlic sauce-spicy northern style $13.95, Peking Duck (whole) with 12 thin pancakes $36.00, Baked Sesame Pocket Buns stuffed Peking style with minced pork and mustard stem $6.95, Maine Lobster $16/#, Dungeness Crab $16/#
Dessert: Sesame Mochi Balls in Red Bean Soup $2.95, Green Tea Ice Cream $3.25, Lychee Sherbet $3.25, Almond Tofu with fruit cocktail $2.95

Impressions:

Entering this cool, dark restaurant after leaving the bright, bustling world of South Beretania is a study in contrast. This traditionally decorated dining spot serves authentic Szechuan, Hunan, Peking, and Cantonese cuisine. Live seafood is king here and would be a wise choice for the discriminating diner. Note the late night dining hours. You can get lost in the Waianae's and still make it back in time for dinner. This is one of those places where valet parking is a must.

Oahu Dining

Windward

Koa House
46-126 Kahuhipa
Kaneohe, HI 96744
808-235-5772
Web: None
Hours: BL 6:30 AM-2:00 PM
Cards: MC V
Dress: Casual
Style: Amer/Isl $

Menu Sampler:

Breakfast:
Eggs: served with choice of three pancakes or rice or toast or home fried
potatoes, Corned Beef Hash & Eggs, Vienna Sausage & Eggs, Spam & Eggs, or
Hamburger Patty & Eggs 4.60, Portuguese Sausage & Eggs 4.75, Canadian
Bacon & Eggs 4.95, Steak & Eggs 5.95, Scottish Bangers & Eggs 4.75,
Mahimahi & Eggs 5.25, Kalbi & Eggs 6.50, Eggs Benedict 5.50/6.50, Vinha
D'alhos & Eggs- Portuguese marinated pork 5.75
Griddle: Sweet Bread French Toast 4.00, Banana or Blueberry Pancakes
3.00/3.75, Pecan Waffles 3.50, Crepe Suzettes-Sour Cream & Lemon 4.75
Lunch:
Sandwiches & Burgers: choice of tossed salad, potato salad, macaroni salad or
home fries, Fried Shrimp, Bacon & Cheese Sandwich 5.75, Chili Burger 4.25,
Mushroom Burger 4.50, Shrimp Burger 4.75, BLT 3.90, Steak Sandwich 5.50
Entrees: served with a hot vegetable and choice of French bread or rice, tossed
salad, potato salad, macaroni salad, or home fries; Shrimp and Mahi, Fried 6.25,
Mahi Juhn-lightly breaded in egg batter 5.50, Beef Teriyaki 5.25, Hamburger
Steak with Brown Gravy 4.95, Vinha D'alhos (Portuguese marinated pork) 5.95,
Chicken Cutlet 4.95, Koa House Combo Special-choice of two-Kal-Bi (beef
short rib), Bar-B-Q Beef, Bar-B-Q Chicken, Mahi Mahi, Chicken Cutlet, Fried
Shrimp 5.75, Chili & Spaghetti served with French Bread 4.25

Impressions:

If you're driving around the island, take the Kahuhipa turn-off from the Kahekili
Highway and look on the right hand side for Koa House. This local favorite has
been around for a long time as witnessed by the priceless koa wood interior that
gives the restaurant its name. The menu has international influences designed to
please a wide range of tastes. Locals consider this to be a top budget choice as
the pricing is very reasonable. Even the lunchtime entrees come in below six
dollars. There's a small lot in front, but be prepared to park along the street.

Hawaii Kai

Kona Brewing Company

Koko Marina Center
Kalanianole Highway
Honolulu, HI 96825
808-394-5662
www.KonaBrewingCo.com
Hours: LD 11:00 AM-9:00 PM Su-Th
        LD 11:00 AM-10:00 PM FrSa
Cards: DC DIS MC V
Dress: Casual
Style: Amer/Isl $$

Menu Sampler:

Breakfast:
N/A

Lunch/Dinner:
Pupu: Roasted Garlic served with toasted spent grain focaccia and warmed creamy Gorgonzola cheese $5.99, Pele's Fire Wings-Fire Rock Marinated Wings with a spicy teriyaki glaze, side of Ranch $6.49, Cheesy Garlic Bread with fresh garlic aioli, mozzarella & Parmesan with a side of marinara $3.99

Salads: Greek Salad with cucumbers, Kalamata olives, Maui onions, pepperoncini, tomatoes & feta cheese atop Kahuku romaine with balsamic vinaigrette $6.49/$9.49, Strawberry Spinach Salad with toasted macadamia nuts, Gorgonzola, Maui onions, and strawberry vinaigrette $7.99/$9.99

Sandwiches: All are served with Kettle Chips, substitute salad for $1.99. Porterhouse Dip of roast beef marinated and cooked in our Black Sand Porter, topped with roasted red onions and melted cheddar & mozzarella cheeses, Porter au jus for dipping $9.99, Imu Style Kalua Pork Sandwich with cabbage, pineapple mesquite BBQ sauce, roasted onions, cheddar & mozzarella $8.99

Gourmet Pizzas: Small 10", Medium 12", and Large 14". All pizzas are available as Calzones. Kona Wild Mushroom Pizza-garlic infused olive oil base, mozzarella & chevre, wild mushrooms, roasted garlic, roasted onions & red peppers, Thai Chicken or Shrimp with spicy peanut Thai base, roasted red peppers, mozzarella, green onions, sesame seeds, $13.99/$17.99/$20.99

Impressions:

The Kona Brewing Company has brought its Big Island charm, handcrafted beer and fun food menu to the Koko Marina Center at Hawaii Kai. This dockside bar and grill targets grazers looking for light bites and a party atmosphere. Those returning from Hanauma Bay will appreciate this casual lunch stop.

North Shore

Kua 'Aina Sandwich Shop
66-160 Kamehameha Highway
Haleiwa, HI 96712
808-637-6067
Web: None
Hours: LD 11:00 AM-8:00 PM
Cards: None
Dress: Casual
Style: Amer $

Menu Sampler:

Breakfast:
N/A

Lunch/Dinner:
Salads: Tossed Green $2.85/$3.75, Tuna or Turkey Salad $5.30
Kua Aina Burgers-Choice of bread or rolls- ⅓lb/ ½ lb- Hamburger $5.30/$5.70, Cheeseburger $5.60/$6.00, Bacon Burger $5.70/$6.10, Ortega Burger $5.60/$6.00, Avocado Burger $6.00/$6.35, Pineapple Burger $5.60/$6.00, Kiddie Burger $3.20, Extra toppings available.
Sandwiches: Mahi Mahi $5.80, Teri Chicken $5.80, BLT $5.00, Hot Roast Beef $5.25, Cold Roast Turkey $5.25, Mahi, Ortega & Cheese $6.40, Roast Beef & Avocado $6.15, Grilled Eggplant & Peppers $5.30, Turkey & Avocado $6.15
Sides: French Fries $1.65/$2.40, Cole Slaw $.55, Pickle $.25, Pepperoncini $.55
Cold Drinks: Small $.95, Medium $1.10, Large $1.25, BYOB Free

Impressions:

There are times when only a burger will do. If that mood strikes you, go for the best. Cruise on up to the North Shore to the small village of Haleiwa and try Kua'Aina Sandwich Shop. The food here has always been top-notch but until recently was difficult to get because of diminutive premises. Kua 'Aina has moved into new digs a couple hundred yards down the street. Now they have plenty of seating outside on the porch or yard and in the dining room. Just step inside and place your order at the counter before finding a table. When your name is called pick up your food. Your burgers will come with ⅓# or ½# patties served medium unless otherwise requested on a choice of Kaiser roll or breads and a variety of toppings. The fries are great. A single basket easily shares for two. Gourmet sandwiches are also available. There's free parking in the rear of the building. Take note that no credit cards are accepted, so bring cash!

Waikiki

Kyoya
2057 Kalakaua Ave.
Honolulu, HI 96815
808-947-3911
Web: None
Hours: L 11:00 AM-1:45 PM XSu
         D 5:30 PM-9:30 PM
Cards: AE DC DIS JCB MC V
Dress: Resort Casual
Style: Japan $$$$
         Ent Card

Menu Sampler:

Breakfast:
N/A
Lunch:
Teishoku-All include by kobachi, salad, tsukemono, misoshiru & rice. Shrimp
Tempura & Butterfish Misoyaki $14, Chicken Katsu $12,Tonkatsu $13, Sashimi
$20, Beef Teriyaki $14, Tempura Soba or Udon $11, Sushi & Sashimi
Nabemono-Shabu Shabu or Beef Sukiyaki, Udonsuki-min. two $25/person
Dessert: Papaya $4, Ice Cream $3, Iced Coffee $5
Dinner:
Teishoku-All accompanied by salad, tsukemono, misoshiru, rice & dessert.
Sashimi $28, Butterfish Misoyaki $24, Tonkatsu $24, Beef Teriyaki $25,
Nabemono-Shabu Shabu-slices of beef, fresh vegetables, and long rice
simmered in a kobu broth and served with two dipping sauces, Sukiyaki-slices
of beef & fresh vegetables cooked in a tasty Sukiyaki sauce, or Udonsuki-thick
udon noodles, chicken, shellfish & vegetables all simmered in a light broth-
Prepared at your table w/accompanying dishes and dessert- $35/$45/$55
Ala Carte: Beef Teriyaki $18, Soft Shell Crab $17, Shrimp and Vegetables
Tempura $15.00, Edamame $7, Tsukemono $7/$12, Sunomono $8, Wafu Steak
$20, Chicken Karaage $10, Salmon Shioyaki $14, Maguro Poki $6
Sake Samplers: Reishu or Atsukan-five samples in each group $10.00

Impressions:

Everything about Kyoya is classic Japanese. This Waikiki tradition has been
around for fifty years, so you know it works. The menu offers patrons a choice
of dining styles as well as dining rooms. Different moods and different times of
day call for different approaches. This upscale restaurant does it all well.

Honolulu

La Mariana Sailing Club

50 Sand Island Access Road
Honolulu, HI 96817
808-848-2800
Web: None
Hours: L 11:00 AM-3:00 PM
        D 5:00 PM-9:00 PM
Cards: AE MC V
Dress: Casual
Style: Isl/Sea $$

Menu Sampler:

Breakfast:
N/A
Lunch:
Salads: Salad Platter with Tomato & Hard Boiled Egg & Garlic Bread $5.25, topped with Shrimp, Turkey, or Chicken $8.75, Tuna $7.75, Avocado $7.50
Sandwiches: Bacon or Bay Shrimp & Avocado on wheat bread with alfalfa sprouts, tomato $7.75, Mahi Mahi Fish & Chips $8.25, Club Special $8.25
Entrees: 6 oz NY Steak Sandwich with cole slaw $9.50, Linguini in Garlic Butter, Parmesan Cheese & Garlic Bread $7.25, French Dip au jus $8.25
Specials: All are served with vegetable & choice of starch. Mahi Mahi Sautéed, Broiled or Cajun Style $9.00, Shrimp Curry with Vegetables $9.00, Ahi or Calamari Steak-choice of prep $Mkt, Eggs Benedict with Sautéed Tender Island Chicken Ham & Turkey on English Muffin $5.00/$9.25
Dinner:
Appetizers: Mushrooms sautéed w/garlic & white wine $8.75, Tako Poke $9.50
Seafood Specialties: Shrimp Scampi $16.25, Seafood Brochette of shrimp, scallop, mahi mahi, onion, green pepper, tomato $17.00Ahi Cajun Black & Blue New Orleans Style $Mkt, Stuffed (with seafood) Eggplant au Gratin $17.00
Meat & Poultry: Prime Rib $16.75/$17.75, Garlic Steak with Anchovies $16.75, Pork Tenderloin with Rib roasted with herbs in a mushroom sherry sauce $16.75

Impressions:

Have you ever wondered where the objets d'art migrate to after a legendary Honolulu hot spot closes? La Mariana has often been the answer. This kitschy, comfortable collection of bamboo, fish tanks and Hawaiiana is located in the midst of the commercial/industrial bustle on Sand Island. The menu offers a variety of fare, but we favor the very reasonably priced fresh fish. Ask about the daily specials before ordering. Parking is tight at lunch. Go early.

Waikiki

La Mer
Halekulani Hotel
2199 Kalia Road
Honolulu, HI 96815
808-923-2311
www.halekulani.com
Hours: D 6:00 PM-10:00 PM
Cards: AE DC DIS JCB MC V
Dress: Formal
Style: Fre $$$$

Menu Sampler:

Breakfast/Lunch:
N/A

Dinner:
Starters: Tartare of Hamachi, Ahi and Salmon with Three Caviars and Three Coulis 23.00, Soup of Mussels and Moano Fillets with saffron and chanterelles 14.00, Escargot in the manner of Provence 18.00, Gourmand Selection 36.00
Entrées: Lobster "Galette" of Basmati Rice and Roasted Opakapaka Sausage 43.00, Crispy Skin Fillet of Onaga with Truffle Jus, Tomato Confit and Fried Basil 39.00, Roasted Salmon and Salmon Tartare with a Meaux Mustard Sauce and Bouquet of Greens 36.00, Bouillabaise La Mer Style in a Puff Pastry 40.00, Kobe Style Filet of Beef Three Ways-Beef Carpaccio with a Parmesan Shaving, Tournedos of Beef with Bone marrow and Bordelaise Sauce, Sliced Filet of Beef on a Truffle Jus with Provencale Vegetables 48.00, Rack of Lamb with a Dijon Mustard Crust, Provencale Style Vegetables and Creamy Potatoes 43.00, Barbary Duck Breast Roasted with Lavender Honey, thigh Confit, Thyme and Garlic, Braised Belgian Endives 38.00, Selection of French Cheeses 14.00
Desserts: Painter's Palette with Almond Florentine, five sorbets, seasonal fruit and freshly pureed coulis: Pineapple Crème with lilikoi jaconde and sorbet $15

Impressions:

This restaurant is the premier venue in the Halekulani's dining collection. The hotel complex is an oasis in the heart of bustling Waikiki Beach, and La Mer is positioned to take advantage of all the grounds have to offer. Here Chef Yves Garnier combines classic techniques with French, Mediterranean, and island influences to create stellar results. No attention to detail is spared in presenting these masterpieces. Service at La Mer is second to none. This has long been the ultimate fine dining spot on Waikiki Beach. Reservations are imperative.

Oahu Dining

Niu Valley

Le Bistro
Niu Valley Shopping Center
5730 Kalanianole Hwy
Honolulu, HI 96821
808-373-7990
Web: None
Hours: D 5:30 PM-9:00 PM XTu
Cards: AE MC V
Dress: Resort Casual
Style: Cont/Ec $$$

Menu Sampler:

Breakfast/Lunch:
N/A
Dinner:
Appetizers: Escargot De Bourgogne 7.8, Fricassee of Fresh Manila Clams 8.8, Today's Soupe 3.9, French Onion Soupe 5.8,Caesar Salade 5.8
Takanohana Grill: Takanohana Grilled Chicken w/white rice 14.8/16.8, Black Angus Beef skewers w/a light red wine sauce, white rice 14.8/16.8
Le Bistro Pastas: Gorgonzola Spaghettini with slivered almonds & cracked black pepper 13.8, Penne Pasta with Italian Sausage, spinach 14.8
Les Entrées: New Orleans "Miro Street" Style Scallops seared with a rich black pepper sauce 16.8/19.8, Classic French Bistro Steak-Rib Eye w/cognac, Roquefort Butter 21.8/25.8, Barbequed Lamb Chops glazed with Balsamic Vinegar 25.8, Seabass in Morels 25.8, Opakapaka Prossecco 25.8, Grilled Paillard of Chicken, Mushroom & Bacon w/garlic roasted potatoes 14.8/16.8, Salmon Grenobloise, North Atlantic, with white wine and capers 19.8, Lemon, Rosemary & Thyme Grilled Chicken with garlic roasted potatoes 14.8/16.8
Weekly Specials: Sunday-Osso Bucco, Monday-Surprise, Wednesday-Veal w/ wild mushrooms, cognac sauce, Thursday-Live Maine Lobster

Impressions:

On the mauka side of the highway between Diamond Head and Hawaii Kai there's a small shopping venue that houses a couple of great little restaurants. There in the Niu Valley Shopping Center you'll find Le Bistro serving upscale, eclectic continental cuisine to an equally upscale and eclectic crowd. Although the menu isn't extensive, it is well rounded, and everyone in your party should be able to find something to please. This is a chef owned and operated restaurant which accounts for the consistency in the quality of food and service.

Oahu Dining

Chinatown

Legend Seafood Restaurant
Chinatown Cultural Plaza
100 N. Beretania Street
Honolulu, HI 96817
808-532-1868
www.legendseafood.com
Hours: BL 8:00 AM-2:00 PM SaSu
          BL 10:30 AM-2:00 PM Mo-Fr
          D 5:30 PM-10:00 PM
Cards: AE DC JCB MC V
Dress: Casual
Style: Chi $$

Menu Sampler:

Breakfast/Lunch:
Dim Sum Service-Prices per Plate $2.15-$4.75
Dinner:
Appetizer: Chinese Chicken Salad with Jellyfish $11.95, Deep Fried Sliced Squid with Spicy Salt $7.95, Drunken Chicken $7.25, Crispy Spring Rolls $5.95
Soup: Shark's Fin Soup with Seafood $16.95, Conpoy Thick Soup $9.95
Entrées: Sautéed Sliced Beef with ginger & green onion on sizzling platter $8.95, Braised Tenderloin Chinese Style $11.95, Baked Live Lobster with butter $Mkt, Sautéed Seafood in Taro Basket $13.95, Sautéed Scallop Szechuan Style $13.95, Stir Fried Shredded Chicken with Spicy Sauce $8.50, Roast Duck (1/2) $11.50, Deep Fried Chicken Stuffed with Minced Shrimp (half) $18.00
Vegetable & Tofu: Stir Fried Ong Choy with Shredded Pepper & Preserved Bean Curd $7.50, Steamed Tofu w/shrimp, shrimp roe and shrimp sauce $9.50
Funn/Noodle/Rice: Stir Fried Look Funn with Beef and Black Bean Sauce $7.50, Fried Rice, Yong Chow Style $7.50, Malaysian Style Chow Funn $7.50

Impressions:

Imagine a bustling, Asian crowd filling a large dining room where English is definitely a second language, and you'll get a pretty close feel for the scene at Legend Seafood Restaurant. This is even more obvious on Saturday and Sunday mornings when the dim sum service starts at 8 AM. When the food carts come around, just point! Not only will the friendly staff help you make selections, but fellow diners will also offer their recommendations. We view this as the perfect lunch spot after spending a morning in the Chinatown markets. Be sure to use the parking deck IN the Chinese Cultural Plaza and get your ticket validated.

Kapahulu

Leonard's Bakery
933 Kapahulu Ave
Honolulu, HI 96815
808-737-5591
Web: None
Hours: 6:00 AM-9:00 PM
Cards: None
Dress: Casual
Style: Spec $

Menu Sampler:

Breakfast/Lunch/Dinner:
Malasadas $.66, Pastries such as Fruit & Custard Danish $.70, Donuts $.48-$.82 each, Pies-whole-Custard, Pumpkin, and Apple $5, Cream Pies $6.75, Cookies in packages $1.30-$3.50, Coffee, Tea, Bottled Water

Impressions:

Leonard's Bakery is a Honolulu institution. Besides their wonderful pastries, cakes, and pies they are renowned for making great malasadas. It seems that everyone in Hawaii needs a malasada fix now and then, and at a price of just sixty-six cents no one should go without! This treat can be compared to a rich donut minus the hole that is deep-fried and then sprinkled with sugar. Malasadas eaten hot with a cup of coffee or tea make a great breakfast.

Chinatown

Little Village Noodle Shop
1113 Smith Street
Honolulu, HI 96817
808-545-3008
Web: None
Hours: LD 10:00 AM-Midnight
Cards: AE MC V
Dress: Casual
Style: Chi $

Menu Sampler:

Breakfast:
N/A
Lunch/Dinner:
Specialty: Shrimp Won Ton Mein $4.95, Duck Noodles Oahu Style $6.25
Traditional Northern Style: Hot & Sour Soup $6.25, Soft Noodles in hot peanut sauce $4.50, Chicken Chives Potstickers (8) $5.25, Sweet Crepe w/red beans $3.95, Shanghai Fried Noodles $6.95, Sesame Pancakes (2) $3.50
Greens & Healths: Steamed Ong Choy with bean curd sauce $4.50, Eggplant w/garlic sauce $6.95, Mu Shui Vegetables w/pancake $6.95, Ma Po Tofu $6.95
Canton Style: Fish Cake noodle $4.95, Boneless Chicken Noodle w/black bean sauce $6.25, Salted Fish w/chicken fried rice $7.25, Seafood Congee $5.75
Chef's Specialty: Steamed Kahuku Shrimp $9.95, Chili Shrimp Sizzling $12.95, Stir-Fried Clams with lemon grass $9.95, Szechuan Spicy Chicken $7.95, Beef w/black pepper sauce $7.95, Roasted Pork w/Taro $7.25, Orange Chicken $7.95, Stir-Fried Lamb with leek and chili $10.95, Mu Shu Pork $7.25
Hong Kong Style: Char Siu $5.95, Grilled Chicken Wings (6 pcs) $3.95
Dessert: Sweet Steamed Egg w/milk $2.75, Tapioca with Taro $1.50

Impressions:

Through the years many of the Chinese eateries in Honolulu's Chinatown have given way to people from other parts of Asia as the original proprietors moved on to other pursuits. Not so up on Smith Street. Here the Little Village Noodle House keeps the old traditions alive serving a very reasonably priced mixed Chinese menu. We like the décor which is simple yet pleasant. Then, there's the waiter who stood ready to make sure that two visitors from another island ordered a balanced lunch. Finally, of course, comes the food, which is tasty, light, and plentiful. Parking is available on the street or in a lot behind the shop.

Oahu Dining

Honolulu

Longhi's Ala Moana
1450 Ala Moana Blvd.
Honolulu, HI 96814
808-947-9899
www.longhis.com
Hours: B 8:00 AM-11:00 AM Mo-Fr
          B 7:30 AM-11:00 AM SaSu
          L 11:00 AM-5:00 PM
          D 5:00 PM-10:00 PM
Cards: AE JCB MC V
Dress: Casual
Style: Pac Rim $$$

Menu Sampler:

Breakfast:
Baked Italian Frittata with Meat & Vegetables or Vegetables with hollandaise on toasted French bread 10.00, Today's Quiche 9.00, French Toast with Grand Marnier, powdered sugar butter and maple syrup 9.25

Lunch:
Appetizers: Grilled Portobello Mushroom w/basil goat cheese pesto, roasted red bell peppers & imported goat cheese 9.00, Ahi Carpaccio on Bruschetta 15.00
Entrees: Belgian Endive Salad with gorgonzola cheese, caramelized macadamia nuts and scallion mint vinaigrette 10.25, Peking Duck Sandwich with hoisin sauce on our scallion roll 10.00, Chicken Picatta Open Faced Sandwich 13.00, Fresh Island Fish Longhi Style sautéed in butter, white wine & lemon with diced tomatoes & basil over garlic toast 14.00, Lobster Cannelloni w/béchamel 14.50

Dinner:
Appetizers: Frutti Di Mare-Poached Shrimp, Scallops, and Calamari, marinated in extra virgin olive oil, garlic, fresh herbs, roasted Mancini peppers, & Kalamata olives-served chilled 16.50, pacific Manila Clams in broth 14.50
Entrees: Prawns Amaretto-sautéed in Amaretto, brandy, fresh orange juice and cream 29, Seared Ahi Au Poivre with shiitake mushrooms in a garlic, green peppercorn, and brandy sauté 30, Lamb Chops (2) w/a raspberry-mint sauce 31
Desserts: Hot Chocolate Soufflé, flowing chocolate center, Haagen-Dazs 12

Impressions:

Bob Longhi has brought his formula of old world style and new world cuisine to the Ala Moana Shopping Center. Looking for an upscale breakfast or lunch in an open-air setting? You'll find it here. Then stop by later for tapas and cocktails or make reservations for a romantic dinner. Celebrity watching can be a plus!

Windward

Lucy's Grill N' Bar
33 Aulike Street
Kailua, HI 96734
808-230-8188
Web: None
Hours: B SuBru 9:30 AM-1:30PM
            D 5:00 PM-10:00 PM
Cards: MC V
Dress: Resort Casual
Style: Ec/Pac Rim $$$

Menu Sampler:

Breakfast:
Fresh Fish Benedict with spinach, poached egg, English muffin, papaya hollandaise $15.00, Sweet Bread Mac Nut French Toast $6.00
Dinner:
Appetizers: Crispy Kalua Pig Triangles with mascarpone & sweet sour Mandarin orange plum sauce $6, Coconut Crusted Shrimp w/sweet Asian chili beurre blanc $10Roast Pacific Oysters w/Mongolian garlic butter $10
Pizza: Kalua Pig Pizza w/red onions, hoisin sesame, mozzarella $11
Salads: Grilled Caesar Salad with fresh papaya, Reggiano, and crouton $8, Pick-It Salad with hearts of romaine, gorgonzola, caramelized walnuts, oil and vinegar $8, Romaine, rock shrimp, crab, avocado, egg, bacon, tomato $18
Entrées: Includes starch and vegetable. $3 charge for splits and special orders. Pan Seared, Pepper Crusted Ahi with wasabi miso beurre blanc $24, Lemongrass Crusted Scallops with green papaya salad, yellow Thai curry $23, Pulehu Style Baby Lamb Chops (6), green papaya chutney, lilikoi demi $24, Crispy Gingered Chicken w/Lucy's Hong Kong style noodles $16
Sides: Brown & White Rice Mix $2, Lucy's Mash Potatoes $3
Desserts: Crème Brulee $6, Dark Chocolate Soufflé Cake with chocolate truffle center and vanilla ice cream $8, Raspberry or Mango Sorbet $4, Gelato $4

Impressions:

Just behind McDonald's on the main highway coming into Kailua, you'll find Lucy's Grill N' Bar. This casually upscale dining spot offers tables inside and out and features a display kitchen preparing an eclectic island menu. We found the tastes to be complex to the point of addiction. Lucy's is quite the hangout for local patrons of all ages and can get busy. The creative fusion menu and upbeat atmosphere are conducive to good dining and lots of fun. This is a great place for an early dinner before heading back across the Pali. Check out the fish tanks!

Oahu Dining

Honolulu

L'Uraku
1341 Kapiolani Blvd
Honolulu, HI 96814
808-955-0552
www.luraku.com
Hours: L 11:00 AM-2:00 PM
         D 5:30 PM-10:00 PM
Cards: AE DC JCB MC V
Dress: Resort Casual
Style: Euro/Japan $$$

Menu Sampler:

Breakfast:
N/A
Lunch:
Baby Spinach & Garlic Shrimp with crispy bacon & mustard sesame vinaigrette
$9.50, Panko Shrimp Katsu $12.75, "Crunchy" Soft Shell Crab BLT with
avocado, Japanese cucumber and citrus aioli on foccacia $13.00, Pork Loin
Rack sautéed & served with stir fried vegetables, tomato lomi, rice $15.00
Weekender Lunch served on Saturday, Sunday & certain holidays only: Four-
course meal for $16 includes three courses (choice of entrée) plus dessert.
Dinner:
Starters: Bento Box Sampler of baked oyster, ahi tartare, crab cake, salmon
sushi $12.95, Ahi Tartare $8.95, Sizzlin' Moi Carpaccio w/Big Island ginger,
tofu, tomato concasse, peppered ponzu vinaigrette & julienned nori $6.95
Entrées: Miso-Yaki Butterfish served on 'Nalo pea sprouts & pickled red
ginger $19.25, Pan Roasted Pork Chop & "Crunchy" Shrimp w/garlic mashed
potato, Hauula tomato lomi & wasabi ketchup $20.50, Garlic Ribeye Steak with
roasted garlic, steamed vegetables, light teriyaki sauce $24.00, Pan roasted
Onaga served w/Manila clams & spicy clam broth $26.25, Filet Mignon $28.50

Impressions:

The high ceilings of this upscale restaurant are adorned with hand-painted
umbrellas for a whimsical East meets West atmosphere that carries all the way
through the menu. This is pupu heaven. The tastes at L'Uraku are exquisite.
Chef Hiroshi Fukui starts with high quality ingredients and gives all of the
preparations a pronounced Japanese twist. His take on fusion cuisine has won
many awards and secured him a position among the Hawaiian Island Chefs. The
one-way streets can make driving a challenge so consider taking a cab.

Honolulu

Maple Garden
909 Isenberg St
Honolulu, HI 96826
808-941-6641
Web: None
Hours: L 11:00 AM-2:00 PM
         D 5:30 PM-10:00 PM
Cards: AE DC DIS JCB MC V
Dress: Casual
Style: Chi $$

Menu Sampler:

Breakfast:
N/A

Lunch/Dinner:
Appetizers: Fried Won Ton $5.25, Spring Roll-House Specialty-$5.95, Wonderful Taste Chicken (hot)-House Specialty-$6.95, Szechuan Cabbage (hot) $2.95, Jelly Fish $6.50, Shredded Chicken w/sesame sauce (hot!) $6.50
Soup: Sour Hot Soup $6.50, Tofu & Oyster Soup $7.95, Winter Melon Soup $5.75, Shredded Pork with Szechuan Cabbage $5.75, Egg Flower Soup $5.75
Vegetables: Creamed Tientsin Cabbage $6.75, Sautéed Crispy String Beans-House Specialty-$6.95, Fried Soft Tofu Ala Maple Garden $7.95
Entrées: Shrimp Maple Garden $8.75, Shrimp with Hot Peppers $8.25, Oysters with Ginger Sauce-House Specialty-$9.50, braised Salmon $9.95, Fish with chili sauce (hot) $8.25, Diced Chicken with Chili (hot) $7.95, Beef & Squid Szechuan Style-House Specialty-$8.25, Hot Garlic Chicken $8.50, Shredded Pork with Dry Tofu-House Specialty-$7.75, Singing Rice with Pork & Vegetables $8.75, Fried Soft Tofu Ala Maple Garden $7.95, Curried Beef $7.75
Dessert: Almond Beancurd $1.75, Pearl Dumplings-House Specialty- $2.50

Impressions:

Maple Garden is a small neighborhood restaurant located on Isenberg between Kapiolani Boulevard and South King Street. This family-owned establishment serves excellent Szechuan cuisine at reasonable prices. Some of the dishes are mildly zesty, while others are best described as peppery hot. Regardless, this is substantial food that satisfies. Besides the ala carte items they offer daily lunch specials at prices under $8.00. Although the clientele are mainly local residents, you'll find akamai visitors dining at Maple Garden as well. There's a small lot next to the building, but you may have to park along the street.

Oahu Dining

Honolulu

Marbella
1680 Kapiolani Blvd.
Honolulu, HI 96814
808-943-4353
Web: None
Hours: L 11:30 AM-2:00 PM Mo-Fr
        D 5:30 PM-10:00 PM
Dress: Resort Casual
Style: Med $$$

Menu Sampler:

Breakfast:
N/A
Lunch:
Pizzas: Artichoke Tuscan with Spinach, Chicken and garlic cream sauce 9.00
Pastas: Fettucine with Calamari and Prawns in a Putanesca sauce 9.75
Sandwiches: Eggplant red pepper & zucchini w/spiced goat cheese 7.50
Dinner:
Soups: Lentil Soup with cumin essence and garlic chips 6.50
Salads: Spanish Composed Salad with oranges, goat cheese & cherry tomatoes 6.75, Mixed Green with granny smith apple brulee and Gorgonzola 7.00
Appetizers: Caramelized Onion Tart with goat cheese, olive tapenade and arugula 8.00, Marbella Spanokopita Filo Pastry with spinach, feta cheese & leek with yogurt sauce 7.50, Grilled Salmon stuffed in grape leaves 8.50
Main Course: Grilled Balsamic Chicken with red wine potato puree and ratatouille 16.00, Saffron Risotto with Daily Fresh Medley Fish, basil oil & garlic shrimp pil pil 18.50, Salmon Wellington with parmesan crusted sea scallops, red wine and beurre blanc 19.00, Oven Baked Cumin Crusted Whole Moi with roasted garlic potatoes and green beans 18.00
Desserts: Chocolate Ganache Stuffed Beignet 8.50, Granny Smith Apple Galette w/Gelato 7.00, and Molten Center Chocolate Cake w/vanilla gelato 5.50

Impressions:

Marbella has brought an intriguing blend of Mediterranean flavors and casual sophistication to the Honolulu dining scene. The ambitious menu draws from numerous sources and provides diners with choices not normally found in this Asian cuisine dominated city. Another big plus is the pricing, which is really quite reasonable considering the high level of this dining experience. Parking can be hard to come by in this busy area, so we recommend taking a cab.

Oahu Dining

Honolulu

Mariposa
Neiman Marcus
Ala Moana Shopping Center
Honolulu, HI 96814
808-951-3420
www.neimanmarcus.com
Hours: Su Bru 11:00 AM-3:00 PM
           L 11:00 AM-3:00 PM XSu
           D 5:00 PM-9:00 PM
Cards: AE DC JCB MC V
Dress: Casual
Style: Ec/Euro-Asian $$$

Menu Sampler:

Breakfast:
Brunch: Caesar Salad $12.00, with chicken $15.00, Housemade Corned Beef Hash & Eggs $10.00, Char Siu & Eggs with Fried Rice $9.00
Entrées: Sautéed Opakapaka with seasonal vegetables, Yukon Gold potatoes and a three pepper vinaigrette $Market Price, Thai Yellow Seafood Curry $18
Lunch:
Entrées: Steamed Manila clams in an herbed miso broth with toasted baguette $15.00, Barbecued Beef Brisket with cole slaw, garlic mashed potatoes and crispy tobacco onions $17.00, Kahuku Corn Chowder $5.00/$6.00
Sandwiches: Slow Smoked Beef Brisket w/tomatoes, lettuce, herb aioli $11.00
Dinner:
Appetizers: Vegetarian Lumpia with Nuoc Cham dipping sauce $8.00, Lobster Katsu w/mango-chile-lime sauce $14.00, Sesame Ahi Tartare w/tobiko $13.00
Entrées: Pan Seared Sea Scallops with herb and garlic pappardelle, sautéed spinach and Portobello mushrooms $25.00, Pulehu Steak Alae, mashed potatoes, seasonal vegetables and red wine demi glace $29.00, Almond-Herb Risotto in roasted garlic vegetable stock, crimini mushrooms, tomato concasse, Olde Amsterdam Gouda and Maui onion jus $18.00, Braised Duck Leg $24.00

Impressions:

Chef Douglas Lum presides over this highly regarded restaurant. Here on the third floor of Neiman Marcus in the Ala Moana Shopping Center, he serves an intriguing menu of fusion cuisine. Besides the wide variety of ala carte items, High Tea is served on Sunday afternoons from 2-5 PM ($16) with English tea, sandwiches, and pastries available for a special treat while shopping.

North Shore

Matsumoto Store
66-087 Kamehameha Hwy
Haleiwa, HI 96712
808-637-4827
www.matsumotoshaveice.com
Hours: 8:30 AM-6:00 PM
Cards: AE DC DIS JCB MC V
Dress: Casual
Style: Spec $

Menu Sampler:

Breakfast/Lunch/Dinner:
Shave Ice in a large selection of local and traditional flavors:
Small Shave Ice $1.20, Large Shave Ice $1.40. Shave Ice with ice cream: Small $1.60, Large $1.80. Shave Ice with Azuki beans: Small $1.60, Large $1.80. Shave Ice with ice cream and azuki beans: Small $1.80, Large $2.00.

Impressions:

Haleiwa is a quaint beachside village on the north shore of Oahu. Here you will find the Matsumoto Store serving that island favorite--shave ice. Since 1951 the Matsumoto's have served this local treat that is similar to a snow cone but with a finer texture. After shaving the ice off a block, they stack it high in a paper cone and add your choice of flavored syrups. For those with more experienced tastes, they offer sweet azuki beans or premium ice cream as add-ons. It can get busy here, but the line moves quickly. There's plenty of parking alongside the store.

Waikiki

Matteo's
364 Seaside Ave
Honolulu, HI 96815
808-922-5551
Web: None
Hours: D 5:30 PM-11:00 PM
Cards: AE DC DIS JCB MC V
Dress: Evening Aloha
Style: Ital $$$$
        Ent Card

Menu Sampler:

Breakfast/Lunch:
N/A

Dinner:
Antipasto: Escargots-baked in a garlic Dijon & fresh herb butter $10.95, Calamari Fritti $7.95, Artichokes alla Matteo's in a garlic butter with white wine and lemon $7.75, Seafood Medley Vinaigrette w/vegetables and noodles $12.95
Salads and Soups: Parma Onion Soup topped with French bread croutons, Italian cheeses & prosciutto $7.50, Salad Caprese with fresh buffalo mozzarella, Roma tomato, grilled fennel, greens and balsamic-basil vinaigrette $7.95, Zuppe Di Clams $10.95, Minestrone Milanese $5.25, Seasonal Soup $5.50
Entrées: Grenadine of Beef Tenderloin topped with a red wine sauce and mushrooms $26.95, Veal Osso Bucco Milanese braised in a rich red wine sauce with saffron risotto and topped with a citrus gremolata $29.50, Cioppino alla Livornese with lobster, clams, mussels, shrimp, scallops, calamari and fresh fish poached in an Italian saffron, tomato and vegetable broth $32.50, Chicken Florentine on spinach with a chardonnay-garlic butter sauce $22.95, Eggplant Parmigiana Dinner $19.95, Veal Saltimbocca $26.95, Fresh Fish Dore Style-battered in egg and topped with a lemon-butter caper sauce $Market Price.
Pasta: Four Cheese Ravioli with Marinara drizzled with roasted garlic cream and macadamia nut pesto $17.95, Seafood Puttanesca on linguine$22.95
Dessert: Pastry & Dessert Tray $6.95, Bananas Foster "Frank Sinatra" with Curacao, rum over ice cream $10.95, Espresso, Cappuccino, Coffees $2-$5.50

Impressions:

Matteo's has been a local favorite for so long it's hard to remember when it opened. This restaurant serves classic Italian cuisine in a traditional atmosphere and does it well. Besides the fine menu, they offer an excellent wine list. It's a little congested in this part of Waikiki, so it would be wise to walk or take a cab.

Oahu Dining

Chinatown

Mei Sum Dim Sum
65 N. Pauahi St.
Honolulu, HI 96817
808-531-3268
Web: None
Hours: BLD 7:00 AM-9:00 PM
Cards: MC V
Dress: Casual
Style: Chi $

Menu Sampler:

Breakfast/Lunch/Dinner:
Dim Sum-wonderful variety and quality-Sweet Sesame Ball $1.95, Mochi Puff $1.95, Shrimp Dumpling $2.35, Shrimp Pork Hash $2.35, Custard Tart $1.95, Mochi Rice in Lotus Leaf $2.35, Lotus Sugar Bow $2.35, Beef Ball $2.35, Steamed Look Funn w/BBQ Pork $3.15, Steamed Look Funn w/ Scallop $3.15
Appetizer: Shrimp Canton $8.50, Pepper Salt Squid $7.95, Drunken Chicken $6.95, Spring Rolls (4 pcs) $3.95, Deep Fried Stuffed Tofu $6.95
Soup: Seaweed Tofu Soup $5.95, Egg Drop Soup $4.50, Won Ton Soup $4.25, Seafood Rice Soup $6.95, Meat Ball Rice Soup $4.95, Rice Soup $2.50
Entrées: Jumbo Scallop with Black Bean Sauce $8.95, Seabass w/Ginger Onion $8.50, Szechuan Style Shrimp $8.50, Seafood Tofu Casserole $8.95, Oyster & Shredded Pork w/Szechuan Sauce $9.50, Beef w/Satay Sauce $7.95, Roasted Duck $6.95, Chicken w/Black Mushroom $7.95 Pork Ong Choy w/Shrimp Paste or Pork Kau Yuk w/Mui Choy $6.95, Scallop Fried Rice $9.50
Vegetables: Chinese Broccoli w/Dried Flounder $6.95, Choy Sum w/Garlic Sauce $5.25, Dried Tofu w/Bean Sprout $5.95, Black Mushroom w/Vegetables $6.95, Steamed Stuffed Tofu $6.95, Braised Mixed Vegetables $5.95
Look Funn: Seafood Noodle in Soup $6.95, Wor Won Ton Mein $4.95, Roast Duck with noodle in soup $5.95, Beef Brisket Noodle in soup $4.95

Impressions:

If you're looking for great dim sum or a Hong Kong style menu served in an authentic yet quieter setting, head up to the corner of Smith and Pauahi in Chinatown. There you'll find Mei Sum Dim Sum. This simple eatery doesn't make a show of things, but the kitchen consistently delivers. Where most places only serve dim sum as a late breakfast, lunch, or teatime treat, Mei Sum offers these delicacies throughout the day. Make sure to look under the glass top on your table for the day's specials. After deciding we couldn't pass any of them by, we ordered way too much, but that was part of the fun of it!

Honolulu

Mekong II
1726 S. King
Honolulu, HI 96814
808-941-6184
Web: None
Hours: L 11 AM-2 PM XSaSu
        D 5-9:30 PM XSaSu
Cards: AE DC JCB MC V
Dress: Casual
Style: Thai $$

Menu Sampler:

Breakfast:
N/A
Lunch/Dinner:
Appetizers: Spring Rolls $6.50, Sa-Teh Chicken with spicy peanut sauce $7.95, Bangkok Wings $6.95, Thai Crispy Noodles $5.95, Fish Patties $6.95
Salads: Green Papaya Salad-shredded papaya with tomatoes, red chili, spices and lime juice $5.95, Calamari Salad-calamari, mint leaves, cucumber, celery, red onion, and lemon grass in a roasted chili dressing $7.95, Thai Beef $6.95
Soups: Spicy Seafood Soup $4.50, Spicy Chicken Soup $3.75, Spicy Fish $3.95
Entrées: Thai Noodles with Chicken-Pad Thai-$6.95, Evil Jungle Prince $7.50, Beef Basil $7.50, Ong Choi (Asian watercress) with Chicken $7.50, Yellow Seafood Curry $11.95, Thai Garlic Chicken $7.50, Long Rice w/Shrimp $8.95
Vegetarian Entrees: Mixed Vegetable Thai Curry with Thai red curry and basil $7.25, Ginger String Beans $7.25, Tofu with Bean Sauce and ginger $7.25
Rice and Noodles: Water Chestnut Fried Rice $6.95, Shrimp Fried Rice $8.95, Thai Broccoli Noodles with beef, chicken or pork $6.95, Brown Rice $1.25
Desserts: Lychee or Mango Sorbet $3.95, Thai Apple-Banana Coconut with Tapioca $3.25, Thai Iced Tea $1.50, Thai Tapioca Pudding $2.95

Impressions:

This small neighborhood restaurant is part of Keo's family of Thai eateries. Although the atmosphere at Mekong II might be a little more basic than some, it's hard to beat the prices. In this part of Honolulu everyone has to keep their overhead down, so if you are trying to do the same this would be a good call. Mekong II offers a good selection of quality Thai specialties including a tasty vegetarian menu. Parking can be a problem here. There's a small lot behind the building, but if that's full you'll have to look along the street.

Oahu Dining

Honolulu

Meritage

Restaurant Row
500 Ala Moana Blvd.
Honolulu, HI 96813
808-529-8686
www.meritagehawaii.com
Hours: L 11:00 AM-2:00 PM Tu-Fr
           D 5:00 PM-9:00 PM Tu-Th, 5:00 PM-11:00 PM Fr-Su
Cards: AE MC V
Dress: Resort Casual
Style: Cont/Pac-Rim $$
           Ent Card

Menu Sampler:

Breakfast:
N/A
Lunch:
Appetizers: Wild Mushrooms Gratinee in a Brandy Basil Cream 5.5
Soups/Salads: French Onion Soup 4.5, Warm Guava Prawn Spinach Salad 9.5
Entrées: Herb Crusted Fish Sandwich 7.5, Lobster & Wild Mushroom Pizza
11.5, Beef Bourguignon 12, Grilled Honey Basil Salmon 12, Clam Linguini 14.5
Dinner:
First Taste: Baked Oysters En Croute with Wild Mushroom Duxelle and
Fennel 10, French Foie Gras w/Caramelized Pears and Balsamic Port Syrup 17
Soups and Salads: Soup of the Day 5, Warm Spinach Salad w/Pistachios 7
Main Attraction: Grilled long Island Duck Confit with Balsamic Syrup, Figs
and Ginger Pear Sauce 17, Grilled Filet Mignon Steak Madison with Rondele
Cheese, Bourgouinone Sauce and Potato Pancake 27, Sautéed Rock Shrimp
Risotto with Asparagus and Wild Mushrooms 17, Meritage Bouillabaise 20
Grand Finale: Passionfruit Cheesecake w/Mascarpone Cheese & Vanilla
Anglaise 5, Macadamia Nut Mocha Mousse Cake 5, Soufflé of the Day 7

Impressions:

Meritage is an interesting little place. It is at once classy yet unpretentious. The
lively clientele matches the surroundings and the eclectic, ambitious menu. Any
foodie couldn't help but appreciate the rich tastes offered here. In some ways
they're European, but in others they're definitely Pacific-Rim. During lunch the
place is full of local business types who work nearby. Later during dinner the
pace slows down as locals and visitors alike come in for an evening of relaxed,
fine dining. Park in the center's deck and make sure to get your ticket validated.

Waikiki

Michel's

2895 Kalakaua Ave
Honolulu, HI 96815
808-923-6552
www.michelshawaii.com
Hours: Su Bru 9:00 AM-Noon, D 5:30 PM-9:30 PM
Cards: AE DC DIS JCB MC V
Dress: Evening Aloha
Style: Fre $$$$

Menu Sampler:

Breakfast/Lunch:

Sunday Brunch 9 AM-Noon (Last Seating)-Eggs Benedict with artichokes and Dungeness crab meat $36, Lobster, Shrimp, Scallop Omelette $34

Dinner:

Appetizers: Ahi Carpaccio off bigeye tuna in a truffle vinaigrette w/a slaw of cucumber, tomato, & daikon $14, Burgundy Escargot in herb garlic butter $13, House Smoked Salmon w/warm potato pancake & grilled apple, greens and Waldorf salad $16, Fresh Oysters with shallot vinaigrette $16

Soups & Salads: Creamy Lobster Bisque with fresh Maine lobster meat flamed in Cognac at your table $9, Sweet Maui Onion soup with caramelized Maui onion with three cheeses under a crisp puff pastry crust $9, Belgian Endive Shrimp Salad w/ gorgonzola, toasted almonds & tomato w/vinaigrette $14

Entrées: Filet "Rossini" style-grilled beef tenderloin on sautéed spinach & fresh foie gras terrine, truffled mashed potato, mango-papaya chutney & Madeira sauce $48, Duckling a l'Orange with red cabbage, mashed potatoes & classic duck-orange jus $34, Goat Cheese-crusted Rack of Lamb with au gratin potatoes, bacon wrapped haricot verts & zinfandel sauce $38, Crab-Stuffed Maine Lobster baked & served w/saffron pilaf, black bean & white wine sauce $48, Potato Crusted Onaga on sautéed orzo & spinach, sweet rock shrimp, tomato coulis, garlic cream $28, Chateaubriand for Two $42/person

Dessert: Chocolate or Grand Marnier Souffle-20 minute preparation

Impressions:

Located in the Colony Surf Condominiums at the quiet Diamond Head end of Waikiki, you'll find one of Honolulu's long time favorite restaurants. This gracious dining room sits on the beach and provides fabulous views all the way down to its sister restaurant, John Dominis. Michel's presents classic French Continental cuisine at its finest with standards of service to match. Reservations are a must at this popular dining spot. Take a cab and avoid the parking hassle.

Waikiki

Miyako

The New Otani Kaimana Beach Hotel
2863 Kalakaua Ave
Honolulu, HI 96815
808-923-1555
www.kaimana.com
Hours: 5:30 PM-9:00 PM
Cards: AE DC DIS JCB MC V
Dress: Resort Casual
Style: Japan $$$
            Ent Card

Menu Sampler:

Breakfast/Lunch:
N/A
Dinner:
Appetizers: Edamame 3.00, Mozuku-seaweed in a shoyu vinaigrette 6.00, Maguro Yamakake-fresh island tuna with Japanese yam 8.00
Grilled Dishes: Sirloin Steak Miyako Style 18.00, Chicken Kushiyaki 12.00, Oyster Platter w/butter herb sauce, special mayonnaise topping 9.50
Vinegared/Fried Dishes: Assorted Sunomono 9.50, Lobster Tempura 18.00
Sashimi: Maguro 15.00, Amaebi 16.50, Beef Tataki with ponzu sauce 14.50
Steamed Dishes/Tofu/Salad: Chawan Mushi-steamed egg custard with shrimp, chicken and mushroom 8.50, Cold Tofu with condiments 4.25, Hot Tofu with condiments 6.50, Wafu Salad of green with sesame dressing 6.50
Rice/Soup: Ume Chazuke-pickled plum over rice in soup 7.50, Sake Chazuke-salmon over rice in soup 8.00, Cha Soba-cold green tea buckwheat noodle 7.25, Clear Soup 3.50, Soybean Soup 2.50, Red Soybean Soup 3.00, Rice 1.50
Sushi: Ala Carte-Tuna 3.00, Salmon Roe 3.50, Eel 2.50, Fatty Tuna Mkt $, Rainbow Roll 12.50, California Roll 11.50, Tekka Roll 5.00, Kappa Roll 4.00
Special Kaiseki Dinner: includes appetizer, soup, entrees, dessert $28.00/$38.00/$43.00/$65.00, Special Nabe Dinners-Sukiyaki $30.00, Shabu Shabu $33.00, Udonsuki $38.00-Minimum of two orders

Impressions:

Miyako is located on the quiet Diamond Head end of Waikiki overlooking San Souci Beach. It would be easy for diners to get caught up in the lovely views, but the excellent food and service rule here. This dignified restaurant offers a wide-ranging menu of Japanese specialties served by kimono-clad waitresses. Plan on spending your evening enjoying this gracious cultural experience.

Oahu Dining

Waikiki

Momoyama
Sheraton Princess Kaiulani Hotel
120 Kaiulani Ave
Honolulu, HI 96815
808-923-4678
Web: None
Hours: D 5.45PM-9:30 PM
Cards: AE DC DIS JCB MC V
Dress: Resort Casual
Style: Japan $$$$
         Ent Card

Menu Sampler:

Breakfast/Lunch:
N/A
Dinner:
Appetizer Specials: Edamame $3.95, Ahi Shioyaki $7.95, Deep Fried Oyster $4.95, Deep Fried Octopus $4.95, Sashimi $5.95, Marinated Pork $4.95, Asari Soup $5.95, Ohitashi $3.95, Agedashi Tofu $5.50, Tako Sunomono $4.95, Soft Shell Crab Karaage $7.95, Tsukemono $4.50, Hiyayakko $3.95
Sushi: Omikase Deluxe Combination $32.00, Chirashi-sushi rice topped with assorted seafood $27.95, California Temaki-crabmeat and avocado $6.95, Toro Temaki $6.95, Firecracker-spicy tuna $6.95, Hamachi Nigiri $7.95, Rainbow Maki $10.95, Shrimp Tempura Maki $7.95, Ume Shiso Maki $4.50
Golden Combinations: served with wafu salad, zensai, tsukemono, rice, miso soup and ice cream-Ikizukuri Lobster or Steamed Lobster w/seafood sashimi & NY steak or fish Misoyaki $62.00, Momoyama Royal-Lobster tail, traditional style w/broiled NY steak $42.00, Matsutake Kamameshi Teishoku- w/salad, tsukemono, tako sunomono, sashimi, tempura, miso soup & ice cream $45.00 Chef Yamada's "Kaiseki Special"-check with your server!

Impressions:

Momoyama is owned by Kyoya, which is a signal to veteran Honolulu foodies that it has got to be good. This venerable establishment offers a wonderful list of set dinners complemented by fine appetizers and sushi. Diners new to the world of Japanese cuisine need not be concerned. The menu translates very well both in language and selection. A professional wait staff is on hand to assure that your experience will be memorable. Watch for promotional discounts as they are often available and can place Momoyama within many budgets.

Honolulu

Morton's of Chicago
Ala Moana Shopping Center
1450 Ala Moana Blvd.
Honolulu, HI 96814
808-949-1300
www.mortons.com
Hours: D 5:00 PM-11:00 PM Mo-Sa
         D 5:00 PM-10:00 PM Su
Cards: AE DC JCB MC V
Dress: Evening Aloha
Style: Stk $$$$

Menu Sampler:

Breakfast/Lunch:
N/A
Dinner:
Appetizers: Smoked Pacific Salmon $12.50, Jumbo Lump Crabmeat Cocktail with mustard mayonnaise $13.95, Broiled Sea Scallops wrapped in Bacon with apricot chutney $13.95, Sautéed Wild Mushrooms $8.95, Lobster Bisque $10.95
Salads: Morton's Spinach Salad $7.95, Sliced Beefsteak Tomato $8.95
Entrées: Double Filet Mignon, Sauce Béarnaise $37.95, Porterhouse Steak $37.95, New York Strip Sirloin $37.95, Rib Eye Steak Cajun or Broiled $31.95, Sicilian Style or Broiled Veal Chop $30.95, Domestic Double Rib Lamb Chops $33.95, Colossal Shrimp Alexander with Sauce Beurre Blanc $31.95, Chicken Christopher, Garlic Beurre Blanc Sauce $21.95, Broiled Salmon $25.95
Vegetables: Sautéed Fresh Spinach & Mushrooms, Creamed Spinach, Sautéed Wild Mushrooms, Sautéed Onions, Baked Idaho Potato, Lyonnaise Potatoes, Mashed Potatoes, Steamed Fresh Broccoli with Sauce Hollandaise $6.75-$8.95
Desserts: A wonderful selection including the house specialty of a Chocolate, Raspberry, Grand Marnier or Lemon Soufflé $12.95, Espresso or Cappucino

Impressions:

Morton's of Chicago is known for its top quality prime USDA beef, but the menu doesn't stop there. Excellent veal, lamb, chicken, and seafood dishes are available as well. But this is a steak house, and the steak had better be done right. Morton's answer to that is broiling the carefully aged meat at 1200 degrees to sear it and seal in its juices. Drive up to the second level of the Ala Moana Shopping Center on the ocean side and you will find the entrance located between Neiman Marcus and Sears. There is a valet, but parking is no problem.

Kapahulu

Mr. Ojisan
Kilohana Square
1018 Kapahulu Ave
Honolulu, HI 96816
808-735-4455
Hours: L 11:00 AM-2:00 PM Mo-Fr
          D 5:30 PM-11:00 PM Mo-Th
          D 5:30 PM-1:00 AM FrSa
Cards: MC V
Dress: Casual
Style: Japan $$

Menu Sampler:

Breakfast:
N/A
Lunch:
Appetizer: Assorted Sashimi $16.95, Tako Wasabi $3.95, Tako Sashimi $8.25, Yamakake (wild yam) $6.95, Kimpira Gobo-fried seasoned burdock $4.50, Clam with butter $6.75, Broiled Salmon $6.95, Fried Tofu $5.95, Gyoza $3.25
A la Carte: Wafu Steak $12.95, Shrimp Tempura $10.95, Vegetable Tempura $7.95, Chicken Katsu $6.95, Pork Ginger $7.25, Soft Shell Crab $6.25
Side Dishes: Oshinko Mori $3.95, Musubi-Plain $1.95, Miso Soup $1.75
Special Combination Dinners include miso soup, oshinko, kobachi, rice & dessert $15.95, choice of two items-Assorted Sashimi, Shrimp & Vegetable Tempura, Tonkatsu, Chicken Katsu, Chicken Teriyaki, Beef Teriyaki, Broiled Saba, Broiled Salmon, Broiled Sanma, Deep Fried Soft Shell Crab.
Sukiyaki $18.95, $34.00 for two, includes kobachi, rice, oshinko, dessert
Yose-Nabe $18.95, $34.00 for two-one pot cooking with seafood, chicken, vegetables & kobachi, rice oshinko, dessert, Teishoku dinners $8.95-$16.95
Dinner:
All the above selections plus Udon $7.25-10.95, & Wafu Steak Teishoku $14.95

Impressions:

If you'd like to experience the Honolulu version of a Japanese neighborhood tavern, take a ride out Kapahulu to Mr. Ojisan. True to its roots, this place has the comfort of a well-worn pair of shoes. Inside, the small tables are continually being rearranged to suit the needs of the upbeat crowd. The menu does a great job covering the Japanese culinary waterfront. The only thing missing is a sushi bar. Although taking a cab always makes sense when visiting the Kapahulu restaurants, there is a parking lot in the courtyard behind the building.

Oahu Dining

Honolulu

Murphy's Bar & Grill

2 Merchant St
Honolulu, HI 96817
808-531-0422
Web: None
Hours: L 11:30 AM-2:30 PM Mo-Fr
         D 5:00 PM-10:00 PM Mo-Sa
Cards: AE DC DIS MC V
Dress: Casual
Style: Irish $$

Menu Sampler:

Breakfast:
N/A
Lunch/Dinner:
Appetizers: Salmon Pâté with minced onion, capers, sour cream, toasted rounds crackers $7.00
Specials: Pizza on Friday nights.
Entrées: Fish & Chips-fresh cod and French fries served with malt vinegar $8.25, Crab & Shrimp grilled on sourdough $9.50, Gaelic Steak-NY Steak with green peppercorn sauce, mashed potatoes and vegetable $11.50, Burgers, Pot Roast or Corned Beef & Cabbage $10.50, Ask about the daily specials.
Beverages: A rack of single malt scotches and draught beers.

Impressions:

Between Chinatown and the financial district you'll find a wonderfully authentic Irish pub. This is the kind of place you go when you feel the need to drink beer, talk loud, throw darts, or play a round of shuffleboard. The menu offers classic pub food with meat and potato dishes heading the list. For the purist, fish and chips are available as well. There's seating in an attractive dining area at the front of the building or in the bar toward the back. If you've had enough sun, sand, and surf to hold you, this is a pleasant place to while away some time.

Oahu Dining

Waikiki

Musashi

Hyatt Regency Waikiki & Spa
2424 Kalakaua Ave
Honolulu, HI 96815
808-923-1234
www.hyatt.com
Hours: B 5:30 AM-10:30 AM
            D 6:00 PM-10:00 PM
Cards: AE DC DIS JCB MC V
Dress: Evening Aloha
Style: Japan $$$$

Menu Sampler:

Breakfast:
Meals: Yakizakana-scrambled eggs, chilled tofu, broiled salmon, miso soup, rice, pickled vegetables $16.00, Zosui-rice soup served with Japanese pickled plum, pickled vegetables and Hawaiian fruit with kani (crab) $12.95, tamago (egg) $11.95, yasai (vegetables) $10.95
Lunch:
N/A
Dinner:
Appetizers: Hamachi Yellow Tail flown in daily from Japan served in a traditional manner $9.25, Assorted Sashimi of fish & seafood $12.50, Cold Tofu w/grated ginger, bonito flakes & spring onions $6.50, Maguro Sashimi $9.00
Soups & Salads: Miso Soup with spring onions, mushrooms, and seaweed $3.00, Egg Custard with chicken, shrimp, and Japanese vegetables $6.25
Sushi Bar: Super Deluxe Assortment of Nigiri & Tekka Maki $32.00
Dinners: Assorted Fish Tempura $27.00, Shabu Shabu w/Prime Sirloin-cooked tableside $29.00, Sukiyaki $29.00, Kaiseki Style Dinner-Steak & Lobster $75.00
Teppanyaki Dinners served from 6-9PM with seating on the hour. Musashi special of Filet Mignon, Lobster and Scallop $47.00, Steak & Prawns $37.00

Impressions:

On the third floor of the Hyatt Regency you'll find a Japanese restaurant where 99% of the patrons come from Japan. That could be intimidating or exciting depending on one's point of view. We prefer the later and see Musashi as an adventure not to be missed. The room isn't particularly large, but the menu covers the traditional Japanese dining styles with grace and style. Let the hostess know what you are interested in so she can seat you properly.

Oahu Dining

Waikiki

Neptune's Garden
Pacific Beach Hotel
2490 Kalakaua Ave
Honolulu, HI 96815
808-921-6112
www.pacificbeachhotel.com
Hours: D 5:30 PM-9:30 PM Tu-Sa
Cards: AE DC DIS JCB MC V
Dress: Evening Aloha
Style: Cont/Sea/Stk $$$$
        Ent Card

Menu Sampler:

Breakfast/Lunch:
N/A

Dinner:
Starters: Phyllo Prawns wrapped in ribbon pastry crust & crisp fried with a starfruit & Ewa watermelon "Lacquer" $10.95, Steamed California Artichoke with lemon-garlic butter sauce, topped with fre4sh Parmigiano Reggiano cheese $9.00, Togarashi Pepper Seared Scallops, grilled polenta cake, greens $9.75
Soups & Salads: Fresh Lehua Taro Vichyssoise with lomi tomato puree $7.75, Kona Lobster Bisque with mushroom fricassee $6.75, Hirabara Farms Baby Romaine Caesar with parmesan crisp $7.75, Tropical Seafood Cobb with shrimp, scallops, & lobster claw, avocado, mango, hearts of palm, tomato, crisp plantain chips, served with Mai Tai Louie Dressing $12.00, Baby Greens $6.50
Entrées: Pan Fried Big Island Moi with rice cracker riso and light shiso butter nage $31.50, Seafood Bouillabaisse with aioli and garlic crostini $29.50, Thai Salmon Shioyaki with green curry, kaffir lime, & lemongrass $25.00, Steamed or Grilled One and One Half Pound Live Lobster with steamed rice & Ponzu Wasabi Butter Sauce $33.50, 12 Oz, Prime Filet Mignon $36.50, Chinese Style Roast Duck with Pohaberry and Mango Sauce $25.50, Fish Trilogy $38.00
Degustation Menus: $65.00, $75.00, and $85.00 per person

Impressions:

There is no such thing as a bad table at Neptune's. The entire dining room is built around the hotel's beautiful three-story 280,000-gallon aquarium. As one might expect, in this fine restaurant seafood holds center stage. However, just so all tastes are covered, Neptune's also offers a variety of superlative meat and poultry dishes. It would be hard to find a more tranquil dining setting anywhere.

Waikiki

Nick's Fishmarket Waikiki
2070 Kalakaua Ave
Honolulu, HI 96815
808-955-6333
www.nicksfishmarketwaikiki.com
Hours: D 5:30 PM-10:00 PM
Cards: AE DC DIS JCB MC V
Dress: Evening Aloha
Style: Sea $$$$
         Ent Card

Menu Sampler:

Breakfast/Lunch:
N/A
Dinner:
Appetizers: Coconut Shrimp served with a mango cocktail sauce $11.45, Oysters Rockefeller $11.25, Calamari Fritti $10.45, Scampi in garlic butter $11.25, Crab Seafood Cake served with an Oriental cole slaw & a spicy red bell pepper sauce $11.45, Blackened Sashimi sliced rare served with a shoyu mustard sauce $13.95, New Zealand Pacific Oysters, fresh, on ice $11.45
Entrées: Fresh Shellfish Bouillabaisse with spiny lobster tail, king crab legs, shrimp, mussels, clams and fresh Hawaiian fish in a saffron broth $39.45, Norwegian Salmon marinated in honey and sake wine, grilled and served with white rice, tomato confit and chili butter $30.95, Hawaiian Mahi Mahi grilled and glazed with a sweet chili, cilantro, sesame marinade and served with a tropical salsa and roasted yellow pepper sauce $30.95, Mixed Seafood Grill of shrimp, scallops, salmon, Caribbean lobster tail and island fish served with oven roasted tomato and basil mashed potatoes and pesto butter $38.95, Lobster Thermidor $48.95, Filet Mignon (8oz) rolled in cracked black pepper and served with au gratin potatoes and a cognac cream demi glace sauce $31.45
Watch for the **Chef's Specials** of complete dinners for $29.95(4 course) or $35.00 (5-course) Early Dining Specials $19.99, 2-For-1 Coupons, Keiki Menu

Impressions:

This fine dining restaurant has been a Waikiki landmark for over 30 years. Success speaks for itself as diners return to enjoy the excellent menu and fine service. As the name would suggest, the specialty of the house is seafood. The approach is Pacific Rim with island flair. Besides their dinner selections, they also offer a late night menu as well as half-price pupu and drink specials in the lounge. Live entertainment is a regular feature. Reservations are recommended.

Oahu Dining

Waikiki

Oceanarium Restaurant

Pacific Beach Hotel
2490 Kalakaua Ave
Honolulu, HI 96815
808-921-6111
www.pacificbeachhotel.com
Hours: Su Bru Buf 10:00 AM-2:30 PM
           B 6:00 AM-11:00 AM, XSu 6:00 AM-8:30 AM
           L 11:00 AM-2:00 PM XSu
           D 5:00 PM-9:30 PM
Cards: AE DC DIS JCB MC V
Dress: Casual
Style: Amer/Isl $$

Menu Sampler:

Breakfast:
Sunday Brunch: prime rib & fresh seafood bar including oysters & sashimi, salad & appetizer bar, entrees and desserts bar- adults $20.95/children $10.50
Weekday Breakfast Buffet: Wide selection plus Fried Rice $12.95
Continental Breakfast: $7.50 a la carte/$9.50 buffet or A la Carte Menu
Lunch:
Thin Sliced Roast Prime Rib of Beef and melted cheddar cheese on sourdough with au jus and fries, garlic fries or onion rings $7.95, Saimin Noodles and Oxtail in broth with ginger and cilantro $7.95, Caesar Salad $6.75
Dinner:
Prime Rib & Seafood Nightly Dinner Buffet 5-9:30 PM: Fresh Oysters and Mussels on the half shell, shrimp, sashimi, poke, salads, kim chee, tsukemono, cheese, fruit, crackers, clam chowder, carved prime rib, steamed snow crab legs, fresh fish of the day, chef's specials, mahimahi with chef's sauce, chef's chicken, roasted pork loin, vegetables, salads, rice, potatoes, seafood pasta station, pastry dessert selections $29.95 for adults, $15.25, children 5-10 years

Impressions:

One wall of this popular family restaurant is a huge three-story aquarium. That might be enough to capture an audience but the Oceanarium works to keep them by providing a solid menu of quality selections at reasonable prices. Buffet style breakfasts are served daily. However, Sundays are special, so the Sunday brunch takes things up a notch. For added affordability early bird specials and a 10-and-under children's menu are available. This is a good stop on the way to the zoo.

Diamond Head

Olive Tree Café
Kahala Mall
4614 Kilauea Ave
Honolulu, HI 96816
808-737-0303
Web: None
Hours: D 5:00 PM-10:00 PM Mo-Su
Cards: None
Dress: Casual
Style: Greek $$

Menu Sampler:

Breakfast:
N/A

Lunch/Dinner:
Soup: Avgo Lemeno-Chicken broth with egg and lemon flavors $2.88, Fresh Pumpkin and Mung Bean $2.88, Lamb Lentil & Vegetable $3.84
Appetizers: Hommus-ground garbanzo, tahini, garlic spread $3.84, Mussel Ceviche-mussels with lemon/lime, capers, olive oil, herbs $4.80, Bean Salad-large bean (Egantes), mixed with fresh herbs, diced tomatoes & pita bread $4.80, Dolmatakia-stuffed grape leaves with rice, herbs, olive oil with tzatziki $4.80, Baba Ghanoosh-pureed broiled eggplant, takini, garlic with pita $4.80
Salads: Greek Salad with Kalamata olives and feta cheese $5.76, Tabule Salad of cracked bulgar wheat, diced tomatoes, cucumbers, onions with lemon-mint dressing on mixed greens $4.80, Feta Cheese & Kalamata Olives $4.80
Entrées: Souvlaki-kebabs served in pita bread with tzatziki (mint, cucumber, yogurt sauce-Fresh Fish $8.64, Chicken $6.72, Lamb $8.64, Falafel of ground vegetables and garbanzo beans, deep fried in pita bread w/tahini $5.76. Spanokopita-spinach with sheep cheese wrapped in filo dough $8.64, Imam Biyildi-half baked eggplant stuffed with tomatoes, herbs and feta cheese $9.60
Dessert: Baklava $1.92, Galatoboriko-Lemon Custard layered with Filo $1.92 Fresh Pumpkin Baklava $1.92. Check the board on the wall for daily specials.

Impressions:

Located at the Kahala Mall this indoor/outdoor café might be a bit small in size, but it's long on good food and friendly atmosphere. The authentic Greek cuisine is fresh and flavorful, and the self-service is fast and efficient. This is a popular dining spot with local residents so go early or late to get a table. You can BYOB without a corkage fee. If the lot is full, park your car down the side street.

Honolulu

OnJin's Café
401 Kamake'e St
Honolulu, HI 96814
808-589-1666
Web: None
Hours: L 11:00 AM-10:00 PM Mo-Sa
          D 5:00 PM-10:00 PM Mo-Sa
Cards: AE DIS MC V
Dress: Resort Casual
Style: Eurasian $$$

Menu Sampler:

Breakfast:
N/A
Lunch:
Starters: Ahi Karaage in a sweet sour chili sauce $7.50, French Onion Soup with melted Swiss cheese and crouton $4.50, Crab Cakes with two tomato sauce and momiji aioli $9.00, Korean Style Potato and Shrimp Pancake made with mochi-ko and kochijon $7.50, Crispy Chicken Wings with spicy aioli $6.75
Entrees: Open Face Crab and Cheese Melt on onion bun $7.50, Boolgogi and Kimchi Sandwich-grilled Korean style beef and kimchi on a bun $6.25, Crispy Snapper drizzled with lemon caper beurre blanc $6.95, Baby Back Ribs-4 piece $9.50, 7 piece $18.00, Curried Chicken Salad lightly spiced with raisins and apples $6.75, Shrimp and Couscous Salad-semolina tossed in a light dressing of herbs $7.95, Grilled New York Steak w/garlic mashed 6 oz-$9.50, 10 oz $16.00
Dinner:
Appetizers: All of the above plus Escargot En Croute-French snails in a puff pastry $6.75, Charred Ahi-spicy ahi with soy lilikoi beurre blanc $6.75
Entrées: All of the above plus Bouillabaise de Chef Onjin flavored w/saffron, lemon grass, & plum tomatoes $20.95, Rack of Lamb-Dijon & rosemary $21.00
Desserts: Cheesecake with Fruit Sauce $3.75, Caramel Custard $3.25

Impressions:

Chef OnJin has been part of the Honolulu fine dining scene for quite some time now. Her spins on Eurasian cuisine lead to plate lunch combinations you won't find on a kau kau wagon! Recently she extended her hours and realigned her menu so patrons can partake of her creations throughout the day. A few special items are added during dinner hours to enhance an already enticing menu. We view OnJin's as an exceptional value in a market where exceptions are the rule.

Kapahulu

Ono Hawaiian Foods
726 Kapahulu Ave.
Honolulu, HI 96815
808-737-2275
Web: None
Hours: L/D 11:00 AM-7:45 PM XSu
Cards: None
Dress: Casual
Style: Haw $

Menu Sampler:

Breakfast:
N/A

Lunch/Dinner:
Ono Hawaiian Foods Special Plates: All plates include Pipikaula, Lomi Salmon, Haupia, Rice or Poi. Kalua Pig Plate $8.70, Laulau Plate $8.70, Chicken Long Rice Plate $8.70, Combination Plate w/Kalua Pig & Laulau $11.50. No substitutions except for rice or poi. Take out boxes available.
Ala Carte: Kalua Pig $5.05, Laulau or Chicken Laulau $4.55, Squid, Chicken, or Butterfish Luau $4.55, Pipikaula $5.20, Hua Kai (Egg Soup) $3.10, Chicken Long Rice Soup $4.55, Salt Meat Luau or Salt Meat Watercress $8.50, Sardine Watercress $4.55, Chicken Watercress Soup $4.55, Chop Steak (Monday only) $6.50, Plain Butterfish (boiled) $4.55, Beef Stew (except Tuesday) or Beef Curry $4.30, Tripe Stew $5.20, Lomi Salmon $3.05/$4.55, Poke Squid (Tako) $7.00, Portuguese Sausage $2.60, Spam $2.60, Poi $2.15/$2.40, Rice $1.65, Sweet Potato (2 pcs) $1.65, Haupia (3 pcs) $0.75, Kim Chee $1.45, Opihi $4.70, Fried Fish, Lomi Fish & Onion, or Poke Fish $Prices Vary
Sodas $1.10

Impressions:

Would you like to try authentic Hawaiian food without attending an expensive luau? Then take a ride out Kapahulu to Ono Hawaiian Foods. This diminutive eatery is popular with locals and visitors alike. Out in front you'll see a sign that states, "No Get Mad—Make Line To Right". That pretty well tells you that you'll have to wait for a seat during busy times. However, it becomes obvious that the extra time invested is well spent after the waitress covers your table with bowls and plates. Parking in this area is dicey so we'd recommend taking a cab. Then, after "eating until you're tired", you'll appreciate the walk home!

Oahu Dining

Waikiki

Orchids

Halekulani Hotel
2199 Kalia Road
Honolulu, HI 96815
808-923-2311
www.halekulani.com
Hours: SuBruBuf 9:30 AM-2:30 PM
         B 7:30-11:00 AM XSu
         L 11:30 AM-2:00 PM XSu
         D 6:00 PM-10:00 PM
Cards: AE DC DIS JCB MC V
Dress: Evening Aloha
Style: Cont $$$$

Menu Sampler:

Breakfast:
Sunday Brunch Buffet: Bountiful variety of hot & cold sushi, poke, sashimi vegetable and meat salads, fruit, smoked fish, traditional breakfast items, roast meats, pastas, popovers, crepes, soup and desserts $39.50/adults, $24/children
Regular Menu: Eggs Benedict $13.00, with Scottish smoked salmon $14.50, with Alaskan king crab cake $16.00, Poi Pancakes $9.00, Haupia Bread French Toast $9.00 **American Breakfast:** $20.50   **Japanese Breakfast:** $24.50
Lunch:
Soups, Salads & Appetizers: Maryland Jumbo Lump Crab Cake with a chili yogurt and chive dressing $10.50, Portuguese Bean Soup $6.00, Caesar $9.00
Entrées: Seared Ahi Nicoise Salad $20.00, Madras Seafood Curry over jasmine rice with pineapple chutney $18.00, Ahi over macadamia nut fried rice $19.00
Dinner:
Appetizers: Crispy Soft Shell Crab with wasabi cream $8.50, Sautéed Jumbo Sea Scallops topped with Osetra caviar and butter-chive sauce $16.00, Ahi seared with Cajun spices, sesame seeds and lilikoi aioli $14.00
Entrées: Steamed Onaga Oriental Style with shiitake mushrooms $33.00, Filet Mignon or NY Steak with a portobello mushroom sauce $29.50
Desserts: Hazelnut Dacquoise with a chocolate cream and mocha sauce $8.00

Impressions:

Orchids combines a beautiful setting, wonderful service, and an exceptional menu to create one of the finest dining experiences in Hawaii. This is a must.

Oahu Dining

Waikiki

Padovani's Restaurant & Wine Bar

DoubleTree Alana Waikiki Hotel
1956 Ala Moana Blvd
Honolulu, HI 96815
808-946-3456
www.padovanirestaurants.com
Hours: B 6:30 AM-10:00 AM
        L 11:30 AM-2:00 PM
        D 6:00 PM-9:30 PM
Cards: AE DC DIS JCB MC V
Dress: Evening Aloha
Style: Fre/Med $$$$

Menu Sampler:

Breakfast:

Upside Down Pancakes (Pineapple, Coconut, Banana, Macadamia Nut) $7.95, Continental Breakfast $12, Full American $17.95, Mini-American $7.95

Lunch:

Appetizers: Mesclun Salad with Jerez vinaigrette $10, Onion Soup Gratinee $9, Sweet Corn Clam Chowder $10, Risotto of Shrimp & Asparagus $14

Entrées: Hawaiian Salad & Sautéed Shrimp w/avocado, papaya, mango & mac nuts w/ sweet & sour vinaigrette $16, Pappardelle Pasta, Seasonal Mushrooms, Herb Sauce $13/$19, Crispy Confit of Duck Leg w/ragout of vegetables vinaigrette $22, Fresh Baked Pizza of the Day $12, Fresh Catch $Mkt

Dinner:

Appetizers: Vichyssoise of kiawe smoked salmon & crab $16, Sautéed Portabella & Polenta, marmalade of onions, truffle oil vinaigrette $15, Parfait of Avocado & Dungeness Crab in fresh artichoke hearts $15

Main Course: Roasted Muscovy Duck Breast, sautéed endive, ginger jus & grapes $32, Roasted Quail stuffed with mushrooms & marmalade of onions, garlic jus $30, Grilled John Dory, fresh asparagus, tomatoes, capers & Nicoise olive vinaigrette $32, Pan-Fried Scallops with creamy cilantro curry sauce $33

Desserts: Strawberry Sunburst $14, Hawaiian Vintage Chocolate Mousse $14

Impressions:

Padovani's has a dual identity. The downstairs dining room offers an amazing collection of Continental dishes. Then, upstairs in the Wine Bar you'll find a lighter, less expensive menu accompanied by over 570 different wines. This very Continental restaurant provides some of the finest dining of its type in the islands. Proper attire is de rigueur.

Oahu Dining

Honolulu

Pagoda Hotel's Floating Restaurant
1525 Rycroft St
Honolulu, HI 96814
808-941-6611
www.pagodahotel.com
Hours: Su Bru 10:00 AM-2:00 PM
           L 11:00 AM-2:00 PM XSu
           D 4:30 PM-9:30 PM
Cards: AE DC DIS JCB MC V
Dress: Resort Casual
Style: Amer/Japan $$
        Ent Card

Menu Sampler:

Breakfast:
Sunday Brunch Buffet: Prime Rib Carving Station, seafood, chicken and fish specialties, poached eggs Florentine, scrambled eggs, bacon, sausage, omelet station (10 fillings), sushi, shrimp and vegetable tempura, crepes, local dishes, French Toast and Belgium waffles, desserts- $17.95/adults, $8.95/children(5-10)

Lunch:
Kama'aina Lunch Buffet: Shrimp and Vegetable Tempura, sushi, poke, four entrees, wok fried noodles, potatoes, salad bar, desserts including soft serve ice cream-adults $11.95/children $5.95. On Saturday, this lunch buffet adds Carved Roast Sirloin of Beef and more special entrées- $14.95/adults, $6.95/children

Dinner:
International Buffet-Monday-Friday-adults $21.95/children $9.95 featuring Roast Prime Rib Au Jus, Snow Crab Legs, Shrimp and Vegetable Tempura
International Buffet-Saturday–Sunday- adults $22.95/children $10.95 featuring Roast Prime Rib of Beef Au Jus, Shrimp & Vegetable Tempura, Island Sashimi, Special Fish prepared local style, & three of the chef's special entrées.

Impressions:

We don't usually endorse buffets, but this is one we can get behind. Pagoda's offerings have a higher level of sophistication than you'll find in most places of this type. Better yet, diners are offered a variety of themes on different days, so you can choose your specialty. The setting is interesting, as this restaurant seems to float on an ornamental fishpond in a charming Japanese garden. Leave the tourist haunts behind and go rub elbows with the locals at the Pagoda!

Windward

Pah Ke's Chinese Restaurant
46-018 Kamehameha Hwy
Kaneohe, HI 96744
808-235-4505
Web: None
Hours: LD 10:30 AM-9:00 PM
Cards: AE MC V
Dress: Casual
Style: Chi $

Menu Sampler:

Breakfast:
N/A
Lunch/Dinner:
Appetizer: Crispy Won Ton $3.50, Crispy Gau Gee $4.50, Deep Fried Scallops with Taro $7.50, Pah Ke's Chicken Salad $5.95, Squid with Salt & Pepper $6.25
Roast Meat: Whole Peking Duck with 18 buns $26.00, Half Roast Duck $9.00, Shoyu Chicken $5.75, Char Siu $5.25, Roast meat Combination $10.25
Soup: Watercress with Pork or Beef Soup $5.75, Bird Nest with Shredded Chicken Soup $10.00, Hot & Sour Soup $5.50, Egg Flower Soup $5.00
Entrees: Sautéed Beef with Ginger & Green Onions $5.75, Pork with Bitter Melon $6.25, Mongolian Beef $5.95, Steamed Porkhash with salted fish $6.75, Sautéed Pork with Shrimp Sauce $5.50, Chicken with Cashew Nuts $6.95, Chicken with Oyster Sauce $5.95, Fresh Scallops with Chinese Peas $8.95, Fish Fillet with Sweet & Sour Sauce $7.95, Sautéed Shrimps Szechuan Style $8.50, Abalone with Black Mushrooms $22.00, Lobster Tails with Vegetables $16.00
Sizzling Platters: BBQ Sizzling Beef $8.50, Seafood Satay $8.95
Casseroles: Pot Roast Pork with Taro $6.95, Seafood Combination $9.75
Eggs: Char Siu Egg Fu Yung $4.95, Shrimp Fu Yung $6.25
Noodles: Seafood Combination Fried Noodles $7.50, Hung To Mein $6.95

Impressions:

Aficionados of road tripping and health-centered Chinese cuisine will appreciate Pah Ke's in Kaneohe. Sure, it might take a little bit of effort to get there, but we guarantee you'll enjoy the drive. Then after you arrive your meal will complete the scene. All the usual Hong Kong favorites are offered along with some spicier dishes for accent. Local products are used whenever possible and absolutely no MSG finds its way into the preparations. Although it's located in the corner of a strip mall, Pah Ke's attracts an upscale local crowd. No one should feel out of place. With Pah-Ke's reasonable pricing, neither should their wallets!

Oahu Dining

Honolulu

Palomino Restaurant

66 Queen St
Honolulu, HI 96814
808-528-2400
Web: None
Hours: L 11:15 AM-2:30 PM Mo-Fr
          D 5:00 PM-10:00 PM
Cards: AE DC DIS MC V
Dress: Evening Aloha
Style: Amer/Euro/Med $$$

Menu Sampler:

Breakfast:
N/A
Lunch:
Soups and Salads: Local Style Portuguese Bean Soup $5.25, Creamy Bleu
Cheese Salad with Toasted Hazelnuts, romaine, bacon, tomato $6.95
Sandwiches: Cheddar Burger with Pepper Bacon on toasted sesame roll $8.95
Pasta: Lobster Ravioli with herb mascarpone $16.95, Carbonara $12.95
Entrées: Spit Roasted Pork Loin with herb crust & wild mushroom sauce
$15.50, Grilled Wild Mushroom Salad w/toasted walnuts, Gorgonzola $12.95
Dinner:
Starters: Dungeness Crab Dip with artichoke hearts, sweet onions, Parmesan,
cracked pizza crisps $12.50, Smoked Salmon Bruschetta w/goat cheese $9.50
Entrées: Asiago-Almond Crusted Sea Scallops, caramelized sweet onions,
roasted red peppers and asparagus, Gloria Ferrer Cuvee beurre blanc $22.95,
Huli Huli Chicken, Lemon & Sage or Garlic & Rosemary $16.95, Kabocha
Pumpkin Ravioli w/sage pasta, Chinese kale, toasted hazelnuts, sage brown
butter $15.95, Spit Roasted Chicken Cannelloni w/roasted garlic cream $15.95

Impressions:

Palomino is the glamour queen of downtown Honolulu restaurants. This upscale
dining spot and watering hole overlooks the Honolulu Harbor and busy Nimitz
Highway. The menu has a Mediterranean base with a Continental twist.
Rotisserie-roasted meats and innovative pupus complement the great seafood
choices offered on the ever-changing menu. Great signature drinks and a solid
wine list make this happening place a popular after-work choice for the
downtown business crowd. Palomino is a very cool choice for lunch or dinner.
The parking deck in the building is a big plus. Enter off Bethel Street.

Oahu Dining

Honolulu

Pineapple Room
Macy's
Ala Moana Shopping Center
Honolulu, HI 96814
808-945-8881
www.alanwongs.com
Hours: B 9:00 AM-10:45 AM SaSu
   L 11:00 AM-3:00 PM
   D 4:00 PM-8:30 PM XSu
Cards: AE DC DIS JCB MC V
Dress: Resort Casual
Style: Haw-Reg/Pac-Rim $$$

Menu Sampler:

Breakfast:
House Made Corned Beef Hash and two eggs with Pineapple Room ketchup
$7.50, Spicy Chorizo Scrambled Eggs on vegetable & cheese quesadilla $10.50,
Big G's Taco Omelet with avocado salsa and chili sour cream $10.50, Hawaiian
Style Eggs Benedict-poached eggs on Kalua pig taro hash cake with lomi
tomatoes and luau leaf hollandaise $9.00, Loco-Moke-O w/veal jus $12.50
Lunch:
Thai Style Chicken Cobb Salad w/lemongrass basil dressing $12.50, Korean
BBQ'ed Chicken Sandwich, kim chee, bean sprouts, marinated watercress
$12.50, Sweet Chili Glazed Mahimahi, w/miso togarashi butter sauce $15.00
Dinner:
Entrées: Guava and Pecan Glazed Lamb, baby vegetables, taro mashed potato,
natural jus $32.00, Miso Glazed Salmon w/stir fried vegetables, kim chee
vinaigrette $21.00, Pineapple BBQ'ed Baby Back Ribs w/garlic mashed
potatoes, sautéed beans, sweet corn $24.50, Seared Peppered Ahi w/roasted
garlic potato, haricot vert, bacon, whole grain mustard vinaigrette $25.00, Kiawe
Grilled NY Striploin, garlic mashed potatoes, green peppercorn sauce $28.00

Impressions:

Pineapple Room is one of Alan Wong's ventures with Chef de Cuisine Steven
Ariel presiding. The menu contains a wonderfully eclectic group of fresh island
dishes prepared with classic touches. There are very few department store dining
rooms that approach this level of sophistication. Wong's genius and Ariel's
expertise combine to make any meal served here an event. Drive up to the third
floor parking level of the Ala Moana deck and you can walk in and be seated.

Oahu Dining

Waikiki

Prince Court Restaurant
Westin Hawaii Prince Hotel
100 Holomoana St
Honolulu, HI 96815/808-944-4494
www.westinhawaiiprincehotel.com
Hours: B 6:00 AM-10:30 AM
           SaSuBru 11:15 AM-1:00 PM
           L Mo-Fr 11:30 AM-2:00 PM
           D 6:00 PM-9:30 PM
Cards: AE DIS JCB MC V
Dress: Evening Aloha
Style: Amer/Japan $$$ Ent Card

Menu Sampler:

Breakfast:
Daily Buffet: 6-10:30 AM-- $21.95 with miso soup with toppings, salads, fruit, cereal, granola, eggs, meats, waffles, traditional and Japanese breakfast entrees
Sa & Su Brunch Buffet: 11:15AM-1PM-- $27.50 with special weekly entrees, saimin, sushi, sashimi, omelet station, antipasti, pasta, crab legs, prime rib
Lunch:
Weekday Buffet: $23.50-'East Meets West" tempura, sushi, shabu shabu. A la Carte-Soba Noodles w/Seared Ahi $10.50, Traditional Curries $12.50
Dinner:
Seafood Dinner Buffet: FrSaSu--$42.00 with crab, sashimi, assorted poke, grilled salmon, prime rib, roasted pig, ahi cakes, stir-fry's, and dessert specials
A la CarteOfferings: Appetizers: Portobello Mushroom and Crab Hash Napoleon with wilted spinach and roasted garlic butter, Cabernet reduction $13.50. **Entrees:** Fresh Pacific Snapper with wild mushroom and lobster ragout $29.00, Grilled Rib Eye Steak w/oven dried tomato & shiitake mushroom relish with redskin mashed potato $29.00, Lobster Tail, Shrimp & Sea Scallops w/grilled vegetables & snap peas, coconut saffron cream $30.00

Impressions:

This is a lovely room with a great view. Outside, the Ala Wai Boat Harbor forms a beautiful backdrop. Inside, you'll find high quality meats, seafood, and produce served in upscale preparations. Although an ala carte menu is always available, many choose to partake in the wonderful buffets and weekend brunches. Chef Goran Streng maintains high standards in all regards. Reservations are suggested, especially for the popular weekend brunch.

Windward

Punalu'u Restaurant & Tundaleo's Bar
53-146 Kamehameha Hwy
Punalu'u, HI 96717
808-237-8474
Web: None
Hours: LD 11:00 AM-8:00 PM
Cards: MC V
Dress: Casual
Style: Isl/Sea $$

Menu Sampler:

Breakfast:
N/A

Lunch/Dinner:
30 Shrimp prepared a variety of ways-Shrimp Scampi, Coconut Shrimp, Coconut & Basil (coconut milk & basil), Tempura, Hot & Spicy, Pineapple Shrimp (sautéed in garlic & olive oil), Li Hing Mui Shrimp (sautéed with pineapple & li hing mui) $14.95, for another $2.00 choice the meal and add vegetables, bread, and rice, fries or mashed potatoes
Seafood Entrees $12.95-Mahi or Ono with white sauce $12.95, Seafood Platter $12.95, New York Steak $12.95, Hamburger with fries $5.50, Mushroom Cheeseburger with fries $5.95

Impressions:

Punalu'u Restaurant has roots that go back to when it was known as Ahi's in Kahuku. After that venerable establishment burned, owner Logan Ahi moved his operation to this site. Other endeavors beckoned and the original owner sold the business that we now know as Punalu'u Restaurant. Today this rambling old roadhouse makes a great stop for those driving this misty windward highway. If you're looking for Old Hawaii, here is one place you can find it.

Punalu'u's specialty is locally raised shrimp served in various fashions. They're all great in their own way, but don't get caught up trying to determine which sounds best and miss a couple of very important points. First, if you order a shrimp dish by itself, all you will get is lots of shrimp on a plate of chopped cabbage. This might be great for sharing as a pupu, but if you plan on eating the entire serving yourself, be sure to ask for the meal version to round things out. Then, if making a selection proves difficult, go with a combination, which allows you to request two or even four preparations on a single plate.

Waikiki

Restaurant Suntory
Royal Hawaiian Shopping Center
2233 Kalakaua Ave
Honolulu, HI 96815
808-922-5511
www.suntory.co.jp/restaurants/index.html
Hours: L 11:30 AM-1:30 PM Mo-Fr, 12:00 PM-2:00 PM SaSu
           D 5:30 PM-9:30 PM
Cards: AE DC DIS JCB MC V
Dress: Resort Casual
Style: Japan $$$$

Menu Sampler:

Breakfast:
N/A
Lunch:
Teppan-yaki Service: All Teppan entrées include salad, miso soup, vegetables, and white rice. Shrimp & Scallops $15.50, New York Steak or Sirloin $16.00, Filet $16.00, Chicken $10.50, Garlic Rice $3.00
Washoku Teishoku: Entrées include salad. Sashimi Teishoku $16.00, Sukiyaki Teishoku $15.00, Tempura Zarusoba $12.50, Tempura Teishoku $12.50
Dinner:
Appetizers: Chawan-mushi, the chef's creation of shrimp, chicken, and vegetables steamed in creamy egg custard $4.50, Ebi tempura $12.50
Teppan-yaki Courses: $59.00-$120.00 includes appetizer, salad, One or more entrées such as lobster or filet, rice, tsukemono, miso soup, ice cream
Shabu-Shabu or Sukiyaki: $39.00 includes assorted appetizers, rice, tsukemono, Shabu-Shabu/Sukiyaki and ice cream.
Sushi Bar Service

Impressions:

Like everywhere else, modern Japanese dining habits have evolved through contact with other cultures. Restaurant Suntory goes against this trend by offering traditional Japanese dishes free from outside influences. The pursuit of authenticity continues as the chef at the teppanyaki table prepares your meal in true Japanese style rather than putting on a display of fancy knife work and pyrotechnics. Dinner can get a little pricey, but lunch is quite affordable. Parking is available in the Royal Hawaiian Shopping Center deck behind the complex. Make sure to get your parking ticket validated!

Honolulu

Royal Garden
Ala Moana Hotel
410 Atkinson Drive
Honolulu, HI 96814
808-942-7788
www.royalgardens.com
Hours: L 11:00 AM-2:00 PM
            D 5:30 PM-10:00 PM
Cards: AE DC DIS JCB MC V
Dress: Evening Aloha
Style: Chi $$$

Menu Sampler:

Breakfast:
N/A
Lunch:
Dim Sum- Extensive selections of steamed items and regular menu service.
Lunch/Dinner:
Appetizers: Deep Fried Taro Ball with crab meat filling $14.95, Char Siu-barbeque fillet pork $9.50, Deep Fried Spring Roll $8.50, Cold Jelly Fish $9.50
Soup: Crab Meat, Pork and Diced Melon Soup $8.95, Hot & Sour Soup $9.50, Chicken Cream Corn Soup $8.95, Seafood with Vegetable Soup $10.95
Entrées: Fried Stuffed Scallop with minced shrimp paste (house specialty) $14.95, Minced Pork and Chinese Sausage & spinach $9.95, Sauteed Shrimp with Szechuan Sauce $15.95, Whole Peking Duck $40.00, Almond Chicken $10.50, Beef with green onion and ginger $10.95, Shredded Pork with bell pepper & chili $9.95, Fried Milk with King Crab Meat (house specialty) $12.95
Casseroles: Abalone & Duck's Webs $29.50, Hawaiian Prawns w/long rice $17.95, Roast Pork & Tofu in Shrimp Sauce $10.95, Braised Chicken $10.95
Dessert: Lychee Sorbet $3.50, Red Bean with Milk in Ice $12.95, Red Bean Soup $2.95, Almond Float w/Fruit Cocktail $2.95, Green Tea Ice Cream $3.50

Impressions:

The Royal Garden offers excellent Chinese cuisine, but the dim sum lunch service is a special cultural treat. Just sit back and watch the parade of carts move around the tables and point to your selections. Although there is a bit of a communication barrier, sign language seems to work. Just be careful when they start passing out the chicken feet! Park on the second floor of Ala Moana.

Hawaii Kai

Roy's
6600 Kalanianole Hwy
Hawaii Kai Corporate Plaza
Honolulu, HI 96825
808-396-7697
www.roysrestaurant.com
Hours: D 5:30 PM-9:30 PM
Cards: AE DC DIS JCB MC V
Dress: Evening Aloha
Style: Haw-Reg/Pac-Rim $$$$

Menu Sampler:

Breakfast/Lunch:
N/A
Dinner:
Appetizer: Hawaii Kai Style Crispy Crab Cakes, spicy sesame beurre blanc $11.50, Wood Grilled Szechuan Spiced Baby Back Ribs $9.50, Seared Shrimp On A Stick, cucumber namasu, kim chee, spicy wasabi cocktail sauce $8.50
Imu Oven Pizzas: Hoisin Barbecued Duck Pizza with Bermuda onions, cilantro & slivered scallions $7.50, Shrimp Caesar Pizza w/macadamia nut pesto $8.50
Salads and Vegetables: Mongolian Grilled Chicken Salad with Maui butter lettuce, candied pecans & sesame soy emulsion $8.50, Crispy Calamari & Asian Glass Noodle Salad w/Thai style vinaigrette $8.50, Mixed Greens $6.50
Entrées: Hibachi Grilled Salmon, spun vegetable salad, ponzu sauce $10.50/$25.50, Roy's original Blackened Island Ahi, spicy hot soy mustard butter sauce $13.50/$27.50, Japanese Style Misoyaki Butterfish, sweet ginger wasabi butter sauce $13.50/$27.50, Char Broiled Honey Mustard Short Rib of Beef, Scalloped Potatoes, Poi, Lomi-lomi Tomatoes $26.50, Shiso & Garlic Seared Large Shrimp, Maine lobster white truffle essence $21.50, Roy's Meatloaf, crispy onion rings, natural mushroom gravy $7.50/$15.50

Impressions:

West of Koko Head in the Hawaii Kai Town Center you'll find the original home of the now global Roy's restaurant chain. Roy Yamaguchi was one of the founders of the Hawaii Regional Cuisine movement. Flavors and ingredients are combined in intriguing ways at all of his restaurants. The ever-changing innovative menu coupled with an interesting and affordable wine list makes dinner at any of them a special experience. Look for Roy's along the highway on the Honolulu side of the lagoon. There's plenty of parking in the lot.

Oahu Dining

Honolulu

Ruth's Chris
Restaurant Row
500 Ala Moana Blvd
Honolulu, HI 96813
808-599-3860
www.ruthschris.com
Hours:　D 5:00 PM-10:00 PM
Cards:　AE DC JCB MC V
Dress:　Evening Aloha
Style:　Stk $$$$

Menu Sampler:

Breakfast/Lunch
N/A

Dinner:
Appetizers: Barbecued Shrimp with white wine, butter, garlic and spices $10.50, Onion Soup Au Gratin $6.50, Mushrooms Stuffed With Crabmeat $10.50, French Fried Maui Onion Rings $4.75, Seared Ahi Tuna $ Market Price

Salads: Caesar $6.95, Fresh Asparagus & Hearts of Palm $6.95, Sliced Tomato & Maui Onion, crumbled blue cheese & vinaigrette $6.95, Spinach Salad $5.95

Entrées: Filet $29.95, Petite Filet $26.95, Rib Eye $30.95, New York Strip $32.95, T Bone $36.95, Veal Chop with hot and sweet peppers $29.95, Broiled Marinated Chicken $19.95, Center Cut Pork Chops $23.95, Lamb Chops (3) with mint jelly $30.95, Steak & Lobster $Market Price, Fresh Catch of the Day- ask your server about selections, $Market Price, Lobster Tails $Market Price

Side Orders: Au Gratin Potatoes $5.95, Shoestring Potatoes $5.95, Lyonnaise $5.95, Cottage Fries $5.95, Baked-1#-$5.95, Sautéed Mushrooms $6.50, Creamed Fresh Spinach $5.95, Fresh Spinach or Broccoli Au Gratin $6.50, Fresh Asparagus with Hollandaise $7.50, Broiled Tomatoes $5.95

Desserts: Bread Pudding w/ Whiskey Sauce $5.95, Crème Brulee $6.95

Impressions:

Ruth's Chris operates a chain of upscale steak houses offering high quality food and service. The Honolulu location can be found in Restaurant Row overlooking Ala Moana Boulevard. Their ala carte menu specializes in custom-aged beef broiled at 1800 degrees and served sizzling at your table. When the waiter informs you that they only use salt and pepper, we suggest ordering your steak well seasoned. The rich side dishes are ample enough to share. Great wine list! Park in the deck at the rear of the building and get your ticket validated.

Oahu Dining

Honolulu

Ryan's Grill
Ward Centre
1200 Ala Moana Blvd.
Honolulu, HI 96813
808-591-9023
Web: None
Hours: Bru 10:00 AM-3:00 PM Su
        L 11:15 AM-5:00 PM Mo-Sa
        D 5:00 PM-1:00 AM Mo-Sa 3:00 PM-1:00 AM Su
Cards: AE DC MC V
Dress: Resort Casual
Style: Amer/Ec $$

Menu Sampler:

Brunch:
Punaluu Sweet Bread French Toast $14.95, Huevos Rancheros Wrap with chicken and black bean salsa $14.95, Ryan's Loco Moco with two eggs $11.95, Eggs Benedict $15.95, Smithfield Ham and Tillamook Cheddar Omelet $16.95
Lunch/Dinner:
Pupus: Jamaican Jerk Fries with a sweet-hot Thai chili and coconut aioli $5.50, Oyster Shooters each $1.95, Chicken Egg Rolls with spicy peanut dipping sauce $7.95, Hot Dungeness Crab & Artichoke Dip with focaccia bread $11.95
Soups & Salads: Classic Caesar w/garlic croutons $5.95, French Onion Soup with Emmenthaler $5.95, House Salad w/Mandarin oranges and sweet-hot vinaigrette $6.50, Chicken Salad w/sesame dressing & won ton strips $6.50
Entrées: Hot Dungeness Crab Sandwich $11.95, Bay Shrimp Fettucine w/mushrooms & marsala $12.50, Guava-Glazed Baby Back BBQ Ribs $12.95, Kiawe Grilled Salmon & Chili-Rubbed Prawns w/BBQ hollandaise $25.95, Top Sirloin w/Crispy Fried Maui Onions $18.95, Vegetable Pizza $10.95
Desserts: Key Lime Pie $4.95, Haupia Crème Brulee $5.95, Fruit Sorbet $4.95

Impressions:

At Ryan's Grill the entire menu is served all day long until 1:00 AM. This can be great news for travelers who arrive in Hawaii many time zones away from home. The menu is an interesting mix of traditional mainland fare with eclectic spins. Complete bar service and creative pupus complete the scene. This is a popular spot for happy hour. Parking is available in the Ward Centre lot.

Honolulu

Sam Choy's Breakfast, Lunch & Crab
580 Nimitz Hwy
Honolulu, HI 96817
808-545-7979
www.samchoy.com
Hours: B 6:30 AM-10:30 AM Mo-Fr
          B SuBuf 9:00 AM-12:00 PM
          L 11:30 AM-4:00 PM
          D 5:00 PM-10:00 PM
Cards: AE DC DIS JCB MC V
Dress: Casual
Style: Isl $$$

Menu Sampler:

Breakfast:
Homemade Corned Beef Hash & Eggs $6.25, Omelets $6.25-$11.95, Belgian
Waffle $4.95, Fried Rice topped w/two eggs $5.75, French Toast Platter $7.25
Sunday Buffet: $13.95/adults, $5.95/children-omelet station, mixed green salad
with Sam's Creamy Oriental Dressing, fresh fruit tray, muffins, several hot
entrees and rice, Home Fries, bacon, sausage, two special hot entrees
Lunch:
"BLC" bacon, lettuce & crab sandwich $10.50, Sam's Favorite Burger $7.50,
Kona Flaming Wok with chicken, beef, or vegetarian $8.95, Paniolo Steak with
grilled onion $10.95, Moi-Moi Saimin $11.50, Fried Poke Lunch $9.50
Dinner:
Pupus: Fried Calamari with kim chee furikake $7.95, Korean Spicy Chicken
Wings $6.95, Sam's Original Fried Poke $7.95, Wok of Manila Clams $8.95
Entrées: Wok Fried Ginger-Onion Maine Lobster on buttered garlic pasta
$27.95, Garlic Roasted Island Chicken with garlic mashed potatoes $16.95, Our
Own Ehu Ale Beer Batter Fish with fries and cole slaw $14.95, Chowder $3.95

Impressions:

Sam Choy made his mark by taking local favorites up market. What better place
to showcase this approach than in an old factory along the Nimitz Hwy. Inside, a
huge display kitchen serves three "local kine" meals a day. The concepts might
be simple, but the presentations aren't. Basics are fused together creating layers
of flavor that never would have been dreamed of on the old plantations. Due to
its location this Sam Choy restaurant has a heavily local trade. Visitors will find
it convenient on their way to and from the airport.

Kapahulu

Sam Choy's Diamond Head Restaurant
449 Kapahulu
Honolulu, HI 96815
808-732-8645
www.samchoy.com
Hours: D 5:30 PM-9:00 PM
               SuBruBuf 9:30 AM-1:30 PM
Cards: AE DC DIS JCB MC V
Dress: Resort Casual
Style: Haw-Reg $$$

Menu Sampler:

Breakfast:
Big Aloha Sunday Brunch Buffet: $21.95/adults, age 5-12 $1/year. Many vegetable, pasta and fruit salads, pokes, hot entrees, curries, prime rib, five spice roast duck, fresh island fish, omelet station, stir-fries, flambé station, desserts

Lunch:
N/A

Dinner:
Pupus: Brie Cheese Wontons with homemade pineapple papaya marmalade $7.50, Seared Ahi Sashimi $10.95, "Potholes", rock lobster tail with tarragon jus, shrimp with garlic butter, and jumbo escargot with escargot butter-all in puff pastry $8.95, Fried Poke-traditional poke seared on a hot grill $8.95

Entrées: Seafood Laulau with mahi, shrimp, scallops and vegetables wrapped in ti leaves and steamed $25.95, Macadamia Nut Crusted Chicken Breast with a shiitake mushroom cream sauce and papaya pineapple marmalade $19.95, Hawaiian Style Seafood Bouillabaisse of half Maine lobster, Alaskan king crab leg, scallops, shrimp, & fresh fish simmered in an aromatic tomato broth $31.95

Desserts: Lemongrass Crème Brulee $6.50, Pineapple Cheesecake $6.75

Impressions:

Sam Choy always manages to include local comfort food in his creative menu. What would dinner at Sam's be without some kind of laulau on the table? To get a better picture of his creative style you can check out his web site, catch one of his guest appearances with Emeril, or watch "Sam Choy's Kitchen" on the local stations. Expect to experience that around-the-kitchen-table feel. Sam's personal warmth, generosity, and love of creative food are always extended to the public. Hawaiians call that Aloha! Parking is provided under the building.

Honolulu

Sansei Seafood Restaurant & Sushi Bar
Restaurant Row
500 Ala Moana Blvd
Honolulu, HI 96814
808-536-6286
www.sanseihawaii.com
Hours: L 11:00 AM-2:00 PM Mo-Fr
          D 5:00 PM-10:30 PM
Cards: AE DIS JCB MC V
Dress: Evening Aloha
Style: Pac-Rim/Sea $$$

Menu Sampler:

Breakfast:
N/A
Lunch:
Quality Plate Lunches in mini ($3.95) or regular ($6.95) including rice and special mac salad, Soups, Big Salads, Gourmet Wraps with Jalapeño Tortilla Wraps, Sandwiches, Domburis, Bentos, Sushi, and numerous sides
Dinner:
Pupus: Sansei's Rock Shrimp Dynamite with creamy masago aioli $8.95, Grilled Misoyaki Chicken over Oriental Cabbage $5.95, Teriyaki Beef $7.95
Appetizers and Salads: Broiled Miso Garlic Prawns (4) over Kula greens with spicy Japanese umeboshi vinaigrette $8.95, Asian Rock Shrimp Cake crusted with crispy Chinese noodles with ginger-lime chili butter & cilantro pesto $6.95, Fresh Hawaiian Ahi Carpaccio w/fresh cilantro & Thai vinaigrette $9.95
Entrées: Roasted Peking Duck Breast over wild mushroom & potato risotto with a rich foie gras demi glaze $24.95, Sansei's Seafood Pasta of black tiger prawns & sweet ocean scallops with Japanese papardelle noodles and fresh veggies tossed in spicy black bean chili butter $19.95, Pepper Crusted Pork Tenderloins over roasted garlic mashed potatoes in an Asian Fig Chutney $18.95
Desserts: Banana Cake and Crispy Banana Lumpia w/caramel sauce $6.95

Impressions:

A few years ago chef/owner D. K. Kodama opened a new Sansei location on Restaurant Row. Building on the success of his original Maui location, D.K. set about creating a place where sushi ruled side by side with Pacific Rim Cuisine. The results are outstanding and well worth checking out. We consider a trip to Sansei to be one of the ultimate grazing experiences in Hawaii.

Oahu Dining

Waikiki

Sarento's Top of The "I"
Ilikai Hotel
1777 Ala Moana Boulevard
Honolulu, HI 96814
808-955-5559
www.tri-star-restaurants.com
Hours: D 5:30 PM-9:15 PM
Cards: AE DC DIS JCB MC V
Dress: Evening Aloha
Style: Ital $$$$

Menu Sampler:

Breakfast/Lunch:
N/A
Dinner:
Appetizers: Escargot Alla Sarento's with roasted garlic and fresh herb butter $10.95, Gamberoni Con Pancetta-grilled prawns with pancetta $11.95
Soup & Salad: Minestrone $5.50, Caesar Salad with capers $6.95, Salad Gabriella with grilled marinated baby artichokes, tomatoes, goat cheese $10.95
Entrées: Opakapaka Portofino-sautéed with rock shrimp, asparagus tips, mushrooms served in a lemon dill butter sauce $28.95, Salmone Con Arrosto Pomodori-pan seared salmon, roasted tomatoes & pesto risotto with a warm balsamic dressing $23.95, Veal Saltimboca with prosciutto, Bel Paese Cheese, shiitake mushrooms $26.95, Filet Marc Anthony brushed with Italian country mustard, buffalo mozzarella & crispy Maui onions, served in a porcini mushroom sauce $27.95, Lamb Chops Mediterranean marinated & grilled-served with feta cheese, Kalamata olives, Maui onions and Roma tomatoes $29.95, Rigatoni Alla Vodka with pancetta, Bermuda onions, spicy vodka cream & tomato sauce $18.95, Penne Calabrese with fresh basil, diced eggplant, tomatoes, Italian sausage & goat cheese $20.95

Impressions:

Food enthusiasts are naturally skeptical of dining rooms located on top of tall buildings. Why? History has shown us that the view often comes first, leaving the food and service to bring up the rear. We're happy to report that this is not the case at Sarento's. The first thing one notices after getting past the power of the room and location is the polite, attentive service. Then comes dinner. You'll find an impressive menu to choose from, leaving the only problem being what to order. This also applies to the wine list where the selections seem endless. Plan to arrive before sunset and get the best of the daytime and evening vistas.

Waikiki

Seafood Village

Hyatt Regency Waikiki
2424 Kalakaua Avenue
Honolulu, HI 96815
808-971-1818
www.seafoodvillage.com
Hours: L 11:00 AM-2:00 PM
         D 5:30 PM-10:00 PM
Cards: AE CB DC JCB MC V
Dress: Resort Casual
Style: Chi $$
         Ent Card

Menu Sampler:

Breakfast:
N/A
Lunch:
Cantonese Dinner menu plus the Hong Kong style dim sum service. Char Siu Bao, Spring Rolls, Shrimp Dumplings, Manapua, Shrimp Shu Mai, Pork Hash, Half Moon, Taro Puff, Won Ton, Seafood and custard tarts at reasonable prices.
Dinner:
Appetizers: Crispy Spring Rolls (3) $4.95, Fried Stuffed Crab Claws (2) $8.95
Salads: Oriental Chicken Salad $4.50, Fresh Roast Duck Salad $4.95
Soup: Lobster & Spinach Soup $8.95, Seafood Hot & Sour Soup $3.75, Chicken & Shiitake Mushroom $4.50, Braised Top Grade Shark's Fin $88.00
Entrées: Sizzling Tenderloin Black Pepper Sauce $18.95, Honey Garlic Tangerine Beef $13.95, Twin Vegetables with Bamboo Fungus $12.50, Fresh Kahuku Shrimp Peppery Salt $17.95, Boneless Chicken Kung Pao Style $10.95
Rice & Noodles: Shrimp and Vegetable Fried Noodles $18.95, Char Siu Fried Rice $12.95, Seafood Combination Noodles $18.95, Garlic & Duck Meat Fried Rice $14.95, Lobster Meat & Vegetables Noodles $28.95, Broccoli with Tofu in wine sauce $10.95, Shanghai Cabbage with Virginia Ham $10.95

Impressions:

On the Ewa side of the Hyatt Regency entrance there's a staircase leading downstairs to a special Chinese dining experience. At lunch their Hong Kong style dim sum service is fun and affordable. The dinner menu is truly massive and features the live seafood for which the restaurant is named. This is fine Cantonese dining within walking distance of all the central Waikiki hotels.

Waikiki

Shogun

Pacific Beach Hotel
2490 Kalakaua Ave
Honolulu, HI 96815
808-921-6113
www.pacificbeachhotel.com
Hours: B 6:00 AM-10:00 AM
           L 11:00 AM-2:00 PM
           D 5:30 PM-10:00 PM
Cards: AE DC DIS JCB MC V
Dress: Evening Aloha
Style: Japan $$$

Menu Sampler:

Breakfast:
Daily Buffet: $17.50/adults, $9.25children -American and Japanese traditional menu items-fruits, scrambled eggs, meats, fish, nori, tofu, croissants, Danish
Lunch:
Weekday Lunch Buffet: $10.95/adults, $6.95/ children, featuring three hot entrees, sushi, poke, sashimi, tako poki, shrimp tempura, yaki soba, rice, oshinko, lomi lomi salmon, salad bar, dessert table and soft serve ice cream
Weekend Lunch Buffet: $15.95/adults, $9.00/children, all of the above plus snow crab legs, beef or seafood teppan, and three "chef special" hot entrees
Dinner:
Sushi Bar Dinner Special-5:30-10 PM- All you can eat Nigiri Sushi with a one and a half hour limit. Seating available only at the sushi counter $39.95
Tea House Style Dinners-5:30-10 PM-only with 48 hour advance ordering- private rooms-minimum party of ten-three entrees, adult $19.95/children$11.95, four entrees, plus Kobachi, tsukemono, rice & tea $21.95/adult, $13.95/children
Dinner Specials-all include miso soup, tsukemono, kobachi, rice and tea. $12.95-$22.95 offering dishes such as salmon misoyaki, tonkatsu, spicy garlic chicken, butterfish misoyaki, cold beef shabu shabu, sukiyaki

Impressions:

Shogun serves authentic Japanese cuisine either buffet style or as a complete dinner. Along one wall you'll find the top of a three-story aquarium, and on the other there's a sushi bar. Sounds sensible enough! After dinner karaoke becomes part of the fun. Lunch at Shogun is a culinary adventure at reasonable prices.

Oahu Dining

Honolulu

Side Street Inn
1225 Hopaka Street
Honolulu, HI 96814
808-591-0253
Web:	None
Hours:	L 10:30 AM-1:30 PM Mo-Fr
	D 4:00 PM-12:30 AM
Cards:	None
Dress:	Casual
Style:	Isl/Pac Rim $$

Menu Sampler:

Breakfast:
N/A
Lunch:
Pan Fried Island Pork Chops 9.00, Teriyaki Rib Eye 7.25, Broiled Mahi 6.50, Chicken or Tofu Vegetable Stir-Fry 6.25, Yakisoba 5.75, Saimin 4.00
Sandwiches: Cheeseburger 4.50, Teriyaki Chicken 4.25, Grilled Mahimahi Deluxe 4.75, Smoked Turkey Deluxe 4.75, Chicken Cutlet 4.25
Salads: Cold Somen Salad 5.00, Shrimp Caesar Salad 6.50, Cobb Salad 7.00
Daily Specials-all plates come with rice and choice of tossed or mac salad-Furikake Catch Mkt $, Chicken Hekka 4.50/5.50/6.00, Mochiko Chicken 4.75/5.75/6.00, Spicy Pork Eggplant 4.50/5,50/6.00, Chinese Style Steamed Catch Mkt $, Hawaiian Plate 7.25, Misoyaki Chicken 4.75/5.75/6.00
Dinner:
Asian Grilled Lamb Chops $21.00, Hoisin or Lilikoi Baby Back Ribs $13.50, Chinese Style Crispy Chicken $8.50, Kal Bi with Kim Chee $15.50, 12 oz New York Steak $18.00, Pan Fried Ahi Belly Mkt $, Deep Fried Calamari $9.75, Broiled Ika $8.75, Soy Beans $6.50, Musubi $2.25, Kim Chee $2.25

Impressions:

This unassuming establishment came by its name honestly. It truly is a rambling little inn and is definitely located on a side street. We first heard about this place from an airline crew who spend their layover eating and relaxing in its friendly confines. One visit convinced us that they had found something special.

Side Street Inn is a pupu lovers delight. Every day at 4 PM the kitchen starts turning out an amazing variety of ala carte specialties. Any one of these could be a meal in itself, so sharing makes tremendous sense. Quality and originality are hallmarks witnessed by the local chefs who appear here after their own closings.

Waikiki

Singha Thai
1910 Ala Moana Blvd.
Honolulu, HI 96815
808-941-2898
www.singhathai.com
Hours: D 4:00 PM-11:00 PM
Cards: AE CB DC DIS JCB MC V
Dress: Evening Aloha
Style: Thai $$$

Menu Sampler:

Breakfast/Lunch:
N/A
Dinner:
Appetizers: Shrimp Spring Rolls with shrimp, minced pork, vermicelli noodles, mushrooms, onions and carrots in crispy rice paper $7.95, Grilled Beef Salad with lemongrass garlic dressing-mild, medium, or hot $8.95, Crispy Duck Lumpia with spicy hoisin sauce $8.95, Curry Puffs with dressing $7.95
Soups: Tom Yum Kung (for two)-spicy lemongrass soup with shrimp, mushrooms, chili paste, cilantro and lime juice- mild, medium or hot $9.95, Ginseng Chicken Soup with Chinese herbs and Ginseng (for two) $9.95
Curries: Baked Boneless Breast of Duck with panang curry sauce $18.95
Noodles: Pad Thai with chicken breast, tamarind sauce & peanuts $12.95
Rice: Vegetarian Fried Rice with mixed vegetables and egg $10.95
Entrées: Siamese Fighting Fish-crispy whole fish served with spicy Thai chili lime sauce $29.95, Asian Style Osso Buco with pearl onions, diced pumpkin and chestnuts $25.95, Singha Steak & Prawns w/sweet potato cake $30.95. Sample Chef Chai's Award-Winning Thai Chili Ginger Sauce or Thai Light Black Bean Sauce over chicken, sea scallops, lobster tail or fresh local fish $15.95-$30.95

Impressions:

Chef Chai Chaowasaree excels at preparing traditional Thai dishes, but also creates wonderful contemporary Pacific Rim cuisine. You'll find a little of both at Singha Thai. Using fresh, locally grown organic ingredients, he serves a light, healthy cuisine that doesn't lack for flavor. Try Chai's recommended food and wine pairings served family style for a diverse sampling of exotic tastes. As an added treat the Royal Thai Dancers perform nightly from 7 to 9 PM.

Kaimuki

Sis Kitchen
1137 11th Avenue
Honolulu, HI 96816
808-732-0902
www.siskitchen.com
Hours: LD 11:00 AM-9:00 PM XTuSu
         D 4:00 PM-9:00 PM Su
Cards: MC V
Dress: Casual
Style: Korean $$

Menu Sampler:

Breakfast:
N/A
Lunch/Dinner:
Lunch Specials: Served 11:00 AM-2:00 PM Mo-Fr. The following are served with side vegetables and rice; Bulgogi (sliced rib-eye steak) 5.95, Dak Gui (BBQ Chicken) mild or spicy 5.95, Bento (Miso Butterfish) 6.95
Appetizers: Mandoo-dumplings, steamed or fried 5.95, House Salad with grilled chicken breast with our homemade dressing 7.95
Soups and Noodles: Dduk Mandoo Kook-dumplings & sliced rice cake served in mild homemade broth 7.95, Hot Kooksoo-noodles in homemade broth 7.95
Rice: Bibimbop-seasoned shredded vegetables, beef and fried egg over rice 7.95, Kim Chee Fried Rice with chopped kim chee, onion and Spam 7.95
Entrees: Served with rice and side dishes. Kim chee Jigae-hot and spicy kim chee pot stew 8.95, Soft Tofu Jigae- soft tofu stone pot stew 8.95, Grilled Miso Butterfish 12.95, Garlic Shrimp sautéed to golden brown in garlic butter sauce 12.95, Croaker grilled or deep-fried 10.95, Spicy Squid and assorted vegetables stir fried in hot chili pepper sauce 9.95, Meat Jun (fritter) 9.95, Bulgogi & Dak Gui 11.95, Kalbi-marinated beef short ribs 12.95, Combination of Bulgogi, Dak Gui, Kalbi 14.95, Spicy Marinated BBQ Sliced Pork 10.95

Impressions:

The Kaimuki area of Honolulu is gathering a fine collection of quality ethnic eateries of which Sis kitchen is a valued new addition. This is dining Korean style with a healthy, fresh approach. Portions are quite large, so be careful not to over order. Sis Kitchen is located in the same block as the Waialae Avenue restaurant row spots and shares the city parking lot behind the buildings.

Oahu Dining

Honolulu

Sorabol

805 Keeaumoku St
Honolulu, HI 96814
808-947-3113
Web: None
Hours: 24/7
Cards: AE DC JCB MC V
Dress: Casual
Style: Kor $$

Menu Sampler:

Breakfast:
$5.95-Kim Chee Pot Stew, Soft Tofu Pot Stew, Char Broiled Mackerel Pike, Bean Sprout Soup, Beef and Vegetable Soup (spicy), Bean-Sprout Soup

Lunch:
Plate style with steamed rice, kim chee, and vegetables. Barbecued Marinated Pork/Chicken $7.50, Barbecued Marinated Prime Ribeye $8.00, Fish Fritter or Beef Fritter Plate $7.50, Combination lunch plates are available $9.50
Special Lunch: BBQ Pork Baby Back Ribs $12.50, Sushi Regular $20.00

Dinner:
All are served with pickled vegetables, kim chee, steamed rice and soup. Bul Go Ki (barbecued marinated ribeyes) $14.95, Marinated and Seasoned Sirloin $16.95, Char-Broiled Hairtail Fish $13.95, Steamed Halibut $13.95, Dumplings in beef soup $8.50, Seaweed Soup $7.50, Chicken Soup with Ginseng and Sweet Rice $14.95, Noodles mixed with beef and vegetables $8.50, Sliced Pork and Kim Chee with spicy sauce $11.95, Char-Broiled Mackerel Fish $10.95, Marinated and Seasoned Tripe $16.95, side orders of sushi available.

Impressions:

If you would like to have an authentic Korean dining experience, pay a visit to Sorabol. Menus of this type can be a bit intimidating with listings of variety meats and unfamiliar fish, but if you stay with the marinated and barbecued dinners you just might find yourself singing its praises. Most dishes are accompanied by an assortment of pickled vegetables including kim chee, which is a zesty salsa made from coarsely chopped cabbage and chili peppers. Spicy! Steamed rice is a complementary neutral flavor that offsets the excitement in the rest of your meal. The restaurant is roomy, casual, and bustles with activity 24 hours a day. There's plenty of free parking in the lot beside the building.

Honolulu

Sunset Grill

Restaurant Row
500 Ala Moana Blvd
Honolulu, HI 96813
808-521-4409
Web: None
Hours: L 11:00 AM-4:00 PM XSaSu
         D 5:00 PM-10:00 PM
Cards: AE DC DIS JCB MC V
Dress: Evening Aloha
Style: Ec/Pac-Rim $$$ Ent Card

Menu Sampler:

Breakfast:
N/A
Lunch:
Pupus: Caesar Salad $8.95, Fried Lobster Ravioli w/roasted garlic &
Gorgonzola sauce $9.95, Grilled Marinated Duck Breast Salad $14.95
Pastas: Scampi over Linguine $18.95, Blue Crab Amontillado w/asparagus
flamed over penne pasta and a garlic cream sauce $18.95, primavera $16.95
Sandwiches: Reuben with Swiss cheese & sauerkraut on Molasses Bread $9.95
Entrées: includes vegetables. Hoisin Barbecue Pacific Salmon with jasmine rice
$18.95, St. Louis Ribs with garlic mashed potatoes $18.95, Petite Filet $17.95
Dinner:
Pupus: House Made Cured Salmon Carpaccio with crostini $12.95, Ahi Poke
local style with Maui onions and macadamia nuts $Market, Calamari $7.95
Salads: Chicken & Gorgonzola with greens, candied walnuts, Granny Smith
apples with a red wine vinaigrette $13.95, Blackened Salmon Spinach $13.95
Pastas: Scampi $18.95, Kiawe Grilled Chicken Primavera over linguine with
roasted tomato sauce $18.95, Spicy Sausage & Tiger Shrimp over penne $21.95
Entrées: Kiawe Grilled Filet Mignon with garlic mashed potatoes and Zinfandel
reduction demi glace $25.95, Seafood Mixed Grill of Shrimp, Salmon, and
Scallops w/a champagne mustard sauce on basil pesto linguine $18.95

Impressions:

Sunset Grill draws its ideas and ingredients from around the world. Your dining
partners are just as likely to have lamb from Colorado as clams from Manila.
Throw in a little Tex-Mex seasoning and hoisin sauce and the kitchen becomes a
pretty wild place. Wine enthusiasts will love this place.

Oahu Dining

Waikiki

Surf Room
The Royal Hawaiian
2259 Kalakaua Ave
Honolulu, HI 96815
808-923-7311
www.royal-hawaiian.com
Hours: SuBru 11:00 AM-2:30 PM
        B Buf 6:30 AM-11:30 AM
        L 11:30 AM-2:30 PM XSu
        D 6:00 PM-10:00 PM
Cards: AE DC DIS JCB MC V
Dress: Evening Aloha
Style: Pac-Rim $$$$

Menu Sampler:

Breakfast:
Sunday Champagne Brunch: carved meats, hot entrees, traditional breakfast items, seafood, salads, fruits, desserts $33.95/adults, $23.95/children
Breakfast Buffet: Traditional breakfast items buffet style $22.25 or a la carte: Pecan Waffle $10.75, Three Egg Gourmet Omelet with hash browns $16.25
Lunch:
Salads & Soups: Roast Five-Spice Chicken Salad with Mac Nuts and Crispy Noodles $12.95, Chilled Light Creamy Maui Onion Soup w/onion rings $6.25
Entrées: Sauteed Mahi Mahi with baby spinach, mango-jicama salsa and jasmine rice $16.25, Royal Hawaiian Seafood Melt Sandwich $13.95
Dinner:
Appetizers: Pepper Spiced Gravlox Summer Roll $10.50, Pan Seared Sea Scallops $13.50, The Royal Sampler $18.00, Shrimp Cocktail $13.00
Salads: Baby Romaine Salad $8.00, Spinach Salad with Fresh Tuna Confit $12.00, Lobster Nicoise Salad & Kahuku Corn Pancake $14.00
Entrées: Teriyaki Glazed Grilled Ahi Fillet $28.00, Sautéed Garlic Jumbo Prawns $32.00, Broiled Beef Tenderloin $36.00, Fresh Maine Lobster $46.00, Royal Hukilau Seafood Bounty – as an entrée $44.50, w/any entrée $16.50

Impressions:

The Surf Room flows from a lovely indoor dining room to a beachfront terrace. Likewise offerings run from the daily resort mega breakfast buffet to romantic Pacific Rim dining. Such is the life of the signature restaurant at the Pink Palace. Stop by and experience the lifestyle at this Waikiki Beach landmark.

Niu Valley

Swiss Haus
Niu Valley Shopping Center
5730 Kalanianole Hwy
Honolulu, HI 96821
808-377-5447
swisshausllc@juno.com
Hours: SuBru 10:30 AM-1:00 PM
              D 5:30 PM-9:00 PM XMo
Cards: AE DC DIS JCB MC V
Dress: Resort Casual
Style: Euro $$

Menu Sampler:

Breakfast:
Sunday Brunch: $16-salads, cold cuts, hot dishes, assorted desserts
Lunch:
N/A
Dinner:
Appetizers: Croute Emmental-creamed mushrooms on toast with sliced ham, glazed with Swiss cheese $5.00, Fresh Steamed Clams $8.50, Escargot $6.75
Soups: Swiss Onion Soup glazed w/Swiss cheese $4.25, Soup of the day $2.00
Salads: Spinach Salad with lemon and olive oil dressing, bacon bits and chopped egg whites $4.25, Salat Teller-assorted salad plate $6.75, Swiss Haus Salad of mixed greens, mushrooms, tomatoes tossed with house dressing $3.25
Complete Dinners: include soup of the day, salad, vegetable and coffee or tea. Veal Medallions Florentine-sautéed veal on a bed of spinach topped with bacon and glazed with Swiss cheese with rosti potatoes $19.50, Entrecote Café de Paris-New York Steak sautéed with special herb-butter sauce with baked potato or French fries $24.50, Trout Caprice-fillets of sautéed fresh rainbow trout on a bed of creamed mushrooms, topped with banana, parsley potatoes $18.50
Light Dinners: Bratwurst $7.50, Vegetarian Pasta with garlic cream sauce $9.75, Weinerli-a European style frankfurter with Swiss potato salad or French fries $6.25, Croute Emmental-creamed mushrooms on toast with ham $8.75

Impressions:

For a change of pace, try this affordable dining spot east of Diamond Head. Swiss Haus features authentic European cuisine that you just don't see offered around Honolulu. It's located in the Niu Valley Shopping Center past Kahala on the main highway and is really quite easy to find. Wait until rush hour is over.

Oahu Dining

Waikiki

Tanaka of Tokyo
Renaissance Ilikai Waikiki Hotel
1777 Ala Moana Blvd
Honolulu, HI 96815
808-945-3443
www.tanakaoftokyo.com
Hours: L 11:30 AM-2:00 PM Mo-Fr
        D 5:30 PM-Closing
Cards: AE DC DIS JCB MC V
Dress: Resort Casual
Style: Japan $$$
        Ent Card

Menu Sampler:

Breakfast:
N/A
Lunch:
Appetizers: Calamari Appetizer with butter and lemon $5.50, Teppan Fried Rice with egg $1.50, Miso Soup $1.50, Sautéed Scallop Appetizer $3.75
Entrées: Tanaka Sirloin Special $13.75, Seafood Combination (shrimp and scallops) with sauce $11.25, Salmon Steak $12.75, Chicken Teriyaki $9.00, Sukiyaki Steak $10.25, Shrimps $10.75, Scallops $11.75, Filet $14.25
Dinner:
Appetizers: Alaskan King Crab steamed in a ti leaf wrap on your teppan grill $12.00, Shrimp grilled and flambéed at your table $5.50, Blackened Ahi $9.75
Entrées: All come with pickled vegetables, tossed salad, miso soup, steamed rice, grilled shrimp appetizer, teppan vegetables, Japanese green tea and dessert. Shogun-combination of prime filet, whole lobster tail and scallops $58.00, Tanaka Sirloin $24.50, Teppanyaki Salmon $19.25, Shrimp $19.25, Chicken Teriyaki $15.50, Lobster-large tail served in shell $36.50, Scallops $20.75
Dessert: Vanilla, Green Tea, or Watermelon Sherbet or Kona Coffee $1.50

Impressions:

Teppanyaki dining has long been a special occasion favorite with eastern and western diners. At Tanaka Of Tokyo chefs prepare dinner with flashing knives and showman-style flair while verbally interacting with the diners. Of course talking story with others around your table is part of the fun. If you don't know, ask and someone is sure to help you. This is a great place for bargain hunters. Lunch is an unbeatable value, and coupons abound for dinnertime specials.

Diamond Head

Tavola Tavola
3106 Monsarrat Avenue
Honolulu, HI 96815
808-737-6600
Web: None
Hours: D 5:30 PM-9:30 PM
           D 5:30 PM-10:00 PM FrSa
Cards: AE DC JCB MC V
Dress: Evening Aloha
Style: Ital $$$

Menu Sampler:

Breakfast/Lunch:
N/A

Dinner:
Antipasti: Fried Calamari and Zucchini with Tartar Sauce $12, Marinated Seafood Salad $12, Salmon Balloon filled with fresh diced vegetables $13, Crepes topped with Salmon and Creamy Sauce $13, Sautéed Squid in tomato sauce $14, Raw Albacore Tuna with arugula, balsamic & olive oil $11
Pasta: Spaghetti with small sausage meatballs and tomato sauce $13, Soft Polenta with a zucchini and calamari sauce and truffle essence $16, Spinach Lasagna with meat sauce $12, Homemade Spinach Pasta with shrimp and cherry tomatoes $15, Homemade Pasta with fresh clams in white wine sauce $16, Homemade Wide Pasta with medley of mushrooms & Bolognaise sauce $15, Shrimp Risotto with asparagus $17, Asparagus Soup $9
Secondi: Today's Fresh Fish with sautéed vegetables and aromatic olive oil $25, Butterfly Shrimp grilled with fresh herb olive oil $19, Grilled Baby Lamb Chops with spinach and roasted potatoes $27, Grilled Ribeye Steak with spinach and roasted potatoes $25, Lamb Stew with green beans $21, Grilled Sausage Patties with soft polenta $19, Four Course Degustation Meal $50

Impressions:

Tavola Tavola is located in a classy little building up near the base of Diamond Head. There behind Kapiolani Park, an Italian-trained Japanese chef prepares an interesting array of southern Italian dishes. Don't expect to see pasta with heavy sauces coming out of his kitchen. In this fine dining establishment the flavors of the ingredients are allowed to come through naturally. Everything from the table service to the house made pastries is strictly upscale, but the atmosphere remains comfortable and welcoming. The parking area is small, so look across the street.

Hawaii Kai

Teddy's Bigger Burgers
Koko Head Marina
7192 Kalanianole Hwy
Honolulu, HI 96825
808-394-9100
Web: None
Hours: LD 10:30 AM-9:00 PM
Cards: None
Dress: Casual
Style: Amer $

Menu Sampler:

Breakfast:
N/A

Lunch/Dinner:
Teddy's Burgers-Big 5 oz-Bigger 7 oz-Biggest 9 oz. and are served with Special Sauce, Lettuce, Tomato, Onions, Pickles. Additional Toppings are Cheese $.40, Bacon $.80, Avocado $.80, Pineapple $.80, Mushrooms $1.00, Chili $1.00 Teddy's Original Burger 4.15/4.95/5.75, Teddy's Teri Burger 4.70/5.45/6.25, Teddy's Spud Burger (Hashbrown patty added) 4.70/5.45/6.25, Teddy's Monster Double 5.95/7.30/8.35
Other Items: Grilled Chicken Breast-plain, teri, garlic or Cajun, Veggie Burger, Fish Sandwich 5.25, Salad 3.00, Grilled Chicken Salad 5.50, Fries 1.50/2.00, Spicy, Garlic or Cheese Fries 2.00/2.55, Onion Rings 2.55
Fountain: Sodas 1.30/1.80, Floats 2.75, Extra Thick Shakes 3.75, Malts + .35

Impressions:

The formula for Teddy's Bigger Burgers was worked out here on Oahu by a couple of guys who really didn't want to live anywhere else. Things started out on a backyard grill and moved up to a small sandwich shop near Diamond Head. Recently Teddy's went mainstream and opened the new Koko Marina location.

The heart of the menu is Teddy's burger served medium with a "special" sauce. These juicy sandwiches come in three sizes suitable for just about any appetite. Backing the headliner comes some great fries and shakes. Additional specialties are offered to suit the tastes of the non-burger crowd. Teddy's is conveniently located near Hanauma Bay and welcomes returning water sports enthusiasts.

Waikiki

The Banyan Veranda
Sheraton Moana Surfrider
2365 Kalakaua Ave
Honolulu, HI 96815
808-922-3111
www.sheraton-hawaii.com
Hours: SuBru 9:00 AM-1:00 PM
           B 7:00 AM-11:00 AM Mo-Sa
           D 5:30 PM-9:00 PM
Cards: AE DC DIS JCB MC V
Dress: Evening Aloha
Style: Asian/Cont $$$

Menu Sampler:

Breakfast:
Sunday Brunch: $36.50/adults, $17.50/children. Soups, salads, fish, sushi, carved meats, seafood, hot entrees, omelet/waffle stations, pastries & desserts
Fixed Price Breakfast: $24.50-Juice, platter of fruits, muffins & breads served tableside. Choice of three entrees, Mac Nut or Banana Pancakes, Omelet, Eggs
Lunch:
N/A
Afternoon Tea: Mo-Sa 1 PM-4:30 PM, Su 3-4:30 PM, Earl Grey, Jasmine, Darjeeling and English Breakfast, or Our House Blends made with local flowers, plants and berries, large selection of teas, scones with Devonshire Cream and preserves, finger sandwiches, salmon roll and sweet pastries $21. Tea & Champagne (Two glasses) $27.
Dinner:
Entrees: Baked Lobster Tail with Shrimps, Scallops and Clams on creamy mushroom risotto $29, New York Steak with herb butter & cognac flamed demi glace $28.25, Pan Roasted Chicken Breast on spinach & artichoke hearts $25

Impressions:

This hotel is referred to as the "First Lady of Waikiki" as it was built when very little else was out here. Sitting in a rocking chair on the front veranda watching Kalakaua Avenue go by gives one an "anachronistic rush" of looking both backward and forward in time. The Banyan Veranda is located in a lovely courtyard facing the beach. The brunch and buffet items reflect the culinary traditions of the many cultures whose paths have crossed in the islands. Of course, afternoon tea is served. This is a wonderful place to dine.

Oahu Dining

Honolulu

The Bistro at Century Center
1750 Kalakaua Ave.-Third Floor
Honolulu, HI 96826
808-943-6500
Web: None
Hours: L 11:00 AM-2:00 PM Mo-Fr
         D 5:30 PM-10:00 PM Su, Tu-Th
         D 5:30 PM-12:00 AM FrSa
Cards: AE DIS JCB MC V
Dress: Evening Aloha
Style: Cont $$$$

Menu Sampler:

Breakfast:
N/A

Lunch:
Appetizers: Slices of Scottish Salmon served over crème fraiche with ikura, caper berries, dill, onions, and assorted dark breads $9.00, Eggplant and Goat Cheese Soufflé over an oven roasted tomato fondue $9.00
Salads: Bistro Salad w/Maui onions, Kamuela tomatoes & choice of vinaigrette-roasted shallot, raspberry, or balsamic $7.00, Caesar Salad $9.00
Entrees: Ahi Nicoise prepared with seared sashimi grade (#1) yellow fin tuna $15.00, Portobello Mushroom Wellington baked in puff pastry, over fresh spinach $15.00, Gnocchi of spinach & potato over roasted tomato coulis $14.00
Dinner:
Appetizers: Escargot A La Bistro-chanterelles & morels done Duxelle with asparagus coulis and Maryland Crab $11.95, Foie Gras-seared $19.95
Entrees: Steak Diane-brandy flambé presentation with potato gnocchi $29.95, Australian Rack of Lamb carved tableside with dauphine potatoes, fresh artichoke, and pomegranate au jus $38.95, Duck A L'Orange $28.95
Desserts: Bananas Flambé $10.95, Crème Brulee $7.50, Tiramisu $7.95

Impressions:

If you're looking for a taste of yesteryear with a foot firmly in the present, The Bistro is it. You'll find a menu with definite Continental roots dusted with island ingredients served in a luxurious atmosphere of thick carpets, tuxedoed waiters, candlelight, and tableside preparations. This is an experience to savor; one to share with that special someone. Located on the third floor of a high-rise across from the Hard Rock Café, The Bistro at Century Center is a separate world from the bustle outside its doors. Use the validated deck parking or valet service.

Oahu Dining

Waikiki

The Cheesecake Factory
2301 Kalakaua Ave.
Honolulu, HI 96815
808-924-5001
www.thecheesecakefactory.com
Hours: 11:00 AM-11:00 PM Mo-Sa
         10:00 AM-11:00 PM Su
Cards: AE DC DIS JCB MC V
Dress: Casual
Style: Ecl $$

Menu Sampler:

Breakfast:
Sunday Brunch: served until 2:00 PM, Eggs Benedict with Canadian bacon 10.95, with fresh spinach, bacon and tomato 11.50, French Toast Napoleon of grilled brioche bread with strawberries, pecans, chantilly cream 9.95
Lunch/Dinner:
Appetizers: Fire Roasted Fresh Artichoke with spicy vinaigrette and garlic dip 8.50, Thai Lettuce Wraps with satay chicken strips, carrots, bean sprouts, and coconut curry noodles wrapped in lettuce leaves with three sauces 10.95
Appetizer Salads: Endive, Pecan and Blue Cheese in light vinaigrette 8.50
Pizza: Pesto Chicken Pizza with oven-dried tomatoes and pine nuts 9.95
Specialties: Grilled Portabella on a Bun with grilled red onion, cheese, spicy mayo, fries 9.50, Spicy Cashew Chicken over rice 14.50, Bistro Shrimp Pasta with basil-garlic-lemon cream sauce 15.95, Herb Crusted Filet of Salmon with lemon sauce, asparagus and mashed potatoes 17.50, Shepherd's Pie with mashed potato topping and parmesan cheese 13.50, Chino-Latino Steak with a Thai Tamarind Sauce, grilled red onion, tomato and steamed white rice 17.95
Salads: Barbeque Ranch Chicken Salad w/crispy fried onion strings 12.95
Sandwiches: Grilled Japanese Eggplant Sandwich, garlic aioli, fries 9.95
Desserts: Black-Out Cake-fudgy chocolate cake, chocolate chips, almonds 6.50
Cheesecakes: 36 kinds by the slice 5.95-7.50, or whole pies at the counter

Impressions:

Though we tend to shy away from Mainland "chain gangs", this is one we endorse. The Cheesecake Factory's sharing-size portions of tasty menu items offer diners a higher than expected level of culinary depth. The restaurant's artfully designed layout maintains a feeling of intimacy in this otherwise oversized facility. Valet parking is available, but if you park in the deck make sure to have your ticket validated because this one can be really expensive!

Hawaii Kai

The Chef's Table
Hawaii Kai Towne Center
333 Keahole
Honolulu, HI 96825
808-394-2433
Web: None
Hours: L 11:30 AM-2:00 PM XMo
         D 5:30 PM-9:00 PM XMo
Cards: MC V
Dress: Resort Casual
Style: Austrian $$$

Menu Sampler:

Breakfast:
N/A
Lunch:
Dinner:
Small Beginnings: Roasted Mushrooms in Cheeses and Walnut Sauce $6.00, Garlic Steamed Clams in sweet butter wine and herb sauce $9.00, Wine Country Escargots baked in herb and garlic butter $8.50, Jumbo Shrimp Cocktail $6.00
Soups: Special $2.75, Roasted Onion Beet Soup glazed with smoked cheese $4.75, Gulyas Soup "Gypsy Style"-paprika beef and potato soup $5.00
Salads: Spinach and Mushroom Salad with hot bacon vinaigrette $5.50, Chef's Table Mixed Salad of greens, mushrooms and shrimp in House dressing $4.00
Austrian Specialties: Wienerschnitzel-pan fried veal cutlet and onion potatoes $17.50, Jaegerschnitzel- sautéed pork steak in mushroom sauce and spetzli $17.00, Sauerbraten, red cabbage, and spetzli $20.00, Beef Goulash $16.50
Fish and Shellfish: Salmon Steak, grilled, pan-fried, or poached, with lemon caper butter $17.00, Trout Fillet baked with mushroom in green peppercorn sauce $18.00, Pan Seared Scallops, mushroom butter sauce, pasta, veg $19.00

Impressions:

We refer to The Chef's Table as a strip mall surprise. Located in the very same shopping center as Hawaii Kai's Costco you'll find a gourmet restaurant with an Austrian chef serving upscale Bavarian cuisine. Inside this lovely room an open display kitchen turns out rich, flavorful dishes using only prime ingredients. The daily specials are particularly interesting, so be sure to ask what's available. This restaurant provides a wonderful contrast to the fusion cuisine offered in so many of Hawaii's better dining spots. Free parking is plentiful in the lot out front.

Oahu Dining

Honolulu

The Contemporary Museum Café
2411 Makiki Heights Drive
Honolulu, HI 96822
808-523-3362
www.tcmhi.org
Hours: L 11:30 AM-2:30 PM XMo
         L 12:00 PM-2:30 PM Su
         Desserts 2:00 PM-3:00 PM
Cards: AE DC DIS JCB MC V
Dress: Resort Casual
Style: Ec $$

Menu Sampler:

Breakfast:
N/A
Lunch:
Appetizers: Hummus & Warm Pita $4.50, Crostini of the Day-baguette toasts
with a ramekin of various toppings $3.75, Poached Shrimp in a spicy remoulade
$7.50, Smoked Salmon Plate w/red onions capers $7.95
Soups & Salads: Ancho Chicken Taco Salad $9.50, Soup du Jour $2.95/$4.95,
Bread $1.00, Asian Chop Salad with hoisin chicken or baked tofu with won ton
strips $9.25, The Un-Caesar Salad-romaine w/creamy gorgonzola & pears
topped with spiced pecans $8.25, with grilled chicken $9.25, Tony's Greek
Shrimp & Pasta Salad with lemon vinaigrette and feta cheese $9.50
Sandwiches: Served with tortilla chips and hummus. Portabello Mushroom
Sandwich with artichoke-pepper relish and sun-dried tomato mayonnaise on
focaccia $8.95, Seared Ahi Sandwich, rare, w/spicy remoulade on a Kaiser roll
$9.50, Hijiki Tofu Burger-seaweed, carrots, green onions & miso w/wasabi
mayo tomato & slaw on wheat bun $7.75, Ancho Chili Chicken Wrap $9.25
Desserts: Changing Menu Daily of homemade delicacies.
Dinner:
N/A

Impressions:

If you like cuisine with your culture or vice versa you'll enjoy a visit to The
Contemporary Museum Café. The culinary style here is eclectic with fresh
flavorful ingredients made into soups, salads, sandwiches, and desserts. The
museum is a former family estate with 3 ½ acres of gardens set on a ridge
overlooking the city. For current exhibitions you can check the web site at
www.tcmhi.org. Don't forget to stop at the unique gift shop before you leave.

Oahu Dining

Waikiki

The Hanohano Room
Sheraton Waikiki Hotel
2255 Kalakaua Ave
Honolulu, HI 96815
808-922-4422
www.sheraton-hawaii.com
Hours: D 5:30 PM-9:30 PM
Cards: AE DC DIS JCB MC V
Dress: Evening Aloha
Style: Cont/Pac-Rim $$$$

Menu Sampler:

Breakfast/Lunch:
N/A
Dinner:
Starters: Kataiffi Wrapped Kauai Shrimp with shredded filo, fried crisp, with ginger remoulade on seaweed salad 11, Escargot with macadamia nuts and Parmesan cheese 11, Miyagi Oysters with salsa, pickled Maui onion, ogo, and Japanese cucumber ponzu 13, Pan Seared Scallops with champagne sauce 12
Soups and Salads: Maui Onion Soup with Gruyere cheese 8, New England Style Clam Chowder with sweet Kahuku corn and sourdough croutons 8, Waimanalo Valley Salad with champagne vinaigrette 8, Fresh Spinach Salad topped with apple-smoked bacon, Hamakua mushrooms (for two) 24
Entrées: Garlic and Rosemary Roasted Chicken with morel sauce 29, Lemongrass Crusted Onaga baked with taro in a ginger cream, Waimanalo Swiss chard, ruby port gastrique 33, Steamed Moi with Waimanalo Herbs and yuzu sesame soy sauce 33, Garlic Marinated Rack of Lamb with a Dijon mustard crust and pineapple sage jus 39, Fire Roasted Veal Chop marinated in rosemary and served with morel sauce 35, Sautéed Onaga in beurre blanc 35
Desserts: White Chocolate Fondue 8, Tahitian Vanilla Bean Brulee Melon Compote 8, Kula Strawberries Sabayon 8, and Kona Coffee Tiramisu 8

Impressions:

Dining on top of tall buildings has always been an attraction. The view might bring people in, but it takes good food to keep them. This 30th floor restaurant gets things done both ways. The chef blends Continental techniques with what the Sheraton calls the "Flavors of Hawaii" to create a memorable dining experience. Although we find the menu a little hard to define we can't help but like it. Just take the glass express elevator to the top of the Sheraton Waikiki.

Honolulu

The Original OnOn
1110 McCully Street
Honolulu, HI 96826
808-946-8833
Web: None
Hours: LD 10:00 AM-9:00 PM
Cards: MC V
Dress: Casual
Style: Chi $$

Menu Sampler:

Breakfast:
N/A
Lunch:
Specials: 11 AM-2 PM, Soft Duck & Won Ton Noodle in Soup $8.25, Special Seafood Fried Rice $8.25, Seabass Fillet w/ginger & onion on rice $7.75
Lunch/Dinner:
Appetizer Pupu: Pepper Salt Chicken Wings (8) $8.25, Egg Roll $7.25
Northern Chinese Cuisine: Spicy Pork Eggplant $7.25, Kung Pao Chicken $7.95, Mu Shu Pork $8.75, Spicy Shredded Pork $7.25, Mixed Vegetables $7.25
Casserole: Oyster & Pot Roast Pork Casserole $12.50, Lup Cheong, Chicken with Black Mushroom Casserole $10.75, Beef Stew w/Lettuce Casserole $9.50
Soup: Scallop with Egg $9.25, Seaweed with Fishcake $7.95, Hot and Sour Soup $7.50, Chicken Cream Corn $7.25, Green Pea with Egg Blossom $7.25
Entrées: Pork Hash with black bean $7.95, Island Pork Chop Peking Style $8.75, Sweet and Sour Pork $7.25, Stuffed Bittermelon $7.95, Roast Duck $7.95, Chicken with Pea Pod $7.95, Lobster with Cashew Nuts $16.50, Cuttlefish with shrimp sauce $8.95, Fresh Scallop with Chinese Pea Pod $9.95, Fish Cake with Sour Cabbage $7.95, Fried Shrimp with green onion $9.75
Egg: Egg Fu Yung $7.25, Salted Duck $1.65, Sweet Pork Fu Yung $7.25
Chop Suey: Choy Sum w/Oyster Sauce $6.50, House Special Chop Suey $7.25

Impressions:

Those who want to experience a little Honolulu neighborhood culture should enjoy a visit to The Original OnOn. This casual eatery bustles throughout the day as local families and businessmen stop by to partake and talk story. The menu is decidedly Chinese with regional orientation designed to satisfy Oahu appetites. Lunch specials and affordable combination plates are offered for the budget minded. Look for OnOn at the corner of Young and McCully.

Diamond Head

The Patisserie
Kahala Mall Shopping Center
4211 Waialae Avenue
Honolulu, HI 96816
808-735-4402
www.ThePatisserie.com
Hours: B 7:00 AM-10:00 AM
          L 10:00 AM-5:00 PM
          D 5:00 PM-8:30 PM XSu
Cards: AE MC V
Dress: Casual
Style: Amer/Ger $$

Menu Sampler:

Breakfast:
Popover $.85, Two Egg Ham & Cheese Omelette with toast & jelly $3.95, Eierpfannkuchen-thin German pancake with orange maple syrup- 1 pancake $2.45, 2 pancakes $3.75, Buttermilk Shortstack (3) $2.45

Lunch:
House Specialties: Meatloaf Sandwich $4.95, Assorted Quiche $3.95, Sausage with potato salad & sauerkraut $6.50, Lasagna & tossed greens $3.95
Sandwiches: Bavarian Loaf $4.25, Danish Ham $3.95, Roast Beef $4.50, Pastrami $4.95, Avocado BLT $4.95, Smoked Turkey $4.75, Chicken $4.25
Beverages: Coffee $.87, Cappucino $1.85, Café Latte $1.85, Espresso $1.35

Dinner:
All entrées include tossed salad with creamy ginger dressing, tangy red cabbage & steamed vegetables, rolls & butter. Sauerbraten with bread dumplings $14.00, Oven Braised Lamb Shank with Cabernet Sauce with roasted potatoes $15.00, Pork Tenderloin with Peppercorn and roast potatoes $15.00, Rahm Schnitzel with veal, spaetzle and a chardonnay cream sauce $15.00
Desserts: Tiramisu $1.75, Apple Tart $2.75, Napoleon $1.85, Éclair $1.85

Impressions:

The Patisserie is an anomaly in a land of anomalies. Where else would you find an exceptional bakery serving great German food in a shopping mall? Maybe in Munich but definitely not in Hawaii! Breakfast and lunch are served deli style, but dinner is a sit-down affair complete with tablecloths and wait staff. This is a popular evening spot with the Kahala crowd making reservations a must. The Kahala Mall sits on the east end of the H1 making this an easy place to find.

Honolulu

The Pavilion Café
The Honolulu Academy of Arts
900 S. Beretania Avenue
Honolulu, Hawaii 96826
808-532-8734
www.honoluluacademy.org
Hours: L 11:30 AM-2:00 PM Tu-Sa
Cards: AE JCB MC V
Dress: Resort Casual
Style: Amer/Ec $

Menu Sampler:

Breakfast:
N/A
Lunch:
Soup of the Day $3.50, White Bean Salad on Arugula and Wilted Radicchio
with shiitake mushrooms, balsamic vinaigrette and Reggiano $8.95, Beef
Tenderloin Sandwich with red onion Dijon & caper relish $10.95, Warm Big
Island Goat Cheese & Nalo Green Salad with seasonal fruit and honey-thyme
vinaigrette $9.95, Roast Turkey Breast Sandwich with Emmenthaler Swiss
cheese & house made chutney on whole wheat bread $8.50, Feta, Tapenade &
Hau'ula Tomato Sandwich on house made focaccia $8.95, Piadina of flatbread,
arugula, chopped tomatoes, basil, fresh mozzarella & prosciutto $8.95
Wine Carte: Whites-glass $4.50/$5.50, bottles $18.50-$39.50, Reds-glass
$5.50, bottles $19.50-$32.50, Café Wines-glass $4.50/$5.50, bottles $17.50-
$34.50, Signature Wine Selections-bottles up to $25.00, corkage $10/bottle
Desserts: Sorbets, gelatos, ice creams $3.00, Dessert Specials such as Chocolate
Pot de Crème, Fresh Fruit Crisp or Tart, Chocolate Walnut Torte $5.95
Dinner:
N/A

Impressions:

The Honolulu Academy of Arts has many treasures inside, and one of them is
The Pavilion Café. This open-air dining spot with its contemporary decor is
located in the interior courtyard of the museum. Seating about 120, The Pavilion
Café offers a short menu that is long on interesting flavor combinations. The
chef prides himself on using only the freshest of ingredients and it shows.
Because of the popularity of the café, reservations are recommended and
accepted at 15-minute intervals. Validated parking is available.

Kapahulu

The Pyramids
758-B Kapahulu Ave.
Honolulu, HI 96816
808-737-2900
Web: None
Hours: L Buf 11:00 AM-2:00 PM Mo-Sa
         D 5:30 PM-10:00 PM Mo-Sa
         D 5:00 PM-9:00 PM Su
Cards: AE DC DIS JCB MC V
Dress: Casual
Style: Med $$

Menu Sampler:

Breakfast:
N/A
Lunch:
All You Can Eat Buffet $8.95-Chicken, Lamb & Beef Shawerma, Rice, Fries, Greek Salad, Pita, Potato Salad, Tomato Salad, Rice Pudding, Falafel
Dinner:
Appetizers: Baba Ghanouj-baked onions and eggplant with tahini, lemon, cumin, and fresh garlic $6.95, Spanakopita (Spinach Pie) with Egyptian Salad $3.95, Stuffed Grape Leaves served with yogurt sauce (10) $11.95, (5) $6.95, Feta Salad $4.95, Pyramids Special of hommos, tabbouleh, falafel, baba ghanouj and grape leaves (4 persons) $19.95, Feta Salad with tomato & cucumber $4.95
Entrées: All are served with salad and pita bread. Kosa-layers of zucchini, onion rings, mushrooms & tomato slices topped with a creamy béchamel $12.95, Mousaka with fried eggplant, ground beef and béchamel $14.95, Kebbeh-marinated ground lamb & beef, cracked wheat, onions, raisins and pine nuts $14.95, Reiash-lamb ribs marinated for two days then charbroiled over low heat $18.95, Chef's Complete Dinner/person (minimum of two) $26.95

Impressions:

Before anyone makes any comments about curb appeal, let's just say we passed The Pyramids by a few times before venturing inside. That first visit was an eye opener. After stepping through the door, a tastefully decorated room greeted us with some of the best Egyptian and Mediterranean cuisine we've had anywhere. Lunchtime is a particularly good value. For a small price, patrons can sample a variety of dishes from a buffet. Then at dinner authentic belly dancers complete the mood. Parking is a problem. Do yourself a favor and take a cab.

Oahu Dining

Honolulu

The Willows
901 Hausten Street
Honolulu, HI 96826
808-952-9200
www.willowshawaii.com
Hours: Bru Buf 10:00 AM-2:30 PM Su
        L Buf 11:00 AM-2:00 PM Mo-Fr
        L Buf 10:00 AM-2:30 PM Sa
        D Buf 5:30 PM-9:00 PM
Cards: AE DC DIS JCB MC V
Dress: Resort Casual
Style: Amer/Haw $$$

Menu Sampler:

Breakfast:
Sunday Brunch Buffet-Belgian Waffle Station, Salads, Prime Rib, Baked Whole Snapper, The Willows Famous Curry, Seafood Bar, Entrees, Dessert Station $25.95, Keiki 4-10 $12.95, Seniors 65+ 10% off

Lunch:
Buffet Mo-Fr $15.95, Keiki 4-10 $7.95, Seniors 65+ 10% off. Soup Station, Salads, Carving Station with Roast Turkey & Prime Rib, The Willows Famous Curry, Saimin Station, Entrees, Dessert Station; Saturday Lunch Buffet $18.95, Keiki 4-10 $9.50, Seniors 65+ 10% off, adds a Japanese Sushi Bar and Seafood Station (Snow Crab Legs) to the weekly menu.

Dinner:
Dinner Buffet Mo-Fr 5:30 PM-9:00 PM, SaSu 5:00 PM-9:00 PM $25.95, Keiki 4-10 $12.95, Seniors 65+ 10% off. Soup Station, Salads, Carving Station of Roast Turkey & Prime Rib, The Willows Roasted Portobello Mushrooms with Balsamic Beurre Blanc, Saimin Station, Suckling Pig, Entrees, Dessert Station.
The Rainbow Room: Ala Carte Dinner We-Su 5:30 PM-9:00 PM. Pupu sized portions of entrees: Steamed Moi with Spicy Garlic Edamame, Asian slaw, miso sauce $8.95, Pan Roasted Scallops with Truffle Caviar Beurre Blanc and sesame crostini $9.95, Wild Mushroom Sampler $6.95, Pan Roasted Venison with Roasted Garlic Miso Butter, potato and stilton croquette $9.95
Pupu Bar for $10, Monday through Friday, call for hours

Impressions:

For a glimpse into the lives of local people as they celebrate milestones in life come to The Willows. Here you'll have your choice of crowd-pleasing buffets served in a lovely garden setting or tapas style dining in the Rainbow Room.

Waikiki

Tiki's Grill & Bar
Aston Waikiki Beach Hotel
2570 Kalakaua Ave.
Honolulu, HI 96815
808-923-8454
www.tikisgrill.com
Hours: LD 10:30 AM-Midnight
Cards: AE DC DIS JCB MC V
Dress: Casual
Style: Amer/Asian/Isl $$

Menu Sampler:

Breakfast:
N/A
Lunch:
Appetizers: Coconut Shrimp $8.95, Steamed Manila Clams & saffron coconut cream sauce $8.95, Kauai Shrimp Summer Rolls w/peanut dipping sauce $5.95
Soups & Salads: Island Fish & Clam Chowder $4.95, Warm Spinach Salad w/mac nut crusted goat cheese $6.95, Curried Pea/Water Chestnut Salad $5.95
Entrées & Sandwiches: Kalua Pig Sandwich w/caramelized Maui Onions & guava BBQ sauce $8.95, Grilled Monchong w/pineapple chutney & rice $14.95
Dinner:
Appetizers: Calamari Katsu-panko crusted w/lemon grass beurre blanc sauce $7.95, Kalua Pig Quesadilla w/ jack cheese, corn relish & guacamole $6.95
Soups & Salads: Oriental Chicken Chop Salad w/sweet-sour sesame dressing $7.95, Island Nicoise Salad with medium rare seared ahi $10.95
Entrées: Chef's Signature King Salmon glazed and served with a lemon grass beurre blanc sauce, mashed sweet potatoes & Asian slaw $15.95, Filet Mignon with grilled onions, mushrooms & roasted garlic butter, mashed potatoes $22.95, Pan Seared Ahi with Cajun spices over Kalua pig mashed potatoes $16.95, Tiki's Cheeseburger-1/2# chuck on house-made Kaiser roll $7.95

Impressions:

There's a new "in" place to go on Waikiki Beach known as Tiki's Grill & Bar. The proprietors positioned Tiki's to appeal to locals and visitors alike. First, they started off with a great chef and an imaginative menu. Then, they added a large bar serving all kinds of drinks and pupus. Finally, they located the place on the third floor of a hotel overlooking the ocean. The mix seems to be working as the crowds have been coming since the day Tiki's opened. Both lunch and dinner can be casual affairs, or you can step up in the evening to more complex entrées.

Chinatown

To Chau Restaurant
1007 River Street
Honolulu, HI 96814
808-533-4549
Web: None
Hours: 8:00 AM- 2:30 PM
Cards: None
Dress: Casual
Style: Viet $

Menu Sampler:

Breakfast/Lunch:
Pho: Vietnamese Beef Soup consisting of a clear, rich beef broth garnished with slices of rare steak and well cooked brisket, flank, tendon, tripe, fresh herbs and vegetables over rice noodles in three sizes: X-Large Bowl $5.50, Medium Bowl $4.50, Regular Bowl $4.00. Different combinations of meat for the pho are from the above list plus beef balls. Fresh basil, bean sprouts, jalapenos included.
Appetizers: Shrimp Rolls (2) of shrimp, pork, fresh herbs, and vermicelli rolled in rice paper with special sauce $3.50, Spring Rolls (6) of minced pork, crab, shrimp, and mushrooms wrapped in rice paper and deep fried $6.00
Plates: BBQ Chicken Rice Plate $6.00, Pork Chop Rice Plate $6.00
Beverages: French Filtered Coffee Hot or Iced $1.50, Hot Jasmine Tea $.50, French Filtered Coffee w/Condensed Milk $2.00, Fresh Lemonade Juice $1.50, Lemonade w/soda water $1.55, Salty Lemonade $1.50, Soy Bean Milk $1.00
Dinner:
N/A

Impressions:

At first glance, the plain unadorned storefront of To Chau might easily be passed by as a bit too "provincial". That is until you get to the head of the line and the door opens. Then the aroma of rich broth and fresh herbs surrounds you and pulls you in. Pho (fuh) shops are a staple in Vietnam. People from all walks of life slurp the rich soup for breakfast and lunch. First, you select the type of meat you want in your pho, and then a generous bowl of beef broth loaded with rice noodles arrives. Alongside the bowl you'll receive a plate of fresh herbs and bean sprouts. These are added gradually as the soup is eaten. To add them all at once would cool the soup and dull the bright flavor of the herbs. Garnish your pho with lime and chilies, add your favorite sauce, and join the party!

Waikiki

Todai
1910 Ala Moana Blvd
Honolulu, HI 96815
808-947-1000
www.todai.com
Hours: L 11:30 AM-2:30 PM
           D 5:30 PM-9:30 PM
Cards: AE MC V
Dress: Resort Casual
Style: Japan/Sea $$$

Menu Sampler:

Breakfast:
N/A
Lunch/Dinner:
Buffet Style serving over 40 kinds of sushi, 15 hot meat & seafood entrees, tempura, salads, and 20+ bite-sized desserts and a crepe station.
Lunch: $14.95 Monday-Friday, $16.95 Saturday and Sunday
Dinner: $25.95 Monday-Friday, $26.95 Saturday and Sunday
Dinner service adds mussels, clams, jumbo shrimp, snow crab legs to the buffet.
Children less than 5 feet tall are 50% off; Seniors 65+ are 20% off

Impressions:

Todai is Waikiki's ultimate Japanese buffet. People wait at the door before they open to get in line for the abundance waiting inside. The assortment of dishes is nearly overwhelming. They offer over forty different kinds of sushi alone! The main buffet is 160-feet long and has an amazing variety of choices. You can't do it all so don't try. All of the dishes are labeled to help the uninitiated better enjoy this dining experience. To finish things up they have a dessert buffet and a crepe station. Lunch is a great value. Although the price goes up, seafood lovers can go crazy at dinner when a variety of shellfish dishes are added to the display.

Diamond Head

Tokyo Tokyo
Kahala Mandarin Oriental Hawaii Hotel
5000 Kahala Avenue
Honolulu, HI 96816
808-739-1500
Web: None
Hours: L 11:00 AM-2:30 PM XSa
         D 5:30 PM-10:00 PM
Cards: AE DC DIS JCB MC V
Dress: Resort Casual
Style: Japan $$$

Menu Sampler:

Breakfast:
N/A
Lunch:
Japanese Buffet: Featuring sushi, tempura, sashimi $28.75
Dinner:
Appetizers: Sashimi Moriawase-a daily selection of fresh prime sashimi $32.50, Tokyo Tokyo Sampler of Kumi's Special, shrimp & scallop gyoza, maguro poke, rainbow roll, beef dengaku $18.50, Ahi Tataki Salad with a sesame-miso vinaigrette $12.50, Salmon with Grated Radish $11.50, Shrimp Tempura $12.50, Small Scallop Kakiage $9.25, Soybean $5.00
Soups & Salads: Seasonal Tomato Salad with Ogo Vinaigrette and Nalo Greens $8.50, Green Papaya Tofu Salad $8.50, Miso Soup $3.50, Soup of the Day $7.50
Entrées: All selections are served with Nalo Green Salad, Kobachi, Miso Soup, Oshinko and Rice. Butterfish Misoyaki $26.75, Fire Roasted Tenderloin of Beef with ginger sauce $34.50, Teriyaki Chicken $23.25, Tonkatsu $24.50
Kaiseki: Chef's Selection with King Crab Motoyaki, Beef Tenderloin, and tempura $75.00 and up; add a flight of three wine or sake pairings $10.00

Impressions:

As you enter the Kahala Mandarin you'll see a casual yet upscale dining venue featuring both traditional and contemporary Japanese cuisine. The owner of this fine dining restaurant is known for teasing patrons with contrasting tastes that work. The purveyor of these delicacies also owns the famous Wasabi Bistro on Kapahulu. We are big fans of both establishments and recommend them highly. Visitor parking is available in the deck, but it is quite expensive so make sure to get your ticket validated.

Waikiki

Trattoria
2168 Kalia Road
Honolulu, HI 96815
808-923-8415
Web: None
Hours: D 5:30 PM-10:00 PM
Cards: AE DC DIS JCB MC V
Dress: Evening Aloha
Style: Ital $$$
        Ent Card

Menu Sampler:

Breakfast/Lunch:
N/A
Dinner:
Alla Carta/Antipasti: Caesar Salad (tableside prep) $7.95, Chef's Special Green Salad $6.25, Stracciatella of chicken broth, Parmesan cheese, egg and fresh parsley $3.50/$4.50, Fresh Clams steamed in white wine, garlic, shallots and herbs with red or white sauce $9.25, Broiled Scampi Prawns $9.95
Pasta: Canneloni alla Milanese-crepes wrapped around a combination of veal, chicken and beef baked and topped with layers of marinara, Bolognese, and cream sauce $14.95, Lasagna al Forno Fatta in Casa $13.95, Sauce choices— Pesto Genovese –a creamy sauce of olive oil, garlic, fresh basil and roasted nuts $13.95, Salsiccie alla Calabrese-medium hot Italian sausages with anise seeds, cooked in marinara sauce $16.95, Puttanesca-sauteed anchovies in melted butter, cooked in hot sauce with tomatoes, black olives and pimientoes $13.25
Entrées: Served with vegetables and the chef's pasta of the day. Veal Marsala with mushrooms $23.95, Chicken Parmesan $22.75, New York Steak seared & topped with butter, garlic and shallots sauce $26.95, Scampi alla Trattoria $24.75, Pescatora-fresh clams in the shell, garlic, herbs, your choice of pasta with white or red sauce $18.95, Aragosta alla Fra Diavolo-Lobster sauteed in olive oil with shallots, tomato, white wine and spices served in the shell $25.95

Impressions:

Trattoria is a long-time Waikiki favorite. Although the entrance suggests informality, inside you'll find starched white tablecloths and hand-painted frescoes. The kitchen's approach is more fine dining than pasta with marinara. We view veal to be a benchmark in Italian restaurants and theirs is of good quality and well prepared. It can get busy in this area so make reservations.

Oahu Dining

North Shore

Turtle Bay Resort Restaurants
57-091 Kamehameha Highway
Kahuku, HI 96731
808-293-8811
www.turtlebayhotel.com
Hours: See Below
Cards: AE DC DIS JCB MC V
Dress: See Below
Style: Diverse

Menu Sampler:

Palm Terrace Café: Casual Dress
B: 7 AM-11 AM, Menu: Sweet Bread French Toast with Coconut Syrup and Macadamia Nut Butter $7.95, Eggs Benedict $11.25, Poached Eggs on Shrimp and Crab Hash with Papaya Salsa $12.50, Hawaiian Silk Smoothie $4.50
L: Lunch Buffet 11 AM-2 PM (if available), menu 11 AM-5 PM, BBQ Chicken Breast Sandwich with grilled apples and cheddar cheese, fries $9.25, Beer Battered Fish & Chips with Hawaiian slaw $12.50, Portuguese Bean Soup $5.25
D: Dinner 5 PM-10 PM, Spinach Linguini with grilled vegetables and chicken in roasted garlic sauce $13.75, Pan Seared Mahi Mahi with aged sherry and roasted red pepper coulis $19.50, Veal Scaloppini with Marsala-Mushrooms $17.50

Sea Tide Room: Resort Casual
Sunday Brunch: 10 AM-2 PM $21.95/adults, $19.95/62+, $12.50/age 4-11. Lavish selection of fruits, omelets, waffles, traditional breakfast items, vegetables, carved meats and seafood with a beautiful panoramic view of Kahuku Point and Turtle Bay. Reservations not required but recommended.

21° North: Evening Aloha
D: Friday and Saturday nights 6 PM-9:30 PM. Reservations required. Appetizer of Tataki of Hawaiian Ahi on mushroom-olive crostini with sundried tomato goat cheese filled rigatoni & charred island ratatouille $13. Entrées of Tarragon Butter Braised Kona Lobster over orzo risotto, asparagus tips, slow roasted shallots & grapefruit butter sauce $32, Grilled Tenderloin of Beef over garlic whipped potato $29. Dessert of Banana Cream Charlotte w/guava sauce $6.00

Impressions:

The Turtle Bay Resort has recently undergone an extensive renovation, and the results were worth the wait. All three restaurants offer patrons stunning ocean views and progressive levels of dining sophistication. These rooms attract an interesting mix of customers from around the north shore as well as around the globe. This diversity is evident in the menus as well as through the clientele.

Kaimuki

Verbano Italiano Ristorante
3571 Waialae Avenue, #101
Honolulu, HI 96816
808-735-1777
www.verbanohawaii.com
Hours: L 11:00 AM-2:30 PM Mo-Fr
           D 5:00 PM-10:00 PM
Cards: AE DIS MC V
Dress: Casual
Style: Ital $$ Ent Card

Menu Sampler:

Breakfast:
N/A
Lunch:
Appetizers: Bruschetta-grilled homemade bread, eggplant, ricotta cheese, fresh tomato, basil, olive oil & balsamic $5.90, Calamari Fritti $7.90
Salads: Spicy Spinach Seafood Salad with shrimp, scallops, & calamari $9.90
Pasta: Fettuccini Carbonara $8.90, Linguini Chicken Anchovies Olio $9.90, Pollo & Melanzane Di Casino of sautéed chicken with bacon, ham, spinach, baked eggplant & mushrooms, garlic, pasta & cheese $10.90
Dinner:
All of the above items plus the following:
Appetizers: Escargot sautéed with fresh garlic, lemon, butter & wine $6.90, Clams Florentina of baked clams, fresh garlic, spinach, bacon, butter & wine $8.90, Roast Peppers with Anchovies $6.90, Carpaccio $7.90
Salads: Caesar Salad $4.90, Italian Salad of romaine, pickled carrot & celery, tomato, pepperoncini, salami, black olives, anchovies, cheese $3.90
Entrees: Steak Tuscana of grilled steak topped with mushrooms, anchovies, capers, chili pepper sauce in olive oil $15.90, Fettuccini Carbonara with sautéed onion, bacon, ham, tossed with egg & butter or marinara $11.90, Vongole Di Tuscan of chopped clams sautéed with garlic, onions; served with spicy tomato sauce $11.90, Veal Marsala with mushrooms, butter & marsala wine $14.90, Seafood Ravioli of homemade pasta with mixed seafood items; your choice of tomato, cream or pesto sauce $13.90

Impressions:

Verbano is one of those special finds that combines a solid menu, pleasant atmosphere, and reasonable prices. The mood here is a step above the casual neighborhood Italian eatery, so dress accordingly. A local favorite!

Waikiki

Wailana Coffee House

1860 Ala Moana Blvd
Honolulu, HI 96815
808-955-1764
Web: None
Hours: 24/7
Cards: AE DIS JCB MC V
Dress: Casual
Style: Amer/Isl $

Menu Sampler:

Breakfast:
Corned Beef Hash, two eggs, butter grilled banana & toast $6.95, Three Egg Omelets $6.25-$7.25, Eggs Benedict with smoked ham and turkey, hashed browns $7.75, Belgian Waffle $4.95, Blueberry Pancakes $4.95, Papaya $3.50
Lunch:
Burgers-served on a toasted bun with lettuce and pickle. Mushroom Burger $5.50, Paniolo Burger with chili beans and chopped onions $5.95, Patty Melt on European Rye with chopped onions and French fries $6.50, BBQ Pork on a toasted bun w/French fries $6.25, Salad Bar w/any sandwich $3.25, Mahi Mahi Sandwich with French fries $6.50, Fisherman's Wharf Salad w/asparagus $8.50
Dinner:
Choice of soup, salad bar or minted fruit cocktail, French fries, whipped potatoes or steamed rice (baked potato 5-10 PM) & roll. Oriental Stir-Fry with beef or chicken & vegetables on bed of noodles $9.25, Teriyaki Steak w/soup, salad bar, or minted fruit cocktail, choice of starch & roll $10.50, Broasted Chicken (4 pcs) w/fries & cole slaw $8.75, Deep Fried Scallops $9.95, Fish & Chips w/tartar sauce $7.75, Fried Saimin $5.25, Spicy Battered Butterfly Shrimp $10.75, Breaded Tenderloin Cutlet w/mushroom sauce $9.25
Happy Hour: 12-9-Mai Tai $2.50, Karaoke 9-1, live music 6-9PM ThFr
Desserts: Hot Fudge Ice Cream Cake $3.75, High Rise Ice Cream Pie $4.50

Impressions:

This bustling restaurant should be franchised and sent to the neighbor islands. They offer good food at reasonable prices in pleasant surroundings and have 24/7 service for the entire menu. What more can you ask for? The choices are extensive and there's something to please just about everyone in your group. An attractive lounge with TVs for viewing sporting events is located right across from the entrance. This dining spot is especially kind to travelers whose body clocks are totally out of whack and want something to eat at 4 AM!

Oahu Dining

Kapahulu

Wasabi Bistro
1006 Kapahulu Ave.
Honolulu, HI 96816
808-735-2800
Web: None
Hours: L 11:00 AM-2:00 PM Mo-Sa
         D 5:30 PM-10:00 PM
Cards: AE JCB MC V
Dress: Casual
Style: Japan $$

Menu Sampler:

Breakfast:
N/A
Lunch:
Starters: Tofu Salad $6.75, Maui Onion Tempura $5.50, Fried Gyoza $3.75,
Entrées: Includes miso soup, green salad, Japanese pickles & rice-Chicken
Teriyaki $8.25, Braised Fish of the Day $11.25, Pork Tenderloin Cutlets $11.00,
Baked Scallops Special $10.00, Soft Shell Crab $6.95, Beef Katsu $10.00
Lunch Combinations: include miso soup, salad, pickles & rice-choice of two
items-Chicken Teriyaki, California Roll, Shrimp & Veg. Tempura, etc. $10.95
Dinner:
Cold Starters: Seafood Sunomono $5.50, Maguro Tataki-seared tuna $8.95
Hot Starters: Calamari Salad $7.25, Soft Shell Crab with ponzu sauce $7.75
Special Starters: Filet of Ahi Wasabi $12.00, Papaya Seafood Motoyaki $8.95
Dinner Entrées: include soup, salad, pickles & rice-Rib Eye Beef $20.75,
Butterfish Yakizakana $20.75, Una-Juu broiled eel over steamed rice $18.50
Sushi: Rainbow Roll (8 pcs) $11.50, Shrimp Tempura Roll $9.25,
Signature Dishes: King Crab Motoyaki $13.00, Trio of Maguro (tuna) $12.00

Impressions:

Kapahulu has its own little restaurant row and right in the middle of it sits the
Wasabi Bistro. This Tokyo style Japanese takes things up a notch. Not only do
they serve some of the best starters and sushi you'll find in Waikiki, but they
also offer a full gamut of traditional entrees and combinations. Those who'd like
to experience fine Japanese cuisine without a high price tag would do well to try
lunch here. You won't be giving that much up since the mid-day menu is nearly
as extensive as that at dinner. Parking is available on premises or by valet.

Chinatown

Won Kee Seafood
Chinatown Cultural Plaza
100 N. Beretania St
Honolulu, HI 96817
808-524-6877
Web: None
Hours: L 11:00 AM-2:30 PM
        D 5:00 PM-10:00 PM
Cards: AE DIS JCB MC V
Dress: Casual
Style: Chi $$
        Ent Card

Menu Sampler:

Breakfast:
N/A
Lunch/Dinner:
Appetizers: Crispy Egg Rolls (3) $4.50, Roast Pork Char Siu $4.50, Steamed Clams $12.00, Wine Chicken and Jelly Fish $9.50, Fresh Oyster $2.00
Soup: Hot & Sour Soup $3.00, Chicken Corn Soup $2.50, Abalone Soup $5.50, Beef Egg Drop Soup $2.50, Steamed Abalone and Shark Fin Soup $20.00
Entrées: Sautéed Scallop with Vegetable $12.95, Jumbo Shrimp braised with curry sauce $16.00, Roast Duck w/plum sauce $9.50, Fresh Clam w/ginger and scallion $12.00, Spicy Deep Fried Pork Ribs $9.50, Cold Ginger Chicken $9.500
Seafood: Sweet and Sour Crispy Shrimp $12.95, Island Prawns Braised with Curry Sauce $18.00, Oyster with Scallion and Ginger Sauce $12.00, Deep Fried Spicy Squid $10.50, Mixed Seafood in Taro Basket $12.95
Meats, Poultry: Sizzling Beef with Maui Onions $10.50, Spicy Garlic Chicken $9.50, Spicy Deep Fried Pork Ribs $9.50, Pepper Steak in Taro Basket $9.50
Noodles & Rice: Fried Noodle or Chow Funn with Seafood $9.00, Yong Chow Fried Rice $8.00, Pan Fried Chow Funn with shrimp and chicken $8.00

Impressions:

When you walk into Won Kee, the first thing you'll notice is the fish tanks along the wall. Many Chinese restaurants utilize in-house tanks to ensure absolute freshness for their more particular patrons. This is a fine dining establishment with massive hand carved furniture and a menu to match. Seafood is their mainstay, but they offer a variety of other traditional dishes as well. Parking is available across the street or in the cultural center deck.

Oahu Dining

Honolulu

Yanagi Sushi
762 Kapiolani Blvd.
Honolulu, HI 96813
808-597-1525
www.yanagisushihawaii.com
Hours: L 11:00 AM-2:00 PM
             D 5:30 PM-2:00 AM Mo-Sa
             D 5:30 PM-10:00 PM Su
Cards: AE DC DIS JCB MC V
Dress: Casual
Style: Japan $$

Menu Sampler:

Breakfast:
N/A
Lunch:
Double Combination Lunch-served with miso soup, rice & pickled vegetables-Tempura, Chicken Teriyaki $7.45, Broiled Salmon, Chicken Teriyaki $7.75
Special Combination Lunch-served with salad, appetizer, miso soup, rice, pickled vegetables & ice cream-choice of two entrées $14.95, three $17.95
Dinner:
Pupus: Toro (ahi belly) Tataki $7.50, Fried Prawn $3.75, Dynamite $6.95
Soups & Salads: Lobster Miso Soup $6.50, Sashimi Salad $9.95
Nabemono: Shabu Shabu of strip loin, vegetables & noodles $19.95, Shabu Shabu Deluxe adds assorted fresh seafood $23.95, Sukiyaki $19.95
Broiled Fishes: Butterfish $9.75, Ahi Teriyaki $7.95, Yakitori $3.75/$7.25
Tempura: Ala Carte-Shrimp $8.25, Vegetable $7.25, Tonkatsu $8.45
Roll Sushi: Honeymoon Roll-unagi, shrimp, avocado, crab eggs, sesame seeds $8.50, Spicy Tuna Roll $4.95, Salmon Skin $4.95, Spider Roll $7.50

Impressions:

Want to join the local movers and shakers for some Japanese cuisine? Get that car out of the garage and head downtown. There at the intersection of Clayton and Kapiolani you'll find the home of Yanagi Sushi. When you arrive, give your keys to the valet and he'll take care of the parking situation. Then, get ready to enjoy a great dining experience. Inside you'll have your choice of seats at the sushi bar or in the dining room maze. There's just about everything Japanese on the menu throughout the day and until very late in the evening. You can't get a Sunday lunch here, but otherwise it's all-day every-day. We really like this one!

Diamond Head

Yen King
Kahala Mall Shopping Center
4211 Waialae Ave.
Honolulu, HI 96816
808-732-5505
Web: None
Hours: LD 10:00 AM-9:30 PM
Cards: AE MC V
Dress: Casual
Style: Chi $$

Menu Sampler:

Breakfast:
N/A
Lunch/Dinner:
Gourmet Buffets: 11 AM-2 PM $9.50/adults, $6.00/children age 3-12;
5 PM-9 PM $13.95/adults, $7.50/children age 3-12
Soup: Hot & Sour Soup $4.50, Won Ton Soup $5.95, Sizzling Rice Soup $5.95
Entrées: Mongolian Beef (hot) $7.50, Peppery Beef Sizzling Platter $8.50, Mu Shu Pork $7.95, Sweet and Sour Pork $7.50, Dry Fried Chicken (hot) $7.95, Crackling Chicken (1/2) $8.95, Peking Duck (1/2) $15.00, Kung Pao Squid (hot) $8.95, Shrimp with Tofu $8.95, Velvet Shrimp $10.50, Happy Family $9.95, Oyster Sautéed in Ginger & Onion Sauce $10.50, Crispy Fried Scallop $11.50, Hot Eggplant with Scallop $11.50, Braised Whole Fish $Mkt
Vegetarian: Egg Fu Yong $5.95, Spinach, Garlic & Wine Sautéed $7.95, Black Mushroom & Chinese Green $5.95, Vegetarian E-Mein Sautéed $6.95
Noodles & Rice: Yen King Chow Mein or Fried Rice $5.95
Dessert: Almond Tofu $1.95, Glazed Banana or Glazed Apple $4.50
Daily Lunch Plates: includes hot & sour soup & rice-2 items $6.25/3- $7.95
Daily Dinner Specials: includes spring roll & won ton, hot sour soup, rice, and almond tofu dessert-2 items $9.75/ 3-$11.50

Impressions:

Yen King does a couple of things very well. First, you'll have to go some to find better Szechuan cooking. If you like a little zip on your plate you'll really enjoy the spicy hot specialties. Then, if grazing is more your style give the buffet a try. This isn't your neighborhood hot bar. Howard calls it his gourmet buffet, and he doesn't miss the mark by much. Kahala Mall shoppers appreciate being able to sit down to an excellent meal without spending much of their time or budget. Daily specials make for a value priced alternative at both lunch and dinner.

Waikiki

Youme.n

Hyatt Regency Waikiki
2424 Kalakaua Ave.
Honolulu, HI 96815
808-922-4991
www.youme-n.com
Hours: D 5:30 PM-10:30 PM
Cards: AE DIS JCB MC V
Dress: Resort Casual
Style: Japan $$

Menu Sampler:

Breakfast/Lunch:
N/A
Dinner:
Sushi: California Roll $6.50, Spicy Tuna Roll $6.00, Philadelphia Roll $7.00, Tempura Roll $11.00, Unagi Avocado Roll $13.50, Special Pinky Roll $19.00, Rainbow Roll $15.00, Shrimp Tempura Tomato Roll $14.50, Sushi By The Piece $2.00 each-Tuna, Eel, Cuttlefish, Salmon, Snapper, Yellow Tail, Beef
Pop Japanese Style Dining: Famous Maui Onion Salad with soy sauce & vinegar dressing $4.50, Fruit & Vegetable Salad $5.00, Hawaiian Poke Poke $6.50, Hawaiian Ahi with soy sauce & mustard $7.00, Deep Fried Chicken $5.00, Baked Oyster (3) with mayonnaise, crab & avocado $12.00, Chicken Teriyaki $12.00, Shrimp Tempura $18.50, Black Peppercorn Steak $21.00

Impressions:

What is Pop Japanese? As near as we can figure it departs from the more traditional, formally structured Japanese dining by showcasing innovative sushi, fun, almost-snack foods, and Japanese tastes applied to an eclectic collection of bites and bits-sort of… At any rate, it takes a creative guy to pull this off in Honolulu, and Kiyoshi, a well-recognized chef/artist, is just the fellow to do it. Upon entering Youme.n you'll be surrounded by a fantasy of swirling color and fanciful forms, all of which were designed by Kiyoshi. Décor aside, wait till you try his menu! Artistic ensembles of poke, sushi rolls and entrees grace your plate and tease your palate! To find the entrance to this colorful establishment, locate the Hyatt Regency on Kalakaua Avenue in Waikiki. In the Diamond Head half of the hotel look for the staircase heading under the building. Walk down those stairs and you'll discover Pop Japanese! Valet parking is available at the hotel.

Oahu Dining

Honolulu

Zaffron
69 N. King St
Honolulu, HI 96817
808-533-6635
www.zaffronhawaii.com
Hours: L 11:00 AM-2:00 PM XSaSu
        D Buf 5:00 PM-9:00 PM We-Sa
Cards: AE DIS MC V
Dress: Resort Casual
Style: Ind $$

Menu Sampler:

Breakfast:
N/A
Lunch:
Plate Orders: Chicken Curry-chicken, chole, aloo sabzi, biryani rice, naan $7.00, Mixed Plate of chicken curry, keema mixed vegetable, chole, aloo sabzi, chicken biryani rice, naan $7.50, Vegetarian Curry w/vegetables & rice $7.00
A la carte: Tandoori Chicken $4.50, Peanut Butter Naan $2.00, Beef Curry $5.50, Chole (chick pea curry) $3.00, Fish Curry $6.00, Dhal (lentils) $3.00
Dinner:
Buffet: adults $14.40/children $7.20, Buffet consists of **Four Meat Choices-** Beef Curry, Spicy Beef Keema, Chicken Curry, Tandoori Chicken, Egg Curry, Goat Curry, Kofta, Lamb Curry-**Six Vegetable Choices-** Bean, Bell Pepper, Cauliflower, Bhindi, Choley, Dal, Eggplant Curry, Gobi, Mixed Vegetables, Squash Curry, **Extras-** Fresh Naan Bread, Vegetable Samosa, Vegetable Salad, Raeta, Hot Mint Chutney, **Two Desserts-** Halawa and Kheer
Iced Tea $1.00, Indian Hot Tea $1.25, juices $1.00, & Milk Shakes $3.00
Canned drinks & bottled water are $1.00 each, Lassis (sweet, salty, mango) $3

Impressions:

If you haven't tried Indian cuisine, you can do so now in Honolulu. Dishes like Tandoori chicken and beef curry can open new doors for someone who's had all the fusion cuisine that they care to eat for a while. The lunch plates are quite reasonably priced and very popular. Their dinner buffets are particularly good for the newcomer, because you can sample many new and different items. In keeping with Islamic tradition alcohol is not served at this establishment.

DINING BY REGION

BIG ISLAND DINING BY REGION

Kohala

Kona

KAUAI DINING BY REGION

West Side

South Shore

Lihue

East Coast

North Shore

LANAI DINING BY REGION

Manele Bay Hotel

Lanai City

The Lodge at Koele

Central Valley

Kihei

MOLOKAI DINING BY REGION

Kaunakakai

West Molokai

OAHU DINING BY REGION

Honolulu

Chinatown

Waikiki

Manoa Valley

Kapahulu

Diamond Head

Leeward

Hawaii Regional Cuisine Chefs

The roster of Hawaii Regional Cuisine Chefs reads like an all-star team of the Hawaii culinary scene. Back in the 1980's these people were all working in big-name resorts and hotels. Their movement began as informal get-togethers where they shared information on local sources for ingredients needed in their kitchens. They then combined their own cultural and professional experience with local dining tradition to create what is now known as Hawaii Regional Cuisine. Not only do these people offer some of the finest dining experiences in the islands, they mentor young chefs-in-training and appear without charge at charity events. Aloha lives in this ohana!

Sam Choy
>Sam Choy's Breakfast, Lunch and Crab-Honolulu
>Sam Choy's Diamond Head Restaurant-Honolulu

Roger Dikon
>PGA National Resort & Spa-Palm Beach Gardens, Florida

Mark Ellman
>Penne Pasta Café-Maui

Amy Ferguson-Ota
>Oodles of Noodles-Big Island

Beverly Gannon
>Hali'imaile General Store-Maui

Jean Marie Josselin
>A Pacific Café-Kauai

George Mavrothalassitis
>Chef Mavro-Honolulu

Peter Merriman
>Merriman's Restaurant-Big Island
>Hula Grill-Maui

Philippe Padovani
>Padovani's Restaurant & Wine Bar-Waikiki

Gary Strehl
>Loews Hotel-Washington, D.C.

Alan Wong
>Alan Wong's Restaurant-Honolulu

Roy Yamaguchi
>Roy's Restaurants-Hawaii

Hawaiian Island Chefs

In 1999 a group of fifteen dynamic young chefs banded together to provide a forum for their creative energies. Each draws from their own culture and then blends techniques and ingredients from other regions to create unique fusion cuisine. The culinary niches they have craved give jaded foodies new frontiers to explore. As you travel around the islands, make sure to give these venues a try.

Steven Ariel
> The Pineapple Room-Honolulu

Chai Chaowasaree
> Chai's Island Bistro, Singha Thai-Honolulu, Waikiki

Hiroshi Fukui
> L'Uraku-Honolulu

Teresa "Cheech" Gannon
> Haliimaile General Store-Maui

George Gomes
> Sarento's On The Beach-Maui

Wayne Hirabayashi
> Hoku's-Kahala Mandarin-Honolulu

D.K. Kodama
> Sansei Seafood Restaurant & Sushi Bar-Maui, Honolulu

Lance Kosaka
> Alan Wong's Restaurant-Honolulu

Jaqueline Lau
> Roy's Waikoloa Bar & Grill-Big Island

Douglas Lum
> Mariposa Restaurant-Honolulu

James McDonald
> Pacific 'O, I'O, The Feast at Lele-Maui

Mark Okumura
> The Pineapple Room-Honolulu

Russell Siu
> 3660 On The Rise-Honolulu

Goran Streng
> Prince Court-Hawaii Prince Hotel Waikiki-Honolulu

Corey Waite
> Five Palms Beach Grill-Maui

HAWAIIAN FISH & SEAFOOD GLOSSARY

Hawaii IS the island state and what could be a more fitting headliner on a Hawaiian menu than the bounty of the sea? Just like everything else found in this Pacific paradise there are unique spins to the fish and seafood offerings. With this in mind we have created a separate glossary to help you explore and better appreciate the aquatic offerings found in Hawaii's dining spots.

Visitors need to be aware that finfish are nearly always listed by their Hawaiian names on island menus. That's no problem for those who grew up in Hawaii, but the rest of us would do well to brush up on the subject first. How else would you know that an ahi is a prize big eye or yellow fin tuna, and that a tako isn't the same as a taco? The word tako in Hawaii means octopus, and receiving one instead of the other could come as quite a surprise!

Most people don't realize that longliners stay out for several days at a time, but trollers come in every night and that the difference in the quality and freshness of their catch can be noticed. If you are paying for fresh island fish you want to make sure that you get it. You might see the term "day boat" used in some of the finer restaurants to describe the freshest of fresh fish and seafood. Regardless, make sure to ask and always insist on fish that has never been frozen.

As long as we're on the subject of getting what you're paying for, let's take a look at the economics of fish and seafood in Hawaii. There's a misconception that just because people see "water water everywhere", the aquatic resources must be limitless and the prices low. Nothing could be farther from the truth. The high cost of production through aquaculture and harvest in the wild along with huge local and foreign demand drive prices to the upper limit of the menu.

In closing, when you decide to take the plunge and go out for fish or seafood, make it a point to trust the recommendations at the restaurant. The chef knows how to match species and preparations for the best possible results. Just let your waiter know what you have in mind and listen to his suggestions. You'll be far happier in the end if you go with the flow than if you try to have it your way.

ahi	big eye or yellow fin tuna
aku	skipjack tuna, most common spring through early fall, robust flavor, firm texture, often served as poke or in sushi, primarily caught by commercial pole-and-line fishermen and recreational trollers
akule	big-eyed scad, a local favorite, primarily caught by netting or by hook-and-line fishermen

ama ebi

sweet shrimp or langoustines, harvested with traps from deep water, available locally but often imported

a'u

billfish of any type

big eye ahi

big eye tuna, most common from mid-fall through mid-spring, moderate beef-like flavor, medium firm texture, favored for sashimi and poke, primarily caught by long-line boats

ehu

red snapper, moderate flavor, most common during winter, medium firm texture, primarily caught by deepwater hook-and-line fishermen

hapu'upu'u

grouper or sea bass, most common spring and fall, moderate flavor, medium firm texture, primarily caught by deepwater hook-and-line fishermen

hebi

shortbill spearfish, most common mid-spring through early fall, moderate flavor, medium firm texture, primarily caught by commercial long-line boats

kajiki

pacific blue marlin, most common summer through fall, moderate flavor, firm texture, primarily caught by commercial long-line boats and recreational trollers

Keahole lobster

clawed "Maine" lobsters raised on the Big Island through aquaculture, available all year

Kona lobster

spiny or rock lobster, primarily caught by divers working the reef or by trapping, usually imported, available all year

lehi

silver mouth snapper, most common during late fall and winter, moderate flavor, medium texture, primarily caught by deepwater hook-and-line fishermen

mahimahi

dolphinfish, most common spring and fall, moderate almost sweet flavor, medium texture, ask if the fish is fresh "island fish", primarily caught by commercial and recreational trollers

moi

pacific threadfin, the royal fish, now raised locally through aquaculture, mild flavor, delicate texture, available all year

monchong

bigscale or sickle pomfret, available all year, robust flavor, medium firm texture, primarily caught as a by-catch of tuna long-liners and deepwater hook-and-line fishermen.

nairagi

striped marlin, most common winter and spring, moderate flavor, medium firm texture, primarily caught by commercial long-line boats and recreational trollers

onaga

ruby or long-tailed red snapper, most common late fall and winter, mild flavor, medium texture, primarily caught by deepwater hook-and-line fishermen

ono

wahoo, most common late spring through early fall, mild almost citrus-like flavor, medium firm texture, primarily caught by commercial and recreational trollers with part of the catch harvested by commercial long-line fishermen

opae

shrimp, now raised locally through aquaculture, available all year

opah

moonfish, most common spring through summer, robust flavor, medium texture, primarily caught by commercial long-line fishermen fishing over seamounts

opakapaka

crimson snapper, most common fall and winter, mild flavor, delicate texture, primarily caught by deepwater hook-and-line fishermen

| **opihi** | small limpet, found on coastal rock faces in the surf zone, eaten raw with salt as "Hawaiian escargot" |

| **papio** | juvenile pompano or crevally, medium flavor, firm texture, caught by shore casters, shallow water trollers, and bottom fishermen |

| **shutome** | broadbill swordfish, most common spring and summer, moderate flavor, medium firm texture, caught at night by commercial long-line fishermen |

| **tako** | octopus or squid, primarily caught by divers working in shallow water or by jigging |

| **tombo** | albacore or "white meat" tuna, most common mid-spring through mid-fall, moderate flavor, medium texture, primarily caught by commercial long-line fishermen and small-boat hand line fishermen |

| **uku** | grey snapper, most common mid-spring through mid-fall, moderate flavor, medium firm texture, primarily caught in deep water by hook-and-line fishermen but is also caught near the surface by recreational trollers |

| **ula** | spiny or rock lobster, primarily caught by divers working the reef or by trapping |

| **ula papapa** | slipper lobster, primarily caught by divers working the reef or by trapping |

| **ulua** | adult pompano or crevally, medium flavor, firm texture, caught by shore casters, shallow water trollers, and bottom fishermen |

| **yellow fin ahi** | yellow fin tuna, most common mid-spring through mid-fall, moderate beef-like flavor, medium firm texture, favored for sashimi and poke, primarily caught by commercial long-line boats and commercial and recreational trollers |

FOOD & CULTURAL TERMS GLOSSARY

a'a	rough clinker lava
aina	the land
abalone	large saltwater mollusk
aburage	deep-fried tofu
adobo	marinated Filipino chicken and/or pork stew
agemono	Japanese cooking method of preparing meats and vegetables by deep-frying
ahi	yellowfin tuna, often served raw as sashimi on a bed of Chinese cabbage with a wasabi and shoyu dipping sauce
ahupua'a	a land division used in old Hawaii consisting of all the lands between two adjoining ridges from the top of the mountain to the ocean
akamai	clever or smart
akua	spirit or god
ali'i	chief or noble
aloha	versatile term that can mean hello, good-bye, and love
Aloha Friday	casual dress day or more importantly the first day of the weekend party that actually starts Thursday afternoon
arroz	rice
arugula	peppery flavored greens
aumakua	guardian spirit
auntie	any older lady, a term of respect

| **'awa** | kava, a beverage made from the ground roots of the intoxicating pepper |

azuki   red beans

banh hoi   Vietnamese meat and vegetable roll-up

barbecue stick   char grilled teriyaki meat stick

bean curd   tofu

bean threads   fine thin noodles made from mung bean starch, long rice

bento   Japanese box lunch

black beans   fermented beans used in Chinese sauces

bok choy   a tall variety of cabbage with white celery like stems and dark green leaves

bulgoki   Korean teriyaki barbecue beef

bun   thin soft Vietnamese rice noodles

butterfish   black cod, has a smooth silky texture

carne   meat

cascaron   Filipino fried sweet dumpling

char siu   sweet marinated barbecued pork

chili oil   liquid fire made from chili peppers and oil

Chinese cabbage   a compact variety of cabbage with white celery-like stems and pale green leaves, also known as Napa cabbage or won bok

chorizo   hot and spicy sausage

chow   stir-fry

chow fun   cooked noodles combined with green onions and bits of meat or seafood then stir-fried with sesame oil

chun

Korean method of frying using flour followed by an egg wash

cilantro

Chinese parsley

coconut creme

thick creamy layer on top of a can of coconut milk

coconut milk

liquid extracted by squeezing grated coconut meat

crack seed

sweet or sour snack foods made from preserved fruits and seeds

da kine

what-cha-ma-call-it

daikon

large white Asian root vegetable commonly used as a garnish

dashi

broth made from dried seaweed and flakes of dried bonito

Diamond Head

directional term used on Oahu meaning to go east in the direction of Diamond Head or "Go Diamond Head"

dim sum

Chinese style dumplings

doce

sweet

donburi

thinly sliced meat, vegetables, and coddled egg served in a deep bowl over rice

edamame

lightly salted and boiled young soybeans

egg roll

fried pastry roll with various meat and vegetable fillings

Ewa

directional term used on Oahu meaning to go west in the direction of Ewa or "Go Ewa" which is opposite from Diamond Head and toward Pearl Harbor

fish cake

ground white fish, starch, and salt cooked together by steaming or frying

fish sauce

potent seasoning made from salt and fish

five spice powder	mixture of several spices that usually includes fennel, peppercorns, cinnamon, cloves, and star anise.
furikake	a dry condiment used on rice dishes
fusion cuisine	layers of flavor, texture, temperatures, and techniques created by combining elements from the cuisines of different cultures
ginger	spicy pungent root vegetable used as a flavoring in Asian cooking
gobo	burdock root
grinds	food
guava	sweet red tropical fruit
guisates	Filipino pork or chicken dish made with peas and pimento in a tomato based sauce
hale	house or building
halo halo	tropical fruit sundae made with ice, milk and sugar instead of ice cream
ham har	fermented dried shrimp paste, very funky, a little goes a long way
hana	work
hana hou	do it one more time/encore!
haole	Caucasian
hapa	half as in hapa-haole or half-Caucasian
haupia	coconut custard dessert
Hawaii Regional Cuisine	movement started in the late '80's/early '90's by young local chefs combining island cooking styles and classic techniques with fresh local products to create an exciting new fusion cuisine

This collection of poems morphed from the event of Hurricane Frances lurking off our shores in Florida in September 2004, and evolved into a compilation of happenings in and around my family of eight siblings and our offspring. It touches on the Iraq war, the terrorists, and Hurricane Katrina. Although I had never written a poem before Frances, except in my "roses are red" era, I now seem unable to stop!

In this book, I have shared my philosophies, my optimism, and at times, my faith. Most of the poems tell a short story in simple rhyme that often end with an uplifting message. I've discovered that I am at long last looking around and within and beginning to see "the forest for the trees." It's a joyous experience!

I'm the second child in a family of eight, raised in a small town in the Mohawk Valley of New York State. We had meager circumstances, but a wealth of family experiences! Retiring from the corporate world, I found a life filled with writing, acting, and adventures with my great-granddaughter.

ica.com

Hawaiian chili water	liquid heat made with Hawaiian chili peppers, water, and salt
Hawaiian rock salt	coarse white or pink rock salt
Hawaiian time	later rather than sooner
heiau	ancient Hawaiian stone temple
hekka	a stir-fry dish made with meat and vegetables in a shoyu-based sauce
hibachi	small charcoal cooker
hoisin sauce	thick, sweet, but pungent sauce used in Chinese cooking
holoholo	pleasure trip, to go "holoholo"
hono	bay
honu	turtle
hukilau	pulling of a large fish net by a group
hui	club or association
hula	Hawaiian native dance
huli huli	"turn turn" as in grilling chicken
imu	Hawaiian underground oven made by digging a pit and lining it with hot lava rocks covered by banana plants and food and burying it for several hours, used at luaus for making kalua pork, laulau, sweet potatoes, etc.
inari sushi	cone sushi made by filling fried tofu pockets with sweet vinegar flavored rice
ipo	sweetheart
kaffir lime leaves	leaves of the kaffir lime tree used as flavoring in Thai cooking

| **kahuna** | priest or skilled person |

| **kai** | the sea |

| **kaiseki** | Japanese fine dining in courses |

| **kal bi ribs** | Korean teriyaki beef short ribs |

| **kale** | Portuguese cabbage |

| **kalo** | taro |

| **kalua pork** | shredded pork prepared luau style in an imu pit, also known locally as kalua pig |

| **kama'aina** | long time resident or someone who was born in Hawaii |

| **kamaboko** | Japanese fish cake |

| **kane** | man |

| **kapu** | forbidden |

| **kapuna** | grandparent or wise older person |

| **katsu** | breaded cutlet |

| **kau kau** | food, a place to eat |

| **keiki** | child |

| **kiawe** | dry land hardwood used in smoking and grilling meats |

| **ki'i** | statue or image |

| **kim chee** | spicy Korean condiment made from fermented cabbage and peppers |

| **koa** | valuable hardwood tree, warrior |

| **Koko Head** | directional term used on Oahu meaning to go in the direction of Koko Head or "Go Koko Head" |

| **kokua** | help |

kona	leeward
kona wind	muggy airflow from the equator
kukui	candlenut tree, the source of kukui nut oil
Kula	a truck gardening district in Upcountry Maui
kulolo	sweet pudding made with poi
kumu	teacher as in kumu hula
lanai	deck or patio
lau hala	woven mats
lau lau	flavored meat mixed with taro leaves and wrapped in ti leaves then steamed, often in an imu
laver	purple seaweed used in making nori
lechon	roasted pig
lei	garland of flowers
lemon grass	woody lemon flavored grass used as flavoring in Southeast Asian cooking
li hing mui	sweet and sour seasoning made from dried plums and salt
lilikoi	passion fruit
limu	edible seaweed
linguica	spicy Portuguese pork sausage seasoned with garlic and paprika
loa	long
loco moco	local dish consisting of rice, a large hamburger patty or slices of Spam, and fried eggs with lots of brown gravy over all
lolo	crazy

lomi	to knead or massage
lomi lomi salmon	salted salmon finely diced with tomatoes and green onions
long rice	clear noodles cooked in broth
lua	restroom
luau	Hawaiian feast, also a dish made from taro leaves, coconut crème, and meat
lulu	calm
lumpia	fried spring roll with meat, vegetable, or dessert fillings
lup cheong	Chinese pork sausage
lychee	sweet white fruit
macadamia nuts	small round nut with creamy but crunchy texture
mac salad	macaroni and mayonnaise
mahalo	thank you
mainland	North America
makai	directional term that is helpful on an island meaning to turn or look toward the ocean
maki sushi	sushi rolled in nori
malasada	wonderful sweet brought here by the Portuguese similar to a fresh sugar donut but minus the hole
malihini	newcomer
malo	loincloth
mana	power or energy from the spirit world
manapua	steamed pork bun

mandoo	Korean dumplings with meat and vegetable fillings
mango	golden fleshed tropical fruit
mano	shark
Manoa	a gardening district near Honolulu, the Manoa Valley
mauka	directional term meaning to look or turn toward the mountain or uphill part of an island
mauna	mountain
mein	Chinese noodles
mele	chant or song
menehune	legendary "little people" of Hawaii
mirin	sweet rice cooking wine
miso	fermented soybean paste
miso soup	light Japanese soup made from soybean paste and garnished with tofu, kamaboko, daikon, green onions, and wakame
mixed plate	plate lunch version of a mixed grill
moa	native Polynesian chicken
moana	ocean
mochi	rice cake
mochiko	sweet rice flour
mo'o	lizard or water spirit
musubi	rice ball
muu muu	loose fitting ankle length dress

naan	Indian flatbread
nabemono	Japanese cooking method of preparing thin slices of meat and vegetables in a hot broth
'Nalo	As in Waimanalo, a garden district on the Windward side of Oahu
nam pla	Thai fish sauce
nam prik	Thai hot sauce
nani	beautiful
nene	Hawaiian goose
nigiri sushi	oblong sushi
niu	coconut
noni	native shrub bearing medicinal fruit
nori	roasted seaweed pressed into sheets
norimaki	sushi rolled in nori
nui	big or great
nuoc mam	Vietnamese fish sauce
off-island	in the islands one does not go "out of town" they go "off-island"
ogo	type of seaweed favored by the Japanese
ohana	extended family
ohelo	native shrub bearing edible berries
okazuya	a Japanese delicatessen where fast foods and snacks are served buffet style
ono	delicious
opae	shrimp

opihi	Hawaiian escargot harvested from rocks along the ocean and eaten raw with salt
oyster sauce	thick brown sauce made from oysters and shoyu often used in stir fry dishes
Pacific Rim Cuisine	a fusion of cuisines involving methods and ingredients from the countries around the Pacific Ocean
pad thai	Thai noodles
pahoehoe	smooth ropey lava
pakalolo	crazy smoke, marijuana, buds; something to decline when offered
pali	cliff
pancit	Filipino noodles
paniolo	Hawaiian cowboy
panko	Japanese breadcrumbs
pao	bread
pao doce	Portuguese sweet bread
papaya	smooth skinned orange-fleshed tropical fruit that can also be used green when peeled and shredded in a salad
pasteles	similar to a tamale except made with bananas instead of corn flour
patis	Filipino fish sauce
pau	finished
pau hana	finished working
pho	Vietnamese noodle soup
pidgin	Hawaiian Creole English
pipi kaula	Hawaiian beef jerky

plantain	cooking banana
plate lunch	island style blue plate special with a main entrée such as teriyaki beef or chicken, two scoops of white rice, and a scoop of macaroni salad
poi	glutinous paste made by pounding steamed taro root, the Hawaiian staple starch
poke	ceviche dish made with cubed fish or sliced octopus mixed with onion and seaweed then marinated in shoyu and spices
pono	righteous
ponzu	tart Japanese citrus sauce
Portuguese sausage	spicy garlic and paprika flavored pork sausage, linguica
pua	flower
pua'a	pig
pueo	owl
puka	hole
pupu	appetizer
pu'u	hill
ramen	curly Japanese wheat noodles
rice noodle	noodles made with rice flour
rice paper	round rice flour wrapper that is soaked in hot water to soften before use
saimin	island noodle soup that has many variations and broths--extras may include Spam, teriyaki beef, green onions, vegetables, hard-cooked eggs, and fish cake

sake	Japanese rice wine
sashimi	raw fish sliced very thin and served with spicy condiments and dipping sauce
satay	tender chicken or beef strips marinated in coconut milk and spices then skewered and grilled
sesame oil	aromatic oil made from sesame seeds used sparingly to flavor Asian dishes
shabu shabu	chafing dish cookery involving thinly sliced meats and vegetables simmered in broth usually with a tabletop preparation
shaka	hand signal using the thumb and little finger used as a greeting
shave ice	similar to a snow cone except there is no crunch as the ice is shaved instead of crushed, can be topped with wonderful tropical flavored syrups and served with ice cream and azuki beans
shoyu	Japanese soy sauce, Aloha Brand is preferred in the islands as it is not as salty as some other types
soba	Japanese buckwheat noodles
somen	thin Japanese wheat noodles
Spam	canned spiced pork lunchmeat
spring roll	fried rice paper roll with various fillings
starch	rice or potatoes
sukiyaki	Japanese beef, tofu, vegetable, and noodle dish with shoyu based sauce commonly cooked at the table
summer roll	fresh rice paper roll with various fillings
sushi	small slices of vegetables, fruits, fish, or meat combined with tangy rice

sweet bread	rich egg bread commonly called Molokai or Portuguese sweet bread
sweet rice	also known as sticky rice or glutinous rice
tako	octopus
talk story	to have a casual conversation
tapa	cloth made from pounded tree bark
taro	starchy root plant used in making poi
teri	teriyaki
teishoku	a complete Japanese meal including soup, salad, entrée, pickled vegetables, and rice
tempura	meat, seafood, or vegetables fried in a light batter coating
tendon	meat and vegetable tempura served over rice
teppanyaki	Japanese cooking method of grilling vegetables, seafood, meat and rice tableside by a knife-wielding chef, very entertaining
teriyaki	sweet tangy shoyu based marinade
Thai basil	herb used in Thai cooking, has a purple flower and sharper taste than sweet basil
ti	broad-leafed plant whose leaves are used for plates, hula skirts, and for wrapping foods and religious offerings
tobiko	flying fish roe, caviar
tofu	soybean curd available fresh or fermented
tom yum	spicy Thai soup
tonkatsu	fried cutlet
tsukemono	pickled vegetables

tuong ot	Vietnamese hot sauce
tutu	grandmother
two scoop rice	two scoops of cooked white rice
uala	sweet potato
udon	thick Japanese wheat noodles
ulu	breadfruit
vertical food	a physical manifestation of fusion cuisine where the elements of the dish are stacked
wahine	woman
wai	water
wakame	a seaweed condiment
wasabi	spicy Japanese horseradish paste often combined sparingly with shoyu to make a dipping sauce for sushi and sashimi
wiki wiki	hurry up, very fast
wok	round bottomed cooking pot used over very high heat to quick sear or stir-fry chopped meats and vegetables
won bok	Chinese cabbage
won ton	Chinese meat dumplings
wor	vegetables
yakimono	Japanese cooking method of preparing meats and vegetables by broiling or grilling
yakiniku	tabletop grilling
yakisoba	grilled noodles
yakitori	grilled meat and vegetable kebabs

NOTES

NOTES

Printed in the United States
20532LVS00001B/262-273